THE AMERICAN NATION

STRAIT OF JUAN DE FUCA

PUGET SOUND

LAKE WINNIPEG

LAKE MANITOBA

LAKE OF THE WOODS

Red R. of the North

Continental Divide

R
O
C
K
Y

Columbia R.

Blue Mts.

Bitterroot Ra.

Yellowstone R.

Y

Snake R.

Teton Ra.

Wind River Ra.

Big Horn Mts.

Black Hills

Badlands

M

CASCADES

Cape Mendocino

GREAT SALT LAKE

Wasatch Ra.

Wyoming Basin

Green R.

Uinta Mts.

Medicine Bow Ra.

Laramie Ra.

Sand Hills

O

Sacramento R.

Great Salt Lake Desert

U

Front Ra.

Platte R.

San Francisco Bay

SIERRA NEVADA

Sawatch Ra.

N

High Plains

Monterey Bay

San Joaquin R.

T

Sangre de Cristo Ra.

Kansas R.

PACIFIC OCEAN

Mojave Desert

Colorado R.

Painted Desert

A

Continental Divide

I

Staked Plains

Canadian R.

Red R.

Quachita Mts.

Gila R.

N

S

Brazos R.

Baja California

Rio Grande

Pecos R.

Trinity R.

PRINCIPAL ISLANDS OF HAWAII

Kauai I.

Niihau I.

Oahu I.

Molokai I.

Maui I.

Hawaii I.

0   100   200
MILES

Seward Peninsula

Brooks Ra.

Yukon R.

Rio Grande

Nueces R.

BERING SEA

Coast Ranges

Aleutian Islands

Alaska Peninsula

Kodiak I.

ALASKA

0   200   400
MILES

Missouri R.

PHYSICAL MAP
OF
THE UNITED STATES

LAKE SUPERIOR

Georgian Bay

LAKE HURON

LAKE MICHIGAN

LAKE ONTARIO

LAKE ERIE

St. Lawrence R.

White Mts.

Prince Edward I.

Cape Breton I.

Bay of Fundy

Nova Scotia

Cape Cod

Adirondack Mts.

Mohawk R.

Green Mts.

Connecticut R.

Hudson R.

Long Island

Delaware R.

DELAWARE BAY

Susquehanna R.

Allegheny Mts.

Potomac R.

Cape Charles

CHESAPEAKE BAY

James R.

Appalachian Mts.

Cape Hatteras

Mississippi R.

Till Prairies

Illinois R.

Drift Plains

Wabash R.

Ohio R.

Ohio R.

Ozark Mts.

Cumberland R.

Cumberland Plateau

Great Smoky Mts.

Blue Ridge Mts.

PIEDMONT

Cape Lookout

Cape Fear

Arkansas R.

Mississippi R.

Tennessee R.

Savannah R.

Red R.

Sabine R.

Alabama R.

Mobile Bay

Cape Canaveral

Mississippi Delta

Tampa Bay

LAKE OKEECHOBEE

The Everglades

GULF OF MEXICO

Florida Keys

ATLANTIC OCEAN

0   100   200   300   400
MILES

St. Thomas I.

St. John I.

St. Croix I.

PUERTO RICO
AND
VIRGIN ISLANDS

0   40   80
MILES

THE AMERICAN NATION

A History of the United States to 1877

VOLUME ONE

Fifth Edition

John A. Garraty

COLUMBIA UNIVERSITY

HARPER & ROW, PUBLISHERS, New York
Cambridge, Philadelphia, San Francisco,
London, Mexico City, São Paulo, Sydney

Sponsoring Editor: Jean Hurtado
Special Projects Editor: Mary Lou Mosher
Project Editor: Beena Kamlani
Designer: Robert Sugar
Production Manager: Willie Lane
Photo Researcher: Mira Schachne
Portfolio Two: Alden Vaughan, Elliot Epstein. Picture research by Ann Novotny
    of Research Reports
Compositor: Lehigh/Rocappi, Inc.
Printer and Binder: R. R. Donnelley & Sons, Co.
Art Studio: Vantage Art, Inc.

The author makes grateful acknowledgment to:

Professor George W. Pierson, Yale University, for permission to quote from *Tocqueville and Beaumont in America,* Oxford University Press, 1938. Copyright 1938 by George W. Pierson.

Cover: Painting of a Pennsylvania farm. The New York Public Library, Astor, Lenox and Tilden Foundation, Stokes Collection. Cover title letter forms: Ray Barber

THE AMERICAN NATION: A History of the United States to 1877
Fifth Edition

Library of Congress Cataloging in Publication Data

Garraty, John Arthur, 1920–
    The American Nation.

    Includes indexes.
    Contents: v. 1. A history of the United States to
1877—v. 2. A history of the United States since 1865.
    1. United States—History. I. Title.
[E178.1.G24 1982]   973   82–15567
ISBN 0-06-042274-2 (v. 1)

For Kathy, Jack, and Sarah

Contents

Maps and Graphs

Maps

Graphs

Preface

Once again, in this fifth edition of *The American Nation* I have tried to present my personal view of American history, while at the same time paying proper attention to the most important books and articles on this immense subject that have come out during the past four years. I have taken a fresh look at each chapter and topic in this book, questioning each general statement and interpretation and seeking to satisfy myself that it fairly represents the best thinking of the profession today.

By far the most extensive changes involve the post World War II period. The passage of time since the book was first published in 1966 has altered my perspective considerably. Some of the events, laws, and people that seemed important then now appear less significant. Other matters that I dismissed (or was unaware of) have been proved by later developments to merit extensive discussion. I have integrated the treatment of domestic and foreign affairs that previously were described in separate chapters. In the process of these changes I have combined four chapters into three, while at the same time carrying the story through the first years of the Reagan administration. Some sections dealing with social and cultural developments have been moved forward to the interwar chapters. I believe these extensive alterations make the account of modern history clearer.

I have also made important changes in the treatment of the era of the American Revolution, changes which stress the effects of domestic events on the causes and course of that conflict. There is a new portfolio dealing with the various patterns of colonial family life. But there are changes of one kind or another on nearly every page. Although I have always been at pains to write as clearly and interestingly as I can, I continue to make small changes that I think improve the flow of the narrative.

However, I do not believe that my basic approach to my subject has changed. This edition has been constructed on the same principles as its predecessors. It assumes, to begin with, that American history is important for its own sake—an epic and unique tale of human experience in a vast land, almost uninhabited at the start, now teeming with more than 200 million people. Beyond this, our history provides an object lesson in how the past affects the present, or rather, how a series of pasts has changed a series of presents in an unending pattern of development. Thus, while historians have never been any better at foretelling the future than politicians, economists, or soothsayers, good ones have always been able to illuminate their own times, adding depth and perspective to their readers' understanding of how they got to be where they were at any particular point.

I have attempted to tell the story of the American past clearly and intelligibly, with adequate attention to its complexities and subtleties. Of course, it is not the final word—that will never be written. It is, however, up-to-date and as accurate and thoughtful and wide-ranging as I could make it. Though I reject the theory that a few great individuals, cut from larger cloth than the general run of human beings, have shaped the destiny of humankind, as a biographer, I think that history becomes more vivid and comprehensible when attention is paid to how the major figures on the historical stage have reacted to events and to one another. I have attempted to portray the leading actors in my account as distinct individuals and to explain how their personal qualities influenced the course of history.

I also believe that generalizations require concrete illustration if they are to be grasped fully. Readers will find many anecdotes and quotations in the following pages along with the facts and dates and statistics that every good history must contain. I am confident that most of this illustrative material is interesting, but I think that it is instructive too. Above all, I have sought to keep in mind the grandeur of my subject. One need not be an uncritical admirer of the American nation and its people to recognize that, as I have said, the history of the United States is a great epic. I have tried to treat this history with the dignity and respect that it deserves, believing, however, that a subject of such magnitude is not well served by foolish praise or by slighting or excusing its many dark and even discreditable aspects.

John A. Garraty

1/THE AGE OF DISCOVERY AND SETTLEMENT

 History sometimes chooses its heroes strangely. The first human beings to set foot in the New World were the ancestors of the American Indians. These people came from Asia, entering the North American continent many thousands of years ago when a land bridge connected northeastern Asia and Alaska. However, they were not in their own minds discoverers or explorers. Being hunters or herders, they were merely moving from camp to camp in search of game and green grass. Almost certainly they were unaware that they were entering new territory. So we must look elsewhere (and much later in time) for the discoverers of America.

Leif Ericson ventured before the day of the compass into the void of the North Atlantic and, around the year 1000, found the shores of Labrador, the first European to reach the New World. Yet Ericson's discovery passed practically unnoticed for centuries, and to most modern inhabitants of the New World he lives only in legend.

Amerigo Vespucci, a clever Italian with an eye for publicity, visited the northern coast of South America in 1499. He wrote an account of his experiences that was widely circulated. In 1507, after reading a distorted copy of Vespucci's tale, a German geographer, Martin Waldseemüller, concluded that the author was the discoverer of the New World and suggested that it be named America in his honor. Today millions call themselves Americans, but few know much about Amerigo Vespucci.

Another Italian mariner, Cristoforo Colombo, brave, persistent, an inspired sailor but a fumbling administrator, an impractical dreamer, and (fortunately) a poor judge of distances, spent a decade cruising in the Caribbean Sea under the mistaken impression that he was next door to China. He killed some natives, established a few rickety settlements, ventured no nearer to North America than Cuba, and died poor, embittered, and frustrated, hotly denying that he had found anything more than a new route to the Orient. Today, whether he be known as Colombo, Colón, or Columbus, he is revered in the Old World and the New as the discoverer of the Western Hemisphere.

Why Columbus rather than Ericson, the real European pioneer, or Vespucci, whose name has become immortal? The answer is that Ericson came upon the scene too soon and Vespucci too late. Europe in the year 1000 was not yet ready to find the New World, and by 1499 it had already found it. Amerigo Vespucci gave his name to the region, but the adventures of Christopher Columbus inspired the development of the whole area between Hudson Bay and the Strait of Magellan.

Columbus and the Discovery of America

About two o'clock on the morning of October 12, 1492, a sailor named Roderigo de Triana, clinging in a gale to the mast of the ship *Pinta,* saw a gleam of white on the moonlit horizon and shouted: *"Tierra! Tierra!"* The land he had spied was an island in the West Indies called Guanahaní by its inhabitants, a place distinguished neither for beauty nor size. Nevertheless, when Triana's master, Christopher Columbus, went ashore bearing the flag of Castile, he named it San Salvador, or Holy Saviour. Columbus selected this imposing name for the island out of gratitude and wonder at having found it—he had sailed with three frail vessels more than 3,000 miles for 33 days without sight of land. The name was appropriate, too, from history's far larger viewpoint. Neither Columbus nor any of his men suspected it, but the discovery of San Salvador was probably the most important event in the history of western civilization since the birth of Christ.

San Salvador was the gateway to two continents. Columbus did not know it, and he refused to learn the truth, but his voyage threw open to exploitation by the peoples of western Europe a region of more than 16 million square miles, an area lushly endowed with every imaginable resource. He made possible a mass movement from Europe (and later from Africa and to a lesser extent from other regions) into the New World. Gathering force rapidly, this movement did not slacken until the present century, and it still has not ceased entirely; something on the order of 70 million persons have been involved in the migration.

Columbus was an intelligent as well as a dedicated and skillful mariner. He failed to grasp the significance of his accomplishment because he had no idea that he was on the edge of two huge continents previously unknown to Europeans. He was seeking a way to China and Japan and the Indies, the amazing countries described by the Venetian Marco Polo in the late 13th century.

Having read carefully Marco Polo's account of his adventures in the service of Kublai Khan, Columbus had decided that these rich lands could be reached by sailing directly west from Europe. The idea was not original, but while others merely talked about it (in the jawbreaking phrase of one scholar, experts had been slow to consider "the cosmographical implications of the earth's sphericity"), Columbus pursued it with brilliant persistence.

If one could sail to Asia directly, the trading possibilities and the resulting profits would be limitless. Oriental products were highly valued all over Europe. Spices such as pepper, cinnamon,

■ In 1590 Theodor de Bry issued a volume of engravings, *America*. It was largely based on John White's watercolors (look at his skillful animal drawings on page 13). This de Bry engraving shows the steps followed by Virginia Indians in forming a dugout canoe, including burning the base of a tree to make it fall (upper right), and reaming out the canoe's interior by a process of slow burning and scraping with shells. The accompanying text concludes: "Thus god endoweth this savage people with sufficient reason to make things necessary to serve their turns."

ginger, nutmeg, and cloves were of first importance, their role being not so much to titillate the palate as to disguise the taste of spoiled meats in regions that had little ice. Europeans also prized such tropical foods as rice, figs, and oranges, as well as perfumes (often used as a substitute for soap), silk and cotton, rugs, textiles such as muslin and damask, dyestuffs, fine steel products, precious stones, and various drugs.

These products flowed into western Europe by way of the Italian city-states. By the 11th century Venice had established a thriving trade with Constantinople, shipping large quantities of European foodstuffs to the great metropolis on the Bosporus. The Venetians also supplied young Slavs, captured or purchased along the nearby Dalmatian coast, to the harems of Egypt and Syria (the word *slave* originally meant a Slav).

The Venetians brought back oriental products from these voyages, and the effect was like that of tossing a stone into a pond. Europeans bestirred

themselves, searching for more goods to offer in exchange. They possessed surpluses of grain and food, but these bulky products were expensive to transport over long distances. However, in Flanders, in the Low Countries, woolen cloth of high quality was being manufactured. Other areas were producing furs and lumber. Demand led to increased output; thus the flow of commerce stimulated manufacturing, which in turn spurred the growth of towns. As towns became larger and more numerous, the market for food expanded and surrounding rural areas increased their agricultural output.

Urban growth also created a demand for more clothmakers. The resulting labor shortage in both town and country produced important changes in the structure of medieval society. The manorial system, based on serfdom, soon began to change. As their labor became more valuable, serfs won the right to pay off their traditional obligations in money rather than in service and to leave the

3

manors and move to the towns or to newly opened farmland. The lords themselves often instituted this change, for they wished to increase agricultural output by draining swamps and clearing forests, and they willingly granted freedom to serfs who would move to the new lands. And they needed money rather than the services of serfs to buy the expensive oriental luxuries being dangled before their eyes by traders.

The Crusades further accelerated the tempo of this new activity. Genuine religious motives seem to have inspired these mighty efforts, protracted over two centuries from 1095 to about 1290, to drive the Moslems from the Holy Land. Once the crusading armies had won a foothold in Asia Minor, the commerce of Venice and of other Italian cities increased still more, and their merchant fleets expanded. The business of transporting and supplying the European armies was itself extremely profitable. Furthermore, when the waves of Crusaders returned home, they brought with them more oriental products and a taste for these things that persisted after the goods themselves had been consumed.

The volume of this trade cannot be exactly determined. It was large enough to keep the fleets of the thriving Italian cities busy, and it tended to grow with the years. Yet it was not impressive by modern standards; the great Belgian historian Henri Pirenne estimated that the entire tonnage of the 13th-century Venetian fleet would scarcely fill a large 20th-century freighter. Nor did the increase in trade cause universal prosperity or even a steady economic expansion in western Europe. In fact the period of the 14th and early 15th centuries seems to have been marked by depression and economic decline in the West.

This decline resulted principally from the terrible losses occasioned by the plague known as the Black Death, which ravaged Europe in the mid 14th century. Part of the difficulty, however, stemmed from the steady drain of precious metals to the Orient (because of the unfavorable balance of east-west trade) and from the high cost of oriental goods. It was easy to blame this on the greed of the Italians, who monopolized east-west trade. Certainly the Venetians have never possessed a reputation for altruism nor the Pisans for being poor businessmen. However, even if the Italians had labored only for the joy of serving their fellow human beings, or if other merchants had been able to break the Italian monopoly, the cost of eastern products would have remained high. To transport spices from the Indies, silk from China, or rugs, cloth, and steel from the Middle East was extremely costly. The combined sea-land routes were long and complicated—across strange seas, through deserts, over high mountain passes—with pirates or highwaymen a constant threat. Every petty tyrant through whose domain the caravans passed levied taxes, a quasi-legal form of robbery. Few merchants operated on a continental scale; typically, goods passed from hand to hand and were loaded and unloaded many times between eastern producer and western consumer, with each middleman exacting as large a profit as he could. In the end the western European consumer had to pay for all this.

As time went on, merchants in the West began to cast about for a cheaper way of obtaining oriental products. If they could be carried by sea by one merchant in one ship, the cost would be far less, for the goods would be loaded and unloaded only once. A small number of sailors could provide all the necessary labor, and the free wind would supply the power to move the cargo to its destination. By the 15th century, this idea was beginning to be transformed into action.

The great figure in the transformation was Prince Henry the Navigator, third son of John I, king of Portugal. After distinguishing himself in 1415 in the capture of Ceuta, on the African side of the Strait of Gibraltar, he became interested in navigation and exploration. Sailing a vessel out of sight of land was still, in Henry's day, more an art than a science and was extremely hazardous. Ships were small and clumsy. Primitive compasses and instruments for reckoning latitude existed, but under shipboard conditions they were very inaccurate. Navigators could determine longitude only by keeping track of direction and estimating speed; even the most skilled could place little faith in their estimates.

Henry attempted to improve and codify navigational knowledge. To his court at Sagres, hard by Cape St. Vincent, the extreme southwestern point of Europe, he brought geographers, astronomers, and mapmakers, along with Arab and Jewish mathematicians. He built an observatory and supervised the preparation of tables measuring the declination of the sun and other navigational data. Searching for a new route to the Orient, Henry's

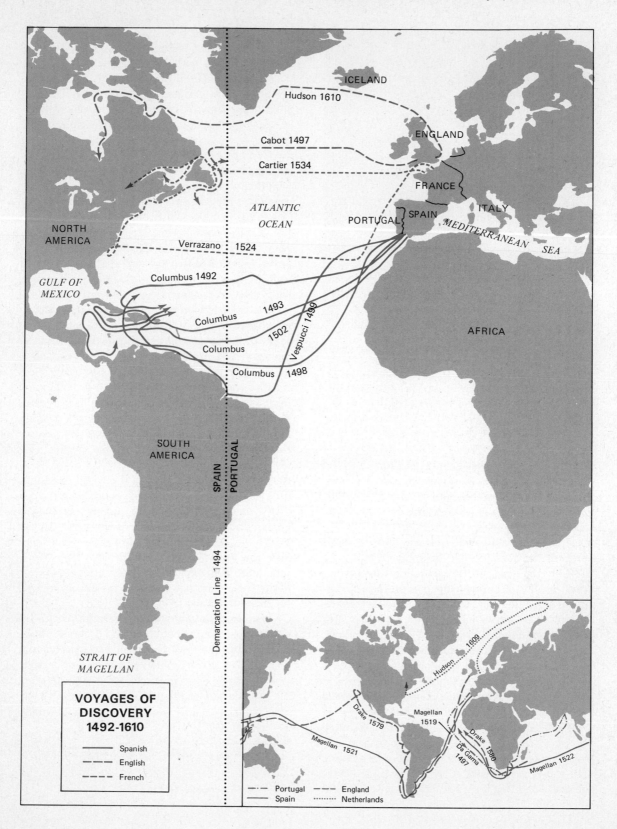

ICELAND

Hudson 1610

ENGLAND

Cabot 1497

Cartier 1534

FRANCE

ITALY

PORTUGAL SPAIN

MEDITERRANEAN SEA

ATLANTIC OCEAN

NORTH AMERICA

Verrazano 1524

GULF OF MEXICO

Columbus 1492

Columbus 1493

1502

Vespucci 1499

Columbus

Columbus 1498

AFRICA

SOUTH AMERICA

SPAIN PORTUGAL

Demarcation Line 1494

STRAIT OF MAGELLAN

VOYAGES OF DISCOVERY 1492-1610

——— Spanish
— — — English
- - - - French

Hudson 1609

Drake 1579

Magellan 1519

Drake 1580

Magellan 1521

Da Gama 1497

Magellan 1522

Portugal — - — England — — —
Spain ——— Netherlands · · · · · ·

■ A portrait which is assumed to be of Columbus, with his hair turning white and his face showing signs of age "after years of great anxiety." He was about 55 years old when he died. In fact, as far as we now know, none of the existing Columbus portraits were painted during his lifetime.

captains sailed westward to the Madeiras and the Canaries and south along the coast of Africa, seeking a way around that continent. In 1445 Dinis Dias reached Cape Verde, site of present-day Dakar.

Henry was interested in trade, but he cared more for the advancement of knowledge, for the glory of Portugal, and for spreading Christianity. When his explorers developed a profitable business in slaves, he tried to stop it. Nevertheless, the movement he began had, like the Crusades, important commercial overtones. Probably half of the Portuguese voyages were undertaken by private merchants. Without the gold, ivory, and other African goods, which brought great prosperity to Portugal, the explorers would probably not have been so bold and persistent. Yet, like Henry, they were idealists, by and large. The Age of Discovery was in a sense the last Crusade; its leaders displayed mixed religious and material motives along with a love of adventure. In any case the Portuguese realized that if they could find a way around

Africa, they might well sail directly to India and the Spice Islands.* The profits from such a voyage would surely be spectacular.

For 20 years after Henry's death in 1460, the Portuguese concentrated on exploiting his discoveries. In the 1480s King John II undertook systematic new explorations focused on reaching India. Gradually his caravels probed southward along the sweltering coast—to the equator, to the region of Angola, and beyond.

Into this bustling, prosperous, expectant little country in the corner of Europe came Christopher Columbus in 1476. Columbus was a weaver's son from Genoa, born in 1451. He had taken to the sea early, ranging widely in the Mediterranean. His arrival in Portugal was unplanned, since it resulted from the loss of his ship in a battle off the coast. For a time he became a chartmaker in Lisbon. He married a local woman. Then he was again at sea. He cruised northward, perhaps as far as Iceland, south to the equator, westward in the Atlantic to the Azores. Had his interest lain in that direction, he might well have been the first person to reach Asia by way of Africa, for in 1488, in Lisbon, he met and talked with Bartholomeu Dias, just returned from his voyage around the southern tip of Africa, which had demonstrated that the way lay clear for a voyage to the Indies. But by this time Columbus had committed himself to the westward route. When King John II refused to finance him, he turned to the Spanish court, where, after many disappointments, he finally persuaded Queen Isabella to equip his expedition. In August 1492 he set out from the port of Palos with his tiny fleet, the *Santa María,* the *Pinta,* and the *Niña.* A little more than two months later, after a stopover in the Canary Islands to repair the *Pinta's* rudder, his lookout sighted land.

Columbus' success was due in large part to his single-minded conviction that the Indies could be reached by sailing westward for a relatively short distance and that a profitable trade would develop over this route. He had persuaded Isabella to grant him, in addition to the title Admiral of the Ocean Sea, political control over all the lands he might

---

*The Moluccas, west of New Guinea. In the geography of the 15th century the Spice Islands were part of the Indies, a vague term that encompassed the southeast rim of Asia from India to what is now Indonesia.

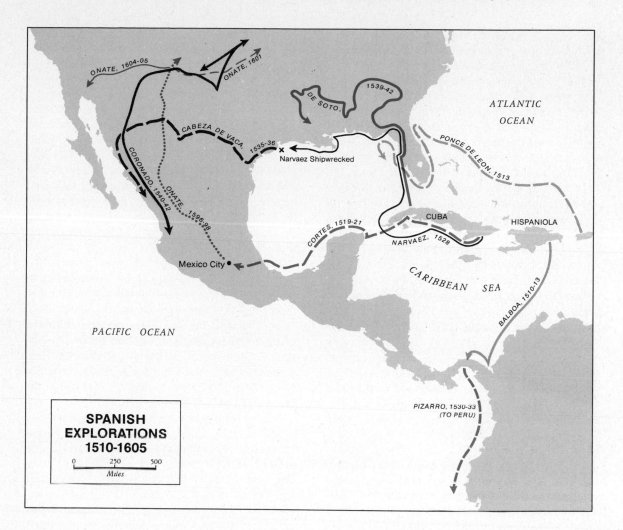

ONATE, 1604-05
ONATE, 1601
DE SOTO, 1539-42
CABEZA DE VACA, 1535-36
CORONADO, 1540-42
ONATE, 1596-98
× Narvaez Shipwrecked
CORTES, 1519-21
NARVAEZ, 1528
CUBA
HISPANIOLA
PONCE DE LEON, 1513
ATLANTIC OCEAN
CARIBBEAN SEA
BALBOA, 1510-13
Mexico City •
PACIFIC OCEAN
PIZARRO, 1530-33 (TO PERU)

SPANISH EXPLORATIONS 1510-1605

0   250   500
Miles

discover and 10 percent of the profits of the trade that would follow in the wake of his expedition. Now his conviction cost him dearly. He refused to accept the plain evidence, which everywhere confronted him, that this was an entirely new world. All about were strange plants, known neither to Europe nor to Asia. The copper-colored people who paddled out to inspect his fleet could no more follow the Arabic widely understood in the East than they could Spanish. Yet Columbus, consulting his charts, convinced himself that he had reached the Indies. That is why he called the natives Indians.

Searching for treasure, he pushed on to Cuba. When he heard the native word *Cubanocan*, meaning "middle of Cuba," he mistook it for *El Gran*

Can (Marco Polo's "Grand Khan") and sent emissaries on a fruitless search through the tropical jungle for the khan's palace. He finally returned to Spain relatively empty-handed but certain that he had explored the edge of Asia. Three later voyages failed to shake his conviction.

Columbus died in 1506, and by that time other captains had taken up the work, most of them more willing than he to accept the New World on its own terms. As early as 1493, Pope Alexander VI had divided the non-Christian world between Spain and Portugal. The next year, in the Treaty of Tordesillas, these powers negotiated an agreement about exploiting the new discoveries. In effect, Portugal continued to concentrate on Africa, leaving the New World, except for what eventually became Brazil, to the Spanish. Thereafter, from their base on Hispaniola (Santo Domingo), founded by Columbus, the Spaniards quickly fanned out through the Caribbean and then over large parts of the two continents that bordered it.

In 1513 Juan Ponce de León made the first Spanish landing on the mainland of North America, exploring the east coast of Florida. In the same year Vasco Nuñez de Balboa crossed the Isthmus of Panama and discovered the Pacific Ocean. In 1519 Hernán Cortés landed an army in Mexico and overran the empire of the Aztecs, rich in gold and silver. That same year Ferdinand Magellan set out on his epic three-year voyage around the world. By discovering the strait that bears his name, at the southern tip of South America, he gave the Spanish a clear idea of the size of the continent. In the 1530s Francisco Pizarro subdued the Inca empire in Peru, providing the Spaniards with still more treasure, drawn chiefly from the silver mines of Potosí. In 1536 Buenos Aires was founded by Pedro de Mendoza. Within another decade Francisco Vásquez de Coronado had marched as far north as Kansas and west to the Grand Canyon, and Hernando de Soto had discovered the Mississippi River. Fifty years after Columbus' first landfall, Spain was master of a huge American empire.

What explains this mighty surge of exploration and conquest? Greed for gold and power, a sense of adventure, the desire to Christianize the Indians—mixed motives propelled the *conquistadores* onward. Most saw the New World as a reincarnation of the Garden of Eden, a kind of fairyland of infinite promise. Ponce de León and many others actually expected to find the Fountain of Youth in America. Their vision, at once so selfish and so exalted, reveals the central paradox of New World history. This immense land brought out both the best and the worst in human beings. Virgin America—like all virgins—inspired conflicting feelings in men's hearts. They worshiped it for its purity and promise, yet they could not resist the opportunity to take advantage of its innocence.

The Indian and the European

The *conquistadores* were brave and imaginative men, well worthy of their fame. It must not, however, be forgotten that they wrenched their empire from innocent hands; in an important sense, the settlement of the New World, which the historian Francis Jennings has called "the invasion of America," ranks among the most flagrant examples of unprovoked aggression in human history. When Columbus landed on San Salvador he planted a cross, "as a sign," he explained to Ferdinand and Isabella, "that your Highnesses held this land as your own." Of the Lucayans, the native inhabitants of San Salvador, Columbus wrote: "The people of this island . . . are artless and generous with what they have, to such a degree as no one would believe. . . . If it be asked for, they never say no, but rather invite the person to accept it, and show as much lovingness as though they would give their hearts."

The Indians behaved this way because the Spaniards seemed the very gods. "All believe that power and goodness dwell in the sky," Columbus reported, "and they are firmly convinced that I have come from the sky." The products of Europe fascinated them. For a bit of sheet copper an inch square, they would part with a bushel of corn, while iron tools and weapons were beyond price to a people whose own technology was still in the Stone Age.

But the Spaniards would not settle for the better of the bargain. Columbus also remarked of the Lucayans: "These people are very unskilled in arms . . . with fifty men they could all be subjected and made to do all that one wished." He and his compatriots tricked and cheated the Indians at every turn. Before entering a new area, Spanish generals customarily read a *Requerimiento* (requirement) to the inhabitants. This long-winded document recited a Spanish version of the history of the human race from the Creation to the division of the non-Christian world by Pope Alexander VI and then called upon the Indians to recognize the sovereignty of the reigning Spanish monarch. ("If you do so . . . we shall receive you in all love and charity.") If this demand was rejected, "we shall powerfully enter into your country, and . . . shall take you, your wives, and your children, and shall make slaves of them. . . . The death and losses which shall accrue from this are your fault." This arrogant harangue was read in Spanish and often out of earshot of the Indians. When they responded by fighting, the Spaniards decimated them, drove them from their lands, and held the broken survivors in contempt. As a priest among them said, the *conquistadores* behaved "like

■ Spanish mistreatment of the Indians was condemned by the crusading priest Bartolomé de Las Casas, who won partial reforms. He often exaggerated for effect, however, resulting in a "Black Legend" widely exploited by Spain's enemies. These watercolors, showing alleged Spanish atrocities, were done for a 1582 French edition of his *Very Brief Account of the Destruction of the Indies.*

the most cruel Tygres, Wolves, and Lions, enrag'd with a sharp and tedious hunger."

All the colonizing powers mistreated the natives. When the Portuguese reached Africa, they carried off thousands into slavery. The Dutch behaved shamefully in the East Indies, as did the French in their colonial possessions—although, in North America at least, the French record was better than most.

English settlers described the Indians as being "of a tractable, free, and loving nature, without guile or treachery," yet in most instances they exploited and all but exterminated them. "Why should you take by force from us that which you can obtain by love?" one puzzled chieftain asked an early Virginia colonist, according to the latter's own account. The first settlers of New England dealt fairly with the local inhabitants. They made honest, if somewhat misguided, efforts to Christianize and educate them and to respect their rights. But within a few years their relations with the Indians deteriorated, and in King Philip's War (1675–1676), proportionately the bloodiest in American history, they destroyed the tribes as independent powers.

Of course the victims of white cruelty were not innocent "noble savages." During thousands of years they had spread throughout the hemisphere from Alaska to Tierra del Fuego. Some were nomads who traveled in small bands and lived by hunting and fishing. Others lived settled lives based on farming, while still others, such as the

Aztecs, were master builders and artists who ruled empires. Indians spoke many languages, and their cultures were almost as different one from the other as Spanish is from Chinese. They worshiped many different gods and in numerous ways. Some Indians were peaceful, some bloodthirsty. Some lived in tents called tepees, others in log houses. The Incas of the South American Andes constructed edifices of immense stones that still stand.

Certain traits they held in common, and some of them the Europeans shared. Being human, Indians suffered from all the human failings in one form or another. The well-meaning Spanish priest who wrote that Indians were "without evil and without guile" was as far off the mark as the one who claimed that they indulged in "every kind of intemperance and wicked lust." They were by our standards terrible male chauvinists. Except for hunting and fishing—which they regarded as sports—most of the labor in Indian communities was performed by women. Indeed, when Indians observed European men working in the fields they scoffed at them for being effeminate. "Having acquired a wife," a modern student of the Indians of Virginia writes, "a man counted on her to support him." Cruelty and war, slavery and plunder, existed in the New World long before Columbus.

Most of the terrible decimation that was everywhere the Indians' fate was caused by European diseases such as smallpox and measles against which they had no natural immunity. The population of Mexico was at least 20 million when Cortés

9

invaded the country and only 6 million a century later. European germs killed far more Mexicans than did European gunpowder and steel. The Arawak population of Hispaniola fell from perhaps 8 million when Columbus first touched there to a couple of hundred 50 years later. The fact remains that in conflicts between Indians and whites, the whites were in nearly every case the aggressors.

Narrow cultural nationalism, not greed or callousness, best explains both the Indians' and the settlers' behavior. The relativity of cultural values escaped all but a handful. If the American Indians were naive in thinking that the invaders, with their huge ships and their potent firesticks, were gods, these "gods" were equally naive in their thinking. In general Indians preferred a slow-paced, even existence to the amassing of material goods. This led Europeans to conclude that they were childlike creatures not to be treated as equals. "[Indians] do but run over the grass, as do also the foxes and wild beasts," an Englishman wrote in 1622, "so it is lawful now to take a land, which none useth, and make use of it." Despite much elevated talk about spreading Christianity, laboriously spelled out in charters and grants, many Europeans thought the native populations incapable of becoming true believers. It took a papal bull to establish the Indians' right to be converted, and when Spain introduced the Inquisition into its colonies in 1569, the natives were exempted from its control on the ground that they were incapable of rational judgment and thus were not responsible for their heretical religious beliefs.

Other troubles came from similar misunderstandings. English colonists assumed that Indian chieftains ruled with the same authority as their own kings; when tribesmen sometimes failed to honor commitments made by their leaders, the English accused them of treachery. The European inability to grasp the communal nature of land tenure among Indians also led to innumerable quarrels.

Europeans assumed that differences meant inferiority. This was their fatal error, their fundamental sin. Apparently their prejudices were not originally racial; although the record is not entirely clear, the earliest colonists seem to have considered Indians members of the white race whose skin had been darkened by exposure to the elements. The term *red man* did not become current until the 18th century.

The Spanish Decline

While Spain waxed fat on the wealth of the Americas, the other nations of western Europe did little. In 1497 and 1498 King Henry VII of England sent John Cabot to the New World. Cabot visited Newfoundland and the northeastern coast of the continent. His explorations formed the basis for later British claims in North America, but they were not followed up for many decades. In 1524 Giovanni da Verrazano made a similar voyage for France, coasting the continent from Carolina to Nova Scotia. Some ten years later the Frenchman Jacques Cartier explored the St. Lawrence River as far inland as present-day Montreal. During the 16th century fishermen from France, Spain, Portugal, and England began exploiting the limitless supplies of cod and other fish they found in the cold waters off Newfoundland. They landed at many points along the mainland coast from Nova Scotia to Labrador to collect water and wood and to dry their catches, but they made no permanent settlements until the next century.

There were many reasons for this delay, the most important probably the fact that Spain had achieved a large measure of internal tranquillity by the 16th century, while France and England were still torn by serious religious and political conflicts. The Spanish also profited from having seized upon those areas in America best suited to producing quick returns. Furthermore, in the first half of the 16th century Spain, under Charles V, dominated Europe as well as America. Charles controlled the Low Countries, most of central Europe, and part of Italy. Reinforced by the treasure of the Aztecs and the Incas, Spain seemed too mighty to be challenged in either the New World or the Old.

Under Philip II, who succeeded Charles in 1556, Spanish strength seemed at its peak, especially after Philip added Portugal to his domain in 1580. But beneath the pomp and splendor (so well captured by such painters as Velázquez and El Greco) the great empire was in trouble. The corruption and vacuity of the Spanish court had much to do with this. So did the ever increasing dependence of Spain upon the gold and silver of its colonies, which tended to undermine the local Spanish economy. Even more important was the disruption of the Catholic church throughout Europe by the Protestant Reformation.

The drive to reform and "purify" Christianity, begun by Martin Luther and carried on by men like John Calvin, had taken on important political overtones. In 1534 King Henry VIII threw off papal control and established himself as head of an *English* church. In the Low Countries resentment at Philip's attempt to suppress religious dissent was buttressed by a nationalistic desire for political independence. Philip was a religious zealot; the Spanish Inquisition crushed every glimmering of heresy at home and sought to do the same throughout the empire. At the same time Philip allowed religious issues to dominate his relations with foreign powers. Thus he supported the claims of Mary Queen of Scots to the throne of England against Queen Elizabeth I primarily because Mary was a Catholic and Elizabeth a Protestant. Elizabeth perforce became anti-Spanish. She aided the Dutch rebels and encouraged her sailors to attack Spanish shipping and challenge Spain's monopoly in the New World.

The growing political and religious conflict had economic overtones. Modern students have exploded the theory that the merchant classes were attracted to Protestantism because the Catholic church, preaching outdated concepts like "just price" and frowning on the accumulation of wealth as an end in itself, stifled their acquisitiveness. Few merchants were more devoted to the quests for riches than the Italians, for example, yet they remained loyal Catholics. So did the wool merchants of Flanders, among the most important in all Europe. Nonetheless, in some lands the business classes tended to support Protestant leaders, in part because the new sects, stressing simplicity, made fewer financial demands upon the faithful than the Catholics did. Merchants generally supported Elizabeth against the Catholic Mary in England, and the friends of independence against Philip in the Low Countries.

As the commercial classes rose to positions of influence, England, France, and the United Provinces of the Netherlands experienced a flowering of trade and industry. The Dutch built the largest merchant fleet in the world. Dutch traders captured most of the Far Eastern business once monopolized by the Portuguese and infiltrated Spain's Caribbean stronghold. A number of English merchant companies, soon to play a vital role as colonizers, sprang up in the last half of the 16th century. These joint-stock companies, ancestors of the modern corporation, enabled groups of investors to pool their capital and limit their individual responsibilities to the sums actually invested—a very important protection in such risky enterprises. The Muscovy Company, the Levant Company, and the East India Company were the most important of these ventures.

English Beginnings in America

English merchants took part in many kinds of international activity. The Muscovy Company spent large sums searching for a passage to China around Scandinavia and dispatched six overland expeditions in an effort to reach the Orient by way of Russia and Persia. In the 1570s Martin Frobisher made three voyages across the Atlantic, hoping to discover a northwest passage to the Orient or new gold-bearing lands.

Such projects, particularly in the area of America, received strong but concealed support from the Crown. Queen Elizabeth I invested heavily in Frobisher's expeditions. England was still too weak to challenge Spain openly, but Elizabeth hoped to break its overseas monopoly just the same. She encouraged her boldest sea dogs to plunder Spanish merchantmen on the high seas. When Captain Francis Drake was about to set sail on his fabulous round-the-world voyage in 1577, the queen said to him: "Drake! . . . I would gladly be revenged on the King of Spain for divers injuries that I have received." Drake, who hated the Spaniards because of a treacherous attack they had once made on the fleet of his kinsman and former chief, Sir John Hawkins, took her at her word. He sailed through the Strait of Magellan and terrorized the west coast of South America, capturing the Spanish treasure ship *Cacafuego*, heavily laden with Peruvian silver. After exploring the coast of California, which he claimed for England, Drake crossed the Pacific and went on to circumnavigate the globe, returning home in triumph in 1580. Although Elizabeth took pains to deny it to the Spanish ambassador, Drake's voyage was officially sponsored. Elizabeth being the principal shareholder in the venture, most of the ill-gotten Spanish bullion went into the Royal Treasury rather than Drake's pocket.

When schemes to place settlers in the New

■ The swashbuckling Raleigh posed with his son Wat in 1602.

World began to mature at about this time, the queen again became involved. The first English effort was led by Sir Humphrey Gilbert, an Oxford-educated soldier and courtier with a lifelong interest in far-off places. Gilbert owned a share of the Muscovy Company; as early as 1566 he was trying to get a royal grant for an expedition in search of a northeast passage to the Orient. But soon his interests concentrated on the northwest route. He read widely in navigational and geographical lore and in 1576 wrote a persuasive *Discourse . . . to prove a passage by the north west to Cathaia.* Two years later the queen authorized him to explore and colonize "heathen lands not actually possessed by any Christian prince."

We know almost nothing about Gilbert's first attempt except that it occurred in 1578–1579; in 1583 he set sail again with five ships and over two hundred settlers. He landed them on Newfound-

land, then evidently decided to seek a more congenial site farther south. However, no colony was established, and on his way back to England his ship went down in a storm off the Azores.

Gilbert's half brother, Sir Walter Raleigh, took up the work. Handsome, ambitious, and impulsive, Raleigh was a great favorite of Elizabeth. He sent a number of expeditions to explore the east coast of North America, a land he named Virginia in honor of his unmarried sovereign. In 1585 he settled about a hundred men on Roanoke Island, off the North Carolina coast, but these settlers returned home the next year. In 1587 Raleigh sent another group to Roanoke, including a number of women and children. Unfortunately, the supply ships sent to the colony in 1588 failed to arrive; when help did get there in 1590, not a soul could be found. The fate of these pioneers has never been determined.

One reason for the delay in getting aid to the Roanoke colonists was the attack of the Spanish Armada on England in 1588. Angered by English raids on his shipping and by the assistance Elizabeth was giving to the rebels in the Netherlands, King Philip II had decided to invade England. His motives were religious as well as political and economic, for England was now seemingly committed to Protestantism. His great fleet of some 130 ships bore huge crosses on the sails as if on another crusade. The Armada carried 30,000 men and 2,400 guns, the largest naval force ever assembled up to that time. However, the English fleet badly mauled this armada, and a series of storms completed its destruction. Thereafter, although the war continued and Spanish sea power remained formidable, Spain could no longer block English penetration of the New World.

Experience had shown that the cost of planting settlements in a wilderness 3,000 miles from England was more than any individual purse could bear. (Raleigh lost about £40,000 in his overseas ventures; early in the game he began to advocate government support of colonization.) As early as 1584 Richard Hakluyt, England's foremost authority on the Americas, made a convincing case for royal aid. In his *Discourse on Western Planting,* Hakluyt stressed the military advantages of building "two or three strong fortes" along the Atlantic coast of North America. Ships operating from such bases would make life uncomfortable for "king Phillipe" by intercepting his treasure fleets—a matter, Hakluyt added coolly, "that toucheth him indeede to the quicke." Colonies in America would also provide a market for English woolens, bring in valuable tax revenues, and perhaps offer employment for the swarms of "lustie youthes that be turned to no provitable use" at home. From the great American forests would come the timber and naval stores needed to build a bigger navy and merchant marine.

Queen Elizabeth read Hakluyt's essay, but she was too cautious and too devious to act boldly on his suggestions. Only after her death in 1603 did full-scale efforts to found English colonies in America begin, and even then the organizing force came from merchant capitalists, not from the Crown. This was unfortunate, because the search for material rewards, and especially for quick profits, dominated the thinking of these enterprisers. Larger national ends (while not neglected, because the Crown was always involved) were subordinated. On the other hand, if private investors had not taken the lead, no colony would have been established at this time.

■ This sampling of the first authentic views of New World wildlife is the work of John White, an English watercolorist who was with Raleigh's Roanoke colonists in 1585 and who later served as governor of the ill-fated colony. White sketched the box tortoise at Roanoke. The flamingo was drawn in the Caribbean, where the Raleigh colonists stopped on their voyage to Roanoke.

The Settlement of Virginia

In September 1605 two groups of English merchants petitioned the new king, James I, for a license to colonize Virginia, as the whole area claimed by England was then named. This was granted the following April, and two joint-stock companies were organized, one controlled by London merchants, the other by a group from the area around Plymouth and Bristol.* Both were under the control of a Royal Council for Virginia, but James appointed prominent stockholders to the council, which meant that the companies had considerable independence.

This first charter revealed the commercial motivation of both king and company in the plainest terms. Although it spoke of spreading Christianity and bringing "the Infidels and Savages, living in those Parts, to human Civility," it stressed the right "to dig, mine, and search for all Manner of

---

*The London Company was to colonize south Virginia, while the Plymouth Company, the Plymouth-Bristol group of merchants, was granted northern Virginia.

Mines of Gold, Silver, and Copper." On December 20, 1606, the London Company dispatched about a hundred settlers aboard the *Susan Constant, Discovery,* and *Godspeed.* This little band reached the Chesapeake Bay area in May 1607 and founded Jamestown, the first permanent English colony in the New World.

From the start everything seemed to go wrong. The immigrants established themselves in what was practically a malarial swamp simply because it appeared easily defensible against Indian attack. They failed to get a crop in the ground because of the lateness of the season and were soon almost without food. Their leaders, mere deputies of the London merchants, did not respond to the challenges of the wilderness. The settlers lacked the skills that pioneers need. More than a third of them were "gentlemen" unused to manual labor, and many of the rest were the gentlemen's body servants, almost equally unequipped for the task of colony building. During the first winter more than half of the settlers died.

All the land belonged to the company, and aside from the gentlemen and their retainers, most of the settlers were only hired laborers who had contracted to work for it for seven years. This was most unfortunate. The situation demanded people skilled in agriculture, and the tragedy was that such a labor force was available. In England times were bad. The growth of the textile industry had led to an increased demand for wool, and great landowners were dismissing laborers and tenant farmers and shifting from labor-intensive agriculture to sheep raising. Inflation, caused by a shortage of goods to supply the needs of a growing population and by the influx of large amounts of American silver into Europe, worsened the plight of the dispossessed. Many landless farmers were eager to migrate if offered a decent opportunity to obtain land and make new lives for themselves.

The merchant directors of the London Company, knowing little or nothing about Virginia, failed to provide the colony with effective guidance. They set up a council of settlers, but they kept all real power in their own hands. Instead of stressing farming and public improvements, they directed the energies of the colonists into such futile labors as searching for gold (the first supply ship devoted precious space to two goldsmiths and two "refiners"), glass blowing, silk raising, wine making, and exploring the local rivers in hopes of finding a water route to the Pacific and the riches of China.

One colonist, Captain John Smith, tried to stop some of this foolishness. Smith had come to Virginia after a fantastic career as a soldier of fortune in eastern Europe, where he had fought many battles, been enslaved by a Turkish pasha, and triumphed in a variety of adventures, military and amorous. Quickly realizing that finding food was the job of first importance, he developed into an expert forager and Indian trader. "A plaine soldier that can use a pickaxe and a spade is better than five knights," Smith said. Toward Indians he was stern but by his standards fair. He sought to control what he called the "proud Savages" yet to avoid bloodshed. Whether he was actually rescued from death at the hands of the Indians by the princess Pocahontas is not certain, but there is little doubt that without him the colony would have perished in the early days. However, he stayed in Virginia only two years.

Lacking intelligent direction and faced with appalling hardships, the colonists failed to develop a sufficient sense of common purpose. Each year they died in wholesale lots. The causes of death were disease, starvation (there was even a case of cannibalism among the desperate survivors), Indian attack, and above all, ignorance and folly. Between 1606 and 1622 the London Company invested more than £160,000 in Virginia and sent over about 6,000 settlers. Yet no dividends were ever earned, and of the 6,000, fewer than 2,000 were still alive in 1622. In 1625 the population was down to about 1,300. The only profits were those taken by certain shrewd investors who had organized a joint-stock company to transport women to Virginia "to be made wives" by the colonists.

One major problem, the mishandling of the local Indians, was largely the colonists' doing. It is quite likely that the settlement would not have survived if the Powhatan Indians had not given the colonists food in the first hard winters, taught them the ways of the forest, introduced them to valuable new crops such as corn and yams, and showed them how to clear dense timber by girdling the trees and burning them down after they were dead. The settlers accepted Indian aid, then took whatever else they wanted by force. "[They] conciliated the Powhatan people while they were of use," one historian has written, "and pressed them remorselessly, facelessly, mechanically, as

■ Engravings from Captain John Smith's *General Historie Of Virginia . . .* (1624) show Smith captured by Indians (left) and being rescued by Pocahontas (right). The engraver was indebted for his setting and figures to de Bry's *America*. The scene at left, for example, is a composite of no less than four de Bry engravings, with Smith, seated in the foreground, as a later addition.

innocent of conscious ill will as a turning wheel, when they became of less value than their land." The Indians did not submit meekly to such treatment. They proved brave, skillful, and ferocious fighters, once they understood that their very existence was at stake. The burden of Indian fighting might easily have been more than the frail settlement could bear.

What saved the Virginians was not the brushing aside of the Indians but their gradual realization that they must produce their own food—cattle raising was especially important—and the cultivation of tobacco, which flourished there and could be sold profitably in England. Once the settlers discovered tobacco, no amount of company pressure could keep them at wasteful tasks like looking for gold. The "restraint of plantinge Tobacco," one company official commented, "is a thing so distastefull to them that they will with no patience indure to heare of it."

John Rolfe, who is also famous for marrying Pocahontas, introduced West Indian tobacco—much milder than the local "weed" and thus more valuable—in 1612. With money earned from the sale of tobacco, the colonists could buy the manufactured articles they could not produce in a raw new country; this freed them from dependence on outside subsidies. It did not mean profit for the London Company, however, for by the time to-

bacco caught on, the surviving original colonists had served their seven years and were no longer hired hands. To attract more settlers, the company had permitted first tenancy and then outright ownership of farms. Thus the profits of tobacco went largely to the planters, not to the "adventurers" who had organized the colony.

Important administrative reforms helped Virginia to forge ahead. A revised charter in 1612 extended the London Company's control over its own affairs in Virginia. Despite serious intracompany rivalry between groups headed by Sir Thomas Smythe and Sir Edwin Sandys, a somewhat more intelligent direction of Virginia's affairs resulted. First the merchants appointed a single resident governor and gave him sufficient authority to control the settlers. Then they made it much easier for settlers to obtain land of their own. In 1619 a rudimentary form of self-government was instituted: a House of Burgesses, consisting of delegates chosen in each district, met at Jamestown to advise the governor on local problems. The company was not bound by the actions of the burgesses, but from this seed sprang the system of representative government that became the American pattern.

These reforms, however, came too late to save the fortunes of the London Company. In 1619 the Sandys faction won control and started an extensive development program, but in 1622 a bloody Indian attack took the lives of 347 colonists. Morale sank and James I, who disliked Sandys, decided that the colony was being badly managed. In 1624 the charter was revoked and Virginia became a royal colony. As a financial proposition the company was a fiasco; the shareholders lost every penny they had invested. Nonetheless, by 1624 Virginia was firmly established and beginning to prosper.

The sociologist Sigmund Diamond has offered an interesting theoretical explanation of how and why the Virginia colony changed from a mere commercial organization to a real society. In the beginning, he asserts, there was no cement binding the colonists into a community; either employees or bosses, they were all oriented toward company headquarters in London. In order to attract more settlers and motivate them to work, the company had to grant them special privileges and status, such as political power and the right to own land, which had the effect of making them more dependent upon one another. By thus destroying the reliance of the colonists on the company, these actions undermined company control over the colonists. "The new relationships in which [the Virginians] were now involved," Diamond explains, "were of greater importance than the company relationship. . . . It was the company's fate to have created a country and to have destroyed itself in the process."

The Pilgrims of Plymouth Plantation

While the Virginia colony limped along under merchant control, a community of English people living in Holland approached Sir Edwin Sandys, seeking permission to establish a settlement near the mouth of the Hudson River, which was within the London Company's grant. This group of religious dissenters, called Pilgrims, had fled England in 1608 to escape persecution and had settled in Leyden. Now, a decade later, distressed by Spanish-Dutch religious conflicts and by the fact that their children were losing contact with their English traditions, they had decided to seek a place to live and worship as they pleased in the emptiness of the New World—another example of the hope that America inspired in the hearts of Europeans.

Sandys, while not sympathetic to their religious views, appreciated their inherent worth and saw to it that their wish was granted. Since the Pilgrims lacked financial resources, they formed a joint-stock company with other prospective emigrants and some optimistic investors who paid their expenses in return for half the profits of their labor. In September 1620, about a hundred strong—only 35 of them were Pilgrims from Leyden—the group set out from Plymouth, England, on the ship *Mayflower*.

These were the first settlers to leave the mother country primarily for religious reasons. In England the Protestant Reformation, while based on real differences of religious principle, never escaped completely from the political motives that had led King Henry VIII to break with the Catholic church. Henry had revolted chiefly in order to rid himself of a wife who had not borne him male heirs and to strengthen his control of the realm. Nor did his daughter Elizabeth adhere to the new order primarily for reasons of conscience; power politics—particularly the enmity of Catholic Spain and the strategic importance of the Protestant rebels in the Low Countries—dictated her stand on religious questions.

However, most of Elizabeth's subjects were not so callous about philosophical and spiritual issues. Many remained steadfastly Catholic. Others considered the state-sponsored Anglican church too "popish" and hoped to push the Reformation further. While professing to be good Anglicans, they wanted to "purify" their church by ridding it of Roman Catholic vestiges. Services should be simpler, they believed, all the higher clergy should be eliminated, and each parish should have more to say about local church affairs.

Unlike these Puritans, the Separatists thought the Anglican church too corrupt for salvage. Each congregation ought to run its own affairs, and church members must decide for themselves their own religious beliefs. In the England of James I, Puritans could satisfy both Crown and conscience, but Separatists like the Pilgrims had to go underground or flee. Having tried both alternatives without finding peace, the Pilgrims were now seeking a third way out in America.

Had the *Mayflower* reached its intended destination, the Pilgrims might have been soon forgotten. Instead the ship touched America slightly to the north, on Cape Cod Bay. Unwilling to remain

The Anabaptist.   The Brownist.

The Familist.   The Papist.

■ A 1641 English cartoon comments on the religious turmoil of the period. The Roman Catholic, "The Papist," at lower right joins in a game of "abusing" the Bible along with three Protestant sects opposed to the Church of England.

Arriving on the bleak Massachusetts shore in December, at a place they called Plymouth, the settlers had to endure a winter of desperate hunger. About half of them died. But in the spring the local Indians provided food and advice. After a bountiful harvest the following November, they celebrated the first Thanksgiving feast, thereby establishing another tradition. Although they grew neither rich nor numerous on the thin New England soil, the Pilgrims' place in history was assured. They won their battles not with sword and gunpowder like Cortés nor with bulldozers and dynamite like modern pioneers, but with simple courage and practical piety. The story of their trials and eventual triumphs has been preserved in *History of Plimmoth Plantation,* the first American history, written by William Bradford, who served 30 terms as governor.

Massachusetts Bay Puritans

The Pilgrims were not the first English colonists to inhabit the northern regions. The Plymouth Company had settled a group on the Kennebec River in 1607. These colonists gave up after a few months, but fishermen and traders continued to visit the area, which was christened New England by Captain John Smith after an expedition there in 1614. Several more or less permanent trading posts were founded. Then, in 1620, the Plymouth Company was reorganized as the Council for New England. More interested in real estate deals than in colonizing, the council disposed of a number of tracts in the area north of Cape Cod, including a large grant in 1622 to its most influential member, Sir Ferdinando Gorges, and his friend John Mason, former governor of an English settlement on Newfoundland. Their domain included a considerable part of what is now Maine and New Hampshire. The most significant of these grants was a very small one made to a group of Puritans from Dorchester, who established a settlement at Salem. In 1629 the "Dorchester Adventurers" organized the Massachusetts Bay Company and obtained a royal grant to the area between the Charles and Merrimack rivers.

The Massachusetts Bay Company was conceived as another commercial venture, but England had become a difficult place for the Puritans by this time. Charles I was now king, and

longer at the mercy of storm-tossed December seas, the settlers decided to remain. Since they were outside the jurisdiction of the London Company, some members of the group claimed to be free of all governmental control. Therefore, before going ashore, the Pilgrims drew up the Mayflower Compact. "We whose names are underwritten," the Compact ran, "do by these Presents, solemnly and mutually in the presence of God and one another covenant and combine ourselves under into a civil Body Politick . . . and by Virtue hereof do enact . . . such just and equal Laws . . . as shall be thought most meet and convenient for the general Good of the Colony."

In this simple manner, ordinary people created a government. The Compact, prototype of many similar covenants, some explicit, others existing by tacit agreement, illustrates the impact of the immense emptiness of the New World on pioneers. Alone in the wilderness, they recognized their interdependence and came to see the need for social and political organizations. This realization had much to do with the development of American republican government and democracy.

■ An engraving of John Winthrop, based on a portrait in the Massachusetts Senate chamber, shows the great Puritan at the height of his moral and intellectual power.

he was much influenced in religious matters by William Laud, the staunch Anglican cleric. Laud strengthened the elaborate ritual and tight central control that the Puritans found so distasteful in the Anglican church. With the king's support, he removed from their pulpits ministers with Puritan leanings. Since it was no longer possible for conscientious Puritans to remain within the fold, the leaders of the Massachusetts Bay Company decided to migrate to America in force. Taking their charter with them—a crucial step which meant that their colony became practically self-governing—they set out in the summer of 1630 with almost a thousand settlers. By fall they had founded Boston and a number of other towns, and the Puritan commonwealth was under way.

The settlers suffered fewer hardships in the early years than had the early Jamestown and Plymouth colonists, and they were immensely aided by a constant influx of new recruits. Continuing bad times and the persecution of Puritans at home led to the Great Migration of the 1630s. Only a minority came to Massachusetts (many thousands poured into the new English colonies in the West Indies), but by 1640 well over 10,000 had arrived. This concentrated group of industrious and fairly prosperous colonists made possible the early development of a complex civilization. Agriculture, while essential, was not particularly profitable; therefore many settlers turned to fishing, the fur trade, and shipbuilding.

The directors of the Massachusetts Bay Company believed they were engaged in a divinely inspired enterprise and saw themselves as governing the settlement as God's agents. That religion and politics were interrelated they regarded as axiomatic. Before leaving England, the stockholders had elected John Winthrop governor of the colony. Winthrop had a profound faith in the Puritan experiment. Their settlement would be like "a city upon a hill," he said. "The eyes of all the people are upon us." Being a practical man who preferred to achieve his ends by negotiation and persuasion, he realized that the handful of men who held power under the charter could not govern effectively without popular support. A broad-based authority was essential to growth and social harmony. He and the other leaders soon decided to make about a hundred of the adult male settlers "freemen" of the commonwealth, thereby permitting them to participate in political affairs.

Apparently some of these men were not church members, but thereafter nonmembers were specifically barred from freemanship. The freemen quickly won the right to choose the governor and to elect representatives to a local legislature called the General Court. Although the system was not democratic in the modern sense, as long as the community retained a high degree of cohesiveness and commitment to Puritan beliefs, it worked well. While ministers were prestigious figures, they were ultimately subject to the control of their parishioners; questions of church policy were decided by the majority vote of members of the congregation.

Other New England Colonies

From the successful Massachusetts Bay colony, settlement radiated outward to other areas of New England because of population growth and Puritan intolerance. In 1629 Sir Ferdinando Gorges and John Mason divided their holdings, Gorges taking the Maine section (enlarged in 1639) and

Mason New Hampshire, but neither succeeded in making much of his claim. Massachusetts gradually took over these areas. The heirs of Gorges and Mason managed to regain legal possession briefly in the 1670s, but Massachusetts bought title to Maine for a pittance (£1,250) in 1677. New Hampshire became a royal colony in 1680.

Meanwhile, beginning in 1635, a number of Massachusetts congregations had pushed southwestward into the fertile valley of the Connecticut River. A group headed by the Reverend Thomas Hooker founded Hartford in 1636. Hooker was influential in the drafting of the Fundamental Orders, a sort of constitution creating a government for the valley towns, in 1639. The Fundamental Orders resembled the Massachusetts system, except that they did not limit voting to church members. Other groups of Puritans came directly from England to settle towns in and around New Haven in the 1630s. These were incorporated into Connecticut shortly after the Hooker colony obtained a royal charter in 1662.

Competition between Connecticut and Massachusetts Bay over land led to quarrels that exacerbated Indian troubles, and Hooker and some of the other Connecticut pioneers quarreled with the Massachusetts leaders about religious questions. They did not differ over basic principles. This was not true, however, in the case of all early settlers, and when real dissenters spoke up, the majority harshly repressed them. Roger Williams, a Salem minister, was a religious zealot even by Puritan standards. His belief in the freedom of individuals to practice their own faith led him to object to the alliance between the church and the civil government in Massachusetts Bay. Since "forced religion stinks in God's nostrils," magistrates should have no authority in religious affairs, he insisted. Williams advanced the radical idea that it was "a National sinne" for the colonists (or for that matter the king) to take possession of any American land until they had bought it from the Indians. When he persisted in advocating these heresies, he was banished. He took refuge in the Narragansett Bay area with a group of his followers, founding Providence in 1636.

Anne Hutchinson, wife of a prominent Boston settler, also got into trouble with the dominant clique in Massachusetts. A headstrong, rather opinionated woman, she presumed to discuss and sometimes to disagree with the sermons of her minister. Her own mystical brand of Puritanism, a variety of Antinomianism, denied any necessary relation between moral conduct and salvation. Possession of God's grace, not mere good behavior, was the key to the gates of Heaven. Even the authority of the Bible, she argued, let alone that of the ministry, must yield to insights directly inspired by God in the individual. Anne Hutchinson's loose and intellectually imprecise interpretation of "salvation by grace" attracted many followers but clashed with the official theology. She too was banished. Her group settled near Providence, and soon other dissidents collected in the area.

In 1644 Williams obtained a charter for these settlements. The colony was called the Rhode Island and Providence Plantation. Its government was relatively democratic, with religious freedom allowed to all and a rigid separation of church and state maintained. After Charles II became king in 1660, a new charter substantially confirmed Rhode Island's liberal system.

French and Dutch Settlements

While the English were settling Virginia and New England, other European powers were challenging Spain's monopoly in the New World. French explorers had pushed up the St. Lawrence as far as the site of Montreal in the 1530s, and beginning in 1603, Samuel de Champlain made several voyages to the region. In 1608 he founded Quebec, and he had penetrated as far inland as Lake Huron before the Pilgrims left Leyden. The French also planted colonies in St. Christopher, Guadeloupe, Martinique, and other islands in the West Indies after 1625.

Through their West India Company, the Dutch also established themselves in the West Indies. On the mainland they founded New Netherland in the Hudson Valley, basing their claim to the region on the explorations of Henry Hudson in 1609. As early as 1624 there was a Dutch outpost, Fort Orange, on the site of present-day Albany. Two years later New Amsterdam was located at the mouth of the Hudson River, and Manhattan Island was purchased from the Indians by Peter Minuit, the director-general of the West India Company, for trading goods worth about 60 guilders.

NORTH AMERICAN COLONIES TO 1650

- English
- French
- Dutch
- Swedish
- Spanish

The Dutch traded with the Indians for furs and plundered Spanish colonial commerce enthusiastically. Through the Charter of Privileges of Patroons, which authorized large grants of land to individuals who would bring over 50 settlers, they tried to encourage large-scale agriculture. Only one such estate, Rensselaerswyck, on the Hudson south of Fort Orange, owned by the rich Amsterdam merchant Kiliaen Van Rensselaer, was successful. Peter Minuit, who was removed from his post in New Amsterdam in 1631, organized a group of Swedish settlers several years later and founded the colony of New Sweden on the lower reaches of the Delaware River. New Sweden was in constant conflict with the Dutch, who finally overran it in 1655. But the Dutch were never deeply committed to colonizing America; their chief activity was in the Far East, where they took over the role formerly played by the Portuguese.

Maryland and the Carolinas

The Virginia and New England colonies were essentially corporate ventures. Most of the other English colonies in America were founded by individuals or by a handful of partners who obtained charters from the ruling sovereign. It was becoming easier to establish settlements in America, for experience had taught the English a great deal about the colonization process. Settlers knew better what to bring with them and what to do after they arrived. Moreover, the psychological barrier was much less formidable. Like a modern athlete seeking to run a mile in less than four minutes, colonizers knew after about 1630 that what they were attempting *could* be accomplished. And conditions in Europe in the mid 17th century encouraged thousands to migrate. Both in England and on the Continent the economic future seemed unpromising, while political and religious persecution erupted in one country after another, each time supplying America with new waves of refugees.

Numbers of influential Englishmen were eager to try their luck as colonizers. The grants they received made them "proprietors" of great estates which were, at least in theory, their personal property. By granting land to settlers in return for a small annual rent, they hoped to obtain a steadily increasing income while holding a valuable specu-

■ This view of Charleston, dating from the 1730s, is a so-called commercial print, many of which were issued in England to attract settlers to the colonies. The caption under the print comments on "the agreeable and wholesome" climate and the "very great & flourishing Town adorned with handsome and commodious buildings."

lative interest in all undeveloped land. At the same time their political power, guaranteed by charter, would become increasingly important as their colonies expanded. In practice, however, the realities of life in America limited their freedom of action and their profits.

One of the first of the proprietary colonies was Maryland, granted by Charles I to George Calvert, Lord Baltimore. Calvert had a deep interest in America, being a member both of the London Company and of the Council for New England and owner of a colony called Avalon in Newfoundland. He hoped to profit financially from Maryland but, since he was a Catholic, he also intended the colony to be a haven for his coreligionists.

Calvert died shortly before Charles approved his charter, so the grant went to his son Cecilius. The first settlers arrived in 1634, founding St. Mary's just north of the Potomac. The presence of the now well-established Virginia colony nearby greatly aided the Marylanders; they had little difficulty in getting started and in developing an economy based, like Virginia's, on tobacco. However, an acrimonious dispute raged for some years between the two colonies over their common boundary. Despite the emptiness of the American wilderness, settlers could squabble over a few acres as bitterly as any European peasants.

The Maryland charter was similar to that of the isolated county palatine of Durham in the north of England, whose bishop-overlords had almost regal authority. Lord Baltimore had the right to establish feudal manors, hold people in serfdom, make laws, and set up his own courts. He soon discovered, however, that to attract settlers he had to allow them to own their farms and that to maintain any political influence at all he had to give the settlers considerable say in local affairs. Other wise concessions marked his handling of the religious question. He would have preferred an exclusively Catholic colony, but while Catholics did go to Maryland, there existed from the beginning a large Protestant majority. Baltimore solved this problem by "accepting" a Toleration Act (1649) that guaranteed freedom of religion to anyone "professing to believe in Jesus Christ." Because the Calverts adjusted their pretensions to American realities, they made a fortune out of Maryland and maintained an influence in the colony until the Revolution.

During the period of the English Civil War and Oliver Cromwell's Protectorate, no important new colonial enterprises were undertaken. With the restoration of the monarchy in 1660 came a new wave of settlement, for the government wished to expand and strengthen its hold on North America. To do so, it granted generous terms to settlers—

21

easy access to land, religious toleration, and political rights—all far more extensive than those available in England.

Most of the earlier colonies were organized by groups of merchants; those of the Restoration period reflected the concerns of great English landowners. The first new venture involved a huge grant south of Virginia to eight proprietors with large interests in colonial affairs, including the Earl of Clarendon, Sir Anthony Ashley Cooper, and Sir William Berkeley, a former governor of Virginia. These men did not intend to recruit large numbers of European settlers, depending instead upon the "excess" population of New England, Virginia, and the West Indies. They (and the Crown) hoped for a diversified economy, the charter granting tax concessions to exporters of wine, silk, oil, olives, and other exotic products. The region was called Carolina in honor of Charles I.

The Carolina charter, like that of Maryland, accorded the proprietors wide authority. With the help of the political philosopher John Locke, they drafted a grandiose plan of government called the Fundamental Constitutions, which created a hereditary nobility and provided for huge paper land grants to a hierarchy headed by the lords proprietors and lesser "landgraves" and "caciques." The manpower to support the feudal society was to be supplied by peasants called "leet-men."

This pretentious system proved unworkable. The landgraves and caciques got grants, but they could not find leet-men willing to toil on their domains. Probably the purpose of all this elaborate feudal nonsense was promotional; the proprietors hoped to convince investors that they could make fortunes in Carolina rivaling those of English lords. In reality, life followed the pattern established in Virginia and Maryland, with nearly all white men owning their own property and possessing a good deal of political power.

The first settlers arrived in 1670, most of them from the sugar plantations of Barbados, where slave labor was driving out small independent farmers. Charles Town (now Charleston) was founded in 1680. Another center of population sprang up in the Albemarle district, just south of Virginia, settled largely by individuals from that colony. Two quite different societies grew up in these areas. The Charleston colony, with an economy based on a thriving trade in furs and on the export of foodstuffs to the West Indies, was pros-

perous and cosmopolitan. The Albemarle settlement was poorer and more "backwoodsy." Eventually, in 1712, the two were formally separated, becoming North and South Carolina.

The Middle Colonies

Gradually it became clear that the English would dominate the entire stretch of coast between the St. Lawrence Valley and Florida. After 1660 only the Dutch challenged their monopoly. The two nations, once allies against Spain, had fallen out because of the fierce competition of their textile manufacturers and merchants. England's efforts to bar Dutch merchant vessels from its colonial trade also brought them into conflict in America. Charles II precipitated a showdown by granting his brother James, Duke of York, the entire area between Connecticut and Maryland. This was tantamount to declaring war. In 1664 English forces captured New Amsterdam without a fight—there were only 1,500 people in the town—and soon the rest of the Dutch settlements capitulated. New Amsterdam became New York. The duke did not interfere much with the way of life of the Dutch settlers, and they were quickly reconciled to English rule. New York had no local assembly until the 1680s, but this had been equally true under the Dutch.

In 1664, even before the capture of New Amsterdam, the Duke of York gave New Jersey, the region between the Hudson and the Delaware, to John, Lord Berkeley and Sir George Carteret. To attract settlers, these proprietors offered land on easy terms and established freedom of religion and a democratic system of local government. A considerable number of Puritans from New England and Long Island moved to the new province.

In 1674 Berkeley sold his interest in New Jersey to two Quakers. The Quakers were left-wing Separatists who believed that they could communicate directly with their Maker; their religion required neither ritual nor ministers. Originally a sect emotional to the point of fanaticism, by the 1670s the Quakers had come to stress the doctrine of the Inner Light—the direct, mystical experience of religious truth—which they believed possible for all persons. They were at once humble and fiercely proud, pacifistic yet unwilling to bow before any person or to surrender their right to worship as they pleased. They distrusted the intellect in religious matters and, while ardent proselytizers of their own beliefs, they tolerated those of others cheerfully. When faced with opposition, they resorted to passive resistance, a tactic that embroiled them in grave difficulties in England and in most of the American colonies. In Massachusetts Bay, for example, six Quakers were executed when they refused either to conform to Puritan ideas or to leave the colony.

The acquisition of New Jersey (when Sir George Carteret died in 1680, they purchased the rest of the colony) gave the Quakers a place where they could practice their religion in peace. The proprietors, in keeping with their principles, drafted an extremely liberal constitution for the colony, the Concessions and Agreements of 1677, which created an autonomous legislature and guaranteed settlers freedom of conscience, the right of trial by jury, and other civil rights.

The main Quaker effort at colonization came in the region immediately west of New Jersey, a fertile area belonging to William Penn, the son of a wealthy English admiral. Penn had early rejected a life of ease and had become a Quaker missionary. As a result, he was twice jailed. Yet he possessed qualities that enabled him to hold the respect and friendship of people who found his ideas abhorrent. From his father, Penn had inherited a claim to £16,000 that the admiral had lent Charles II. The king, reluctant to part with that much cash, paid off the debt in 1681 by giving Penn the region north of Maryland and west of the Delaware River, insisting only that it be named Pennsylvania, in honor of the admiral. The Duke of York then added Delaware, the region between Maryland and Delaware Bay, to Penn's holdings.

William Penn considered his colony a "Holy Experiment." He treated the Indians fairly, buying title to their lands and trying to protect them in their dealings with settlers and traders. Anyone who believed in "one Almighty and Eternal God" was entitled to freedom of worship. His political ideas were paternalistic rather than democratic—the assembly he established could only approve or reject laws proposed by the governor and council—but individual rights were as well protected in Pennsylvania as in New Jersey.

Penn's altruism, however, did not prevent him from taking excellent care of his own interests. He sold land to settlers large and small on easy terms but reserved huge tracts for himself and attached quitrents (see page 31) to that which he disposed of. He promoted Pennsylvania tirelessly, writing a series of glowing, although perfectly honest, descriptions of the colony which were circulated widely in England and, in translation, on the Continent. These attracted many settlers, including large numbers of Germans—the Pennsylvania "Dutch" (a corruption of *Deutsch,* meaning "German").

Penn was neither a doctrinaire nor an ivory-tower philosopher. He came himself to Pennsylvania and agreed to adjustments in his first Frame of Government when local conditions demonstrated the need for change. His combination of wisdom, liberality, and good salesmanship helped the colony to prosper and grow rapidly. Of course the presence of well-settled colonies on all sides and the richness of the soil had much to do with this happy state of affairs. By 1685 there were almost 9,000 settlers in Pennsylvania, and by 1700 twice that number, a heartening contrast to the early history of Virginia and Plymouth. Pennsylvania produced wheat, corn, rye, and other crops in abundance and found a ready market for its surpluses on the sugar plantations of the West Indies.

The Settlement of Georgia

Nearly 50 years after the settlement of Pennsylvania, a final English colony was established. This was Georgia, and the circumstances of its founding were most unusual. A group of London philanthropists concerned over the plight of honest persons imprisoned for debt conceived of settling these unfortunates in the New World, where they might make a fresh start. (Here is striking proof that Europeans were still beguiled by the prospect of regenerating their society in the New World.) They petitioned for a grant south of the Carolinas, and the government, eager to create a buffer between South Carolina and the hostile Spanish in Florida, readily granted a charter (1732) to a group of "trustees" who were to manage the colony without profit to themselves for a period of 21 years.

In 1733 the leader of the trustees, James Oglethorpe, founded Savannah. Oglethorpe was a complicated person, vain, high-handed, and straitlaced, yet hardworking and idealistic. He hoped to people the colony with sober and industrious yeomen farmers. Land grants were limited to 50 acres and made nontransferable. To insure sobriety, rum and other "Spirits and Strong Waters" were banned. To guarantee that the colonists would have to work hard, the entry of "any Black . . . Negroe" was prohibited. The Indian trade was to be strictly regulated in the interest of fair dealing. Oglethorpe intended that silk, wine, and olive oil be the main products—none of which, unfortunately, could be profitably produced in Georgia.

His noble intentions came to naught. The settlers refused to endure the Spartan existence he envisaged; they swiftly found ways to circumvent all restrictions. Rum flowed, lawyers argued, slaves were imported, large landholdings were amassed, and Georgia developed an economy much like South Carolina's. Oglethorpe returned to England in 1743; in 1752 the trustees, disillusioned, abandoned their responsibilities. Georgia then became a royal colony.

SUPPLEMENTARY READING

Titles marked with an asterisk have been published in paperback

On the explorers and the world they opened up, see D. B. Quinn, **North America from Earliest Discovery to First Settlements*** (1977), S. E. Morison, **The European Discovery of America** (1971–1974), and C. O. Sauer, **Sixteenth-Century North America*** (1971). Morison's biography of Columbus, **Admiral of the Ocean Sea** (1942), is a model of sound scholarship and good writing.

The European background of colonization is discussed in W. C. Abbott's **Expansion of Europe** (1938). Fuller accounts of the English background can be found in Wallace Notestein, **The English People on the Eve of Colonization*** (1954), A. L. Rowse, **The Elizabethans and America*** (1959), and Carl Bridenbaugh, **Vexed and Troubled Englishmen*** (1968). J. H. Elliott, **The Old World and the New*** (1970), analyzes the impact of America on Europe.

On French and Spanish colonization, see W. J. Eccles, **France in America*** (1972), and Charles Gibson, **Spain in America*** (1966). On the interactions of European and Indian civilizations, consult A. W. Crosly, Jr., **The Columbian Exchange: Biological and Cultural Consequences of 1492*** (1972), and R. F. Berkhofer, Jr., **The White Man's Indian** (1978). Full discussions of the culture and history of the American Indians are provided by W. E. Washburn, **The Indian in America*** (1975), and William Brandon, **The American Heritage Book of Indians*** (1961), the latter profusely illustrated and covering the tribes of the entire hemisphere. Francis Jennings, **The Invasion of America*** (1975), is extremely critical of white dealings with the Indians. A. T. Vaughan, **New England Frontier*** (1965), argues that New Englanders treated the Indians fairly. On the African background of black slaves, see B. Davison and K. Buah, **History of West Africa to the 19th Century*** (1967); on the slave trade, P. D. Curtin, **The Atlantic Slave Trade*** (1970), and H. S. Klein, **The Middle Passage** (1978).

The finest general account of the history of English colonization is C. M. Andrews' **The Colonial Period of American History*** (1934–1938). T. J. Wertenbaker's **The First Americans*** (1927) is a brief summary, and W. F. Craven's **The Colonies in Transition*** (1968) is a first-rate study of late 17th- and early 18th-century developments. On the southern colonies, W. F. Craven's **The Southern Colonies in the Seventeenth Century*** (1949) is excellent, while G. F. Willison's **Behold Virginia** (1951) is popular history at its best. Willison's **Saints and Strangers*** (1945) is an equally good study of the Pilgrims.

Historians have always been of two minds about the Puritan colonies. S. E. Morison, in **Builders of the Bay Colony*** (1930), presents a favorable account; J. T. Adams presents an anti-Puritan interpretation in **The Founding of New England*** (1921). For the middle colonies, see T. J. Wertenbaker, **The Founding of American Civilization: The Middle Colonies** (1938). The Georgia experiment is covered well in Phinizy Spalding, **Oglethorpe in America** (1977). No student should miss at least dipping into the works of Francis Parkman on the French in America. His **Pioneers of France in the New World** (1855) covers the early period.

Biographies worth noting include P. L. Barbour, **The Three Worlds of Captain John Smith** (1964), A. T. Vaughan, **American Genesis: Captain John Smith*** (1975), E. S. Morgan, **The Puritan Dilemma: The Story of John Winthrop*** (1958), Morgan's **Roger Williams: The Church and the States*** (1967), and C. O. Peare, **William Penn: A Biography*** (1957).

SAHARA DESERT

KANEM

Senegal R.

GHANA

FULANI

Gambia R.

MALI

L. TCHAD

BAGA

MALINKE

BAMBARA

BOBO

SENUFO

YORUBA

OYO

Benne R.

MENDE

VoltaR.

DAHOMEY

BENIN

ASHANTI

Kumasi

FON

Benin City

IBO

Cross R.

ASHANTI

Ouidah

BINI

Aro

GREBO

FANTI

Niger

IBIBIO

Old Calabar

KRU

Delta

Bonny

A

WINDWARD COAST

T

IVORY COAST

GOLD COAST

SLAVE COAST

L

Ubangi R.

A

Congo R.

N

Equator

KOTA

T

Congo R.

TEKE

Kasai R.

I

C

KONGO

KONGO

YAKA

Cuanza R.

MBUNDU

ANGOLA

Niger R.

THE WEST COAST OF AFRICA

GHANA — kingdoms
FULANI — peoples
Bonny — cities

Portfolio One

THE HERITAGE OF AFRICA

Although the Portuguese who began inching their way down the west coast of Africa in the 15th century were searching for a new route to the Indies, they were willing to be distracted by whatever trade prospects appeared on the horizon—including 29 black men kidnaped near Arguin in 1443 and sold in the markets of Lisbon. For centuries the trans-Saharan trade had enriched such inland empires as Ghana and Kanem; now, as trade with Europe increased, new states emerged nearer the coast. The reshaping of these societies under the warping pressures of the slave trade, examined in the following pages, contributed to the demise of some, the growth of others.

By coincidence, the slave trade was concentrated on those peoples most productive of art; that artistic talent, examples of which illustrate this portfolio, was one more victim of the institution of human bondage.

From the Senegal to the Gambia

Among the emerging coastal societies were the peoples of Senegambia (the area between the Senegal and Gambia rivers), heirs to the ancient western Sudanic empires. For example, a group of Fulani, in alliance with some of the Malinke, conquered the area along the south bank of the Senegal in 1559. Previously nomadic herders, the Fulani now settled in neat, well-ordered towns like the one shown below.

Senegambia was the first sub-Saharan area to experience contact with Europeans. By 1500, gold, ivory, pepper, gum arabic—and some slaves—were being exported in exchange for horses, fabrics, and metalware. All this changed when the Spanish Caribbean islands began to raise sugar on a large scale in the mid 17th century; to meet the insatiable demand for labor, slaves became Africa's most important export. Senegambia was profoundly affected. Bondage had existed there only as a semifeudal relationship, and slaves were rarely sold. Once slavery became commercially profitable, Senegambians built up an "inventory" by making enslavement the legal punishment for most crimes and by earmarking for export captives taken in warfare with their neighbors.

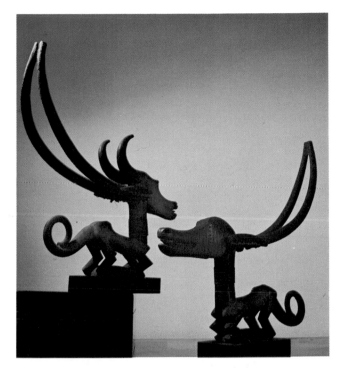

■ The antelope headdresses of the Bambara people, above and below, were worn by masked young men in agricultural rites. They always appeared in pairs, representing male and female, in leaping dances on the newly sown fields. They memorialized Chi Wara, half man and half animal, who in myth had taught man how to cultivate. Bambara empire-building wars in the 1730s resulted in the export of many war captives, often by Malinke merchants. Figures such as the one at left were given to Malinke girls to carry in dances celebrating their coming of age. This one is decorated on the arms and head with precious cowry shells from the Indian Ocean, a form of currency used in many parts of Africa.

■ The helmet mask above belonged to the women's secret society of the Mende people, the only known instance in Africa of female masking. The crested hairdo and exaggerated high forehead were marks of beauty.

■ The tall Baga serpent spirit of the waters at left presided over initiation rituals. The streamlined mask above may have represented a water spirit of the coastal Grebo or Kru, who were expert boat handlers.

The Windward Coast

Religion was a pervasive force among the peoples of Africa, affecting, as the examples at left of sculpture from the societies of the Windward Coast reveal, all aspects of social, economic, and cultural life. Most Africans believed in a creator god who was worshiped directly by the individual but who could be influenced only through the intercession of a pantheon of lesser, specialized deities. The goals of religious practices were increase and fertility. All material things, animate and inanimate, were believed to be imbued with spirits, and death or destruction did not extinguish their vital forces. Thus ancestors, recent or remote, remained influential in the affairs of the living through the activities of cults.

The role of ancestor cults varied. In monarchies they became virtually a state religion glorifying the legendary, heroic, semidivine origins of the ruling dynasty. Among the smaller societies, such as those of the Windward Coast, where life was regulated by men's secret societies, these cults stressed the continuance, unity, and order of the clan.

African art embodied all these ideas. The creator god was never portrayed, and only rarely were the lesser deities depicted, for the gods were considered too abstract for visualization. Rather, sculptures such as those shown here were expressionistic images of nature or ancestor spirits.

■ The Senufo "fire-spitter" mask above is a dynamic composite of animal features. Its visual complexity reflects its symbolic character; in ritual use it incarnated a spirit force capable of protecting the people from a variety of evils. The many-beaked Bobo bird mask at right was worn in ritual dances to promote agricultural fertility. Both these inland peoples were probably enslaved and exported by the Kru or the Ashanti.

The Gold Coast

The Ashanti people probably migrated in the 17th century to the area of present-day Ghana, where they quickly subdued and organized the numerous small states of the area into a loose confederation. About 1700, Osei Tutu, who reigned in the principal state of Kumasi, summoned a council of all the rulers. The assembled throng witnessed the appearance of a Golden Stool, or throne, the repository of the nation's soul and symbolic of Osei Tutu's supreme authority as Asantehene, king of kings. At the same time, a civil and moral code of 77 laws was sanctified.

The Ashanti nation flourished, principally because of its valuable gold resources and its strong, well-organized military caste. All the gold, which symbolized royalty and the sun, belonged to the Asantehene, though it circulated as currency in the form of dust and nuggets. The provinces paid tribute, and the Asantehene collected duties on trade. All the gold of deceased or disgraced persons reverted to his coffers, as did any dust or nuggets dropped during trading in the marketplace.

Gold had drawn merchants across the Sahara for centuries, and it was the first attraction for European traders. Later a slave trade developed, supplied by tribute from vassal states and by prisoners of war. The Ashanti were generally content to allow the coastal Fanti people to act as their middlemen in the sale of captives to the Europeans. T. E. Bowdich, an 1817 visitor, observed that the Ashanti did not engage in commerce "lest their genius for war . . . be enervated." They did trade for guns, however, which they were careful to prohibit being traded further so as to retain their military ascendancy over neighboring states.

Bowdich, among the first group of Europeans to visit Kumasi, witnessed the great annual festival celebrating the yam harvest. All the provincial rulers gathered for several days of religious ceremonies, festivities, and the promulgation of new laws. Above right is a detail from Bowdich's portrayal of the festival. The Asantehene (under the red umbrella) and his captains watch the dancing, served by attendants carrying gold regalia and elephant-tail fly whisks.

■ The stools crafted by the Ashanti were thought to be the habitations of their spirits, and those belonging to clan founders and kings were cherished as altars for ancestor cults. The royal Golden Stool was (and still is) kept in a sacred secret place and rarely seen. The example above, decorated in silver, belonged to the Asantehene Kofi Karikari, and the gold mask on the opposite page is from his treasury. It may be a depiction of the ruler of a conquered people.

The Fon of Dahomey

The Fon peoples of Dahomey began moving inland to the Abomey plateau around 1600, probably seeking to escape the instability brought on by the Dutch presence on the coast. By 1645 the Fon had founded a strong monarchy based on a concept of government, unique in Africa, that stressed the individual's responsibility to the king. This idea, open to all peoples, ran counter to traditional African theories of a feudal monarchy which considered the king the "father" of his subjects and vassal states. Dahomey was a military state, and when it entered the slave trade, its war captives formed a ready source of supply. Guns traded for slaves strengthened the might of its standing army. As the Fon kingdom expanded, rebellions broke out among its subject peoples, fomented by devotees of the indigenous gods. The revolts failed and whole cult groups were sold into slavery, the exiles carrying their gods with them to the West Indies, Brazil, and Louisiana.

Meanwhile, the nearby coastal kingdoms were being reshaped by the competition for European trade and by the Europeans' meddling in political affairs. The kingdom of Ouidah tried unsuccessfully to monopolize the trade by building a free port, with separate mud-walled compounds for each foreign company engaged in trade. Ouidah's port, opposite, was drawn in 1725 by the captain of a French slaver.

By this time Dahomey was encroaching upon the coastal states. In the 1720s King Agaja took advantage of their dynastic and internal squabbling and made them his vassals. There is evidence that Agaja sought to end the slave trade; certainly the business declined in these years. If this was his intention, it was not to be realized. Outraged by Agaja's repudiation of its traditional feudal relations to these states and threatened by his limitations on access to the sea trade, the powerful neighboring Oyo nation swept down on Dahomey. By 1730 Agaja, chastened by four years of devastating campaigns, was back in the slave trade.

■ In the Fon pantheon, Gu (opposite) was the most important son of the creator sky gods, who delegated him to make the earth habitable for people. Gu was also the *vodu* (god) of war and metal, a fitting deity for the bellicose Fon. This monumental shrine image is made of iron. Art was also produced to serve the Dahomean court. Appliqué cloth tapestries depicting the exploits of the kings decorated the palace walls. Below is a detail from a cloth commemorating one of Agaja's victories. The insignia of office often incorporated complex symbolism; the motif decorating the staff at right, a serpent swallowing its tail, is simultaneously a symbol of infinity and a word play on the name *Dahomey*.

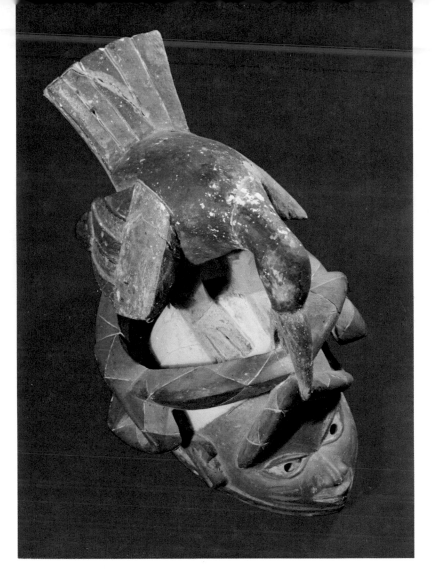

■ The Yoruba *gelede* society was devoted to counteracting the evil work of witches. Some of its masks were used in sacred rituals held at night. Others, like the painted, figured one at left, were used the following day in secular plays, often humorous tales of human foibles.

The Yoruba of Oyo

In legend, Oranmiyan, Prince of Ife, founded Oyo and its ruling line around 1200 after establishing a dynasty in Benin. In his person Oranmiyan symbolized the familial relationship of the Yoruba kings and the peoples of over 20 separate states. Although very junior in this "family," Oyo by 1700 dominated the lands from Dahomey to Benin. The Yoruba were markedly urban, and trades and crafts—notably sculpture—flourished in their towns. Oyo's strengths were its stable, limited monarchy and its favorable position to trade for horses raised on the northern grasslands. The powerful Oyo cavalry was feared throughout the region. By the late 1600s Oyo was exporting many slaves through its vassals, Allada and Ouidah. When King Agaja of Dahomey menaced this trade, the Oyo cavalry overran Dahomey and made it tributary. Although Oyo was at its zenith for the rest of the 18th century, state policy was the subject of bitter debate between the leading commercial and military families. The commercial interests won out: the army was allowed to decline while trade, particularly in slaves, increased. (Oyo never imported firearms in quantity and seemed not to have grasped their significance.) In the slave trade lay the seeds of ruin, and Oyo's collapse was swift. It was beset simultaneously by slave rebellions, revolts of subject territories, and attacks by neighboring states armed with guns. With the Oyo cavalry no longer a match for any enemy, the nation disintegrated; by 1850 even the once-thriving capital lay deserted.

■ Oyo was the center of the cult of the legendary king Shango, a major deity in the Yoruba pantheon. He ruled thunder, lightning, and rain—and, consequently, fertility. The shrine figure of a mother and child at left represented Shango's power to cure barrenness. His devotees wore a headdress shaped like a double ax, symbolizing his thunderbolts. The mounted warrior above decorated an *oshe shango,* a staff carried by worshipers when Shango "rode their heads." Below, a warrior in padded armor is carried on the shoulders of a retainer.

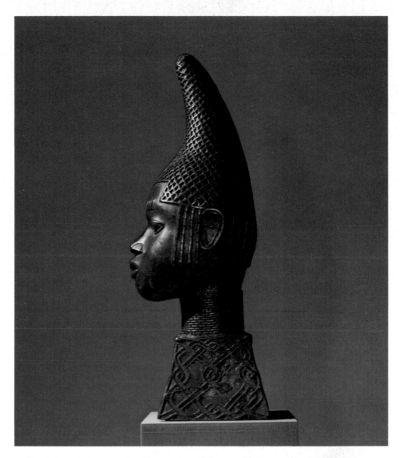

■ Benin's artists were in the service of its semidivine rulers. Leopards, symbols of the oba, were kept at court and immortalized in bronze (left). Above is a queen mother wearing a headdress of precious coral beads.

The Empire of Benin

According to Benin's oral traditions, the Bini people asked the ruler of Ife to send one of his sons to them. In about 1200 Prince Oranmiyan founded Benin's ruling line of obas, or kings. Six generations later the oba sent to Ife again for a smith to teach the use of brass to Benin's sculptors, so that they could cast memorial heads like the one above for the oba's ancestor altars. The semidivine oba devoted much of his time to ceremonies honoring his ancestors, and an analogous ancestor worship was observed in families and craft guilds.

Benin's history is one of steady expansion and the development of a strongly centralized government. Rulers of villages and provinces had to be initiated into the Palace Society before assuming power. Benin City had some 40 craft guilds, each with its highest-ranking members in the Palace Society.

Benin's most glorious era was the 15th and 16th centuries. It was known as "a time of much brass"—obtained through trade and used in sculpture. The Portuguese arrived in 1485 to offer diplomatic and trade relations as well as Christianity. The oba's response was measured; he placed strict controls on the European trade and very early decreed that no male Bini could be sold for export (although, as elsewhere, criminals and prisoners of war were "commercial items"). This measure limited commerce for a time, but many of Benin's provinces, seeing the chance for profit and independence, entered the slave trade readily, exchanging captives for firearms. Thereafter, Benin's decline was inevitable.

■ The walls of the oba's palace—a city within a city—were of red clay, polished so that they shone like marble. The brass box above, representing a part of the palace, bears copper birds and a python that ornamented its wooden roof. The men may represent Portuguese musketeers who aided Benin's army in several campaigns.

■ Interior galleries of the palace were hung with hundreds of these bronze plaques, a form which may have been suggested to Benin's artists by Portuguese paintings. They are records of court life and rituals. At left, the seated oba is attended by two of his chieftains, all bedecked in heavy, coral-beaded ceremonial dress (the small Portuguese figures are decorative motifs). At center, three helmeted hunters go forth armed with spears. At right, a court musician, perhaps a slave, plays Efik-style drums made from hollow logs.

■ All ivory belonged to the oba; this pectoral mask was probably part of his regalia. The crest alternates Portuguese faces and mudfish, both associated with the god of the sea and wealth.

■ The Ibo family group above is part of a terra-cotta altar dedicated to the spirit of the yam—the staple of life. The most important force among these peoples was the men's secret societies, such as the Ibo *mmwo* and the Ekoi *ekpe*. Deriving their authority from ancestor spirits, they used their power to keep peace. The mask at upper left represented a female spirit in the *mmwo* ritual (white symbolized death). The Ekoi mask at left portrayed deceased society members.

Bonny and Old Calabar

In contrast to the great kingdoms that rose nearby, the peoples of the Niger Delta formed small political groups. This reflected the fragmented character of the land itself, heavily forested and crisscrossed by river tributaries and lagoons. Traditionally linked to Benin, they were interrelated economically by the river trade and socially by their similar institutions.

The coastal city-states, particularly Old Calabar and Bonny, prospered in the slave trade. The Efik clan of the Ibibio people, whose name derived from the Ibibio word *oppress*, monopolized Old Calabar's trade, usually supplying upcountry peoples, bought or kidnaped, to the slavers. On one occasion, however, when trade rivalries were acute, one section of the town conspired to sell its neighbors.

The inland Ibo of Aro capitalized on their famous oracle of the god Chukwu. Aro's emissaries acted both as the oracle's spokesmen and as merchants, manipulating the power of the oracle to exact fines and payments in slaves to be "eaten by Chukwu." In reality, these unfortunates filled the slave ships at Bonny.

The efficient river ports became a major center of the slave trade in its later years. So important was the trade to the local economy that the king of Bonny vigorously protested its abolition. "We think that this trade must go on," he insisted. "That also is the verdict of our oracle and the priests. They say that your country [Great Britain], however great, can never stop a trade ordained by God himself."

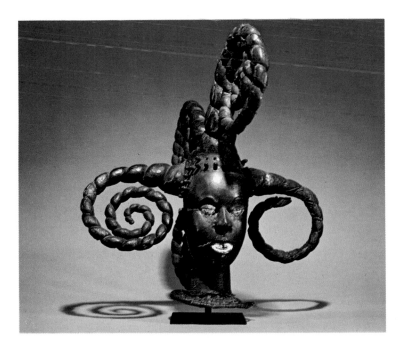

■ Two Ibibio clans, the Efik and Oron, lived in the Cross River area. The Efik of Old Calabar kept order among freemen and slaves through the *ekpe* society; at left is a ritual skin-covered headdress. The Oron people made dignified bearded figures, like that above, for their ancestors' graves.

The Kingdom of Kongo

The first Portuguese mission to Kongo, in 1485, found a well-established state. Its ruler, the Mani Kongo, welcomed missionaries, diplomats, and merchants, and his successor, Mvemba Nzinga, was converted to Christianity and baptized Affonso I. Affonso was a believer in the benefits to be derived from European ways. He corresponded with his "royal brother," the king of Portugal, requesting priests, teachers, and doctors. Paid in slaves, they quickly became traders. By 1526 Affonso was writing to his royal brother: ". . . we cannot reckon how great the damage is, since the . . . merchants are taking every day our natives, sons of the land. . . . So great, Sir, is the corruption and licentiousness that our country is being completely depopulated. . . . It is *our will that in these kingdoms there should not be any trade of slaves nor outlet for them.*"

But the trade did not stop; it was too profitable. By the 1530s most slaves were drawn from beyond the Kongo kingdom—Teke from the north, Mbundu from the south. This led to border tensions and raids, and these, combined with Portuguese intrigues, so weakened Kongo that it could offer little resistance when, in 1568, the warlike Yaka swept through the country. The Portuguese, alarmed by the chaos they themselves had engendered and attracted by rumors of silver mines, turned their attention to the south.

■ Stone grave guardians like the one at left commemorated Kongo kings and chiefs and symbolized the continuity of government. They were said to be "thinking of the welfare of the people." The Kongo-made cast brass crucifix above dates from the Portuguese era. Even after their meaning had been forgotten, such crosses were carried by chiefs as power emblems.

■ The fierce aspect of the Yaka mask at left suggests the terror they inspired. Such masks, surmounted by legendary characters, were worn by young men during celebrations of their initiation into status as adults.

■ The Kota effigy above is a *mbulungulu*, which guarded ancestral relics and protected their vital force. The Kota people lived north of the Teke and may have obtained the copper and brass used to plate these images through the network of Kongo trade routes—in exchange for bondsmen.

■ The Teke worshiped nature spirits and the shades of the recent dead. The mysterious, highly abstract face mask at left is a rare Teke spirit mask; its meaning and use are not known. The Teke furnished the Kongo with copper and ivory for trade with the Portuguese before slaves surpassed these items in value.

Town of Ropass on the Rio Nuniez

"Traffick in Men"

"I must own . . . that I was first kidnaped and betrayed by [those of] my own complexion, who were the first cause of my exile and slavery," an ex-slave wrote in 1787. "But if there were no buyers, there would be no sellers." The earliest buyers were the Portuguese, but by 1600 the Dutch, French, and English had also realized the profits in "man-stealing." They were soon followed by the Prussians, Danes, Swedes, and Genoese. Never was there more than a handful of Europeans in the trading stations. Business was conducted directly at the major ports or through the "trust trade"—giving local merchants goods to barter inland for slaves. For the Europeans it was a killing business; only one out of two survived the climate and local diseases. Living arrangements were ramshackle: a warehouse on a malarial river island, as above, or a rotting ship anchored in an estuary. Only on the Gold Coast did the kings lease land for a few of the traders' "castles" which, in European imaginations, rimmed the African shores. The local king dictated the rules of trade and filled a slave ship in his own good time. The Europeans' power lay in the insidious luxuries which became necessities: liquor and firearms. In 1723 New England merchants, lately come to the trade, introduced rum to Africa; soon it was more popular than French brandy or English gin. "The kings of Africa," a Swedish observer commented, "incited by the merchandise shown them, which consists principally of strong liquors, give orders to . . . attack their own villages at night."

■ The pigtailed European trader above right, an 18th-century ivory from Kongo, proffers a "dash" of liquor. Below is a slave coffle en route to a coastal slave market. The captives were beset by terrors of the unknown. "I was . . . persuaded," one said, "that I had got into a world of bad spirits . . . I asked the others if we were not to be eaten by those white men with horrible looks, red faces, and long hair. . . ."

■ The slave brig *Marie Séraphique* rides at anchor off Haiti in 1773, as planters inspect her cargo. This delicate rococo painting commemorated a successful passage from Angola. Its mood is sharply at variance with the grimmer realities evident in the deck-packing plan opposite, which illustrated a 1792 report on the slave trade.

"These Valuable People"

"There is no buying slaves here [the Gold Coast] without you give two ounces of gold on each . . . and you may think yourself happy to get [them] even at that rate," a trader wrote in 1772. The going price in another port for "these valuable people" was 115 gallons of rum for a healthy man, 95 for a woman. Market preferences varied; some peoples were esteemed as house servants, others as field workers. The Ibo were considered melancholy and suicidal in slavery, the Ashanti rebellious. The French favored Dahomeans; the Spanish, Yoruba; the English, the Gold Coast peoples. The Portuguese concentrated on the peoples farther south. The Portuguese at least did not deny that Africans had souls; their unique rationalization for slavery was "redemption" in a Christian land, and the ports of the Congo and Angola witnessed mass baptisms of human cargoes before shipment.

The terror and dehumanization of the Middle Passage exceeded even that of the slave markets. This second leg of the triangular trade generally took two or three months—longer from East Africa. In the West Indies the cargoes were either sold or disembarked for "seasoning"—acclimatization—before being sent on to North or South America. Statistics on the slave trade before 1700 are scanty at best and incomplete for the 18th century. Conservative estimates on the number of Africans sold range from 10 to 20 million; the mortality on the Middle Passage may have averaged 20 to 30 percent. This varied considerably depending on the length of the voyage, and the situation was aggravated by the fact that the cargoes tended to rebel or commit suicide if allowed topside. The obvious solution was to confine them below, on decks about five feet high, layered "in two rows, one above the other like books on a shelf" and packed, one trader said, as close as spoons fitting together.

"The stench of the hold while we were on the coast was intolerably loathsome," an ex-slave recalled. "But now that the whole ship's cargo were confined there together it became absolutely pestilential. The closeness of the place and the heat of the climate, added to the number in the ship, was . . . aggravated by the galling of the chains . . . and the filth of the necessary tubs, into which the children often fell. . . ." "They had not so much room as a man in his coffin," according to testimony taken from a ship's surgeon. "He has known them to go down apparently in good health at night and be found dead in the morning . . . and therefore concludes [they] died of suffocation." Another surgeon complained of the difficulty of treating the captives below decks because of air so foul and heat "so excessive . . . that a candle would not burn."

"The sights I witnessed may I never look on such again," wrote the captain of a slaver after his first voyage. "This is a dreadful trade." Yet such were the profits to be earned on the Middle Passage that he remained in the trade for more than 20 years.

2/THE COLONIAL WORLD

 The colonies were settled chiefly by English people at first, with a leavening of Germans, Scots, Scotch-Irish, Dutch, French, Swedes, Finns, Portuguese, a scattering of other nationalities, and a gradually increasing number of black African slaves. The cultures these people brought with them varied according to the nationality, social status, intelligence, and taste of the individual. They never lost this heritage entirely, but they—and certainly their descendants—became something quite different from their relatives who remained in the Old World. They became what we call Americans.

26

An American Civilization

The subtle but profound change that occurred when the Europeans moved to the New World was hardly self-willed. Most of the settlers came, it is true, hoping for circumstances different from those they left behind—for a more bountiful existence, sometimes also for nonmaterialistic reasons, such as the opportunity to practice a religion barred to them at home. Even the poorest and the most rebellious seldom intended to develop a new civilization; rather they wished to reconstruct the old on terms more favorable to themselves. Nor did the "American" type result from the selection of particular kinds of Europeans as colonizers. The typical settler was young and unmarried, yet persons from every walk of life entered the emigrating stream (and probably in rough proportion to their numbers in Europe if we exclude the very highest and lowest social strata). Certainly there was no selection of the finest grain to provide seed for cultivating the wilderness.

Why then did America become something more than another Europe? Why, for example, was New England not merely a new England? The chief reason is that their physical surroundings transformed the people. America was isolated from Europe by 3,000 miles of ocean. The Atlantic served as an umbilical cord but also as a barrier; it was practically closed to commerce during the stormy winter months and dangerous enough in any season. The crossing took anywhere from a few weeks to several months, depending on wind and weather. No one undertook an ocean voyage lightly in colonial times, and few who made the westward crossing ever thought seriously of returning. The modern mind can scarcely grasp the awful isolation that enveloped the settler, the sense of being alone, of having cut all ties with home and past. One had to face forward (westward) and construct a new life or perish—if not of hunger, then of loneliness.

One may see in these circumstances the roots of the Americans' celebrated self-reliance and individualism. Americans were free in the sense of being uninhibited—no effective power fettered them. They were largely self-governing not because they were too proud to submit to dictation but because the mother country was too far away to govern them effectively. "The Trustees wanted to be privy to every decision taken in Georgia," a recent biographer of James Oglethorpe explains. "Oglethorpe found this quite impossible because of the multitude of day-to-day determinations that had to be made on the spot. . . . By the time the Trustees had been consulted the circumstances might have changed drastically."

The isolation of America serves equally well to explain some less attractive elements of the national character. The early colonists habitually carried weapons during every waking hour. They became inured to violence, to settling disagreements directly and by force, to seizing the main chance, to thrusting aside anything and anyone who stood in their way.

The emptiness of the continent also changed the colonists. In Europe land was scarce and labor plentiful. In America conditions were exactly the opposite; any settler—or rather, any *white* settler—who did not own land had at least a reasonable expectation of owning some. Colonists, at least in the early days, had to be their own landlords, artisans, surveyors, doctors, and explorers, not because of any inherent versatility but because their primitive world did not permit them to specialize. By the time a more complicated society had evolved, the new pattern of thinking—an American pattern—was well established.

Once the colonies were on their feet, the fertile soil of America and the abundance of fish and game supplied settlers with unlimited amounts of food. Few persons went hungry. Within a few generations observers were noticing that Americans were generally bigger than their European cousins, and there can be little doubt that the plenitude of calories and proteins affected the colonists not only physically but psychologically.

Even geography wielded a considerable influence, largely negative, on early American history. Civilized societies overcome physical obstacles. They bridge streams, irrigate deserts, drain swamps, carve roads through forests and over mountains. In the formative years such tasks were beyond the colonists' resources. They had to adjust to the contours of their new home before they could grow strong enough to alter them.

The Appalachian range is not particularly impressive as mountains go, but it affected formidably the life that evolved along its eastern slopes. Its grandest manifestation can be seen in the difference between French and English colonists in America. The French funneled through the St.

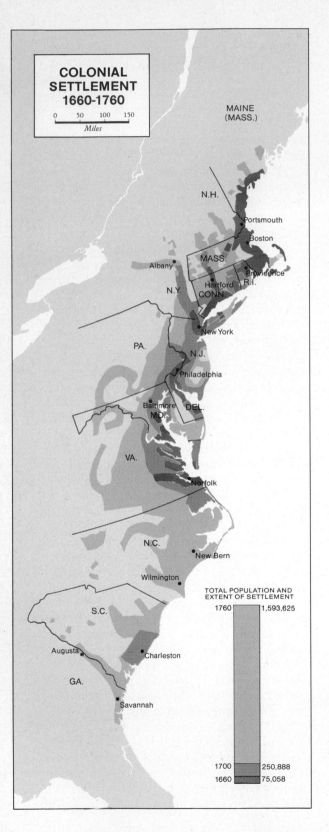

COLONIAL SETTLEMENT 1660-1760

0   50   100   150
Miles

MAINE (MASS.)

N.H.

Portsmouth

Boston

Albany

MASS.

N.Y.

Hartford   Providence
CONN.   R.I.

New York

PA.

N.J.

Philadelphia

Baltimore   DEL.
MD.

VA.

Norfolk

N.C.

New Bern

Wilmington

TOTAL POPULATION AND
EXTENT OF SETTLEMENT

1760   1,593,625

S.C.

Augusta
Charleston

GA.

Savannah

1700   250,888
1660   75,058

Lawrence Valley behind the mountains and into the heart of the continent. While some became farmers, many others followed the rich fur trade over thousands of miles. They became creatures of the woods who lived (and thought) more like Indians than Europeans. The English, blocked from easy penetration inland in most areas, had to settle down to farming.

Within British America the effect of the Appalachians varied according to the region. In Virginia the mountains are set well back from the sea; the rivers flow gently to the Atlantic. Navigable far inland, they became the roads of the tobacco colonies. Farms sprang up in Maryland and Virginia along the banks of rivers. Merchant vessels delivered European products to farmers at their own docks and took away their produce in exchange. There were few seaports because seaports were not needed as depots and centers of commerce. Civilization fanned out thinly along every navigable tributary; life was rural. "Southern hospitality," the slowness of the region to develop a school system, the scarcity of artisans—factors as disparate as these can be explained at least in part in geographical terms.

In the northern regions no such network of navigable streams existed. Seacoast towns grew up where sheltered harbors provided space for the loading and unloading of ships. To reach them the inland settlers had to build roads, and since roads were expensive, settlement tended to be compact. Villages quickly dotted the farmlands, and village life differed profoundly from life in the south. That southerners had no inherent dislike of urban ways was proved as soon as settlement spread upstream beyond the limits of navigation. Towns like Richmond (on the James), Fredericksburg (on the Rappahannock), and Wilmington (on the Cape Fear, in North Carolina) all mark points where oceangoing ships must stop or run aground. They

■ The multicolored bar gives two types of information. The three color blocks are used in the map to show the extent of settlement, with dark gray representing the extent of settlement in about 1660, the darker color areas that of 1700, and the more extensive light color areas that of 1760. The relative size of the color blocks within the bar reflect the size and growth of population, from about 75,000 settlers in 1600 to well over one and a half million in 1760. Colonial population increased more than six fold between 1700 and 1760.

were founded to serve as centers of trade for farmers farther inland.

Geography was far from being the only influence on the shape of colonial societies. Religious differences, the quirks of individual leaders, pure chance, and many other factors affected regional patterns. But geography was important in the vital early years. The Hudson-Mohawk Valley, allowing easy access to the interior, made possible the extensive fur trade of New York. Everywhere rapids and waterfalls accounted for the location of grist and lumber mills.

The Colonial Family

Still another important influence was the way American conditions affected relationships between the sexes. In nearly every colony most of the first settlers were young males. It quickly became obvious that their individual "need" for women coincided with the larger interests of the colonial community and those of European promoters. As Sir Edwin Sandys put it with regard to the Jamestown settlement, the introduction of women colonists would "make the men more setled." He and other colonizers worked incessantly to recruit unmarried women, shipping them over in batches of a hundred or more. Almost invariably these women "found husbands" in short order, the eager bridegrooms paying the company 120 pounds of prime tobacco to cover the cost of transportation. Throughout the colonial period an unmarried woman was almost an oddity—it was possible to refer to a woman of 20 as an "antique virgin" and a single woman over 25 tended to be seen as an old maid.

European society was organized on paternalistic lines, and this pattern was reproduced in America. The historian Julia Spruill has summarized the role of women in colonial society:

> Wifehood and motherhood . . . were held before the colonial woman as the purpose of her being, and home as the sphere of all her actions. Her mission in life was, first, to get a husband and then keep him pleased, and her duties were bearing and rearing children, and caring for her household.

Nevertheless, a distinctly American pattern of family life emerged, one in which woman's status was higher than in European families. Observers began to notice that American men, despite their crude manners and rough ways, were respectful of women in general and loving, considerate, and—at least by European standards—loyal and faithful to their wives.

The chronic shortage of labor best explains the American attitude toward women and also toward children, who, being easy to feed and highly useful, were treated—again, by European standards of the times—tenderly and indulgently. Very large families were not unusual; Benjamin Franklin, for example, was the youngest of 17 children, and broods of a dozen or more were quite common. Being objects of love and respect did not free American women and children from the necessity of extremely hard work or from most of the legal inequities suffered by their English, French, or German counterparts. Colonial women, the historian Eleanor Flexner writes, "had many duties, but few rights." Rich or poor, their lives were an endless round of labor. Even in the 18th century one of the richest men in Virginia proudly described his daughters as "every Day up to their Elbows in Housewifery."

For exceptional women the labor shortage created opportunities to develop their talents. Some managed large plantations; Eliza Lucas ran three in South Carolina for her absent father while still in her teens, and after the death of her husband, Charles Pinckney, she successfully managed his large properties. Other able colonial women ran newspapers, served as teachers and doctors, and operated shops in the towns. Margarett Brent, probably the first American feminist, was a leading figure in Maryland in the late 1640s. Brent straightened out the affairs of Governor Leonard Calvert after his death, and by her intervention prevented a mutiny among the local militia.

But such cases were rare. Married women could not own property or sign contracts as individuals; even their own earnings belonged technically to their husbands. Nor, with only a handful of exceptions, could women vote, and they were everywhere held by law and religion to stricter moral standards in matters involving sex. Divorces were difficult to obtain. Yet on balance colonial conditions worked to advance the status of women and to provide children with the emotional security that comes from being wanted. Life was hard but its burdens were fairly shared, at least in comparison to the old country. Much of the confidence

■ David, Joanna, and Abigail Mason posed for their portrait by an unknown itinerant painter in Massachusetts about 1670. As is often true with primitive portraits, the children's faces appear older than their physical sizes would warrant, but even so they seem touchingly childlike.

and spontaneity of the "American character" that struck foreign commentators probably rose from this source.

The basic structure of American families was, of course, the same as the European. Aside from its primary functions of child rearing and feeding and sheltering its members, the family was a center for work, religious observance, and the maintenance of social order, in the words of the historian John Demos, "an absolutely central agency of economic production and exchange." In some ways American conditions acted to increase these family responsibilities. In sparsely settled regions there were few community services, and education as well as the care of the ill, the aged, and the incompetent were usually managed in the home. But in the long run, the colonial situation tended to weaken family ties. In a land of large opportunities and rapid change, young people were less likely to respect parental authority based on traditions and experiences that were not relevant to the new conditions. The physical expansion of the colonies almost required the fragmentation of extended family groupings, but even in settled areas

the typical family was nuclear: children tended to set up their own homes as soon as possible after marriage.

Southern Land and Labor

Two patterns of life sprang up in British America. Maryland, Virginia, the Carolinas, and Georgia followed one path. Pennsylvania and those colonies to the north followed another.

Agriculture was the bulwark of southern life; the tragic experiences of the Jamestown settlers revealed this quickly enough. Jamestown also suggested that a colony could not succeed unless its inhabitants were allowed to own their own land. The first colonists, it will be recalled, were employees of the London Company who had agreed to work for seven years in return for a share of the profits. When their contracts expired there were no profits. To satisfy these settlers and to attract new capital, the company declared a "dividend" of land, its only asset. The surviving colonists each received 100 acres. Thereafter, as prospects continued poor, the company relied more and more on grants of land to attract both capital and labor. A number of wealthy Englishmen were given immense tracts, some running to several hundred thousand acres. Lesser persons willing to settle in Virginia received more modest grants. Whether dangled before a great tycoon, a country squire, or a poor farmer, the offer of land had the effect of encouraging migration to the colony. This was a much-desired end, for without the labor to develop it the land was worthless.

Soon what was known as the headright system became entrenched in Virginia, and when the Crown took over in 1624 the system was not disturbed. Behind it lay the eminently sound principle that land should be parceled out according to the availability of labor to cultivate it. For each "head" entering the colony the government issued a "right" to take any 50 acres of unoccupied land. To "seat" a claim and receive title to the property, the holder of the headright had to mark out its boundaries, plant a crop, and construct some sort of habitation. This system was adopted in all the southern colonies and in Pennsylvania and New Jersey.

The first headrights were issued with no strings attached, but generally the grantor demanded a small annual payment called a quitrent. A quitrent was not rent at all, for the person who paid it was not a tenant. It was a tax, perhaps a shilling for 50 acres, which provided a way for the proprietors to derive incomes from their colonies. By the middle of the 18th century the Calvert family was collecting over £4,000 a year in Maryland from this source.

A quitrent differed from a modern tax in that it bore little relation to the value of the property and was not assessed to pay for public services. It was a tribute paid in recognition of the "sovereignty" of the grantor, a commutation of feudal obligations that had never really existed in America. Quitrents were therefore resented and always hard to collect.

The headright system encouraged landless Europeans to migrate to America. More often than not, however, those most eager to come could not afford passage across the Atlantic. In order to bring together those with money who sought land and labor and those without funds who wanted to go to America, the indentured servant system was developed. Indentured servants resembled apprentices. In return for transportation they agreed to work for a stated period, usually about five years. During that time they were subject to strict control by the master and received no compensation beyond their keep. Servants therefore lacked any incentive to work hard, whereas masters tended to "abuse their servantes . . . with intollerable oppression." In this clash of wills the advantage lay with the master; servants lacked full political and civil rights, and masters could administer physical punishment and otherwise abuse them with almost total impunity.

After the servant completed his years of labor, he became free. Usually he was entitled to an "outfit" (a suit of clothes, some farm tools, seed, and perhaps a gun) that would enable him to take up farming on his own. Custom varied from colony to colony and according to the bargain struck by the two parties when the indenture was signed. In the Carolinas and in Pennsylvania, for example, servants received small grants of land from the colony when their service was completed.

The headrights issued when indentured servants entered the colonies went to whoever paid their passage, not to the servants. Thus the system gave a double reward to capital—land and labor for the price of the labor alone. Since well over half of the white settlers of the southern colonies came as indentured servants, the effect on the structure of southern society was enormous. Most servants eventually became landowners, but with the passage of time their lot became harder. The best land belonged to the large planters, and low tobacco prices and high local taxes combined to keep many ex-servants in dire poverty. Some were forced to become "squatters" on land along the fringes of settlement that no one had yet claimed. Squatting often led to trouble; eventually someone was sure to turn up with a legal title to the squatter's property. Squatters then demanded what they called squatters' rights, the privilege of buying the land from the legal owner without paying for the improvements they had made upon it. This led to arguments, lawsuits, and sometimes to violence.

About the time that the earliest indentured servants appeared, African blacks were brought to North America. The first blacks arrived on a Dutch ship and were sold at Jamestown in 1619. Early records are vague and incomplete, so it is

TO BE SOLD on board the Ship *Bance-Island*, on tuesday the 6th of *May* next, at *Ashley-Ferry*; a choice cargo of about 250 fine healthy

NEGROES,

just arrived from the Windward & Rice Coast. —The utmost care has already been taken, and shall be continued, to keep them free from the least danger of being infected with the SMALL-POX, no boat having been on board, and all other communication with people from *Charles-Town* prevented.

Austin, Laurens, & Appleby.

N. B. Full one Half of the above Negroes have had the SMALL-POX in their own Country.

■ This notice of a slave auction appeared in a Charleston newspaper in 1763. The danger of smallpox infection was very real; slave ships often carried the disease.

not possible to say whether these Africans were treated as slaves or freed after a period of years like indentured servants. What is certain is that by about 1640 *some* Virginia blacks were slaves (a few, with equal certainty, were free) and that by the 1660s local statutes had firmly established the institution in Virginia.

Whether slavery produced race prejudice in America or prejudice slavery is a hotly debated, important, and difficult-to-answer question. Most 17th-century Europeans were prejudiced against Africans; the usual reasons that led them to look down on "heathens" with customs other than their own were in the case of Africans greatly reinforced by their blackness, which the English equated with dirt, the Devil, danger, and death. "Black is the Colour of Night, Frightful, Dark and Horrid," a popular disquisition of 1704 proclaimed. That Africa was also the habitat of the great apes suggested, furthermore, that blacks were somehow related to these human-appearing creatures and were thus inherently bestial and inferior.

Yet the English knew that the Portuguese and Spaniards had enslaved blacks—*negro* is Spanish for black. Since the English adopted the word as a name for Africans, their treatment of Africans in the New World may also have derived from the Spanish.

Probably the Africans' blackness lay at the root of the tragedy. Winthrop D. Jordan, whose researches have added enormously to our understanding of the question, stresses the process by which prejudice and existing enslavement interacted with each other as both cause and effect, leading to the total debasement of the African.

> The concept of Negro slavery [in the tobacco colonies] . . . was neither borrowed from foreigners, nor extracted from books, nor invented out of whole cloth, nor extrapolated from servitude, nor generated by English reaction to Negroes as such, nor necessitated by the exigencies of the New World. Not any one of these made the Negro a slave, *but all.*

Slavery took root throughout English America. As early as 1626 there were 11 slaves in New Netherland, and when the English conquered the colony in 1664 there were 700 slaves in a population of about 8,000. The Massachusetts Body of Liberties of 1641—strange title—provided that "there shall never be any bond-slavery . . . amongst us; unless it be lawful captives taken in just warrs [*i.e.*, Indians] and such strangers as willingly sell themselves, or *are solde* to us." However, relatively few blacks were imported until late in the 17th century, even in the southern colonies. In 1650 there were only 300 of them in Virginia and as late as 1670 no more than 2,000.

White servants were much more highly prized. The African, after all, was utterly alien to both the European and the American ways of life. In a country starved for capital, the cost of slaves—roughly five times that of servants—was another disadvantage. In 1664 the governor of Maryland informed Lord Baltimore that local planters would use more "neigros" "if our purses would endure it."

For these reasons, so long as white servants could be had in sufficient numbers, there were few slaves in British America. Eventually, however, the growing number of white servants who had fulfilled their indentures caused social problems. They found it progressively more difficult (though not impossible) to obtain land. Most were young and because of the scarcity of women in the 17th century, unmarried. They tended to be dissatisfied and to make trouble for established planter interests. This situation contributed to the shift toward slave labor in the last quarter of the century; slaves did not compete with the planters for land, and they lacked the political rights of freemen.

Agriculture in the South

Land and labor made agriculture possible, but it was necessary to find a market for American crops in the Old World if the colonists were to enjoy anything but the crudest sort of existence. They could not begin to manufacture all the articles they required; to obtain from England such items as plows and muskets and books and chinaware, they had to have something to offer in exchange. Fortune favored the southern colonies in this search for a "cash crop."

The founders of Virginia tried to produce all sorts of things that were needed in the old country: grapes and silk in particular, indigo, cotton, oranges, olives, sugar, and many other plants. But it was tobacco, unwanted, even strongly opposed at first, that became Virginia's great staple during the colonial period.

Tobacco was unknown in Europe until Spanish explorers brought it back from the West Indies. It was not common in England until the time of Sir Walter Raleigh. Then it quickly proved irresistible to thousands of devotees. However, since it clearly contained some habit-forming drug, many people opposed its use.

At first the London Company discouraged the colonists from growing tobacco. King James I wrote a pamphlet attacking the weed, in which, among other things, he anticipated modern cancer researchers by saying that smoking was a "vile and stinking" habit "dangerous to the Lungs." But English smokers and partakers of snuff ignored their king, and the Virginia colonists ignored their company. By 1617 a pound of tobacco was worth more than five shillings in London. Company and Crown then changed their tune, granting the colonists a monopoly and encouraging them in every way. Little wonder that production in America leaped from 2,500 pounds in 1616 to 500,000 in 1627 and to nearly 30 million a year in the late 17th century. By the 1770s production exceeded 100 million pounds. Of course such a tremendous expansion of the supply caused the price to plummet. By the middle of the 17th century the English market was glutted and the colonists were seeking desperately to curb production.

The low price of tobacco in the last decades of the 17th century did not stop the growth of the tobacco colonies, but it did alter the structure of their society. Small farmers found it more difficult to make a decent living. At the same time a number of favored individuals were accumulating large tracts of land by grant and purchase. If well managed, a big plantation gave its owner important competitive advantages over the small farmer. Tobacco was notorious for the speed with which it exhausted the fertility of the soil—the grower with large holdings could shift frequently to new fields and thus maintain a high yield. Nevertheless, while no exact statistics exist, it is probably true that throughout the 17th and 18th centuries small farmers controlling no more than four or five slaves or servants raised well over half the tobacco crop of Virginia and Maryland.

In South Carolina, after a few decades in which furs and cereals were the chief products, Madagascar rice was introduced into the low-lying coastal areas in 1696. It quickly proved its worth as a cash crop. By 1700 almost 100,000 pounds were being exported annually; by the eve of the Revolution rice exports from South Carolina and Georgia exceeded 65 million pounds a year.

Rice culture required water for flooding the fields. At first freshwater swamps were adapted to the crop, but by the middle of the 18th century the chief rice fields lay along the tidal rivers and inlets. A series of dikes and floodgates allowed fresh water to pour across the fields with the rising tide; when the tide fell, the gates closed automatically to keep the water in. The process was reversed when it was necessary to drain the land. Then the water ran out as the tide ebbed, and the pressure of the next flood pushed the gates shut.

In the 1740s a second cash crop, indigo, was introduced in South Carolina by Eliza Lucas. Indigo did not compete with rice either for land or labor. It prospered on high ground and needed care in seasons when the slaves were not busy in the rice paddies. The British were delighted to have a new source of indigo because the blue dye was important in their woolens industry. Parliament quickly placed a bounty on it to stimulate production.

The production of tobacco, rice, and indigo, along with furs and forest products such as tar and resin, meant that the southern colonies had no difficulty in obtaining manufactured articles from abroad. Planters dealt with agents in England, called factors, who managed the sale of their crops, filled their orders for manufactures, and supplied them with credit.

This was a great convenience but not necessarily an advantage, for it made the colonists dependent upon European middlemen, who naturally exacted a price for their services. It tended to prevent the development of a diversified economy. Throughout the colonial era, while small-scale manufacturing was flourishing in the north, it was stillborn in the south. Even in the decade before the Revolution it was not unheard of for a Virginia planter to send a fine piece of silk—itself an import—all the way to London to be dyed because it had become soiled. There were some local businesses such as iron mining, flour milling, lumbering, and barrelmaking (the largest southern craft). But according to Carl Bridenbaugh's study, *The Colonial Craftsman*, even Charleston, a thriving community of 12,000, "did not nourish an outstanding craft or produce a single eminent workman before the Revolution." Despite its rich export trade, its fine harbor, and the easy availability of excellent lumber, Charleston's shipbuilding industry never remotely rivaled that of northern parts.

Southern society was agricultural and therefore rural. Charleston was the only city of importance in the region, and even in Charleston the dominant elements were rice planters who maintained town houses in order to escape the unhealthy conditions of their swampy domains in summer. Small farmers made up the majority, especially along the westward-moving edge of settlement. But the planters, with their slaves, Georgian mansions, and broad acres, set the tone of society and provided political leadership.

By 1700 declining prices in the tobacco colonies had combined with the opening up of fertile lands in Pennsylvania to reduce the attractiveness of the south to indentured servants. Yet tobacco cultivation required a great deal of labor. Its tiny seeds—10,000 in a teaspoonful—were sown in special beds, and after sprouting, each little plant was moved to the fields. Constant weeding was essential. During the growing period, shoots ("suckers") had to be removed and the top bud clipped off at the proper time or the plant would become a spindly "Frenchman" instead of a valuable broadleaved specimen. When the supply of servants dwindled, the planters turned to slaves, more readily available after the formation of the Royal African Company in 1672, and this accelerated the trend toward large-scale agriculture.

On the South Carolina rice plantations slave labor predominated from the beginning, for free workers would not submit to its backbreaking and unhealthy regimen. The first quarter of the 18th century saw an enormous influx of Africans. By

A MAP of
the moſt INHABITED part of
VIRGINIA
containing the whole PROVINCE of
MARYLAND
with Part of
PENSILVANIA, NEW JERSEY AND NORTH CAROLINA
Drawn by
Joshua Fry & Peter Jefferson
in 1775.

■ These scenes decorated colonial maps made in the 1770s. At left is a South Carolina indigo plantation, showing the method of extracting the dye. Right, a lordly tobacco planter ships his crop. The Peter Jefferson mentioned in the printed title was Thomas Jefferson's father.

1730 about 30 percent of the population south of Pennsylvania was black, and in some districts the concentration was far higher. By the latter part of the century blacks outnumbered whites in South Carolina by nearly two to one.

Given the existing race prejudice and the degrading impact of slavery, this demographic change had an enormous effect on southern life—all the more drastic because it occurred without plan and with little understanding of its significance on the part of whites. In each colony regulations governing the behavior of blacks, both slave and free, were gradually worked out. These increased in severity as one moved southward, that is, as the density of the black population increased. They were at their worst in the West Indies, where blacks were a majority of the population. The blacks had no civil rights under these codes, and punishments for violations were sickeningly severe. Whipping—the biblical 39 stripes—was common for minor offenses, death by hanging or by being burned alive for serious crimes. Blacks were sometimes castrated for sexual offenses—even for lewd talk about white women—or for repeated attempts to escape. The following eyewitness description of the execution of a slave in English Jamaica comes from a letter from an overseer to his employer and thus cannot be written off as humanitarian propaganda or journalistic sensationalism:

> His leggs and armes was first brocken in peeces with stakes, after which he was fasten'd upon his back to the Ground—a fire was first made to his feete and burn'd uppe by degrees; I heard him speake severall words when the fire consum'd all his lower parts as far as his Navill. The fire was upon his breast (he was burning neere 3 houres) before he dy'd.

That blacks resented slavery goes without saying, but since slavery did not mean the same thing to all of them, their reactions to it varied. Throughout the 18th century a constant stream of new slaves was arriving from Africa. These "outlandish" blacks tended to respond differently than American-born slaves. Among the latter, field hands experienced a different kind of slavery than did household servants, and skilled artisans faced still another set of circumstances. In short, a slave's place in society influenced his behavior.

The master race sought to acculturate the slaves in order to make them more efficient workers. A slave who could understand English was easier to order about; one who could handle farm tools or wait on table was more useful than one who could not; a carpenter or a mason was more valuable still. But acculturation increased the slave's independence and mobility, and this posed problems. Field hands seldom tried to escape; they expressed their dissatisfactions by pilferage and petty sabotage, by laziness, or by feigning stupidity. Most runaways were artisans who hoped to "pass" as free in a nearby town. It was one of the many paradoxes of slavery that the more valuable a slave became, the harder that slave was to control.

On the other hand, few runaway slaves became rebels. Indeed, organized slave rebellions were rare, and while individual assaults by blacks on whites were common enough, it must be remembered that personal violence was common among whites throughout American history. But the masters had sound reasons for fearing their slaves; the particular viciousness of the system lay in the fact that oppression bred resentment, which in turn produced still greater oppression.

What is superficially astonishing is that the whites—absolute masters of their human property—grossly exaggerated the danger of slave revolts. They pictured the black as a kind of malevolent ogre, powerful, bestial, and lascivious, a caldron of animal emotions that had to be restrained at any cost. Probably the characteristics they attributed to the blacks were really projections of their own passions. The most striking illustration of this process was the universal white fear of the "mongrelization" of the race: if blacks were free, they would breed with whites. Yet in practice the interbreeding, which indeed took place, was almost exclusively the result of white men using their power as masters to impregnate female slaves.

Thus the "peculiar institution" was fastened upon America with economic, social, and psychic barbs. Ignorance and self-interest, lust for gold and for the flesh, primitive prejudices and complex social and legal ties, all combined to convince the whites that black slavery was not so much good as a fact of life. With the passage of time a barely perceptible trend toward ameliorating the harshness of bondage emerged, but talk of abolishing slavery was almost nonexistent until the eve of the Revolution. A few isolated reformers, mostly Quakers, attacked the institution on the religious ground that all human beings are equal before God: "*Christ* dyed for all, both *Turks, Barbarians, Tartarians,* and *Ethyopians.*" Yet a few Quakers owned slaves, and even the majority who did not usually succumbed to color prejudice. Blackness was a defect, but it was no justification for enslavement, they argued. And they attracted little attention anywhere—none in areas where slavery was important.

Southern Intellectual and Religious Trends

The disruptions in England caused by the Civil War and the great interest that the English gentry took in America after the restoration of the monarchy brought many wealthy and educated persons to the southern colonies, and they unquestionably impressed their values on the region. Prosperity and the social implications of a system that allowed a fortunate few to exploit the labor of great numbers of slaves encouraged some large planters to "indulge their propensity to consume," but at least until late in the colonial period most of them led busy, fruitful, and interesting lives. The great landowner William Byrd II (1674–1744) often rose at 3 A.M. in order to catch up on his reading before beginning his daily rounds. Besides his tobacco fields, Byrd operated a sawmill and a gristmill, dabbled in politics, engaged in the Indian trade, planted orchards, and prospected for iron, coal, and copper.

"New" men were constantly on the rise; by their industry and ambition they gave society a tone of bustle and drive. Daniel Dulany of Maryland offers a good example of the type. He arrived in Maryland in 1703 as an indentured servant. Ten years later he was a lawyer and landowner. He married well and prospered. Soon he was reaping rewards in land speculation. His descendants, one historian writes, "made up a dynasty of social significance in the colony."

Large planters could be said to predominate in the southern colonies but not to dominate them. Gradations of wealth and status did not in themselves produce conflicts of interest. As Aubrey C. Land, an authority on the social structure of the colonial south, has put it, "probably never since . . . have the favored few enjoyed such harmony with the less fortunate." *Class* harmony did not, however (as we shall see), mean the absence of social conflict.

Slavery, of course, was not an equalizing or harmonizing force, for it increased the psychological barrier between rich and poor by degrading labor and accustoming the colonists to draw invidious comparisons between one type of human being and another. Slave labor never drove the small farmer out of business, however. The widespread use of slaves was the *result*, not the cause, of falling tobacco prices. Slaves were cheap enough in the colonial era to be owned by persons of only middling wealth, and the great plantation employing 50 or more blacks was always the exception.

Colonists north and south continued to look to the mother country for intellectual and cultural leadership. This was especially true of southerners because of their close economic ties with the homeland. Wealthy planters wore imported clothes, drove about the countryside in English coaches, used fine imported china and furniture, and built first-rate libraries of English and continental books. Many sent their children abroad to be educated.

In matters of education there was a tremendous gap in the south, not only between rich and poor but between the rich and the moderately successful majority. It is true that the College of William and Mary was established at Williamsburg, Virginia, in 1693, but almost no primary or secondary schools existed in the southern colonies. The rural nature of society, with the population scattered along countless rivers and bays, helps account for this unfortunate fact. Well-to-do planters could afford private tutors for their children, and occasionally two or three families combined to hire a teacher, but many small farmers (and nearly all of the slaves) remained unlettered.

By the middle of the 18th century the Anglican church had been established in all the southern colonies, which meant that it was the official religion, its ministers supported by public funds. The

Virginia assembly had made attendance at Anglican services compulsory in 1619, and in later years it deprived dissenters of the right to vote. Many non-Anglicans were driven from the colony. In Maryland, Lord Baltimore, although intolerant of non-Christians, had sought to persuade the Protestant majority to adopt a live-and-let-live attitude toward Catholics by imposing stiff fines on individuals who used terms like "heretick" and "papist" in what his Toleration Act defined as "a reproachful manner." This law did not survive the invasion of the colony by militant Puritans. It was repealed in 1654 during the Cromwellian period, reenacted in 1657, then repealed again in 1692 when the Anglican church was established. Catholics, who made up less than ten percent of Maryland's population, were repeatedly discriminated against: in 1704 priests were forbidden to say mass and in 1718 Catholics lost the right to vote. In the Carolinas the proprietors' original desire to encourage the immigration of people of all faiths—including Jews and Quakers—could not be carried out in practice. The Anglican church was established in 1706. In Georgia, where no state religion existed at the start, Anglicanism was established in 1758.

The Anglican church was not a very powerful force in the south. The scattering of population militated against organized religion just as it did against schools, and the English hierarchy made matters worse by neglecting their American parishes. Since there was no Anglican bishop in the colonies, novices had to sail to England to be ordained, something few colonists were willing to do. Those English pastors who migrated to America were mostly second-rate men unable to obtain a decent living at home; they and their American flocks were in almost constant conflict.

■ A tutor's advertisement in a Williamsburg newspaper in 1752 suggests the kind of education that was available to the children of wealthy southern planters.

In Virginia Anglican ministers were usually paid in tobacco vouchers worth the market value of 17,280 pounds of the crop. In 1758, after a drought drove up the price of tobacco, the House of Burgesses passed a law providing that "tobacco debts" for the year 1759 be honored at a rate of two pence per pound. Since tobacco was selling at more than twice that price in 1759, this Two-Penny Act deprived the ministers of a much-desired windfall.

Indignant clergymen appealed to the Privy Council in London, which voided the law. Thereupon several ministers went to court to sue for back pay. One test case, involving the claim of the Reverend James Maury, revealed how thoroughly the Anglican clergy had failed to win the respect of the populace. The judge ruled in Maury's favor, but a young lawyer, Patrick Henry, beclouded the issue with oratorical pyrotechnics, attacking the clergy as unpatriotic, money-grubbing "enemies of the community." The jury awarded Maury only one penny in damages. The "Parson's Cause," settled in 1763, has long been regarded as one of the earliest portents of the Revolution, for it demonstrated that in a clash of royal and local authority, most Americans would stand by their local leaders.

Agriculture in the North

North of Maryland the vast majority of people were also farmers in the colonial era, but the society that grew up there was quite different. Sugar, rice, and indigo could not be grown in the northern colonies. Except in a few limited areas, most notably in the Connecticut River valley, tobacco did not flourish either. Farmers raised the standard cereal crops, and in the 17th and 18th centuries even England normally harvested more than it needed of such grains as wheat and barley and oats. Aside from furs, forest products, and a few minor items, there was little demand in Europe for the products of the northern colonies.

Nevertheless, the facts of colonial life made it inevitable that most northern settlers become farmers. Indian corn was their principal crop for many decades, for it was easily cultivated and its yield per acre under rough frontier conditions was far higher than that of other grains. It was a versatile product, nutritious and tasty when prepared in a variety of ways for human consumption and an excellent fodder for livestock. In the form of corn liquor it was easy to store and to transport. In all the colonies, south as well as north, corn became the basic food of the early settlers.

However, once land was cleared and fenced, other grains could be produced in quantity. Wheat was the most important, especially in Pennsylvania. In New England wheat suffered greatly from a disease called the blast, so rye, oats, barley, and other grains were cultivated, as were other European vegetables and native plants such as pumpkins and potatoes. The northern colonists did a great deal of fishing, for the offshore reaches from below Cape Cod to Newfoundland constituted one of the finest fishing grounds in the world. Yet the market for colonial fish in northern Europe was no better than the market for grain.

Thus, while the northern colonists could feed themselves without difficulty, they had no direct way of turning their surpluses into the European manufactured products they desired. English ships did not flock to northern waters as they did to the tidal streams of the south and to the West Indian sugar ports.

Northern Manufacturing and Commerce

The northerners found ways to surmount this problem. During the long winter months farm families manufactured all kinds of objects, from bone buttons to leather breeches and hemp-string bags. Nearly everyone raised a few sheep, and spinning wheels were almost as ubiquitous in northern farmhouses as tables, chairs, and beds. The weaving of linen from local flax was widespread. As late as 1750, 90 percent of the farmers of Pennsylvania made most of their own clothing.

Under such conditions, families began to specialize, for no one could master all the manufacturing skills. Specialization meant producing goods for sale and exchange. Both specialization and producing for a market tended to increase the quality as well as the quantity of manufactures. The expansion of northern manufacturing and the general colonial shortage of labor redounded to the advantage of workers. Richard B. Morris, the leading authority on early American labor, estimates that real wages in the colonies averaged between 30 and 100 percent higher than in England.

Local manufacturing could not possibly supply all the goods that the colonists needed, however, and there remained the problem of disposing of surplus farm products in an overwhelmingly rural society. The solution was to seek out markets in far corners of the earth. This necessitated the building of a merchant fleet.

Fortunately, the colonists had at hand some of the finest timber in the world. Boston, Salem, Newport, Portsmouth, Philadelphia, and other northern ports became centers of shipbuilding. American vessels were soon ranging the Atlantic. A Boston skipper might take a cargo of dried fish, lumber, and wheat to the West Indies, where the one-crop sugar economy made the planters dependent upon the outside world for their needs. In the Indies he could fill his hold with sugar and then make sail for England, there to exchange the sugar for the manufactured goods that the northern colonists craved.

This triangular, or better, multiangular trade took many forms. West Indian planters produced large quantities of molasses, a by-product of sugar refining. Merchants soon discovered that they could exchange American products for molasses, which they sold to New England distillers who turned the molasses into rum, creating still another local industry. Not all of this rum was consumed in America—although mighty efforts were made in that direction. Most of the surplus was shipped to Africa and exchanged for slaves, who were carried to the Indies, thereby completing the cycle. A number of Yankees made fortunes by engaging in this noxious but profitable commerce. Foreign trade led to increased local trade too; English manufactured goods sometimes found their way to the tobacco colonies by way of northern ports, while northern fishermen, kept from the stormy Atlantic in winter, frequently went off on coasting voyages in that season laden with mixed cargoes of local products to exchange for tobacco and rice.

So trade became the key to prosperity in the northern colonies, important all out of proportion to its immediate value and to the number of per-

■ The naval stores mentioned in the map legend were products such as tar and turpentine obtained from the resin of pine trees and other evergreens. They were essential for the upkeep of wooden ships.

COLONIAL ECONOMY

Cattle and Grain   Tobacco   Rice and Indigo

Furs and Skins   Naval Stores

Fishing   Ironworks

Lumber and Timber   Rum Distilleries

Trading and Shipping   Shipbuilding

MAINE (MASS.)

N.H.

Portsmouth

Boston

Albany

MASS.

N.Y.

CONN.

R.I.

Newport

New London

PA.

N.J.

New York

Philadelphia

Baltimore

DEL.

MD.

VA.

Norfolk

N.C.

New Bern

Wilmington

S.C.

Augusta

Charleston

GA.

Savannah

0   50   100   150   200
Miles

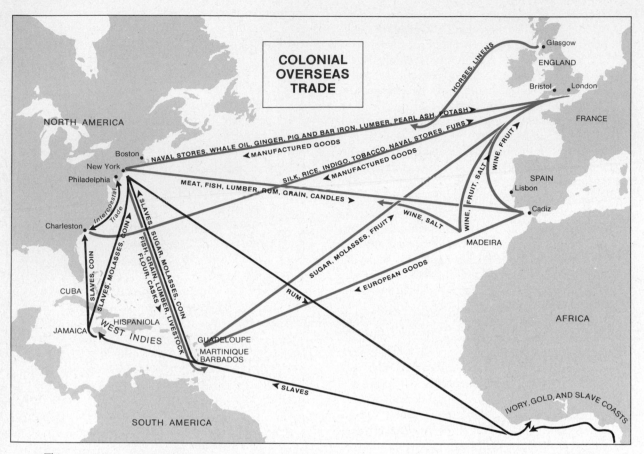

COLONIAL
OVERSEAS
TRADE

■ This map summarizes the chief routes of colonial trade in the 1700s. The triangular slave trade is in black for clarity. Most southern exports went to England, but a lack of suitable English markets led the northern and middle colonies to seek outlets for their products in the West Indies and southern Europe.

sons engaged in it. This explains why northern merchants were the leaders and trendmakers of that region, just as a relative handful of great planters set the tone for society in the south.

In 1690 Boston had fewer than 7,000 inhabitants, New York some 4,500, Philadelphia little more than 2,000. Fifty years later Boston's population had risen to 16,000, Philadelphia's to 13,000, New York's to 11,000.* Into these communities flowed the manufactured goods and luxury prod-

ucts of Europe and the grain, fur, and lumber of America. The resulting interchanges supported a host of profitable enterprises. Besides the merchants and sailors and the many employers and artisans engaged in the building of ships, wholesalers and retailers flourished, together with carpenters, silversmiths, tailors, and other craftsmen, even dancing masters. Of course, not everyone prospered. Perhaps a third of the townspeople were unskilled laborers and their families; they earned enough to live on but accumulated little property.

Most colonial cities were crowded and dirty. Being seaports, they were always full of sailors on leave and other transients bent on having a good time. Crime and vice vexed civic-minded citizens; even Puritan Boston had at least a dozen prosti-

---

*After 1740 Boston stopped expanding until after the Revolution, but in 1775 Philadelphia had 40,000 inhabitants and New York 25,000. The only important southern city, Charleston, grew from 6,800 to 12,000 between 1740 and 1775. On the eve of the Revolution at least eight other towns, including Baltimore, Newport, and New Haven, had populations of over 5,000.

tutes as early as the 1670s, and every town had a well-populated, if not always very secure, jail. Many aspects of the modern "problem of the cities" existed in miniature in these towns.

In 1700 not a single newspaper was published in the colonies, but by the middle of the century every large colonial community had one, and in some towns books were published. Taverns served as meeting places for serious clubs and as centers for intellectual and political discussions, as well as for drinking, gambling, and other forms of dalliance. The cities were intellectual centers. Books and ideas from all over Europe entered America through the seaport towns. As early as 1660 the Dutch governor of New Netherland claimed that 18 languages could be heard in and around New Amsterdam. In the towns the most ambitious and intelligent colonials—Benjamin Franklin is only the most famous of many—made their fortunes and thought their thoughts. The magnetic attraction of urban life, which was to become so powerful in the 19th and 20th centuries, was already exerting its force. It must be kept in mind, however, that all the colonies were overwhelmingly rural. As late as 1775 no more than 5 percent of the population lived in the towns.

Land and Labor in the North

Despite the importance of commerce in the northern colonies, independent farmers were the backbone of the region. In many areas they obtained land the same way that southerners did. The headright system flourished in Pennsylvania and New Jersey. The proprietor's easy terms and the rich soils of the region made Pennsylvania particularly attractive to 18th-century immigrants, both those who paid their own way and those who arrived as indentured servants. Many Scotch-Irish settlers (Presbyterian Scots whose ancestors had migrated to northern Ireland in the 17th century) flocked in beginning about 1700. The Scotch-Irish pushed west to the valleys of the Appalachian range and then funneled southward into the back country of Virginia and the Carolinas. Often they became squatters, for difficult conditions did not dismay them, and they felt perfectly capable of fighting for their "rights" when challenged. In New York a few great families like the Van Rens-

selaers had engrossed huge areas; tenant farming was common there as nowhere else in British America. Since decent freeholds were not easy to obtain, the colony grew slowly.

The New England colonies adopted a different method of land disposal, one that reflected the community-mindedness of the settlers and in turn had an important impact on local life. Instead of encouraging individual pioneers, the New England colonial governments (which held legal title to all wilderness property within their boundaries) granted land in 36-square-mile blocks called townships to *groups* of settlers.

When the grant had been made, these town "proprietors" chose a suitable location for a village. Around a square held in common, each family selected a plot of land large enough for a house and a good-sized vegetable garden. Beyond this village center the settlers cleared fields for farming. The fields were privately owned, but they were divided into many small strips so that no one individual would get all the best soil. Usually the leading families and the local minister were awarded extra-large allotments, but each family received enough land to provide for its needs. No one could engross large tracts, and no one had to pay for the land. The rest of the township belonged to the community as a whole. All residents had the right to pasture livestock and to use the timber and other forest products on the common land.

This system made for compact expansion, since the legislatures assigned townships in an orderly manner along the edge of settlement. It also insured the quick establishment of community life. Each village soon boasted at least a church and a school, and around these centers other activities could grow. Every kind of craftsman could be found in the towns: carpenters, tailors, glaziers, masons, weavers, blacksmiths, and many others. Towns vied with one another to attract skilled workers. It was not unusual for the citizenry to build a house for a trained workman in return for his promise to practice his craft in the community for a period of years.

As trades prospered they inspired local specialization. By the 1760s, Lynn, Massachusetts, was turning out 80,000 pairs of shoes a year. Specialization also fostered new trades; the development of shoemaking, for example, led to a demand for tanners. Life was dynamic in the New England village; all residents profited from the presence of so many individuals of different training and interests.

The town government provided services such as road building that further strengthened each citizen's sense of belonging to the group, and the system made for orderly expansion within the community. Newly arrived settlers could be admitted to citizenship only by vote in town meeting. Then they received house plots and land for cultivation, carved from the common holdings. The new resident was acutely conscious of becoming a part of a going social organization and of sharing the privileges and responsibilities that this entailed. Beyond question, the tone of society was influenced by the institutional framework within which settlement took place.

The largest New England towns seldom held more than 2,500 persons in the colonial period. But as they grew, the communal character of life began to break down. Compact and relatively isolated family farms sprang up around the periphery of the villages. As population expanded, the remaining commons shrank and tended to rise in value. To protect their privileged positions, older residents sometimes tried to deny political rights to newcomers. Such actions created social as well as economic distinctions in town life.

As expansion went on, the colonial governments began to treat the wilderness lands somewhat differently too. By the 1720s they were selling townships to speculators, a reversal of the original policy of making land available without charge to settlers of good character who could use it. Persons of wealth and political influence could obtain whole towns or shares in several towns. Ezra Stiles—minister, scholar, and later president of Yale College—owned shares in perhaps a dozen townships in several colonies, and he bought and sold these holdings much as a modern investor trades in stocks.

Nevertheless, the township way of life was essentially democratic. Local issues were settled by majority vote in town meetings. The towns in turn sent representatives to the colonial legislature, thus insuring a roughly equal distribution of political power in the larger community. If the grandchildren of original proprietors tended to scorn newcomers and to use their control of the machinery of local government to withhold economic and political privileges, they were seldom able to do so for very long. The logic of the system was against them to begin with, and in a Puritan *commonwealth* the force of logic generated considerable moral pressures. Probably more important, the law of supply and demand was against them. As in other parts of America, labor was needed more than land. Although gradations of wealth and personal influence existed in every community and everyone was acutely conscious of the difference, say, between a "gentleman" and a "goodman" and between the latter and a mere servant, the beckoning frontier precluded the growth of an underprivileged *class*. Towns that held too tightly to their commons and denied newcomers a voice at meetings simply ceased to grow.

Although slavery existed in every northern colony, it was nowhere as important as it was in the south. Of the 150,000 blacks in the colonies in 1740, only about 18,000 lived north of Maryland. The absence of staple crops that could be cultivated by gang labor and the long winters when the need for farm labor was minimal militated against the importation of Africans in large numbers. Most northern blacks, slave and free, worked as household servants or held menial jobs in the towns. New York City's population in the 18th century was about 15 percent black, Boston's about 8 percent.

Life for northern slaves was on the average easier than it was in the plantation colonies, but not because masters were more humane. The governing factor everywhere was the ratio of black to white. Nor did the somewhat more relaxed attitude of northerners toward blacks reflect a different evaluation of the race; northern prejudices and misconceptions were just as irrational, passions just as easily stirred. Free blacks were not usually denied the right to vote by law, but if property qualifications did not disfranchise them, local "custom" did. And when northern blacks caused trouble, or when northern whites *thought* they were causing trouble, they were subjected to punishments as severe and cruel as any devised by southerners. After subduing a genuine uprising of New York City slaves in 1712, in which 9 whites were killed, the authorities hanged 13 slaves, burned 4 alive—one over a slow fire—broke one on the wheel, and left one to starve to death in chains. Another "plot" in New York in 1741, possibly a figment of overheated white imaginations, led to the execution of 31 blacks, 13 by fire.

The Impact of Puritanism

Conditions of soil and climate affected the economy of New England, and the township system shaped the social and political history of the region, but Puritanism, both as a religion and as a way of thinking, permeated every aspect of New England life.

The Puritans had come to America to establish a "purer" church than existed anywhere in Christendom. They believed people to be essentially sinful; they could be regenerated or "saved" only by the grace of God. Since the Deity did not dispense this grace lightly, the majority of the human race was doomed to roast forever in Hell. Each person's fate, according to Puritan logic, was foreordained, for an omniscient God must know in advance the future of every soul. Yet life was not without hope; one must never give up seeking salvation. "We must look upon ourselves," a judge remarked, "as under a solemn divine Probation."

God's blessings being material as well as spiritual, success in the accumulation of worldly goods was a likely, although not a necessary, indication of salvation. Thus hard work, thrift, and strict attention to business were qualities to be cultivated by those who hoped to enter Heaven. The Puritans, in other words, were preeminently behavioralists; they wanted to create a "visible" kingdom of God on earth.

Nevertheless, they believed that good behavior, like material success, was an indication, not a guarantee, of salvation. The best evidence of grace was to have had some extraordinary emotional experience, some mystical sign of intimate contact with God. Those who had had such an experience proclaimed that fact in church, and if they convinced the congregation that the experience had been genuine, they were elected to church membership. Their combination of elitism and zeal meant that the Puritans had little interest in converting sinners. Since few could achieve salvation in any case, there was no point in being concerned with the rest except to punish their transgressions.

These miserable souls might—indeed they must—attend church, but only the elect of God had a say in the affairs of His house.

Church and state were not separated in the modern sense in most of the colonies. In Massachusetts Bay and, except for Rhode Island, in the rest of New England, the tie between the churches and the civil government was extremely close, going far beyond the mere use of public funds to support a particular religion. In early Massachusetts church attendance was compulsory, and magistrates enforced moral as well as civil law. Although clergymen could not hold office, they played a large role in nonreligious affairs, advising the magistrates, supervising the social activities of the people, and pontificating on everything from the harvesting of crops to the meaning of such natural phenomena as storms and droughts.

Religious toleration being inconceivable to most 17th-century Christians, all the colonies refused to tolerate unbelievers. Since they were driven by such a tremendous sense of their own mission, the Puritans were especially hard on dissenters. That they had themselves been victims of persecution did not make them any less inclined to persecute others. This was particularly unfortunate because many settlers could not in conscience subscribe to all the Puritan tenets. By the 1670s at least half—estimates run as high as four-fifths—of the residents of Massachusetts Bay were "unregenerate." They were not church members and could not vote in civil elections.

Puritanism was often too intense, too inhibiting, too smug. It bred in some of its devotees a narrow, almost psychopathic harshness and rigidity, an overconcern with sin that approached relish. For those who dissented—zealots like Anne Hutchinson, pious individuals of independent mind like Roger Williams, or characters like the roistering Thomas Morton, who danced with his followers around a maypole—the Puritan response was jail, banishment, and even, for a few stubborn Quakers, death.

Yet there was more to Puritanism than bigotry and repression. Puritans opposed not enjoyment but frivolity—not wine, for example, but drunkenness. ("Drink," said one early Puritan divine, "is in itself a good creature of God . . . but the abuse of drink is from Satan.") While intolerant of other religions, Puritans examined every nook and cranny of their own beliefs, testing them always against reason as well as Scripture, never content with oversimplified answers to hard philosophical questions. They detested the "ignorant sinner" almost as much for the ignorance as for the sin. Despite the rigors of life in the wilderness, they insisted upon educating their children, for how could the next generation achieve salvation if it could not read the Bible? They considered a learned ministry vital, for ordinary citizens needed expert guidance if they hoped to understand the complexities of their faith; thus, within six years of the founding of Boston, the Puritans had created a college (Harvard), certainly one of the most remarkable achievements in the history of colonization.

In the 18th and 19th centuries optimists tended to deride Puritan talk about the weakness and sinfulness of human beings. The Puritans, one 19th-century New Englander claimed, had "regarded human existence itself as a ghastly risk, and, in the case of the vast majority of human beings, an inconceivable misfortune." Our own century, enlightened by the beams that Freud projected into the dark corners of the mind and chastened by the failure of reason and science to make a universal Eden of the globe, has viewed the Puritan evaluation of human nature more respectfully. If to be saved by God's grace means to achieve peace of mind through self-understanding, then salvation is as rare in the 20th century as the Puritans thought it was in the 17th century. Looking about in their wilderness Zion, the Puritans saw that most people were weak and sinful, that nature was capricious, that fate was blind. Their glory was twofold: they accepted this sad reality without self-delusion and then struggled to rise above personal limitations, subdue savage surroundings, and be worthy of whatever fortune came their way.

The Puritan faith was another reason why New England village life was so stimulating and dynamic. The town was the battlefield on which the struggle for eternal salvation was fought. Its inhabitants were alert, assertive, self-conscious citizens, not the simple peasants of European village communities. While philosophically undemocratic, Puritanism contributed to the development of American political institutions, particularly by its stress on *limited* government (since human beings are sinful by nature, they cannot be trusted with much power over their fellows), on *self*-government (the basic principle of congregationalism), on individualism (everyone must be able to read and interpret the Bible), and on the right of the community to control its members in the common interest.

The contradictions inherent in these concepts have never been resolved; probably they never can be. The tensions they produced in colonial New England have persisted. Are individuals morally bound to obey laws they consider evil? Which shall take precedence, the will of the majority or the liberties of an individual? Such questions were asked during the American Revolution, during the Civil War—and they are being asked today.

The heyday of New England Puritanism was short. Class antagonisms and westward expansion gradually weakened community solidarity, and economic prosperity worked in subtle ways to undermine the church-centered community. The most devout merchant often found that business interests conflicted with such Puritan concepts as just price. Religious intolerance discouraged immigration (thereby restricting the growth of domestic markets) and gave New England merchants a bad reputation in other regions. More generally, the success of the merchants inevitably brought them prestige and power, destroying the preeminence of the clergy. And for all Puritans, prosperity made it increasingly difficult to distinguish between praiseworthy thriftiness and excessive acquisitiveness, the "Cursed Hunger for Riches."

The Puritan communities were not riddled with vice and greed, although the clergy, assembled at Boston in 1679, produced a long and circumstantial catalogue of such transgressions, ranging from Sabbath breaking and extravagance of dress to "the sinn of whoredom." The majority of the settlers remained hardworking, clean living, and pious. But the Puritan virtues led to the amassing of wealth, to expansion, and to diversity—all changes that undermined the Puritan commonwealth. "Religion brought forth prosperity," the Reverend Cotton Mather explained, "and the daughter destroyed the mother." This was an overstatement, but religious attitudes did change.

Orthodox Puritan theology taught that children of the elect could be baptized but could not become full church members and partake of communion until they personally had experienced God's grace. Many, as they became adults, had not. Therefore, in 1662, this strict rule was modified by the Half-Way Covenant, which permitted these persons to submit their own children for baptizing and to remain themselves as "half-way" members of the church.

This concession implied that church membership and attendance at organized services were at least partial substitutes for God-given grace. From the point of view of the elect, the compromise was both humane and politically essential. They were not prepared to see their grandchildren grow up under the stigma of Adam's sin; as Cotton Mather wrote, "The good old generation could not, without uncomfortable apprehensions, behold their offspring excluded from the baptism of Christianity." At the same time the elect made sure that the church would not simply die of old age and (incidentally) that the half-way members, being still "members," could continue to vote in civil elections. On the other hand, the covenant extended the power of the clergy over the third generation, binding the young to submit to church discipline.

Not even this compromise could long preserve the monopoly of the original "visible saints." The conflict between the idea of a powerful clergy and the belief that everyone must personally understand the meaning of Holy Writ was bound to weaken the church. So did the confusion between the intellectual and the emotional sides of Puritanism. The Puritan must *understand* yet also *feel* to be saved. Which was more important? Puritans walked different paths in search of the answer. In the end some became Unitarians, embracing a religion so highly intellectualized as to seem to some not a religion at all. Others took the less taxing path that led to the evangelical faiths, with their stress on hymn singing, camp meetings, and inspirational preaching.

By the time Charles II ascended the throne in 1660, orthodox Puritans were bemoaning the decay of religious standards in New England. Thereafter, the resurgent royal authority added to their woes. In 1684 the Massachusetts Bay charter was annulled, and soon all the colonies north and east of Pennsylvania were brought into the Dominion of New England under one powerful governor, Sir Edmund Andros. Although Puritan Congregationalism remained the established religion, the loss of the charter weakened the political influence of the clergy. Church membership ceased to be a requirement for voting, and Governor Andros even

forced the congregation of the Old South Meeting House in Boston to permit its use for Anglican services. Fearing that Andros intended to establish the Anglican church in Massachusetts, the Puritan hierarchy thereafter adopted a more tolerant attitude.

When news of the Glorious Revolution and the accession of William and Mary to the English throne reached the colonies, Andros was overthrown and the Dominion dissolved, but Massachusetts never recovered its original charter. The former "Bible commonwealth" became a Crown colony in 1691. The Puritan clergy continued to fight religious laxity and the secularization of life with a zealous "counterreformation"—which may have inadvertently contributed to the Salem witchcraft mania of 1692, in which 20 miserable "witches" were put to death. When this hysteria had spent itself, the shamefaced general public blamed the trouble on the orthodox clergy, especially on Cotton Mather, who had published a book on witchcraft a few years earlier. This was unfair, for nearly everyone believed in witches in the 17th century. In the 18th century, as settlement spread westward and strip farming around a village center gave way to consolidated farms scattered through the townships, both church attendance and the quality of the clergy declined. The average person's intensity of interest and conviction in religious matters slackened.

The Great Awakening

In all the colonies, religious fervor had slackened somewhat in the early 18th century, but the right of local communities to provide public support for the predominant faith was beginning to be accepted. Immigration produced a proliferation of religions (Quakers, Mennonites, Lutherans, and Presbyterians in Pennsylvania, Dutch Reformed in New York, Baptists in Rhode Island, pockets of Jews and Catholics in the seaboard cities, and so on), and this, together with the developing worship of reason that characterized the 18th-century Enlightenment, seems to have fostered skepticism in many quarters. Many Puritans were tempted by Arminianism, a vague creed that played down hellfire and predestination and argued that a life of good works and quiet respectability was enough to assure salvation. People could save

■He had a squint in his left eye and was not imposing physically, but his contemporaries were overwhelmed by evangelist George Whitefield's magnetic voice and dramatic presence in the pulpit. The portrait was painted by John Wollaston.

their souls, as it were, by an act of will. On the other hand, the multiplication of religions did not make for harmonious relations between groups. The stress on local self-determination produced sects, congregations that believed that they alone knew all the answers, that all others were professing false creeds.

This state of affairs was modified in the 1740s by a mass movement known as the Great Awakening. Sporadic revivals of intense religious feeling had been common in the colonies before that time. As early as 1733 a brilliant theologian named Jonathan Edwards had deeply stirred his congregation in Northampton, Massachusetts. A tall, slender figure, with piercing eyes and a thin but arresting voice, Edwards preached the power of God and the depravity of humankind. Although he was not characteristically a hellfire-and-brimstone preacher, he could picture the tortures of eternal damnation vividly when necessary. His parishioners, even little children, were soon trembling over the fate of their eternal souls and experiencing repentance and "conversion" in whole-

sale lots. Emotional appeals of this sort tended to divide congregations; often what today would be called a generation gap appeared. The older people wished to preserve past forms, the younger ones espoused the new emotional approach to salvation. In some sections economics reinforced the gap. The shrinking supply of undeveloped land and a period of hard times reduced opportunities for the young and made them eager for change.

The explosion of the Great Awakening, which tipped the balance in favor of the new, was set off by a young English minister, George Whitefield, who was already famous in the mother country as an inspired preacher. Beginning in November 1739, Whitefield toured America, releasing everywhere an epidemic of religious emotionalism. Although not nearly Edwards' equal as a thinker—Whitefield's theology, one authority wrote, was "scaled down to the comprehension of twelve-year-olds"—he had few peers as an orator and actor. David Garrick, king of the London stage, is supposed to have said that he would give a hundred guineas to be able to say "Oh" as Whitefield did.

His oratorical brilliance aside, Whitefield succeeded because his message was well suited to American ears. He attacked the narrowness of the sects, calling for unity among believers. "God help us to forget party names and become Christians in deed and truth," he prayed. While not denying the truth of predestination, he hinted that God could be persuaded to open the gates of Heaven to all good and faithful Christians.*

Whitefield attracted dozens of disciples and imitators among the clergy, including some who were plainly mentally unbalanced. According to the historian Ola Winslow, "Scores of parishes became centers of religious frenzy. Sermons were preached every night in the week, and there were private gatherings at all hours of the day. Meetinghouses were packed; conversion was the theme of the hour." Whitefield had his greatest impact in the south and in frontier regions, but even in New England he caused a storm. In Boston 19,000 people (more than the population of the town) thronged to hear him during a three-day visit.

The Awakening flared sporadically for nearly a

---

*A widespread diphtheria epidemic in the 1730s, which killed thousands of children, may account for some of the intense concern about salvation at the time.

decade. A typical highpoint occurred at Enfield, Connecticut, on July 8, 1741, when Edwards delivered his famous sermon "Sinners in the Hands of an Angry God." As Edwards warned, "O sinner! Consider the fearful danger you are in: it is a great furnace of wrath, a wide and bottomless pit, full of the fire of wrath, that you are held over," a great moaning reverberated through the church. People cried out: "What shall I do to be saved?" and "O, I am going to Hell." As one witness later recorded, "the shrieks & crys were piercing & Amazing."

When imposed upon the conflict in Puritan theology between reason and emotion and upon the strains on community unity generated by expansion and increasing wealth, the Awakening caused what the historian Richard L. Bushman has called a "psychological earthquake." Persons chafing under the restraints of Puritan authoritarianism and made guilt-ridden by their rebellious feelings now found release. For some the release was more than spiritual; Timothy Cutler, a conservative Anglican clergyman, complained that as a result of the Awakening "our presses are forever teeming with books and our women with bastards."

Whether or not Cutler was correct, the Great Awakening helped many people to rid themselves of the idea that disobedience of authority entailed damnation. Anything that God justified, human law could not condemn. Of course this idea had social and political as well as religious implications. In the hands of some of Whitefield's disciples, the message became openly radical. The rich, one spellbinder claimed, "grow in Wickedness in Proportion to the Increase in their Wealth."

The excesses of the Great Awakening disgusted many people, and this led to factional disputes in many congregations. Conservatives began by questioning the emotionalism of "New Light" preachers like Whitefield and ended by challenging the idea of predestination on the ground that it was unreasonable to believe that a benevolent God would not be swayed by the actual behavior of His creatures. In a general atmosphere of hysteria, basic religious values were unlikely to flourish. Edwards, for example, broke with his church and became first a missionary among the Indians and then president of the College of New Jersey, now Princeton.

While it caused divisions, the Awakening also fostered toleration. Whitefield and his followers preached wherever they could find an audience. Their efforts caused the idea of denominationalism to flourish among Protestants. If one group claimed the right to have its own forms and ideas, how could it deny to other Protestant churches equal freedom to practice the common faith as they wished? The Awakening turned Protestants away from reliance upon state support on the theory that politics was a divisive and corrupting influence in religion. There followed the founding of church-financed colleges (Brown, Dartmouth, and Rutgers, for example) and many other institutions such as orphanages and Indian missions.

The Great Awakening was one of the first truly national events in colonial history. Thirteen isolated settlements, expanding north and south as well as westward, were becoming one. Powerful bonds were being forged. Intercolonial trade expanded. Increasingly the British tried to centralize the administration and regulation of this trade. As early as 1691, there was a rudimentary colonial postal system. In 1754, not long after the Great Awakening, the farsighted Benjamin Franklin advanced his Albany Plan for a colonial union to deal with common problems such as defense against the Indians.

The Impact of the Enlightenment

These stirrings of national self-consciousness did not mean that Americans were escaping from European influences; their culture was heavily derivative throughout the colonial period and for decades thereafter. The 18th-century European Enlightenment had an enormous impact. The founders of the colonies were contemporaries of the astronomer Galileo (1564–1642), the philosopher-mathematician René Descartes (1596–1650), and Sir Isaac Newton (1642–1727), the genius who revealed to the world the workings of gravity and the other laws of motion. American society matured amid the excitement generated by these great discoverers, who provided both a new understanding of the natural world and a new mode of thought. Instead of seeing a universe responding to the caprice of an omnipotent and sometimes wrathful Deity, people began to envisage a universe based on impersonal, scientific laws that governed the behavior of all matter, animate

■ The pioneering work of the naturalist John Bartram was carried on, after his death, by his son William. These drawings by William show a study of snails and Florida alligators.

and inanimate. Earth and the heavens, human beings and the lower animals—all seemed parts of an immense, intricate machine. God was the master technician (the divine watchmaker) who had created the marvelous structure and who now watched over it, but who never interfered with its immutable operation.

It therefore appeared that human reasoning power rather than God's revelations was the key to knowledge; it followed that knowledge of the laws of nature, by enabling people to understand the workings of the universe, would enable them to master their surroundings.

Most creative thinkers of the Enlightenment realized that human beings were not entirely rational and that complete understanding of the physical world was impossible. Readers of their works tended to ignore the qualifying phrases. By the 18th century European and American intellectuals were responding eagerly to the new view of the world. They scanned stellar space and scoured the earth, collecting and cataloguing masses of data, sure that no mystery could long elude their search for truth. Their faith produced the so-called Age of Reason, and while their confidence in human rationality seems to us naive and the "laws" they formulated no longer appear so mechanically perfect (the universe is far less orderly than they imagined), they added immensely to knowledge.

Americans accepted the underlying assumptions of the Age of Reason wholeheartedly. The inevitability of progress seemed self-evident to a people who were so successfully transforming a wilderness into a rich and civilized society (the immensity of the task only strengthened their belief that the task could be accomplished). That human beings were capable of self-improvement appeared axiomatic in the flexible and dynamic colonial environment. Deism, a faith that revered God for the marvels of His universe rather than for His power over humankind, was especially popular in America, attracting thousands of converts among the educated minority.

Colonial America produced no Galileo or Newton, but it contributed significantly to the collection of scientific knowledge. The unexplored continent provided a great laboratory for the study of natural phenomena. John Bartram, a Philadelphia Quaker who flourished in the middle years of the 18th century, ranged from Florida to the Great Lakes, gathering and classifying hundreds of American plants. Bartram also studied the Indians closely, speculating about their origins and collecting information about their ways of life. Cadwallader Colden, lieutenant governor of New York from 1761 to 1776, made important contributions to the systematic study of American flora and fauna and carried on an extensive correspondence with the Swedish botanist Linnaeus and other noted European scientists.

Professor John Winthrop of Harvard, a descendant of the first governor of the Massachusetts Bay colony, measured the earth's distance from the sun with an accuracy of over 98 percent. David Rittenhouse constructed the first orrery (a mechanical model of the solar system) in America in 1767. Even the Puritan divine Cotton Mather, was an avid scientist. He helped introduce smallpox inoculation in America, having no patience with the belief of many religious persons that it was sacrilegious to interfere with the unfathomable workings of God's will. Science strengthened religion, he insisted. "Gravity," he wrote, "leads us to God, and brings us very near to Him." In addition, Mather wrote about subjects as diverse as rattlesnakes, magnetism, and church history; his massive *Magnalia Christi Americana* (1702) is an attic of miscellaneous information. The planter William Byrd dabbled in medicine, amassed a library of over 3,600 volumes, and collected botanical specimens for British scientists in the Royal Society, of which he was an active member.

Benjamin Franklin is the most famous American example of the Enlightenment type. He was born in 1706, the son of a soap and candle maker. He learned the printer's trade and at the age of 17 moved from his native Boston to Philadelphia. By the time he was 20 he owned his own newspaper, the Pennsylvania *Gazette*. A few years later he began publishing *Poor Richard's Almanack*, which with its wise sayings, homespun advice stressing hard work and thrift, and an endless supply of miscellaneous information, became an annual best seller.

When he was in his early forties, Franklin retired from business to concentrate on his many other interests. One of his biographers has called him a "harmonious human multitude." Besides his famous kite experiment, which proved that lightning was in fact electricity, he invented the

■ Rittenhouse built two orreries as teaching tools for Princeton and the University of Pennsylvania; this one is at Princeton, and was restored in the 1950s. In a letter he remarked: "I am so taken with optics, that I do not know whether, if the enemy should invade this part of the country, as Archimedes was slain while making geometrical figures, so I should die making a telescope."

■ An unfamiliar view of Ben Franklin, painted by Matthew Pratt in 1756 when Franklin was 50 years old. He is wearing a full-bottomed wig. The more familiar later portraits show Franklin with his own sparse gray hair.

lightning rod, the iron Franklin stove (a far more efficient way of heating a room than an open fireplace), bifocal spectacles, and other ingenious devices. His scientific work made him world famous. In addition, he served for 14 years (1751–1764) in the Pennsylvania Assembly and for part of that time was the agent of the colony in London. He founded a debating club named the Junto, a circulating library, and in 1743 the American Philosophical Society. He set up an academy for young artisans that later became the University of Pennsylvania. He helped get the first hospital in Philadelphia built, and he was an organizer of a volunteer fire company. In his spare time he taught himself Latin, French, Spanish, and Italian.

Franklin wrote so much about the virtues of hard work and thrift that some historians have described him as stuffy and straitlaced. Nothing could be further from the truth. He saw the social value of conventional behavior, but he was no slave to convention. He fathered two illegitimate children, wrote humorous essays on such subjects as the advantage of having affairs with older and plain-looking women (who were, he claimed, more likely to appreciate the attention). Above all,

he was open-minded and imaginative as well as shrewd and judicious—an unbeatable combination.

Although Thomas Jefferson made no single contribution to the advancement of knowledge that was equal to some of Franklin's, he represents the culmination of the American Enlightenment: linguist, bibliophile, political scientist, architect, inventor, scientific farmer, and—above all—apostle of reason. "Fix reason firmly in her seat," Jefferson wrote, "and call to her tribunal every fact, every opinion."

Of course the ordinary settler was not a scientist, a philosopher, or even much of a reader; few colonial homes contained many books other than the Bible. Most Americans were practical rather than speculative types, tinkerers rather than constructors of grand designs, and they were little concerned with intellectual questions. As one 18th-century observer noted, they were easily diverted "by Business or Inclination from profound Study, and prying into the Depth of Things." They had neither time nor patience for searching out large generalizations. Nevertheless, by the mid 18th century the intellectual climate in the colonies was one of eager curiosity, flexibility of outlook, and confidence.

Social Mobility

Clear social and economic lines of demarcation existed in the colonial world. Blacks, even those who were not slaves, were discriminated against both legally and socially. The wealthy had status denied the common run of colonists, most of whom deferred automatically to those they considered their betters, as their ancestors in Europe had done for centuries past. Of the white population, perhaps 20 percent could be described as poor (far less than in Europe), and many of the poor were recent immigrants, apprentices, indentured servants, and others whose prospects of improvement were quite good. It was a socially mobile environment—most people who were willing to work hard could rise in the world. "A society with an endemic labor shortage," one social historian writes, "could always find a useful place for young, able-bodied persons." Germantown, Pennsylvania, with a population of about 2,700, had in 1790 only 12 people, all aged, in its poorhouse.

In bad times poverty became a serious social problem in the larger towns. About one thousand of the 15,000 residents of Boston were receiving public relief in the late 1750s. In the towns the gap between rich and poor was substantial and growing by that time. The richest 5 percent of all Bostonians owned half the wealth, and they were beginning to display their prosperity by building big houses filled with imported furnishings and by driving about town in gorgeous coaches and carriages.

In rural areas differences were much smaller and the colonies were still overwhelmingly rural. In general, the bulk of the white population—roughly three of every four families, according to the best estimates—possessed "middling" wealth. While some colonists were very rich, the most opulent lived quite modestly compared with a peer of the realm or a great merchant prince in England. Whatever their condition, most settlers took it for granted that only persons with some material stake in the country could be counted upon to preserve the social order. For this reason, all the colonial governments established property qualifications for voting and somewhat higher qualifications for holding office.

Nevertheless, in all the colonies property was so widely held that large numbers of ordinary citizens could vote. The charter of Massachusetts Bay provided that only men owning a "40 shilling freehold" (land that would rent for 40 shillings a year) or other property valued at £50 could vote in provincial elections. However, as Robert E. Brown's exhaustive researches in Massachusetts town records have shown, most settlers could meet one or the other of these requirements. In Virginia the situation was similar; few white men failed to fulfill the voting requirements: owning 25 acres of improved land, 100 acres of unoccupied land, or a house and lot in a town. Even in colonies like South Carolina and New York, where property qualifications were stiffer, a much larger percentage of the people could vote than in England. It also seems clear that in the larger towns where many citizens could not meet the property requirements for voting, the requirements were simply ignored.

European visitors, accustomed to a more hierarchical world, frequently marveled at the ease and informality of American society. The ordinary citizen displays "no knavish reverence" of his rich neighbor, the German traveler Johann Schoepf reported. Rather he "treats him with an open, but seemly, familiarity." It would be incorrect, however, to describe colonial society as democratic in the modern sense. Practical democracy was far in advance of popular thinking about democracy throughout America. The plain farmer and artisan did not consider themselves the equal, socially or politically, of the great planter or merchant. In Virginia the political leaders of the colony were nearly all what we would call aristocrats, typified by men like Washington and Jefferson. At one point six members of the Lee family held seats in the House of Burgesses. The mass of ordinary farmers in the colony could have voted these men out of office; instead they freely chose their "betters" to represent them. "People in general have a predilection for the great, and are ever fond of bestowing the highest offices upon them," a Philadelphia writer explained.

Social distinctions were far less rigid than in Europe and more directly related to material wealth, for there was no native nobility, no *permanently* privileged class. The undeveloped, expanding country offered almost unlimited opportunities for the ambitious to grow rich, and with wealth, as in any society, came social status. Colonial politics were characteristically chaotic for this reason. The elite might rule, but new elites emerged at every turn—great "new" planters in Virginia in the middle of the 17th century, merchant princes in booming Baltimore a hundred years later. While still prisoners of European social and political ideas, while aping, as provincials nearly always do, the standards of the homeland, the Americans were establishing a way of life more flexible and more democratic than any in the world. Americans respected people for what they were and for what they had done, not for the achievements of some forgotten ancestor.

Sectional Conflicts

In part because of the opportunities available and the lack of social rigidity, sharp conflicts often broke out between sections. America was a huge land, travel between distant regions slow, uncomfortable, and expensive. Relatively few persons had firsthand knowledge of districts other than their own. The residents of one colony found it difficult to believe they had much in common with strangers hundreds of miles away in another settlement. The historical accident that led to the establishment on the continent of 13 separate political units bound together only indirectly through the Crown and the royal bureaucracy prevented the colonists from thinking in national terms. In their own eyes they were Virginians or New Yorkers or, at most, New Englanders. Beyond that they saw themselves as subjects of the king. "American" was not a term with much political significance even in the mid 18th century, although recent studies suggest that by that time the people were beginning to feel a sense of community, a kind of latent nationalism.

Perhaps because the settlers were not yet accustomed to thinking in continental terms, few important intercolonial conflicts disrupted Britain's American empire. Occasionally, nasty quarrels over boundaries arose, but they rarely became critical. The conflicting claims of Massachusetts, Connecticut, New York, Pennsylvania, and Virginia to the Ohio Valley were only beginning to assume serious proportions in the mid 18th century. They were overshadowed by the common threat to these claims posed by the French. Slavery, the great disruptive force of the following century, did not arouse much controversy in the colonial era.

Between different regions of individual colonies, relations were not always serene. Sectionalism, a national disease in the 19th century, was a local scourge in the 18th. To some extent regional conflicts were inevitable, being based on fundamental clashes of economic interests. Principally these flared up between eastern and western sections, between the older, settled areas and the frontier. Westerners wanted land policies that encouraged rapid expansion. Easterners tended to disagree, fearing that the opening up of new land

■ The "Indian menace" was always uppermost in the minds of those living on the frontier. A drawing made in 1711 by Christopher von Graffenried, the founder of a Swiss-German colony in North Carolina, shows Graffenried, his surveyor, and their black servant held captive by the Tuscarora. A tribal dance (right) was followed by the torture of the bound prisoners. Graffenried and his companions were later ransomed.

would depress the value of their own holdings. Westerners wished to spend public money on the construction of roads and what later came to be called "internal improvements"; in the developed areas most people objected to such expenditures. Westerners were *always* anti-Indian. A state of almost perpetual warfare existed along the frontier, where the jagged teeth of settlement chewed inexorably into the Indians' hunting grounds. Even in times superficially calm the threat of Indian attack never vanished in the western districts. Yet eastern colonists, far removed from danger, urged restraint upon western settlers because warfare was a costly drain upon the whole community. When easterners sanctimoniously advised their western cousins to live at peace with the Indians or offered Indians firearms and liquor in order to obtain furs on the best terms, the westerners became as hostile toward the easterners as toward the Indians.

Geographical conflicts were complicated by counterforces within each region. Eastern land speculators favored the rapid growth of the west as much as western farmers, while eastern fur traders, eager to preserve the western wilderness as a hunting ground, had enthusiastic allies in the frontier districts. Eastern merchants joined their western customers in demanding better roads. Descriptions of colonial conflicts phrased only in terms of east versus west are usually oversimplifications. The headstrong, on-the-make attitude of both frontier settlers and members of the eastern establishments had a great deal to do with most of the clashes of the colonial era.

When trouble occurred, the fact that the newer western counties were denied equal representation in the provincial legislatures was usually involved. Beginning with the first meeting of the Virginia House of Burgesses in 1619, colonials apportioned seats in legislative bodies on a geographical basis. Each lawmaker represented an area of land, not a specific number of people. So long as the districts were of roughly equal size and the population spread evenly over the entire area, the system worked well. But as civilization moved westward, some colonial legislatures discriminated against settlers in the newer regions by giving them far less representation than their numbers warranted. This was easily done, since the older areas controlled the machinery by which

new districts were established. In North Carolina at the time of the Revolution, the seaboard counties still elected two-thirds of the members of the legislature. In Pennsylvania the area around Philadelphia exercised even more striking control over political affairs.

Western settlers were therefore unable to back their views with appropriate political force. When conflicts of interest sprang up over such things as Indian policy, they were overwhelmingly outvoted. In a democratic system the losers may grumble, but they respect the right of the majority to prevail. When a minority makes the decision, however, they are righteously wrathful. And when one element easily predominates, it tends to become contemptuous of other interests. The give-and-take of democratic debate, which settles conflicts by compromise, does not take place. This unfortunate state of affairs aggravated colonial social and economic conflicts; tempers flared, and sometimes it led to armed revolt.

Troubles caused by eastern disregard for western interests can be spotted throughout colonial history. In Virginia, for example, a major explosion led by an impetuous and ambitious young planter named Nathaniel Bacon took place in 1676. Despite western growth, there had been no election in Virginia since 1662, and a clique in the entourage of the royal governor, Sir William Berkeley, held most of the government jobs in the colony. When Indians ravaged the frontier early in 1676, Berkeley, who was generally sympathetic toward them, insisted that reprisals be confined to those tribes that had caused the trouble.

Bacon, although wealthy and a member of the Virginia upper crust, was with regard to Indians a typical frontiersman: he did not relish such fine distinctions. He raised an extralegal army, killed some peaceful local tribesmen, and then turned on the colonial government at Jamestown. After a spectacular series of ups and downs in which Jamestown was burned and a number of the rebels executed, some important reforms were enacted. Right and justice were by no means entirely on the side of Bacon and his followers, either before or during the troubles. The conflict was as much between rival groups of large landowners as between small farmers and the eastern establishment. The rebels were neither democrats nor opposed to English rule. Yet the uprising might

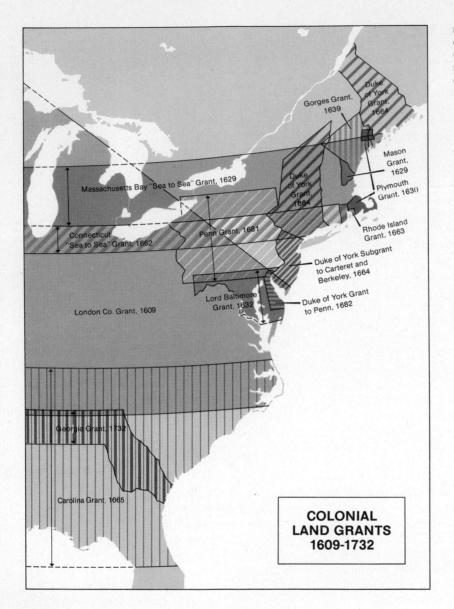

■ A welter of conflicting and overlapping colonial grants (only the more important are shown here) caused boundary disputes that dragged on well into the 19th century.

COLONIAL LAND GRANTS 1609-1732

never have occurred if the colonial government had been more representative of the opinions of all sections and interests.

The 1763 uprising of the "Paxton Boys" in Pennsylvania, though less complicated, was also triggered by eastern indifference to Indian attacks on the frontier—an indifference made possible by the fact that the east outnumbered the west in the assembly, 26 to 10. Fuming because they could obtain no help from Philadelphia against the Indians, a group of Scotch-Irish from Lancaster county fell upon a village of peaceful Conestoga Indians and murdered them in cold blood. Then these Paxton Boys marched on the capital, several hundred strong. Fortunately a delegation of burghers, headed by Benjamin Franklin, talked them out of attacking the town, partly by promising to vote a bounty on Indian scalps!*

In 1771 a somewhat different uprising pitted rich against poor and easterner against westerner in North Carolina. A pitched battle was fought in

---

*Yet fairer representation did not come in Pennsylvania until the Revolution.

the western part of the colony between frontiersmen calling themselves "Regulators" and government troops. The Regulators were crushed and their leaders executed.

The New England frontier, by contrast, did not suffer from eastern domination. Each township was represented in the legislature, and since all townships were the same size, no great disproportion could arise. If anything, western communities, being less thickly settled, were overrepresented; the seaport towns of the Massachusetts Bay colony, for example, had only 14 representatives in a legislature of nearly 200. In all New England, although conflicts of interest between east and west arose from time to time, no Bacons, no Paxton Boys, no Regulators took up arms against the government.

While colonial history is full of broils and tumults, in a significant sense social relations were remarkably harmonious. People competed fiercely for wealth and status, yet save for the shameful subordination of the black populace (an important exception), the rules of the competition were reasonably fair and the prizes so abundant that few losers retired empty-handed from the contest. Americans were a happy people, taken all in all. Though still relatively few in number and legally subordinate to Great Britain, they were growing steadily more prosperous and more powerful; during the 18th century, the population doubled every 20 years. Staggering tasks faced them as they labored to make a garden of their continental wilderness, but the future was clear to all but the most obtuse. It was a pleasing prospect indeed.

SUPPLEMENTARY READING

Titles marked with an asterisk have been published in paperback

Among general interpretations of colonial life, D. J. Boorstin's **The Americans: The Colonial Experience*** (1958) and H. M. Jones' **O Strange New World*** (1964) are stimulating. David Hawke, **The Colonial Experience** (1966), is a general survey of colonial history. J. A. Henretta, **The Evolution of American Society*** (1973) synthesizes much recent research on the period. Richard Hofstadter, **America at 1750*** (1971), is a magisterial view of the state of the colonies. The writings of F. J. Turner on the influence of the frontier on American history, collected in R. A. Billington (ed.), **Frontier and Section*** (1961), are particularly applicable to the colonial era. D. M. Potter's **People of Plenty*** (1954) is another general interpretation of American civilization that is especially convincing when tested against the facts of colonial life. Carl Bridenbaugh's **Myths and Realities: Societies of the Colonial South*** (1952), T. J. Wertenbaker's **The First Americans*** (1972), J. T. Adams' **Provincial Society*** (1927), and D. J. Lovejoy's **The Glorious Revolution in America** (1972) are very useful.

On economic conditions, E. J. Perkins, **The Economy of Colonial America** (1980), is an up-to-date survey. Three older works provide a mass of detail: L. C. Gray, **History of Agriculture in the Southern United States** (1933), P. W. Bidwell and J. I. Falconer, **History of Agriculture in the Northern United States** (1925), and E. R. Johnson et al., **History of the Domestic and Foreign Commerce of the United States** (1922). On colonial land disposal, see Marshall Harris, **Origin of the Land Tenure System in the United States** (1953). R. B. Morris, **Government and Labor in Early America*** (1946), is

a standard work, while A. E. Smith, **Colonists in Bondage*** (1947), is a good study of indentured servitude. On slavery, see Herbert Klein, **The Middle Passage** (1978), D. B. Davis, **The Problem of Slavery in Western Culture*** (1966), W. D. Jordan, **White Over Black: American Attitudes Toward the Negro*** (1968), and Lorenzo Greene, **The Negro in Colonial New England*** (1942). On life in New England, see D. R. Rutman, **Winthrop's Boston*** (1965), John Demos, **A Little Commonwealth: Family Life in Plymouth Colony*** (1970), R. L. Bushman, **From Puritan to Yankee: Character and Social Order in Connecticut*** (1967), K. A. Lockridge, **A New England Town: The First Hundred Years*** (1970), and Philip Greven, **Four Generations** (1970). J. C. Spruill, **Women's Life and Work in the Southern Colonies*** (1972), is useful. Stuart Bruchey, **The Roots of American Economic Growth*** (1965), explores the dynamics of American economic development.

Bernard Bailyn, **The New England Merchants in the 17th Century*** (1955), is an excellent study, as are F. B. Tolles, **Meeting House and Counting House: The Quaker Merchants of Colonial Philadelphia*** (1948), S. G. Wolf, **Urban Village: Population, Community, and Family Structure in Germantown, Pennsylvania** (1977), and L. B. Wright, **The First Gentlemen of Virginia*** (1940). R. M. Tryon, **Household Manufactures in the United States** (1917), is still the best survey of the subject, while Carl Bridenbaugh, **The Colonial Craftsman*** (1950), is full of interesting information. Bridenbaugh's **Cities in the Wilderness*** (1938) is the best source of information on colonial urban life up to about

1740, while his **Cities in Revolt*** (1955) deals with the immediate pre-Revolutionary years. On class conflict, see G. B. Nash, **The Urban Crucible*** (1979).

On cultural history, see L. B. Wright, **The Cultural Life of the American Colonies*** (1957). A standard study of colonial religion is W. W. Sweet, **Religion in Colonial America** (1942). Of the many books on the Puritans, Alan Simpson, **Puritanism in Old and New England*** (1955), and D. R. Rutman, **American Puritanism*** (1970), are good introductions. The works of Perry Miller are outstanding. See especially his **Errand into the Wilderness*** (1956), **Orthodoxy in Massachusetts** (1933), **The New England Mind: The 17th Century*** (1939), and **The New England Mind: From Colony to Province*** (1953). S. E. Morison, **The Intellectual Life of Colonial New England*** (1956), E. S. Morgan, **The Puritan Family*** (1965) and **Visible Saints*** (1963), are valuable. On the Anne Hutchinson controversy, see Emery Battis, **Saints and Sectaries** (1962). For the Great Awakening, consult E. S. Gaustad, **The Great Awakening in New England*** (1957), and W. M. Gewehr, **The Great Awakening in Virginia** (1930). The best biography of Jonathan Edwards is O. E. Winslow, **Jonathan Edwards*** (1940). Bernhard Knollenberg provides an excellent brief discussion of the Parson's Cause in **Origin of the American Revolution*** (1960). Other important studies of colonial religion and its relation to broader developments are Allan Heimert, **Religion and the American Mind from the Great Awakening to the Revolution** (1966), and Carl Bridenbaugh, **Mitre and Sceptre: Transatlantic Faiths, Ideas, Personalities, and Politics*** (1962).

Colonial education is treated in two excellent books, Bernard Bailyn, **Education in the Forming of American Society*** (1960), and, in more detail, L. A. Cremin, **American Education: The Colonial Experience** (1970).

On the Enlightenment in America, see H. F. May, **The Enlightenment in America** (1976), H. S. Commager, **The Empire of Reason*** (1977), Max Savelle, **Seeds of Liberty*** (1948), and Brooke Hindle, **The Pursuit of Science in Revolutionary America*** (1956). The definitive biography of Franklin is Carl Van Doren, **Benjamin Franklin*** (1938), but V. W. Crane's brief **Benjamin Franklin and a Rising People*** (1954) is also first-rate. E. T. Martin, **Thomas Jefferson: Scientist*** (1952), is a useful summary.

Voting in colonial America and its relation to social structure has been subject to intensive examination. R. E. Brown has made the most important contribution with his **Middle-Class Democracy and the Revolution in Massachusetts*** (1955) and, with B. K. Brown, has also produced **Virginia: Democracy or Aristocracy?** (1964). J. T. Main, **The Social Structure of Revolutionary America*** (1965), sees colonial society as prosperous and highly mobile. Other studies of the suffrage include C. S. Sydnor, **Gentlemen Freeholders** (1952) (published in paperback as **American Revolutionaries in the Making**), on Virginia, R. P. McCormick, **The History of Voting in New Jersey** (1953), and Theodore Thayer, **Pennsylvania Politics and the Growth of Democracy** (1953). A more general treatment is Chilton Williamson, **American Suffrage: From Property to Democracy*** (1960). The writings of F. J. Turner, already mentioned, are full of material for the study of sectionalism in the colonies. On Bacon's rebellion, see Wilcomb Washburn, **The Governor and the Rebel*** (1957).

3/AMERICA AND THE BRITISH EMPIRE

 Since the colonies were founded piecemeal by persons with varying motives and backgrounds, common traditions and loyalties developed slowly. For the same reason, the British government was slow to think of its American possessions as a unit or to deal with them in any centralized way. From the time in 1497 when Henry VII authorized John Cabot and his sons to search out new lands, the "rule, title, and jurisdiction" over these lands had resided in the Crown. They were the *king's* possessions. As a good sovereign he was obligated to use them in a manner consonant with the national interest, but it was left to him and his advisers to decide what that interest was. No authority challenged his right to dispose of one section of his American domain to this group of merchants under such-and-such terms and another to that personal friend or creditor under a different arrangement. The specific form of each colony's government and the degree of local independence permitted it depended on how this was done.

The British Colonial System

There was a pattern basic to all colonial governments and a general framework of imperial control for all the king's overseas plantations. English political and legal institutions (common law, private property, more or less representative legislative assemblies, systems of local administration) took hold everywhere in British America. While the colonists and the home authorities often had different motives in establishing new settlements, they were seldom conflicting motives. Colonists might leave home with grievances, bent on securing certain rights denied them in England, but prosperity, political and economic expansion, and the reproduction of Old World civilization were aims common to ruler and ruled, to Englishman and American.

In the earliest days of any settlement, the need to rely upon home authorities was so obvious that few questioned England's political sovereignty. Thereafter, as the fledglings grew strong enough to think of using their own wings, distance and British political inefficiency combined to allow them a great deal of freedom. Although royal representatives in America tried to direct policy, the Crown generally yielded the initiative in local matters to the colonies while reserving the right to veto actions it deemed to be against the national interest. External affairs were controlled entirely in London.

Each colony had a governor. By the 18th century he was an appointed official, except in Rhode Island and Connecticut. Governors were chosen by the king in the case of the royal colonies and by the proprietors of Maryland, Delaware, and Pennsylvania. Their powers were much like those of the king in Great Britain. They executed the local laws, appointed many minor officials, summoned and dismissed the colonial assemblies, and proposed legislation to them. They possessed the right to veto colonial laws, but in most colonies,

again like the king, they were financially dependent on their "subjects."

Each colony also had a legislature. Except in Pennsylvania, these assemblies consisted of two houses. The lower house, chosen by qualified voters, had general legislative powers, including control of the purse. In all the royal colonies except Massachusetts, members of the upper house, or council, were appointed by the king. They functioned primarily as advisers, although they possessed some judicial and legislative powers. Judges were appointed by the king and served at his pleasure. Yet both councilors and judges were normally selected from among the leaders of the local communities; London had neither the time nor the will to investigate their political beliefs. The system, therefore, tended to strengthen the influence of the entrenched colonials.

Although the power of the lower houses of the legislatures was severely restricted in theory, the assemblies tended to dominate the government in nearly every colony. Financial power—including the right to set the governor's salary—gave them some importance, and the fact that the assemblies usually had the backing of public opinion was significant. As Jack P. Greene has demonstrated in his important study *The Quest for Power*, most colonial legislators were, in the main, pragmatists. Knowing their own interests, they pursued them steadily, without much regard for political theories or the desires of the royal authorities. In the words of one Virginia governor, they were "Expedient Mongers in the highest Degree." They extended their influence by slow accretion. Governors came and went, but the lawmakers remained, accumulating experience, building upon precedent, widening decade by decade their control over colonial affairs.

The official representatives of the Crown, whatever their powers, whatever their intentions, were prisoners of their surroundings. A royal governor lived thousands of miles from London, alone in a *colonial* world. To defend the British position at every turn when one had to make one's life amid a vigorous and strong-willed people, who usually had solid practical arguments to buttress their side if it clashed with the Crown's, was no easy task. Governors had no security of tenure; they served at the whim of the government in London. In their dealings with the assemblies they were often bound by rigid and impractical royal instructions that restricted their ability to maneuver. They had few jobs and favors to offer in their efforts to influence the legislators. Judges might interpret the law according to English precedents, but in local matters colonial juries had the final say. And juries were seldom awed by precedents that clashed with their own conceptions of justice.

Within the British government the king's Privy Council had the responsibility for establishing colonial policy. It did so on an ad hoc basis, treating each situation as it arose and seldom generalizing. Everything was decentralized: the Treasury had charge of financial matters, the army of military affairs, and so on. The Privy Council could and did disallow (annul) specific colonial laws, but it did not proclaim constitutional principles to which all colonial legislatures must conform. It acted as a court of last appeal in colonial disputes and handled each case individually. One day the council might issue a set of instructions to the governor of Virginia, the next a different set to the governor of South Carolina. No one office directed colonial affairs; no one person or committee thought broadly about the administration of the overseas empire. Parliamentary legislation applied to the colonies, yet there was little distinctively *American* legislation. For example, Parliament passed laws regulating the trade of the entire British empire and until late in the colonial period directed its attention specifically to North American conditions only on rare occasions.

At times the British authorities, uneasy about their lack of control over the colonies, attempted to create a more effective system. Whenever possible the original, broadly worded charters were revoked. To transform proprietary and corporate colonies into royal colonies (whose chief officials were appointed by the king) seems to have been London's official policy by the late 17th century. The Privy Council appointed a number of subcommittees to advise it on colonial affairs at this time. The most important was the Lords of Trade, which had its own staff and archives and wielded great influence. In the 1680s James II made a massive attempt to strengthen and centralize royal control. He brought New York, New Jersey, and all of New England under one administration, the Dominion of New England, and apparently planned to unify the southern colonies in a similar

manner. James' actions were deeply resented by the colonists, and when he was deposed in the Glorious Revolution, the Dominion collapsed. Thereafter there were no large-scale efforts at unification; indeed, the tendency was in the other direction. Delaware at least partially separated from Pennsylvania in 1704, and the two Carolinas formally split in 1712.

In 1696 a new Board of Trade took over the functions of the Lords of Trade and expanded them considerably. It nominated colonial governors and other high officials. It reviewed all the laws passed by the colonial legislatures, recommending the disallowance of those that seemed to conflict with imperial policy. The efficiency, assiduousness, and wisdom of the Board of Trade fluctuated over the years, but the Privy Council and the Crown nearly always accepted its recommendations.

Colonists naturally disliked having their laws disallowed, and London exercised this power with considerable restraint; only about 5 percent of the laws reviewed were rejected. Furthermore, the board served as an important intermediary for colonists seeking to influence king and Parliament. All the colonies in the 18th century maintained agents in London to present the colonial point of view before board members. The most famous colonial agent was Benjamin Franklin, who represented Pennsylvania, Georgia, New Jersey, and Massachusetts at various times during his long career.

The British never developed an effective, centralized government for the American colonies. Probably this fact more than any other explains our present federal system and the wide areas in which the state governments are sovereign and independent. Local and colonywide government in America evolved from English models. Had a rational central authority been superimposed in the early days, the colonies would almost certainly have accepted it. Then, even in revolt, they would probably have followed a different path.

The Theory of Mercantilism

The Board of Trade, as its name implies, was concerned with commerce as well as colonial administration. According to prevailing European opinion, colonies were important chiefly for economic reasons. The 17th century being a period of hard times and considerable unemployment, some authorities saw the colonies as excellent dumping grounds for surplus people. If only two idlers in each parish were shipped overseas, one clergyman calculated in 1624, England would be rid of 16,000 undesirables. But most 17th-century economic thinkers envisaged colonies more as potential sources of raw materials, particularly gold and silver, the possession of which they considered the best barometer of national prosperity. They adopted what has been called the theory of mercantilism.

Since gold and silver could not be mined in significant amounts in western Europe, every early colonist dreamed of finding "El Dorado." The Spanish were the winners in this search; from the mines of Mexico and South America a treasure in gold and silver poured into the Iberian Peninsula. Failing to control the precious metals at the source, the other powers tried to obtain them by guile and warfare (witness the exploits of Francis Drake). In the mid 17th century another method, less hazardous and in the long run far more profitable, called itself to the attention of the statesmen of western Europe.

If a country could make itself as nearly self-sufficient as possible and at the same time keep all its citizens busy producing items marketable in other lands, it could sell more abroad than it imported. This state of affairs was known as "having a favorable balance of trade." The term is misleading; in reality trade, which means exchange, always balances unless one party simply gives its goods away (a practice never recommended by the mercantilists). A country with a favorable balance in effect imported gold or silver instead of other commodities. Nevertheless, mercantilism came to mean concentrating on producing for export and limiting imports of ordinary goods and services in every way possible. Colonies that did not have deposits of precious metals were well worth having if they yielded raw materials that would otherwise have to be purchased from foreign sources, or if they provided markets for the manufactured products of the mother country.

Of the English colonies in the New World, those in tropical and subtropical climes were valued for their raw materials. The more northerly ones were important as markets, but because they were small in the 17th century, in English eyes they took second place. In 1680 the sugar imported from the single West Indian island of Barbados was worth more than the goods sent to England by all the mainland colonies.

If the possession of gold and silver signified wealth to a mercantilist, trade was the path that led to riches and merchants the guides who would pilot the ship of state to prosperity. "Trade is the Wealth of the World," Daniel Defoe wrote in 1728. "Trade makes the difference as to Rich and Poor, between one Nation and another; Trade nourishes Industry . . . and Trade raises new Species of Wealth, which Nature knew nothing of. . . ." One must, of course, have something to sell, so internal production must be stimulated. Parliament placed heavy duties on foreign foodstuffs and enacted all kinds of tariffs and subsidies to encourage the manufacture of textiles, iron, and other products.

The nurture of commerce was fundamental. Toward this end Parliament enacted the Navigation Acts. These laws, put into effect over a period of half a century and more, were designed to develop the imperial merchant fleet, to channel the flow of colonial raw materials into England, and to keep foreign goods and vessels out of colonial ports (since the employment of foreign ships in the carrying trade was as much an import as the consumption of foreign wheat or wool).

The Navigation Acts

The system originated in the 1650s during the Cromwell period in response to the stiff commercial competition offered by the Dutch. Having won their independence from Spain, the Dutch had constructed a magnificent merchant fleet of more than 10,000 ships. Their sailors roamed the world's oceans in search of business. They dominated the coastal trade of France, threatened to do the same with that of England, and practically monopolized the whale fisheries of the North Atlantic. They established themselves in South America, in India, and in the East and West Indies. Before 1650 a large share of the produce of the English colonies in America reached Europe in Dutch vessels; the first slaves in Virginia, it will be recalled, arrived on a Dutch ship and were doubtless paid for in tobacco that was later burned in the clay pipes of the burghers of Amsterdam and Rotterdam.

Dismayed by this trend, Parliament in 1650 and 1651 barred foreign ships from the English colonies (except when specially licensed) and prohibited the importation into England of goods that were not carried in English ships or those of the country where the goods had been originally produced. All foreign vessels were excluded from the English coastal trade. Although phrased in general terms, this legislation struck primarily at the Dutch, and in 1652 the English provoked the first of three wars with the Dutch Republic that were only extensions of the policy laid down in the first Navigation Acts.

The laws of 1650–1651 could not be rigidly enforced, for England did not have enough ships to supply its overseas possessions. The colonies protested vigorously and then ignored the regulations. Nevertheless, the English persisted. New laws were passed after the accession of Charles II in 1660, and as the merchant marine expanded (tonnage doubled between 1660 and 1688) and the Royal Navy gradually reduced Dutch power in the New World, enforcement became fairly effective.

The Navigation Act of 1660 reserved the entire trade of the colonies to English ships and required that the captain and three-quarters of his crew be English. (Colonists, of course, were English, and their ships were treated on the same terms as those sailing out of London or Liverpool.) The act also provided that certain colonial "enumerated articles"— sugar, tobacco, cotton, ginger, and dyes like indigo and fustic—could not be "shipped, carried, conveyed or transported" outside the empire. Three years later Parliament required that with trifling exceptions all European products destined for the colonies be brought to England before being shipped across the Atlantic. Since trade between England and the colonies was reserved to English vessels, this meant that the goods would have to be unloaded and reloaded in England. Legislation in 1673 and 1696 was concerned with enforcing these laws: it dealt with the posting of bonds, the registration of vessels, and the appointment of customs officials. Early in the 18th century the list of enumerated articles was expanded to include rice, molasses, naval stores, furs, and copper.

English mercantilists looked upon the empire broadly; they envisioned the colonies as part of an economic unit, not as servile dependencies to be exploited for England's selfish benefit. The growing of tobacco in England was prohibited, and valuable bounties were paid to colonial producers of indigo and naval stores. A planned economy, England specializing in manufacturing and the colonies in the production of raw materials, was the grand design. By and large the system suited the realities of life in an underdeveloped country rich in raw materials and suffering from a chronic labor shortage.

Much has been made by some historians of the restrictions that the British placed on colonial manufacturing. The Wool Act of 1699 prohibited the export (but not the manufacture for local sale) of colonial woolen cloth. A similar law regarding hats was passed in 1732, and in 1750 an Iron Act outlawed the construction of new rolling and slitting mills in America. No other restrictions on manufacturing were imposed. At most the Wool Act stifled a potential American industry; the law was directed chiefly at Irish woolens rather than American. The hat industry cannot be considered a major one. Iron, however, was important; by the middle of the 18th century the industry was thriving in Virginia, Maryland, New Jersey, and Pennsylvania. One historian estimates that in 1775 America was turning out one-seventh of the world supply. Yet the Iron Act was designed to steer the American iron industry in a certain direction, not to destroy it. Eager for iron to feed English mills, Parliament eliminated all duties on colonial pig and bar iron entering England, a great stimulus to the basic industry. A similar system had been set up with regard to West Indian sugar as early as 1651, when the English fixed the duty on semirefined sugar at a level more than three times higher than that on raw sugar.

The Effects of Mercantilism

Mercantilism reflected, more than it molded, the imperial economy. The laws encouraged England to be the colonies' main customer and chief supplier of manufactures, but this would have been true in any case, and it remained true after the Revolution, when the Navigation Acts no longer applied to America. The chronic colonial shortage of hard money was superficially caused by the flow of specie to England to meet the "unfavor-

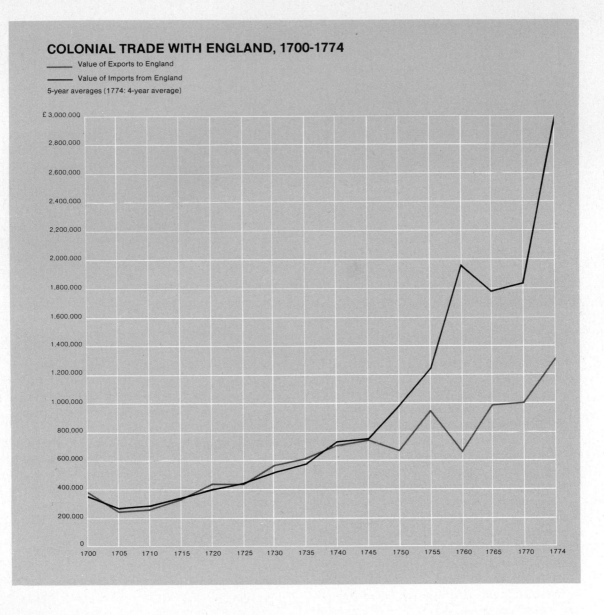

COLONIAL TRADE WITH ENGLAND, 1700-1774

——— Value of Exports to England
——— Value of Imports from England
5-year averages (1774: 4-year average)

able" balance that resulted from this trade, and this, too, reflected natural conditions. The rapidly growing colonial economy consumed far more manufactured products than it could pay for out of current production. To be "in debt" to England really meant that the English were investing capital in America, a state of affairs that continued until World War I.

Important colonial products for which no market existed in England (such as fish, wheat, and corn) were never enumerated and moved freely

and directly to foreign ports. Most colonial manufacturing was untouched by English law. Shipbuilding benefited from the Navigation Acts, since many English merchants bought vessels built in the colonies. Between 1769 and 1771, Massachusetts, New Hampshire, and Rhode Island yards constructed perhaps 250 ships of 100 to 400 tons for transatlantic commerce and twice that many sloops and schooners for fishermen and coastal traders. The manufacture of rum for local consumption and for the slave trade was significant;

■ "Ye Flourishing City of New York" was how William Burgis titled his panoramic drawing, done about 1717. This detail shows the boat basin at the Battery, near the tip of Manhattan Island, with the low hills of New Jersey in the background. The buildings are distinctly Dutch in style.

so were barrelmaking, flour milling, shoemaking, and dozens of other crafts that operated without restriction.

Two forces that worked in opposite directions must be considered before arriving at any judgment about English mercantilism. While the theory presupposed a general imperial interest above that of both colony and mother country, when conflicts of interest arose the latter nearly always predominated. The Hat Act may have been good mercantilism, but Parliament passed it because English feltmakers were concerned over the news that Massachusetts and New York were turning out 10,000 hats a year. The requirement that foreign goods destined for the colonies must first be unloaded in England increased the cost of certain goods to Americans for the benefit of English merchants and dockworkers. The enumeration of tobacco and other colonial products meant that English merchants could profit by reexporting surpluses to the Continent; by 1700 this reexport trade amounted to 30 percent of the value of all England's exports.

Whenever Parliament or the Board of Trade resolved an Anglo-American disagreement, the colonists tended to lose out. "It cannot be expected," the Board of Trade announced in 1706, "that encouragement should be given by law to the making of any manufactures made by England in the plantations, it being against the advantage of England." Complementary interests conspired to keep conflicts at a minimum, but in the long run, as the American economy became more complex, the colonies would have been seriously hampered and much more trouble would have occurred had the system continued to operate.

On the other hand, the restrictions of English mercantilism were greatly lessened by inefficiency. The English government was by modern standards incredibly cumbersome and corrupt. The king and his ministers handed out government posts to win political favor or to repay political debts, regardless of the recipient's ability to perform the duties of the office. Transported to remote America, this bumbling and cynical system scarcely functioned at all when local opinion resisted it. Smuggling became a respected profession, bribery of English officials standard practice. Despite a supposedly prohibitive duty of sixpence a gallon imposed by the Molasses Act of 1733, molasses from the French West Indies continued to be imported. The duty was seldom collected. A customs officer in Salem offered to pass French molasses for 10 percent of the legal tax, and in

New Jersey the collectors "entered into a composition with the Merchants and took a Dollar a Hogshead or some such small matter."

Mercantilism hurt certain colonial interests (the tobacco planters were the most important of these), but it helped others, and most people proved adept at getting around those aspects of the system that threatened them. In any case, the colonies enjoyed almost continuous prosperity in the years between 1650 and the Revolution, as even so dedicated a foe of mercantilism as Adam Smith admitted.

By the same token England profited greatly from its overseas possessions. With all its inefficiencies, mercantilism worked. Prime Minister Sir Robert Walpole's famous policy of "salutary neglect," which involved looking the other way when Americans violated the Navigation Acts, was partly a bowing to the inevitable, partly the result of complacency. English manufactures were better and cheaper than those of other nations. This fact, together with ties of language and a common heritage, predisposed Americans toward doing business in England. All else followed naturally; the mercantilistic laws merely steered the American economy in a direction it had already taken. At least this was the case until the end of the French and Indian War.

As the colonies matured, their relations with Crown and Parliament remained reasonably harmonious. The great majority of the settlers were of British descent, and their interests generally coincided with those of their cousins in the mother country. This was fortunate because the British authorities were poorly equipped to deal with trouble in America. As one leading authority on 18th-century English politics has said, there was "immense ignorance and even vaster indifference" in the government with regard to all American questions. When trouble did come, intelligence and diligence would be called for—and found lacking.

Early Colonial Wars

The British colonies were part of a great empire that was part of a still larger world. Seemingly isolated in their remote communities, scattered like a broken string of beads between the wide Atlantic and the trackless Appalachian forests, Americans were constantly affected by outside events both in the Old World and in the New. Under the spell of mercantilistic logic, the western European nations competed fiercely for markets and colonial raw materials. War—hot and cold, declared and undeclared—was almost a permanent condition of 17th- and 18th-century life, and when the powers clashed they fought wherever they could get at one another, in America, in Europe, and elsewhere.

Although the American colonies were minor pieces in the game and were sometimes casually exchanged or sacrificed by the masterminds in London, Paris, and Madrid in pursuit of some supposedly more important objective, the colonists quickly generated their own international animosities. North America, a huge and almost empty stage, evidently did not provide enough room for French, Dutch, Spanish, and English companies to perform. Frenchmen and Spaniards clashed savagely in Florida in the 16th century. Before the landing of the Pilgrims, Samuel Argall of Virginia was sacking French settlements in Maine and carrying off Jesuit priests into captivity at Jamestown. Instead of fostering tranquillity and generosity, the abundance of America seemed to make the settlers belligerent and greedy.

The North Atlantic fisheries quickly became a source of trouble between Canadian and New England colonists, despite the fact that the waters of the Grand Banks teemed with cod and other fish. To dry and salt their catch the fishermen needed land bases, and French and English Americans struggled constantly over the harbors of Maine, Nova Scotia, and Newfoundland.

Even more troublesome was the fur trade. The yield of the forest was easily exhausted by indiscriminate slaughter, and traders contended bitterly to control valuable hunting grounds. The French in Canada conducted their fur trading through tribes such as the Algonquins and the Hurons. This brought them into conflict with the Five Nations, the powerful Iroquois confederation centered in what is now New York State. As early as 1609 the Five Nations were at war with the French and their Indian allies. For decades this struggle flared sporadically, the Iroquois more than holding their own both as fighters and as traders. They combined, according to one contemporary French account, the stealth and craftiness of the fox, the ferocity and courage of the lion,

■ Corn Planter (Ki-on-twog-ky), a Seneca chief of the late 18th century, in a romantic portrait by F. Bartoli. The European influence on the Iroquois culture shows especially here in the chief's elaborate, heavy metal jewelry.

and the speed of a bird in flight. They brought quantities of beaver pelts to the Dutch and later the English at Albany. They preyed on pro-French tribes north of Lake Ontario and dickered with Indian trappers in far-off Michigan, "to carry," as one indignant French official complained, "the furs of our land to the Dutch." When the English took over the New Amsterdam colony they eagerly adopted the Iroquois as allies, buying their furs and supplying them with guns.

The French managed to bypass the Iroquois by sending their trappers into the Illinois country and even beyond the Mississippi in search of skins, but they never conquered or neutralized them. In the final showdown for control of North America the friendship of the Iroquois was vitally important to the English.

By the last decade of the 17th century it had become clear that the Netherlands lacked the strength to maintain a big empire and that Spain was fast declining. The future, especially in North America, belonged to England and France. In the wars of the next 125 years European alliances shifted dramatically, yet the English and what

John Adams called "the turbulent Gallicks" were always on opposite sides.

In the first three of these conflicts colonists played only minor parts. The fighting in America consisted chiefly of sneak attacks on isolated outposts. In King William's War (1689–1697), the American phase of the War of the League of Augsburg, French forces raided Schenectady in New York and frontier settlements in New England. English colonists retaliated by capturing Port Royal, Nova Scotia, only to lose that outpost in a counterattack in 1691. The Peace of Ryswick in 1697 restored all captured territory in America to the original owners.

The next struggle was the War of the Spanish Succession (1702–1713), fought to prevent the union of Spain and France under the Bourbons. The Americans named this conflict Queen Anne's War. French-inspired Abenaki Indians razed Deerfield, Massachusetts. A party of Carolinians burned St. Augustine in Spanish Florida. The New Englanders retook Port Royal. However, in Europe the forces of England, Holland, and Austria, led by the Duke of Marlborough, won a series of decisive victories. In the Treaty of Utrecht in 1713, France yielded Nova Scotia, Newfoundland, and the Hudson Bay region to Great Britain.

If the colonies were mere pawns in these wars, the people of New England (and of Canada) paid heavily in them. Many frontier settlers were killed in the raids. Hundreds of townsmen died during the campaigns in Nova Scotia. Massachusetts taxes went up sharply and the colony issued large amounts of paper currency to pay its bills, causing an inflation that ate into the living standards of wage earners.

The American phase of the third Anglo-French conflict, the War of the Austrian Succession (1740–1748), was called King George's War. The usual Indian raids were launched in both directions across the lonely forests that separated the St. Lawrence settlements from the New York and New England frontier. A New England force captured the strategic fortress of Louisbourg on Cape Breton Island, guarding the entrance to the Gulf of St. Lawrence. The Treaty of Aix-la-Chapelle in 1748, however, required the return of Louisbourg, much to the chagrin of the New Englanders.

As this incident suggests, the colonial wars generated a certain amount of trouble between England and the colonies; matters that seemed unim-

■ The French-Indian attack on Deerfield during Queen Anne's War typified the savagery of frontier warfare. The raiders killed 53 and carried off 111 captives to Canada. This scene is from a 19th-century edition of an eyewitness account.

portant in London might loom large in American eyes, and vice versa. But the conflicts were seldom serious. The wars did, however, increase the bad feelings between settlers north and south of the St. Lawrence. Every Indian raid was attributed to French provocateurs, although more often than not the English colonists themselves were responsible for the Indian troubles. Conflicting land claims further aggravated the situation. Massachusetts, Connecticut, and Virginia possessed overlapping claims to the Ohio Valley, and Pennsylvania and New York also had pretensions in the region. Yet the French, ranging broadly across the midcontinent, insisted that the Ohio country was exclusively theirs.

The Great War for the Empire

In this beautiful, almost untouched land, a handful of individuals determined the future of the continent. Over the years the French had established a chain of forts and trading posts running from Mackinac Island in northern Michigan to Kaskaskia on the Mississippi and Vincennes on the Wabash, and from Niagara in the east to the Bourbon River, near Lake Winnipeg, in the west. By the 1740s, however, Pennsylvania fur traders, led by George Croghan, a rugged Irishman, were setting up posts north of the Ohio River and dickering with Miami and Huron Indians who ordinarily sold their furs to the French. In 1748 Croghan

built a fort at Pickawillany, deep in the Miami country, in what is now western Ohio. That same year agents of a group of Virginia land speculators who had recently organized what they called the Ohio Company reached this area.

With trifling exceptions, an insulating band of wilderness had always separated the French and English in America. Now the two powers came into contact. The immediate result was a showdown battle for control of North America, the "great war for the empire." Thoroughly alarmed by the presence of the English on land they had long considered their own, the French struck hard. Attacking suddenly in 1752, they wiped out Croghan's post at Pickawillany and drove his traders back into Pennsylvania. Then they built a string of barrier forts south from Lake Erie along the Pennsylvania line: Fort Presque Isle, Fort Le Boeuf, Fort Venango. The Pennsylvania authorities chose to ignore this action, but Lieutenant Governor Robert Dinwiddie of Virginia (who was an investor in the Ohio Company) dispatched a 21-year-old surveyor named George Washington to warn the French that they were trespassing on Virginia territory.

Washington, a gangling, inarticulate, yet courageous and intensely ambitious young planter, made his way northwest in the fall of 1753 and delivered Dinwiddie's message to the commandant at Fort Le Boeuf. It made no impression. "[The French] told me," Washington reported, "that it was their absolute Design to take Posses-

sion of the *Ohio*, and by G–– they would do it."
Governor Dinwiddie thereupon promoted Washington to lieutenant colonel and sent him back in
the spring of 1754 with 150 men to seize a strategic junction south of the new French forts, where
the Allegheny and Monongahela rivers join to
form the Ohio.

Eager but inexperienced in battle, young Washington botched his assignment. As his force labored painfully through the tangled mountain
country southeast of the fork of the Ohio, he received word that the French had already occupied
the position and were constructing a powerful
post, Fort Duquesne. Outnumbered by perhaps
four to one, Washington foolishly pushed on. He
surprised and routed a French reconnaissance
party, but this brought upon him the main body of
enemy troops.

Hastily he threw up a defensive position, aptly
named Fort Necessity, but the ground was ill chosen; the French easily surrounded the fort and
Washington had to surrender. After tricking the
young officer, who could not read French, into
signing an admission that he had "assassinated"
the leader of the reconnaissance party, his captors,
with the gateway to the Ohio country firmly in
their hands, permitted him and his men to march
off. Nevertheless, Washington returned to Virginia a hero, for although still undeclared, this was
war, and he had struck the first blow against the
hated French.

In the resulting conflict—which they named the
French and Indian War—the English colonists
outnumbered the French by about 1.5 million to
90,000. But the English were divided and disorganized, the French disciplined and united. The
French controlled the disputed territory, and most
of the Indians took their side. With an ignorance
and arrogance typical of 18th-century colonial administration, the British mismanaged the war and
failed to make effective use of local resources. For
several years they stumbled from one defeat to
another.

General Edward Braddock, a competent but un-
inspired soldier, was dispatched to Virginia to
take command. In June 1755 he marched against
Fort Duquesne with 1,400 Redcoats and a smaller
number of colonials, only to be ambushed and
decisively defeated by a much smaller force of
French and Indians. Braddock died bravely in bat-

tle, and only 500 of his men, led by Colonel
Washington, who was serving as his aide-de-
camp, made their way back to Virginia.

Elsewhere Anglo-American arms fared little
better in the early years of the war. Expeditions
against Fort Niagara, key to all French defenses in
the west, and Crown Point, gateway to Montreal,
bogged down. Meanwhile the Indians, armed by
the French, bathed the frontier in blood. Venting
the frustrations caused by 150 years of white advance, they attacked defenseless outposts with un-
believable brutality. Crazed with hatred, they
poured molten lead into their victims' wounds,
ripped off the fingernails of captives, raped, kidnaped—even drank the blood of the brave who
endured their tortures stoically. The most feared
of the "French" Indians were the Delawares, a
once peaceful Pennsylvania tribe that had been
harried from their homelands by English and Iroquois. General Braddock paid his Indian allies
only £5 each for French scalps but offered £200 for
the hair of Shinngass, the Delaware chieftain.

In 1756 the conflict spread to Europe to become
the Seven Years' War. Prussia sided with Great
Britain, Austria with the French. On the world
stage, too, things went badly for the British. Finally, in 1757, as defeat succeeded defeat, King
George II was forced to allow William Pitt, whom
he detested, to take over leadership of the war
effort. Pitt, grandson of "Diamond" Pitt, a *nouveau
riche* East India merchant, was an unstable man
who spent much of his life on the verge of mad-
ness, but he was an imaginative planner and a
passionate orator, capable of inspiring the entire
nation in its hour of trial.

Pitt recognized, as few contemporaries did, the
potential value of North America. Instead of relying on the tightfisted and shortsighted colonial assemblies for men and money, he poured regiment
after regiment of British regulars and the full resources of the British treasury into the contest,
mortgaging the future recklessly to secure the
prize. Grasping the importance of sea power in
fighting a war on the other side of the Atlantic, he
used the British navy to bottle up the enemy fleet
and hamper French communications with Canada.
He possessed a keen eye for military genius, and
when he discovered it, he ignored seniority and
the outraged feelings of mediocre generals and
promoted talented young officers to top com-

■ This watercolor of Amherst's seizure of the French fortress of Louisbourg in 1758 is the work of Thomas Davies, an English artillery officer. Louisbourg is at center, under attack from Amherst's seige lines at right and Admiral Boscawen's British fleet lying offshore. French ships are aflame in the harbor.

mands. His greatest find was James Wolfe, whom he made a brigadier at 31. Wolfe and Major General Jeffrey Amherst, only ten years his senior and another of Pitt's discoveries, recaptured the Louisbourg fortress in July 1758.

That winter, as Pitt's grand strategy matured, Fort Duquesne fell. It was appropriately renamed Fort Pitt, the present Pittsburgh. The following summer Fort Niagara was overrun. Amherst took Crown Point, and Wolfe sailed up the St. Lawrence to Quebec. There the French General Montcalm had prepared a formidable defense, but after months of probing and planning Wolfe found and exploited a chink in the city's armor and on the Plains of Abraham defeated the French—although both he and Montcalm died in the battle. In 1760 Montreal fell and the French abandoned all Canada to the British.

Spain attempted to stem the British advance but failed utterly. A Far Eastern fleet captured Manila in 1762, and another British force took Cuba. The French sugar islands in the West Indies were also captured, while in India British troops reduced the French posts one by one.

Peace was restored in 1763 by the Treaty of Paris. Its terms were moderate considering the extent of the British triumph. France abandoned all claim to North America except two small islands near Newfoundland; Great Britain took over Canada and the eastern half of the Mississippi Valley, Spain (in a separate treaty) the area west of the great river and New Orleans. Guadeloupe and Martinique, the French sugar islands, were returned by the British, as were some of the captured French possessions in India and Africa. Spain got back both the Philippine Islands and Cuba; in exchange the Spanish ceded East and West Florida to Great Britain. France and Spain thus remained important colonial powers.

"Half the continent," the great historian Francis Parkman wrote, "had changed hands at the scratch of a pen." From the point of view of the English colonists in America, the victory was overwhelming. All threat to their frontiers seemed to have been swept away. Surely, they believed in the first happy moments of victory, their peaceful and prosperous expansion was assured for countless generations.

And no honest American could deny that the victory had been won chiefly by British troops and with British gold. Colonial militiamen fought well in defense of their homes or when some highly prized objective seemed ripe for the plucking; they lacked discipline and determination when required to fight far from home and under commanders they did not know. As one American official admitted to the British commander in chief, it was difficult to get New Englanders to enlist "unless assurances can be given that they shall not march to the southward of certain limits." General Wolfe characterized colonial troops as "the dirtiest, most contemptible cowardly dogs you can conceive," and another English officer compared the ordinary run to "broken innkeepers, horse jockeys and Indian traders."

Colonials did not accept this evaluation, though they were happy enough to see scarlet-clad British regulars bear the brunt of the fighting and happier still when the Crown shouldered most of the financial burden of the long struggle. The local assemblies contributed to the cost, but except for Massachusetts and Virginia their outlays were trivial compared with the £82 million poured into the worldwide conflict by the British.

Little wonder that the great victory produced a burst of praise for king and mother country throughout America. Parades, cannonading, fireworks, banquets, the pealing of churchbells—these were the order of the day in every colonial town. Ezra Stiles, later president of Yale, extolled "the illustrious House of Hanover," whose new head, the young George III, had inherited the

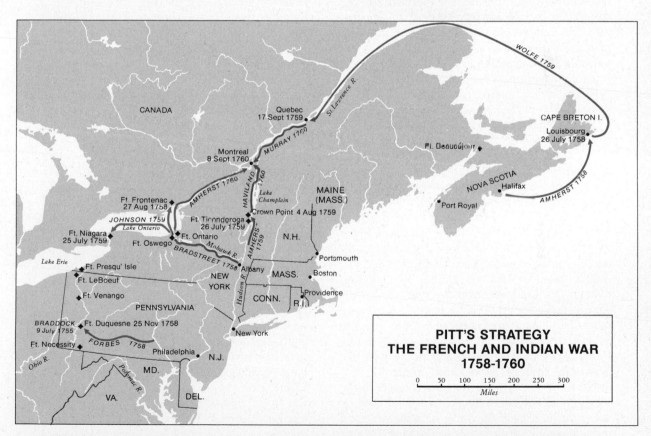

**PITT'S STRATEGY
THE FRENCH AND INDIAN WAR
1758-1760**

0   50   100   150   200   250   300
Miles

■ A key phase of Pitt's American strategy involved capturing the French strongpoints guarding the approaches to Canada: Louisbourg, protecting the St. Lawrence; Fort Ticonderoga and Crown Point, on Lake Champlain; and Fort Duquesne, in the Ohio Country. Colonial forces played a significant role in this strategy, with John Forbes seizing Fort Duquesne, John Bradstreet winning control of Lake Ontario, and William Johnson taking Fort Niagara.

throne in 1760. "Nothing," said Thomas Pownall, wartime governor of Massachusetts and a student of colonial administration, "can eradicate from [the colonists'] hearts their natural, almost mechanical affection to Great Britain."

Postwar Problems

In London peace proved a time for reassessment; that the empire of 1763 was not the same as the empire of 1754 was obvious. The new, far larger dominion would be much more expensive to maintain. Pitt had spent a huge sum winning and securing it, much of it borrowed money. Great Britain's national debt had doubled between 1754 and 1763. Now this debt must be serviced and repaid, and the strain that this would place upon the economy was clear to all. Furthermore, the day-to-day cost of administering an empire that extended from Hudson Bay to India was far larger than that which the already burdened British taxpayer could be expected to bear. Before the great war for the empire, Britain's North American possessions were administered for about £70,000 a year; after 1763 the cost was five times as much.

The American empire had also grown far more complex. A system of administration that treated it as a string of separate plantations struggling to exist on the edge of the forest would no longer suffice. The war had been fought for control of the Ohio Valley, but it had not decided who would govern the region or what was to be done with it. Seven years of Indian warfare had dammed up the westward movement. Now pressures were mounting for renewed expansion. Conflicting colonial claims, based on charters drafted by men who thought the Pacific lay over the next hill, threatened to make the great valley a battleground once more. The Indians remained unpacified, urged to fight on by Spaniards in the area around New Orleans who sought to check and throw back the American advance. Rival land companies contested for charters, while fur traders, eager to absorb the riches formerly controlled by France, strove to hold back the wave of settlement that must inevitably destroy the world of the beaver and the deer. One Englishman who traveled through America at this time predicted that if the colonists were left to their own devices, "there would soon be civil war from one end of the continent to the other."

Apparently only Great Britain could deal with these problems and rivalries, for when a far-sighted man like Franklin had proposed a rudimentary form of colonial union—the Albany Plan of 1754—it was almost universally rejected by the Americans. Unfortunately, the British government did not rise to the challenge. Perhaps this was to be expected, given the singularly ineffective character of 18th-century British politics. The government, according to the historian J. H. Plumb, was "an extremely complex system of political bargaining and blackmail." A handful of aristocrats (fewer than 150 peers were active in government affairs) dominated politics, and they were more concerned with local offices and personal advantage than with large questions of policy. An American who spent some time in London in 1764 trying to obtain approval for a plan for the development of the west reported: "The people hear Spend thire time in Nothing but abuseing one Another and Striveing who shall be in power with a view to Serve themselves and Thire friends." George I and George II were not indifferent to national affairs and George III was not a tyrant, as once was commonly believed, but the first two were stupid and the third at best an inept politician.

Even the best-educated English leaders were nearly all monumentally ignorant of American conditions. The British imperial system lacked effective channels of communication. Information about American attitudes came from royal officials in the colonies and others with special interests to protect or advance, or from the colonial agents and merchants in London, whose information was often out of date. Serene in their ignorance, most English leaders insisted that colonials were uncouth and generally inferior beings. During the French and Indian War, any officer with a royal commission outranked all officers of the colonial militia, regardless of title. Young Colonel Washington, for example, had to travel all the way from Virginia to the headquarters of the commander in chief in Boston to establish his precedence over one Captain John Dagworthy, a Maryland officer who had *formerly* held a royal commission and who did not propose to let a mere colonial colonel outrank him.

Many English people resented the colonists because they were rapidly becoming rich and powerful. Shortly after the war, John Adams predicted that within a century America would be wealthier and more populous than Great Britain.* If the English did not say much about this possibility, they too considered it from time to time—without Adams' relish.

Tightening Imperial Controls

The attempt of the inefficient, ignorant, envious, and indignant British government to deal with the intricate colonial problems that resulted from the great war for the empire led to the American Revolution—a rebellion that was costly and unnecessary but which produced excellent results for the colonists, for Great Britain, for the rest of the empire, and eventually for the entire world. The trouble resulted from the decision of British authorities after the war to intervene more actively in American affairs. Theoretically the colonies were entirely subordinate to Crown and Parliament, yet after the disastrous failure of the Dominion of New England to centralize control of the colonies in the 1680s they had been allowed a remarkable degree of freedom to manage their own affairs. Of course they had come to expect this as their right.

Parliament had never attempted to raise a revenue in America. "Compelling the colonies to pay money without their consent would be rather like raising contributions in an enemy's country than taxing Englishmen for their own benefit," Benjamin Franklin wrote. That shrewd judge of human nature, Sir Robert Walpole, initiator of the policy of salutary neglect, recognized the colonial viewpoint. He responded to a suggestion that Parliament tax the colonies by saying: "I will leave that for some of my successors, who may have more courage than I have." Nevertheless, the *legality* of parliamentary taxation, or of other parliamentary intervention in colonial affairs, had not been seriously contested. During King George's War and

again during the French and Indian War many British officials in America suggested that Parliament tax the colonies.

Nothing was done until 1759, when British victories had made ultimate triumph sure. Then a general tightening of imperial regulations began. Important Virginia and South Carolina laws were disallowed and royal control over colonial courts was strengthened. In Massachusetts the use of general search warrants (writs of assistance) was authorized in 1761. These writs enabled customs officers searching for smuggled goods to invade homes and warehouses without evidence or specific court orders. The British believed this necessary because many colonial merchants were trading shamelessly with the French in the West Indies. With French shipping driven from the seas by the Royal Navy and American privateers, the price of food and other necessities in the Indies soared, and some Americans could not resist the opportunities that resulted. But nearly all Americans resented the invasions of privacy that the writs caused. In 1761 a Boston lawyer, James Otis, argued in a case involving 63 merchants that the writs were "against the Constitution" and therefore void. Otis lost the case, but by suggesting that Parliament's authority over the colonies was not absolute, he became a colonial hero.

After the signing of the peace treaty in 1763, events pushed the British authorities to still more vigorous activity in America. Freed of the restraint imposed by French competition, Englishman and colonist increased their pressure on the Indians. Cynical fur traders now cheated them outrageously, while callous military men hoped to exterminate them like vermin. The British commander in the west, Lord Jeffrey Amherst, suggested infecting the Indians with smallpox; another officer expressed the wish that they could be hunted down with dogs.

Led by an Ottawa chief named Pontiac, the desperate tribes made one last effort to drive the white men back across the mountains. Pontiac's Rebellion caused much havoc, but it failed. By 1764 most of the western tribes had accepted the peace terms offered by a royal commissioner, Sir William Johnson, one of the few who understood and sympathized with the Indians. The British government then decided to maintain 15 regiments, some 6,000 soldiers, in posts along the en-

---

*As early as 1751, Franklin predicted that in a century "the greatest number of Englishmen will be on this Side of the Water."

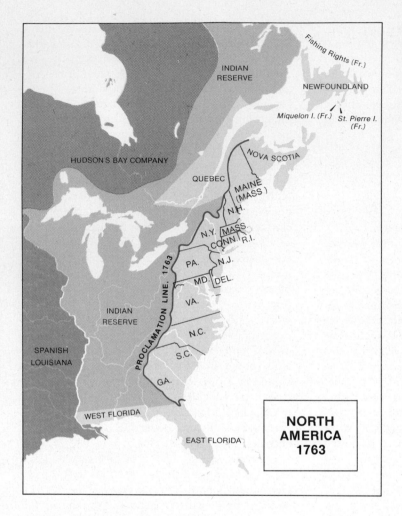

■ North America 1763. George III's Proclamation of 1763 in effect reserved for the Indians the vast area across the Appalachians (except for the new royal colonies of Quebec, East Florida, and West Florida) as far west as Spanish Louisiana and as far north as the Hudson's Bay Company preserve.

tire arc of the frontier, as much to protect the Indians from the settlers as the settlers from the Indians. It proclaimed a new western policy: no settlers were to cross the Appalachian divide. Only licensed traders might do business with the Indians beyond that line. The purchase of Indian land was outlawed. In compensation, three new colonies—Quebec, East Florida, and West Florida—were created, but they were not permitted to set up local assemblies.

This Proclamation of 1763 excited much indignation in America. The frustration of dozens of schemes for land development in the Ohio Valley angered many influential colonists. Colonel Washington referred to the proclamation contemptuously as "a temporary expedient to quiet the minds of Indians," and he continued to stake out claims to western lands. The licensing of fur

traders aroused opposition, especially when the British mishandled the task of regulating the trade.

Originally the British had intended the proclamation to be temporary. With the passage of time, however, sentiment for maintaining it increased; checking the westward expansion of the colonies seemed a good way of keeping them tied closely to the mother country. The proclamation line, the Board of Trade declared, was "necessary for the preservation of the colonies in due subordination."* Naturally this attitude caused resentment

---

*The British were particularly concerned about preserving the colonies as markets for their manufactures. They feared that the spread of population beyond the mountains would stimulate local manufacturing because the high cost of land transportation would make British goods prohibitively expensive.

in America. To close off the west temporarily in order to pacify the Indians made some sense; to keep it closed was like trying to contain a tidal wave.

Beginnings of the Great Debate

Americans disliked the new western policy but realized that the problems were knotty and that no simple solution existed. Their protests were somewhat muted. Great Britain's effort to raise money in America to help support the increased cost of colonial administration caused far more vehement complaints. George Grenville, who became prime minister in 1763, was a fairly able man, although long-winded and rather narrow in outlook. His reputation as a financial expert was based chiefly on his eagerness to reduce government spending. Under his leadership Parliament passed, in April 1764, the so-called Sugar Act. This law placed tariffs on sugar, coffee, wines, and many other products imported into America in substantial amounts. Taxes on European products imported by way of Great Britain were doubled, and the enumerated articles list was extended to include iron, raw silk, potash, and several other items. The sixpence-per-gallon tax on foreign molasses, imposed in 1733 and designed to be prohibitively high, was reduced to threepence, at which level the foreign product could compete with molasses from the British West Indies.

At the same time, new measures aimed at enforcing all the trade laws were put into effect. (A threepenny molasses duty would not produce much revenue if it were as easy to avoid as the old levy had been.) Those accused of violating the Sugar Act were to be tried before British naval officers in vice-admiralty courts. Grenville was determined to end both smuggling and the corruption and inefficiency that had plagued the customs service for decades. Soon the customs service was collecting each year 15 times as much in duties as it had before the war.

The Sugar Act and the decision of the government in London to restrict the printing of paper money in the colonies disturbed Americans deeply. Throughout the 18th century local assemblies had issued paper currency in anticipation of tax payments to finance emergencies such as wars.

The act of 1764 merely imposed restrictions on colonial paper; it did not prevent its use. But it came at a bad time. During the war the seaports prospered mightily, and shipbuilding boomed. Merchants earned fat profits supplying the British forces with food and other goods. British soldiers and sailors, 40,000 of them, spent most of their wages in the colonies.

When the fighting shifted to the Caribbean after the fall of Canada, most of this spending stopped. The soldiers "are gone to drink [rum] in a warmer Region, the place of its production," a New York merchant mourned. A depression resulted which the new laws made worse. Hard-hit merchants and artisans found British policy alarming.

Far more alarming was the nature of the Sugar Act and the manner of its passage. The Navigation Acts had imposed duties of many kinds, but they had been intended to regulate commerce and the sums collected had been trivial. Indeed, the Navigation Acts might well be considered an instrument of imperial foreign policy, an area of government that everyone willingly conceded to London. Yet few Americans were willing to concede that Parliament had the right to tax them. As *Englishmen* (and as readers of John Locke) they believed that no one should be deprived arbitrarily of his property and that, as James Otis put it in his stirring pamphlet *The Rights of the British Colonies Asserted and Proved*, everyone should be "free from all taxes but what he consents to in person, or by his representative." Locke had made clear in his *Second Treatise of Government* (1690) that property ought never be taken from people without their consent, not because material values transcend all others but because human liberty can never be secure when arbitrary power of any kind exists. "If our Trade may be taxed why not our Lands?" the Boston town meeting asked when news of the Sugar Act reached America. "Why not the produce of our Lands and every Thing we possess or make use of?"

To most people in Great Britain the colonial protest against taxation without representation seemed a hypocritical quibble. The distinction between tax laws and other types of legislation was artificial, they reasoned. Either Parliament was sovereign in America or it was not, and only a fool or a traitor would argue that it was not. If the colonists were loyal subjects of George III, as they claimed, they should bear cheerfully their fair share of the cost of governing his widespread dominions. As to representation, the colonies *were* represented in Parliament; every member of that body stood for the interests of the entire empire. If Americans had no say in the election of members of Commons, neither did most Englishmen.

This concept of "virtual" representation accurately described the British system. But it made no sense in America, where from the time of the first settlements members of the colonial assemblies had represented the people of the districts in which they stood for office. The confusion between virtual and "direct" (geographically based) representation revealed the extent to which colonial and British political practices had diverged over the years.

The British were partly correct in concluding that selfish motives influenced colonial objections to the Sugar Act. The colonists denounced taxation without representation, but they would have rejected the offer of a reasonable number of seats in Parliament if it had been made, and they would probably have complained about paying taxes to support imperial administration even if imposed by their own assemblies. American abundance and the simplicity of colonial life had enabled them to prosper without assuming any considerable tax burden. Now their maturing society was beginning to require communal rather than individual solutions to the problems of existence. Not many of them were prepared to face up to this hard truth.

Over the course of colonial history Americans had taken a singularly narrow view of imperial concerns. They had avoided complying with the Navigation Acts whenever they could profit by doing so. Colonial militiamen had compiled a sorry record when asked to fight for Britain or even for the inhabitants of colonies other than their own. True, most Americans professed loyalty to the Crown, but not many would voluntarily open their purses except to benefit themselves. In short they were provincials, in attitude and in fact. Many of the difficulties they faced after they won their independence resulted from this narrowness of outlook.

Nevertheless, the colonists were genuinely concerned about the principle of taxation without representation. They failed, however, to agree upon a common plan of resistance. Many of the assemblies drafted protests, but these varied in force as well as in form. Merchant groups that tried to organize boycotts of products subject to the new taxes met with indifferent success. Then in 1765 Parliament provided the flux necessary for welding colonial opinion by passing the Stamp Act.

The Stamp Act Crisis

The Stamp Act placed stiff excise taxes on virtually all kinds of printed matter—colonial newspapers, legal documents, licenses, even playing cards. Stamp duties were supposed to be relatively painless and cheap to collect; in England similar taxes brought in about £100,000 annually. Grenville hoped the Stamp Act would produce £60,000 a year in America, and the law provided that all revenue should be applied to "defraying the necessary expenses of defending, protecting, and securing, the . . . colonies."

Hardly a farthing was collected. As the clergyman Jonathan Mayhew explained, "almost every British American . . . considered it as an infraction of their rights, or their dearly purchased privileges." The Sugar Act had been related to Parliament's uncontested power to control colonial trade, but the Stamp Act was a direct tax. When Parliament ignored the politely phrased petitions of the colonial assemblies, more vigorous protests quickly followed.

Virginia took the lead. In late May 1765 Patrick Henry, fresh from his triumph in the Parson's Cause controversy, introduced resolutions asserting redundantly that the House of Burgesses possessed "the only and sole and exclusive right and power to lay taxes" on Virginians and suggesting that Parliament had no legal authority to tax the colonies at all. Henry spoke for what the royal governor called the "Young, hot and Giddy Members" of the legislature. The more extreme of his resolutions failed of enactment, but the debate they occasioned attracted wide and favorable attention. On June 6 the Massachusetts assembly proposed an intercolonial Stamp Act Congress, which, when it met in October, passed another series of resolutions of protest.

During the summer an irregular organization known as the Sons of Liberty began to agitate against the act. Although led by men of character

■ A woodcut reveals the unsubtle methods used by New Hampshire protestors to intimidate a stamp master. As his effigy is stoned and jeered, a mock funeral procession (at left) begins.

and position, the "Liberty Boys" frequently resorted to violence to achieve their aims. In Boston they staged vicious riots, looting and then wantonly vandalizing the houses of the stamp master and the lieutenant governor and destroying important government records. In Connecticut the stamp master Jared Ingersoll, a man of great courage and dignity, faced an angry mob demanding his resignation. When threatened with death if he refused, he coolly replied that he was prepared to die "perhaps as well now as another Time." Probably his life was not really in danger, but the size and determination of the crowd convinced him that resistance was useless, and he capitulated.

The stamps were printed in England and shipped to stamp masters (all Americans) in the colonies well in advance of November 1, 1765, the date the law was to go into effect. The New York stamp master had resigned, but the stamps were stored in the city under military guard. Radicals distributed placards reading, "The first Man that either distributes or makes use of Stampt Paper let him take care of his House, Person, and Effects. We dare." When Major Thomas James, the officer who had charge of the stamps, promised that "the stamps would be crammed down New Yorkers' throats," a mob responded by breaking into his house, drinking all his wine, and smashing his furniture and china, reducing the place to a shambles.

In some colonies the stamps were snatched by mobs and put to the torch amid rejoicing. Elsewhere they were locked up in secret by British officials or held on shipboard. For a time no business requiring stamped paper was transacted; then, gradually, people began to defy the law by issuing and accepting unstamped documents.

Threatened by mob action should they resist, British officials stood by helplessly. The law was a dead letter.

The looting associated with this crisis raises a question: Was the protest aimed at the wealthy and powerful in America as well as at British tyranny? That many of the poor resented the colonial elite goes without saying, as does the fact that in many instances the rioting got out of hand and took on a social as well as a political character. Times were hard, and the colonial elite, including most of the leading critics of British policy, had little compassion for the poor, whom they feared could be corrupted by anyone who offered them a square meal or a glass of rum. Once roused, laborers and artisans may well have directed their energies toward righting what they considered local wrongs.

Yet the mass of the people, being owners of property and capable of influencing political decisions, were not social revolutionaries. They might envy and resent the wealth and power of the great landowners and merchants, but there is no evidence that they wished to overthrow the established order.

The British were not surprised that Americans disliked the Stamp Act. They had not anticipated, however, that Americans would react so violently and so unanimously. Americans did so for many reasons. Business continued poor in 1765, and the stamp taxes (20 shillings for a liquor license, 5 shillings for a will, 2 shillings for an advertisement in a newspaper) represented a heavy burden. The taxes would hurt the business of lawyers, merchants, newspaper editors, and tavernkeepers. Even clergymen dealt with papers requiring stamps. The protests of such influential and articulate people had a powerful impact on public opinion.

The greatest cause of alarm to the colonists was Great Britain's flat rejection of the principle of no taxation without representation. To buy a stamp was to surrender all claim to self-government. Almost no colonist in 1765 wished to be independent of Great Britain, but all valued highly their local autonomy and what they called "the rights of Englishmen." They saw the Stamp Act as only the worst in a series of invasions of these rights. Already Parliament had passed still another measure, the Quartering Act, requiring local legislatures to house and feed new British troops sent to the colonies. Reluctantly, many Americans were beginning to fear that the British authorities had organized a conspiracy to deprive them of their liberties—indeed, to subvert the liberties of all English subjects.

In the 18th century the English and their American cousins considered themselves, with justice, the freest people in the world. They attributed their freedom to what they called their balanced government. In England power appeared to be shared by the Crown, the House of Lords (representing the aristocracy), and the House of Commons (representing the rest of the realm). The governors, councils, and assemblies seemed to play analogous roles in the colonies. In reality this balance of separate forces never existed, either in Britain or in America. The apparent harmony of society was in both instances the product of a lack of seriously divisive issues, not of dynamic tension between rival forces. But the new laws seemed to Americans to threaten the balance, and this idea was reinforced by their observations of the corruption of English elections. Benjamin Franklin, being a colonial agent in London, knew British politics well. He complained that the entire country was "at market" and "might be bought . . . by the Devil himself" for about £2 million. A clique seeking unlimited power was trying to destroy balanced government in Britain and in America, or so many colonists thought.

There was no such conspiracy; yet to the question, Were American rights actually in danger? no certain answer can be made. Grenville and his successors were English politicians, not tyrants. They looked down on bumptious colonials but surely had no wish to destroy either them or their prosperity. The British attitude was like that of a parent making a recalcitrant youngster swallow a bitter medicine: protests were understandable, but in the patient's own interest they must·be ignored.

On the other hand, British leaders believed that the time had come to assert royal authority and centralize imperial power at the expense of colonial autonomy. The need to maintain a substantial British army in America to control the western Indians tempted the government to use some of the troops to "control" white Americans as well. And psychologically they were not ready to deal with Americans as equals or to consider American interests on a par with their own. In the long run, American liberty would be destroyed if this attitude were not changed.

Besides refusing to use stamps, Americans responded to the Stamp Act by boycotting British goods. Nearly a thousand merchants signed nonimportation agreements. These struck British merchants hard in their pocketbooks, and they in turn began to bring pressure on Parliament for repeal. After a hot debate—Grenville, whose ministry had fallen over another issue, advocated using the army to enforce the act—the hated law was repealed in March 1766. In America there was jubilation at the news. The ban on British goods was lifted at once. Colonists congratulated themselves on having stood fast in defense of a principle and having won their point.

The Declaratory Act

The great controversy over the constitutional relationship of colony to mother country was only beginning. The same day that it repealed the Stamp Act, Parliament passed a Declaratory Act stating that the colonies were "subordinate" and that Parliament could enact any law it wished "to bind the colonies and people of *America*."

To most Americans this bald statement of parliamentary authority seemed unconstitutional—a flagrant violation of their conception of how the British imperial system worked. Actually the Declaratory Act highlighted the degree to which British and American views of the system had drifted apart. The English and the colonials were using the same words but giving them different meanings. Their conflicting definitions of the word *representation* was a case in point. Another involved

A LIST of the Names of *those* who AUDACIOUSLY continue to counteract the UNITED SENTIMENTS of the BODY of Merchants thro'out NORTH-AMERICA ; by importing British Goods contrary to the Agreement.

John Bernard,
(In King-Street, almoſt oppoſite Vernon's Head.

James McMaſters,
(On Treat's Wharf.

Patrick McMaſters,
(Oppoſite the Sign of the Lamb.

John Mein,
(Oppoſite the White-Horſe, and in King-Street.

Nathaniel Rogers,
(Oppoſite Mr. Henderſon Inches Store lower End King-Street.

William Jackſon,
At the Brazen Head, Cornhill, near the Town-Houſe.

Theophilus Lillie,
(Near Mr. Pemberton's Meeting-Houſe, North-End.

John Taylor,
(Nearly oppoſite the Heart and Crown in Cornhill.

Ame & Elizabeth Cummings,
(Oppoſite the Old Brick Meeting Houſe, all of Boſton.

Iſrael Williams, Eſq; & Son,
(Traders in the Town of Hatfield.

And, *Henry Barnes,*
(Trader in the Town of Marlboro'.

The following Names ſhould have been i ſerted in the Liſt of Juſtices.

County of Middleſex.	County of Lincoln.
Samuel Hendley	
John Borland	John Kingſbury
Henry Barnes	
Richard Cary	County of Berkſhire.
County of Briſtol.	Mark Hopkins
George Brightman	Elijah Dwight
County of Worceſter.	Iſrael Stoddard
Daniel Bliſs	

■ The "blacklist" from the *North-American Almanack* was intended to put pressure on merchants in and around Boston who refused to sign nonimportation agreements. Whether they signed or not, merchants suffered economic losses.

the word *constitution.* To the British the Constitution meant the totality of laws, customs, and institutions that had developed over time and under which the nation functioned. In America, partly because governments were based upon specific charters, the word meant a written document or contract spelling out, and thus limiting, the powers of government. If in England Parliament passed an "unconstitutional" law, the result might be rebellion, but that the law existed none would deny. "If the parliament will positively enact a thing to be done which is unreasonable," the great

18th-century English legal authority Sir William Blackstone wrote, "I know of no power that can control it." In America people were beginning to think that an unconstitutional law simply had no force.

Even more basic were the differing meanings that English and Americans were giving to the word *sovereignty.* As Bernard Bailyn has explained in *The Ideological Origins of the American Revolution,* 18th-century English political thinkers believed that sovereignty (ultimate political power) could not be divided. Government and law being based ultimately on force, some "final, unqualified, indivisible" authority had to exist if social order was to be preserved. The Glorious Revolution in England had settled the question of where sovereignty resided—in Parliament. The Declaratory Act, so obnoxious to Americans, seemed to the English the mere explication of the obvious. That colonial governments had passed local laws the English did not deny, but they had done so at the sufferance of the sovereign legislative power, Parliament.

Given these ideas and the long tradition out of which they had sprung, one can sympathize with the British failure to follow the colonists' reasoning (which had not yet evolved into a specific proposal for constitutional reform). But most responsible British officials refused even to listen to the American argument.

The Townshend Acts

Despite the repeal of the Stamp Act, the British did not abandon the idea of taxing the colonies. If direct taxes were inexpedient, indirect ones like the Sugar Act certainly were not. To persuade Parliament to repeal the Stamp Act, some Americans (most notably Benjamin Franklin) had claimed that the colonists objected only to direct taxes. To draw such a distinction as a matter of principle was absurd, and in fact few colonists had done so. British leaders saw the absurdity but easily convinced themselves that Americans were making the distinction.

The government was hard pressed for funds to cover an annual budget of over £8.5 million. Therefore, in June 1767, the chancellor of the exchequer, Charles Townshend, introduced a series of new levies on glass, lead, paints, paper, and tea imported into the colonies. Townshend was a

■ In Copley's flattering portrait, painted in 1771, Samuel Adams points to the Massachusetts charter as if reminding Great Britain of the colonists' rights.

charming and witty man experienced in colonial administration, but he was something of a play-boy (his nickname was Champagne Charlie), and he lacked both integrity and common sense. He liked to think of Americans as ungrateful brats; he once said he would rather see the colonies turned into "Primitive Desarts" than treat them as equals. Townshend thought it "perfect nonsense" to draw a distinction between direct and indirect taxation, yet in his arrogance he believed the colonists were stupid enough to do so.

By this time the colonists were thoroughly on guard, and they responded quickly to the Townshend levies with a new boycott of British goods. In addition they made elaborate efforts to stimulate colonial manufacturing. By the end of 1769 imports from the mother country had been almost halved. Meanwhile, administrative measures enacted along with the Townshend duties were creating more ill will. A Board of Customs Commissioners, with headquarters in Boston, took charge of enforcing the trade laws, and new vice-admiralty courts were set up at Halifax, Boston, Phila-delphia, and Charleston to handle violations. These courts operated without juries, and the new commissioners proved to be a gang of rapacious racketeers who systematically attempted to obtain judgments against honest merchants in order to collect the huge forfeitures—one-third of the value of ship and cargo—that were their share of all seizures.

The struggle forced Americans to do some deep thinking about both American and imperial political affairs. The colonies' common interests and growing economic and social interrelationships probably made some kind of union inevitable. Trouble with England speeded the process. In 1765 the Stamp Act Congress had brought the delegates of nine colonies to New York. Now, in 1768, the Massachusetts General Court took the next step. It sent the legislatures of the other colonies a "Circular Letter" summarizing Massachusetts' feelings about the Townshend Acts and soliciting suggestions as to what should be done. The question of the limits of British power in America was much debated, and this too was no doubt inevitable, again because of change and growth. As the colonies matured, the balance of Anglo-American power *had* to shift or the system would become tyrannical. Even in the 17th century the attitude that led Parliament to pass the Declaratory Act would have been both insupportable and unrealistic. By 1766 it would have been vicious were it not absurd.

After the passage of the Townshend Acts, a lawyer named John Dickinson wrote a series of *Letters from a Farmer in Pennsylvania to the Inhabitants of the British Colonies*. Dickinson considered himself a loyal British subject trying to find a solution to colonial troubles. "Let us behave like dutiful children, who have received unmerited blows from a beloved parent," he wrote. Nevertheless, he stated plainly that while Parliament was sovereign, it had no right to tax the colonies, though it might collect incidental revenues in the process of regulating commerce.

Some Americans were much more radical than Dickinson. Samuel Adams of Boston, a genuine revolutionary agitator, believed by 1768 that Parliament had no right at all to legislate for the colonies. If few were ready to go that far, fewer still accepted the reasoning behind the Declaratory Act.

The British ignored American thinking. The

The BLOODY MASSACRE perpetrated in King—t—Street BOSTON on March 5th 1770 by a party of the 29th REGT

Engrav'd Printed & Sold by PAUL REVERE BOSTON

Unhappy Boston! see thy Sons deplore,
Thy hallow'd Walks besmear'd with guiltless Gore.
While faithless P—n and his savage Bands,
With murd'rous Rancour stretch their bloody Hands,
Like fierce Barbarians grinning o'er their Prey,
Approve the Carnage, and enjoy the Day.

If scalding drops from Rage from Anguish Wrung,
If speechless Sorrows lab'ring for a Tongue,
Or if a weeping World can ought appease
The plaintive Ghosts of Victims such as these;
The Patriot's copious Tears for each are shed,
A glorious Tribute which embalms the Dead.

But know, FATE summons to that awful Goal,
Where JUSTICE strips the Murd'rer of his Soul:
Should venal C—ts the scandal of the Land,
Snatch the relentless Villain from her Hand,
Keen Execrations on this Plate inscrib'd,
Shall reach a JUDGE who never can be brib'd.

The unhappy Sufferers were Mess.rs Sam.l GRAY SAM.l MAVERICK, JAM.s CALDWELL, CRISPUS ATTUCKS & PAT.k CARR
Killed. Six wounded; two of them (CHRIST.r MONK & JOHN CLARK) Mortally

■ Revere's famous engraving of the Boston Massacre was potent propaganda fully exploited by the Boston radicals. Many copies were made. His view of a deliberately ordered, concerted volley fired into a group of innocent citizens bore slight resemblance to fact. At the trial of the British soldiers, the jury was warned against "the prints exhibited in our houses" that added "wings to fancy." Two soldiers were punished mildly, the rest acquitted.

Massachusetts Circular Letter had been framed in moderate language and clearly reflected the convictions of most of the people in the Bay colony, yet when news of it reached England, the secretary of state for the colonies, Lord Hillsborough, ordered the governor to dissolve the legislature. Two regiments of British troops were transferred from the frontier to Boston, part of the aforementioned policy of bringing the army closer to the centers of colonial unrest.

These acts convinced more Americans that the British were conspiring to destroy their liberties. Bostonians found it galling that Redcoats should patrol their streets with the country at peace and no enemy in sight. A series of petty incidents between soldiers and townspeople, culminating in the Boston Massacre (March 1770), in which Redcoats fired into an angry crowd, killing five, exacerbated public feeling. Such violence played into the hands of radicals like Samuel Adams.

The British authorities finally gave up trying to raise revenue in the colonies. In April 1770 all the Townshend duties except the threepenny tax on tea were repealed. The tea tax was maintained as a matter of principle. "A peppercorn in acknowledgment of the right was of more value than millions without it," one British peer declared smugly—a glib fallacy.

At this point the nonimportation movement collapsed; although the boycott on tea was continued, many merchants imported British tea and paid the tax too. "Drank green tea," one patriot wrote in describing an afternoon at the merchant John Hancock's. "From Holland, I hope, but don't know." During the next two years no serious crisis erupted. Imports of British goods were nearly 50 percent higher than before the nonimportation agreement. So long as the British continued to be conciliatory, the colonists seemed satisfied with their place in the empire.

In 1772 new troubles broke out. The first was plainly the fault of the colonists involved. Early in June the British patrol boat *Gaspee* ran aground in Narragansett Bay, south of Providence, while pursuing a suspected smuggler. The *Gaspee*'s commander, Lieutenant Dudingston, had antagonized everyone in the area by his officiousness and zeal; that night a gang of local people boarded the helpless *Gaspee* and put it to the torch. This action was clearly criminal, but when the British attempted to bring the culprits to justice no one would testify

against them. The British, frustrated and angry, were strengthened in their conviction that the colonists were utterly lawless.

Then Governor Thomas Hutchinson of Massachusetts suddenly announced that henceforth the Crown rather than the local legislature would pay his salary. Since control over the salaries of royal officials gave the legislature a powerful hold on them, this development was disturbing. Colonial suspicions of British motives mounted again, especially after it was revealed that judges would also be paid by the London government. Groups of radicals formed "committees of correspondence" and stepped up communications with one another, planning joint action in case of trouble.

The Tea Act Crisis

In the spring of 1773 an entirely unrelated event precipitated the final crisis. The British East India Company held a monopoly of all trade between India and the rest of the empire. This monopoly had yielded fabulous returns, but decades of cor-

BOSTON, December 2, 1773.

WHEREAS it has been reported that a Permit will be given by the Custom-House for Landing the Tea now on Board a Veſſel laying in this Harbour, commanded by Capt. HALL : THIS is to Remind the Publick, That it was ſolemnly voted by the Body of the People of this and the neighbouring Towns aſſembled at the Old-South Meeting-Houſe on Tueſday the 30th Day of *November*, that the ſaid Tea never ſhould be landed in this Province, or pay one Farthing of Duty : And as the aiding or aſſiſting in procuring or granting any ſuch Permit for landing the ſaid Tea or any other Tea ſo circumſtanced, or in offering any Permit when obtained to the Maſter or Commander of the ſaid Ship, or any other Ship in the ſame Situation, muſt betray an inhuman Thirſt for Blood, and will alſo in a great Meaſure accelerate Confuſion and Civil War : This is to aſſure ſuch public Enemies of this Country, that they will be conſidered and treated as Wretches unworthy to live, and will be made the firſt Victims of our juſt Reſentment.

The PEOPLE.

N. B. Captain *Bruce* is arrived laden with the ſame deteſtable Commodity ; and 'tis peremptorily demanded of him, and all concerned, that they comply with the ſame Requiſitions.

■ The inflammatory handbill at right, attributing to the "Enemies of this Country" an "inhuman Thirst for Blood," typified the propaganda that flooded Boston from the presses of the Sons of Liberty during the tea crisis. The city was virtually under mob rule; two weeks later the Tea Party (left) took place. This sketch is by German artist Johann Ramberg.

ruption and inefficiency together with heavy military expenses in recent years had weakened the company until it was almost bankrupt.

Among the assets of this venerable institution were some 17 million pounds of tea stored in English warehouses. The decline of the American market, a result first of the boycott and then of the smuggling of cheaper Dutch tea, partly accounted for the glut. Normally, East India Company tea was sold to English wholesalers. They in turn sold it to American wholesalers, who distributed it to local merchants for sale to the consumer. A substantial British tax was levied on the tea as well as the threepenny Townshend duty. Now Lord North, the new prime minister, decided to remit the British tax and to allow the company to sell directly in America through its own agents. The savings would permit a sharp reduction of the retail price and at the same time yield a nice profit to the company. The Townshend tax was retained, however, to preserve (as Lord North said when the East India Company directors suggested its repeal) the principle of Parliament's right to tax the colonies.

The company then shipped 1,700 chests of tea to colonial ports. Though the idea of high-quality tea offered at bargain prices was tempting, after a little thought nearly everyone in America appreciated the dangers involved in buying it. If Parliament could grant the East India Company a monopoly of the tea trade, it could parcel out all or any part of American commerce to whomever it pleased. More important, the act appeared utterly diabolical, a dastardly trick to trap them into paying the tea tax. The plot seemed obvious: the real price of Lord North's tea was American submission to parliamentary taxation.

Public indignation was so great in New York and Philadelphia that when the tea ships arrived, the authorities ordered them back to England without attempting to unload. The tea could only be landed "under the Protection of the Point of the Bayonet and Muzzle of the Cannon," the governor of New York reported. "Even then," he added, "I do not see how the Sales or Consumption could be effected."

The situation in Boston was different. The tea ship *Dartmouth* arrived on November 27. The people of the region, marshaled by Sam Adams, were determined to prevent it from landing its cargo; Governor Hutchinson was equally determined to collect the tax and enforce the law. For days the town seethed. Thousands milled in the streets, harangued by Adams and his friends, while the *Dartmouth* and two later arrivals lay at their moorings. Then, on the night of December 16, as Hutchinson was preparing to seize the tea for nonpayment of the duty, a band of colonists disguised as Indians boarded the ships and dumped the hated tea chests in the harbor. A huge crowd gathered at wharfside cheered them on.

The destruction of the tea was a serious crime for which many persons, aside from the painted "Patriots" who jettisoned the chests, were responsible. The British burned with indignation when news of the "Tea Party" reached London. People talked (fortunately it was only talk) of flattening Boston with heavy artillery. Nearly everyone agreed that the colonists must be taught a lesson. George III himself said, "We must master them or totally leave them to themselves." What particularly infuriated the British was the certain knowledge that no American jury would render a judgment against the criminals; the memory of the *Gaspee* affair was fresh in everyone's mind in England, as undoubtedly it was in the minds of those Bostonians who, wearing the thinnest of disguises, brazenly destroyed the tea before thousands of witnesses.

Colonies in Revolt

Parliament responded in the spring of 1774 by passing the Coercive Acts. The Boston Port Act closed the harbor of Boston to all commerce until its citizens paid for the tea. The Administration of Justice Act provided for the transfer of cases to courts outside Massachusetts when the governor felt that an impartial trial could not be had within the colony. The Massachusetts Government Act revised the colony's charter drastically, strengthening the power of the governor, weakening that of the local town meetings, making the council appointive rather than elective, and changing the method by which juries were selected. These were unwise laws—they cost Great Britain an empire. All of them, and especially the Port Act, were unjust laws as well. Parliament was punishing a whole people for the crimes of individuals. These were acts of tyranny, a denial of English principles of justice.

The Americans named the laws (together with a new, more extensive Quartering Act and the Quebec Act, an unrelated measure that attached the area north of the Ohio River to Canada and gave the region an authoritarian, centralized government) the Intolerable Acts. That the British answer to the crisis was coercion the Americans found unendurable. The result was revolution.

Who must bear the blame for the rupture? Both sides in part, but the major share belongs on British shoulders. Although no one had thought it through in detail, the Americans were trying to work out a federal system with certain powers centered in London and others in the colonial capitals. Nearly every colonist was willing to see Great Britain continue to control many aspects of American life. Parliament, however—and in the last analysis George III and most Britons—insisted that their authority over the colonies was unlimited. Behind their stubbornness lay the arrogant psychology of the European: *"Colonists are inferior. . . . We own you."*

Lord North directed the Coercive Acts at Massachusetts alone because he thought that the other colonies, profiting from Massachusetts' discomfiture, would not intervene, and because of the British tendency to think of the colonies as separate units connected only through London. His strategy failed because his assumption was incorrect: the colonies began at once to act in concert.

In June 1774 Massachusetts called for a meeting of delegates from all the colonies to consider common action. This First Continental Congress met at Philadelphia in September; only Georgia failed to send delegates. Many points of view were represented, but even the so-called conservative proposal, introduced by Joseph Galloway of Pennsylvania, called for a thorough overhaul of the empire. Galloway suggested an *American* government, consisting of a president general appointed by the king and a grand council chosen by the colonial assemblies, that would manage intercolonial affairs and possess a veto over parliamentary acts affecting the colonies.

This was not what the majority wanted. Prolonged thought and discussion had produced a marked shift in opinion. If taxation without representation was tyranny, so was all legislation.

■ The "American question" was a constant topic of conversation in London, especially after news of the Tea Party crossed the Atlantic. Violence and property destruction dismayed some of the English, but those sympathetic to the colonial plight must have taken great pleasure when these three caricatures were published by the London firm of Sayer and Bennett. "The Alternative of Williamsburg" (above) portrays the tarring and feathering of those refusing to sign the nonimportation agreements; Virginians had taken the cue for the punishing of loyalists from their northern Boston friends. The two prints at the left are acid comments on the situation in Boston. At the top, Sons of Liberty brutalize a tax collector against a backdrop of the Tea Party. In "The Bostonians in Distress" (left) residents caged by the Port Act devour fish supplied by fellow colonists.

Therefore Parliament had no right to legislate in any way for the colonies. James Wilson, born in Scotland and a resident of America for less than a decade, made the argument in a pamphlet, *Considerations on the . . . Legislative Authority of the British Parliament*, published in the summer of 1774. "All the different members of the British empire are distinct states, independent of each other, but connected together under the same sovereign," Wilson insisted. John Adams, a cousin of Samuel and a Boston lawyer, while prepared to *allow* Parliament to regulate colonial trade, now believed that Parliament had no inherent right to control it. "The foundation . . . of all free government," he declared, "is a right in the people to participate in their legislative council." Americans "are entitled to a free and exclusive power of legislation in their several provincial legislatures."

Propelled by the reasoning of Wilson, Adams, and others, the Congress passed a declaration of grievances and resolves that amounted to a complete condemnation of Britain's actions since 1763. A Massachusetts proposal that the people take up arms to defend their rights was endorsed. The delegates also organized a "Continental Associ-

ation" to boycott British goods and to stop all exports to the empire. To enforce this boycott, committees were appointed locally "to observe the conduct of all persons touching this association" and to expose violators to public scorn.

To the extent that the Continental Congress reflected the views of the majority—there is no reason to suspect that it did not—it may be said that by the fall of 1774 the American Revolution had already begun. The committees set up to enforce the boycott were, in a sense, extralegal governments. Americans had decided that drastic changes must be made. Fumblingly yet inexorably, they were becoming aware of their common interests, their *Americanism*. It was not merely a question of mutual defense against the threat of British power, not only (in Franklin's aphorism) a matter of hanging together lest they hang separately. A nation was being born.

Looking back many years later, one of the delegates to the First Continental Congress made just these points. He was John Adams of Massachusetts, and he said: "The revolution was complete, in the minds of the people, and the Union of the colonies, before the war commenced."

SUPPLEMENTARY READING

Titles marked with an asterisk have been published in paperback

The fullest analysis of the British imperial system can be found in the early volumes of L. H. Gipson's **British Empire Before the American Revolution** (1936–1968), while the British political system is described in L. B. Namier, **The Structure of Politics at the Accession of George III*** (1929) and **England in the Age of the American Revolution*** (1930). For a briefer account, see J. H. Plumb, **England in the 18th Century*** (1950). O. M. Dickerson, **American Colonial Government** (1912), is a standard work, as is L. W. Labaree, **Royal Government in America** (1930). See also J. A. Henretta, **Salutary Neglect** (1972). J. P. Greene, **The Quest for Power: The Lower Houses of Assembly in the Southern Royal Colonies*** (1963), describes how the colonists extended their control of political affairs, while R. L. Schuyler, **Parliament and the British Empire** (1929), argues that Great Britain's authority over the colonies was always extensive.

The best study of mercantilism is Eli Heckscher, **Mercantilism** (1935); the fullest analysis of the Navigation Acts is G. L. Beer, **The Origins of the British Colonial System** (1908) and **The Old Colonial System** (1912).

O. M. Dickerson, **The Navigation Acts and the American Revolution*** (1951), claims that mercantilism did not injure the colonial economy, but L. A. Harper, **The English Navigation Laws** (1939), concludes that it did. C. P. Nettels, **The Money Supply of the American Colonies Before 1720** (1934), is an important study.

The colonial wars are vividly described in parts V–VII of Francis Parkman's **France and England in North America** (1877–1892); the best modern account is H. H. Peckham, **The Colonial Wars*** (1963). On the French and Indian War, L. H. Gipson's multivolume work is particularly useful; a brief, popular account is Brian Connell, **The Savage Years** (1959). Washington's role receives full treatment in Volume II of D. S. Freeman, **George Washington** (1948). On the problems posed for the British by the acquisition of French Canada, C. W. Alvord, **The Mississippi Valley in British Politics** (1916), may be supplemented with T. P. Abernethy, **Western Lands and the American Revolution** (1937), and J. M. Sosin, **Whitehall and the Wilderness** (1961).

On the causes of the Revolution, two brief treatments are L. H. Gipson, **The Coming of the Revolution***

(1954), and E. S. Morgan, **The Birth of the Republic*** (1956), a better-balanced analysis. Fuller discussions can be found in Merrill Jensen, **The Founding of a Nation** (1968), J. C. Miller, **Origins of the American Revolution*** (1943), a most entertaining volume, and in Bernhard Knollenberg, **Origin of the American Revolution*** (1960), which is more argumentative but at some points more penetrating. Bernard Bailyn's **The Ideological Origins of the American Revolution*** (1967) and **The Origins of American Politics*** (1968) are brilliant analyses of the political thinking and political structure of 18th-century America, while his edition of the **Pamphlets of the American Revolution** (1965) should be sampled by every student. G. B. Nash, **The Urban Crucible*** (1979), contains valuable data on political, social, and economic conditions in the largest towns, which Nash calls "crucibles of revolutionary agitation." See also Pauline Maier's **From Resistance to Revolution** (1972) and **The Old Revolutionaries** (1980) and A. F. Young (ed.), **The American Revolution: Explorations in the History of American Radicalism*** (1976).

Important special studies of the period include A. M. Schlesinger, **The Colonial Merchants and the American Revolution*** (1918), E. S. and H. M. Morgan, **The Stamp Act Crisis*** (1953), B. W. Labaree, **The Boston Tea Party*** (1964), John Shy, **Toward Lexington: The Role of the British Army in the Coming of the American Revolution*** (1965), J. M. Sosin, **Agents and Merchants: British Colonial Politics and the Origins of the American Revolution** (1965), and M. G. Kammen, **A Rope of Sand: The Colonial Agents, British Politics, and the American Revolution** (1968).

4/THE AMERICAN REVOLUTION

 The actions of the First Continental Congress led the British authorities to force a showdown with their bumptious colonial offspring. "The New England governments are in a state of rebellion," George III announced. "Blows must decide whether they are to be subject to this country or independent." Already General Thomas Gage, veteran of Braddock's ill-fated expedition against Fort Duquesne and now commander in chief of all British forces in North America, had been appointed governor of Massachusetts. New redcoated regiments poured into Boston, camping on the town common once peacefully reserved for the citizens' cows. Parliament echoed with demands for a show of strength in America. General James Grant announced that with a thousand men he "would undertake to go from one end of America to the other, and geld all the males, partly by force and partly by a little coaxing." Some opposed the idea of crushing the Americans, and others believed that it could not be easily managed, but they were a small minority. The House of Commons listened to Edmund Burke's magnificent and sensible speech on conciliating the colonies and then voted 270 to 78 against him.

"The Shot Heard Round the World"

The decision to use troops against Massachusetts was made in January 1775, but the order did not reach General Gage until April. In the interim both sides were active. Parliament voted new troop levies, declared Massachusetts to be in a state of rebellion, and closed the Newfoundland fisheries and all seaports except those in Great Britain and the British West Indies, first to the New England colonies and then to most of the others. The Massachusetts Patriots, as they were now calling themselves, formed an extralegal provincial assembly, reorganized the militia, and began training "Minute Men" and other fighters. Soon companies armed with anything that would shoot were drilling on town commons throughout Massachusetts, and in other colonies too.

When Gage received his orders on April 14, he acted swiftly. The Patriots had been accumulating arms at Concord, some 20 miles west of Boston. On the night of April 18 Gage dispatched 700 crack troops to seize these supplies. The Patriots were forewarned. Paul Revere set out on his famous ride* to alert the countryside and warn John Hancock and Sam Adams, leaders of the provincial assembly, whose arrest had been ordered. When the Redcoats reached Lexington early the next morning, they found the common occupied by about 70 Minute Men. After an argument the Americans began to withdraw. Then someone fired a shot. There was a flurry of gunfire and the Minute Men fled, leaving eight dead.

The British marched on to Concord, where they

---

*William Dawes and Dr. Samuel Prescott helped spread the alarm.

destroyed whatever supplies the Patriots had been unable to carry off. Now militiamen were pouring into the area from all sides. A hot skirmish at Concord's North Bridge forced the Redcoats to yield that position. Somewhat alarmed, they began to march back to Boston. Soon they were being subjected to a withering fire from American irregulars along their line of march. A strange battle developed on a "field" 16 miles long and only a few hundred yards wide. Gage was obliged to send out an additional 1,500 men, and total disaster was avoided only by deploying skirmishers to root out snipers by burning every barn and farmhouse along the road to Boston. When the first day of the Revolutionary War ended, the British had sustained 273 casualties, the Americans less than 100.

For a brief moment of history tiny Massachusetts stood alone at arms against an empire that had humbled France and Spain. Yet Massachusetts assumed the offensive! The provincial government organized an expedition that captured Fort Ticonderoga and Crown Point, on Lake Champlain. The other colonies rallied quickly to Massachusetts' cause, sending reinforcements to the Massachusetts army.

The Second Continental Congress

On May 10 (the day Ticonderoga fell) the Second Continental Congress met in Philadelphia. It was a distinguished group, more radical than the First Congress. Besides John and Sam Adams, Patrick Henry and Richard Henry Lee of Virginia, and Christopher Gadsden of South Carolina, all holdovers from the First Congress, there was Thomas Jefferson, a lanky, sandy-haired young planter from Virginia. Jefferson, an indifferent debater but a brilliant writer, had recently published *A Summary View of the Rights of British America*, an essay criticizing the institution of monarchy and warning George III that "Kings are the servants, not the proprietors of the people." Virginia had also sent George Washington, who could neither write well nor make good speeches, but who knew more than any other colonist about commanding men. He wore his buff and blue colonel's uniform to indicate his willingness to place his skill at the disposal of the Congress. The renowned Benjamin

Plate III. The Engagement at the North Bridge in Concord

1. The Detachment of the Regulars who fired first on the Provincials at the Bridge
2. The Provincials headed by Colonel Robinson & Major Buttrick. 3. The Bridge
A. Doolittle Sculp.

■ On the right, the British forces at the North Bridge in Concord fight a rear-guard action. A line of riflemen hold off the Massachusetts militia on the left, while the mass of the Redcoats retreat toward Boston. An engraving by Amos Doolittle made from a sketch by Ralph Earl.

Franklin was a delegate and moving rapidly to the radical position. The Boston merchant John Hancock was chosen president of the Congress.

This Congress had no legal authority, yet it had to make agonizing decisions under the pressure of rapidly unfolding military events—with the future of every American depending on its actions. Delicate negotiations and honeyed words might yet persuade king and Parliament to change their ways, but precipitate, bold effort was essential to save Massachusetts.

In this predicament Congress naturally dealt first with the military crisis. It formed the forces gathering around Boston into a Continental Army and appointed George Washington commander in chief. After Washington and his assistants left for the front on June 23, the Congress turned to the task of requisitioning men and supplies.

Meanwhile, in Massachusetts the first major battle of the war had been fought. The British position on the peninsula of Boston was impregnable to direct assault, but high ground north and south, at Charlestown and Dorchester Heights, could be used to pound the city with artillery. When the Patriots seized Bunker Hill and Breed's Hill at Charlestown and constructed a redoubt on the latter, Gage determined at once to drive them off. This was accomplished on June 17. Twice the Redcoats marched in close ranks up Breed's Hill, each time being driven back after suffering heavy losses. Stubbornly they came again, and this time they carried the redoubt, for the defenders had run out of ammunition. However, more than a thousand Redcoats fell in a couple of hours, out of a force of some 2,500, while the Patriots lost only 400 men, most of them cut down by British bayonets after the hill was taken.

The British had cleared the Charlestown peninsula, but the victory was really the Americans', for they had proved themselves against professional soldiers and had exacted a terrible toll. "The day ended in glory," a British officer wrote, "but the loss was uncommon in officers for the number engaged."

The Battle of Bunker Hill, as it was called for no good reason, greatly reduced whatever hope remained for a negotiated settlement. The spilling of so much blood left each side determined to force the other's submission. The British recalled General Gage, replacing him with General Sir William Howe, a respected veteran of the French and Indian War, and George III formally proclaimed the colonies to be "in open rebellion." The Continental Congress dispatched one last plea to the king (the Olive Branch Petition), but this was a sop to the moderates. Immediately thereafter it adopted the "Declaration of the Causes and Necessity of Taking Up Arms," which condemned everything the British had done since 1763. Americans were "a people attacked by unprovoked enemies"; the time had come to choose between "submission" to "tyranny" and "resistance by force." Congress then ordered an attack on Canada and created a special committee to seek foreign aid and another to buy munitions abroad. It authorized the outfitting of a navy under Commodore Esek Hopkins of Rhode Island.

Congress (and the bulk of the people) still hung back from a break with the Crown. To declare for independence would be to burn the last bridge, to become traitors in the eyes of the mother country. Aside from the word's ugly associations, everyone knew what happened to traitors when their efforts failed. It was sobering to think of casting off everything that being English meant: love of king, the traditions of a great nation, pride in the power of a mighty empire. "Where shall we find another Britain?" John Dickinson asked at the time of the Townshend Acts crisis. "Torn from the body to which we are united by religion, liberty, laws, af-fections, relation, language and commerce, we must bleed at every vein."

Then, too, rebellion might end in horrors worse than submission to *British* tyranny. The disturbances following the Stamp Act and the Tea Act had revealed an alarming fact about American society. The organizers of the protests, mostly persons of wealth and status, had thought in terms of "ordered resistance." They countenanced violence only as a means of forcing the British authorities to pay attention to their complaints. But protest meetings and mob actions had brought out every thief, every ne'er-do-well, every demagogue in the colonies. Property had been destroyed, not all of it owned by Loyalists and British officials. Too much exalted talk about "rights" and "liberties" might well give the poor (to say nothing of the slaves) an exaggerated impression of their importance. Finally, in a world where every country had some kind of monarch, could common people *really* govern themselves? The most ardent defender of American rights might well hesitate after considering all the implications of independence.

The Great Declaration

Independence was probably inevitable by the end of 1775. The belief that George III had been misled by evil or stupid advisers on both sides of the Atlantic became progressively more difficult to sustain. Mistrust of Parliament—indeed, of the whole of British society—grew apace.

Two events in January 1776 pushed the colonies a long step toward a final break. First came the news that the British were sending hired Hessian soldiers to fight against them. Colonists associated mercenaries with looting and rape and feared that the German-speaking Hessians would run amok among them. Such callousness on the part of Britain made reconciliation seem out of the question.

The second decisive event was the publication of *Common Sense*. This tract was written by Thomas Paine, a onetime English corsetmaker and civil servant turned pamphleteer, a man who had been in America scarcely a year. *Common Sense* called boldly for complete independence. It attacked not only George III but the idea of monarchy itself. Paine applied the uncomplicated logic of the zealot to the recent history of America. Where the colonists had been humbly petitioning George III and swallowing their resentment when he ignored them, Paine called George a "Royal Brute" and "the hardened sullen-tempered Pharaoh of England." Where many Americans had wanted to control their own affairs but feared the instability of untried republican government, Paine stated plainly that monarchy was a corrupt institution. "A government of our own is our natural right," he insisted. "O! ye that love mankind! Ye that dare oppose not only tyranny but the tyrant, stand forth!"

Virtually everyone in the colonies must have read *Common Sense* or heard it explained and discussed. About 150,000 copies were sold in the critical period between January and July.*

The tone of the debate changed sharply as Paine's slashing attack had its effect. The Continental Congress began to act more boldly. In March it unleashed privateers against British commerce; in April it opened American ports to foreign shipping; in May it urged the provincial assemblies to frame constitutions and establish state governments.

On June 7 Richard Henry Lee of Virginia introduced a resolution:

RESOLVED: That these United Colonies are, and of right ought to be, free and independent States, that they are absolved from all allegiance to the British Crown, and that all political connection between them and the State of Great Britain is, and ought to be, totally dissolved.

This momentous resolution was not passed at once; Congress first appointed a committee consisting of Thomas Jefferson, Benjamin Franklin, John Adams, Roger Sherman, and Robert Livingston to frame a suitable justification of independence. Livingston, a member of one of the great New York landowning families, was put on the committee in an effort to push New York toward independence. Sherman, a self-educated Connecticut lawyer and merchant, was a conservative who opposed parliamentary control over colonial affairs. Franklin, the best known of all Americans and an experienced writer, was a natural choice; so was John Adams, whose devotion to the cause

of independence combined with his solid conservative qualities made him perhaps the typical man of the Revolution.

Thomas Jefferson was probably placed on the committee because politics required that a Virginian be included and because of his literary skill and quality of mind. Aside from writing *A Summary View of the Rights of British America,* he had done little to attract notice. At 33 he was the youngest member of the Continental Congress and was only marginally interested in its deliberations. He had been slow to take his seat in the fall of 1775, and he had gone home to Virginia before Christmas. He put off returning several times and arrived in Philadelphia only on May 14. Had he delayed another month, someone else would have written the Declaration of Independence. Nevertheless the committee asked Jefferson to prepare a draft. (Jefferson wanted John Adams to do it, but Adams refused, saying: "You can write ten times better than I can.") His draft, with a few amendments made by Franklin and Adams and somewhat toned down by the whole Congress, was officially adopted by the delegates on July 4, 1776.

Jefferson's Declaration consisted of two parts. The first was by way of introduction: it justified the abstract right of any people to revolt and described the theory on which the Americans based their creation of a new, republican government. The second, much longer, section was a list of the "injuries and usurpations" of George III, a bill of indictment explaining why the colonists felt driven to exercise the rights outlined in the first part of the document. Here Jefferson stressed George's interference with the functioning of representative government in America, his harsh administration of colonial affairs, his restrictions on civil rights, and his maintenance of troops in the colonies without their consent. The king was blamed for Parliament's efforts to tax the colonies and to restrict their trade. Jefferson sought to marshal every possible evidence of British perfidy and to make the king, rather than Parliament, the villain. He held George III responsible for many actions by subordinates that George had never deliberately authorized and for some things that never happened. The long bill of particulars reads more like a lawyer's brief than a careful analysis; it holds relatively little interest for the modern reader.

Jefferson's general statement of the right of

---

*If a comparable portion of today's population purchased such a work, its sale would be in the neighborhood of 11 million copies!

■ A detail from John Trumbull's *Declaration of Independence* (reproduced here in actual size) portrays the five-man drafting committee presenting its handiwork to the Congress. From left, Massachusetts' John Adams, Connecticut's Roger Sherman, New York's Robert Livingston, Virginia's Thomas Jefferson, and Pennsylvania's Benjamin Franklin. Trumbull's skillful composition "ranks" the contributors, with Jefferson dominating.

revolution, however, has inspired oppressed peoples all over the world for more than 200 years:

> We hold these truths to be self-evident, that all men are created equal, that they are endowed by their Creator with certain unalienable Rights, that among these are Life, Liberty and the pursuit of Happiness. That to secure these rights, Governments are instituted among Men, deriving their just powers from the consent of the governed, That whenever any Form of Government becomes destructive of these ends, it is the Right of the People to alter or to abolish it, and to institute new Government. . . .

Why has this statement had so much influence on modern history? Not because the thought was original with Jefferson. As John Adams later pointed out—Adams viewed his great contemporary with a mixture of affection, respect, and jealousy—the basic idea was commonplace among 18th-century liberals.* "I did not consider it any part of my charge to invent new ideas," Jefferson explained, "but to place before mankind the common sense of the subject, in terms so plain and firm as to command their assent. . . . It was intended to be an expression of the American mind."

Revolution was not new, but the spectacle of a people solemnly explaining and justifying their right, in an orderly manner, to throw off their oppressors and establish a new system on their own

---

*Adams also dismissed Paine's *Common Sense* as "a tolerable summary of arguments which I had been repeating again and again in Congress for nine months."

authority was almost without precedent. Soon the French would be drawing upon this example in their revolution, and rebels everywhere have since done likewise. And if Jefferson did not create the concept, he gave it a nearly perfect form. The French historian Gilbert Chinard has said: "The Declaration of Independence is not only a historical document, it is the first and to this day the most outstanding monument in American literature."

1776: The Balance of Forces

A formal declaration of independence merely cleared the way for tackling the problems of founding a new nation and maintaining it in defiance of Great Britain. Lacking both traditions and authority based in law, the Congress had to create political institutions and a new national spirit—all in the midst of war.

Always the military situation took precedence over other tasks, for a single disastrous setback might make everything else meaningless. At the start the Americans had a great military advantage, for they already possessed their lands (except for the few square miles occupied by British troops). Although thousands of colonists fought for George III, the British soon learned that to put down the American rebellion they would have to bring in men and supplies from bases on the other side of the Atlantic. This was a most formidable task.

Meanwhile, the initiative remained with the Americans. An expedition under General Richard Montgomery had captured Montreal in November 1775, and another small force under Benedict Arnold advanced to the gates of Quebec after a grueling march across the wilderness from Maine. Montgomery and Arnold attempted to storm the Quebec defenses on December 31, 1775, but were repulsed with heavy losses. Even so, the British troops in Canada could not drive the remnants of the American army—perhaps 500 men in all—out of the province until reinforcements arrived in the spring.

Certain long-run factors operated in America's favor. Although His Majesty's soldiers were brave and well disciplined, the army was as inefficient and ill directed as the rest of the British government. Whereas nearly everyone in Great Britain wanted to crack down on Boston after the Tea Party, many boggled at engaging in a full-scale war against all the colonies. Aside from a reluctance to spill so much blood, there was the question of expense. Finally, the idea of dispatching the cream of the British army to America while powerful enemies on the Continent still smarted from past defeats seemed dangerous. For all these reasons the British approached gingerly the task of subduing the rebellion. When Washington fortified Dorchester Heights overlooking Boston, General Howe withdrew his troops to Halifax rather than risk another Bunker Hill. On March 17, 1776, Washington marched his troops into the city. For the moment the 13 colony-states were clear of Redcoats.

Awareness of Britain's problems undoubtedly spurred the Continental Congress to the bold actions of the spring of 1776. However, on the very day that Congress voted for independence (July 2), General Howe was back on American soil, landing in force on Staten Island in New York harbor in preparation for an assault on the city. Soon Howe had at hand 32,000 well-equipped troops and a powerful fleet commanded by his brother, Richard, Lord Howe. Washington realized that if the British controlled New York City and the Hudson River they could "stop intercourse between the northern and southern Colonies, upon which depends the Safety of America."

Suddenly the full strength of the empire seemed to have descended on the Americans. Superior British resources (a population of 9 million to the colonies' 2.5 million, large stocks of war materials and the industrial capacity to boost them further, mastery of the seas, a well-trained and experienced army, a highly centralized and, when necessary, ruthless government) were now all too evident.

The demonstration of British might accentuated American military and economic weaknesses: both money and the tools of war were continually in short supply in a predominantly agricultural country. Many of Washington's soldiers were armed with weapons no more lethal than spears and tomahawks. Few had proper uniforms. Even the most patriotic resisted conforming to the conventions of military discipline; the men hated drilling and all parade ground formality.

Supply problems were handled inefficiently and often corruptly. Few officers knew much about such mundane but vital matters as how to construct and maintain proper sanitary facilities when large numbers of soldiers were camped at one place for extended periods of time. What was inelegantly known as "the Itch" afflicted soldiers throughout the war.

Behind the lines, the country was far from united. Whereas nearly all colonists had objected to British policies after the French and Indian War, many still hesitated to take up arms against the mother country. Even Massachusetts harbored many Loyalists, or Tories, as they were called; about a thousand Americans fled Boston with General Howe, abandoning their homes rather than submit to the rebel army.

No one knows exactly how the colonists divided on the question of independence; what is certain is that the people did divide and that the divisions cut across geographic, social, and economic lines. The most explicit estimate places Tory strength between 7.6 and 18 percent of the white population; the "hard-core" Tories who left America during and after the war numbered between 60,000 and 100,000. The Patriots were much more numerous, but large elements, perhaps a majority of the people, were more or less indifferent to the conflict or, in Tom Paine's famous phrase, were summer soldiers and sunshine patriots—they supported the Revolution when all was going well and lost their enthusiasm in difficult hours. A high proportion of those holding royal appointments and many Anglican clergymen remained loyal to King George, as did numbers of merchants with close connections in Britain. There were important pockets of Tory strength in rural sections of New York, in the North Carolina back country, and among persons of non-English origin and other minority groups who tended to count on London for protection against the local majority.

Many became Tories simply out of distaste for change or because they were pessimistic about the condition of society and the possibility of improving it. "What is the whole history of human life," wrote the Tory clergyman and schoolmaster Jonathan Boucher of Virginia, "but a series of disappointments?" Still others believed that the actions of the British, however unfair and misguided, did not justify rebellion. Knowing that they possessed a remarkably free and equitable system of government, they could not stomach shedding blood

merely to avoid paying a few new taxes or to escape from what they considered minor restrictions on their activities. "The Annals of no Country can produce an Instance of so virulent a Rebellion . . . originating from such trivial Causes," one Loyalist complained.

The Tories lacked organization; many of their "leaders" did not know one another, and they had no central committee to lay plans or coordinate their efforts. Some Tories fled, others sought the protection of the British army, others took up arms, others accommodated themselves silently to Patriot pressures. The British, overestimating both the number of Loyalists and their own ability to crush the rebels, supplied little support or direction to the Tories before 1778. The leading Patriots, of course, worked closely together, but many of them suffered from a lack of *national* feeling. As in the colonial wars against the French, those who would fight stoutly when their own district was threatened frequently refused to make sacrifices to help Americans in other regions.

If the differences separating Patriot from Loyalist are unclear, feelings were nonetheless bitter. Battles between Tory units and the Continental Army were often exceptionally bloody. "Neighbor was against neighbor, father against son and son against father," one Connecticut Tory reported. "He that would not thrust his own blade through his brother's heart was called an infamous villain."

General Howe's campaign against New York brought to light another American weakness—the lack of military experience. Washington, expecting Howe to attack New York, had moved south to meet the threat, but both he and his men failed badly in this first major test. Late in August Howe crossed from Staten Island to Brooklyn. In the Battle of Long Island he easily outflanked and defeated Washington's army. Had he acted decisively, he could probably have ended the war on the spot, but Howe, who could not make up his mind whether to be a peacemaker or a conqueror, was not decisive. When he hesitated in consolidating his gains, Washington managed to withdraw his troops to Manhattan Island.

Howe could have trapped Washington simply by using his fleet to land troops on the northern end of Manhattan; instead he attacked New York City directly, leaving the Americans an escape route to the north. Again Patriot troops proved no

NEW YORK-NEW JERSEY CAMPAIGNS 1776-1777

← American Forces

← British Forces

0   5   10   15
Miles

NEW YORK

Peekskill

Hudson R.

White Plains
28 Oct 1776

HOWE

Hackensack

Ft. Lee   Ft. Washington

Morristown
(Winter Quarters)

Harlem Heights
16 Sept 1776

Newark

East R.

New York

NEW JERSEY

Passaic R.

WASHINGTON

CORNWALLIS

Staten
Island

Long Island
27 Aug 1776

SIR WILLIAM HOWE

ADMIRAL LORD HOWE

Rariton R.

New Brunswick

CLINTON

3 Jan 1777
Princeton

ATLANTIC
OCEAN

Newton   Trenton
26 Dec 1776

PENNSYLVANIA   Allentown

Delaware R.

■ The events in and around New York, so nearly disastrous to Washington and his army, are detailed in this map.

match for British regulars. Though Washington threw his hat to the ground in a rage and threatened to shoot cowardly Connecticut soldiers as they fled the battlefield, he could not stop the rout and had to fall back on Harlem Heights in upper Manhattan. And once more Howe failed to pursue his advantage promptly.

Still Washington refused to see the peril in remaining on an island while the enemy commanded the surrounding waters. Only when Howe shifted a powerful force to Westchester, directly threatening his rear, did Washington move north to the mainland. Finally, after several narrow escapes, he crossed the Hudson River to New

Jersey, where the British could not use their naval superiority against him.

The battles in and around New York City seemed to presage an easy British triumph. Yet somehow Washington salvaged a moral victory from these ignominious defeats. He learned rapidly; seldom thereafter did he place his troops in such vulnerable positions. And his men, in spite of repeated failure, had become an army. In November and December 1776 they retreated across New Jersey and into Pennsylvania. General Howe then abandoned the campaign, going into winter quarters in New York but posting garrisons at Trenton, Princeton, and other strategic points. The troops at Trenton were hated Hessian mercenaries, and Washington decided to attack them. He crossed the ice-clogged Delaware River with 2,400 men on Christmas night during a wild storm. The little army then marched 9 miles to Trenton, arriving at daybreak in the midst of a sleet storm. The Hessians were taken completely by surprise. Those who could fled in disorder, the rest—900 of them—surrendered.

The Hessians were first-class professional soldiers, probably the most competent troops in Europe at that time. The victory gave a boost to American morale. A few days later Washington outmaneuvered General Cornwallis, who had rushed to Trenton with reinforcements, and won another battle at Princeton. These engagements had little strategic importance, since both armies then went into winter quarters. Without them, however, there might not have been an army to resume the war in the spring.

Forming State Governments

The efforts of the states and the Continental Congress to establish new governments can only be understood against the background of military events. Defeats led to confusion and bickering, and hopes for the rapid establishment of a legal central government were dashed. A draft constitution prepared by John Dickinson in July 1776 ran into trouble: the larger states objected to equal representation of all the states, and the states with large western land claims refused to cede them to the central government. It was not until November 1777 that the Articles of Confederation were submitted to the states for ratification.

Besides struggling to frame a constitution, the Congress had to run the war and perform all the executive functions of government. It did so through a host of committees (the indefatigable John Adams served on more than 80). Congress managed to carry on fruitful diplomatic negotiations with France and other powers, borrow large sums, issue Continental currency, requisition money and supplies from the states, organize a postal system, and supervise Washington's conduct of the war.

One difficulty in the way of establishing a central government was the lack of precedent: there

had never been an *American* government. Another was suspicion of authority imposed from above. British oppression had forced the colonies to combine, but it had strengthened their conviction that local control of political power was vital. Remembering Parliament's treatment of them, they refused to give any central authority the right to tax.

Neither problem blocked the creation of effective state governments. In an important sense the *real* revolution occurred when the individual colonies broke the official ties with Great Britain. Using their colonial charters as a basis, the states began framing new constitutions even before the Declaration of Independence. By early 1777 all but Connecticut and Rhode Island, which continued under their colonial charters well into the 19th century, had taken this decisive step.

On the surface the new governments were not drastically different from those they replaced. The most significant change was the removal of *outside* control, which had the effect of making the governments more responsive to public opinion. Gone were the times when a governor could be appointed and maintained in office by orders from London. Each new constitution provided for an elected legislature, an executive, and a system of courts. In general the powers of the governor and of judges were limited, the theory being that elected rulers no less than those appointed by kings were subject to the temptations of authority, that, as one Patriot put it, all men are "tyrants enough at heart." The typical governor had no voice in legislation and little in appointments. Pennsylvania went so far as to eliminate the office of governor, replacing it with an elected council of 12.

The locus of power was in the legislature, which the people had come to count on to defend their interests. In addition to the lawmaking authority exercised by the colonial assemblies, the state constitutions gave the legislatures the power to declare war, conduct foreign relations, control the courts, and perform many other essentially executive functions. While continuing to require that voters be property owners or taxpayers, the constitution makers remained suspicious even of the legislature. The British concept of virtual representation they rejected out of hand. They saw legislators as *representatives*, that is, agents carrying out the wishes of the voters of a particular district rather than superior persons chosen to decide public issues according to their own best judgment. Gordon S. Wood, whose *The Creation of the American Republic* throws much light on the political thinking of the period, describes the concept as "acutely actual representation." Where political power was involved, the common American principle was every man for himself. The constitutions contained bills of rights protecting the people's civil liberties against all branches of the government. In Britain such guarantees checked only the Crown; the Americans invoked them against their own elected representatives as well.

The state governments combined the best of the British system, including its respect for fairness and due process, with the uniquely American stress on individualism and a healthy dislike of too much authority. The idea of drafting written frames of government—contracts between the people and their representatives that carefully spelled out the powers and duties of the latter—grew out of the experience of the colonists after 1763, when the vagueness of the unwritten British Constitution had caused so much controversy, and from the compact principle described in the Declaration of Independence. It represented one of the most important innovations of the Revolutionary era: a peaceful method for altering the political system. In the midst of violence the states changed their frames of government in an orderly, legal manner—a truly remarkable achievement that became a beacon of hope to reformers all over the world.

Social Reform

Many states seized the occasion of constitution making to introduce important reforms.* In Pennsylvania, Virginia, North Carolina, and other states the seats in the legislature were reapportioned in order to give the western districts their fair share. Primogeniture, entail (the right of an owner of property to prevent his heirs from ever disposing of it), and quitrents were abolished wherever they had existed. Steps toward greater freedom of religion were taken, especially in states where the Anglican church had enjoyed a privileged position. While most states continued to support religion after independence was won, they usually distributed the money roughly in accordance with the numerical strength of the various Protestant denominations.

Many states moved tentatively against slavery. In attacking British policy after 1763, colonists had frequently claimed that Parliament was trying to make slaves of them. No less a personage than George Washington wrote in 1774: "We must assert our rights, or submit to every imposition, that can be heaped upon us, till custom and use shall make us tame and abject slaves." However exaggerated the language, such reasoning led to denunciations of slavery, often vague but significant in their effects on public opinion. The fact that practically every important thinker of the European Enlightenment had criticized slavery on moral and economic grounds (Montesquieu, Voltaire, Diderot, and Rousseau in France, David Hume, Dr. Johnson,* and Adam Smith in England, to name a few) had an impact on educated opinion. Then, too, the forthright statements in the Declaration of Independence about liberty and equality seemed impossible to reconcile with slaveholding.

The war opened direct paths to freedom for some slaves. In November 1775 Lord Dunmore, the royal governor of Virginia, proclaimed that all slaves "able and willing to bear arms" for the British would be liberated. In fact, the British treated slaves as captured property, seizing them by the thousands in their campaigns in the south. The fate of these blacks is obscure. Some ended up in the West Indies, still slaves. Others were evacuated to Canada and liberated, and some of them settled the British colony of Sierra Leone in West Africa, founded in 1787. Probably many more escaped from bondage by running away during the confusion accompanying the British campaigns in the south.

About 5,000 blacks served in the Patriot army and navy. Most black soldiers were assigned noncombat duties, but some fought bravely in every major battle from Lexington to Yorktown.

---

*In fact the process of constitution making and reform took many years and was not completed until well after the war had ended.

*"How is it," asked Dr. Johnson, who opposed independence vehemently, "that we hear the loudest *yelps* for liberty among the drivers of negroes?"

Beginning with Pennsylvania in 1780, the northern states all did away with slavery. In most cases slaves born after a certain date were to become free upon reaching maturity. Since New Jersey did not pass its emancipation act until 1804, there were numbers of slaves in the so-called free states well into the 19th century—more than 3,500 as late as 1830. But the institution was on its way toward extinction. All the states prohibited the importation of slaves from abroad, and except for Georgia and South Carolina, the southern states passed laws removing restrictions on the right of individual owners to free their slaves. The greatest success of voluntary emancipation came in Virginia, where, between 1782 and 1790, 10,000 blacks were freed.

These advances encouraged foes of slavery to hope that the institution would soon disappear. But slavery died only where it was not economically important. Except for owners whose slaves were "carried off" by the British, only in Massachusetts, where the state supreme court ruled slavery unconstitutional in 1783, were owners deprived of existing slaves against their will.

Little of the social or economic upheaval usually associated with revolutions occurred after 1776. The property of Tories was frequently seized by the state governments, but almost never with the idea of redistributing wealth or providing the poor with land. While some large Tory estates were broken up and sold to small farmers, others passed intact to wealthy individuals or to groups of speculators. The war disrupted many traditional business relationships. Some merchants were unable to cope with the changes; others adapted well and grew rich. But the changes occurred without regard for the political beliefs or social values of either those who profited or those who lost.

That the new governments were liberal but moderate reflected the spirit of the times, a spirit typified by Thomas Jefferson, who had great faith in the democratic process yet owned a large estate and many slaves and had never suggested a drastic social revolution. More individuals of middling wealth were elected to the legislatures than in colonial times because the Revolution stimulated popular interest in politics and republican forms subtly undermined the tendency of farmers and artisans to defer automatically to great planters

and merchants. Few of these "ordinary" people, however, wanted radical changes. If they were becoming more skeptical about "their betters," they remained scornful of unskilled laborers, servants, and others lower than they on the social ladder. There were three classes in Philadelphia society, a writer in the Pennsylvania *Packet* noted in 1781: "The first class consists of commercial projectors . . . speculators, riotous livers, and a kind of loungers . . . The second class are a set of honest sober men, who mind their business . . . The third class are thieves, pick-pockets, low-cheats and dirty sots."

In the late 18th century there was a trend, barely perceptible at the time, toward increasing the legal rights of married women. It became somewhat easier for women to obtain divorces. In 1791 a South Carolina judge went so far as to say that the law protecting "the absolute dominion" of husbands was "the offspring of a rude and barbarous age." The "progress of civilization," he continued, "has tended to ameliorate the condition of women, and to allow even to wives, something like personal identity." As the tone of this "liberal" opinion indicates, no basic change in male attitudes took place because of the Revolution. Indeed, much of the change that did occur resulted from American judges following evolving British precedents after independence was won.

Attitudes towards the education of women changed because of the Revolution. According to the best estimates, at least half the white women in America could not read or write as late as the 1780s. But as the historian Linda K. Kerber writes, "the republican experiment demanded a well-educated citizenry." In a land of opportunity like the United States, women seemed particularly important because of their role in training the young. "You distribute 'mental nourishment' along with physical," one orator told the women of America in 1795. "The reformation of the world is in your power. . . . The solidity and stability of your country rest with you." Therefore the idea of female education began to catch on. Schools for girls were founded and the level of female literacy gradually rose.

During the war conflicts erupted over economic issues involving land and taxation, yet no single class or interest triumphed in all the states or in the national government. In Pennsylvania, where the western radical element was strong, the constitution was extremely democratic; in South Carolina the conservative tidewater planters maintained control handily. Many great landowners were ardent Patriots; others became Tories—and so did many small farmers.

In some cases the state legislatures wrote the new constitutions. In others the legislatures ordered special elections to choose delegates to conventions empowered to draft the charters. The convention method was a further important product of the Revolutionary era, an additional illustration of the idea that constitutions are contracts between the people and their leaders. Massachusetts even required that its new constitution be ratified by the people after it was drafted. All in all, the Revolution produced a more nearly democratic society, not one that satisfies modern standards of fairness and justice entirely, but a distinct advance toward popular rule.

Financing the War

All internal conflicts save the political one between Tory and Patriot were muted by the presence of British troops on American soil. The Continental Congress and the states carried on the war cooperatively. General officers were appointed by the Congress, lesser ones locally. The Continental Army, small but increasingly effective, was the backbone of Washington's force. The states raised militia chiefly for short-term service. Militiamen fought well at times but often proved unreliable. Washington continually fretted about their "dirty, mercenary spirit" and their "intractable" nature, yet he could not have won the war without them.

The fact that Congress' requisitions of money often went unhonored by the states does not mean that the states failed to contribute heavily to the war effort. Altogether they spent about $5.8 million in hard money, and they met Congress' demands for beef, corn, rum, fodder, and other military supplies. In addition Congress raised large sums by borrowing. Americans bought bonds worth between $7 and $8 million during the war. Foreign governments lent another $8 million, most of this furnished by France. Congress issued more than $240 million in paper money, the states over $200 million more. This currency fell rapidly in

■ Washington issued this blunt requisition order the day after his army limped into its Valley Forge encampment. The army's supply problems were intensified by the weakness of its transportation system.

value, resulting in an inflation that caused hardship and grumbling. The people, in effect, paid much of the cost of the war through the depreciation of their savings, but it is hard to see how else the war could have been financed, given the prejudice of the populace against paying taxes to fight a war against British taxation.

Other help in the struggle came from France and Spain. Beginning in the 1760s, France, hoping for trouble between the British and their American colonies, had maintained secret agents in America to report on developments. When trouble came, the Comte de Vergennes, French foreign minister, hastened to take advantage of it. By early May 1776 he had persuaded Louis XVI to authorize the expenditure of a million livres for munitions for America, and more was added the following year. Spain also contributed to the cause. Soon vital supplies were being funneled secretly to the rebels through a dummy trading company, Roderigue Hortalez et Cie. Without this aid the Americans could not have paid for the war materials they so desperately needed.

Saratoga and the French Alliance

When spring reached New Jersey in April 1777, Washington had fewer than 5,000 men under arms. Great plans—far too many and too complicated, as it turned out—were afoot in the British camp. The strategy called for General John Burgoyne to lead a large army from Canada down Lake Champlain toward Albany, while a smaller force under Lieutenant Colonel Barry St. Leger pushed eastward toward Albany from Fort Oswego on Lake Ontario. General Howe was to lead a third force north up the Hudson. Patriot resistance would be smashed between these three armies and the New England states isolated from the rest. Before participating in this campaign, Howe decided to attack Philadelphia. He hoped that, besides keeping Washington occupied, the presence of Redcoats in Pennsylvania would encourage local Tories to rise, thereby speeding the disintegration of the American forces.

As a venture in coordinated military tactics the British campaign of 1777 was a fiasco. General "Gentleman Johnny" Burgoyne, a charming if somewhat bombastic character, part politician, part poet, part gambler, part ladies' man, yet also a brave soldier who respected and was loved and admired by his men, began his march from Canada in mid June. By early July his army, which consisted of 500 Indians, 650 Loyalists, and 6,000 regulars, had captured Fort Ticonderoga, at the southern end of Lake Champlain. He quickly pushed beyond Lake George, but then bogged down. Burdened by a huge baggage train that included 138 pieces of generally useless artillery, more than 30 carts laden with his personal wardrobe and supply of champagne, and his mistress,* he could advance at but a snail's pace through the dense woods north of Saratoga. Patriot forces, mainly militia, impeded his way by felling trees across the forest trails.

General Howe, in the meantime, wasted valu-

able weeks trying to trap Washington into exposing his army in New Jersey. This enabled Washington, who by June had 9,000 regulars and large militia elements at his disposal, to send some of his regulars to buttress the militia forming in Burgoyne's path. On July 23 Howe sailed from New York with the bulk of his army to attack Philadelphia, reaching the Chesapeake Bay area on August 25. Only a small force under General Sir Henry Clinton remained in the New York area to aid Burgoyne.

St. Leger were also slow in carrying out his part of the grand design. He did not leave Fort Oswego until July 26, and then he too bogged down at Fort Stanwix, about a third of the way to Albany. He placed the fort under siege early in August, but General Benedict Arnold marched westward with a thousand men from the army resisting Burgoyne and drove St. Leger back to his base at Oswego.

By the end of August the British plan had been completely disrupted. The drive from Canada had stalled, the push from the west had been turned back, that from New York City had been stillborn. American militiamen were filtering into the area north of Albany. Although he was too vain to realize it, Burgoyne was in serious trouble.

With magnificent disregard for the rest of the war, Howe now proceeded to move against Philadelphia. He taught Washington, who had moved south to oppose him, a series of lessons in tactics, defeating him at the Battle of Brandywine on September 11, feinting him out of position before Philadelphia, and moving unopposed into that city on September 26. Yet he failed to destroy Washington's army, which attacked him sharply at Germantown early in October. This attack was almost successful; when Howe finally repelled it, winning another useless victory, Washington was able to retreat in an orderly fashion.

Meanwhile, disaster befell General Burgoyne. The American forces under Philip Schuyler and later under Horatio Gates and Benedict Arnold had erected formidable defenses immediately south of Saratoga near the town of Stillwater. Burgoyne struck at this position on September 19 and again on October 7 and was thrown back each time with heavy losses. Each day more local militia swelled the American forces. Soon Burgoyne was under siege, his troops pinned down by withering fire from every direction, unable even to bury their dead. The only hope was General Clin-

---

*Many soldiers, enlisted men as well as officers, took their wives or other women along on campaigns. More than 2,000 accompanied the Burgoyne expedition. At one point Washington complained of "the multitude of women . . . especially those who are pregnant, or have children [that] clog upon every movement." Actually, women in 18th century armies worked hard, doing most of the cooking, washing, and other "housekeeping" tasks.

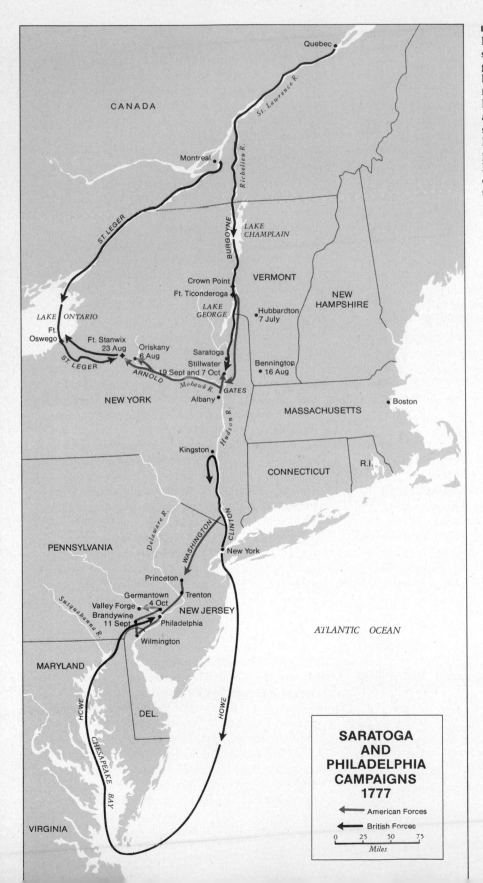

■ Howe's attack on Philadelphia and Burgoyne's simultaneous fatal attempt at grand strategy are shown here. Lacking definite orders from London to participate in Burgoyne's campaign, and already resentful that his own strategic plans were ignored, Howe set sail for the Chesapeake, leaving behind in New York a token force to cooperate with Burgoyne to the north.

SARATOGA
AND
PHILADELPHIA
CAMPAIGNS
1777

→ American Forces

➤ British Forces

0   25   50   75

Miles

ton, who had finally started up the Hudson from New York. Clinton got as far as Kingston, about 80 miles below Saratoga, but on October 16 he decided to return to New York for reinforcements. The next day, at Saratoga, Burgoyne surrendered. Some 5,700 British prisoners were marched off to Virginia.

This overwhelming triumph probably decided the war, for when news of the victory reached France, Louis XVI immediately recognized the United States. By February 1778 Vergennes and three American commissioners in Paris, Benjamin Franklin, Arthur Lee, and Silas Deane, had drafted a commercial treaty and a formal treaty of alliance. The two nations agreed to make "common cause and aid each other mutually" should war "break out" between France and Great Britain. Meanwhile, France guaranteed "the sovereignty and independence absolute and unlimited" of the United States.

When the news of Saratoga reached England,

Lord North realized that a Franco-American alliance would probably follow. To forestall it he was ready to give in on all the issues that had agitated the colonies before 1775. Both the Coercive Acts and the Tea Act would be repealed; Parliament would pledge never to tax the colonies.

Instead of implementing this proposal promptly, Parliament did not act until March 1778. Royal Peace Commissioners did not reach Philadelphia until June, a month after Congress had ratified the French treaty. The British proposals were icily rejected, and while the peace commissioners were still in Philadelphia war broke out between France and Great Britain.

The war, however, was far from won. After the Battle of Germantown, Washington had settled his army for the winter at Valley Forge, 20 miles northwest of Philadelphia. The army's supply system collapsed. According to the Marquis de Lafayette, one of many European liberals who volunteered to fight on the American side, "the

■ A widely circulated European cartoon (this is a Dutch version) inspired by the events of 1777. England's cow of commerce is milked by France, Spain, and Holland, while America saws off its horns and John Bull with his dog fails to rouse the British lion. Behind them, the Howe brothers nod over a punch bowl in Philadelphia.

unfortunate solders . . . had neither coats, nor hats, nor shirts, nor shoes; their feet and legs froze till they grew black, and it was often necessary to ampute them." Often the men had nothing to eat but "Fire Cake," a mixture of ground grain and water molded on a stick or in a pan and baked in the campfire.

To make matters worse, there was grumbling in Congress over Washington's failure to win victories and talk of replacing him as commander in chief with Horatio Gates, the "hero" of Saratoga. (In fact Gates was an indifferent soldier, lacking in decisiveness and unable to instill confidence in his subordinates. "Historical accounts of the Saratoga campaign have given abundant reasons for the American victory other than the military skill of Horatio Gates," one of his biographers has confessed.)

As the winter dragged on, the Continental Army melted away. So many officers resigned that Washington was heard to say that he was afraid of "being left Alone with the Soldiers only." Since enlisted men could not legally resign, they deserted by the hundreds. Yet somehow the army survived. Gradually the soldiers who remained became a tough, professional fighting force. Their spirit has been described by the historian Charles Royster as a "mixture of patriotism, resentment, and fatalism."

The War in the South

Spring brought a revival of American hopes in the form of more supplies, new recruits, and, above all, word of the French alliance. In May the British replaced General Howe as commander with General Clinton, who decided to transfer his base back to New York. While he was moving across New Jersey, Washington attacked him at Monmouth Court House. The fight was inconclusive, but the Americans held the field when they day ended and were able to claim a victory. Clinton marched on to New York.

Thereafter British strategy changed. Fighting in the northern states practically ceased. Instead, relying on sea power and the supposed presence of many Tories in the south, the British concentrated their efforts in South Carolina and Georgia. Savannah fell late in 1778 and most of the settled parts of Georgia were overrun during 1779. In

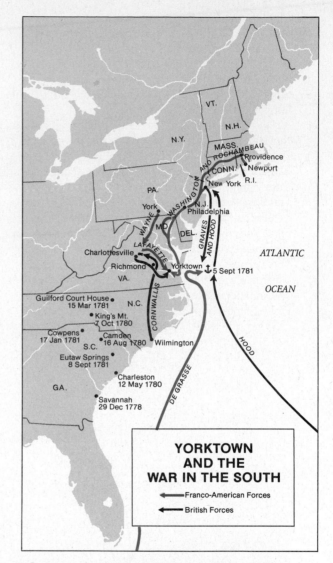

YORKTOWN AND THE WAR IN THE SOUTH

◄—— Franco-American Forces

◄—— British Forces

■ In an era when communications were slow and erratic at best, the coordination between the American and French land and naval forces that sealed up Cornwallis in Yorktown was nothing short of remarkable.

1780 Clinton led a massive expedition against Charleston. When the city surrendered in May, more than 3,000 soldiers were captured, the most overwhelming American defeat of the war. Leaving General Cornwallis and some 8,000 men to carry on the campaign, Clinton sailed back to New York.

The Tories of South Carolina and Georgia came closer to meeting British expectations than did those of any other region. Nevertheless, the callous behavior of the British troops rapidly persuaded large numbers of hesitating citizens to join the Patriot cause. Guerrilla bands led by men like Francis Marion, the "Swamp Fox," and Thomas Sumter, after whom Fort Sumter, famous in the Civil War, was named, provided a nucleus of resistance in areas that had supposedly been subdued.

In June 1780 Congress placed the highly regarded Horatio Gates in charge of a southern army consisting of the irregular militia units and a hard core of Continentals transferred from Washington's command. Gates encountered Cornwallis at Camden, South Carolina. Foolishly, he entrusted a key sector of his line to untrained militiamen, who promptly panicked when the British charged with fixed bayonets. Gates suffered heavy losses and had to fall back. Congress then recalled him, sensibly permitting Washington to replace him with General Nathanael Greene, a first-rate officer.

A band of militiamen had trapped a contingent of Tories at King's Mountain and forced its surrender. Greene, avoiding a major engagement with Cornwallis' superior numbers, divided his troops and staged a series of raids on scattered points. In January 1781, at the Battle of Cowpens in northwestern South Carolina, General Daniel Morgan inflicted a costly defeat on Colonel Banastre Tarleton, one of Cornwallis' best officers. Cornwallis pursued Morgan hotly, but the American rejoined Greene and at Guilford Court House they inflicted heavy losses on the British. Then Cornwallis withdrew to Wilmington, North Carolina, where he could rely on the fleet for support and reinforcements. Greene's Patriots quickly regained control of the Carolina back country.

Victory at Yorktown

Seeing no future in the Carolinas and unwilling to vegetate at Wilmington, Cornwallis marched north into Virginia, where he joined forces with troops under Benedict Arnold. (Disaffected by what he considered unjust criticism of his general-

■A French view of DeGrasse's fleet blockading the bay at Yorktown. The French ships, in the right foreground, have long pennants streaming from their masts.

ship, Arnold had sold out to the British in 1780. He intended to betray the bastion of West Point on the Hudson River. The scheme was foiled when incriminating papers were found on the person of a British spy, Major John André. Arnold fled to the British and André was hanged.) As in the Carolina campaign, the British had numerical superiority at first but lost it rapidly when local militia and Continental forces concentrated against them. Cornwallis soon discovered that Virginia Tories were of little help in such a situation. "When a Storm threatens, our friends disappear," he grumbled.

General Clinton ordered Cornwallis to take up a defensive position at Yorktown, where he could be supplied by sea. Cornwallis objected; Yorktown, he said, was "an unhealthy swamp" where his army would be "liable to become a prey to a Foreign enemy with a temporary superiority at sea." But Clinton insisted.

It was a terrible mistake. The British navy in American waters far outnumbered American and French vessels, but the Atlantic is wide, and in those days communication was slow. The French had a fleet in the West Indies under Admiral De Grasse and another squadron at Newport, Rhode Island, where a French army was stationed. In the summer of 1781 Washington, De Grasse, and the Comte de Rochambeau, commander of French land forces, designed and carried out with an efficiency unparalleled in 18th-century warfare a complex plan to bottle up Cornwallis.

The British navy in the West Indies and at New York might have forestalled this scheme had it moved promptly and in force. But Admiral Sir George Rodney sent only part of his Indies fleet. As a result De Grasse, after a battle with a British fleet commanded by Admiral Thomas Graves, won control of the Chesapeake and cut Cornwallis off from the sea.

The next move was up to Washington, and this was his finest hour as a commander. He desperately wanted to attack the British base at New York, but at the urging of Rochambeau he agreed instead to strike at Yorktown. After tricking Clinton into thinking he was going to strike at New York, he pushed boldly south. In early September he reached Yorktown and joined up with an army commanded by Lafayette and troops from De Grasse's fleet. He soon had nearly 17,000 French and American veterans in position.

Cornwallis was helpless. He held out until October 17 and then asked for terms. On the 19th more than 7,000 British soldiers marched out of their lines and laid down their arms while their band played "The World Turned Upside Down." Then the jubilant Lafayette ordered his military band to play "Yankee Doodle."

The Articles of Confederation

Although there were no major battles after Yorktown, the signing of a peace treaty lay well in the future. Meanwhile, the nation struggled to establish itself. A great forward step had been taken in 1781 when the Articles of Confederation were ratified. When the Articles were first submitted in November 1777, the states had offered a host of petty objections and suggestions. Congress sensibly stood firm, and most of them accepted the document. By the beginning of 1779 only Maryland had not ratified it.

Maryland held out in order to force a change that would authorize Congress to determine the western limits of states with land claims beyond the Appalachians. There were many good reasons why this should be done. The state claims to the west were overlapping, vaguely defined, and in some instances preposterous (see map, page 54). To have permitted a few states to monopolize the west would have unbalanced the union from the start.

Many people in the "landed" states recognized the justice of Maryland's suggestion, yet Maryland had a more selfish motive. Land speculators in the state had obtained from the Indians rights to large tracts in the Ohio Valley claimed by Virginia. Under Virginia, the Maryland titles would be worthless, but under a national administration they might be made to stand up.

Virginia resented its neighbor's efforts to grasp these valuable lands by indirection, but with the British about to advance into the state, Virginia agreed to surrender its claim to all land west and north of the Ohio River. It thwarted the Maryland speculators by insisting that all titles based on Indian purchases be declared void. Maryland then had no recourse but to ratify the Articles, and the new national government was officially proclaimed on March 1, 1781.

The Articles merely provided a legal basis for authority that the Continental Congress had already been exercising. Each state, regardless of size, was to have but one vote; the union was only a "league of friendship." Article II defined the limit of national power: "Each state retains its sovereignty, freedom, and independence, and every Power, Jurisdiction, and right, which is not by this confederation expressly delegated to the United States, in Congress assembled." Time would prove this an inadequate arrangement, chiefly because the central government had no way of enforcing its authority. As the historian David Ramsay explained in 1789, "No coercive power was given to the general government, nor was it invested with any legislative power over individuals."

However, the central government had been strong enough to carry on the war, and this charter added to its prestige. At about the same time Congress increased its effectiveness by establishing departments of Foreign Affairs, War, and Finance, with individual heads responsible to it. The most important of the new department heads was the superintendent of finance, a Philadelphia merchant named Robert Morris. When Morris took office, the Continental dollar was worthless, the system of supplying the army chaotic, the credit of the government exhausted. He set up an efficient method of obtaining food and uniforms for the army, persuaded Congress to charter a national Bank of North America, and somehow—aided by the slackening of military activity after Yorktown—got the country back on a specie basis. New foreign loans were obtained, partly because Morris' efficiency and industry inspired confidence.

The Peace of Paris

These developments strengthened the new United States, but the event that confirmed its existence was the signing of a peace treaty with Great Britain. Yorktown had been only one of a string of defeats suffered by British arms in the Mediterranean, the West Indies, Africa, and Asia. The national debt had doubled again since 1775. In March 1782 Lord North resigned after Parliament renounced all further efforts to coerce the colonies. At once the new ministry of Lord Rockingham attempted to negotiate a peace settlement with America.

The problem of peacemaking was complicated. The United States and France had pledged not to make a separate peace. Spain, at war with Great Britain since 1779, was allied with France but not with America. Although eager to profit at British expense, the Spanish hoped to limit American expansion beyond the Appalachians, for they had ambitions of their own in the eastern half of the Mississippi Valley. France, while ready enough to see America independent, did not want the new country to become *too* powerful; in a conflict of interest between America and Spain, France tended to support Spain.

The Continental Congress, grateful for French aid, overestimated both French power and French loyalty to America. In 1779 it had appointed John Adams minister plenipotentiary to conduct peace negotiations. Almost from the moment of his arrival in Paris, Adams came into conflict with Foreign Minister Vergennes. "He means to keep his hand under our chin to prevent us from drowning, but not to lift our head out of the water," the shrewd Adams noted. Vergennes was subtle, intelligent, and unscrupulous. When he discovered that Adams was neither pliable nor naive, he used his influence to have him replaced by a five-man commission, consisting of—in addition to Adams—Franklin, Jefferson, John Jay, and Henry Laurens. Congress went so far as to instruct the commissioners to rely entirely upon the advice of Vergennes in negotiations, subject only to the limitation that they must hold out at all costs for independence. This occurred in June 1781.

When the commissioners discovered that Vergennes was not the perfect friend of America that Congress believed him to be, they did not hesitate to violate their instructions.* Franklin, perhaps because as a famous scientist and sage he was wined and dined by the cream of Paris and petted and fussed over by some of the city's most beautiful women, was neither aggressive nor suspicious enough to press fully the American point of view. John Jay, who had spent two years dealing with Spanish duplicity as unacknowledged American minister in Madrid, was more tough-minded. When he realized that Spain and France were less than entirely committed to American interests, he

---

*Jefferson did not take part in the negotiations, and Adams and Laurens played relatively minor roles. Franklin and Jay did most of the work of drafting the treaty.

■ To his niece, Franklin wrote from Paris: "Somebody, it seems, gave it out that I lov'd Ladies; and then every body presented me their ladies . . ." Here, one of the aristocratic French "Ladies" is crowning Franklin with a hero's laurel wreath.

took Franklin aside and convinced him they must stop consulting Vergennes at every step. They hinted to the British representative, Richard Oswald, that they would consider a separate peace if it were a generous one and suggested that Great Britain would be far better off with America, a nation that favored free trade, in control of the trans-Appalachian region than with a mercantilist power like Spain.

The British government reacted favorably, authorizing Oswald "to treat with the Commissioners appointed by the Colonys, under the title of Thirteen United States." Soon the Americans were deep in negotiations with Oswald. They told Vergennes what they were doing but did not discuss details.

Oswald was cooperative, and the Americans drove a hard bargain. One scrap of conversation reveals the tenor of the talks.

OSWALD: We can never be such damned sots as to disturb you.

ADAMS: Thank you. . . . But nations don't feel as you and I do, and your nation, when it gets a little refreshed from the fatigues of the war, and when men and money become plentiful, and allies at hand, will not feel as it does now.

OSWALD: We can never be such damned sots as to think of differing again with you.

ADAMS: Why, in truth I have never been able to comprehend the reason why you ever thought of differing with us.

By the end of November 1782 a preliminary treaty had been signed. "His Britannic Majesty," Article I began, "acknowledges the said United States . . . to be free, sovereign and independent States." Other terms were equally in line with American hopes and objectives. The boundaries of the nation were set at the Great Lakes, the Mississippi River, and 31° north latitude (roughly the northern boundary of Florida). Britain recognized the right of Americans to take fish on the Grand Banks off Newfoundland and—far more important—to dry and cure their catch on unsettled beaches in Labrador and Nova Scotia. The British agreed to withdraw their troops from American soil "with all convenient speed." Where the touchy problem of Tory property seized during the Revolution was concerned, the Americans agreed only that Congress would "earnestly recommend" that the states "provide for the restitution of all estates, rights and properties which have been confiscated." They promised to prevent further property confiscation and prosecutions of Tories—certainly a wise as well as a humane policy—and they agreed not to impede the collection of debts owed British subjects. Vergennes was flabbergasted by the success of the Americans. "The English buy the peace more than they make it," he wrote. "Their concessions . . . exceed all that I should have thought possible."

The American commissioners obtained favorable terms because they were shrewd diplomats, and because of the rivalries that existed among the great European powers. In the last analysis Britain preferred to have a weak nation of English-speaking people in command of the Mississippi Valley rather than France or Spain. From their experience at the peace talks, the American leaders learned the importance of playing one power against another without committing themselves completely to any.

This policy became the basis of what later was known as American isolationism, though in the 1780s it was anything but that. It demanded constant contact with European affairs and skill at adjusting policies to changes in the European balance of power. And it enabled the United States, a young and relatively feeble country, to grow and prosper.

Growth of American Nationalism

American independence and control of a wide and rich domain were the most obvious results of the Revolution. Changes in the structure of society, as we have seen, were relatively minor. Economic developments, such as the growth of new trade connections and the expansion of manufacturing in an effort to replace British goods, were of only modest significance. By far the most important so-

cial and economic changes involved the Tories and were thus by-products of the political revolution rather than a determined reorganization of a people's way of life.

There was another important result of the Revolution: the growth of American nationalism. Most modern revolutions have been *caused* by nationalism and have *resulted* in independence. In the case of the American Revolution the desire to be free antedated any very intense national feeling. The colonies entered into a political union not because they felt an overwhelming desire to bring all Americans under one rule but because unity offered the only hope of winning a war against Great Britain. That they remained united after throwing off British rule reflects the degree to which nationalism had developed during the conflict.

By the middle of the 18th century the colonists had begun to think of themselves as a separate society distinct from Europe and even from Britain. Benjamin Franklin described himself not as a British subject but as "an American subject of the King," and in 1750 a Boston newspaper could urge its readers to drink "American" beer in order to free themselves from being "beholden to Foreigners" for their alcoholic beverages. Little political nationalism existed before the Revolution, however. Local ties remained predominant. A few might say, with Patrick Henry in 1774, "The distinctions between Virginians, Pennsylvanians, New Yorkers, and New Englanders are no more. I am not a Virginian, but an American." But such people were rare before the final break with Great Britain.

The new nationalism rose from a number of sources and expressed itself in different ways. Common sacrifices in war certainly played a part; the soldiers of the Continental Army fought in the summer heat of the Carolinas for the same cause that had led them to brave the ice floes of the Delaware in order to surprise the Hessians. Such men lost interest in state boundary lines; they became Americans. John Marshall of Fauquier County, Virginia, for example, was a 20-year-old militiaman in 1775. The next year he joined the Continental Army. He served in Pennsylvania, New Jersey, and New York and endured the winter of 1777–1778 at Valley Forge. "I found myself associated with brave men from different states who were risking life and everything valuable in a common cause," he later wrote. "I was confirmed in the habit of considering America as my country and Congress as my government." Andrew Jackson, child of the Carolina frontier, was only 9 when the Revolution broke out. One brother was killed in battle, another died as a result of untreated wounds. Young Andrew took up arms and was captured by the Redcoats. A British officer ordered Jackson to black his boots and, when the boy refused, struck him across the face with the flat of his sword. Jackson bore the scar to his grave—and became an ardent nationalist on the spot. He and Marshall had very different ideas and came to be bitter enemies in later life. Nevertheless they were both American nationalists—and for the same reason.

Civilians as well as soldiers reacted in this way. A Carolina farmer whose home and barn were protected against British looters by men who spoke with the harsh nasal twang of New England adopted a broader outlook toward politics. When the news came that thousands of Redcoats had stacked their arms in defeat after Yorktown, few people cared what state or section had made the victory possible—it was an American triumph.

The war caused many people to move from place to place. Soldiers traveled as the tide of war fluctuated; so too—far more than in earlier times—did prominent leaders. Members of Congress from every state had to travel to Philadelphia; in the process they saw much of the country and the people who inhabited it. Listening to their fellows and serving with them on committees almost inevitably broadened these men, most of them highly influential in their local communities.

With its 13 stars and 13 stripes representing the states, the American flag symbolized national unity and reflected the common feeling that such a symbol was necessary. After much experimentation (one version pictured the Union as a snake made up of 13 segments), the Continental Congress adopted the basic pattern in June 1777.

Certain practical problems that demanded common solutions also drew the states together. No one seriously considered having 13 postal systems or 13 sets of diplomatic representatives abroad. Every new diplomatic appointment, every treaty of friendship or commerce signed, committed all to a common policy and thus bound them more closely together. And economic developments had

a unifying effect. Cutting off English goods encouraged manufacturing, making America more self-sufficient and stimulating both interstate trade and national pride.

The Great Land Ordinances

The western lands, which had divided the states in the beginning, became a force for unity once they had been ceded to the national government. Everyone realized what a priceless national asset they were, and while many greedily sought to possess them by fair means or foul, all now understood that no one state could determine the future of the west.

The politicians argued hotly about how these lands should be developed. Some advocated selling the land in township units in the traditional New England manner to groups or companies; others favored letting individual pioneers stake out farms in the helter-skelter manner common in the colonial south. The decision was a compromise. The Land Ordinance of 1785 provided for surveying western territories into six-mile-square townships before sale. Every other township was to be further subdivided into 36 sections of 640 acres (one square mile) each. The land was sold at auction at a minimum price of one dollar an acre. The law favored speculative land-development companies, for even the 640-acre units were far too large and expensive for the typical frontier family. But the fact that the land was to be surveyed and sold by the central government was a nationalizing force. Congress set aside the sixteenth section of every township for the maintenance of schools, another important and farsighted decision.

Still more significant was the Northwest Ordinance of 1787, which established governments for the west. As early as 1780 Congress had resolved that all lands ceded to the nation by the states should be "formed into distinct republican States" with "the same rights of sovereignty, freedom and independence" as the original 13. In 1784 a committee headed by Thomas Jefferson worked out a plan for doing this, and in 1787 it was enacted into law. The area bounded by the Ohio, the Mississippi, and the Great Lakes was to be carved into not less than three or more than five territories. Until the adult male population of the entire area

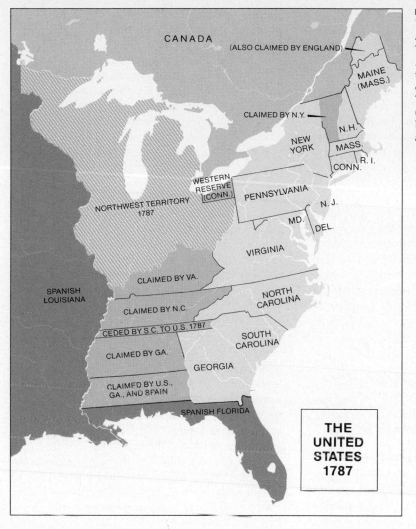

CANADA
(ALSO CLAIMED BY ENGLAND)

MAINE
(MASS.)

CLAIMED BY N.Y.

N.H.

NEW
YORK

MASS.

R. I.

CONN.

WESTERN
RESERVE
(CONN.)

PENNSYLVANIA

N. J.

NORTHWEST TERRITORY
1787

MD.

DEL.

VIRGINIA

CLAIMED BY VA.

SPANISH
LOUISIANA

CLAIMED BY N.C.

NORTH
CAROLINA

CEDED BY S.C. TO U.S. 1787

CLAIMED BY GA.

SOUTH
CAROLINA

CLAIMED BY U.S.,
GA., AND SPAIN

GEORGIA

SPANISH FLORIDA

**THE
UNITED
STATES
1787**

■ The giving up by New York and Virginia of their claims to the vast area that became the Northwest Territory set a precedent for trans-Appalachian land policy. By 1802 the various state claims had been ceded to the national government. The original Northwest Territory (the Old Northwest) was bounded by the Ohio River, the Mississippi, and the Great Lakes.

reached 5,000, it was to be ruled by a governor and three judges, all appointed by Congress. Acting together, these officials would make and enforce the necessary laws. When 5,000 men of voting age had settled in the territory, the ordinance authorized them to elect a legislature and send a nonvoting delegate to Congress. Finally, when 60,000 persons had settled in any one of the political subdivisions, it was to become a state. It could draft a constitution and operate in any way it wished, save that the government had to be "republican" and that slavery was prohibited.

Seldom has a legislative body acted more wisely. That the western districts must become states everyone conceded from the start. The peo-

ple had had their fill of colonialism under British rule, and the rebellious temper of frontier settlers made it impossible even to consider maintaining the west in a dependent status. (When North Carolina ceded its trans-Appalachian lands to the United States in 1784, the settlers there, uncertain how they would fare under federal rule, hastily organized an extralegal "State of Franklin," and it was not until 1789 that the national government obtained control.) On the other hand, it would have been unfair to turn the territories over to the first-comers, who would have been unable to manage such large domains and who would surely have taken advantage of their priority to dictate to later arrivals. A period of tutelage was necessary, a period when the "mother country" must guide and nourish its growing offspring.

Thus the intermediate territorial governments corresponded almost exactly to the governments of British royal colonies. The appointed governors could veto acts of the assemblies and could "convene, prorogue, and dissolve" them at their discretion. The territorial delegates to Congress were not unlike colonial agents. Yet it was vital that this intermediate stage end and that its end be determined in advance so that no argument could develop over when the territory was ready for statehood.

The system worked well and was applied to nearly all the regions absorbed by the nation as it advanced westward. Together with the Ordinance of 1785, which branded its checkerboard pattern on the physical shape of the west, this law gave the growing country a unity essential to the growth of a national spirit.

National Heroes

The Revolution further fostered nationalism by giving the people their first commonly revered heroes. Benjamin Franklin was widely known before the break with Great Britain through his experiments with electricity, his immensely successful *Poor Richard's Almanack,* and his invention of the Franklin stove. His staunch support of the Patriot cause, his work in the Continental Congress, and his diplomatic successes in France, where he was extravagantly admired, added to his fame. Franklin demonstrated, to Europeans and to Americans themselves, that all Americans need not be ignorant rustics.

Thomas Jefferson was also a national figure by the 1780s. His writing of the Declaration of Independence (to which, it will be recalled, Franklin contributed) made him a hero to all Americans. When in retrospect the boldness of the document and its felicity of expression could be fully appreciated, and when the success of the revolt made it even more significant, the Declaration and its author were revered in every state.

Most notable of all was Washington, "the chief human symbol of a common Americanism." Stern, cold, inarticulate, the great Virginian did not seem a likely candidate for hero worship. Yet he had qualities that made people name babies after him and call him "the Father of his Country" long before the war was won: his personal sacrifices in the cause of independence, his integrity, his devotion to duty, his commanding presence, and above all, perhaps, his obvious desire to retire to his Mount Vernon estate (for many Americans feared *any* powerful leader and worried lest Washington seek to become a dictator). He was, one contemporary explained, "discreet and Virtuous, no harum Starum ranting Swearing fellow but Sober, steady, and Calm."

As a general, Washington was not a brilliant strategist like Napoleon, although his design for the complicated Yorktown campaign was superb. Neither was he a tactician of the quality of Caesar or Robert E. Lee. His lack of genius made his achievements all the more impressive. He held his forces together in adversity, avoiding both useless slaughter and catastrophic defeat. He learned from experience and won the respect—if not the love—of his men and the cooperation of Congress and his French allies. People of all sections, from every walk of life, looked upon Washington as the embodiment of American virtues: a man of deeds rather than words; a man of substance accustomed to luxury yet capable of enduring great hardships stoically and as much at home in the wilderness as an Indian; a bold Patriot, quick to take arms against British tyranny, yet eminently respectable. The Revolution might have been won without Washington, but it is unlikely that the free United States would have become so easily a true nation had he not existed.

A National Culture

Breaking away from Great Britain accentuated certain trends toward social and intellectual independence and strengthened the national desire to create an *American* culture. The Anglican church in America had to form a new organization once the connection with the Crown was severed; in 1786 it became the Protestant Episcopal church. The Dutch and German Reformed churches also became independent of their European connections. Roman Catholics in America had been under the administration of the vicar apostolic of England; after the Revolution Father John Carroll of Baltimore assumed these duties, and in 1789 he became the first American Roman Catholic bishop.

The impact of post-Revolutionary nationalism on American education was best reflected in the immense success of the textbooks of Noah Webster, later famous for his American dictionary. The first of these, the famous *Spelling Book,* which appeared in 1783 when Webster was a young schoolteacher in Goshen, New York, emphasized American forms and usage and contained a patriotic preface urging Americans to pay proper respect to their own literature. Webster's *Reader,* published shortly thereafter, included selections from the speeches of Revolutionary leaders who, according to the compiler, were the equals of Cicero and Demosthenes as orators. Some 15 million copies of the *Speller* were sold in the next five decades, several times that number by 1900. The *Reader* was also a continuing best seller.

Webster's work was not the only sign of nationalism in education. In 1787 John M'Culloch published the first American history textbook. The colleges saw a great outburst of patriotic spirit. King's College (founded in 1754) received a new name, Columbia, in 1784.* Everywhere it was recognized that the republic required educated and cultivated leaders. Many new colleges were founded in the two decades or so following the Revolution, among them the future state universities of Maryland, Georgia, South Carolina, and North Carolina, and such other institutions as Georgetown, St. John's of Annapolis, Williams, and Bowdoin.

Nationalism affected the arts and sciences in the

years after the Revolution. Jedidiah Morse's popular *American Geography* (1789) was a paean in praise of the "astonishing" progress of the country, all the result of the "natural genius of Americans." The American Academy of Arts and Sciences, founded at Boston during the Revolution, was created "to advance the interest, honor, dignity and happiness of a free, independent and virtuous people."

American painters and writers of the period usually chose extremely patriotic themes. John Trumbull helped capture Dorchester Heights and force the evacuation of Boston, took part in the defense of northern New York against Burgoyne, and fought in Pennsylvania and Rhode Island. When he took up painting he produced such pictures as *The Battle of Bunker's Hill, The Surrender of Lord Cornwallis at Yorktown,* and *The Declaration of Independence.* Trumbull referred to these and similar efforts as his "national work." Joel Barlow intended his *Vision of Columbus,* written between 1779 and 1787, to prove that America was "the noblest and most elevated part of the earth." Royall Tyler's play *The Contrast,* which was produced in New York in 1787, compared American virtue (the hero was called Colonel Manly) with British vice and contained such chauvinistic lines as:

Why should our thoughts to distant countries roam
When each refinement may be found at home?

The United States in the 1780s was far from being the powerful centralized nation it has since become. Probably most citizens still gave their first loyalty to their own states. In certain important respects the Confederation was pitifully ineffectual. However, people were increasingly aware of their common interests and increasingly proud of their common heritage. The motto of the new nation, *E pluribus unum*—"from many, one"—perfectly describes a process that was rapidly taking place in the years after Yorktown.

---

*Queen's College (founded in 1766) was not renamed Rutgers until 1825. The other colleges existing at the time of the Revolution were Harvard and William and Mary, both founded in the 17th century; Yale (1701); the College of New Jersey, now Princeton (1746); Franklin's Academy, now the University of Pennsylvania (1751); Rhode Island, now Brown (1764); and Dartmouth (1769).

SUPPLEMENTARY READING
Titles marked with an asterisk have been published in paperback

The best brief survey of the Revolutionary years is E. S. Morgan, **The Birth of the Republic*** (1956). A more detailed (and very lively) treatment is J. C. Miller, **Tri-**

umph of Freedom* (1948). Don Higgenbotham, **The War of American Independence*** (1971), provides an up-to-date account of the military aspects of the Revolution and Charles Royster, **A Revolutionary People at War** (1979), describes the attitudes of soldiers and civilians toward the army. H. S. Commager and R. B. Morris (eds.), **The Spirit of Seventy-Six** (1958), is a rich collection of source materials. For Washington's role, see D. S. Freeman, **George Washington** (1948–1957), and C. P. Nettels, **George Washington and American Independence** (1951).

On the Continental Congress and the Articles of Confederation, see E. C. Burnett, **The Continental Congress*** (1941), and two books by Merrill Jensen, **The Articles of Confederation*** (1940) and **The New Nation*** (1950). Eric Foner, **Tom Paine and Revolutionary America*** (1976), is an excellent brief biography. The classic analysis of the Declaration of Independence is C. L. Becker, **The Declaration of Independence*** (1922). Jefferson's ideas are thoughtfully analyzed in Gilbert Chinard, **Thomas Jefferson: The Apostle of Americanism*** (1929), and Adrienne Koch, **Jefferson and Madison*** (1950).

The early history of the state governments is covered in Elisha P. Douglass, **Rebels and Democrats*** (1955), but Allan Nevins, **The American States During and After the Revolution** (1924), is still indispensable. The development of political ideas is admirably described and analyzed in G. S. Wood, **The Creation of the American Republic*** (1969), and in D. J. Boorstin, **The Genius of American Politics*** (1953). The financial problems of this period are covered in E. J. Ferguson, **The Power of the Purse*** (1968), and Clarence Ver Steeg, **Robert Morris, Revolutionary Financier** (1954). For federal policy toward western lands, see R. M. Robbins, **Our Landed Heritage*** (1942), and W. D. Pattison, **The Beginnings of the American Rectangular Land Survey** (1957).

The classic account of the social and economic effects of the Revolution is J. F. Jameson, **The American Revolution Considered as a Social Movement*** (1926). E. B. Greene, **The Revolutionary Generation** (1943), contains a wealth of material on social and economic developments. R. E. Brown takes issue with Jameson's view in **Middle-Class Democracy and the Revolution in Massachusetts** (1955), as does R. P. McCormick, **Experiment in Independence: New Jersey in the Critical Period** (1950). J. T. Main, **The Social Structure of Revolutionary America*** (1965), provides a general picture against which to evaluate the views of Jameson and his critics. On the Tories, see W. H. Nelson, **The American Tory*** (1962), M. B. Norton, **The British-Americans** (1972), R. M. Calhoun, **The Loyalists in Revolutionary America** (1973), and Wallace Brown, **The King's Friends** (1965). P. H. Smith, **Loyalists and Redcoats*** (1965), treats the fumbling efforts of the British to make use of their American supporters. The effects of the Revolution on slavery are treated in W. D. Jordan, **White Over Black*** (1968), Arthur Zilversmit, **The First Emancipation: The Abolition of Slavery in the North*** (1967), and Benjamin Quarles, **The Negro in the American Revolution*** (1961). L. K. Kerber, **Women of the Republic** (1980), and M. B. Norton, **Liberty's Daughters** (1980), discuss the effects of the Revolution on women.

On the diplomacy of the Revolution, see S. F. Bemis, **The Diplomacy of the American Revolution*** (1935). The definitive account of the peace treaty is R. B. Morris, **The Peacemakers*** (1965).

On the emergence of American nationalism and cultural history generally, see E. B. Greene's **Revolutionary Generation** and R. B. Nye, **The Cultural Life of the New Nation*** (1960). R. L. Merritt, **Symbols of American Community** (1966), concludes from a study of colonial newspapers that a sense of national identity was well developed before 1763. P. C. Nagel, **One Nation Indivisible: The Union in American Thought** (1964), discusses the various views of the nature of the Union advanced in this period, and Paul Varg, **Foreign Policies of the Founding Fathers** (1963), is instructive.

■ This panorama of the Van Bergen farm in New York's Catskill Mountains was painted by an unknown artist about 1735. The entire picture (top) graced the farm's living-room mantel. The enlarged sections (above) show more clearly details of the farm's human and animal inhabitants.

Portfolio Two

COLONIAL LIFE

British America was overwhelmingly rural. The colonial farm, not the bustling seaport, sprawling plantation, or picturesque town, was the center and symbol of colonial life. Farms varied, of course, from frontier clearings to elegant estates, and life-styles varied accordingly. The farm pictured here represents the large middle rank: a solid house of modest proportions, one or more barns and other outbuildings, a numerous family of adults, children, servants, and possibly one or more slaves, and enough land and animals to produce in normal years an adequate, perhaps bountiful, harvest. Most of life's major events occurred on the farm: birth, youth, education (a little book-learning and a lot of social and occupational training), marriage, old age, and death. Occasional trips to nearby towns and a rare excursion to a colonial city or even back to England might interrupt the routine, especially among upperclass males. But by and large, colonial life—at least in Britain's mainland colonies that sprouted along the eastern seaboard in the 17th and 18th centuries—was country life, with all its economic and social implications.

A few Americans—less than 10 percent—lived in cities, but even urban dwellers were never far from the countryside, and many owned livestock and garden plots. Such rural dominance partly explains the pride some Americans took in the success of colonial farming and in supposedly rural virtues. "Everywhere," an 18th-century writer boasted after a trip through the northern colonies, "you saw good houses, well-fenced fields, ample barns, large orchards . . . . Everywhere, you find the strongest marks of industry, activity, and boldness." But city folk could point to signs of their own industry, activity, and boldness. Colonial life partook of town as well as country, even if the latter held greater sway.

Beginnings

In their more pessimistic moods, 17th-century colonists viewed America as "a hideous and desolate wilderness, full of wild beasts and wild men." Early settlers therefore clustered together in fortified outposts where they could aid and protect each other. There they began the difficult and often dangerous first steps toward "taming" the wilderness: felling trees, clearing fields, building shelters, and raising palisades against the Indians, who rightly resented encroachments on their lands. From Virginia and Maryland on Chesapeake Bay to Plymouth and Massachusetts in New England and later to the Carolinas in the deep South, the situation was almost the same. Quasi-military outposts, initially inhabited mostly by men but increasingly too by women and children, imposed their architecture, customs, and ideas on the American landscape.

This modern painting shows Wolstenholme Towne, part of the larger plantation of Martin's Hundred on the James River in Virginia. The community lasted only three years, from 1619 to its destruction by Indians in 1622. Although the details of the earliest settlements are uncertain, this conjectural reconstruction is based on meticulous archeological and historical research. Most early American settlements, and many later frontier outposts, must have resembled this scene.

Life in such crude communities was often bitter, painful, and short as diseases, weather, and enemies—both native and European—took heavy tolls. But the lure of cheap land, high wages, and freedom from many of Europe's restraints kept the flow of immigrants coming.

■ Painting by Richard Schlecht © National Geographic Society.

■ Few colonial families bothered to embroider elaborate "family trees" like the Copps of Stonington, Connecticut (below), but virtually everyone knew by heart several generations of his own tree or could find them inscribed in the family Bible. The Copp tree illustrates a nuclear family of parents and their children. As the names and dates reveal, Samuel Copp married Dolley Brown in December of 1769, when he was 26, she 25—slightly above the average age of marriage for an 18th-century couple but well within the "normal" range. Their first child was born, almost predictably, 10 months later. The Copps had eight more children (slightly above the average number) who were born, according to colonial custom, at approximately two-year intervals. The 42-month gap between Esther's birth and Nancy's suggests that there may have been one or more miscarriages; at the time, Mrs. Copp was about 40 years old. This tree, embroidered some time after Betsey's death in 1794, records that Samuel and Dolley still had five living daughters and three sons, ranging in age from 7 to 24. The ornate needlework and "hearts and flowers" motifs imply a close, affectionate family.

■ The family of Dr. Samuel Cheney and his wife, Rebecca, gathered for this portrait by an unknown artist in the late 18th or early 19th century. Like the Copp family (opposite page), the Cheneys appear to be fairly representative, although their ability to afford a professional portrait and their formal clothing mark them among the upper class. Probably three generations are pictured here. Family genealogies indicate that Samuel's first wife had seven children, his second wife (Rebecca) none. The youngest children are presumably Rebecca's step grandchildren by Samuel's eldest son or daughter.

Family

According to a Puritan clergyman, God "chose to lay the foundations of both State and Church, in a family, making that the Mother Hive out of which both swarms of State and Church, issued forth." Non-Puritans would have said it differently, but virtually all colonists agreed on the fundamental premise: that families—not individuals—were the basic units of society and the core of political and religious life.

Although there were differences here and there throughout the 17th century and well into the 18th, the pattern of family life was fairly consistent. Fathers ruled; wives were important helpmates but clearly subordinate, and children were trained to be obedient and deferential. The family was expected to be orderly, disciplined, and productive. A Puritan pronouncement of 1679 insisted that "Most of the evils that abound amongst us, proceed from defects as to family government." When the family failed, society failed.

Parental authority began to wane in the middle of the 18th century. A father's influence over the selection of his children's mates, occupations, and places of residence diminished, as did the influence of nonparental kin such as grandparents, uncles, aunts, cousins, and siblings. The nuclear family became increasingly autonomous, bonds between its members became more affectionate and sentimental.

■ Infant and childhood deaths were frequent tragedies of colonial life. Families often lost several children to disease, accidents, or medical ignorance, and women often succumbed to the hazards of childbirth. The tombstone above tells one family's poignant story.

Servants and Slaves

"Servants," a Virginian wrote in 1705, "they distinguish by the Names of Slaves for Life, and Servants for a time." He went on to describe the many legal protections enjoyed by servants against abusive masters and provisions for "freedom dues" upon completion of their contracted time. He said nothing about the rights of slaves. They had none.

By 1775, Africans imported to British America and their descendants comprised a fifth of the colonial population. They performed far more than a fifth of the arduous labor. On southern farms they did most of the agricultural and artisan work; in northern seaports they did much of the labor at wharves and warehouses and some of the craft work as well. Every colony had slaves, and in many areas blacks far outnumbered whites. Although they brought important skills and made valuable contributions to colonial culture, few blacks gained freedom and fewer still had legal or political rights.

White servants were sometimes treated as badly as—perhaps worse than—most slaves, but at least they could look forward to eventual freedom. Often, like slaves, they were sold on arrival. "Many parents must sell and trade away their children," lamented a German immigrant, "like so many head of cattle. . . . It often happens that such parents and children, after leaving the ship, do not see each other again for many years, perhaps no more in all their lives." Frequent servant complaints and notices of runaways suggest that conditions were unbearable to many indentured servants. Still, most white Americans swapped several years of their labor for the passage from Europe. The prize seemed worth the price. One immigrant assured his wife, who lived on an island off the Scottish coast, "I yet hope . . . to make you a Virginian Lady among the woods of America which is by far more pleasent than the roaring of the raging seas round abo't Zetland. And yet to make you eat more wheat Bread in your old age than what you have done in your Youth."

■ Most servants signed contracts, usually called "indentures," that specified the length of service and some of the conditions governing both master and servant. So common was indentured servitude that forms, such as the one here, were widely used. Immigrants who arrived without such documents and could not pay the cost of their passage served the number of years required by "the Custom of the Country," usually not more than five years for adults and to age 21 (sometimes 24) for minors.

■ This rare portrait of a colonial servant is known only as "Jersey Nanny." It was engraved in 1748 and presumably shows a northern slave woman who had become an integral part of a white family.

■ Colonial newspapers abounded in ads such as those pictured at left. The lower one offers servants for sale; the ad above it seeks the return of a runaway. Despite detailed descriptions of the fugitives, few were caught. The land was too vast, disguises too handy, and newspapers too scarce.

■ Survivors of the infamous "middle passage" from Africa to America faced the trauma of the slave auction, such as the one shown in this early 19th-century engraving. Families were often separated because buyers selected slaves to fit the needs of the plantation and were rarely motivated by humane concerns.

Housing

"The farmers' houses," observed a French immigrant to Virginia in 1687, "are built entirely of wood, the roofs being made of small boards of chestnut as are also the walls. Those who have some means, cover them inside with a coating of mortar. . . . They build also a separate kitchen, a separate house for Christian [indentured] slaves, one for negro slaves, and several to dry the tobacco, so that when you come to the house of a person of some means, you think you are entering a fairly large village."

This idyllic description of a southern plantation contrasts sharply with a report of Jamestown in 1608. The colonists then were "utterly destitute of houses, not one as yet built, so that they lodged in cabbins and holes within the grounde." Even their "cabbins" were flimsy rows of upright stakes interwoven with smaller sticks and plastered with mud or clay. Roofs were made of turf or straw. Elsewhere, early settlers tried other forms of shelter, including wigwams (oblong, with oval roofs), dugouts, and hastily built cottages meant to last only a few years. Survival, not comfort, was their goal.

As time and circumstances permitted, colonists fashioned more durable dwellings. Almost always their models were the homes they had known in Europe—either their own or those they aspired to. As early as the 1650s, a New Englander could announce that "the Lord hath been pleased to turn all the wigwams, huts, and hovels the English dwelt in at their first coming, into orderly, fair, and well-built houses." Other writers compared colonial homes favorably to London houses. But most colonists lived in modest structures, either in the country or in the seaboard cities.

ca. 1670

ca. 1720

ca. 1760

■ Houses seldom remain unchanged. The house above, owned by the Mott family of Portsmouth, Rhode Island, grew during its first century from a fairly modest building with a small ell to a substantial boxlike building with a rear lean-to. At each stage it was thoroughly "colonial."

In colonial America, as in almost any time and place, the quality and style of a house reflected its owners' economic circumstances, ethnic background, and aesthetic taste. Pictured below is the principal room of a middle-class home in Delaware, built about 1740. The exterior was made of squared logs—a Swedish contribution to American architecture that spread very slowly among other nationalities in the British colonies. The interior, however, closely resembles most small colonial homes. The Virginia plantation "Greenway" (left), suggests a much higher level of wealth and a much larger family. This estate, later owned by President John Tyler, is typical of southern plantations in its large but not ostentatious main house and its numerous outbuildings. Far different were the slave cabins (upper left) of a South Carolina plantation. Although they provided minimum shelter, they offered no opportunity for the occupants to express their individual preferences in location or design. Those pictured appear to have been better than average.

■ Tobacco

■ Sassafras

Farming

"Some few towns excepted," observed an American in the 1770s, "we are all tillers of the earth." Year in and year out, the lives of most colonists—including the women and children of the household as well as servants or slaves—were guided by nature's daily and yearly rhythms as they fed and milked animals, planted seeds, tended fields, and harvested crops. Even leisure time on the farm was dictated more by nature's demands than by the farmers' wishes.

Early 17th-century farmers experimented eagerly with native and imported plants as they searched for crops that would thrive in America and command high prices in Europe. Efforts to raise mulberry trees for silk production were generally unsuccessful, as were most attempts to grow citrus fruits, figs, and other Mediterranean crops. But sassafras was an early and easy success because it was thought to cure syphilis and other ailments and because the tree grew wild along the eastern seaboard. When the medicinal value of sassafras proved illusory, other crops had to be found; most required far more land and labor.

From the Indians, colonists learned about maize, potatoes, squash, and other vegetables that flourished in American soil and quickly became the American farmer's subsistence crops. (Such foodstuffs were generally too perishable for export except to nearby markets; seeds, however,

■ Sugar farming in the West Indies.

■ An 18th-century German plow from New York.

■ Potatoes   ■ Maize

were soon taken to Europe, Africa, and Asia where they made major contributions to "Old World" agriculture.) Colonists learned too about tobacco, which rapidly became the American farmer's most prevalent crop. *American Husbandry* (1774), an exhaustive treatise on colonial farming, reported that tobacco was "cultivated in all parts of North America, from Quebec to Carolina, and even the West Indies. . . . In Maryland, Virginia, and North Carolina . . . it is of immense consequence." Pictured above are illustrations from *The Herbal, or Generall Historie of Plants* (1633 edition) by John Gerard, an English physician and horticulturalist, whose book helped Europeans learn about American plants.

South of the Chesapeake Bay region other cash crops fared better than tobacco: sugar in the West Indies, rice in South Carolina, and indigo (after 1745) in North Carolina. Large plantations, worked by slaves, made handsome profits for their owners, but even in the south most settlers toiled on small farms from sunup to sundown alongside their one or two bond servants. From Pennsylvania northward, most farms were small and most laborers free. The family—father, mother, children, and hired hands—worked together to raise a variety of crops, especially wheat and vegetables; they were generally well fed and mildly prosperous.

■ Slash-and-burn farming on the colonial frontier.

■ Moses Levy (1665–1728), a prominent New York merchant, emigrated from England in 1702 and soon owned several ships that shuttled between American, West Indian, and European ports. Their cargoes were basic, essential goods—bread, tea, lumber, and the like—but profitable. Levy and his relatives formed the nucleus of a prosperous Jewish community in New York that spread during the 18th century to Newport, Philadelphia, and Baltimore. Moses Levy was in many ways a typical colonial merchant: his business grew as the colonies expanded and as his own business acumen led him into lucrative ventures and profitable connections with other merchants.

■ By the eve of the American Revolution, Philadelphia was a thriving port of ca. 30,000 inhabitants, the largest city in British America and the second largest in the British Empire. Almost from its founding in 1682, Pennsylvania's principal community was a major commercial center. This view of the city in 1720 shows its remarkable growth in less than forty years. Like other colonial ports, Philadelphia served simultaneously as its region's entrance point for American and European goods and as the hinterland's window to the outside world.

■ In 1653 Boston merchant Robert Keayne observed in his will that a marketplace in Boston would be "useful for the country people that come with their provisions for the supply of the town, that they may have a place to sit dry in and warm both in cold, rain, and dirty weather, and may have a place to leave their corn or any other things that they cannot sell safe till they come again." Keayne also wanted the building to have meeting rooms and a library for lawmakers, clergymen, and soldiers—a true "Town House." Keayne's bequest of £300 underwrote the construction of the building shown here in a modern drawing based on the original specifications. Keayne's Town House served its intended purposes from 1658 to 1711.

Commerce

In 1740, an English official reported that "the British Empire of America is of inestimable value to the Nation of Great Britain"; the colonies employed over 3,000 ships and 25,000 sailors in the fishing trade alone. And as the mother country prospered, so did the colonies.

Rhode Island's commerce was representative at least of the northern provinces. A visitor in 1760 observed that its merchants imported "from Great Britain, dry goods; from Holland, money; from Africa, slaves; from the West Indies, sugars, coffee, and molasses; and from the neighboring colonies, lumber and provisions: with what they purchase in one place they make their returns in another. . . . By this kind of circular commerce they subsist and grow rich."

Merchant princes, such as Moses Levy, were not solely responsible for colonial America's prosperity. As Robert Keayne implied in his provisions for the Boston marketplace, almost every farmer was also a merchant, selling his surplus produce to get money to buy other goods and services. That was especially true of planters in the south and the West Indies who raised staple crops such as tobacco, sugar, rice, and indigo. They sold their huge surplus harvests to middlemen who carried American produce to markets or sold it to other middlemen. By the late 18th century, many fortunes had been made—and lost—as America's commerce played an increasingly important role in colonial and international life.

■ American craftsmanship, exemplified by this Revere tankard, became widely praised for its simple design and sturdy construction. And like most colonial products, a tankard was eminently useful.

"Colonial craftsmanship," notes the outstanding modern authority on the subject, "came into full bloom in the seaboard cities." Only the cities could support gold refining, silversmithing, and cabinetmaking. Only the cities offered employment for several practitioners of the same craft, which led to a healthy competition in prices and stimulated improvements in design and technology. Benjamin Franklin's career is illustrative; fierce rivalry among printers helped to make Philadelphia the center of American printing.

Even in cities most artisans worked in family units and in their own homes. Apprentices were considered part of the family. The artisan's sons usually worked beside their fathers until they set up shop for themselves—although Franklin, like some youths of his day, was unhappy in his father's craft (tallow chandling) and soon found other employment. Families worked on the ground floor and lived upstairs. The front of the workplace served also as a store, where the artisan sold his wares to customers attracted by signs that often illustrated as well as described the family business. More often, however, artisans made goods to a customer's order; rarely did they keep an inventory of ready-made goods, except in the cities where weavers, ironmongers, jewelers, hatters, and cabinetmakers sometimes advertised an available stock.

■ Long before his famous "midnight ride" in 1775, Paul Revere (1735–1818) was well known as a silversmith and, to a lesser extent, as an engraver. This portrait by John Singleton Copley—one of America's outstanding artists—shows Revere the way his own generation remembered him: a master craftsman who took justifiable pride in the pieces he designed, created, and sold. He had learned the silversmith's craft from his father, who carried on Boston's long tradition, beginning with John Hull in the 1640s, of excellent silversmithing. The younger Revere brought that tradition to new heights of quality and quantity as he shaped Spanish-American silver into handsome, functional objects. He used pewter for less expensive items.

■ Many colonial artisans found work in shipyards (above left), where the demand was high for a wide range of trades: joiners, carvers, painters, anchor smiths, riggers, sailmakers, boatbuilders, oarmakers, and others. Coopers (above right) were among colonial America's most ubiquitous artisans, making kegs to hold fresh water and beer, to store and ship tobacco, and to preserve almost any cargo on land or sea. Almost every community, especially in the south, kept one or more coopers busy the year around. Bookbinders (right) were at the other end of the artisan's spectrum: because most books were imported, American binders were few and limited to the largest towns.

Artisans

Although artisans were only a small fraction of the colonial labor force—far fewer than farmers (some farmers, of course, were also part-time craftsmen) and perhaps fewer than merchants— their importance in colonial life was disproportionately large. American artisans made most of the utensils, furniture, containers, and vehicles that raised colonial life from mere survival to a level that ranged from modest comfort to opulence. Even colonial aristocrats—who imported their coaches, clothes, furniture, and dishes from Europe—could not have accumulated or maintained their wealth without American-made ships, buildings, barrels, crates, harnesses, horseshoes, nails, ropes, and servants' clothes. Imported goods were the veneer, not the substance, of colonial material life.

Colonial craftsmen were encouraged by greater opportunities than Europe offered and by fewer economic restrictions; they could work at their "mysteries," as the crafts were often called, with high expectations of profit and praise. Their work was arduous, however. The age of machinery had not yet arrived; with few exceptions, colonial artisans made their products by hand from cloth, wood, metal, or leather. In every American colony, tailors hand-sewed clothes; cordwainers stitched shoes and boots; weavers wove cloth for clothes, blankets, curtains, and towels; blacksmiths forged iron into useful shapes; glassblowers fashioned goblets, bottles, and windowpanes; coopers fitted together every kind of container; and cabinetmakers shaped furniture of all descriptions. And because each item was the result of individual skill, most artisans took pride in their work. Some, however, did shoddy work or fleeced their customers.

Childhood

Children's principal tasks were educational: learning to read, write, worship, work, and—perhaps most important of all—to accept parental advice without question. Calvinist families took seriously Pastor John Robinson's admonition that children had "a stubbornness, and stoutness of mind arising from natural pride, which must . . . be broken and beaten down." An English mother added "When the will of a child is totally subdued, and it is brought to revere and stand in awe of the parents, then a great many childish follies and inadvertencies may be passed by."

As soon as a child could understand a few words, it was included in family prayers and Bible readings. "Youth" began at age 6 or 7 with more formal religious training, as well as training in secular subjects. Clothing now distinguished boys from girls; until then, both usually wore long robes (see the younger Payne child on the next spread). By this age too, discipline became stricter and punishments more severe, although few colonial parents advocated corporal punishment except in extreme circumstances. More common was Cotton Mather's method. "To be chased for a while out of *my Presence*," he confided to his diary, "I would make to be look'd upon, as the sorest Punishment in the Family."

At the age of 15 or 16, colonial youths took on many adult responsibilities. Most ended their formal schooling, became apprentices (if they hadn't earlier), and were eligible for militia duty. Girls accepted a major share of their mothers' responsibilities at home. But in most colonies, girls did not legally become adults until 18, boys until 21.

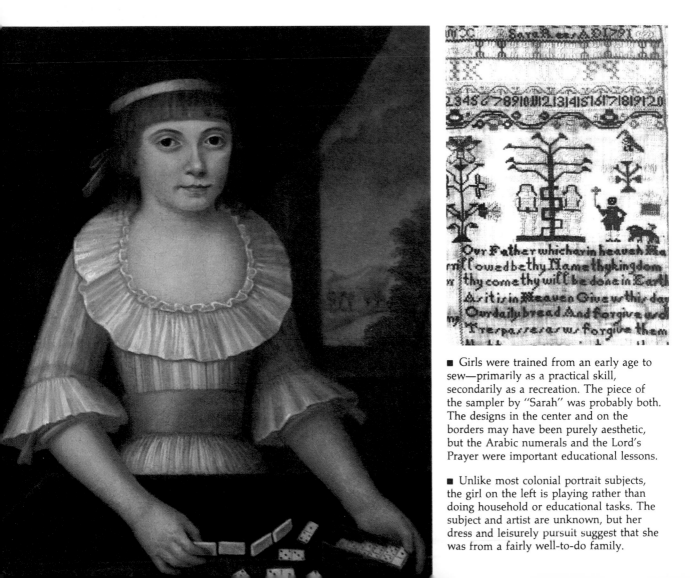

■ Girls were trained from an early age to sew—primarily as a practical skill, secondarily as a recreation. The piece of the sampler by "Sarah" was probably both. The designs in the center and on the borders may have been purely aesthetic, but the Arabic numerals and the Lord's Prayer were important educational lessons.

■ Unlike most colonial portrait subjects, the girl on the left is playing rather than doing household or educational tasks. The subject and artist are unknown, but her dress and leisurely pursuit suggest that she was from a fairly well-to-do family.

■ Historians of colonial childhood believe that infants, if they escaped the prevalent diseases, were by and large happy. They were breast-fed for a year or more, swaddled in soft clothing, rocked in cradles (such as the one below), and given loving attention by parents, siblings, and other relatives. This toddler (right), painted by an unknown artist, seems blissfully content with his or her start in life. The parents, however, knew too well that infancy was life's most dangerous stage. As Reverend John Robinson warned, "After their coming into the world through so many dangers, they come into a world of dangers. In their infancy, how soon is the tender bud nipped, or bruised by sickness or otherwise! Into how many needless dangers do they throw themselves, in which many perish, besides those which God brings them."

Colonial children had few toys. They played instead (as farm children did until the present generation) with household objects such as wooden spoons and balls of yarn, or outdoors with sticks and stones or whatever they could find to amuse themselves. Homemade toys were another alternative, especially straw or rag dolls, kites, and carved animals. The toy shown at bottom left is a combination whistle and horse with wheels that belonged to Robert Livingston of New York.

This handsome portrait of Alexander Spotswood Payne and his younger brother John Robert Dandridge Payne, with their nurse and dog, is a glimpse of youth in an upper-class 18th-century family. Alexander's clothes suggest prosperity, elegance, and "good breeding"; his bow and arrow imply that in the Payne family hunting was a sport rather than a necessity. The presence of a black nurse, moreover, reveals the luxury—and insensitivity—of human bondage. The Paynes no doubt took such privileges for granted; they came from a long aristocratic line. (Alexander was named for his distinguished ancestor, Governor Alexander Spotswood of Virginia.) By the middle of the 18th century, wealthy families throughout British America kept itinerant artists busy with individual and family portraits such as this one by an unidentified limner. It is unusual only in the informality of the scene and the prominent inclusion of a black servant.

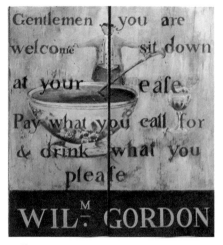

■ Taverns were important to colonial life as centers of conversation, conviviality, and news—both local and international. One customer's bill (left), with a logo engraved by Paul Revere, shows the relative cost of services at a Boston tavern. The sign (above) speaks for itself. Southern gentlemen (below) especially enjoyed fox hunting. It combined English aristocratic attitudes toward hunting with American notions of proper clothing and horsemanship. This painting by an unknown artist depicts an 18th-century Virginia hunt.

Recreation

Even at the busiest times and in the grimmest of years, most colonists found ways to relax. In early Virginia, when the colony was beset by economic crisis and Indian hostility, some settlers bowled in the streets of Jamestown—much to the governor's disgust. Despite Puritan strictures against frivolous recreation, early New Englanders resorted to dice, cards, and tippling. Harvests and other major events were followed by thanksgiving feasts and accompanying merriment.

Other forms of recreation eventually emerged. "The first drudgery of settling colonies, which confines the attention of people to mere necessaries, is now pretty well over," Benjamin Franklin observed in 1743, "and there are many in every province in circumstances that set them at ease, and afford leisure to cultivate the finer arts." Men's clubs were formed in most larger towns for literary purposes, such as Franklin's Junto and Library Company in Philadelphia. Other clubs were less serious. An Annapolis man recounted that "We meet, converse, laugh, talk, smoke, drink, differ, agree, argue, Philosophize, harangue, pun, sing, dance and fiddle together, nay we are really in fact a club." Many colonists enjoyed horse races, cockfights, watering spas, and, late in the century, theaters.

On large southern plantations, life could be a recreational whirl. "Nothing is now to be heard of in conversation," reported a visitor to Virginia, "but the *Balls*, the *Fox-hunts*, the fine *entertainments*, and the *good fellowship*, which are to be exhibited at the approaching *Christmas.*" Slaves were not invited to such events, except as servants, but as the picture below vividly demonstrates, plantation life had more than one entertainment center. Far from the mansion, black men and women fit African songs and instruments to American circumstances. Such gatherings helped to keep alive their African heritage and bring solace to their constricted lives.

Education

Colonial children were educated in many social institutions: family, church, community, and—less often—school. Some youths virtually educated themselves, as Benjamin Franklin's *Autobiography* aptly illustrates. But for most children, including Franklin, indoctrination into the values and knowledge of their society began in the cradle under the guidance of parents and siblings and remained home-centered. Especially on the frontier and on isolated farms, families were almost the only teachers. For the vast majority of teenage boys and almost all girls, formal education ended with a few years at a village common school, at "dame" schools (run by women), or in private lessons. Where schools were not available, and even sometimes where they were, tutors taught whatever they and their employers considered necessary. The tutor might be the local clergyman, or physician, or even an indentured servant.

Students entered college whenever they could meet the requirements, regardless of age. Cotton Mather, for example, went to Harvard at 13. He and his contemporaries demonstrated to the college's satisfaction that they could, in the words of a Kings College (later Columbia) advertisement, "read well, and write a good legible Hand, and . . . be well versed in the Five first Rules in Arithmetic, i.e., as far as *Division* and *Reduction*; and as to *Latin* and *Greek*, . . . have a good Knowledge in the *Grammars*, and . . . give a good Account of two or three of the first Books of *Virgil's Aeneid*, and some of the first Chapters of the *Gospel of St. John*, in *Greek*."

A Princeton freshman described a typical day: Awakened at 5:00 A.M., prayer service at 5:30, study for an hour before breakfast at 8:00, recitation and studying from 9:00 to 1:00 P.M., when dinner was served. Studies resumed from 3:00 to 5:00, followed by evening prayers and then supper at 7:00. At 9:00 P.M. the exhausted scholars could resume studying or go to bed; "to go before is reproachful." After a week of this routine, he concluded that "I am, through divine goodness, . . . more reconciled to rising in the Morning so early than at first."

■ Before they reached school age, New England children learned the elements of literacy and religion from primers, such as the one above, that unabashedly blended moral precepts with basic rules of English grammar. "Horn books"—wooden paddles covered with thin sheets of cattle horn—assured that the Lord's Prayer or some other basic lesson was always handy.

■ William Beekman was a New York lad of 12 when John Durand painted this portrait in 1766. The Latin text in William's hand and the books behind him by Virgil and Ovid reflect the importance of ancient languages to college-bound youths. Three years later, William would enter Princeton.

■ The College of New Jersey, founded in 1746 and eventually located in the town of Princeton, was the fourth colonial college. It had been preceded only by Harvard, William and Mary, and Yale. The center building in this painting, based on a sketch of about 1760, is Nassau Hall, then the largest structure in the colonies. To the right is President John Witherspoon's home. There were then about 60 boys at the college, with two professors and the president as faculty. Tuition, board, and room cost £25 per year. A visitor found the main building to be "extremely convenient, airy, and spacious; and has a chapel and other proper offices. Two students are in each set of apartments, which consists of a large bed-room with a fire-place, and two studies. There is a small collection of books, a few instruments, and some natural curiosities."

Religion

Variety and intensity were the hallmarks of colonial religion. As early as 1686 the governor of New York observed that his colony harbored not only Dutch Calvinists, Dutch Lutherans, French Calvinists, Anglicans, and regular Quakers, but also "Singing Quakers, Ranting Quakers; Sabbatarians; Antisabbatarians; Some Anabaptists; some Independents; some Jews; in short [of] all sorts of opinions there are some . . . ." But even in New York, the widely held belief that a stable society should have an official religion encouraged intolerance of all but the dominant faith. One New Englander bluntly stated, "He that is willing to tolerate any Religion . . . besides his own, unless it be in matters meerly indifferent, either doubts of his own, or is not sincere in it." All who dissented from the prevailing orthodoxy, he proclaimed, had "free Liberty to keep away from us, and such as will come to be gone as fast as they can, the sooner the better." Even on the supposedly egalitarian frontier, adherents of one denomination often abused their religious rivals, as an Anglican missionary discovered in the 1760s when Presbyterians (he charged) let 57 dogs loose in his church to interrupt the service.

Intolerance stemmed partly from the intense piety of many colonists. In an age of high mortality and little scientific understanding of natural phenomena (earthquakes, lightning, eclipses of the sun or moon), belief in an arbitrary deity was hardly surprising. Nor is it surprising that people who left their homelands partly because of religious persecution should cling to their faith with a strong commitment. As late as 1730, a New England preacher insisted that early New England "quickly grew so famous for religion abroad that scarce any other but those who liked it came over for many years." When religious zeal waned throughout the colonies in the early 18th century, a Great Awakening revived lagging spirits. "What shall I do to be saved?" became a frequent and genuine plea. But throughout the colonial era, religious enthusiasm remained high both by the standards of that time and of our own. Religion was the colonial anchor, the one reliable sanctuary in an unpredictable world.

By the second half of the 18th century, denominational rivalries had eased in most areas, and a growing sense of tolerance and Christian community (rarely extended to non-Christians or even to Roman Catholics) helped to bring on a new mood of acceptance and even, some argued, of indifference. In *Letters from An American Farmer* Hector St. John de Crevecoeur described the religious climate of the 1770s: "All sects are mixed as well as all nations; thus religious indifference is imperceptibly disseminated from one end of the continent to the other; which is at present one of the strongest characteristics of the Americans." Compared to the 17th century, that may have been true, at least in the sense that most Americans were indifferent to *other peoples'* opinions. That was a legacy the colonial era would bequeath to the future. Crevecoeur characterized the Americans' religious attitude in the late 18th century as "a perfect freedom of thought . . . which becomes a source of happiness to each individual, to each family, to each district. . . . Here not only every community, but every individual worships God as he thinks it most agreeable to Him. . . ."

■ Richard Mather, shown here in the earliest known American woodcut portrait, was pastor of the Puritan congregation at Dorchester, Massachusetts, from 1636 to 1669. Several of his descendants followed in his clerical footsteps, including son Increase Mather and grandson Cotton Mather.

■ Many colonial American churches survive as examples of early religious architecture and as symbols of colonial America's profound piety. On the opposite page is the Old Swedes' Church (Lutheran) in Wilmington, Delaware, built in 1698 and still in use.

■ The chalice and paten from an Anglican parish (below) in Philadelphia recall some of the differences between the austere Calvinist denominations and the more elaborate rituals of the Anglican Church (or Church of England, later called Episcopalian in the United States). This communion service was presented to Christ's Church by Queen Anne in 1708.

5/NATIONALISM TRIUMPHANT

 Because of the nationalism spawned by the Revolution, large elements in the population resented the constraints imposed by the Articles of Confederation on the power of the central government. On the other hand, when the war ended the need for unity seemed less pressing; sectional conflicts reasserted themselves. Modern research has modified the thesis, advanced by John Fiske in *The Critical Period of American History* (1888), that the government was demoralized and inadequate. If as Washington said it moved "on crutches . . . tottering at every step," it *did* move. The negotiation of a brilliantly successful peace treaty ending the Revolutionary War, the humane and farsighted federal land policies, and even the establishment of a federal bureaucracy to manage routine affairs were remarkable achievements, all carried out under the Articles. Yet the country's evolution placed demands upon the national government that its creators had not anticipated.

Western Tensions

The government had to struggle to win actual control over the territory granted the United States in the treaty ending the Revolution. Both Great Britain and Spain stood in the way of this objective. The British had promised to withdraw all their troops from American soil promptly, and so they did—within the settled portions of the 13 states. Beyond the frontier, however, they had established a string of seven military posts, running from the northern end of Lake Champlain through Niagara and Detroit to the tip of the Michigan peninsula (see map, page 133). These, despite the Treaty of Paris, they refused to surrender. Pressing against America's exposed frontier like hot coals, the posts seared national pride. They threatened to set off another Indian war, for the British intrigued constantly to stir up the tribes against the Americans. The great prize was the rich fur trade of the region, which the British now controlled but which would probably be drained off through Albany and other American centers if British military influence was removed.

The British justified holding on to these positions by citing the failure of the Americans to live up to some terms of the peace treaty. The United States had agreed not to impede British creditors seeking to collect prewar debts in America and to "earnestly recommend" that the states restore Tory property confiscated during the revolt. The national government complied with both requirements (which called for nothing more than words on Congress' part), but the individual states did not cooperate. Many passed laws making it impossible for British creditors to collect debts, and in general the property of Tory émigrés was not returned.

Yet those violations of the peace terms, which resulted more from the state of public opinion than from the weakness of the central authority, had little to do with the continued presence of the British on American soil. They would not have evacuated the posts at this time even if every farthing of the debt had been paid and every acre of

confiscated land restored. Not internal dissension or the absence of congressional determination but the lack of military might accounts for the failure of the United States to compel the British to withdraw. Although Britain had been unable to conquer the colonies, it was a much simpler task to hold posts far removed from centers of American power, and in a region swarming with Indians hostile to settlers but willing to deal with white men interested in buying furs.

Americans found the presence of British troops galling, even in the western wilderness. When the French had pushed a line of forts into the Ohio country in the 1750s, it had seemed to most colonists only a matter of local concern, to be dealt with by Virginia or Pennsylvania. Three decades later the inability to eject the British seemed a national disgrace.

Then there was the question of the Spanish in the southwest. Spain had been a cobelligerent, not an ally, in the war with Great Britain. In the peace negotiations it had won back Florida and the Gulf Coast region east of New Orleans. Spanish troops had captured Natchez during the war, and although the post lay north of the boundary, Spain refused to turn it over to the United States. Far more serious, the Spaniards had closed the lower Mississippi River to American commerce. Because of the prohibitive cost of moving bulky farm produce over the mountains, settlers beyond the Appalachians depended on the Mississippi and its network of tributaries to get their corn, tobacco, and other products to eastern and European markets. If Spain closed the river, or even if it denied them the right to "deposit" goods at New Orleans while awaiting oceangoing transportation, westerners could not sell their surpluses.

Frontier settlers fumed when Congress failed to win concessions from Spain. A few of the unscrupulous and shortsighted among their leaders, such as General James Wilkinson, a handsome, glib, hard-drinking veteran who had moved to Kentucky after the Revolution, accepted Spanish bribes and tried to swing the southwest into the Spanish orbit.

A stronger central government might have ameliorated these foreign problems, but it could not have eliminated them. United or decentralized, America was too weak in the 1780s to challenge a major European nation. Until the country grew

■ The Mississippi teems with commerce in Christophe Colomb's view of about 1790. Two flatboats (on the right) and a keelboat are in the improbably narrow river; in the center left foreground Colomb sits on a log, sketching his father-in-law's plantation house on the other side of the river.

more powerful, or until the Europeans began to fight among themselves, the United States was bound to suffer at their hands.

On the domestic scene, however, difficulties arose that common action could meet. The Confederation strove to meet them but lacked the authority to surmount them. Increasingly large elements in the population came to believe that the authority of the central government should be widened—one more aspect of the growth of nationalism.

Foreign Trade

The fact that the Revolution freed American trade from the restrictions of British mercantilism proved a mixed blessing in the short run. Americans could now trade directly with the continental powers, and commercial treaties were negotiated with a number of them. Beginning in 1784, when the 360-ton *Empress of China* reached Canton with a cargo of furs and cotton to be exchanged for silks, tea, and spices, a valuable Far Eastern trade sprang

up where none had existed before. At the same time, exclusion from Britain's imperial trade union brought serious losses.

Immediately after the Revolution a controversy broke out in Great Britain over fitting the former colonies into the mercantilistic system. Some were beginning to believe generally in free trade, much influenced by Adam Smith's brilliant exposition of the subject in *The Wealth of Nations,* published in 1776. Others, while remaining mercantilists, realized how important the American trade was for British prosperity and argued that special treatment should be afforded the former colonists. Unfortunately, a proud empire recently humbled in war could hardly be expected to exercise such forbearance. Persuaded in part by the reasoning of Lord Sheffield, who claimed that Britain could get all the American commerce it wished without making concessions, Parliament voted to try building up exports to America while holding imports to a minimum, all according to the best tenets of mercantilism.

The British attitude hurt American interests severely. In the southern states the termination of

116

royal bounties hit North Carolina producers of naval stores and South Carolina indigo planters hard, and a new British duty on rice reduced the export of that product by almost 50 percent. Rice and tobacco growers were also afflicted by a labor shortage in the 1780s because of the wartime British seizure of so many slaves.

British Orders in Council in 1783 barring American cured meat, fish, and dairy products from the British West Indies and permitting other American products to enter the islands only in British ships struck at the northern states. The British hoped that Canada and Newfoundland would replace New England as the supplier of food for their sugar islands, and they counted on their own merchant fleet to carry the commerce of the region. Fishermen lost the lucrative West Indian market, merchants a host of profitable opportunities. Shipbuilding slumped because of these facts and because British merchants stopped ordering American-made vessels.

At the same time British merchants, eager to regain markets closed to them during the Revolution, poured low-priced manufactured goods of all kinds into the United States. Americans, long deprived of British products, rushed to take advantage of the bargains. Soon imports of British goods were approaching the levels of the early 1770s, while exports to the empire reached no more than half their earlier volume.

America had always had an unfavorable balance of trade. The economy was essentially colonial; the people produced bulky, relatively cheap raw materials and voraciously consumed expensive manufactured goods. In the first three-quarters of the 18th century, historians estimate, imports exceeded exports by more than £20 million. The growth and development of the country had been greatly aided by the investment of foreign capital, chiefly British. The constant shortage of hard money in colonial times was one result of this condition, since gold and silver tended to flow to Europe to pay interest on loans and to purchase manufactured goods.

The influx of British goods after the Revolution aggravated the situation just when the economy was suffering a certain dislocation as a result of the ending of the war. From 1784 to 1786 the country went through a period of bad times. The inability of the central government to pay its debts undermined confidence and caused grave hard-

ships for veterans and others dependent on the Confederation. In some regions crop failures compounded the difficulties. The depression made the states stingier than ever about supplying the requisitions of Congress; at the same time many of them levied heavy property taxes in order to pay off their own war debts. Everywhere people were hard pressed for cash. "As Money has ever been considered the root of all evils," one Massachusetts man commented sourly, "may we not presage happy times, as this source is almost done away?"

The depression of the mid 1780s was not a major economic collapse by any stretch of the imagination. By 1786 all signs were pointing toward a revival of good times. Nevertheless, dislike of British trade policy remained widespread. The obvious tactic would have been to place tariffs on British goods in order to limit imports or force the British to open the West Indies to all American goods, but the Confederation lacked the authority to do this. When individual states erected tariff barriers, British merchants easily got around them by bringing their goods in through states that did not. The fact that American consumers delighted in the flood of high-quality British manufactured products at low prices complicated the problem. That the central government lacked the power to control commerce disturbed merchants, other businessmen, and the ever increasing number of national-minded citizens in every walk of life.

Thus a movement developed to give the Confederation the power to tax imports. In 1781 Congress sought authority to levy a 5 percent tariff duty. Eleven states agreed—a remarkable indication of the growth of national feeling, considering that local control of taxation and trade had been primary objectives of the Revolution. However, the measure required the unanimous consent of the states and therefore failed. Another request for the same power made in a more moderate form won the approval of all the states by 1786, but conditions imposed by New York were unacceptable to Congress, and again the measure failed.

Defeat of the "impost" pointed up the need for revising the Articles of Confederation, for here was a case where a large percentage of the states were ready to increase the power of the national government yet were unable to do so. Although many individuals in every region were worried about creating a centralized monster that might gobble up the sovereignty of the states, the practical needs of the times convinced most that this risk must be taken. Not a *general* devotion to local sovereignty but the existence of pockets of resistance—as in Rhode Island—to a broader, more national outlook hamstrung the Confederation.

Inflation and Deflation

The depression and the unfavorable balance of trade led to increased pressures in the states for the printing of paper money and the passage of laws designed to make life easier for debtors. Before the Revolution the colonists had grappled with the chronic shortage of hard money in many ways, declaring various staple products such as furs, tobacco, and even Indian wampum to be legal tender, deliberately overvaluing foreign coins to discourage their export, making it illegal to ship coins abroad, and printing paper currency. In response to wartime needs, both the Continental Congress and the states issued large amounts of paper money during the Revolution, with inflationary results (the Continental dollar became utterly worthless by 1781, and Virginia eventually called in its paper at 1,000 to 1).

After the war some states set out to restore their credit by imposing heavy taxes and severely restricting new issues of money. Combined with the postwar depression and the increase in imports, this policy had a powerful deflationary effect on prices and wages. Soon debtors, especially farmers, were crying for relief, both in the form of stay laws designed to make it difficult to collect debts (these laws were popular because of the anti-British feeling of the times) and through the printing of more paper money.

More than half the states yielded to this pressure in 1785 and 1786. Issues in South Carolina, New York, and Pennsylvania were conservatively handled and succeeded, but in some states the money depreciated rapidly: Georgia's currency lost 75 percent of its value in one year, and issues in North Carolina and New Jersey also failed.

The most disastrous experience was that of Rhode Island, where the government attempted to legislate public confidence in £100,000 of paper. Any landowner could borrow a share of this money from the state for 14 years, using his property as security. Creditors feared that the loans would never be repaid and had no confidence in the money, but the legislature established a system of fines in cases where people refused to accept it. When creditors fled the state to avoid being confronted, the legislature authorized debtors to discharge their obligations by turning the necessary currency over to a judge. Of course these measures further weakened public confidence; when the state tried to use paper money to meet its obligations to the federal government, Congress refused to accept it. Indeed, no one accepted the currency freely. The Rhode Island Supreme Court, in *Trevett* v. *Weeden,* declared that it was unconstitutional to fine a creditor for refusing it, and soon there was a reaction.* The element of compulsion was withdrawn, and the paper depreciated rapidly.

Although the Rhode Island case was atypical, it alarmed conservatives. Then, close on its heels, came a disturbing outbreak of violence in Massachusetts. The Massachusetts legislature was determined to pay off the state debt and maintain a sound currency. Taxes amounting to almost £1.9 million were levied between 1780 and 1786, the burden falling most heavily on those of moderate income. The historian Merrill Jensen estimates that the average Massachusetts farmer paid about a third of his income in taxes. Bad times and deflation led to many foreclosures, and the prisons were crowded with honest men unable to pay their debts. "Our Property is torn from us," one town complained, "our Gaols filled & still our Debts are not discharged."

In the summer of 1786 mobs in the western communities began to stop foreclosures by forcibly preventing the courts from holding their sessions. Under the leadership of Daniel Shays, veteran of Bunker Hill, Ticonderoga, and Saratoga, the "rebels" marched on Springfield and prevented the state supreme court from meeting. When the government sent troops against them, they attacked the Springfield arsenal. They were routed, and the uprising then collapsed. Shays fled to Vermont.

In itself, "Shays' Rebellion" did not amount to much. As Thomas Jefferson wittily observed, it was only "a *little* rebellion" and as such "a medi-

---

*This was the first case in which an American court declared a legislative act void on constitutional grounds.

cine necessary for the sound health of government." Shays and his fellows were genuinely exasperated by the refusal of the government even to try to provide relief for their troubles. By taking up arms they forced the authorities to heed them: at its next session the legislature made some concessions to their demands. Good times soon returned and the uprising was forgotten. Yet the episode had an impact far beyond the borders of Massachusetts and all out of proportion to its intrinsic importance. Unlike Jefferson, most well-to-do Americans considered the uprising "Liberty run mad." "What, gracious God, is man! that there should be such inconsistency and perfidiousness in his conduct?" the usually unexcitable George Washington asked when news of the riots reached Virginia. "We are fast verging to anarchy and confusion!" During the crisis, private persons had had to subscribe funds to put the rebels down, and when Massachusetts had appealed to Congress for help there was little Congress could legally do. The lessons seemed plain: liberty must not become an excuse for license; greater authority must be vested in the central government.

The reactions to the Rhode Island excesses and the uprising in Massachusetts illustrated the continuing development of American nationalism. Citizens everywhere were concerned with what was going on in other parts of the country. Newspapers in all the states followed the bizarre spectacle of debtors in Rhode Island pursuing their creditors with fistfuls of paper money. The tragicomic revolt of Daniel Shays worried planters in far-off Virginia and the Carolinas almost as much as it did the merchants of Boston. All were becoming more conscious of their common interests, their national identity. Bacon's Rebellion, a far more serious affair, had evoked no such reaction in the 17th century, nor had the Regulator War in North Carolina as late as 1771.

Drafting the Constitution

If most people wanted to increase the power of Congress, many were afraid to shift the balance too far lest they destroy the sovereignty of the states. The machinery for change established in the Articles of Confederation, which required the unanimous consent of the states for all amendments, posed a particularly delicate problem. Ex-

perience had shown it unworkable, yet to bypass it would be revolutionary and therefore dangerous.

The first fumbling step toward reform was taken in March 1785, when representatives of Virginia and Maryland, meeting at the home of George Washington to settle a dispute over the improvement of navigation on the Potomac River, suggested a conference of all the states to discuss common problems of commerce. In January 1786 the Virginia legislature sent out a formal call for such a gathering, to be held in September at Annapolis. However, the meeting disappointed advocates of reform; delegates from only five states appeared, and being so few they did not feel it worthwhile to propose changes.

Among the delegates was a young New York lawyer named Alexander Hamilton, a brilliant, imaginative, and daring man who was convinced that only drastic centralization would save the nation from disintegration. Instead of giving up, he proposed calling another convention to meet at Philadelphia to deal generally with constitutional reform. Delegates to the new convention should be empowered to work out a broad plan for correcting "such defects as may be discovered to exist" in the Articles of Confederation.

The Annapolis group approved Hamilton's suggestion, and Congress endorsed it. This time all the states but Rhode Island sent delegates. On May 25, 1787, the convention opened its proceedings at the State House in Philadelphia and unanimously elected George Washington its president. When it adjourned four months later, it had drafted the Constitution.

The Philadelphia Convention

As the decades have passed and the Constitution has grown more and more tradition-encrusted without losing any of its flexibility, each generation has tried to explain how a people so young and inexperienced, so free-swinging and unruly, could have produced it. One reason was the ability of those who drafted it. The Founding Fathers were remarkable men. Jefferson, who was on a foreign assignment and did not attend the convention, called them "demigods," though he later had reason to quarrel with certain aspects of their handiwork. Collectively they possessed a rare combination of talents. Amazingly youthful—the youngest man ever elected president, John F. Kennedy, 43 at the time of his inauguration in 1961, was older than the average delegate in 1787—they escaped the weaknesses so often associated with youth: instability, overoptimism, half-cocked radicalism, and the refusal to heed the suggestions of others. The times made them mature beyond their years, for the Revolutionary generation had been inspired by the uniqueness of its opportunities. It was, John Adams wrote, "a time when the greatest lawgivers of antiquity would have wished to live," an opportunity to "establish the wisest and happiest government that human wisdom can contrive."

The delegates were acutely aware of their responsibilities. "We . . . decide for ever the fate of republican government," James Madison said during the deliberations, and if this was an overstatement, it nonetheless represented the opinion of most of those present. At the same time they recognized the difficulties they faced. The ancient Roman republic was their model, and all knew that it had been overthrown by tyrants and eventually overrun by barbarians.

Fortunately, they were nearly all of one mind on basic questions. That there should be a federal system, with both independent state governments and a national government with limited powers to handle matters of common interest, was accepted by all but one or two of them. Republican government, drawing its authority from the people and remaining responsible to them, was a universal assumption. A measure of democracy followed inevitably from this principle, for even the most aristocratic delegates agreed that ordinary citizens should share in the process of selecting those who were to make and execute the laws.

All agreed that no group within society, no matter how numerous, should have *unrestricted* authority. They looked upon political power much as we today view nuclear energy: a force with tremendous potential value for mankind, but one easily misused and therefore dangerous to unleash. People meant well and had limitless possibilities, the constitution makers believed, but they were selfish by nature and could not be counted on to respect the interests of others. The poor, therefore, should have a say in government in order to be able to protect themselves against those who would exploit their weakness, and somehow the majority must be prevented from plundering the

■ James Madison, one of the key figures at the Convention; miniature by Charles Willson Peale, ca. 1783.

rich, for property must be secure or no government could be stable. No single state or section must be allowed to predominate, nor should the legislature be supreme over the executive or the courts. Power, in short, must be divided, and the segments must be balanced one against the other.

Although the level of education among them was high and a number might fairly be described as learned, the delegates' approach was pragmatic rather than theoretical. This was perhaps their most useful asset, for their task called for reconciling clashing interests. It could never have been accomplished without compromise and an acute sense of what was possible (as distinct from what was ideally best).

Early in their deliberations the delegates decided to go beyond their instructions to revise the Articles of Confederation: they would draft an entirely new frame of government. This was a bold, perhaps illegal act, but it was in no way immoral because nothing the convention might recommend was binding on anyone. Alexander Hamilton, eager to scrap the Confederation in favor of a truly national government, captured the mood of the gathering when he said: "We can only propose and recommend—the power of ratifying or rejecting is still in the States. . . . We ought not to sacrifice the public Good to narrow Scruples."

The Settlement

The delegates voted on May 30 that "a *national* Government ought to be established" and then set to work hammering out a specific plan. Two big questions had to be answered. The first—*What powers should this national government be granted?*—occasioned relatively little discussion. The right to levy taxes and to regulate interstate and foreign commerce was assigned to the central government almost without debate. So was the power to raise and maintain an army and navy and to summon the militia of the states to enforce national laws and suppress insurrections. With equal absence of argument, the states were deprived of their rights to issue money, to make treaties, and to tax either imports or exports without the permission of Congress. Thus, in summary fashion, was brought about a massive shift of power, made practicable by the new nationalism of the 1780s.

The second major question—*Who shall control the national government?*—proved more difficult to answer in a manner satisfactory to all. Led by Virginia, the larger states pushed for representation in the national legislature based on population. The smaller states wished to maintain the existing system of equal representation for all. The large states rallied behind the Virginia Plan, drafted by James Madison and presented to the convention by Edmund Randolph, governor of the state. The small states supported the New Jersey Plan, prepared by William Paterson, a former attorney general of that state.

The question was important; equal state representation would have been undemocratic, while a proportional system would have effectively destroyed the influence of all the states *as states*. But the delegates saw it in terms of combinations of large or small states, and this was unrealistic: when the states combined, they did so on geographic, economic, or social grounds that had nothing to do with size. Nevertheless, the debate was long and hot, and for a time it threatened to disrupt the convention. Finally, in mid July, the delegates agreed to what has been called the Great Compromise. In the lower house of the new legislature—the House of Representatives—places were to be assigned according to population and filled by popular vote. In the upper house—the Senate—each state was to have two members, elected by its legislature.

Then a complicated struggle took place between northern and southern delegates, occasioned by the institution of slavery and the differing economic interests of the regions. Northerners contended that slaves should be counted in deciding each state's share of direct federal taxes. Southerners, of course, wanted to exclude slaves from the count. Yet southerners wished to include slaves in determining their representation in the House of Representatives, though they had no intention of permitting the slaves to vote. In the Three-fifths Compromise it was agreed that "three-fifths of all other Persons" should be counted for both purposes. (As it turned out, the compromise was a victory for the southerners, for no direct taxes were ever levied by Congress before the Civil War.) Settlement of the knotty issue of the African slave trade was postponed by a clause making it illegal for Congress to outlaw the trade before 1808. Questions involving the regulation of less controversial commerce also caused sectional disagreement. Southerners disliked export taxes because their staple products were largely sold abroad. In return for a clause prohibiting such taxes, they dropped their demand that all laws regulating foreign commerce be approved by two-thirds of both houses of Congress. Many other differences of opinion were resolved by the give-and-take of practical compromise. As the historian David M. Potter once said, the Constitution was "an exchange of promises" whereby different interests gained large advantages by making large concessions.

The final document, signed on September 17, established a legislature of two houses, an executive consisting of a president with wide powers and a vice-president whose only function was to preside over the Senate, and a national judiciary consisting of a Supreme Court and such "inferior courts" as Congress might decide to create. The lower, popularly elected branch of the Congress was supposed to represent especially the mass of ordinary citizens. It was given the sole right to introduce bills for raising revenue. The 26-member Senate was looked upon by many as a sort of advisory council similar to the upper houses of the colonial legislatures. Its consent was required before any treaty could go into effect and for major presidential appointments. The Founding Fathers also intended the Senate to represent in Congress the interests not only of the separate states but of

■ The room in Independence Hall where the Constitutional Convention was held has been scrupulously restored.

what Hamilton called "the rich and the well-born" as contrasted with "the great mass of the people."

The creation of a powerful president was the most drastic departure from past experience, and it is doubtful that the Founding Fathers would have gone so far had everyone not counted on Washington, a man universally esteemed for character, wisdom, and impartiality, to be the first to occupy the office. Besides giving him general responsibility for executing the laws, the Constitution made the president commander in chief of the armed forces of the nation and general supervisor of its foreign relations. He was to appoint federal judges and other officials, and he might veto any law of Congress, although his veto could be overridden by a two-thirds majority of both houses. While not specifically ordered to submit a program of legislation to Congress, he was to deliver periodic reports on the "State of the Union" and recommend "such Measures as he shall judge necessary and expedient." Most modern presidents have interpreted this requirement as authorizing them to submit detailed legislative proposals and to use the full power and prestige of the office to get Congress to enact them.

Looking beyond Washington, whose choice was

sure to come about under any system, the Constitution established a cumbersome method of electing presidents. Each state was to choose a number of "electors" equal to its representation in Congress. The electors, meeting separately in their own states, were to vote for two persons for president. Supposedly the procedure would prevent anyone less universally admired than Washington from getting a majority in the "electoral college," in which case the House of Representatives would choose the president from among the leading candidates, each state having but one vote. However, the swift rise of national political parties prevented the expected fragmentation of the electors' votes, and only two elections have ever gone to the House for settlement.

The national court system was set up to adjudicate disputes under the laws and treaties of the United States. No such system had existed under the Articles, a major weakness. Although the Constitution did not specifically authorize the courts to declare laws void when they conflicted with the Constitution, the courts soon exercised this right of "judicial review" in cases involving both state and federal laws.

That the Constitution reflected the commonly

held beliefs of its framers is everywhere evident in the document. It greatly expanded the powers of the central government yet did not seriously threaten the independence of the states. Foes of centralization, at the time and ever since, have predicted the imminent disappearance of the states as sovereign bodies. But despite a steady trend toward centralization, probably inevitable as American society has grown ever more complex, the states remain powerful political organizations that are sovereign in many areas of government.

The Founders believed that since the new powers of government might easily be misused, each should be held within safe limits by some countervailing force. The Constitution is full of ingenious devices ("checks and balances") whereby one power controls and limits another without reducing it to impotence. The separation of legislative, executive, and judicial functions is the fundamental example of this principle. Others are the president's veto; Congress' power of impeachment, cleverly divided between House and Senate; the Senate's power over treaties and appointments; judicial review; and the balance between Congress' right to declare war and the president's control of the armed forces.

Ratification of the Constitution

Influenced by the widespread approval of Massachusetts' decision to submit its state constitution of 1780 to the voters for ratification, the framers of the Constitution provided that their handiwork be ratified by special state conventions. This procedure gave the Constitution what Madison called "the highest source of authority"—the endorsement of the people, expressed through representatives chosen specifically to pass upon it. The framers may also have been motivated by a desire to bypass the state legislatures, where many members might resent the reductions being made in state authority. This was not of central importance because the legislatures could have blocked ratification by refusing to call conventions. Only Rhode Island did so, and since the Constitution was to go into operation when nine states had approved it, Rhode Island's stubbornness did no vital harm.

Such a complex and controversial document as the Constitution naturally excited argument throughout the country. Those who favored it were called Federalists, their opponents, Antifederalists.* It is difficult to generalize about the members of these groups. The Federalists tended to be substantial individuals, members of the professions, well-to-do, active in commercial affairs, and somewhat alarmed by the changes wrought by the Revolution. They were more interested, perhaps, in orderly and efficient government than in safeguarding the maximum freedom of individual choice, but they were not necessarily opposed to popular government.

The Antifederalists were more often small farmers, debtors, and persons to whom free choice was more important than power. But many rich and worldly citizens opposed the Constitution, and many poor and obscure persons were for it. It seems likely that most did not support or oppose the new system for narrowly selfish reasons. The contemporary judgment of the historian David Ramsay that "the great body of independent men who saw the necessity of an energetic government" swung the balance in favor of the Constitution is probably correct.

Whether the Antifederalists were more democratic than the Federalists is an interesting question. Those who are loud for local autonomy do not necessarily believe in equal rights for all the locals. Many Antifederalist leaders (more than half, according to the best recent research) had reservations about democracy. On the other hand, even Hamilton, no admirer of democracy, believed that the humblest citizens should have *some* say about their government. In general, practice still stood well ahead of theory when it came to popular participation in politics.

Various Antifederalists criticized many of the specific grants of authority in the new Constitution, some concocting farfetched arguments to show what disasters might ensue should it be put into effect. The routine clause (Article I, Section 4) giving Congress the power to regulate "the times, places, and manner of holding elections" threatened to "destroy representation entirely," a North Carolina Antifederalist claimed. The chief force

---

*In fact the Antifederalists were those who really favored a federal system. The Federalists should more logically have been called Centralists or Nationalists.

behind the opposition was a vague fear that the new system would destroy the independence of the states.

It is important to keep in mind that the country was large and sparsely settled, that communication was primitive, and that the central government did not influence the lives of most people to any great degree. Many persons believed that a centralized republican system would not work in a country so large and with so many varied interests as the United States. Patrick Henry considered the Constitution "horribly frightful." It "squints toward monarchy," he added. That Congress could pass all laws "necessary and proper" to carry out the functions assigned it and legislate for the "general welfare" of the country seemed alarmingly all-inclusive. The first sentence of the Constitution, beginning "We the *people* of the United States" rather than "We the states," convinced many that the document represented centralization run wild. "As I enter the Building I stumble at the Threshhold," Samuel Adams remarked.

Many members of the Convention were well-to-do and stood to profit from the establishment of a sound and conservative government that would honor its obligations, foster economic development, and preserve a stable society. Since the Constitution was designed to do all these things, it has been suggested that the Founders were not true patriots but selfish men out to protect their own interests. Charles A. Beard advanced this thesis over half a century ago in *An Economic Interpretation of the Constitution*, arguing that most members of the Convention owned large amounts of depreciated government securities that were bound to rise in price if the Constitution was approved. The thesis has been thoroughly discredited. The Founders wanted to advance their own interests as every normal human being does. Most of them, however, had no special involvement in securities, being far more concerned with land. The closest thing to a general spirit at Philadelphia was a public spirit. To call men like Washington, Franklin, and Madison self-seeking would be absurd.

Beard's book is important. It provided a necessary corrective to the 19th-century tendency to deify the Founding Fathers, and it called attention to the role of economic motivation in the framing of the Constitution. But it ought not to obscure the greatness of the Constitution or the men who made it.

Very little of the opposition to the Constitution grew out of economic issues. Most people wanted the national debt paid off; nearly everyone opposed an unstable currency; most favored uniform trade policies. Aside from a few doctrinaires, most were ready to give the new government a chance if they could be convinced that it would not destroy the states. When backers agreed to add amendments guaranteeing the civil liberties of the people against invasion by the national government and reserving all unmentioned power to the states, much of the opposition disappeared. Sam Adams ended up voting for the Constitution in the Massachusetts convention after the additions had been promised.

No one knows exactly how public opinion divided on the question of ratification. In nearly every state a large majority of the more articulate people favored the Constitution. The Federalists were usually able to create an impression of strength far beyond their numbers and to overwhelm doubters with the mass of their arguments. They excelled in political organization and in persuasiveness. James Madison, for example, demolished the thesis that a centralized republican government could not function efficiently in a large country. In rule by the majority lay protection against the "cabals" of special interest groups. "Extend the sphere," Madison argued, "and you take in a greater variety of parties and interests; you make it less probable that a majority of the whole will have a common motive to invade the rights of other citizens." Moreover, the management of national affairs would surely attract leaders of greater ability and sounder character to public service than the handling of petty local concerns ever could in a decentralized system.

The Constitution met with remarkably little opposition in most of the state ratifying conventions, considering the importance of the changes it instituted. Delaware acted first, ratifying unanimously on December 7, 1787. Pennsylvania followed a few days later, voting for the document by a two-to-one majority. New Jersey approved unanimously on December 18; so did Georgia on January 2, 1788. A week later Connecticut fell in line, 128 to 40.

The Massachusetts convention provided the first close contest. Early in February, by a vote of

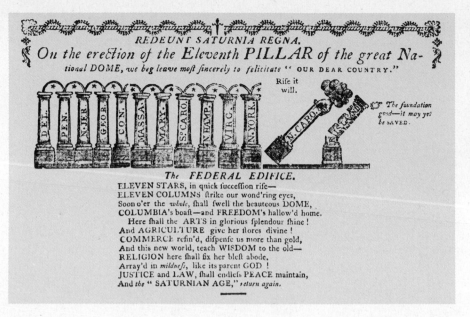

REDEUNT SATURNIA REGNA.

On the erection of the Eleventh PILLAR of the great Na-
tional DOME, we beg leave most sincerely to felicitate " OUR DEAR COUNTRY."

Rise it
will.

The foundation
good—it may yet
be SAVED.

The FEDERAL EDIFICE.
ELEVEN STARS, in quick succession rise—
ELEVEN COLUMNS strike our wond'ring eyes,
Soon o'er the *whole*, shall swell the beauteous DOME,
COLUMBIA's boast—and FREEDOM's hallow'd home.
Here shall the ARTS in glorious splendour shine !
And AGRICULTURE give her stores divine !
COMMERCE refin'd, dispense us more than gold,
And this new world, teach WISDOM to the old—
RELIGION here shall fix her blest abode,
Array'd in *mildness*, like its parent GOD !
JUSTICE and LAW, shall endless PEACE maintain,
And *the* " SATURNIAN AGE," *return again.*

■ New York's approval of the Constitution on July 26, 1788, inspired this cartoon in the Massachusetts *Centinel.* Hope was high that North Carolina would "rise" to ratify, but prospects in Rhode Island were not as bright—and, as it turned out, rightly so.

187 to 168, the delegates decided to ratify. In April Maryland accepted the Constitution by nearly six to one, and in May South Carolina approved, 149 to 73. New Hampshire came along on June 21, voting 57 to 47 for the Constitution. This was the ninth state, making the Constitution legally operative. On June 25, before the news from New Hampshire had spread throughout the country, Virginia voted for ratification, 89 to 79. Aside from Rhode Island, this left only New York and North Carolina outside the Union.

New York politics presented a complex and baffling picture during the entire Revolutionary era. Resistance to independence had been strong there in 1776 and remained a problem all through the war. Although New York was the third largest state, with a population rapidly approaching 340,000, it sided with the small states at Philadelphia, and two of its three delegates (Hamilton was the exception) refused to sign the final document and took the lead in resisting ratification. A handful of great landowning and mercantile families dominated politics, but they were divided into shifting factions. In general, New York City favored ratification and the rural areas were against it.

The Antifederalists, well organized and competently led in New York, won 46 of the 65 seats at the ratifying convention. The New York Federal-

ists had one great asset in the fact that so many states had already ratified and another in the person of Alexander Hamilton. Although contemptuous of the *weakness* of the Constitution, Hamilton supported it with all his energies as being incomparably stronger than the old government. Working with Madison and John Jay, he produced the *Federalist Papers,* a brilliant series of essays explaining and defending the new system. These were published in the local press and later in book form. Although generations of judges and lawyers have treated them almost as parts of the Constitution, their impact on contemporary public opinion was probably slight. Open-minded members of the convention were undoubtedly influenced, but few delegates were open-minded.

Hamilton became virtually a one-man army in defense of the Constitution, plying hesitating delegates with dinners and drinks, facing obstinate ones with the threat that New York City would secede from the state if the Constitution were rejected. He spoke, one of the leading Antifederalists at the convention remarked, "frequently, very long, and very vehemently" on every aspect of the Constitution, posing as a devoted supporter of republican government and scoffing at the idea that the Constitution represented a threat to liberty. Once New Hampshire and Virginia had ratified, opposition in New York became

FEDERAL HALL
The Seat of CONGRESS
Printed & Sold by A Doolittle New Haven 1790

■ His hand on the Bible, Washington takes the presidential oath administered by Robert Livingston on the portico of New York's Federal Hall. Engraving by Amos Doolittle, after a drawing by Peter Lacour.

a good deal less intransigent. In the end, by promising to support a call for a second national convention to consider amendments, the Federalists carried the day, 30 to 27. With New York in the fold, the new government was free to get under way.*

*North Carolina did not ratify until November 1789, and Rhode Island held out until May 1790.

Washington as President

During January and February 1789 elections took place in the states, and by early April enough congressmen had gathered in New York, the temporary national capital, to commence operation. The ballots of the presidential electors were officially counted in the Senate on April 6, Washington being the unanimous choice. John Adams, with 34 electoral votes, won the vice-presidency. On April 30 Washington took the oath of office at Federal Hall.

Washington made a firm, dignified, conscientious, but cautious president. His acute sense of responsibility and his sensitivity to the slightest criticism made it almost impossible for him to relax and enjoy himself while in office. "The eyes of Argus are upon me," he complained, "and no slip will pass unnoticed." Each presidential action must of necessity establish a precedent. Hoping to make the presidency appear respectable in the eyes of the world, he saw to it that his carriage was drawn by six cream-colored horses, and when he rode (he was a magnificent horseman), it was upon a great white charger, with the saddle of leopardskin and the cloth edged in gold. Twenty-one servants (seven of them slaves) attended his needs at the presidential mansion on Broadway. When guests arrived for state functions, they were met at the entry by powdered lackeys.

Washington meticulously avoided treading upon the toes of Congress, for he took seriously the principle of the separation of powers. Never would he speak for or against a candidate for Congress, nor did he think that the president should push or even propose legislation. When he knew a controversial question was to be discussed in Congress, he avoided the subject in his annual message. The veto, he believed, should be employed only when the president considered a bill unconstitutional.

In selecting his Cabinet and other advisers, Washington favored no particular faction.* He insisted only that appointees be competent and "of known attachment to the Government we have chosen." He picked Hamilton for secretary of the treasury, Jefferson for secretary of state, General Henry Knox of Massachusetts for secretary of war, and Edmund Randolph for attorney general. He called upon them for advice according to the logic of his particular needs and frequently without regard for their own specialties. Thus he sometimes consulted Jefferson about financial matters and Hamilton about foreign affairs. This

system caused resentment and confusion, especially when rival factions began to coalesce around Hamilton and Jefferson. Nevertheless, Washington persisted in acting as though no political organizations existed, for he wished to minimize conflict.

Despite his respect for the opinions of others, Washington was a strong chief executive. As Hamilton put it, he "consulted much, pondered much, resolved slowly, resolved surely." His stress on the dignity of his office suited the needs of a new country whose people tended to be perhaps too informal. It was indeed important that the *first* president be particularly concerned about establishing precedents. His scrupulous care lest he overstep the bounds of presidential power helped erase the prejudices of those who feared that republican government must inevitably succumb to dictatorship and tyranny. When each step is an experiment, when foreign dangers loom at the end of every errant path, it is surely wise to go slowly. And no one should forget that Washington's devotion to duty did not always come easily. Occasionally he exploded. Thomas Jefferson has left us a graphic picture of the president at a Cabinet meeting, in a rage because of some unfair criticism, swearing that "by god he had rather be on his farm than to be made *emperor of the world.*"

The Bill of Rights

The first Congress had the task of constructing the machinery of government. By September 1789 it had created the State, Treasury, and War departments and passed a Judiciary Act establishing 13 federal district courts and three circuit courts of appeal. The number of Supreme Court justices was set at six, and Washington named John Jay chief justice.

True to Federalist promises—for a large majority of both houses were friendly to the Constitution—Congress prepared a list of a dozen amendments (10 were ratified) guaranteeing what Representative James Madison, who drafted the amendments, called the "great rights of mankind." These amendments, known as the Bill of Rights, provided that Congress should make no law infringing freedom of speech, the press, or religion. The right of trial by jury was reaffirmed. No one was to be subject to "unreasonable"

---

*The Cabinet was not provided for in the Constitution, but Washington established the system of calling his department heads together for general advice, a practice that was generally followed by his successors.

searches or seizures nor compelled to testify against himself in a criminal case. No one was to "be deprived of life, liberty, or property, without due process of law." The Bill of Rights was unique; the English Bill of Rights of 1689 was much less broad-gauged and, being an act of Parliament, subject to repeal by Parliament at any time. The Tenth Amendment—not, strictly speaking, a part of the Bill of Rights—was designed to mollify those who feared that the states would be destroyed by the new government. It provided that powers not delegated to the United States or denied specifically to the states by the Constitution were to reside either in the states or in the people.

As experts pointed out, the amendments were not logically necessary because the federal government had no authority to act in such matters to begin with. But many had wanted to be reassured. Experience has proved repeatedly that whatever the logic of the situation, the protection afforded individuals by the Bill of Rights has been anything but unnecessary.

The Bill of Rights did much to convince doubters that the new government would not become too powerful. More complex was the task of proving that it was powerful enough to deal with those national problems that the Confederation had not been able to solve: the threat to the west posed by the British, Spaniards, and Indians; the disruption of the pattern of American foreign commerce resulting from independence; the collapse of the financial structure of the country.

Hamilton and Financial Reform

One of the first acts of Congress in 1789 was to employ its new power to tax. The simplest means of raising money seemed to be that first attempted by the British after 1763, a tariff on foreign imports. Congress levied a 5 percent duty on all foreign products entering the United States, applying higher rates to certain products, such as hemp, glass, and nails, as a measure of protection for American producers. The Tariff Act of 1789 also placed heavy tonnage duties on all foreign shipping, a mercantilistic measure designed to stimulate the American merchant marine.

Raising money for current expenses was a small and relatively simple aspect of the financial prob-

lem faced by Washington's administration. The nation's debt was large, its credit shaky, its economic future uncertain. In October 1789 Congress deposited upon the slender shoulders of Secretary of the Treasury Hamilton the task of straightening out the fiscal mess and stimulating the country's economic development.

Hamilton at 34 had already proved himself a remarkable man. Born in the British West Indies, the illegitimate son of a shiftless Scot who was little better than a beachcomber, and raised by his mother's family, he went to New York in 1773 to attend King's College. When the Revolution broke out, he joined the army. At 22 he was a staff colonel, aide-de-camp to Washington. Later, at Yorktown, he led a line regiment, displaying a bravery approaching foolhardiness. He married the daughter of Philip Schuyler, a wealthy and influential New Yorker, and after the Revolution he practiced law in that state.

Hamilton was a bundle of contradictions. Witty, charming, possessed of a mind like a sharp knife, he was sometimes the soul of practicality, sometimes an incurable romantic. No more hard-headed realist ever lived, yet he was quick to resent any slight to his honor, even—tragically—ready to fight a duel though he abhorred the custom of dueling. A self-made man, he admired aristocracy and disparaged the abilities of the common run of mankind who, he said, "seldom judge or determine right." Although granting that Americans must be allowed to govern themselves, he was as apprehensive of the "turbulence" of the masses as a small boy passing a graveyard in the dark. "No popular government was ever without its Catilines and its Caesars," he warned—a typical example of that generation's concern about the fate of the Roman republic.

The country, Hamilton believed, needed a strong national government. "A great Federal Republic," he said, is a "noble and magnificent" thing, whereas "there is something proportionably diminutive and contemptible in the prospect of a number of petty states, with the appearance only of union, jarring, jealous, perverse, without any determined direction." He wished to reduce the states to mere administrative units, like English counties.

As secretary of the treasury Hamilton proved to be a farsighted economic planner. The United States, a "Hercules in the cradle," needed capital to develop its untapped material and human resources. To persuade investors to commit their funds in America, the country would have to convince them that it would meet every obligation in full. His *Report on the Public Credit* outlined the means for accomplishing this objective. The United States owed more than $11 million to foreigners and over $40 million to its own citizens. Hamilton suggested that this debt be funded at par, which meant calling in all outstanding securities and issuing new bonds to the same face value in their stead, and establishing an untouchable sinking fund to assure payment of interest and principal. Further, a large part of the debts of the states should be assumed (taken over) by the United States on the same terms.

While most members of Congress agreed, albeit somewhat grudgingly, that the debt should be funded at par, many believed that at least part of the new issue should go to the original holders of the old securities: the soldiers, farmers, and merchants who had been forced to accept them in lieu of cash for goods and services rendered the Confederation during the Revolution. Many of these people had sold their securities for a fraction of their face value to speculators; under Hamilton's proposal, the speculators would make a killing. To the argument for divided payment, Hamilton answered coldly: "[The speculator] paid what the commodity was worth in the market, and took the risks. . . . He . . . ought to reap the benefit of his hazard."

Hamilton was essentially correct, and in the end Congress had to go along. After all, the speculators had not caused the securities to fall in value; indeed, as a group they had favored sound money and a strong government. The best way to restore the nation's credit was to convince investors that the government would honor all obligations in full. What infuriated his contemporaries and still attracts the scorn of many historians was Hamilton's motive. He deliberately intended his plan to give a special advantage to the rich. The government would be strong, he thought, only if well-to-do Americans enthusiastically supported it. What better way to win them over than to make it worth their while financially to do so?

In part opposition to the funding plan was sectional, for citizens of the northern states held more than four-fifths of the national debt. The scheme for assuming the state debts aggravated the con-

■ "To confess my weakness," Hamilton wrote when he was only 14, "my ambition is prevalent." This pastel drawing by James Sharples was made about 1796.

troversy, since most of the southern states had already paid off much of their Revolutionary War obligations. For months Congress was deadlocked. Finally, in July 1790, Hamilton worked out a compromise with Representative James Madison of Virginia and Secretary of State Jefferson. The two Virginians swung a few southern votes, and Hamilton induced some of his followers to support the southern plan for locating the permanent capital of the Union on the Potomac River.

Jefferson later claimed that Hamilton had hoodwinked him. Having only recently returned from Europe, he said, "I was really a stranger to the whole subject." Hamilton had persuaded him to "rally around" by the false tale that "our Union" was threatened with dissolution. This was nonsense; Jefferson agreed to the compromise because he expected that Virginia and the rest of the south would profit from having the capital so near at hand.

The assumption bill passed, and the entire funding plan was a great success. Soon the United States had the highest possible credit rating in the world's financial centers. Foreign capital poured into the country.

Hamilton next proposed that Congress charter a national bank. Such an institution would provide safe storage for government funds and serve as an agent for the government in the collection, movement, and expenditure of tax money. Most important, it would issue bank notes, thereby providing a vitally needed medium of exchange for the specie-starved economy. This Bank of the United States was to be partly owned by the government, but 80 percent of the $10 million stock issue was to be sold to private individuals.

The country had much to gain from such a bank, but again—Hamilton's devilish cleverness was never more in evidence—the well-to-do commercial classes would gain still more. Government balances in the bank belonging to all the people would earn dividends for a handful of rich investors. Manufacturers and other capitalists would profit from the bank's credit facilities. Public funds would be invested in the bank, but control would remain in private hands, since the government would appoint only 5 of the 25 directors. Nevertheless, the bill creating the bank passed both houses of Congress with relative ease in February 1791.

President Washington, however, hesitated to sign it, for the bill's constitutionality had been questioned during the debate in Congress. Nowhere did the Constitution specifically authorize Congress to charter corporations or engage in the banking business. As was his wont when in doubt, Washington called upon Jefferson and Hamilton for advice.

Hamilton defended the legality of the bank. Since a logical connection existed between the purpose of the bill and powers clearly stated in the Constitution, he wrote, the bill was constitutional. "A bank has a natural relation to the power of collecting taxes—to that of regulating trade to that of providing for the common defence." Jefferson disagreed. Congress could only do what the Constitution specifically authorized, he said. The "elastic clause" granting it the right to pass "all Laws which shall be necessary and proper" to carry out the specified powers must be interpreted literally or Congress would "take possession of a boundless field of power, no longer susceptible to any definition." Because a bank was obviously not *necessary*, it was not authorized.

Although not entirely convinced, Washington accepted Hamilton's reasoning and signed the bill. He could just as easily have followed Jefferson, for the Constitution is not clear. If one stresses *proper*

in the "necessary and proper" clause, one ends up a Hamiltonian; if one stresses *necessary*, then Jefferson's view is correct. Historically (and this is the important point) politicians have nearly always adopted the "loose" Hamiltonian interpretation when they favor a measure and the "strict" Jeffersonian one when they do not. Jefferson disliked the bank; therefore he claimed it was unconstitutional. Had he approved, he doubtless would have taken a different tack. In 1819 the Supreme Court officially sanctioned Hamilton's construction of the "necessary and proper" clause (see pages 204–205), and in general that interpretation has prevailed. Because the majority tends naturally toward an argument that increases its freedom of action, the pressure for this view has been continual and formidable.

The Bank of the United States succeeded from the start. When its stock went on sale, investors snapped up every share in a matter of hours. People eagerly accepted its bank notes at face value. Business ventures of all kinds found it easier to raise new capital. Soon state-chartered banks entered the field. There were only 3 state banks in 1791; by 1801 the number was 32.

Hamilton had not finished. In December 1791 he submitted his *Report on Manufactures*, a bold call for economic planning. The pre-Revolutionary nonimportation agreements and wartime shortages had stimulated interest in manufacturing. Already a number of joint-stock companies had been founded to manufacture textiles, and an elaborate argument for economic diversification had been worked out by American economists such as Tench Coxe and Mathew Carey. Hamilton was familiar with these developments. In his *Report* he called for government tariffs, subsidies, and awards to encourage American manufacturing. He hoped to change an essentially agricultural nation into one with a complex, self-sufficient economy.

Once again business and commercial interests in particular would benefit. They would be protected against foreign competition and otherwise subsidized, whereas the general taxpayer, particularly the farmer, would pay the bill in the form of higher taxes and higher prices on manufactured goods. Hamilton argued that in the long run every interest would profit, and he was undoubtedly sincere, being too much the nationalist to favor one section at the expense of another. A majority of the Congress, however, balked at so broad-gauged a scheme. Hamilton's *Report* was pigeonholed, though many of the specific tariffs he recommended were enacted into law in 1792.

Nevertheless, the secretary of the treasury had managed to transform the financial structure of the country and to prepare the ground for an economic revolution. The constitutional reforms of 1787 had made this possible, and Hamilton turned possibility into reality.

Foreign Problems

The western problems and those related to international trade proved more difficult because foreign powers were involved. The British showed no disposition to evacuate the posts on American soil simply because the American people had decided to strengthen their central government, nor did the western Indians suddenly agree to abandon their hunting grounds to the white invaders. Military campaigns against the Indians were at first unsuccessful. When a bill was introduced in Congress to bring economic pressure on the British by placing discriminatory tonnage duties on British ships, it was defeated because of the opposition of northern business interests.

However, events that had nothing to do with the new Constitution enabled the United States to achieve most of its objectives. In 1789 revolution broke out in France. By 1793 a republic had been proclaimed, King Louis XVI had been beheaded, and France had become embroiled in a war with the chief European nations. The war caused a great deal of trouble for the United States, but it presented the United States with a marvelous opportunity to play one side off against the other.

With France fighting Great Britain and Spain, there arose the question of America's obligations under the Alliance of 1778. That treaty required the United States to defend the French West Indies "forever against all other powers." Suppose the British attacked Martinique; must America then go to war? Morally the United States was so obligated, but no responsible American statesman urged such a policy. With the British in Canada and Spanish forces to the west and south, the nation would be in serious danger if it entered the war. Instead, in April 1793, Washington issued a proclamation of neutrality.*

Meanwhile the French had sent a special representative, Edmond Charles Genet, to the United States to seek support. The French Revolution had excited much enthusiasm in the United States, for it seemed to indicate that American democratic ideas were already engulfing the world. The increasing radicalism in France tended to dampen some of the enthusiasm, yet when "Citizen" Genet landed at Charleston, South Carolina, the majority of Americans probably wished the revolutionaries well. As Genet, a charming, ebullient young man, made his way northward to present his credentials, cheering crowds welcomed him in every town. Quickly concluding that the proclamation of neutrality was "a harmless little pleasantry designed to throw dust in the eyes of the British," he began, in plain violation of American law, to license American vessels to operate as privateers against British shipping and to grant French military commissions to a number of American adventurers in order to mount expeditions against Spanish and British possessions in North America.

Washington received Genet coolly, and soon thereafter he flatly ordered him to stop his illegal activities. Genet, whose capacity for self-deception was monumental, appealed to public opinion over the president's head and continued to commission privateers. Washington then demanded his recall. The incident ended on a ludicrous note. When Genet left France, he had been in the forefront of the Revolution. Now events had marched swiftly leftward, and the new leaders in Paris considered him a dangerous reactionary. His replacement arrived in America with an order for his arrest. To return might well mean the guillotine, so Genet asked the government that was expelling him for political asylum! Washington agreed, for he was not a vindictive man. A few months later the bold revolutionary married the daughter of the governor of New York and settled down to become a farmer on Long Island.

The Genet affair was incidental to a far graver problem. Although the European war increased

---

*The word *neutrality* does not appear in this famous proclamation. Washington spoke rather of "conduct friendly and impartial toward the belligerent powers."

the foreign demand for American products, it also led to attacks on American shipping by both France and Great Britain. Each power captured American vessels headed for the other's ports whenever it could. In 1793 and 1794 perhaps 600 United States ships were seized. The British attacks caused far more damage, both physically and psychologically, because the British fleet was much larger than France's, and France at least professed to be America's friend and to favor freedom of trade for neutrals. In addition the British issued secret orders late in 1793 turning their navy loose on neutral ships headed for the French West Indies. Pouncing without warning, British warships captured about 250 American vessels and sent them off as prizes to British ports. The merchant marine, one American diplomat declared angrily, was being "kicked, cuffed, and plundered all over the Ocean."

The attacks roused a storm in America, reviving hatreds that had been smoldering since the Revolution. The continuing presence of British troops in the northwest (in 1794 the British began to build a *new* fort in the Ohio country) and the restrictions imposed on American trade with the British West Indies raised tempers still further. To try to avoid a war, for he wisely believed that the United States should not become embroiled in the Anglo-French conflict, Washington sent Chief Justice John Jay to London to seek a settlement with the British.

Jay's Treaty

Jay spent months in England in 1794 discussing various issues. The British genuinely wanted to keep the peace—as one minister quipped, the Americans "are so much in debt to this country that we scarcely dare to quarrel with them." At the same time they were concerned about American intentions. Despite Washington's neutrality proclamation, the British feared that the two new republics, France and the United States, would draw together in a battle against Europe's monarchies. Furthermore, the British were riding the crest of a wave of important victories in the war, whereas the United States was pitifully unprepared.

The treaty that Jay brought home contained one major concession: the British agreed to evacuate the posts in the west. They also promised to compensate American shipowners for seizures in the West Indies and to open up their colonies in Asia to American ships. The British conceded nothing, however, to American demands that the rights of neutrals on the high seas be respected; in effect, Jay submitted to the "Rule of 1756," a British regulation stating that neutrals could not trade in wartime with ports normally closed to them by mercantilistic restrictions in time of peace. A provision opening the British West Indies to American commerce was so hedged with qualifications limiting the size of American vessels and the type of goods allowed that the United States refused to accept it. Jay assented to an arrangement that prevented the United States from imposing discriminatory duties on British goods, an idea that a number of congressmen had proposed as a means of forcing Great Britain to treat American commerce more gently. He committed the United States government to paying pre-Revolutionary debts still owed British merchants, a slap in the face to many states whose courts had been impeding their collection. Yet nothing was said about the British paying for the slaves they had "abducted" during the fighting in the south.

Although Jay was perhaps too pro-British to have driven the hardest possible bargain, this was a valuable treaty for the United States. It was also a humiliating one. Most of what the United States gained already legally belonged to it, and the treaty sacrificed principles of tremendous importance to a nation dependent on foreign trade. It seemed certain to be rejected. But Washington realized that he must accept it or fight. Swallowing his disappointment, he submitted the treaty to the Senate, which, after a difficult contest, ratified it on June 24, 1795.

Washington's decision was one of the wisest—and luckiest—of his career. The treaty marked a long step toward the pacification and regularization of Anglo-American relations, essential for both the economic and political security of the nation. Unexpectedly—this was the luck of the decision—the treaty enabled the United States to solve its problems in the southwest. The Spanish, wishing to withdraw from the anti-French coalition and fearing a British attack on their American possessions, interpreted the Jay Treaty as a prelude to a wider Anglo-American entente. They quickly agreed to a treaty (negotiated by Thomas

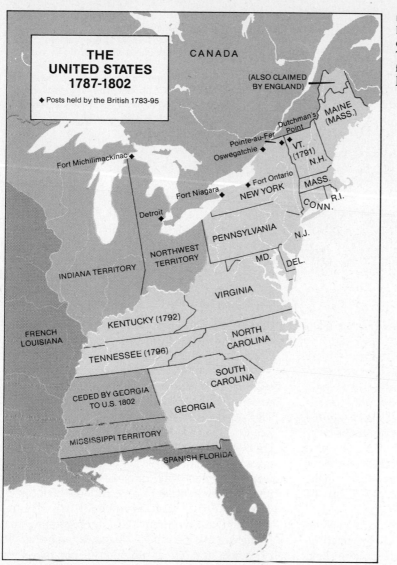

**THE
UNITED STATES
1787-1802**

◆ Posts held by the British 1783-95

CANADA

(ALSO CLAIMED
BY ENGLAND)

Dutchman's
Point

MAINE
(MASS.)

Pointe-au-Fer
Oswegatchie

VT.
(1791)

N.H.

Fort Michilimackinac

Fort Ontario

MASS.

Fort Niagara

NEW YORK

CONN.

R.I.

Detroit

PENNSYLVANIA

N.J.

INDIANA TERRITORY

NORTHWEST
TERRITORY

MD.

DEL.

VIRGINIA

FRENCH
LOUISIANA

KENTUCKY (1792)

NORTH
CAROLINA

TENNESSEE (1796)

SOUTH
CAROLINA

CEDED BY GEORGIA
TO U.S. 1802

GEORGIA

MISSISSIPPI TERRITORY

SPANISH FLORIDA

■ The United States on the eve of the
Louisiana Purchase. In 1804 Georgia's
cession became part of the Mississippi
Territory. The seven British western
forts were evacuated as a result of
Jay's Treaty (1795).

Pinckney) that granted the United States the free
navigation of the Mississippi River and the right
of deposit at New Orleans, and they accepted the
American version of the Florida boundary.

Thus, despite alarms and divisive controversy,
Americans for the first time avoided involvement
in a war between the major powers of Europe. It
had been a close thing, for many believed war on
one side or the other desirable; but the decision
was made by the Americans themselves, not by
persons on the other side of the Atlantic. This was
one of the most important benefits of the Revolution and of independence.

Federalism Victorious

Jay's and Pinckney's treaties cleared the United
States' title to the vast region between the Appalachians and the Great River. At the same time the
long struggle with the Indians, which had consumed a major portion of the government's revenues and had held back settlement of the
Northwest Territory, was finally ended. The government's policy was "expansion with honor,"
with the emphasis on expansion. In 1789 Congress
put Indian relations under the War Department
rather than the State Department, a clear indica-

■ Fort Harmar (named in honor of the Indian fighter Josiah Harmar) was located at the junction of the Ohio and Muskingum Rivers. The tiny cluster of houses on the opposite bank made up the village of Marietta. The Ohio wilderness stretches to the horizon. This scene was drawn around 1790.

tion that force, not diplomacy, would be the main instrument of federal policy.

Trouble came swiftly when white settlers moved onto the land north of the Ohio River in large numbers. The Indians, determined to hold this country at all costs, struck hard at the invaders. In 1790 the Miami chief Little Turtle, a gifted strategist, inflicted a double defeat on troops commanded by General Josiah Harmar. The next year Little Turtle and his men defeated the forces of General Arthur St. Clair still more convincingly. Both Harmar and St. Clair resigned from the army, their careers ruined.

By early 1792 the Indians had driven the whites into "beachheads" at Marietta and Cincinnati on the Ohio. But in August 1794, while Jay was dickering in London for the evacuation of the British forts, General Anthony Wayne defeated the Indians at the Battle of Fallen Timbers, near present-day Toledo. When the British at Fort Miami, who had egged the tribesmen on with promises of aid, now coldly refused to help, the Indians' will to resist was at last broken. In the Treaty of Greenville, signed the following summer, they abandoned their claims to much of the Northwest Territory.

After the events of 1794–1795, settlers poured into the west as water bursts through a broken dike. Kentucky had become a state in 1792; now, in 1796, Tennessee was admitted. Two years later

Mississippi Territory was organized, and at the end of the century, Indiana Territory. The great westward flood reached full tide.

Another event that took place in the west while Jay was negotiating with the British offered further evidence of the growth of American nationalism. This was Washington's suppression of the Whiskey Rebellion. To help pay for the cost of assuming the state debts, Hamilton had persuaded Congress to put a stiff excise tax on whiskey. This hurt western farmers, who turned much of their grain into whiskey in order to cope with the high cost of transportation. When Hamilton frivolously replied to western complaints by suggesting that farmers drank too much to begin with and should cut down on their consumption if they found the tax oppressive, resentment increased. In the summer of 1794 rioting broke out in western Pennsylvania. Much like the Shaysites a few years earlier, the "rebels" interfered with judicial proceedings and terrorized local law enforcement officers. But the new Constitution made possible prompt and effective action against them. Washington, in an uncharacteristically harsh and precipitous decision, called up nearly 13,000 militiamen (more men than he had ever commanded during the Revolution) and marched westward. At this tremendous show of force the rebels vanished. There was no fighting. A few minor figures were thrown in jail, and thereafter the tax was peaceably collected until it was repealed during Jefferson's administration. The contrast with Shays' Rebellion warmed the hearts of all who feared "anarchy." Thus the events of the mid 1790s seemed to demonstrate that independence had been fully established and that the United States at last had become a true nation.

SUPPLEMENTARY READING
Titles marked with an asterisk have been published in paperback

On the "critical period," see Merrill Jensen, **The Articles of Confederation*** (1940) and **The New Nation*** (1950), which attack the Fiske thesis. J. L. Davis, **Sectionalism in American Politics** (1977), is also useful. For the western problems of this period, see B. W. Bond, **The Foundations of Ohio** (1941), A. P. Whitaker, **The Spanish American Frontier*** (1927), and J. A. James, **Life of George Rogers Clark** (1928). On economic problems, E. J. Ferguson, **The Power of the Purse*** (1968), R. A. East, **Business Enterprise in the American Revolutionary Era** (1938), and T. C. Cochran, **New York in the Confederation** (1932), are useful, while C. P. Nettels, **The Emergence of a National Economy*** (1962), puts this subject in the broader perspective of the period 1775–1815. A lively treatment of Shays' Rebellion is M. L. Starkey, **A Little Rebellion** (1955); D. P. Szatmary, **Shays' Rebellion** (1980), is a more recent study.

The political thinking of the period is discussed lucidly in G. S. Wood, **The Creation of the American Republic*** (1969), in Richard Buel, Jr., **Securing the Revolution: Ideology in American Politics*** (1972), and in J. T. Main, **Political Parties Before the Constitution*** (1973). As for the making of the Constitution, the records kept by Madison and other delegates to the Constitutional Convention are reprinted in C. C. Tansill (ed.), **Documents Illustrative of the Formation of the Union . . .** (1927). A good general account of the convention is Clinton Rossiter, **1787: The Grand Convention*** (1966). The best treatment of Alexander Hamilton's connection with the Constitution and of his political views generally is Clinton Rossiter, **Alexander Hamilton and the Constitution** (1964). For Madison, Irving Brant, **James Madison: Father of the Constitution** (1950), provides the fullest account.

C. A. Beard, **An Economic Interpretation of the Constitution*** (1913), caused a veritable revolution in the thinking of historians about the motives of the Founding Fathers, but recent studies have caused a major reaction away from the Beardian interpretation; see especially R. E. Brown, **Charles Beard and the Constitution*** (1956), and a more detailed critique, Forrest McDonald, **We the People: The Economic Origins of the Constitution*** (1958). Two books by R. A. Rutland, **The Birth of the Bill of Rights*** (1955) and **The Ordeal of the Constitution: The Anti-Federalists and the Ratification Struggle** (1966), and also J. T. Main, **The Antifederalists*** (1961), are helpful in understanding the opposition to the Constitution, while the **Federalist Papers*** of Hamilton, Madison, and Jay, available in many editions, are essential for the arguments of the supporters of the new government. For the Bill of Rights, consult Bernard Schwartz, **The Great Rights of Mankind** (1977).

On the organization of the federal government and the history of the Washington administration, see L. D. White, **The Federalists** (1948), an administrative history, and J. C. Miller, **The Federalist Era*** (1960), a more general history of the period. Nathan Schachner, **The Founding Fathers*** (1954), is a somewhat fuller study of these years. Washington's presidency is treated in detail in the latter volumes of D. S. Freeman, **George Washington** (1948–1957). Joseph Charles, **Origins of the American Party System*** (1961), is thought-provoking, and the early chapters of W. N. Chambers, **Political Parties in a New Nation*** (1963), are also useful.

Hamilton's **Reports** as secretary of the treasury are conveniently collected in Samuel McKee, Jr. (ed.), **Papers on Public Credit, Commerce, and Finance by Alexander Hamilton*** (1934). The best of the many biographies of Hamilton are Broadus Mitchell, **Alexander Hamilton*** (1976) and J. C. Miller, **Alexander Hamilton: A Portrait in Paradox*** (1959). For foreign affairs during the Washington administration, see Alexander De Conde, **Entangling Alliance: Politics and Diplomacy under George Washington** (1958), Felix Gilbert, **To the Farewell Address*** (1961), Harry Ammon, **The Genet Mission** (1973), and two volumes by S. F. Bemis, **Jay's Treaty*** (1923) and **Pinckney's Treaty*** (1926). Hannah Arendt, **On Revolution*** (1963), provides an interesting discussion of the relative influence of the French and American revolutions on later history.

6/JEFFERSONIAN DEMOCRACY

 No one had a better right to rejoice in the course of events in the mid 1790s than Alexander Hamilton. His financial reforms had achieved a dramatic success. Jay's Treaty had extinguished the danger of war with Great Britain, a conflict that in his opinion would have been catastrophic. And the Mississippi had been opened, another advance toward the national greatness he desired. Yet Hamilton was far from content, for a formidable opposition to himself and to everything he believed in had developed. The opposition was coalescing into a political party headed by Thomas Jefferson. A savage struggle for power was under way, the prize being the mantle of Washington, who was determined to retire at the end of his second term in 1797.

Thomas Jefferson: Political Theorist

Jefferson hardly seemed cut out for politics. Although in some ways a typical, pleasure-loving southern planter, he had in him something of the Spartan. He grew tobacco but did not smoke, and he partook only sparingly of meat and alcohol. Unlike most planters he never hunted or gambled, though he was a fine horseman and enjoyed dancing, music, and other social diversions. His practical interests ranged enormously—from architecture and geology to natural history and scientific farming—yet he displayed little interest in managing men. Controversy dismayed him, and he tended to avoid it by assigning to some thicker-skinned associate the task of attacking his enemies. Nevertheless, he was not without ambition. He wanted to have a say in shaping the future of the country, and once engaged he fought stubbornly and at times deviously to get and hold power.

Like Hamilton, Jefferson thought human beings basically selfish. "Lions and tigers are mere lambs compared with men," he once said. Yet he believed that "no definite limits can be assigned to the improvability of the human race" and that unless people were free to follow the dictates of reason, the march of civilization would grind quickly to a halt. "To preserve the freedom of the human mind," he wrote, "every spirit should be ready to devote itself to martyrdom." Democracy seemed to him not so much an ideal as a practical necessity. If people could not govern themselves, how could they be expected to govern their fellows? He had no patience with Hamilton's fondness for magnifying the virtues of the rich and the well-born. He believed that "genius" was a rare quality but one "which nature has shown as liberally among poor as rich." When a very old man he wrote: "The mass of mankind has not been born with saddles on their backs, nor a favored few booted and spurred, ready to ride them legitimately, by the grace of God."

Jefferson believed *all* government a necessary evil at best, for by its nature it restricted the freedom of the individual. For this reason, he wanted the United States to remain a society of small independent farmers.* Such a nation did not need much political organization.

Jefferson's main objection to Hamilton was that Hamilton wanted to commercialize and centralize the country. This he feared, for it would mean the growth of cities, which would complicate society and hence require more regulation. "When we get piled upon one another in large cities, as in Europe," he wrote Madison in 1787, "we shall become corrupt as in Europe, and go to eating one another as they do there." He distrusted city workers; since they did not own property, they seemed to have no stake in orderly government. Like Hamilton he believed them easy prey for demagogues. "I consider the class of artificers as the panders of vice, and the instruments by which the liberties of a country are usually overturned," he said. "Those who labor in the earth," he also said, "are the chosen people of God, if ever He had a chosen people."

Jefferson objected to what he considered Hamilton's pro-British orientation. Despite his support of the Revolution, Hamilton admired English society and the orderliness of the British government, and he modeled much of his financial program on the British example. To the author of the Declaration of Independence, these attitudes passed all understanding. Jefferson thought English society immoral and decadent, the British system of government fundamentally corrupt. Toward France, the two took opposite positions. Jefferson was in Paris when the French Revolution broke out; he was delighted to see another blow struck at tyranny. Leading French liberals consulted him at every turn. Later, as secretary of state, he excused the excesses of the French upheaval far more than did most Americans. To Hamilton, the violence and social disruption caused by the Revolution were anathema.

The conflict between Hamilton and Jefferson came to a head slowly. Jefferson went along with Hamilton's funding plan and, as we have seen, traded the assumption of state debts for a capital on the Potomac. However, when Hamilton proposed the Bank of the United States and the Whiskey Tax, he dug in his heels. These measures seemed designed to benefit the northeastern commercial classes at the expense of southern and western farmers. Sensing a dastardly plot to milk

---

*To Jefferson, agriculture was both the fundamental and the noblest of callings. "The greatest service which can be rendered to any country is to add a useful plant to its culture," he once said.

Triumph Government: perish all its enemies.__
Traitors be warned: justice though slow is sure

■ The Federalists often attacked Jefferson for his pro-French attitudes. A dog-eared cartoon ca. 1790 shows Washington in the national chariot leading troops against an invasion of bloodthirsty French "Cannibals" at the left. The figures trying to halt the chariot are, from left, Albert Gallatin, Citizen Genet, holding the spoke of the wheel, and Jefferson.

the producing masses for the benefit of a few capitalists and suspecting that Hamilton wanted to turn America into a monarchy, Jefferson joined the opposition.

Late in the spring of 1791 he and James Madison, the real founder of the anti-Hamilton party, began to sound out other politicians. He appointed a friend of Madison, the poet Philip Freneau, to a minor State Department post. Settling in Philadelphia, the new temporary capital, Freneau established a newspaper, the *National Gazette,* and was soon describing that "illustrious patriot" Thomas Jefferson as the "Colossus of Liberty" and flailing away editorially at Hamilton and his policies. Furious, Hamilton hit back hard at Jefferson through the columns of another Philadelphia paper, John Fenno's *Gazette of the United States.*

As their quarrel became more and more personal, first Jefferson and then Hamilton appealed to Washington for support. The poor president, who hated controversy, tried to get them to bury

their differences—to no avail. The two now agreed on only one thing: Washington, who was in ill health and wished desperately to retire, must serve a second term.

Federalists and Republicans

Around the striking personalities of these quarreling leaders, two political camps began to gather. Congressional supporters of Hamilton, taking the name Federalists, acted increasingly in concert on important questions, while Jefferson's friends, called Democratic Republicans, did likewise. Why national political parties emerged after the ratification of a Constitution that made no provision for such organizations is a question that has long intrigued historians. Probably the main reason was the obvious one: by creating a strong central government the Constitution produced national issues and a focus for national discussion and settlement of these issues. Furthermore, by failing to create

138

machinery for nominating candidates for federal offices, the Constitution left a vacuum which informal party organizations promptly filled.

In the early stages neither the Federalist nor the Democratic Republican was a party in the modern sense; there were no national committees, no conventions, no state "machines." In large measure the two parties were alliances of local and state groups, greatly influenced by parochial issues and the personalities of local leaders. Over time, however, closer-knit organizations developed.

What determined a voter's party allegiance in the 1790s is hard to pin down. No simple dichotomy between Hamiltonian business interests and Jeffersonian agrarian interests makes sense. The divisions were close, and since 90 percent of the citizens were farmers, a sharp commercial-agrarian split would have produced an overwhelming victory for the Democratic Republicans. Farmers who produced for commercial markets were more likely to respond to Federalist arguments, settlers in remote areas to those of the Democratic Republicans. A majority of the privileged group that Hamilton appealed to voted Federalist, but numbers of merchants and other businessmen supported the Jeffersonians. As in the divisions over ratifying the Constitution, individuals of status with established interests tended to be Federalists, while those on the periphery of society (and those on the make) were more often on the other side. The problem is enormously complicated by conditions and traditions in the separate states.

In short, no clear-cut social or economic alignments appeared, although social and economic issues were certainly discussed by the politicians. The parties stood for their leaders more than for principles, and these men, dealing with a series of practical problems, were not always consistent in their attitudes.

The personal nature of early American political controversies goes far toward explaining why the party battles of the era were so bitter. So does the continuing anxiety that plagued partisans of both persuasions about the supposed frailty of a republican government. The United States was still very much an experiment; leaders who sincerely proclaimed their own devotion to its welfare suspected that their opponents wanted to undermine its institutions. Federalists feared that the Jeffersonians sought a dictatorship based on mob rule, Democratic Republicans that the Hamiltonians hid "under the mask of Federalism hearts devoted to monarchy."

The growing controversy over the French Revolution and the resulting war between France and Great Britain widened the split between the parties. After the radicals in France executed Louis XVI and instituted the Reign of Terror, American conservatives were horrified. The Jeffersonians, however, continued to defend the Revolution. Slaveowners could be heard singing the praises of *liberté, égalité, fraternité,* and great southern landlords, whose French counterparts were losing their estates—some their heads—were extolling "the glorious successes of our Gallic brethren." In the same way the Federalists began to idealize the British, whom they considered the embodiment of the forces that were resisting French radicalism.

This created an explosive situation. Enthusiasm for a foreign country might tempt Americans, all unwittingly, to betray their own. Hamilton came to believe that Jefferson was so prejudiced in favor of France as to be unable to conduct foreign affairs rationally, and Jefferson could say contemptuously: "Hamilton is panick struck, if we refuse our breech to every kick which Great Britain may choose to give it."

In fact Jefferson never lost his sense of perspective. When the Anglo-French war erupted, he recommended neutrality. In the Genet affair, although originally sympathetic to the young envoy, Jefferson ended by characterizing him as "hotheaded, all imagination, no judgment, passionate, disrespectful and even indecent." He cordially approved Washington's decision to send Genet packing. Although he objected to the Jay Treaty, he did so not out of fondness for France but because he believed peace with Great Britain could not be purchased by surrendering American rights. "Acquiescence under insult is not the way to escape war," he wrote in 1795.

Hamilton perhaps went a little too far in his friendliness to Great Britain, but the real danger was that some of Hamilton's and Jefferson's excitable followers might become so committed as to forget the true interests of the United States.

Washington's Farewell

As long as Washington remained president, his popularity inhibited the solidification of party lines. On questions of finance and foreign policy he usually sided with Hamilton and thus increasingly incurred the anger of Jefferson. But he was, after all, a Virginian. Only the most rabid partisan could think him a tool of northern commercial interests. He remained as he intended himself to be, a symbol of national unity. But he was determined to put away the cares of office at the end of his second term. In September 1796 he announced his retirement in a "Farewell Address" to the nation.

Washington had found the acrimonious rivalry between Federalists and Republicans very disturbing. "I had no conceptions that Parties would . . . go the length I have been witness to," he complained to Jefferson. Hamilton advocated national unity, yet he seemed prepared to smash any individual or faction that disagreed with his vision of the country's future. Jefferson had risked his neck for independence, but he opposed the economic development needed to make America strong enough to defend that independence. Washington was less brilliant than either Hamilton or Jefferson but wiser. He appreciated how important it was that the new nation remain at peace—with the rest of the world and with itself. In his farewell he deplored the "baneful effects of the spirit of party" that led honest people to use dishonest means to win a mean advantage over fellow Americans. He tried to show how the north benefited from the prosperity of the south, the south from that of the north, and the east and west also, in reciprocal fashion. It is significant that he drew on the suggestions of both Hamilton and Madison in preparing his farewell.

Washington urged the people to avoid both "inveterate antipathies" and "passionate attachments" to any foreign nation. Nothing had alarmed him more than the sight of Americans dividing into "French" and "English" factions. Furthermore, France had repeatedly interfered in American domestic affairs. First there had been Genet, childish and exasperating. Later another French minister, Citizen Adet, had tried to prejudice both Congress and public opinion against the Jay Treaty. Adet had attempted to organize on American soil an expedition to conquer Louisiana for France. "Against the insidious wiles of foreign influence," Washington now warned, "the jealousy of a free people ought to be *constantly* awake." America should develop its foreign trade but steer clear of foreign political connections as far as possible. "Permanent alliances" should be avoided, although "temporary alliances for extraordinary purposes" might sometimes be useful.

Election of 1796

Washington's Farewell Address was destined to have a long and important influence on American thinking, but its immediate impact was small. He had intended it to cool political passions. Instead, in the words of one Federalist congressman, people took it as "a signal, like dropping a hat, for the party racers to start." By the time the presidential campaign had ended, many Federalists and Republicans were refusing to speak to one another.

Jefferson was the only Republican candidate seriously considered in 1796. The logical Federalist was Hamilton, but, as was to happen so often in American history with powerful leaders, he was not considered "available" because his controversial policies had made him many enemies. Gathering in caucus, the Federalists in Congress nominated Vice-President John Adams for the top office and Thomas Pinckney of South Carolina, negotiator of the popular Spanish treaty, for vice-president. In the election the Federalists won a majority.

Hamilton, hoping to run the new administration from the wings, preferred Pinckney, a relatively weak character, to the tough-minded Adams. He arranged for some of the Federalist electors from South Carolina to vote only for Pinckney. Catching wind of this, a number of New England electors retaliated by cutting Pinckney. As a result, Adams won in the electoral college, 71 to 68, over Jefferson, who had the solid support of the Republican electors. Pinckney got only 59 electoral votes. Jefferson thus became vice-president.

The unexpected result seemed to presage a decline in partisanship. Adams actually preferred the Virginian to Pinckney for the vice-presidency, while Jefferson said that if Adams would "relinquish his bias to an English constitution," he might make a fine chief executive. The two had in common a distaste for Hamilton—a powerful bond.

However, the closeness of the election indicated a trend toward the Republicans, who were making constant and effective use of the canard that the Federalists were "monocrats" (monarchists) determined to destroy American liberty. Without Washington to lead them, the Federalist politicians were already quarreling among themselves; honest, able, hard-working John Adams was too caustic and too scathingly frank to unite them. The unpopularity of the Jay Treaty hurt the Federalists further. In March 1797 everything seemed to indicate a Republican victory at the next election.

The XYZ Affair

At this point occurred one of the most remarkable reversals of public feeling in American history. French attacks on American shipping, begun out of irritation at the Jay Treaty and in order to influence the election, continued after Adams took office. Hoping to stop them, Adams appointed three commissioners (Charles Pinckney, United States minister to France and elder brother of Thomas; John Marshall, a prominent Virginia Federalist; and Elbridge Gerry of Massachusetts, a former congressman who was a friend of Jefferson but was not closely identified with either party) to try to negotiate a settlement. Their mission was a fiasco. Talleyrand, the French foreign minister, sent three agents (later spoken of as X, Y, and Z) to demand a huge bribe as the price of making a deal. The Americans refused, more because they suspected Talleyrand's good faith than because of any distaste for bribery. "No, no, not a sixpence," Pinckney told the agents. The talks broke up, and

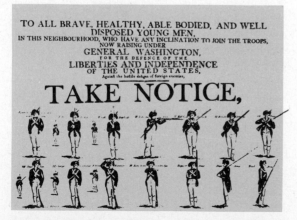

■ A recruiting poster of 1798 appealed for volunteers to defend the nation "against the hostile designs of foreign enemies," the "enemies" being the French.

in April 1798 President Adams released the commissioners' reports.

They caused a sensation. Americans' sense of national honor, perhaps overly tender because the country was so young and insecure, was outraged. Pinckney's laconic refusal to pay a bribe was translated into the grandiose phrase "Millions for defense, but not one cent for tribute!" and broadcast throughout the land. John Adams, never a man with mass appeal, suddenly found himself a national hero. Federalist hotheads burned for a fight. Congress unilaterally abrogated the French Alliance, created a Navy Department, and appropriated enough money to build 40-odd warships and triple the size of the army. Washington came out of retirement to lead the forces, with Hamilton, now a general, as second in command. On the seas American privateers began to attack French shipping.

A declaration of war would have been immensely popular. But perhaps—it is not an entirely illogical surmise about John Adams—the president did not want to be popular. He knew that the United States had only 3,500 men under arms and a navy of exactly three vessels. Instead of calling for war, he contented himself with approving the buildup of the armed forces.

The Republicans, committed to friendship with France, were thrown into consternation. Although angered by the XYZ Affair, they hoped to avoid war and tried, one angry Federalist said, "to clog the wheels of government" by opposing the military appropriations. Their newspapers spewed abuse on Adams and his administration. Benjamin Bache, editor of the Philadelphia *Aurora*, referred to the president as "blind, bald, toothless, querulous," which was three-quarters true but irrelevant. John Daly Burk of the New York *Time Piece* called him a "mock Monarch" surrounded by a "*court* composed of tories and speculators," which was a flat lie.

In light of this virulent reaction, many Federalists expected the Republicans to side with France if war broke out. Hysterical and near panic, these Federalists easily persuaded themselves that the danger of subversion was acute. The French Revolution and the resulting war were churning European society to the depths, stirring the hopes of liberals and striking fear in the hearts of conservatives. Refugees of both persuasions were often forced to flee their homes, and many of them came to the United States. Suddenly the presence of the foreigners seemed threatening to "native" Americans. Benjamin Bache was a grandson of Benjamin Franklin, but Burk, for example, was Irish-born. The most important leader of the Republican opposition in Congress was Albert Gallatin, an immigrant from Switzerland.

Alien and Sedition Acts

Conservative Federalists saw in this situation a chance to smash the opposition. In June and July 1798 they pushed through Congress a series of repressive measures known as the Alien and Sedition Acts. The least offensive of these laws, the Naturalization Act, increased the period a foreigner had to reside in the United States before being eligible for citizenship from 5 to 14 years. The Alien Enemies Act gave the president the power to arrest or expel aliens in time of "declared war," but since the quasi-war with France was never declared, this measure had no practical importance. The Alien Act authorized the president to expel *all* aliens whom he thought "dangerous to the peace and safety of the United States." (Adams never invoked this law, but a number of aliens left the country out of fear that he might.) Finally, there was the Sedition Act. Its first section, making it a crime "to impede the operation of any law" or to attempt to instigate a riot or insurrection, was reasonable enough; but the act made it illegal to publish, or even to utter, any "false, scandalous and malicious" criticism of high government officials.

Although milder than British sedition laws, this proviso rested, as James Madison said, on "the exploded doctrine" that government officials "are the masters and not the servants of the people." To criticize a king is to try to undermine the respect of his subjects for the establishment over which he rules, and that is seditious. To criticize an elected official in a republic is to express dissatisfaction with the way one's agent is performing an assigned task—certainly no threat to the state itself. The difference between the two modes of thought escaped the Federalists of 1798.

This is mere theory; far worse was the Federalists' practice under the Sedition Act. As the election of 1800 approached, they made a systematic attempt to silence the leading Republican newspa-

pers. Twenty-five persons were prosecuted and ten convicted, all in patently unfair trials. In typical cases, the editor Thomas Cooper was sentenced to six months in jail and fined $400, the editor Charles Holt got three months and a $200 fine, the editor James Callender got nine months and a $200 fine. In some instances the criticisms of the Adams administration had been very raw, yet equally harsh things were being said with impunity by Federalist editors about Vice-President Jefferson. When Cooper, a distinguished English-born radical and later president of the University of South Carolina, attempted after serving his sentence to have Hamilton prosecuted for *his* intemperate attacks on President Adams, he got nowhere.

While Thomas Jefferson did not object in principle to *state* sedition laws, he believed that the Alien and Sedition Acts violated the First Amendment's guarantees of freedom of speech and the press and were an invasion of the rights of the states. He conferred with Madison, and they decided to draw up resolutions arguing that the laws were unconstitutional. Madison's draft was presented to the Virginia legislature and Jefferson's to the legislature of Kentucky. Since the Constitution was a compact made by sovereign states, each state had "an equal right to judge for itself" when the compact had been violated, the Kentucky Resolves declared. Thus a state could declare a law of Congress unconstitutional. The Virginia Resolves took an only slightly less forthright position.

Neither Kentucky nor Virginia tried to implement these resolves or to interfere with the enforcement of the Alien and Sedition Acts. Jefferson and Madison were protesting Federalist highhandedness and firing the opening salvo of Jefferson's campaign for the presidency, not advancing a new constitutional theory of extreme states' rights. "Keep away all show of force," Jefferson advised his supporters.

This was sound advice, for events were again playing into the hands of the Republicans. Talleyrand had never wanted war with the United States. When he finally realized how vehemently the Americans had reacted to his little attempt to replenish his personal fortune, depleted during the Revolution, he let Adams know that new negotiators would be properly received.

President Adams quickly grasped the importance of the French change of heart, for like Washington before him he never forgot that the country needed peace and tranquillity in order to grow stronger and more closely knit. Other leading Federalists, however, had lost their heads. By shouting about the French danger, they had roused the country against radicalism, and they did not intend to surrender this advantage tamely. Hamilton in particular wanted war at almost any price—if not against France, then against Spain. He saw himself at the head of the new American army sweeping first across Louisiana and the Floridas, then on to the south. "We ought to squint at South America," he suggested. "Our game will be to attack where we can," he added. "Tempting objects will be without our grasp."

The British cleverly played upon Federalist ambitions, hinting at further commercial concessions, talking of convoying American merchant vessels in case of a Franco-American war, even suggesting to the United States minister in London, Rufus King, the idea of a British-American attack on South America. But the Puritan Adams was a specialist at resisting temptation. He would neither go to war merely to destroy the political opposition in America nor follow "the fools who were intriguing to plunge us into an alliance with England . . . and wild expeditions to South America." Instead he submitted to the Senate the name of a new minister plenipotentiary to France, and when the Federalists tried to block the appointment, he threatened to resign. That would have made Jefferson president! So the furious Federalists had to give in, though they forced Adams to send three men instead of one.

Napoleon had taken over France by the time the Americans arrived, and he drove a harder bargain than Talleyrand would have. In the end he signed an agreement (the Convention of 1800) abrogating the Franco-American treaties of 1778. Nothing was said about the damage done to American shipping by the French, but the war scare was over.

Election of 1800

Suddenly the public realized that the furor over war and subversion had been concocted almost out of thin air. Nevertheless, the presidential contest between Adams and Jefferson was close. Be-

cause of his stand for peace, Adams personally escaped the brunt of popular indignation against the Federalist party. His solid qualities had a strong appeal to conservatives, and fear that the Republicans would introduce radical "French" social reforms did not disappear. Many nationalist-minded voters worried lest the strong government established by the Federalists be weakened by the Jeffersonians in the name of states' rights. The economic progress stimulated by Hamilton's financial reforms also seemed threatened. When the electors' votes were counted in February 1801, the Republicans were discovered to have won narrowly, 73 to 65.

But *which* Republican? The Constitution did not distinguish between presidential and vice-presidential candidates; it provided only that each elector should vote for two candidates, the one with the most votes becoming president and the runner-up vice-president. The vice-presidential candidate of the Republicans was Aaron Burr of New York, a former senator and a rival of Hamilton in law and politics. And Republican party solidarity had been perfect: Jefferson and Burr received 73 votes each. Because of the tie, the House of Representatives (voting by states) had to choose between them.

In the House the Republicans could control only 8 of the 16 state delegations. On the first ballot Jefferson got these 8 votes, one short of election, while 6 states voted for Burr. Two state delegations, being evenly split, lost their votes. Through 35 ballots the deadlock persisted; the Federalists, fearful of Jefferson's radicalism, voted solidly for Burr. Pressures were exerted on both candidates to make deals to win additional support. Officially at least, both refused. Burr put on a great show of remaining above the battle. (Had he been an honorable man, he would have withdrawn, since the voters had clearly intended him for the second spot.) Whether Jefferson made any promises is uncertain; there is some evidence that to break the deadlock he assured the Federalists that he would preserve Hamilton's financial system and continue the Washington-Adams foreign policy. Hamilton played an important part behind the scenes; he detested Burr and threw his weight to Jefferson. Finally, on February 17, 1801, Jefferson was elected. Burr became vice-president.

To make sure that this deadlock would never be repeated, the Twelfth Amendment was drafted, providing for separate balloting in the electoral college for president and vice-president. This change was ratified in 1804, shortly before the next election.

The Federalist Contribution

On March 4, 1801, in the raw new national capital on the Potomac River named in honor of the Father of his Country, Thomas Jefferson took the presidential oath and delivered his inaugural address. The new president believed that a revolution as important as that heralded by his immortal Declaration of Independence had occurred, and

for once most of his enemies agreed with him.

Certainly an era had ended. In the years between the Peace of Paris and Jay's Treaty the Federalists had practically monopolized the political good sense of the nation. In the perspective of history they were "right" in strengthening the federal government, in establishing a sound fiscal system, in trying to diversify the economy, in seeking an accommodation with Great Britain, and in refusing to be carried away with enthusiasm for France despite the bright dreams inspired by the French Revolution. The Federalists had displayed remarkable self-control and moderation at least until 1798. They were nationalists who did not try to destroy local patriotism, aristocrats willing to live

■ Ellicott's engraved map of 1792, based on L'Enfant's original plan, was adopted by Congress as the final plan for the city of Washington, D.C. One notation on this sketch says: "The grand Avenues, and such Streets as lead immediately to Public places, are from 130 to 160 feet wide, and may be conveniently divided into foot ways, walks of trees, and a carriage way."

with the spirit of democracy. The Constitution is their monument, with its wise compromises, its balance of forces, its restraint, its practical concessions to local prejudices.

But the Federalists were unable to face up to defeat. When they saw the Jeffersonians gathering strength by developing clever new techniques of party organization and propaganda, mouthing slogans about "monocrats," glorifying both the past with its satisfying simplicity and the future with its promise of a glorious day when all men would be free, equal, and brothers, they panicked. Abandoning the sober wisdom of their great period, they fought ignobly to save themselves at any cost. The effort turned defeat into rout. Jefferson's victory, fairly close in the electoral college, approached landslide proportions in the congressional elections, where popular feeling could express itself directly.

Jefferson erred, however, in calling this triumph a revolution. The real upheaval had been attempted in 1798; it was Federalist inspired, and it failed. In 1800 the voters expressed a preference for the old over the new, that is, for individual freedom and limited national power. And Jefferson, despite Federalist fears that he would destroy the Constitution and establish a radical social order, presided instead over a regime that confirmed the great achievements of the Federalist era.

What was most significant about the election of 1800 was that it was *not* a revolution. After a bitter contest the Jeffersonians took power and proceeded to change the policy of the government. They did so peacefully. Thus American republican government passed a crucial test: control of its machinery had changed hands in a democratic and orderly way. And only less significant, the informal party system had demonstrated its usefulness. The Jeffersonians had organized popular dissatisfaction with Federalist policies, formulated a platform of reform, chosen leaders to put their plans into effect, and elected those leaders to office.

Jefferson as President

The novelty of the new administration lay in its style and its moderation. Both were apparent in Jefferson's inaugural address. The new president's opening remarks showed that he was neither a demagogue nor a firebrand. "The task is above my talents," he said modestly, "and . . . I approach it with . . . anxious and awful presentiments." The people had spoken, and their voice must be heeded, but the rights of dissenters must be respected. "All . . . will bear in mind this sacred principle," he said, "that though the will of the majority is in all cases to prevail, that will to be rightful must be reasonable; that the minority possess their equal rights, which equal law must protect, and to violate would be oppression."

Jefferson spoke at some length about specific policies. He declared himself against "entangling alliances" and for economy in government, and he promised to pay off the national debt, preserve the government's credit, and stimulate both agriculture and its "handmaid," commerce. His main stress was on the cooling of partisan passions. "Every difference of opinion is not a difference of principle. We have called by different names brethren of the same principle. We are all Republicans—we are all Federalists." And he promised the country "a wise and frugal Government, which shall restrain men from injuring one another . . . [and] leave them otherwise free to regulate their own pursuits."

Jefferson quickly demonstrated the sincerity of his remarks. He saw to it that the Whiskey Tax and other Federalist excises were repealed, and he made sharp cuts in military and naval expenditures to keep the budget in balance. The national debt was reduced from $83 million to $57 million during his eight years in office. The Naturalization Act of 1798 was repealed and the old five years' residence requirement for citizenship restored. The Sedition Act and the Alien Act expired of their own accord in 1801 and 1802.

The changes were not drastic. Jefferson made no effort to tear down the fiscal structure that Hamilton had erected. "We can pay off his debt," the new president confessed, "but we cannot get rid of his financial system." Nor did the author of the Kentucky Resolves try to alter the balance of federal-state power.

Yet there was a different tone to the new regime. Jefferson had no desire to surround himself with pomp and ceremony; the excessive formality and punctilio of the Washington and Adams administrations had been distasteful to him. He made sure that his own household was less cluttered by ritual and display. From the moment of

■ The winning design for the executive mansion, reproduced here, won $500 (a good sum for the times) for Irish-born architect James Hoban. Construction started in 1792, and the building was finished late in John Adams' term; Adams lived there only four months, until March, 1801.

his election he played down the ceremonial aspects of the presidency. He asked that he be notified of his election by mail rather than by a committee, and he would have preferred to have taken the oath at Charlottesville, near Monticello, his home, rather than at Washington. After the inauguration he returned to his boardinghouse on foot and took dinner in his usual seat at the common table.

In the White House he often wore a frayed coat and carpet slippers, even to receive the representatives of foreign powers when they arrived, resplendent with silk ribbons and a sense of their own importance, to present their credentials. At social affairs he paid little heed to the status and seniority of his guests. When dinner was announced, he offered his arm to whichever lady he was talking to at the moment and placed her at his right; other guests were free to sit wherever they found an empty chair. During business hours congressmen, friends, foreign officials, and plain citizens coming to call took their turn in the order of their arrival. "The principle of society with us," Jefferson explained, "is the equal rights of all. . . . Nobody shall be above you, nor you above anybody, *pell-mell* is our law."

"Pell-mell" was also good politics, and Jefferson was a superb politician. He gave dozens of small stag dinner parties for congressmen, serving the food personally from a dumbwaiter connected with the kitchen. The guests, carefully chosen to make congenial groups, were seated at a round table to encourage general conversation; the food and wine were first-class. These were ostensibly social occasions—shoptalk was avoided—yet they paid large political dividends. Jefferson learned to know every congressman personally, Democratic Republican and Federalist alike, and not only their political views but their strengths, their quirks, their flaws. And he worked his personal magic upon them, displaying the breadth of his knowledge, his charm and wit, his lack of pomposity. "You see, we are alone and *our walls have no ears*," he would say, and while the wine flowed and the guests sampled delicacies prepared by Jefferson's French chef, the president manufactured political capital. "You drink as you please and converse at your ease," one guest reported.

Jefferson made effective use of his close supporters in Congress, and of Cabinet members as well, in persuading Congress to go along with his proposals. His state papers were models of sweet reason, minimizing conflicts, stressing areas where all honest people must agree. After all, as he indicated in his inaugural address, nearly all Americans *were* both federalists and republicans; no great principle divided them into irreconcilable camps. Jefferson set out to bring them all into *his* camp, and he succeeded so well in four years that when he ran for reelection against Charles Pinckney, he got 162 of the 176 electoral votes cast. Eventually even John Quincy Adams, son of the second president, became a Jeffersonian.

At the same time Jefferson was anything but nonpartisan in the sense that Washington had been. His Cabinet consisted exclusively of men of his own party. He exerted almost continuous pressure on Congress to make sure that his legislative program was enacted into law. He did not remove many Federalist officeholders, and at one point he remarked ruefully that government officials seldom died and never resigned; but when he could, he used his power of appointment to reward his friends and punish his enemies.

Attack on the Judiciary

Although notably open-minded and tolerant, Jefferson had a few stubborn prejudices. One was against kings, another against the British system of government. A third was against judges, or rather, against entrenched judicial power. While recognizing that judges must have a degree of independence, he feared what he called their "habit of going out of the question before them, to throw an anchor ahead, and grapple further hold for future advances of power." The biased behavior of Federalist judges during the trials under the Sedition Act enormously increased this basic distrust. It burst all bounds when the Federalist majority of the dying Congress rammed through the Judiciary Act of 1801 in a last-ditch effort to "protect" the country against Jeffersonian radicalism.

The Judiciary Act created 6 new circuit courts, presided over by 16 new federal judges, and a small army of attorneys, marshals, and clerks. The expanding country needed the judges, but with the enthusiastic cooperation of President Adams the Federalists made shameless use of the opportunity to fill all the new positions with conservative Federalists, and this angered Jefferson. Adams had also appointed John Marshall of Virginia,

■ Jefferson appears more relaxed and approachable in this drawing by Charles Saint-Mémin than he does in more formal portraits.

whom Jefferson particularly disliked, as chief justice of the United States. The new appointees were dubbed midnight justices because, according to rumor, Adams stayed up till midnight on March 3, his last day as president, feverishly signing their commissions.

The Republicans retaliated as soon as the new Congress met by repealing the Judiciary Act of 1801, but President Jefferson still fumed. Upon taking office he had discovered that in the confusion of Adams' last hours the commissions of a number of justices of the peace for the new District of Columbia had not been distributed. While these were small fry indeed, Jefferson was so angry that he ordered the commissions held up even though they had been signed by Adams. One of the appointees, William Marbury, then petitioned the Supreme Court for a writ of mandamus ordering the new secretary of state, James Madison, to give him his commission.

The case of *Marbury* v. *Madison* placed Chief Justice Marshall in an embarrassing position.

Marbury had a strong claim. If Marshall refused to issue a mandamus, everyone would say he dared not stand up to Jefferson, and the prestige of the Court would suffer. If he issued the writ, he would place the Court in direct conflict with the executive. Madison would probably ignore the order, and in the prevailing state of public opinion nothing would be done to make him act. This would be a still more staggering blow to the judiciary. What should the chief justice do?

Marshall had studied law only briefly and had no judicial experience, but in this crisis he first displayed the genius that was to mark him as a great judge. By right Marbury should have his commission, he announced. However, the Court could not require Madison to give it to him. Marbury's request for a mandamus had been based on an ambiguous clause in the Judiciary Act of 1789. That clause was unconstitutional, Marshall declared, and therefore void. Congress could not legally give the Supreme Court the right to issue writs of mandamus in such circumstances.

With the skill and foresight of a chess grand master, Marshall turned what had looked like a trap into a triumph. By sacrificing the pawn, Marbury, he established the power of the Supreme Court to invalidate federal laws that conflicted with the Constitution. Jefferson could not check him because instead of throwing an anchor ahead, as Jefferson had feared, Marshall had *refused* power. Yet he had certainly grappled a "further hold for future advances of power," and the president could do nothing to stop him.

The Marbury case made Jefferson more determined to strike at the Federalist-dominated courts. He decided to press for the impeachment of some of the more partisan judges. First he had the House of Representatives bring charges against District Judge John Pickering. Pickering was clearly insane—he had frequently delivered profane and drunken harangues from the bench—and the Senate quickly voted to remove him. Then Jefferson went after a much larger fish, Samuel Chase, associate justice of the Supreme Court. Chase had been prominent for decades, an early leader of the Sons of Liberty, a signer of the Declaration of Independence, active in the affairs of the Continental Congress. Washington had named him to the Supreme Court in 1796, and he had delivered a number of important opinions. But his handling of cases under the Sedition Act had been

outrageously high-handed. Defense lawyers had become so exasperated as to throw down their briefs in disgust at some of his prejudiced rulings. But the trial demonstrated that Chase's actions had not constituted the "high crimes and misdemeanors" required by the Constitution to remove a judge. Even Jefferson became disenchanted with the efforts of some of his more extreme followers and accepted Chase's acquittal with equanimity.

The Barbary Pirates

Aside from these perhaps salutary setbacks, Jefferson's first term was a parade of triumphs. Although he cut back the army and navy sharply in order to save money, he temporarily escaped the consequences of leaving the country undefended because of the lull in the European war signalized by the Treaty of Amiens between Great Britain and France in March 1802. Despite the fact that he had only seven frigates in commission, he even managed to fight a small naval war with the Barbary pirates without damage to American interests or prestige.

The North African Arab states of Morocco, Algiers, Tunis, and Tripoli had for decades made a business of piracy, seizing vessels all over the Mediterranean and holding crews and passengers for ransom. The European powers found it simpler to pay them annual protection money than to crush them. Under Washington and Adams, the United States joined in the payment of this tribute; while large, the sums were less than the increased costs of insurance for shippers when the protection was not purchased. Such pusillanimity ran against Jefferson's grain—"When this idea comes across my mind, my faculties are absolutely suspended between indignation and impatience," he said—and when the pasha of Tripoli tried to raise the charges, he balked. Tripoli then declared war in May 1801, and Jefferson dispatched a squadron to the Mediterranean.

In the words of one historian, the action was "halfhearted and ill-starred." The pirates were not overwhelmed, and a major American warship, the frigate *Philadelphia*, had to be destroyed after running aground off the Tripolitanian coast. The payment of tribute continued until 1815. Just the same, America, though far removed from the pirate bases, was the only maritime nation that tried

■ The frigate *Philadelphia* had been captured in October, 1803, by Tripolitanian pirates. In February of 1804, Stephen Decatur managed to steal into the harbor of Tripoli with a small boarding party (the ship at lower left), and set fire to the vessel.

to resist the blackmail. Although the war failed to achieve Jefferson's purpose of ending the payments, its final effect was positive. The pasha agreed to a new treaty more favorable to the United States, and American sailors led by Commodore Edward Preble won valuable experience and a large portion of fame. The greatest hero was Lieutenant Stephen Decatur, who captured two pirate ships, led ten men in a daring raid on another in which he took on a gigantic sailor in a wild battle of cutlass against boarding pike,* and snatched the stricken *Philadelphia* from the pirates by sneaking aboard and setting her afire.

The Louisiana Purchase

The major achievements of Jefferson's first term had to do with the American west, and of these

the greatest by far was the acquisition of the huge area between the Mississippi River and the Rocky Mountains. In a sense the purchase of this region, called Louisiana, was fortuitous, an accidental by-product of European political adjustments and the whim of Napoleon Bonaparte. Certainly Jefferson had not planned it, for in his inaugural address he had expressed the opinion that the country already had all the land it would need for a thousand generations. It was nonetheless the perfectly logical—one might almost say inevitable—result of a long series of events in the history of the Mississippi Valley.

Along with every other American who had even a superficial interest in the west, Jefferson understood that the United States must have access to the mouth of the Mississippi and the city of New Orleans or eventually lose everything beyond the Appalachians. "There is on the globe one single spot, the possessor of which is our natural and habitual enemy," he was soon to write. "It is New Orleans." Thus, when he learned

---

*Decatur killed the pirate by firing a small pistol from his pocket as his opponent was about to skewer him.

EXPLORING THE LOUISIANA PURCHASE

- ◄——— Lewis and Clark, 1804-1805
- ◄-- -- Lewis and Clark, 1806   ◄-·-·- Pike, 1805
- ◄——— Freeman, 1805   ◄-··-·· Pike, 1806-1807

0   250   500
Miles

shortly after his inauguration that Spain had given Louisiana back to France, he was immediately on his guard. Control of Louisiana by Spain, a "feeble" country with "pacific dispositions," could be tolerated; control by a resurgent France dominated by Napoleon, the greatest military genius of the age, was entirely different. Did Napoleon have designs on Canada? Did he perhaps mean to resume the old Spanish and British game of encouraging the Indians to harry the American frontier? And what now would be the status of Pinckney's precious treaty? Deeply worried, the president instructed his minister to France, Robert R. Livingston, to seek assurances that American rights in New Orleans would be respected and to negotiate the purchase of West Florida in case that region had also been turned over to France.

Jefferson's concern was well founded; France was indeed planning new imperial ventures in North America. Immediately after settling its difficulties with the United States through the Convention of 1800, France signed the secret Treaty of San Ildefonso with Spain, which returned Louisiana to France. Napoleon hoped to use this region

■The explorations of Lewis and Clark, as well as those of Freeman and Pike, are traced in the map. The shading shows the Louisiana Purchase as delineated by its "natural" boundaries. On their return journey, Lewis and Clark divided their party to explore more thoroughly the area around the upper Missouri and Yellowstone rivers.

in their hands. The original Napoleon, taking advantage of the slackening of war in Europe, dispatched an army of 20,000 men under General Charles Leclerc to reconquer it.

When Jefferson learned of the Leclerc expedition, he had no trouble divining its relationship to Louisiana. His uneasiness became outright alarm. In April 1802 he again urged Minister Livingston to attempt the purchase of New Orleans and Florida or, as an alternative, to buy a tract of land near the mouth of the Mississippi where a new port could be constructed. Of necessity, the mild-mannered, idealistic president now became an aggressive realist. If the right of deposit could not be preserved through negotiation, it must be purchased with gunpowder, even if that meant acting in conjunction with the despised British. "The day that France takes possession of New Orleans," he warned, "we must marry ourselves to the British fleet and nation."

In October 1802 the Spanish, who had not yet actually turned Louisiana over to France, heightened the tension by suddenly revoking the right of deposit at New Orleans. We now know that the French had no hand in this action, but it was beyond reason to expect Jefferson or the American people to believe it at the time. With the west clamoring for relief, Jefferson appointed his friend and disciple James Monroe minister plenipotentiary and sent him to Paris with instructions to offer up to $10 million for New Orleans and Florida. If France refused, he and Livingston should open negotiations for a "closer connection" with the British.

Before Monroe reached France the tension was broken. General Leclerc's Saint Domingue expedition ended in disaster. Although Toussaint surrendered, Haitian resistance continued. Yellow fever raged through the French army; Leclerc himself fell before the fever, which wiped out practically his entire force.

When news of this calamity reached Napoleon early in 1803, he began to have second thoughts about reviving French imperialism in the New World. Without Saint Domingue the wilderness of Louisiana seemed of little value. Napoleon was preparing to reopen his campaigns in Europe. He could no longer spare troops to recapture a rebellious West Indian island or to hold Louisiana against a possible British attack, and he needed money. For some weeks the commander of the

as a breadbasket for the French West Indian sugar plantations, just as colonies like Pennsylvania and Massachusetts had fed the British sugar islands before the Revolution.

However, the most important French island, Saint Domingue, or Haiti, had slipped from French control. At the time of the French Revolution the slaves of the island had revolted. In 1793 they were granted personal freedom, but they fought on under the leadership of the "Black Napoleon," a self-taught genius named Toussaint L'Ouverture, and by 1801 the island was entirely most powerful army in the world mulled the question without consulting anyone. Then, with characteristic suddenness, he made up his mind. On April 10 he ordered Foreign Minister Talleyrand to offer not merely New Orleans but all of Louisiana to the Americans. The next day Talleyrand summoned Livingston to his office on the rue du Bac and dropped this bombshell. Livingston was almost struck speechless but quickly recovered his composure. When Talleyrand asked what the United States would give for the province, he suggested the French equivalent of about $5 million. Talleyrand pronounced the sum "too low" and urged Livingston to think about the subject for a day or two.

Livingston faced a situation that could never confront a modern diplomat. His instructions said nothing about buying an area almost as large as the entire United States, and there was no time to write home for new instructions. The offer staggered the imagination. Luckily, Monroe arrived the next day to share the responsibility. The two Americans consulted, dickered with the French, and finally agreed—they could scarcely have done otherwise—to accept the proposal. Early in May they signed a treaty. For 60 million francs—about $15 million—the United States was to have all Louisiana.

No one knew exactly how large the region was or what it contained. When Livingston asked Talleyrand about the boundaries of the purchase, he replied: "I can give you no direction. You have made a noble bargain for yourselves, and I suppose you will make the most of it." Never, as the historian Henry Adams wrote, "did the United States government get so much for so little."

Napoleon's unexpected concession caused consternation in America, though there was never real doubt that the treaty would be ratified. Jefferson did not believe that the government had the power under the Constitution to add new territory or to grant American citizenship to the 50,000 residents of Louisiana by executive act, as the treaty required. He even drafted a constitutional amendment: "The province of Louisiana is incorporated with the United States and made part thereof," but his advisers convinced him that it would be dangerous to delay approval of the treaty until an amendment could be acted upon by three-fourths of the states. Jefferson then suggested that the Senate ratify the treaty and submit

an amendment afterward "confirming an act which the nation had not previously authorized." This idea was so obviously illogical that he quickly dropped it. Finally, he came to believe "that the less we say about constitutional difficulties the better." Since what he called "the good sense of our country" clearly wanted Louisiana, he decided to "acquiesce with satisfaction" while Congress overlooked the "metaphysical subtleties" of the problem and ratified the treaty.

Some of the more partisan Federalists, who had been eager to fight Spain for New Orleans, attacked Jefferson for undermining the Constitution. Even Hamilton expressed hesitation about absorbing "this new, immense, unbounded world," though he had dreamed of seizing still larger domains himself. In the end Hamilton's nationalism reasserted itself, and he urged ratification of the treaty, as did such other important Federalists as John Adams and John Marshall. And in a way the Louisiana Purchase was as much Hamilton's doing as Jefferson's. Napoleon accepted payment in United States bonds, which he promptly sold to European investors. If Hamilton had not established the nation's credit so soundly, such a large issue could never have been so easily disposed of.

It was ironic—and a man as perceptive as Hamilton must surely have recognized the irony—that the acquisition of Louisiana assured Jefferson's reelection and further contributed to the collapse of Federalism. The purchase was popular even in the New England bastions of that party. While the negotiations were progressing in Paris, Jefferson had written of partisan political affairs: "If we can settle happily the difficulties of the Mississippi, I think we may promise ourselves smooth seas during our time." These words turned out to be no more accurate than most political predictions, but the Louisiana Purchase drove another spike into Federalism's coffin.

Federalism Discredited

The west and south were solid for Jefferson, and the north was rapidly succumbing to his charm. The addition of new western states would soon further reduce New England's power in national affairs. So complete did the Republican triumph seem that certain die-hard Federalists in New England began to think of secession. Led by former secretary of state Timothy Pickering, a sour, implacable conservative, a group known as the Essex Junto organized in 1804 a scheme to break away from the Union and establish a "Northern Confederacy."

Even within the dwindling Federalist ranks the Junto had little support. Nevertheless, Pickering and his friends pushed ahead, drafting a plan whereby, having captured political control of New York, they would take the entire northeast out of the Union. Since they could not begin to win New York for anyone in their own ranks, they hit on the idea of supporting Vice-President Aaron Burr, who was running against the "regular" Republican candidate for governor of New York. Although Burr did not promise to bring New York into their confederacy if elected, he encouraged them enough to win their backing. The foolishness of the plot was revealed in the April elections: Burr was overwhelmed by the regular Republican. The Junto's scheme collapsed.

The incident, however, had a tragic aftermath. Hamilton had campaigned against Burr, whom he considered "an embryo Caesar." When he continued after the election to cast aspersions on Burr's character (not a very difficult assignment, since Burr frequently violated both the political and sexual mores of the day), Burr challenged him to a duel. It was well known that Hamilton opposed dueling in principle, his own son having been slain in such an affair, and he certainly had no need to prove his courage. But he believed his honor at stake. The two met with pistols on July 11, 1804, at Weehawken, New Jersey, across the Hudson from New York City. Hamilton made no effort to hit the challenger, but Burr took careful aim. Hamilton fell, mortally wounded. Thus a great, if enigmatic, man was cut off in his prime. His work, in a sense, had been completed, and his philosophy of government was being everywhere rejected, yet the nation's loss was large.

Lewis and Clark

While the disgruntled Federalists dreamed of secession, Jefferson was planning the exploration of Louisiana and the region beyond. Early in 1803 he got $2,500 from Congress and obtained the permission of the French to send his exploring party across Louisiana. To command the expedition he appointed his private secretary, Meriwether Lewis, a young Virginian who had seen considerable service with the army in the west and who possessed, according to Jefferson, "a great mass of accurate information on all the subjects of nature." Lewis chose as his companion officer William Clark, another soldier (he had served with General Anthony Wayne at the Battle of Fallen Timbers) who had much experience in negotiating with Indians.

Jefferson, whose interest in the west was scientific as well as political, issued minute instructions to Lewis:

> Other objects worthy of notice will be, the soil and face of the country . . . the remains and accounts of any animals which may be deemed rare or extinct; the mineral productions of every kind, but particularly metals . . . volcanic appearances; climate, as characterized by the thermometer, by the proportion of rainy, cloudy, and clear days, by lightning, hail, snow, ice, by the access and recess of frost, by the winds prevailing at different seasons, the dates at which particular plants put forth or lose their flower or leaf, times of appearance of particular birds, reptiles or insects. . . .

Scientific matters were inextricably intertwined with practical ones, such as the fur trade, for in his nature studies Jefferson concentrated on "useful" plants and animals. He was haunted by imperialistic visions of an expanding America that were not unlike those of Hamilton. After the consummation of the Louisiana Purchase, he instructed Lewis to try to establish official relations with the Indians in the Spanish territories beyond. Lewis should assure the tribes that "they will find in us faithful friends and protectors," Jefferson said. That the expedition would be moving across Spanish territory need not concern the travelers because of "the expiring state of Spain's interests there."

Lewis and Clark gathered a group of 48 experienced men near St. Louis during the winter of 1803–1804. In the spring they set forth, pushing slowly up the Missouri River in a 55-foot keelboat and two dugout canoes called pirogues. By late fall they had reached what is now North Dakota, where they built a small station, Fort Mandan, and spent the winter. In April 1805, having shipped back to the president more than thirty boxes of plants, minerals, animal skins and bones, and In-

■ Lewis and Clark kept meticulous records of the many plants and animals they discovered. The text with this sketch says: ". . . a species of small fish which now begin to run and are taken in great quantities in the Columbia R . . . I have drawn the likeness of them as large as life (8 inches long); it is as perfect as I can make it with my pen."

dian artifacts, they struck out again toward the mountains, accompanied by a Shoshone squaw, Sacagawea, and her French-Canadian husband, who acted as interpreters and guides. They passed the Great Falls of the Missouri and then clambered over the Continental Divide at Lemhi Pass, in southwestern Montana. Soon thereafter the going became easier, and they descended to the Pacific by way of the Clearwater and Columbia rivers, reaching their destination in November. They had hoped to return by ship, but during the

long, damp winter not a single vessel appeared. In the spring of 1806 they headed back by land, reaching St. Louis on September 23.

The country greeted the news of their return with delight. Besides locating several passes across the Rockies, Lewis and Clark had established friendly relations with a great many Indian tribes to whom they presented gifts, medals, American flags, and a sales talk designed to promote peace and the fur trade. They brought back a wealth of data about the country and its resources. The journals kept by members of the group were published and, along with their accurate maps, became major sources for scientists, students, and future explorers. To Jefferson's great personal satisfaction, Lewis provided him with many specimens of the local wildlife, including two grizzly bear cubs, which he kept for a time in a stone pit in the White House lawn.

The success of Lewis and Clark did not open the gates of Louisiana very wide. Other explorers sent out by Jefferson accomplished far less. Thomas Freeman, an Irish-born surveyor, led a small party up the Red River but ran into a powerful Spanish force near the present junction of Arkansas, Oklahoma, and Texas and was forced to retreat. Between 1805 and 1807 Lieutenant Zebulon Pike explored the upper Mississippi Valley and the Colorado region. (He discovered but failed to scale the peak south of Denver that bears his name.) Pike eventually made his way to Santa Fe and the upper reaches of the Rio Grande, but he was not nearly so careful and acute an observer as Lewis and Clark were and consequently brought back much less information. By 1808 fur traders based at St. Louis were beginning to invade the Rockies, and by 1812 there were 75,000 people in the southern section of the new territory. That year it was admitted to the Union as the state of Louisiana. The northern region lay almost untouched until much later.

Jeffersonian Democracy

With the purchase of Louisiana, Jefferson completed the construction of the political institution known as the Republican party and the philosophy of government known as Jeffersonian Democracy. From what sort of materials had he built his juggernaut? In part his success was a matter of personality; in the march of American democracy he stood halfway, temperamentally, between Washington and Andrew Jackson, perfectly in tune with the thinking of his times. The colonial American had practiced democracy without really believing in it; hence, for example, the maintenance of property qualifications for voting in regions where nearly everyone owned property. Stimulated by the libertarian ideas of the Revolution, Americans were rapidly adjusting their beliefs to conform with their practices. However, it took a Jefferson, a man of large estates, possessed of the general prejudice in favor of the old-fashioned citizen rooted in the soil, yet deeply committed to majority rule, to oversee the transition.

Jefferson's marvelous talents as a writer help to explain his success. He expounded his ideas in language that few could resist. He had a remarkable facility for discovering practical arguments to justify his beliefs—as when he suggested that by letting everyone vote, elections would be made more honest because with large numbers going to the polls bribery would become prohibitively expensive.

Jefferson prepared the country for democracy by proving that a democrat could establish and maintain a stable regime. The Federalist tyranny of 1798 was compounded of selfishness and stupidity, but it was also based in part on honest fears that an egalitarian regime would not protect the fabric of society from hotheads and crackpots. The impact of the French Revolution on conservative thinking in the middle 1790s can scarcely be overestimated. America had fought a seven-year revolution without executing a single Tory, yet during the few months that the Terror ravaged France, nearly 17,000 persons were officially put to death for political "crimes," and many thousands more were killed in civil disturbances. Worse, in the opinion of many, the French extremists had attempted to destroy Christianity, substituting for it a "Cult of Reason." They confiscated property, imposed price controls, abolished slavery in the French colonies. Little wonder that many Americans feared that the Jeffersonians, lovers of France and of *liberté, égalité, fraternité,* would try to remodel American society in a similar way.

Jefferson calmed these fears. "Pell-mell" might scandalize the British and Spanish ministers and a few other mossbacks, but it was scarcely revolutionary. The most partisan Federalist was hard put to see a Robespierre in the amiable president scratching out state papers at his desk or chatting with a Kentucky congressman at a "republican" dinner party. Furthermore, Jefferson accepted Federalist ideas on public finance, even learning to live with Hamilton's bank. As a good democrat, he drew a nice distinction between his own opinions and the wishes of the majority, which he felt must always take priority. Even in his first inaugural he admitted that manufacturing and commerce were, along with agriculture, the "pillars of our prosperity," and while believing that these activities would best thrive when "left most free to individual enterprise," he accepted the principle that the government should protect them when necessary from "casual embarrassments." Eventually he gave his backing to modest proposals for spending federal money on roads, canals, and other projects that, according to his political philosophy, ought to have been left to the states and private individuals.

During his term the country grew and prospered, the commercial classes sharing in the bounty along with the farmers so close to Jefferson's heart. Blithely he set out to win the support of all who could vote. "It is material to the safety of Republicanism," he wrote in 1803, "to detach the mercantile interests from its enemies and incorporate them into the body of its friends."

Thus Jefferson undermined the Federalists all along the line. They had said that the country must pay a stiff price for prosperity and orderly government, and they demanded prompt payment in full, both in cash (taxes) and in the form of limitations on human liberty. Under Jefferson these much-desired goals had been achieved cheaply and without sacrificing freedom. A land whose riches could only be guessed at had been obtained without firing a shot and without burdening the people with new taxes. "What farmer, what mechanic, what laborer, ever sees a taxgatherer in the United States?" the president could ask in 1805, without a single Federalist rising to challenge him. Order without discipline, security without a large military establishment, prosperity without regulatory legislation, freedom without license—truly the Sage of Monticello appeared to have led his fellow Americans into a golden age.

Republican virtue seemed to have triumphed, both at home and abroad. "With nations as with individuals," Jefferson proudly proclaimed as he took the oath of office at the start of his second term, "our interests soundly calculated, will ever be found inseparable from our moral duties." And he added more smugly still: "Fellow citizens, you best know whether we have done well or ill."

SUPPLEMENTARY READING

Titles marked with an asterisk have been published in paperback

No student interested in Jefferson's political and social philosophy should miss sampling his writings, of which the best edition, still incomplete, is J. P. Boyd (ed.), **The Papers of Thomas Jefferson** (1950–). A useful compilation of his more important writings is Adrienne Koch and William Peden, **The Life and Selected Writings of Thomas Jefferson** (1944). Koch's **The Philosophy of Thomas Jefferson*** (1943) is valuable, as are Gilbert Chinard, **Thomas Jefferson: The Apostle of Americanism*** (1929), and M. D. Peterson, **Thomas Jefferson and the New Nation*** (1970). The biography of Jefferson by Dumas Malone (1948–1980) provides masses of valuable data.

On the Federalist and Democratic Republican parties, see Joseph Charles, **The Origins of the American Party System*** (1961), M. J. Dauer, **The Adams Federalists*** (1953), N. E. Cunningham, Jr., **The Jeffersonian Republicans*** (1958), and W. N. Chambers, **Political Parties in a New Nation*** (1963). The best biography of John Adams is still Gilbert Chinard, **Honest John Adams*** (1933). Page Smith, **John Adams** (1962), contains a wealth of personal material drawn from the Adams papers but is almost useless for the politics of Adams' presidency. S. G. Kurtz, **The Presidency of John Adams*** (1957), is a solid work, and Peter Shaw, **The Character of John Adams** (1976), is an interesting psychological study.

For the diplomatic conflicts of the late 1790s, see Bradford Perkins, **The First Rapprochement: England and the United States** (1967), Alexander De Conde, **The Quasi-War*** (1966), and William Stinchcombe, **The XYZ Affair** (1980). On the Alien and Sedition Acts, both J. M. Smith, **Freedom's Fetters: The Alien and Sedition Laws and American Civil Liberties*** (1956), and J. C. Miller, **Crisis in Freedom: The Alien and Sedition Acts*** (1951), are excellent. L. W. Levy, **Freedom of Speech and Press in Early American History*** (1963), provides valuable background for understanding the acts, for it demonstrates that modern conceptions of civil liberties are very different from those commonly held in the 18th century. Levy's **Jefferson and Civil Liberties: The Darker Side*** (1963) is a lawyer's brief for the prosecution.

The classic work on Jefferson's presidency, Henry Adams, **History of the United States During the Administration of Jefferson and Madison*** (1889–1891), is strongly anti-Jefferson in orientation. The most recent general treatment of the Jeffersonian era is Marshall Smelser, **The Democratic Republic*** (1968). On the parties of the era, see N. E. Cunningham, Jr., **The Jeffersonian Republicans in Power*** (1963), and D. H. Fischer, **The Revolution of American Conservatism: The Federalist Party in the Era of Jeffersonian Democracy*** (1965); on the structure of Jefferson's administration, L. D. White, **The Jeffersonians*** (1951); on Jefferson's management of the administration and of Congress, J. S. Young, **The Washington Community*** (1966), a fascinating book. Older works of value are C. A. Beard, **Economic Origins of Jeffersonian Democracy*** (1915), and C. G. Bowers, **Jefferson in Power*** (1936), which is a good corrective to the work of Henry Adams because of its pro-Jefferson bias.

Jefferson's battle with the judges can be followed in A. J. Beveridge, **Life of John Marshall** (1916–1919). For *Marbury* v. *Madison,* see J. A. Garraty (ed.), **Quarrels That Have Shaped the Constitution*** (1964), and D. O. Dewey's more detailed **Marshall Versus Jefferson*** (1970).

The war with the Barbary pirates is covered in R. W. Irwin, **The Diplomatic Relations of the United States with the Barbary Powers** (1931). On the Louisiana Purchase, see Henry Adams' **History,** E. W. Lyon, **Louisiana in French Diplomacy*** (1934), A. P. Whitaker, **The Mississippi Question** (1934), Irving Brant, **James Madison: Secretary of State** (1953), and George Dangerfield, **Chancellor Robert R. Livingston of New York** (1960).

Jefferson's interest in the west is discussed in E. T. Martin, **Thomas Jefferson: Scientist*** (1952). An excellent general treatment of western exploration is contained in R. A. Billington, **Westward Expansion** (1967). On Lewis and Clark, see P. R. Cutright, **Lewis and Clark: Pioneering Naturalists** (1976), Richard Dillon, **Meriwether Lewis** (1965), and J. O. Steffen, **William Clark** (1977). The career of Pike is traced in W. E. Hollon, **The Lost Pathfinder: Zebulon Montgomery Pike** (1949).

7 / AMERICA ESCAPES FROM EUROPE

 Smugness and complacency are luxuries that politicians can seldom afford. Jefferson, beginning his second term with pride in the past and confidence in the future and with the mass support of the nation, soon found himself in trouble at home and abroad. In part his difficulties rose from the extent of the Republican victory. In 1805 the Federalists had neither useful ideas nor intelligent leadership nor effective numbers. They held only a quarter of the seats in Congress. As often happens in such situations, lack of opposition weakened party discipline and encouraged factionalism among the Republicans. At the same time, Napoleon's renewed aggressiveness in Europe, to which the sale of Louisiana had been a prelude, produced a tangle of new problems for the neutral United States. Jefferson could not solve these problems merely by being "just" and "moral," as he had suggested in his second inaugural address. At the end of his second term he was suffering from rheumatism and recurrent headaches that were no doubt of psychosomatic origin, and he wrote feelingly to a friend: "Never did a prisoner, released from his chains, feel such relief as I shall on shaking off the shackles of power."

John Randolph of Roanoke

Jefferson's domestic troubles were not of critical importance, but they were vexing. To a considerable extent they resulted from the elements in his makeup that explain his success: his facility in adjusting his principles to practical conditions, his readiness to take over the best of Federalism. This flexibility got him in trouble with some of his disciples, who were less ready than he to surrender principle to expediency.

The most prominent of the Republican critics was John Randolph of Roanoke, congressman from Virginia and majority leader during Jefferson's first term. Randolph was unique. Although he had wit, charm, intelligence, and imagination, his mind was tragically warped; in later life he was periodically insane. He was probably sexually impotent, and frustration made him a sour, vitriolic, and unyielding obstructionist. He made a fetish of preserving states' rights against invasion by the central government. "Asking one of the States to surrender part of her sovereignty is like asking a lady to surrender part of her chastity," he remarked in one of his typical epigrams.

Randolph first clashed with Jefferson in 1804, over an attempted settlement of the so-called Yazoo land frauds. In 1795 the Georgia legislature had sold a huge area in what is now Alabama and Mississippi to four land companies for a tiny fraction of its value, something less than two cents an acre. When it was revealed that many of the legislators had been corrupted, the next legislature canceled the grants, but not before the original grantees had unloaded large tracts on various third parties. These innocents turned to the federal government for relief when the grants were canceled. Jefferson favored a bill giving 5 million acres to these interests, but Randolph would have

■ John Randolph of Roanoke (as he signed his name to avoid confusion with his cousin "Possum" John) was painted in 1805, when he was 32, by Gilbert Stuart.

none of this. Rising in righteous wrath, he denounced in his shrill soprano all those who would countenance such fraud. The compromise bill was defeated.*

By the beginning of Jefferson's second term, Randolph was fretting about how the president's adversaries were taking advantage of his "easy credulity." Then, in December 1805, he broke with the administration over a request that Jefferson had made for $2 million to be used in unspecified dealings designed to obtain West Florida from Spain. Randolph—correctly, it turned out—suspected chicanery and from that date could be counted on to oppose every administration measure. He seldom mustered more than a handful of supporters in Congress, but his stabbing, nerve-shattering assaults grievously disturbed the president's peace of mind.

---

*The controversy then entered the courts, and in 1810 Chief Justice Marshall held in *Fletcher* v. *Peck* that in rescinding the grant Georgia had committed an unconstitutional breach of contract. Before Marshall's ruling, however, the federal grant was finally approved by Congress. Had it not been, *Fletcher* v. *Peck* would have provided the "victims" of the Yazoo frauds with an area considerably larger than the state of Mississippi!

The Burr Conspiracy

Another Republican who caused trouble for Jefferson was Aaron Burr, and again the president was partially to blame for the difficulty. After their contest for the presidency in 1801, Jefferson pursued Burr almost vindictively, depriving him of federal patronage in New York and replacing him as the 1804 Republican vice-presidential candidate with Governor George Clinton, Burr's chief rival in the state.

While still vice-president, Burr began to flirt with treason. He approached Anthony Merry, the British minister in Washington, and offered to "effect a separation of the Western part of the United States." His price was £110,000 and the support of a British fleet off the mouth of the Mississippi. The British did not fall in with his scheme, but he went ahead nonetheless. Exactly what he had in mind has long been in dispute. Certainly he dreamed of acquiring a western empire for himself; whether he intended to wrest it from the United States or from Spanish territories beyond Louisiana is unclear. He joined forces with General James Wilkinson, whom Jefferson unfortunately had appointed governor of Louisiana Territory, and who, it will be recalled, was secretly in the pay of Spain (see page 115).

In 1806 Burr and Wilkinson organized a small force at a place called Blennerhassett Island, in the Ohio River. Some six dozen men began to move downriver toward New Orleans under Burr's command. Whether the objective was New Orleans or some part of Mexico, the scheme was clearly illegal. For some reason, however—possibly because he was incapable of loyalty to anyone*—Wilkinson betrayed Burr to Jefferson at the last moment. The president issued a proclamation warning the nation and ordering Burr's arrest. Burr tried to escape to Spanish Florida but was captured in February 1807, brought to Richmond, Virginia, under guard, and charged with high treason.

Any president will deal summarily with traitors, but Jefferson's attitude during Burr's trial reveals the depth of his hatred. He "made himself a party to the prosecution," personally sending evi-

■ Aaron Burr was sketched during his 1807 treason trial by the French expatriate artist Charles Saint-Mémin, who was well known for his profile portraits. (See the Jefferson portrait on page 147.)

dence to the United States attorney who was handling the case and offering blanket pardons to associates of Burr who would agree to turn state's evidence. On the other hand, Chief Justice Marshall, presiding at the trial in his capacity as judge of the circuit court, repeatedly showed favoritism to the prisoner. The proceedings quickly lost all appearance of impartiality.

In this contest between two great men at their worst, Jefferson as a vindictive executive and Marshall as a prejudiced judge, the victory went to the judge. Organizing "a military assemblage," Marshall declared on his charge to the jury, "was not a levying of war." To "advise or procure treason" was not in itself treason. Unless two independent witnesses testified to an overt act of treason as thus defined, the accused should be declared innocent. In the light of this charge, the jury, deliberating only 25 minutes, found Burr not guilty.

Burr was also tried and acquitted on the charge of conspiring to invade Spanish territory. Throughout his ordeal he never lost his self-possession and seemed to view the proceedings with amiable cynicism. Then, since he was wanted either for murder or for treason in six states, he went into exile in Europe. Some years later he returned to New York, where he spent an unregenerate old age, fathering two illegitimate children in his seventies and being divorced by his second wife on grounds of adultery at 80.

As in his squabble with Randolph, Jefferson

---

*John Randolph said of him: "Wilkinson is the only man that I ever saw who was from the bark to the very core a villain."

suffered no vital setback in the Burr affair. Nevertheless, it was a blow to his prestige, it left him more embittered against Marshall and the federal judiciary, and it added nothing to his reputation as a statesman.

Napoleon and the British

Jefferson's difficulties with Randolph and Burr may be traced at least in part to the purchase of Louisiana. His easy success in obtaining the region encouraged him to think that West Florida could be snapped up with equal ease, and this error brought upon him the shrill wrath of Randolph of Roanoke. Louisiana itself, fat, empty, and unknown, excited the cupidity of men like Burr and Wilkinson. But problems infinitely more serious were also related to Louisiana.

Napoleon had jettisoned Louisiana to clear the decks before resuming the battle for control of Europe. This war had the effect of stimulating the American economy, for the warring powers needed American goods and American vessels. Shipbuilding boomed; foreign trade, which had quintupled since 1793, nearly doubled again between 1803 and 1805. By the summer of 1807, however, the situation had changed: a most unusual stalemate had developed in the war. In October 1805 Britain's Horatio Nelson demolished the combined Spanish and French fleets in the Battle of Trafalgar, off the coast of Spain. Napoleon, now at the summit of his powers, quickly redressed the balance, smashing army after army thrown against him by Great Britain's continental allies. First he attacked the Austrians, capturing 50,000 at Ulm in Bavaria. Then he shattered a great Austrian and Russian army in the Battle of Austerlitz (December 1805), perhaps the most brilliant victory of his career. In 1806 he overwhelmed the Prussians at Jena and the following June, the Russians at Friedland in East Prussia. Thereafter Napoleon was master of Europe, while the British controlled the seas around the Continent. Neither nation could strike directly at the other.

They therefore resorted to commercial warfare, striving to disrupt each other's economy. Napoleon struck first with his Berlin Decree (November 1806), setting up a paper blockade of the British Isles and making "all commerce and correspondence" with Great Britain illegal. The British retaliated with a series of edicts called Orders in Council, blockading most continental ports and barring from them all foreign vessels unless they first stopped at a British port and paid customs duties. Napoleon then issued his Milan Decree (December 1807), declaring any vessel that submitted to the British rules "to have become English property" and thus subject to seizure.

The blockades and counterblockades seemed designed to stop commerce completely, yet this was not the case. Napoleon's "Continental System" was supposed to make Europe self-sufficient and isolate Great Britain, yet he was willing to sell European products to the British (if the price was right); his chief objective was to deprive them of their continental markets. The British were ready to sell anything on the Continent, and to allow others to do so too, provided they first paid a toll. In effect this commercial warfare amounted to the organized exploitation of foreign merchants, who were enjoying unprecedented opportunities for profit because of the prolonged conflict. The Continental System was, in John Quincy Adams' pithy phrase, "Little more than extortion wearing the mask of prohibition," and British policy was equally immoral—a kind of piracy practiced with impunity because the Royal Navy controlled the seas.

When war first broke out between Britain and France in 1792, the colonial trade of both sides had fallen largely into American hands because the danger of capture drove many belligerent merchant vessels from the seas. This commerce had engaged Americans in some rather devious practices. Under the Rule of War of 1756, it will be recalled, the British denied to neutrals the right to engage in trade during time of war from which they were barred by mercantilistic regulations in time of peace. If an American ship carried sugar from the French colony of Martinique to France, for example, the British claimed the right to capture it because such traffic was normally confined to French bottoms by French law.

To avoid this risk, American merchants brought the sugar first to the United States, a legal peacetime voyage under French mercantilism. Then they reshipped it to France as *American* sugar. Since the United States was a neutral and sugar not contraband of war, the Americans expected the British to let their ships pass with impunity. Continental products likewise reached the French West Indies by way of United States ports, and the American government encouraged the traffic in both directions by refunding customs duties on foreign products reshipped within a year. Between 1803 and 1806 the annual value of foreign products reexported from the United States jumped from $13 million to $60 million! In 1806 the United States exported 47 million pounds of coffee—none, of course, of local origin. An example of this type of trade is offered by Samuel Eliot Morison in his *Maritime History of Massachusetts:*

> The brig *Eliza Hardy* of Plymouth enters her home port from Bordeaux, on May 20, 1806, with a cargo of claret wine. Part of it is immediately re-exported to Martinique in the schooner *Pilgrim,* which also carries a consignment of brandy that came from Alicante in the brig *Commerce,* and another of gin that came from Rotterdam in the barque *Hannah* of Plymouth. The rest of the *Eliza Hardy's* claret is taken to Philadelphia by coasters, and thence re-exported in seven different vessels to Havana, Santiago de Cuba, St. Thomas, and Batavia.

This underhanded commerce irritated the British. In the cases of the *Essex* and the *William* (1805–1806) a British judge, Sir William Grant, decreed that American ships could no longer rely on "mere voluntary *ceremonies*" to circumvent the Rule of 1756. Thus, just when Britain and France were cracking down on direct trade by neutrals, Britain determined to halt the American reexport trade, thereby gravely threatening American prosperity.

The Impressment Controversy

More dismaying were the cruel indignities being visited upon American seamen by the British practice of impressment. Under British law, any able-bodied subject could be drafted for service in the Royal Navy in an emergency. Normally, when the commander of a warship found himself short-handed, he put into a British port and sent a "press gang" ashore to round up the necessary men in harborside pubs. When far from home waters he might hail any passing British merchant ship and commandeer the necessary men, though this practice was understandably unpopular in British maritime circles. He might also stop a *neutral* merchantman on the high seas and remove any British subject. Since the United States owned by far the largest merchant fleet among the neutrals, its vessels bore the brunt of this practice.

Impressment had been a cause of Anglo-American conflict for many years; American pride suffered every time a vessel carrying the flag was forced to back topsails and heave to at the command of a British man-of-war. Still more galling was the contemptuous behavior of British officers when they boarded American ships. In 1796 an American captain named Figsby was stopped twice by British warships while carrying a cargo of poultry and other livestock to Guadaloupe. First a privateer, the *Sea Nymph,* impressed two of his crew, confiscated most of his chickens, "abused" him, and stole his ship's flag. Two days later H.M.S. *Unicorn* took another of Figsby's men, the rest of his poultry, four sheep, and three hogs.

Many British captains made little effort to be sure they were impressing British subjects; any likely looking lad might be taken when the need was great. Furthermore, there were legal questions in dispute. When did an English immigrant become an American? When he was naturalized, the United States claimed. Never, the British retorted; "once an Englishman, always an Englishman."

America's lax immigration laws compounded the problem. A foreigner could become a citizen with ridiculous ease; those too impatient to wait the required five years could purchase false naturalization papers for as little as a dollar. Because working conditions in the American merchant marine were superior to those of the British, at least 10,000 British-born tars were serving on American ships. Some became American citizens legally; others obtained false papers; some admitted to being British subjects; some were deserters from the Royal Navy. From the British point of view, all were liable to impressment.

The Jefferson administration conceded the right of the British to impress their own subjects from American merchant ships. When naturalized Americans were impressed, however, the administration was irritated, and when native-born Americans were taken, it became incensed. Impressment, Secretary of State Madison said in

■ At left, the Ograbme ("embargo" spelled backward), a unique snapping turtle created by cartoonist Alexander Anderson, effectively frustrates an American tobacco smuggler.

1807, was "anomalous in principle . . . grievous in practice, and . . . abominable in abuse." Between 1803 and 1812 at least 5,000 sailors were snatched from the decks of United States vessels and forced to serve in the Royal Navy.* Many of them—estimates run as high as three out of every four—were Americans. The British did not claim the right to impress native-born Americans, and when it could be proved that boarding officers had done so, the men in question were released by higher authority. During the course of the controversy, the British authorities freed 3,800 impressed Americans, which suggests that a much larger number were seized. However, the British refused to abandon impressment. "The Pretension advanced by Mr. Madison that the American Flag should protect every Individual sailing under it . . . is too extravagant to require any serious Refutation," one British foreign secretary explained.

The combination of impressment, British interference with the reexport trade, and the general harassment of neutral commerce instituted by both Great Britain and France would have perplexed the most informed and hardheaded of leaders, and in dealing with these problems Jefferson was neither informed nor hardheaded. Funda-

mentally he was an isolationist, ready "to let every treaty we have drop off without renewal"; he even considered closing down all overseas diplomatic missions. He believed it much wiser to stand up for one's rights than to compromise, yet he hated the very thought of war. While the American merchant fleet passed 600,000 tons and continued to grow at an annual rate of over 10 percent, Jefferson kept only a skeleton navy on active service, despite the fact that the great powers were fighting a worldwide, no-holds-barred war. Instead of building a navy that other nations would have to respect, he relied on a tiny fleet of frigates and a swarm of gunboats that were useless against the Royal Navy—"a macabre monument," in the words of one historian, "to his hasty, ill-digested ideas" about defense.*

The Embargo Act

The frailty of Jefferson's policy became obvious once the warring powers began to attack neutral shipping in earnest. Between 1803 and 1807 the British seized over 500 American ships, Napoleon

---

*This is a conservative estimate; some historians place the number at about 9,000.

*The gunboats had performed effectively against the Barbary pirates, but Jefferson was enamored of them mainly because they were cheap. A gunboat cost about $10,000 to build, a frigate well over $300,000.

over 200 more. The United States could do nothing. "We have principles from which we shall never depart," Jefferson boasted. "Our neutrality should be respected." He added immediately: "On the other hand, we do not want war, and all this is very embarrassing."

The ultimate in frustration came on June 22, 1807, off Norfolk, Virginia. The American frigate *Chesapeake* had just left port for patrol duty in the Mediterranean. Among its crew were a British sailor who had deserted from H.M.S. *Halifax* and three Americans who had been illegally impressed by the captain of H.M.S. *Melampus* and had later escaped. The *Chesapeake* was barely out of sight of land when H.M.S. *Leopard* (56 guns) approached and signaled it to heave to. Thinking that *Leopard* wanted to make some routine communication, Captain James Barron did so. A British officer came aboard and demanded that the four "deserters" be handed over to him. Barron refused, whereupon as soon as the Britisher was back on board, *Leopard* opened fire on the unsuspecting American ship, killing three sailors. Barron had to surrender. The "deserters" were seized and then the crippled *Chesapeake* was allowed to limp back to port.

The attack was in violation of international law, for no nation claimed the right to impress sailors from warships. The British government admitted this, though it delayed making restitution for years. The American public clamored for war, but the country had nothing to fight with. Jefferson contented himself with ordering British warships out of American territorial waters. However, he was determined to put a stop to the indignities being heaped upon the flag by Great Britain and France. The result was the Embargo Act.

The Embargo Act prohibited all exports. American vessels could not clear for any foreign port, and foreign vessels could do so only in ballast. Importing was not forbidden, but few foreign ships would come to the United States if they had to return without a cargo. Although the law was sure to injure the American economy, Jefferson hoped that it would work in two ways to benefit the nation. By keeping United States merchant ships off the seas it would end all chance of injury to them and to the national honor. By denying Britain and France American goods and markets, great economic pressure would be put upon them

to moderate policies toward American shipping. The fact that boycotts had repeatedly wrested concessions from the British during the crises preceding the Revolution was certainly in Jefferson's mind when he devised the embargo.

Seldom has a law been so bitterly resented and resisted by a large segment of the public. It demanded of the maritime interests far greater sacrifices than they could reasonably be expected to make. Massachusetts-owned ships alone were earning over $15 million a year in freight charges by 1807, and Bay State merchants were making far larger gains from the buying and selling of goods. Foreign commerce was the most expansive force in the economy, the chief reason for the nation's prosperity. Losses through seizure were exasperating, but they could be guarded against by insurance. Impressment excited universal indignation, but it hit chiefly at the defenseless, the disreputable, and the obscure and never caused a labor shortage in the merchant marine. The profits of commerce were still tremendous. A Massachusetts senator estimated that if only one vessel in three escaped the blockade, the owner came out ahead. Thus the remedy was more harmful than the disease. As John Randolph remarked in a typical sally, the administration was trying "to cure the corns by cutting off the toes."

The Embargo Act had catastrophic effects. Exports fell from $108 million in 1807 to $22 million in 1808, imports from $138 million to less than $57 million. Prices of farm products and manufactured goods reacted violently; seamen were thrown out of work; merchants found their businesses disrupted.

How many Americans violated the law is difficult to determine, but they were ingenious at discovering ways to do so. Many American ships made hastily for blue water before the machinery of enforcement could be put into operation, not to return until the law was repealed. Quantities of goods flowed illegally across the Canadian border. Shipping between American ports had not been outlawed, and coasting vessels were allowed to put into foreign ports when in distress. Suddenly mysterious storms began to drive experienced skippers leagues off their courses, some as far as Europe. The brig *Commerce*, en route from Massachusetts to New Orleans, was "forced" by a shortage of water to make for Havana. Having replen-

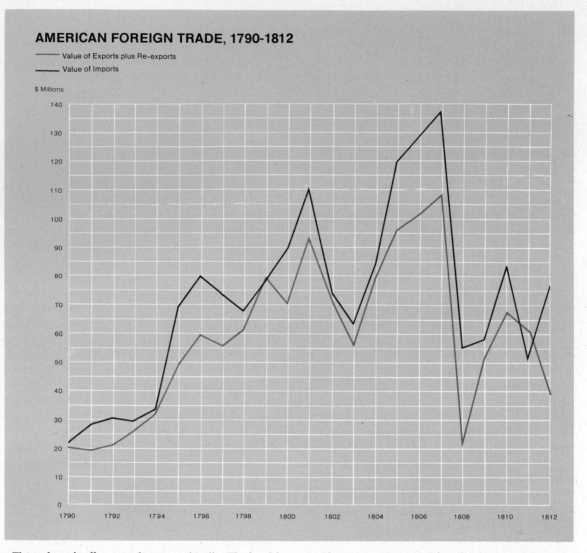

AMERICAN FOREIGN TRADE, 1790-1812
Value of Exports plus Re-exports
Value of Imports

$ Millions

■ The embargo's effects are shown graphically. The brief foreign trade spurt in 1810 was due to congressional passage of Macon's Bill No. 2.

ished her casks, she exchanged her cargo for sugar.

The law permitted merchants with property abroad to send ships to fetch it. About 800 ships went off on such errands. Lawbreakers were difficult to punish. In the seaport towns juries were no more willing to convict men of violating the Embargo Act than their fathers had been to convict those charged with violating the Townshend Acts. A mob at Gloucester, Massachusetts, destroyed a revenue cutter in the same spirit that Rhode Is-

landers exhibited in 1772 when they burned the *Gaspee.*

Surely the embargo was a mistake. The United States ought either to have suffered the indignities heaped upon its vessels for the sake of profits or, by constructing a powerful navy, made it dangerous for the belligerents to treat its merchantmen so roughly. Jefferson was too proud to choose the former alternative, too parsimonious to choose the latter. Instead he applied harsher and harsher regulations in a futile effort to accomplish his purpose. Militiamen patrolled the Canadian border; revenuers searched out smuggled goods without proper warrants. The illegal trade continued, and in his last months as president Jefferson simply gave up. Even then he would not admit that the embargo was a fiasco and urge its repeal. Only in Jefferson's last week in office did a leaderless Congress finally abolish it, substituting the Non-Intercourse Act, which forbade trade only with Great Britain and France and authorized the president to end the boycott against either power by proclamation when and if it stopped violating the rights of Americans.

Madison in Power

It is a measure of Jefferson's popularity that the Republicans won the election of 1808 handily despite the embargo. James Madison got 122 of the 173 electoral votes for the presidency, and the party carried both houses of Congress, although by reduced majorities.

Madison was a small, neat, rather precise person, narrower in his interests than Jefferson but in many ways a deeper thinker. He was more conscientious in the performance of his duties and more consistent in adhering to his principles. Ideologically, however, they were as close as two active and intelligent people could be. Madison had no better solution to offer for the problem of the hour than had Jefferson. The Non-Intercourse Act proved difficult to enforce—once an American ship left port, there was no way to prevent the skipper from steering for England or France—and it exerted little economic pressure on the British, who continued to seize American vessels. Late in 1809, at the urging of Secretary of the Treasury Gallatin, who was concerned because the government was operating at a deficit, Representative Nathaniel Macon of North Carolina introduced a bill permitting American ships to go anywhere but closing United States ports to the ships of Britain and France. After protracted bickering in Congress, this measure was replaced by another, known as Macon's Bill No. 2, which removed all restrictions on commerce with France and Britain, though French and British warships were still barred from American waters. It authorized the president to reapply the principle of noninter-

course to either of the major powers if the other should "cease to violate the neutral commerce of the United States." This bill became law in May 1810.

The volume of United States commerce with the British Isles swiftly zoomed to pre-embargo levels. Trade with France remained much more limited because of the British fleet. Napoleon therefore announced that the Berlin and Milan decrees would be revoked in November on the understanding that Great Britain would abandon its own restrictive policies. Treating this ambiguous proposal as a statement of French policy (which it decidedly was not), Madison reapplied the nonintercourse policy to Great Britain. Napoleon, having thus tricked Madison into closing American ports to British ships and goods, continued to seize American ships and cargoes whenever it suited him to do so.

The British grimly refused to modify the Orders in Council unless it could be shown that the French had actually repealed the Berlin and Milan decrees—and this despite mounting complaints from their own businessmen that the new American nonimportation policy was cutting off a major market for their manufactures. Madison, on the other hand, could not afford either to admit that Napoleon had deceived him or to reverse American policy still another time. Reluctantly he came to the conclusion that unless Britain repealed the Orders, the United States must declare war.

Tecumseh and the Prophet

There were other reasons for fighting besides British violations of neutral rights. The Indians were again making trouble, and western farmers believed that the British in Canada were egging them on. This had been true in the past but was no longer the case in 1811–1812. American domination of the southern Great Lakes region was no longer in question. Canadian officials had no desire to force a showdown between the Indians and the Americans, for that could have but one result. Aware of their own vulnerability, the Canadians wanted to preserve Indian strength in case war should break out between Great Britain and the United States.

American political leaders tended to believe

that Indians should be encouraged to become farmers and to copy the "civilized" ways of whites. However, no government had been able to control the frontiersmen, who by bribery, trickery, and force were driving the tribes back year after year from the rich lands of the Ohio Valley. General William Henry Harrison, governor of Indiana Territory, a relentless, insensitive soldier, kept a constant pressure on them. He wrested land from one tribe by promising it aid against a traditional enemy, from another as a penalty for having murdered a white man, from others by corrupting a few chiefs. Harrison justified his sordid behavior by citing the end in view—that "one of the fairest portions of the globe" be secured as "the seat of civilization, of science, and of true religion." The "wretched savages" should not be allowed to stand in the path of this worthy objective. As early as 1805 it was clear that unless something drastic was done, Harrison's aggressiveness, together with the corroding effects of white civilization, would soon obliterate the tribes.

At this point the Shawnee chief Tecumseh made a bold and imaginative effort to reverse the trend by binding all the tribes east of the Mississippi into a great confederation. Traveling from the Wisconsin country to the Floridas, he persuaded tribe after tribe to join him. "Let the white race perish," Tecumseh declared. "They seize your land; they corrupt your women . . . . Back whence they came, upon a trail of blood, they must be driven!"

To Tecumseh's political movement his brother Tenskwatawa, known as the Prophet, added the force of a moral crusade. Instead of aping white customs, the Prophet said, Indians must give up white ways, white clothes, and white liquor and reinvigorate their own culture. Ceding lands to the whites must stop because the Great Spirit intended that the land be used in common by all.

The Prophet was a fanatic who saw visions and claimed to be able to control the movement of heavenly bodies. Tecumseh, however, possessed true genius. A powerful orator and a great organizer, he had deep insight into the needs of his people. Harrison himself said of Tecumseh: "He is one of those uncommon geniuses which spring up occasionally to produce revolutions and overturn the established order of things." The two brothers made a formidable team. By 1811 thousands of

■ There appears to be no accurate portrait of Tecumseh: this highly romanticized version by an unknown artist shows him in European dress. "Sell (our) country!" he said. "Why not sell the air, the clouds, and the great sea?"

Indians were organizing to drive the whites off their lands. Alarms swept through the west.

With about a thousand soldiers, General Harrison marched boldly against the brothers' camp at Prophetstown, where Tippecanoe Creek joins the Wabash, in Indiana. Tecumseh was away recruiting men, and the Prophet recklessly ordered an assault on Harrison's camp outside the village on November 7, 1811. When the white soldiers held their ground despite the Prophet's magic, the Indians lost confidence and fell back. Harrison then destroyed Prophetstown. While the Battle of Tippecanoe was pretty much a draw, it disillusioned the Indians and shattered their confederation. Frontier warfare continued, but in the disorganized manner of former times. Like all such fighting it was brutal and bloody.

Unwilling as usual to admit that their own excesses were the chief cause of the trouble, the settlers directed their resentment at the British in Canada. "This combination headed by the Shawanese prophet is a British scheme," a resolution adopted by the citizens of Vincennes, Indiana, proclaimed. As a result, the cry for war with Great Britain rang along the frontier.

Depression and Land Hunger

Some westerners pressed for war because they were suffering an agricultural depression. The prices they received for their wheat, tobacco, and other products in the markets of New Orleans were falling, and they attributed the decline to the loss of foreign markets and the depredations of the British. American commercial restrictions had more to do with the western depression than the British, and in any case the slow and cumbersome transportation and distribution system that western farmers were saddled with was the major cause of their difficulties. But the farmers were no more inclined to accept these explanations than they were to absolve the British from responsibility for the Indian difficulties. If only the seas were free, they reasoned, costs would go down, prices would rise, and prosperity would return.

To some extent western expansionism also heightened the war fever. The west contained immense tracts of virgin land, but westerners wanted more. Canada would surely fall to American arms in the event of war, the frontiersmen believed. So, apparently, would Florida, for Spain was now Britain's ally. But it was primarily because Canada was nearby and vulnerable that westerners spoke so heatedly about attacking it; had there been no conflict over neutral rights, Canada would not have been an issue. Florida in itself provided no cause for a war, for it was sure to fall into American hands before long. In 1810 Madison had snapped up the extreme western section without eliciting any effective response from Spain.

Westerners, and many easterners too, were more patriots than imperialists in 1811 and 1812. When the "War Hawks" (their young leaders in Congress) called for war against Great Britain, they did so because they saw no other way to defend the national honor and force repeal of the Orders in Council. The choice seemed to lie between war and surrender of true independence. As Madison put it, to bow to British policy would be to "recolonize" American foreign commerce.

Resistance to War

Powerful interests in the eastern maritime states were dead set against fighting. Some Federalists would have resisted anything the administration proposed, but other people based their objections on economics and a healthy realism. No ship-owner could view with equanimity the idea of taking on the largest navy in the world. Such persons complained sincerely enough about impressment and the Orders in Council, but war seemed worse to them by far. Self-interest led them to urge patience.

Such a policy would have been wise, for Great Britain did not represent a real threat to the United States. British naval officers were high-handed, officials in London complacent, British diplomats in Washington second-rate and obtuse. Yet language, culture, and strong economic ties bound the two countries. Napoleon, on the other hand, represented a tremendous potential danger. He had offhandedly turned over Louisiana, but even Jefferson, the chief beneficiary of his largess, hated everything he stood for. Jefferson called Napoleon "the Attila of the age" and "an unprincipled tyrant who is deluging the continent of Europe with blood."

No one understood the Napoleonic danger to America more clearly than the British; part of the stubbornness and arrogance of their maritime policy grew out of their conviction that Napoleon was a threat to all free nations. The *Times* of London declared: "The Alps and the Apennines of America are the British Navy. If ever that should be removed, a short time will suffice to establish the headquarters of a [French] Duke-Marshal at Washington." Yet by going to war with Britain, the United States was aiding Napoleon.

What made the situation even more unfortunate was the fact that by 1812 conditions had changed in England in a way that made a softening of British maritime policy likely. A depression caused chiefly by the increasing effectiveness of Napoleon's Continental System was plaguing the country. Manufacturers, blaming the slump on the loss of American markets, were urging repeal of the Orders in Council. Gradually, though with exasperating slowness, the government prepared to yield. On June 23, after a change of ministries, the new foreign secretary, Lord Castlereagh, suspended the orders. Five days earlier, alas, the United States had declared war.

The War of 1812

The illogic of the War Hawks in pressing for a fight was exceeded only by their ineffectiveness in planning and managing the struggle. By what possible strategy could the ostensible objective of the war be achieved? To construct a navy capable of challenging the British fleet would have been the work of many years and a more expensive proposition than the War Hawks were willing to consider. So hopeless was that prospect that Congress failed to undertake *any* new construction in the first year of the conflict. Several hundred merchant ships lashed a few cannon to their decks and sailed off as privateers to attack British commerce. The navy's seven modern frigates, built during the war scare after the XYZ Affair, put to sea. But these forces could make no pretense of disputing Britain's mastery of the Atlantic.

For a brief moment the American frigates held center stage, for they were faster, tougher, larger, and more powerfully armed than their British counterparts. Barely two months after the declaration of war, Captain Isaac Hull in U.S.S. *Constitution* chanced upon H.M.S. *Guerrière* in mid-Atlantic, outmaneuvered her brilliantly, brought down her mizzenmast with his first volley, and then gunned her into submission, a hopeless wreck. In October U.S.S. *United States,* captained by Stephen Decatur, hero of the war against the Barbary pirates, caught H.M.S. *Macedonian* off the Madeiras, pounded her unmercifully at long range, and forced her surrender. *Macedonian* was taken into New London as a prize; over a third of her 300-man crew were casualties, while American losses were but a dozen. Then, in December, *Constitution,* now under Captain William Bainbridge, took on the British frigate *Java* off Brazil. "Old Ironsides" shot away the *Java's* mainmast and reduced her to a hulk too battered for salvage.

These victories had little influence on the outcome of the war. The Royal Navy had 34 frigates, 7 more powerful ships of the line, and dozens of smaller vessels. As soon as these forces could concentrate against them, the American frigates were immobilized, forced to spend the war gathering barnacles at their moorings while powerful British squadrons ranged offshore. The privateering merchantmen were more effective because they were so numerous; they captured more than 1,300 British vessels during the war. The best of them—vessels like *America* and *True-Blooded Yankee*—were redesigned, given more sail to increase their speed, and formidably armed. *America* captured 26 prizes valued at more than a million dollars. *True-Blooded Yankee* took 27 and destroyed 7 more in a Scottish harbor.

Great Britain's one weak spot seemed to be Canada. The colony had but half a million inhabitants to oppose 7.5 million Americans. Only 2,257 British regulars guarded the long border from Montreal to Detroit. The Canadian militia was feeble, and many of its members, being American-born, sympathized with the "invaders." Nevertheless it quickly developed that the War Hawk talk was mostly brag and bluster. According to Congressman Henry Clay of Kentucky, the west was one solid horde of ferocious frontiersmen, armed to the teeth and thirsting for Canadian blood. Yet when Congress authorized increasing the army by 25,000 men, Kentucky produced only 400 enlistments.

American military leadership proved extremely disappointing. Madison relied on officers who had served with distinction in the Revolution, but in most cases, as one biographer suggested, their abilities "appeared to have evaporated with age and long disuse." Instead of a concentrated strike against Canada's St. Lawrence River lifeline, the generals planned a complicated three-pronged attack. It was a total failure. In July 1812 General William Hull, veteran of the battles of Trenton, Saratoga, and Monmouth and now governor of Michigan Territory, marched forth with 2,200 men against the Canadian positions facing Detroit. Hoping that the Canadian militia would desert, he delayed his assault, only to find his communications threatened by hostile Indians led by Tecumseh. Hastily he retreated to Detroit, and when the Canadians, under General Isaac Brock, pursued him, he surrendered the fort without firing a shot! In October another force attempted to invade Canada from Fort Niagara. After an initial success it was crushed by superior numbers, while a large contingent of New York militiamen watched from

■ In Ambroise Louis Garneray's painting, Oliver Hazard Perry's squadron (right) drives through the British line in the Battle of Lake Erie. When Perry's flagship *Lawrence* was knocked out of action, he transferred under fire to the *Niagara* and, attacking aggressively, pounded the two largest British vessels into submission.

the east bank of the Niagara River, unwilling to fight outside their own state. The third arm of the American "attack" was equally unsuccessful. Major General Henry Dearborn, who had fought honorably in the Revolution from Bunker Hill to Yorktown but who had grown so fat that he needed a specially designed cart to get from place to place, set out from Plattsburg, New York, at the head of an army of militiamen. Their objective was Montreal, but when they reached the border, the troops refused to cross. Dearborn meekly marched them back to Plattsburg.

Meanwhile, the British had captured Fort Michilimackinac in northern Michigan, and the Indians had taken Fort Dearborn (now Chicago), massacring 85 captives. Instead of sweeping triumphantly through Canada, the Americans found themselves trying desperately to keep the Canadians out of Ohio.

Stirred by these disasters, westerners rallied somewhat in 1813. General Harrison, the victor of Tippecanoe, headed an army of Kentuckians in a series of inconclusive battles against British troops and Indians led by Tecumseh. He found it impossible to recapture Detroit because a British squadron controlling Lake Erie threatened his communications. President Madison, therefore, assigned Captain Oliver Hazard Perry to the task of building a fleet to challenge this force. In September 1813, at Put-in-Bay near the western end of the lake, Perry destroyed the British vessels in a bloody battle in which 85 of the 103 men on Perry's flagship were casualties. "We have met the enemy and they are ours," he reported modestly.*

---

*About a quarter of Perry's 400 men were blacks, which led him to remark that "the color of a man's skin" was no more an indication of his worth than "the cut and trimmings" of his coat.

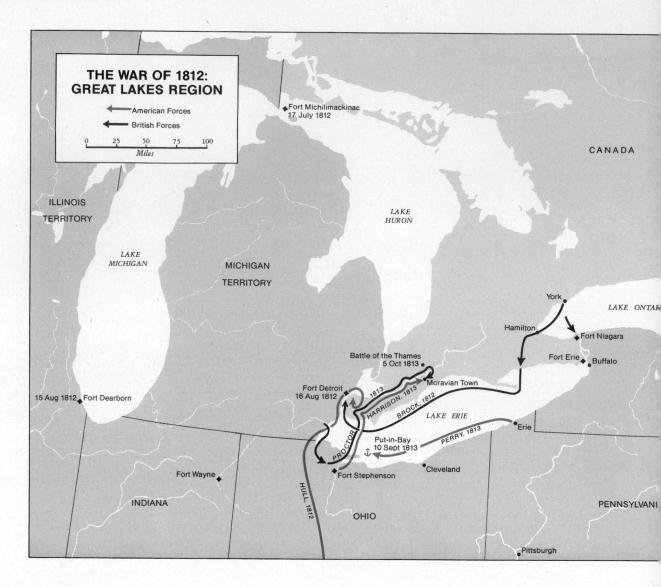

THE WAR OF 1812:
GREAT LAKES REGION

→ American Forces
→ British Forces

0   25   50   75   100
Miles

With the Americans in control of Lake Erie, Detroit became untenable for the British, and when they fell back, Harrison gave chase and defeated them at the Thames River, some 60 miles northeast of Detroit. Although little more than a skirmish, this battle had large repercussions. Tecumseh was among the dead (an eccentric American colonel, Richard Mentor Johnson, was to base a long and successful political career upon his claim of having personally done in the great chief), and without him the Indians lost heart. But American attempts to win control of Lake Ontario and to invade Canada in the Niagara region were again thrown back. Late in 1813 the British captured Fort Niagara and burned the town of Buffalo. The conquest of Canada was as far from accomplishment as ever.

The British fleet had intensified its blockade of American ports, extending its operations to New England waters previously spared to encourage the antiwar sentiments of local maritime interests. All along the coast patrolling cruisers, contemptuous of Jefferson's puny gunboats, captured small craft, raided shore points to commandeer provisions, and collected ransom from port towns by threatening to bombard them. One captain even sent a detail ashore to dig potatoes for his ship's mess.

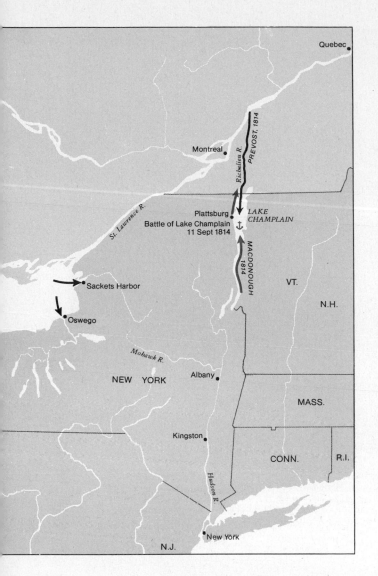

Britain Assumes the Offensive

Until 1814 the British put relatively little effort into the American war, being concerned primarily with the struggle against Napoleon. However, in 1812 Napoleon had invaded Russia and been thrown back; thereafter one by one his European satellites rose against him. Gradually he relinquished his conquests; the Allies marched into France, Paris fell, and in April 1814 the emperor abdicated. Then the British, free to strike hard at the United States, dispatched some 14,000 veterans to Canada.

By the spring of 1814 British strategists had de-vised a master plan for crushing the United States. One army, 11,000 strong, was to march from Montreal, tracing the route that General Burgoyne had followed to disaster in the Revolution. A smaller amphibious force was to make a feint at the Chesapeake Bay area, destroying coastal towns and threatening Washington and Baltimore. A third army was to assemble at Jamaica and sail to attack New Orleans and bottle up the west.

It is necessary, in considering the War of 1812, to remind oneself repeatedly that in the course of the conflict many brave young men lost their lives. Without this sobering reflection it would be easy to dismiss the conflict as a great farce compounded of stupidity, incompetence, and brag. For the British, despite their years of experience against Napoleon, were scarcely more effective than the Americans when they assumed the offensive. They achieved significant success only in the diversionary attack in Chesapeake Bay.

While the main British army was assembling in Canada, 4,000 veterans under General Robert Ross sailed from Bermuda for the Chesapeake. After making a rendezvous with a fleet commanded by Vice Admiral Sir Alexander Cochrane and Rear Admiral Sir George Cockburn, which had been terrorizing the coast, they landed in Maryland at the mouth of the Patuxent River, southeast of Washington. A squadron of gunboats "protecting" the capital promptly withdrew upstream; when the British pursued, their commander ordered them blown up to keep them from being captured.

The British troops marched rapidly toward Washington. At Bladensburg, on the outskirts of the city, they came upon an army twice their number, commanded by General William H. Winder, a Baltimore lawyer who had already been captured and released by the British in the Canadian fighting. While President Madison and other officials watched, the British charged—and Winder's army turned tail almost without firing a shot. The British swarmed into the capital and put most public buildings to the torch. Before personally setting fire to the White House, Admiral Cockburn took one of the president's hats and a cushion from Dolley Madison's chair as souvenirs, and, finding the table set for dinner, derisively drank a toast to "Jemmy's health," adding, an observer coyly recalled, "pleasantries too vulgar for me to repeat."

■ An exaggerated British version of the burning of Washington, issued two months after the event. The small type under the print claims ". . . the property destroyed amounted to thirty Millions of Dollars."

This was the sum of the British success. When they attempted to take Baltimore, they were stopped by a formidable line of defenses devised by General Samuel Smith, a militia officer. General Ross fell in the attack. The fleet then moved up the Patapsco River and pounded Fort McHenry with its cannon, raining perhaps 1,800 shells upon it in a 25-hour bombardment on September 13 and 14. While this attack was in progress, an American civilian, Francis Scott Key, who had been temporarily detained on one of the British ships, watched anxiously through the night. Key had boarded the vessel before the attack in an effort to obtain the release of an American doctor who for some reason had been taken into custody in Washington. As twilight faded, Key had seen the Stars and Stripes flying proudly over the battered fort. During the night the glare of rockets and bursting of bombs gave proof that the defenders were holding out. Then, by the first light of the new day, Key saw again the flag, still waving over Fort McHenry. Drawing an old letter from his pocket, he dashed off the words to "The Star-Spangled Banner," which, when set to music, was to become the national anthem of the United States.

To Key that dawn seemed a turning point in the war. He was roughly correct, for in those last weeks of the summer of 1814 the struggle was indeed being resolved. Unable to crack the defenses of Baltimore, the British withdrew to their ships; shortly after, they sailed to Jamaica to join the forces preparing to attack New Orleans. The destruction of Washington had been a profound shock. Thousands came forward to enlist in the army. The new determination and spirit were strengthened by news from the northern front, where General Sir George Prevost had been leading the main British invasion force south from Montreal. At Plattsburg, on the western shore of Lake Champlain, his 11,000 Redcoats came up against a well-designed defense line manned by 3,300 Americans under General Alexander Macomb. Prevost called up his supporting fleet of four ships and a dozen gunboats. An American fleet of roughly similar strength under Captain Thomas Macdonough, a youthful officer who had served with Decatur against the Barbary pirates, came forward to oppose the British. On September 11, in a brutal battle at point-blank range, Macdonough destroyed the British ships and drove off the gunboats. With the Americans now threatening his flank, Prevost lost heart. Despite his overwhelming numerical superiority, he retreated to Canada.

The Treaty of Ghent

The war should have ended with the battles of Plattsburg, Washington, and Baltimore, for later military developments had no effect on the outcome. Earlier in 1814 both sides had agreed to discuss peace terms. Commissioners were appointed and negotiations begun during the summer at Ghent, in Belgium. The American delegation consisted of former secretary of the treasury Albert Gallatin, Speaker Henry Clay of the House of Representatives, James A. Bayard, a former senator, and two veteran diplomats, Jonathan Russell, minister to Sweden, and John Quincy Adams, minister to Russia. Adams was chairman. The British commissioners were lesser men by far, partly because they could refer important questions to the Foreign Office in nearby London for decision and partly because Britain's topflight diplomats were engaged in settling the future of Europe at the Congress of Vienna.

The talks at Ghent were drawn out and frustrating. The British were in no hurry to sign a treaty, believing that their three-pronged offensive in

1814 would swing the balance in their favor. They demanded at first that the United States abandon practically all the Northwest Territory to the Indians and cede other points along the northern border to Canada. As to impressment and neutral rights, they would make no concessions at all. The Americans would yield no territory, for public opinion at home would have been outraged if they had. Old John Adams, for example, told President Madison at this time, "I would continue this war forever rather than surrender an acre. . . ."

Fortunately, the British came to realize that by pressing this point they would only spur the Americans to fight on. News of the defeat at Plattsburg modified their ambitions, and when the Duke of Wellington advised that from a military point of view they had no case for territorial concessions so long as the United States controlled the Great Lakes, they agreed to settle for *status quo ante bellum,* which is what the Americans sought. The other issues, everyone suddenly realized, had simply evaporated. The mighty war triggered by the French Revolution seemed finally over. The seas were free to all ships, and the Royal Navy no longer had need to snatch sailors from the vessels of the United States or of any other power. On Christmas Eve 1814 the treaty, which merely ended the state of hostilities, was signed. Although, like other members of his family, he was not noted for tact, John Quincy Adams rose to the spirit of the occasion. "I hope," he said, "it will be the last treaty of peace between Great Britain and the United States." And so it was.

The Hartford Convention

Before news of the treaty could cross the Atlantic, two events took place that had important effects but that would not have occurred had the news reached America more rapidly. The first was the Hartford Convention, a meeting of New England Federalists held in December 1814 and January 1815 to protest the war and to plan for a convention of the states to revise the Constitution.

Sentiment in New England had opposed the war from the beginning, and the Federalist party had been quick to employ the discontent to revive its fortunes. Federalist-controlled state administrations refused to provide militia to aid in the fight and discouraged individuals and banks from lending money to the hard-pressed national government. Trade with the enemy flourished as long as the British fleet did not crack down on New England ports, and goods flowed across the Canadian line in as great or greater volume as during Jefferson's embargo.

Their attitude toward the war made the Federalists even more unpopular with the rest of the country, and this in turn encouraged extremists to talk of seceding from the Union. After Massachusetts summoned the meeting of the Hartford Convention, the fear was widespread that the delegates would propose a New England Confederacy, thereby striking at the Union in a moment of great trial.

Luckily for the country, moderate Federalists controlled the convention. They approved a statement that in case of "deliberate, dangerous and palpable infractions of the Constitution" a state has the right "to interpose its authority" to protect itself. This concept, similar to that expressed in the Kentucky and Virginia resolves by the Republicans when they were in the minority, was accompanied by a list of proposed constitutional amendments designed to make the national government conform more closely to the New England ideal. These would have (1) repealed the three-fifths compromise on representation and direct taxes, which favored the slaveholding states, (2) required a two-thirds vote of Congress for the admission of new states and for declaring war, (3) reduced Congress' power to restrict trade by measures such as an embargo, (4) limited presidents to a single term, and (5) made it illegal for naturalized citizens to hold national office. Nothing formally proposed at Hartford was treasonable, but the proceedings were kept secret, and rumors of impending secession were rife. In this atmosphere came the news from Ghent of an honorable peace. The Federalists had been denouncing the war and predicting a British triumph; now they were discredited.

The Battle of New Orleans

Still more discrediting to Federalists was the second event that would not have happened had communications been more rapid: the Battle of New Orleans. During the fall of 1814 the British

had gathered an army at Negril Bay in Jamaica, commanded by Major General Sir Edward Pakenham, brother-in-law of the Duke of Wellington. Late in November an armada of 60 ships set out for New Orleans with 11,000 soldiers. Instead of sailing directly up from the mouth of the Mississippi as the Americans expected, Pakenham approached the city by way of Lake Borgne, to the east. Proceeding through a maze of swamps and bayous, he advanced close to the city's gates before being detected. Early on the afternoon of December 23, three mud-spattered local planters

■ An engineer in the Louisiana militia named Hyacinthe Laclotte painted the Battle of New Orleans from sketches made during the action. The main British thrust is shown in progress against the left side of the American line. In the foreground a column of troops carrying scaling ladders is caught in a withering fire. In addition to turning back the British infantry, Jackson's big guns silenced their artillery.

burst into the headquarters of General Andrew Jackson, commanding the defenses of New Orleans, with the news.

For once in this war of error and incompetence the United States had the right man in the right place at the right time. After his Revolutionary War experiences, Jackson had studied law, then moved west, settling in Nashville, Tennessee. He served briefly in both houses of Congress and was active in Tennessee affairs. Jackson was a hard man and fierce-tempered, frequently involved in brawls and duels, but honest and, by western standards, a good public servant. When the war broke out, he was named major general of volunteers. Almost alone among nonprofessional troops during the conflict, his men won impressive victories, crushing the Creek Indians in a series of battles in Alabama.

Jackson's success was due to his toughness and determination, a determination that his biographer Robert Remini describes as "virtually demonic . . . sheer, total, concentrated." Discipline based on fear, respect, and their awareness of his genuine concern for their well-being made his individualistic frontier militiamen into an army. His men called Jackson Old Hickory; the Indians called him Sharp Knife.

Following these victories, Jackson was assigned the job of defending the Gulf Coast against the expected British strike. Although he had misjudged Pakenham's destination, he was ready when the news of the British arrival reached him. "By the Eternal," he vowed, "they shall not sleep on our soil." "Gentlemen," he told his staff officers, "the British are below, we must fight them tonight."

While the British rested and waited reinforcements, planning to take the city the next morning, Jackson rushed up men and guns. At 7:30 P.M. on December 23 he struck hard, taking the British by surprise. But Pakenham's veterans rallied quickly, and the battle was inconclusive. With Redcoats pouring in from the fleet, Jackson fell back to a point five miles below New Orleans and dug in.

He chose his position wisely. On his right was the Mississippi, on his left an impenetrable swamp, to the front an open field. On the day before Christmas (while the commissioners in Ghent were signing the peace treaty) Jackson's army, which included an excellent segregated unit of free black militiamen, erected an earthen parapet about ten yards behind a dry canal bed. Here the Americans would make their stand.

For two weeks Pakenham probed the American line. Jackson strengthened his defenses daily. At night, patrols of silent Tennesseans slipped out with knife and tomahawk to stalk British sentries. They called this grim game "going hunting." On January 8, 1815, Pakenham ordered an all-out frontal assault. The American position was formidable, but his men had defeated Napoleon. At dawn, through the lowland mists, the Redcoats moved forward with fixed bayonets. Pakenham assumed that the undisciplined Americans—about 4,500 strong—would run at the sight of bare steel.

The Americans did not run. Perhaps they feared the wrath of their commander more than enemy bayonets. Artillery raked the advancing British, and when the range closed to about 150 yards, the riflemen opened up. Jackson had formed his men in three ranks behind the parapet. One rank fired, then stepped down as another took its place. By the time the third had loosed its volley, the first had reloaded and was ready to fire again. Nothing could stand against this rain of

lead. General Pakenham was wounded twice, then killed by a shell fragment while calling up his last reserves. During the battle a single brave British officer reached the top of the parapet. When retreat was finally sounded, the British had suffered almost 2,100 casualties, including nearly 300 killed. Thirteen Americans lost their lives, and 58 more were wounded or missing.

Fruits of "Victory"

Word of Jackson's magnificent triumph reached Washington almost simultaneously with the good news from Ghent. People found it easy to confuse the chronology and consider the war a victory won on the battlefield below New Orleans instead of the standoff it had been. Jackson became the "Hero of New Orleans"; the entire nation rejoiced. One sour Republican complained that the Federalists of Massachusetts had fired off more powder and wounded more men celebrating the victory than they had during the whole course of the conflict. The Senate ratified the peace treaty unanimously, and the frustrations and failures of the past few years were forgotten. Moreover, American success in holding off Great Britain despite internal frictions went a long way toward convincing European nations that both the United States and its republican form of government were here to stay. The powers might accept these truths with less pleasure than the Americans, but accept them they did.

The nation had suffered relatively few casualties and little economic loss, except to the shipping interests. The Indians were the main losers in the contest. When Jackson defeated the Creeks, for example, he forced them to cede 23 million acres to the United States.

The war completed the destruction of the Federalist party. The success of the Jeffersonians' political techniques had inspired younger Federalists in many parts of the country to adopt the rhetoric of democracy and (more important) to perfect local organizations. In 1812 the party made significant gains in the northeast, electing numbers of congressmen and winning many state and local offices. They did not run a candidate for president, but their support enabled the dissident New York Republican De Witt Clinton to obtain 89 electoral votes to Madison's 128.

Their private correspondence reveals that these Federalists were no more enchanted by the virtues of mass democracy than their elders, but by mouthing democratic slogans they revived the party in many districts. Now the results of the war undermined their efforts. They had not supported the war effort; they had argued that the British could not be defeated; they had dealt clandestinely with the enemy; they had even threatened to break up the Union. So long as the issue remained in doubt, these policies won considerable support, but New Orleans made the party an object of ridicule and scorn. It soon disappeared even in New England, swamped beneath a wave of patriotism that flooded the land.

The chief reason for the happy results of the war had little to do with American events. After 1815 Europe settled down to what was to be a century of relative peace. With peace came an end to serious foreign threats to America and a revival of commerce. European emigration to the United States, long held back by the troubled times, spurted ahead, providing the expanding country with its most valuable asset—strong, willing hands to do the work of developing the land. The mood of Jefferson's first term, when democracy had reigned amid peace and plenty, returned with a rush. And the nation, having had its fill of international complications, turned in on itself as Jefferson had wished.

Anglo–American Rapprochement

There remained a few matters to straighten out with Great Britain and Spain. Since no territory had changed hands at Ghent, neither signatory had reason to harbor a grudge. There was no sudden flowering of Anglo-American friendship. British conservatives continued, in the words of the historian George Dangerfield, to view the United States as "little more than a grimy republican thumbprint" on the pages of history, and the device of "twisting the British lion's tail" remained an important tool in the workchest of many an American politician for the rest of the century. Yet for years no serious trouble marred Anglo-American relations. The war had taught the British to respect Americans, if not to love them.

In this atmosphere the two countries worked out peaceful solutions to a number of old problems. In July 1815 they signed a commercial convention ending discriminatory duties and making other adjustments favorable to trade. Boundary difficulties also moved toward resolution. At Ghent the diplomats had created several joint commissions to settle the disputed boundary between the United States and Canada. Many years were to pass before the line was finally drawn, but establishing the principle of defining the border by negotiation was important. In time, a line extending over 3,000 miles was agreed to without the firing of a single shot.

Immediately after the war the British began to rebuild their shattered Great Lakes fleet. Disinclined to engage in a naval arms race, the United States suggested demilitarizing the lakes, and the British agreed. The Rush–Bagot Agreement of 1817 limited each country to one 100-ton vessel armed with a single 18-pounder on Lake Champlain and another on Lake Ontario. They were to have two each for all the other Great Lakes. Gradually, as an outgrowth of this decision, the entire border was demilitarized, a remarkable achievement. In 1818 the two countries agreed to the 49th parallel as the northern boundary of Louisiana Territory between Lake of the Woods and the Rockies, and to the joint control of the Oregon country for ten years. The question of the rights of Americans in the Labrador and Newfoundland fisheries, which had been much disputed during the Ghent negotiations, was settled amicably.

Transcontinental Treaty

The acquisition of Spanish Florida and the settlement of the western boundary of Louisiana were also accomplished as an aftermath of the War of 1812, but in a far different spirit. Spain's control of the Floridas was feeble. West Florida had passed into American hands by 1813, and frontiersmen in Georgia were eyeing East Florida greedily. Indians struck frequently into American territory from Florida, then fled to sanctuary across the line. American slaves who escaped across the border could not be recovered. In 1818 President James Monroe ordered General Andrew Jackson to clear raiding Seminole Indians from American soil and to pursue them into Florida if necessary. Seizing

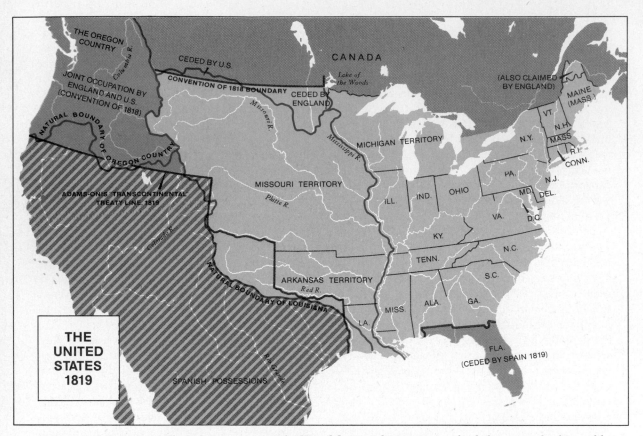

■ The United States, 1819. The light gray areas are the United States and its territories, the darker gray is land owned by Great Britain, and the darker color, land owned by Spain. The Northwest Territory of the 1787 map (see page 133) has been retitled Michigan Territory. The southern part of the jointly-occupied Oregon Country will eventually become the Pacific (or New) Northwest.

on these instructions, Jackson marched into Florida and easily captured two Spanish forts.

Although Jackson eventually withdrew from Florida, the impotence of the Spanish government made it obvious even in Madrid that if nothing were done, the United States would soon fill the power vacuum by seizing the territory. The Spanish also feared for the future of their tottering Latin American empire, especially the northern provinces of Mexico, which stood in the path of American westward expansion. Spain and the United States had never determined where Louisiana Territory ended and Spanish Mexico began. In return for American acceptance of a boundary as far east of the Rio Grande as possible, Spain was ready to surrender Florida.

For these reasons the Spanish minister in

Washington, Luis de Onís, undertook in December 1817 to negotiate a treaty with John Quincy Adams, Monroe's secretary of state. Adams pressed the minister mercilessly on the question of the western boundary, driving a bargain that would have done credit to the most tightfisted of his Yankee ancestors. Onís opened their talks by proposing a line in the middle of what is now Louisiana, and when Adams countered by demanding a boundary running through present-day Texas, Onís professed to be shocked. Abstract right, not power, should determine the settlement, he said. "Truth is of all times, and reason and justice are founded upon immutable principles." To this Adams replied: "That truth is of all times and that reason and justice are founded upon immutable principles has never been contested by the United

States, but neither truth, reason, nor justice consists in stubbornness of assertion, nor in the multiplied repetition of error."

In the end Onís could only yield. He saved Texas for his monarch but accepted a boundary to Louisiana Territory that followed the Sabine, Red, and Arkansas rivers to the Continental Divide and the 42nd parallel to the Pacific, thus abandoning Spain's claim to a huge area beyond the Rockies that had no connection at all with the Louisiana Purchase. Adams even compelled him to agree that when the boundary followed rivers, United States territory was to extend to the farthest bank, not merely to midstream. The United States obtained Florida in return for a mere $5 million, and that paid not to Spain but to Americans who held claims against the Spanish government.

This "Transcontinental Treaty" was signed in 1819, though ratification was delayed until 1821. Most Americans at the time thought the acquisition of Florida the most important part of the treaty, but Adams, whose vision of America's future was truly continental, knew better. "The acquisition of a definite line of boundary to the [Pacific] forms a great epoch in our history," he recorded in his diary.

The Monroe Doctrine

Concern with defining the boundaries of the United States did not reflect a desire to limit expansion, rather the feeling that there should be no more quibbling and quarreling with foreign powers that might distract the people from the great task of national development. The classic enunciation of this point of view, the completion of America's withdrawal from Europe, was the Monroe Doctrine.

Two separate strands met in this pronouncement. The first led from Moscow to Alaska and down the Pacific Coast to the Oregon country. Beginning with the explorations of Vitus Bering in 1741, the Russians had maintained an interest in fishing and fur trading along the northwest coast of North America. In 1821 the czar extended his claim south to the 51st parallel and forbade the ships of other powers to enter coastal waters north of that point. This announcement was disturbing.

The second strand ran from the courts of the European monarchs to Latin America. Between 1817 and 1822 practically all of the region from the Rio Grande to the Strait of Magellan had won its independence. Spain, former master of all the area except Brazil, was too weak to win it back by force, but Austria, Prussia, France, and Russia decided at the Congress of Verona in 1822 to try to regain the area for Spain in the interests of "legitimacy." There was talk of sending a large French army to South America. This possibility also caused grave concern in Washington.

To the Russian threat, Monroe and Secretary of State Adams responded with a terse warning: "The American continents are no longer subjects for any new European colonial establishments." This statement did not impress the Russians, but they had no intention of colonizing the region. In 1824 they signed a treaty with the United States abandoning all claims below the present southern limit of Alaska (54°40' north latitude) and removing their restrictions on foreign shipping.

The Latin American problem was more complex. The United States was not alone in its alarm at the prospect of a revival of French or Spanish power in that region. Great Britain, having profited greatly from the breakup of the mercantilistic Spanish empire by developing a thriving commerce with the new republics, had no intention of permitting a restoration of the old order. But the British monarchy preferred not to recognize the new revolutionary South American republics, for England itself was only beginning to recover from a period of social upheaval as violent as any in its history. Bad times and high food prices had combined to cause riots, conspiracies, and angry demands for parliamentary reform.

In 1823 the British foreign minister, George Canning, suggested to the American minister in London that the United States and Britain issue a joint statement opposing any French interference in South America, pledging that they themselves would never annex any part of Spain's old empire, and saying nothing about recognition of the new republics. This proposal of joint action with the British was flattering to the United States but scarcely in its best interests. The United States had already recognized the new republics, and it had no desire to help Great Britain retain its South American trade. As Secretary Adams pointed out, to agree to the proposal would be to abandon the possibility of someday adding Cuba or any other part of Latin America to the United States. America should act independently, Adams urged. "It would be more candid, as well as more dignified, to avow our principles explicitly . . . than to come in as a cockboat in the wake of the British man-of-war."

Monroe heartily endorsed Adams' argument and decided to include a statement of American policy in his annual message to Congress in December 1823. "The American continents," he wrote, "by the free and independent condition which they have assumed and maintain, are henceforth not to be considered as subjects for future colonization by any European powers." Europe's political system was "essentially different" from that developing in the New World, and the two should not be mixed. The United States would not interfere with existing European colonies in North or South America and would avoid involvement in strictly European affairs, but any attempt to extend European control to countries in the hemisphere that had already won their independence would be considered, Monroe warned, "the manifestation of an unfriendly disposition toward the United States" and consequently a threat to the nation's "peace and safety."

This policy statement—it was not dignified with the title Monroe Doctrine until decades later—attracted little notice in Europe or Latin America and not much more at home. Obviously the United States, whose own capital had been overrun by a mere raiding party less than ten years before, could not police the entire Western Hemisphere. European statesmen dismissed Monroe's message as "arrogant" and "blustering," worthy

only of "the most profound contempt." Latin Americans, while appreciating the intent behind it, knew better than to count on American aid in case of attack.

Nevertheless, the principles laid down by President Monroe so perfectly expressed the wishes of the people of the United States that when the country grew powerful enough to enforce them, there was little need to alter or embellish his pronouncement. However understood at the time, the doctrine may be seen as the final stage in the evolution of American independence.

The famous Declaration of 1776, in this perspective, merely began a process of separation and self-determination. The peace treaty ending the Revolutionary War was a further step, and Washington's neutrality proclamation of 1793 was another, demonstrating as it did the capacity of the United States to determine its own best interests despite the treaty of alliance with France. The removal of British troops from the northwest forts, achieved by the otherwise ignominious Jay Treaty, marked the next stage. Then the Louisiana Purchase made a further advance toward true independence by assuring that the Mississippi River could not be closed to the commerce so vital to the development of the western territories. The stand-off War of 1812 ended any lingering British hope of regaining control of America, and the Transcontinental Treaty pushed the last European power from the path of westward expansion. Monroe's "doctrine" was a kind of public announcement that the sovereign United States had completed its independence and wanted nothing better than to be left alone. Better yet if Europe could be made to allow the entire hemisphere to follow its own path.

SUPPLEMENTARY READING

Titles marked with an asterisk have been published in paperback

Henry Adams' **History of the United States*** and most of the other volumes dealing with Jefferson's first administration mentioned in the previous chapter continue to be useful for this period. On John Randolph, see Henry Adams, **John Randolph*** (1882), and W. C. Bruce, **John Randolph of Roanoke** (1939). C. P. Magrath, **Yazoo: Law and Politics in the New Republic*** (1966), is the best treatment of the case of *Fletcher* v. *Peck.* The best life of Burr is Nathan Schachner, **Aaron Burr*** (1937); the most recent studies of his conspiracy

are T. P. Abernethy, **The Burr Conspiracy** (1954), and F. F. Beirne, **Shout Treason: The Trial of Aaron Burr** (1959). Raymond Walters, Jr., **Albert Gallatin: Jeffersonian Financier and Diplomat*** (1957), is an excellent biography of one of the key figures of the age.

By far the best account of the controversy over neutral rights is Bradford Perkins, **Prologue to War*** (1961), which combines careful research with lucid interpretation. Madison's actions can be followed in Irving Brant, **James Madison: The President** (1956). Both L. M. Sears,

Jefferson and the Embargo (1927), and J. F. Zimmerman, **Impressment of American Seamen** (1925), are solid monographic studies. S. E. Morison, **The Maritime History of Massachusetts*** (1921), contains excellent chapters on the embargo and war periods. J. W. Pratt first played up the role of the west in triggering the War of 1812 in his **Expansionists of 1812** (1925). Pratt's thesis is attacked sharply by A. L. Burt, **The United States, Great Britain, and British North America from the Revolution to the Establishment of Peace After the War of 1812** (1940). Perkins deals with this controversy judiciously in **Prologue to War,*** but see also Reginald Horsman, **The Causes of the War of 1812*** (1962), and R. H. Brown, **The Republic in Peril: 1812*** (1963).

For the war itself, see H. L. Coles, **The War of 1812*** (1965), a good brief account. Irving Brant, **James Madison: Commander-in-Chief** (1961), vigorously defends Madison's handling of the war. Jackson's part in the conflict is described in Marquis James, **Andrew Jackson: The Border Captain** (1933), and R. V. Remini, **Andrew Jackson and the Course of American Empire, 1767–1821** (1977). On the Treaty of Ghent, see F. L. Engelman, **The Peace of Christmas Eve** (1962). Bradford Perkins, **Castlereagh and Adams** (1964), S. F. Bemis, **John Quincy Adams and the Foundations of American Foreign Policy*** (1949), and George Dangerfield, **The Era of Good Feelings*** (1952), also discuss the settlement intelligently. For the Hartford Convention, consult S. E. Morison, **Harrison Gray Otis, 1765–1848** (1969), and Dangerfield's **The Era of Good Feelings.***

For the postwar diplomatic settlements, see Bradford Perkins, **Castlereagh and Adams,** S. F. Bemis, **John Quincy Adams,** and Harry Ammon, **James Monroe: The Quest for National Identity** (1971); for the Monroe Doctrine specifically, see Dexter Perkins, **The Monroe Doctrine: 1823–1826** (1927), and A. P. Whitaker, **The United States and the Independence of Latin America*** (1941).

8/NEW FORCES IN AMERICAN LIFE

James Monroe, of Westmoreland County, Virginia, was a lucky man. He lived a long life in good health; he was happily married to a beautiful and cultivated woman; he saw close up most of the great events in the history of the young republic. Washington looked upon him with favor when Monroe was a youthful soldier and sent him on his first diplomatic mission in 1794. He studied law at the feet of Jefferson, who became his lifelong friend. Like so many Virginians of his generation, Monroe's chief ambition was to serve his country, and this end he achieved in full measure. At the age of 18 he shed his blood for liberty at the glorious Battle of Trenton. He was twice governor of his state, a United States senator, and a Cabinet member. He was at various times the nation's representative in Paris, Madrid, and London. In 1816 he was elected president, defeating Rufus King of New York, 183 electoral votes to 34.

The Era of Good Feelings

As president, Monroe's good fortune continued. The world was finally at peace, the country united and prosperous. A man of good feeling who would keep a steady hand on the helm and hold to the present course seemed called for, and Monroe possessed exactly the qualities that the times required. "He is a man whose soul might be turned wrongside outwards, without discovering a blemish," Jefferson said, and John Quincy Adams, a harsh critic of public figures, praised Monroe's courtesy, sincerity, and sound judgment.

Courtesy and purity of soul do not always suffice to make a good president. In more troubled times Monroe might well have brought disaster, for he was not a forceful leader. He originated few policies, presented few important state papers, organized no personal machine. "The existence of parties is not necessary to free government," he told Andrew Jackson in 1816. The Monroe Doctrine, by far the most significant achievement of his administration, was as much the work of Secretary of State Adams as his own. No one ever claimed that Monroe was better than second-rate, yet when his first term ended, he was reelected without organized opposition.

Monroe seemed to epitomize the resolution of the conflicts that had divided the country between the end of the Revolution and the Peace of Ghent. In his long career he had frequently taken strong positions on controversial issues; always, however, he was a nationalist—his most recent biographer, Harry Ammon, has subtitled the story of Monroe's life "The Quest for National Identity."

By 1817 the divisive issues of earlier days had vanished. Monroe dramatized their disappearance by beginning his first term with a goodwill tour of New England, heartland of the opposition. The tour was a triumph. Everywhere the president was greeted with tremendous enthusiasm. After he visited Boston, once the headquarters and now the graveyard of Federalism, a Federalist newspaperman gave the age its name. Pointing out that the celebrations attending Monroe's visit had brought together in friendly intercourse many persons "whom party politics had long severed," he dubbed the times the "Era of Good Feelings."

It has often been said that the harmony of Monroe's administrations was superficial, that beneath the calm lay potentially disruptive issues that had not yet begun to influence national politics. The dramatic change from the unanimity of Monroe's second election to the fragmentation of four years later, when four candidates divided the vote and the House of Representatives had to choose the president, seems to prove the point.

Nevertheless, the people of the period had good reasons for thinking it extraordinarily harmonious. Peace, prosperity, liberty, and progress: all flourished in 1817 in the United States. The heirs of Jefferson had accepted, with a mixture of resignation and enthusiasm, most of the economic policies advocated by the Hamiltonians. In 1816 Madison put his signature to a bill creating a new national bank almost exactly in the image of Hamilton's, which had expired before the War of 1812, and to a protective tariff which, if less comprehensive than the kind Hamilton had wanted, marked an important concession to the rising manufacturing interests. Monroe accepted the principle of federal aid for transportation projects, approving a bill authorizing Congress to invest $300,000 in the Chesapeake and Delaware Canal Company.

The Jeffersonian balance between individual liberty and responsible government, having survived both bad management and war, had justified itself to the opposition. The new unity was symbolized by the restored friendship of Jefferson and John Adams. In 1801 Adams had slipped sulkily out of Washington without waiting to attend his successor's inauguration, but after ten years of icy silence, the two old collaborators effected a reconciliation. Although they continued to disagree vigorously about matters of philosophy and government, the bitterness between them disappeared entirely. By Monroe's day, Jefferson was writing long letters to "my dear friend" and receiving equally warm and voluminous replies.

When political divisions appeared again, as they soon did, it was not because the old balance had been shaky. Few of the new controversies challenged Republican principles or revived old

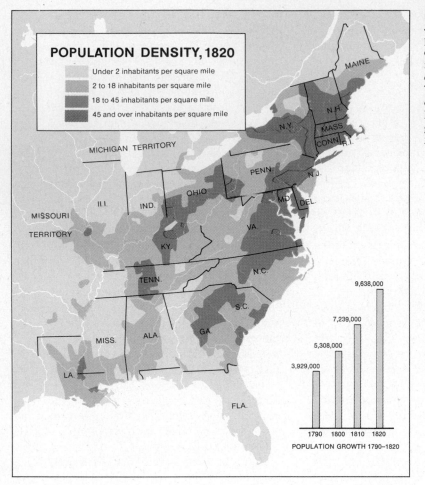

POPULATION DENSITY, 1820

Under 2 inhabitants per square mile

2 to 18 inhabitants per square mile

18 to 45 inhabitants per square mile

45 and over inhabitants per square mile

MAINE

MICHIGAN TERRITORY

N.H.

N.Y.

MASS.

CONN. R.I.

PENN.

N.J.

OHIO

ILL.

IND.

MD. DEL.

MISSOURI

TERRITORY

VA.

KY.

N.C.

TENN.

S.C.

MISS.

ALA.

GA.

LA.

FLA.

3,929,000   5,308,000   7,239,000   9,638,000

1790   1800   1810   1820

POPULATION GROWTH 1790–1820

■ The 1820 census revealed a 33.1 percent increase in national population over the previous census, with some of the largest increases in what was earlier called the Old Northwest. The population of the area comprising Illinois, Indiana, and Michigan Territory, for example, grew some 31,000, to more than 200,000 during the decade.

issues. Instead, these controversies were children of the present and the future, products of the continuing growth of the country.

National unity speeded national expansion, yet expansion, paradoxically, endangered national unity. For as the country grew, new differences appeared within its sections even as the ties binding the parts became stronger and more numerous.

Growth in the 30 years after the ratification of the Constitution had been phenomenal even for a country that took growth for granted. The area of the United States doubled, increasing from 888,811 to 1,788,006 square miles, but this figure is deceptive because very little of the Louisiana Purchase had been settled by 1820. More significant, the population of the nation had more than doubled, from 4 million to 9.6 million. Perhaps the most remarkable feature of this growth was that nearly all of it resulted from natural increase. Only about 250,000 immigrants entered the United States between 1790 and 1820, for the turbulent conditions in Europe during the wars had slowed the flow of humanity across the Atlantic to a trickle. The pace of the westward movement had also quickened; by 1820 more than 2.2 million people had settled in the Mississippi Valley, and the moving edge of the frontier ran in a long, irregular curve from Michigan to Arkansas.

Roots of Economic Growth

To the superficial observer, Americans earned their living in the Era of Good Feelings much as they had in 1790. The country was still overwhelmingly rural. Less than 700,000 people lived in centers of more than 2,500 in 1820, and the percentage of urban dwellers had declined in the ten previous years. But this seemingly stable condition was changing; the nation was on the brink of a major economic readjustment, for certain obscure seeds planted in the early years of the republic had taken root. Almost unnoticed in a country that lived by agriculture and maritime commerce, new ways of producing goods and making a living were beginning to take hold. The industrial revolution was coming to America with a rush.

The growth of industry required certain technological advances and the development of a new type of business organization. Both elements existed in Europe by the time of the Revolution, but it was only after the ratification of the Constitution that they crossed the Atlantic. In 1790 a young English-born genius named Samuel Slater, employed by the Rhode Island merchant firm of Almy & Brown, began to spin cotton thread by machine in the first effective factory in the United States. In 1800 a youthful graduate of Yale College, Eli Whitney, having contracted to make 10,000 rifles for the government, succeeded in manufacturing them by such precise methods that the parts were interchangeable, a major step toward the perfection of the assembly-line system of production. Three years later Oliver Evans, a Philadelphia inventor, had come close to achieving automation in flour milling. A worker poured wheat down a chute at one end of the plant and a second worker headed the barrels of superfine flour which emerged at the other end. The intervening steps of weighing, cleaning, grinding, and packing were all performed by machines.

Other important technological advances included John Fitch's construction and operation of the world's first regularly scheduled steamboat in 1790 and Eli Whitney's invention of the cotton gin in 1793. The steamboat and the gin affected American history almost as much as the factory system and mass production. The former, when employed on western waters, cut the cost of transportation dramatically and brought the west into the national economy. The latter made possible the widespread cultivation of cotton, which transformed the south and fed the cotton factories of the world for decades.

Innovations in the way businesses were orga-

nized and financed accompanied technological developments. The most spectacular step was the sudden flowering of American banking. Here the establishment of the Bank of the United States was of key importance. Aside from aiding government financial operations, the Bank provided an important source of credit for private business. Its success led to the founding of many state-chartered banks. When the great Bank was created in 1791, there were only 3 banks in the entire country. By 1800 there were 29, located in all the major towns and in such minor centers of commerce and industry as Nantucket, Massachusetts, and Hudson, New York. Bank credit, in the historian Bray Hammond's words, "was to Americans a new source of energy, like steam." Yet many citizens failed to grasp this truth. "Every dollar of a bank bill that is issued beyond the quantity of gold and silver in the vaults represents nothing and is therefore a cheat upon somebody," John Adams remarked as late as 1809.

America was not industrialized overnight. Slater's factory did not signal the disappearance of the family spinning wheel or the spread of the factory system to other forms of manufacturing. Most commercial and manufacturing businesses were still managed by a single owner or a few partners. Methods of distributing goods, keeping records, and accounting remained primitive. Interchangeable firing pins for rifles did not lead at once to the spark plug or even to matching pairs of shoes. More than 15 years were to pass after the invention of Fitch's steamboat before it was widely accepted, and it was the better part of another decade before it found its true home beyond the Appalachians.

Birth of the Factory

The stirrings of America's industrial revolution were slow in coming. By the 1770s British manufacturers, especially those in textiles, had made astonishing progress in mechanizing their operations, bringing workers together in buildings called factories where waterpower, and later steam, supplied the force to run new spinning and weaving devices that increased productivity and reduced labor costs. John Kay's flying shuttle, James Hargreaves' spinning jenny, and Richard Arkwright's perfection of the water frame were

■ The restored Old Slater Mill at Pawtucket, R.I., was built and remodeled over the years from 1793 to 1830. The original mill was probably the first building in the United States conceived from the start as a textile factory.

the major technological improvements. Arkwright in particular was responsible for the efficient installation of these machines in factories.

Since machine-spun cotton was cheaper and of better quality than that spun by hand, producers in other countries were eager to adopt British methods. Americans had depended on Great Britain for such products until the Revolution cut off supplies; then the new spirit of nationalism gave impetus to the development of local industry. A number of state legislatures offered bounties to anyone who would introduce the new machinery. The British, however, guarded their secrets vigilantly. It was illegal to export any of the new machines or to send their plans abroad. Workers skilled in their construction and use were forbidden to leave the country. These restrictions were effective for a time; the principles on which the new machines were based were simple enough,

but to construct workable models without plans was another matter. Although a number of persons tried to do so, it was not until Samuel Slater installed his machines in Pawtucket that a successful factory was constructed.

Slater, trained by one of Arkwright's partners, was more than a skillful mechanic. Attracted by stories of the rewards offered in the United States, he slipped out of England in 1789. Not daring to carry any plans, he depended on his memory and his mechanical sense for the complicated specifications of the necessary machines. When Moses Brown brought him to Rhode Island, he insisted on scrapping the crude machinery Almy & Brown had assembled. Then, working in secrecy with a carpenter who was "under bond not to steal the patterns nor disclose the nature of the work," he built and installed Arkwright-type water frames and other machinery. In December 1790 all was ready, and the first American factory began production.

It was a humble beginning indeed. Slater's machines made only cotton thread, which Almy & Brown sold in its Providence store and "put out" to individual artisans, who, working for wages, wove it into cloth in their homes. The machines were tended by a labor force of nine children, for the work was simple and the pace slow. The young operatives' pay ranged from 33 to 67 cents per week, about what a youngster could earn in other occupations.

The factory was profitable from the start. Slater soon branched out on his own, and others trained by him opened their own establishments. By 1800 seven mills possessing 2,000 spindles were in operation; by 1815, after production had been stimulated by the War of 1812, there were 130,000 spindles turning in 213 factories. Many of the new factories were inefficient, but the well-managed ones earned large profits. Slater began with almost nothing. When he died in 1835 he owned mill properties in Rhode Island, Massachusetts, Connecticut, and New Hampshire in addition to other interests, and by the standards of the day he was a rich man.

Before long the Boston Associates, a group of merchants headed by Francis Cabot Lowell, added a new dimension to factory production. Beginning at Waltham, Massachusetts, where the Charles River provided the necessary waterpower, they built between 1813 and 1850 a number of large factories that revolutionized textile production. Some early factory owners had set up hand looms in their plants, but the weavers could not keep pace with the whirring jennies. Lowell, after an extensive study of British mills, smuggled the plans for an efficient power loom into America. His Boston Manufacturing Company at Waltham, capitalized at $300,000, combined machine production, large-scale operation, efficient management, and centralized marketing procedures. It concentrated on the mass production of a standardized product.

Lowell's cloth, though plain and rather coarse, was durable and cheap. His profits averaged almost 20 percent a year during the Era of Good Feelings. In 1823 the Boston Associates began to harness the power of the Merrimack River, setting up a new $600,000 corporation at the sleepy village of East Chelmsford, Massachusetts (population 300), where there was a fall of 32 feet in the river. Within three years the town, appropriately renamed Lowell, had 2,000 inhabitants.

Nonfactory Production

The efficiency of the "Lowell System" was obvious, yet it led to no immediate transformation of American manufacturing. While the embargo and the war with Great Britain aided the new factories by limiting foreign competition, they also stimulated nonfactory production. In Monroe's time the "household-handicraft-mill complex" was still dominant nearly everywhere. Except in the manufacture of textiles, factories employing as many as 50 workers did not exist. Traveling artisans and town craftsmen produced goods ranging from hats, shoes, and other articles of clothing to barrels, clocks, pianos, ship's supplies, cigars, lead pencils, and pottery. Ironworks, brickyards, flour mills, distilleries, and lumberyards could be found even in the most rural parts of the country. The historian George Rogers Taylor reports that in and about a single tiny Ohio town in 1815 more than 30 craftsmen of the shoemaker-baker-druggist type plied their trades.

Nearly all these "manufacturers" produced only to supply local needs, but in some instances large industries grew up without advancing to the factory stage. In the neighborhood of the Connecticut town of Danbury, hundreds of small shops turned out hats by handicraft methods. The hats were sold in all sections of the country, the trade being organized by wholesalers. The shoe industry followed a related pattern, with centers of production in Pennsylvania, New Jersey, and especially eastern Massachusetts. Merchants in these regions bought leather in wholesale lots, had it cut to patterns in central workshops, and then distributed it to craftsmen who made the shoes in their homes or shops on a piecework basis. The finished product was returned to the central shops for inspection and packaging and then shipped throughout the United States. Some strange combinations of production techniques appeared, none more peculiar than in the manufacture of stockings. Frequently the feet and legs were knit by machine in separate factories and then "put out" to handworkers who sewed the parts together in their homes.

Since technology affected American industry unevenly, contemporaries found the changes difficult to evaluate. Few people in the 1820s appreciated how profound the impact of the factory system would be. The city of Lowell seemed remarkable and important but not necessarily a herald of future trends. Yet in nearly every field apparently minor changes were being made. Beginning around 1815, small improvements in the design of water wheels, such as the use of leather transmission belts and metal gears, made possible larger and more efficient machinery in mills and factories. The woolens industry gradually became as mechanized as the cotton. Iron production advanced beyond the stage of the blacksmith's forge and the small foundry only slowly; nevertheless, by 1810 machines were stamping out nails at a third the cost of the hand-forged type, and a few years later sheet iron, formerly hammered out laboriously by hand, was being produced in efficient rolling mills. At about this time the puddling process for refining pig iron made it possible to use coal for fuel instead of expensive charcoal.

Improvements were made soon after the War of 1812 in the manufacture of paper, glass, and pottery. The commercial canning of sterilized foods in airtight containers began about 1820. The invention in that year of a machine for cutting ice, which reduced the cost by over 50 percent, had equally important effects on urban eating habits.

Corporations

Besides the competition of other types of production and the inability of technology to supply instant solutions to every industrial problem, there were other reasons why the factory took hold so slowly in the United States. Mechanization required substantial capital investment, and capital was chronically in short supply. The modern method of organizing large enterprises, the corporation, was rarely used in this period. Between 1781 and 1801 only 326 corporations were chartered by the states, and only a few of them were engaged in manufacturing. The general opinion was that only quasi-public projects, such as roads and waterworks, were entitled to the privilege of incorporation. Anyone interested in organizing a corporation had to obtain a special act of a state legislature. And even among businessmen there

was a tendency to associate corporations with monopoly, with corruption, and with the undermining of individual enterprise. In 1820 the economist Daniel Raymond wrote: "The very object . . . of the act of incorporation is to produce inequality, either in rights, or in the division of property. *Prima facie,* therefore all money corporations are detrimental to national wealth. They are always created for the benefit of the rich. . . ." Such feelings help to explain why as late as the 1860s most manufacturing was being done by unincorporated companies.

Industrial Labor

While the new machines saved immense amounts of labor, a shortage of labor in the United States hampered the spread of the factory system. Most Americans would not work for wages if they could gain a livelihood in some other way. And since the early factories depended on waterpower, they were frequently located far from centers of population. Under the household system the labor force could be widely scattered without inconvenience. Part-time work, so easily adapted to household manufacture, was ill suited to factory conditions.

In the long run the factory revolutionized the lives of workers, but (as with its effect on production) the immediate impact was uneven and not always clear. The majority of nonagricultural workers in the 1820s were either self-employed craftsmen or part of the apprentice-journeyman structure out of which master craftsmen normally emerged. As in colonial times, the average worker, whether a tailor, shoemaker, printer, baker, or carpenter, was apprenticed to a master while still a lad. His training period of five to seven years finished, he became a journeyman, working for wages. Eventually, if he was reasonably talented, frugal, and industrious, he could hope to set up a shop of his own.

The changing nature of production subjected this system to severe strain. It was not so much that the new machines were reducing the need for skilled labor, though in some industries this was certainly a factor. More important was the ever widening spread of markets. As wholesale merchants and budding capitalists took control of the distribution of manufactured goods, they put pressure on producers to decrease costs. In some cases this could be done by lowering wages; more often it was accomplished by cutting corners in the process of manufacture. A cheap, efficient product became more sought after than a finely finished one. The importance of skill (and thus the bargaining power of the worker) declined not so much because machines did the work better but because in many quarters high-quality work ceased to be valued as it had been. The growing shoe industry, for example, concentrated on producing rough brogans for slaves and western farmers. To achieve efficiency, the merchants who controlled the business broke down the work into a series of simple tasks. While shoes continued to be made almost entirely by hand, the degree and variety of skill required by each worker declined, and with it the worker's prestige and importance.

Most factory workers, especially in the textile industry, were drawn from outside the regular labor market. Relatively few hand spinners and weavers became factory workers; indeed, most of them continued to work as they had, for it was many years before the factories could even begin to satisfy the ever increasing demand for cloth. Nor did immigrants attend the new machines. Instead, the operators relied heavily on women and children. The machines lessened the need for both skill and strength, while the labor shortage made it necessary to tap unexploited sources. By the early 1820s about half the cotton textile workers in the factories were children under 16 years of age.

Most people of that generation considered this a good thing, arguing that the work was easy and that it kept the youngsters busy at useful tasks while providing their families with extra income. Roxana Foote, the mother of Harriet Beecher Stowe, author of *Uncle Tom's Cabin*, came from a solid, middle-class family in Guilford, Connecticut. Nevertheless, she worked full-time before her marriage in her grandfather's small spinning mill. "This spinning-mill was a favorite spot," a relative recalled many years later. "Here the girls often received visitors, or read or chatted while they spun." Roxana explained her way of life as a "mill girl" in a casual manner: "I generally rise with the sun, and, after breakfast, take my wheel, which is my daily companion, and the evening is generally devoted to reading, writing, and knitting." A society accustomed to seeing the children of fairly

■ The cover page of a periodical collection of articles by New England "mill girls": the Lowell publishers listed were Misses Curtis and Farley. A prominent feature in the design is the beehive, a popular symbol representing industriousness.

well-to-do farmers working full-time in the fields was not shocked by the sight of children working all day in mills. In some factories laborers were hired in family units. No one member earned very much, but with a couple of adolescent daughters and perhaps a son of 9 or 10 helping out, a family could take home enough to live decently.

Instead of hiring children, the Boston Associates developed the "Waltham System" of employing young, unmarried women and lodging them in company boardinghouses. These were much like small college dormitories, centers of social life and not merely places to eat and sleep. They were strictly supervised; straitlaced New Englanders did not hesitate to permit their daughters to live in them. The regulations laid down by one company, for example, required that all employees "show that they are penetrated by a laudable love of temperance and virtue." "Ardent spirits" were "banished" from company property, "games of hazard and cards" prohibited. A 10 P.M. curfew was enforced.

For a generation the thriving factories of cities like Lowell, Chicopee, and Manchester provided the background for a remarkable industrial idyll. Young women came from farms all over New England to work for a year or two in the mills. They earned about $2.50 or $3 a week and spent perhaps half of that for room and board. Anything but an industrial proletariat, they filled the windows of the factories with flowering plants, organized sewing circles, edited their own literary periodicals, and attended lectures on edifying subjects. That such activity was possible on top of a 70-hour workweek is a commentary on both the resiliency of youth and the leisurely pace of the early factories.

Not considering themselves part of a permanent labor force, they worked to save for a trousseau, to help educate a younger brother, or simply for the experience and excitement of meeting new people and escaping the confining environment of the farm. "The feeling that at this new work the few hours they had of every-day leisure was entirely their own was a satisfaction to them," one Lowell worker recalled. The English novelist Charles Dickens, though scarcely enchanted by American ways, was impressed by a visit to Lowell, which he compared most favorably to "those great haunts of misery," the English manufacturing towns. "They were all well dressed," he wrote of the workers. "They were healthy in appearance, many of them remarkably so, and had the manners and deportment of young women. . . . The rooms in which they worked were as well ordered as themselves."

While the growth of industry did not suddenly revolutionize American life, it reshaped society in

CONSUMER PRICES, 1800-1820

■ This is the first of five charts showing consumer prices from 1800 to 1982. The "index" is very rough for the 19th century, especially before the Civil War, but it gives an approximate idea of what living costs were. The 100 line is the base line; it is the consumer price index for the years 1957–1959, averaged. The data for all Consumer Price charts were supplied by the Bureau of Labor Statistics.

various ways. For many years it lessened the importance of foreign commerce. Some relative decline from the lush years immediately preceding Jefferson's embargo was no doubt inevitable, especially in the fabulously profitable reexport trade, but industrial growth reduced the need for foreign products and thus the business of merchants. Only in the 1850s, when the wealth and population of the United States were more than three times what they had been in the first years of the century, did the value of American exports climb back to the levels of 1807. As the country moved closer to self-sufficiency (a point it never reached), nationalistic and isolationist sentiments were subtly augmented. During the embargo and the War of 1812 a great deal of capital had been transferred from commerce to industry; afterward new capital continued to prefer industry, attracted by the high profits and growing prestige of manufacturing. The rise of manufacturing affected farmers too, for as cities grew in size and number, commercial agriculture flourished. Dairy farming, truck gardening, and fruit growing began to thrive around every manufacturing center.

Cotton Revolutionizes the South

By far the most important indirect effect of industrialization occurred in the south, which soon began to produce cotton to supply the new textile factories of Great Britain and New England. The possibility of growing large amounts of this crop in America had not been seriously considered in colonial times, but by the 1780s the demand for raw cotton to feed the voracious British mills was causing many American farmers to experiment with the crop. Most of the world's cotton at this time came from Egypt, India, and the East Indies. The plant was considered tropical, most varieties being unable to survive the slightest frost. Hamilton, who missed nothing that related to the economic growth of the country, reported: "It has been observed . . . that the nearer the place of growth to the equator, the better the quality of the cotton."

Beginning in 1786, "sea-island" cotton was grown successfully in the mild, humid lowlands and offshore islands along the coasts of Georgia and South Carolina. This was a high-quality cotton, silky and long-fibered like the Egyptian. But its susceptibility to frost severely limited the area of its cultivation. Elsewhere in the south, "green-seed," or upland, cotton flourished, but this plant had little commercial value because the seeds could not be easily separated from the lint. When sea-island cotton was passed between two rollers, its shiny black seeds simply popped out; with upland cotton the seeds were pulled through with the lint and crushed, the oils and broken bits destroying the value of the fiber. To remove the seeds by hand was laborious; a slave working all day could clean scarcely a pound of the white fluff. This made it an uneconomical crop. In 1791 the usually sanguine Hamilton admitted in his *Report on Manufactures* that "the extensive cultivation of cotton can, perhaps, hardly be expected."

Early American cotton manufacturers used the sea-island variety or imported the foreign fiber, in the latter case paying a duty of three cents a pound. However, the planters of South Carolina and Georgia, suffering from hard times after the Revolution, needed a new cash crop. Rice production was not expanding, and indigo, the other staple of the area, had ceased to be profitable when it was no longer possible to claim the British bounty. Cotton seemed an obvious answer. Farmers were experimenting hopefully with varieties of the plant and mulling the problem of how upland cotton could be more easily deseeded.

This was the situation in the spring of 1793, when Eli Whitney was a guest at Mulberry Grove, the plantation of Catherine Greene, widow of General Nathanael Greene, some dozen miles from Savannah.* Whitney had accepted a position as private tutor at 100 guineas a year with a nearby family and had stopped to visit a friend, Phineas Miller, who was overseer of the Greene plantation. While at Mulberry Grove, Whitney, who had never seen a cotton plant before, met a number of the local landowners.

> I heard [he wrote his father] much of the extreme difficulty of ginning Cotton, that is, separating it from its seed. There were a number of very respectable Gentlemen at Mrs. Greene's who all agreed that if a machine could be invented that would clean the Cotton with expedition, it would be a great thing both to the Country and to the inventor.

Whitney thought about the problem for a few days and then "struck out a plan of a machine." He described it to Miller, who enthusiastically offered to finance the invention. Since Whitney had just learned that his job as tutor would pay only 50 guineas, he accepted Miller's proposal.

Within ten days he had solved the problem that had baffled the planters. His gin (engine) consisted of a cylinder covered with rows of wire teeth rotating in a box filled with cotton. As the cylinder turned, the teeth passed through narrow slits in a metal grating. Cotton fibers were caught by the teeth and pulled through the slits. The seeds, too thick to pass through the openings, were left behind. A second cylinder, with brushes rotating in

---

*The property, formerly owned by a prominent Georgia Tory, had been given to Greene by the state in gratitude for his having driven out the British during the Revolution.

COTTON PRODUCTION, 1800-1860

Bales

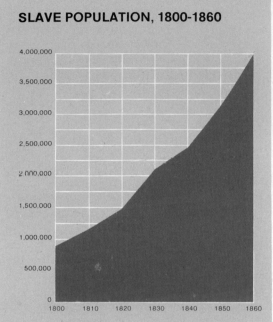

SLAVE POPULATION, 1800-1860

the opposite direction to sweep the cotton from the wires, prevented matting and clogging.

This "absurdly simple contrivance" almost instantly transformed southern agriculture. With a gin a slave could clean 50 times as much cotton as by hand; soon larger models driven by mules and horses were available. The machines were so easy to construct (once the basic idea was understood) that Whitney and Miller were never able to enforce their patent rights effectively. Rival manufacturers shamelessly pirated their work, and countless farmers built gins of their own. Cotton production figures tell the story: in 1790 about 3,000 bales (the average bale weighed 500 pounds) were produced in the United States. In 1793, 10,000 bales were produced; two years later, 17,000; by 1801, 100,000. The embargo and the War of 1812 temporarily checked expansion, but in 1816 output spurted ahead by more than 25 percent, and in the early 1820s annual production averaged well over 400,000 bales.

Despite this avalanche, the price of cotton remained high. During the 1790s it ranged between 26 and 44 cents a pound, a veritable bonanza. In the next decade the price was lower (15 to 19 cents), but it still provided high profits even for

inefficient planters. It was higher again after 1815 and fell below 14 cents only once before 1826. With prices at these levels, profits of $50 an acre were not unusual, and the south boomed.

Upland cotton would grow wherever there were 200 consecutive days without frost and 24 inches of rain. The crop engulfed Georgia and South Carolina and spread north into parts of Virginia. After Andrew Jackson smashed the southwestern Indians during the War of 1812, the rich "Black Belt" area of central Alabama and northern Mississippi and the delta region along the lower Mississippi River were rapidly taken over by the fluffy white staple. In 1821 Alabama alone raised 40,000 bales. Central Tennessee also became important cotton country.

Cotton stimulated the economy of the rest of the nation as well. Most of it was exported, the sale paying for much-needed European products. The transportation, insurance, and final disposition of the crop fell largely into the hands of northern merchants, who profited accordingly. And the surplus corn and hogs of western farmers helped feed the slaves of the new cotton plantations. As Douglass North explained in *The Economic Growth of the United States: 1815–1860*, cotton was "the major expansive force" in the economy for a generation beginning about 1815. "The demands for western foodstuffs and northeastern services and manufactures were basically dependent upon the income received from the cotton trade."

Revival of Slavery

Amid the national rejoicing over this prosperity, one aspect both sad and ominous was easily overlooked. Slavery, a declining or at worst stagnant institution in the decade of the Revolution, was revitalized in the following years.

Libertarian beliefs inspired by the Revolution ran into the roadblock of race prejudice as soon as some of the practical aspects of freedom for blacks became apparent. As disciples of John Locke, the Revolutionary generation had a deep respect for property rights; in the last analysis most white Americans placed these rights ahead of the personal liberty of black Americans in their constellation of values. Forced abolition of slavery therefore attracted few recruits. Moreover, the rhetoric of the Revolution had raised the aspirations of blacks. Increasing signs of rebelliousness appeared among them, especially after the slave uprising in Saint Domingue, which culminated, after a great bloodbath, in the establishment of the black Republic of Haiti in 1804. This example of a successful slave revolt filled white Americans with apprehension. Their fears were irrational (Haitian blacks outnumbered whites and mulattos combined by seven to one) but nonetheless real. And fear led to repression; the exposure of a plot to revolt in Virginia, led by the slave Gabriel, resulted in some three dozen executions even though no actual uprising had occurred.

The mood of the Revolutionary decade had led to the manumission of many slaves; unfortunately this led many whites to have second thoughts about ending slavery. "If the blacks see all of their color slaves, it will seem to them a disposition of Providence, and they will be content," a Virginia legislator, apparently something of an amateur psychologist, claimed. "But if they see others like themselves free . . . they will repine." As the number of free blacks rose, restrictions on them were everywhere tightened.

In the 1780s many opponents of slavery began to think of solving the "Negro problem" by colonizing freed slaves in some distant region—in the western districts or perhaps in Africa. The colonization movement had two aspects. One, a manifestation of an embryonic black nationalism, reflected the disgust of black Americans with local racial attitudes and their interest in African civilization. Paul Cuffe, a Massachusetts Quaker, managed to finance the emigration of 38 of his fellow blacks to Sierra Leone in 1815, but few others followed. The other colonization movement, led by whites, was paternalistic. Some white colonizationists genuinely abhorred slavery. Others could not stomach living with free blacks; to them colonization was merely a polite word for deportation. Most white colonizationists were conservatives who considered themselves realists. Whether they thought blacks degenerate by nature or the victims of their surroundings, they were sure that American conditions gave them no chance to better their lot and that both races would profit from separation.

The colonization idea became popular in Virginia in the 1790s, but nothing was achieved until after the founding of the American Colonization Society in 1817. The society purchased African land and established the Republic of Liberia. However, despite the cooperation of a handful of black nationalists and the patronage of many important white southerners, including presidents Madison and Monroe and Chief Justice Marshall, it accomplished little. Although some white colonizationists expected ex-slaves to go to Africa as enthusiastic Christian missionaries who would convert and "civilize" the natives, few blacks in fact wished to migrate to a land as alien to their own experience as to their masters'. Only about 12,000 went to Liberia, and the toll taken among them by tropical diseases was large. As late as 1850 the black American population of Liberia was only 6,000.

The cotton boom of the early 19th century acted as a brake on the colonization movement. As cotton production expanded, the need for labor in the south grew apace. The price of slaves doubled between 1795 and 1804. As it rose, the inclination of even the most kindhearted masters to free their slaves began to falter. Although the importation of slaves from abroad had been outlawed by all the states, perhaps 25,000 were smuggled into the country in the 1790s. In 1804

■ The colonization movement was in decline when this 1842 membership certificate, featuring an inviting African vista, was issued by a colonization society.

South Carolina reopened the trade, and between that date and 1808, when the constitutional prohibition of importation became effective, some 40,000 were brought in. Thereafter the miserable traffic in human beings continued clandestinely, though on a very small scale (see page 315).

Equally obnoxious was the interstate slave trade that resulted from the cotton boom. While it had always been legal for owners to transport their own slaves to a new state if they were settling there, many states forbade, or at least severely restricted, interstate commercial transactions in human flesh. A Virginia law of 1778, for example, prohibited the importation of slaves for purposes of sale, and persons entering the state with slaves had to swear that they did not intend to sell them. Once cotton became important, these laws were systematically evaded. There was a surplus of slaves in one part of the United States and an acute shortage in another. A migration from the upper south to the cotton lands quickly sprang up.

Slaves from "free" New York and New Jersey and even from New England began to appear on the auction blocks of Savannah and Charleston. Early in the Era of Good Feelings, newspapers in New Orleans were carrying reports such as: "Jersey negroes appear to be particularly adapted to this market. . . . We have the right to calculate on large importations in the future, from the success which hitherto attended the sale."

By about 1820 the letter of the law began to be changed. Soon the slave trade became an organized business, cruel and shameful, frowned on by the "best" people of the south, managed by the depraved and the greedy, yet patronized by nearly anyone who needed labor. "The native land of Washington, Jefferson, and Madison," one disgusted Virginian told a French visitor, "[has] become the Guinea of the United States."

The lot of blacks in the northern states was almost as bad as that of southern free blacks. Except in New England, where there were few of them to begin with, most were denied the vote, either directly or by extralegal pressures. They could not testify in court, intermarry with whites, obtain decent jobs or housing, or get even a rudimentary education. Some states prohibited the migration of free blacks into their territories. Most segregated them in theaters, hospitals, and churches and on public transportation facilities. They were barred from hotels and restaurants patronized by whites.

Northern blacks could at least protest and try to convince the white majority of the injustice of their treatment. These rights were denied their southern brethren. They could and did publish newspapers and pamphlets, organize for political action, petition legislatures and the Congress for redress of grievances—in short, they applied methods of peaceful persuasion in an effort to improve their position in society.

Road Building

Inventions and technological improvements were extremely important in the settlement of the west. On superficial examination, this may not seem to have been the case, for the hordes of settlers who struggled across the mountains immediately after the War of 1812 were no better equipped than their ancestors who had pushed up the eastern slopes in previous generations. Many plodded on

■ About 1820 a young artist named Joshua Shaw journeyed west to the frontier, sketching the pioneers with whom he shared the rigors of travel. As shown here, many carried everything they owned as they struggled along on foot or by mule.

foot over hundreds of miles, dragging crude carts laden with their meager possessions. More fortunate pioneers traveled on horseback or in heavy, cumbersome wagons, the best known being the hearselike, canvas-topped Conestoga "covered wagons," pulled by horses or oxen.

In many cases the pioneers followed trails and roads no better than those of colonial days—quagmires in wet weather, rutted and pitted with potholes a good part of the year. When they settled down, their way of life was no more advanced than that of the Pilgrim fathers. At first they were creatures of the forest, feeding upon its abundance, building their homes and simple furniture with its wood, clothing themselves in the furs of forest animals. They usually planted the first crop in a natural glade; thereafter, year by year, they

pushed back the trees with ax and saw and fire until the land was cleared. Any source of power more complicated than an ox was beyond their ken. Until the population of the territory had grown large enough to support town life, settlers were as dependent on crude household manufactures as any earlier pioneer.

The spread of settlement into the Mississippi Valley created challenges that required technological advances if they were to be met. In the social climate of that age in the United States, these advances were not slow in coming. Most were related to transportation, the major problem for westerners. Without economical means of getting their produce to market, they were condemned to lives of crude self-sufficiency. Everyone recognized that an efficient transportation network would increase land values, stimulate domestic and foreign trade, and strengthen the entire economy.

The Mississippi River and its tributaries provided a natural highway for western commerce and communication, but it was one that had grave disadvantages. Farm products could be floated down to New Orleans on rafts and flatboats, but the descent from Pittsburgh took at least a month. Transportation upstream was out of the question for anything but the lightest and most valuable products, and even for them it was extremely expensive. In any case, the natural flow of trade was between east and west. That is why, from early in the westward movement, much attention was given to building roads linking the Mississippi Valley to the eastern seaboard.

Constructing decent roads over the rugged Appalachians was a formidable task. The steepest grades had to be reduced by cutting through hills and filling in low places, all without modern blast-ing and earth-moving equipment. Streams had to be bridged. Drainage ditches were essential if the roads were not to be washed out by the first rains, and a firm foundation of stones, topped with a well-crowned gravel dressing, had to be provided if they were to stand up under the pounding of heavy wagons. The skills required for building roads of this quality had been developed in Great Britain and France, and the earliest American examples, constructed in the 1790s, were similar to good European highways. The first such road, connecting Philadelphia and Lancaster, Pennsylvania, opened to traffic in 1794.

In heavily populated sections the volume of traffic made good roads worth their cost, which ran to as much as $13,000 a mile where the terrain was difficult, though the average was perhaps half that figure. In some cases good roads ran into fairly remote areas. In New York, always a leading state in the movement for improved transportation, an excellent road had been built all the way

■ The crude state of early 19th-century western roads is vividly portrayed in George Tattersall's watercolor. The expression "to be stumped" stemmed from the frequent plight of wagons and stagecoaches on such roads.

from Albany to Lake Erie by the time of the War of 1812, and by 1821 the state had some 4,000 miles of good roads.

Transportation and the Government

Most of the improved highways and many bridges were built as business ventures by private interests. Promoters charged tolls, the rates being set by the states. Tolls were collected at gates along the way; hinged poles suspended across the road were turned back by a guard after receipt of the toll. Hence these thoroughfares were known as turnpikes, or simply pikes.

The profits earned by a few early turnpikes, such as the one between Philadelphia and Lancaster, caused the boom in private road building, but even the most fortunate of the turnpike companies did not make much money. Maintenance was expensive, traffic spotty. (Ordinary public roads paralleling turnpikes were sometimes called "shunpikes" because penny-pinching travelers used them to avoid the tolls.) Some states bought stock to bolster weak companies, and others built and operated turnpikes as public enterprises. Local governments everywhere provided considerable support, for every town was eager to develop efficient communication with its neighbors.

Despite much talk about individual self-reliance and free enterprise, local, state, and national governments, contributed heavily to the development of what in the jargon of the day were called "internal improvements." They served as "primary entrepreneurs," supplying capital for risky but socially desirable enterprises, with the result that a fascinating mixture of private and public energy went into the building of these institutions. At the federal level even the parsimonious Jeffersonians became deeply involved. In 1808 Secretary of the Treasury Albert Gallatin drafted a comprehensive plan for constructing much-needed roads at a cost of $16 million. This proposal was not adopted, but the government poured money in an erratic and unending stream into turnpike companies and other organizations created to improve transportation.

Logically, the major highways, especially those over the mountains, should have been built by the national government. Strategic military requirements alone would have justified such a program. One major artery, the Old National Road, running from Cumberland, Maryland, to Wheeling, in western Virginia, was constructed by the United States between 1811 and 1818. In time it was extended as far west as Vandalia, Illinois. However, further federal road building was hampered by political squabbles in Congress, usually phrased in constitutional terms but in fact based on sectional rivalries and other economic conflicts. Thus no comprehensive highway program was undertaken in the 19th century.

While the National Road, the New York Pike, and other, rougher trails such as the Wilderness Road into the Kentucky country were adequate for the movement of settlers, they did not begin to answer the west's need for cheap and efficient transportation. Wagon freight rates averaged at least 30 cents a ton-mile around 1815. At such rates, to transport a ton of oats from Buffalo to New York would have cost 12 times the value of the oats! To put the problem another way, four horses could haul a ton and a half of oats about 18 or 20 miles a day over a good road. If they could obtain half their feed by grazing, the horses would still consume about 50 pounds of oats a day. It requires little mathematics to figure out how much oats would be left in the wagon when it reached New York City, almost 400 miles away.

Turnpikes made it possible to transport such goods as clothing, hardware, coffee, and books across the Appalachians, but the expense was considerable. It cost more to ship a ton of freight 300 miles over the mountains from Philadelphia to Pittsburgh than from Pittsburgh to Philadelphia by way of New Orleans, more than ten times as far. Until the coming of the railroad, which was just being introduced in England in 1825, shipping bulky goods by land over the great distances common in America was uneconomical. Businessmen and inventors concentrated instead on improving water transport, first by designing better boats and then by developing artificial waterways.

Steamboats and the West

Rafts and flatboats were adequate for downstream travel, but the only practical solution to upstream travel was the steamboat. After John Fitch's work around 1790, a number of others made important

■ This pencil sketch of Robert Fulton was done about 1803 in Paris by the American artist John Vanderlyn, who was studying abroad under the patronage of Aaron Burr.

contributions to the development of steam navigation. One early enthusiast was John Stevens, a wealthy New Jerseyite, who designed an improved steam boiler for which he received one of the first patents issued by the United States. Stevens got his brother-in-law, Robert R. Livingston, interested in the problem, and the latter used his political influence to obtain an exclusive charter to operate steamboats on New York waters. In 1802, while in France trying to buy New Orleans from Napoleon, Livingston got to know Robert Fulton, a young American artist and engineer who was experimenting with steam navigation, and agreed to finance his work. In 1807, after returning to New York, Fulton constructed the *North River Steam Boat*, famous to history as the *Clermont*.

The *Clermont* was 142 feet long, 18 feet abeam, and drew 7 feet of water. With its towering stack belching black smoke, its side wheels could push it along at a steady five miles an hour. Nothing about it was radically new, but Fulton brought the essentials—engine, boiler, paddle wheels, and hull—into proper balance and thereby produced an efficient vessel.

No one could patent a steamboat; soon the new vessels were plying the waters of every navigable river from the Mississippi east. After 1815 steamers were making the run from New Orleans as far as Ohio. By 1820 at least 60 vessels were operating between New Orleans and Louisville, and by the end of the decade there were more than 200 steamers on the Mississippi.

The day of the steamboat had dawned, and although the following generation would experience its high noon, even in the 1820s its major effects were clear. The great Mississippi Valley, in the full tide of its development, was immensely enriched. Produce poured down to New Orleans, which soon ranked with New York and Liverpool among the world's great ports. Only 80,000 tons of freight reached New Orleans from the interior in 1816–1817, more than 542,000 tons in 1840–1841. Upriver traffic was affected even more spectacularly. Freight charges plummeted, in some cases to a tenth of what they had been after the War of 1812. Around 1818 coffee cost 16 cents a pound more in Cincinnati than in New Orleans, a decade later less than 3 cents more. The northwest emerged from self-sufficiency with a rush and became part of the national market.

Steamboats were far more comfortable than any contemporary form of land transportation, and competition soon led builders to make them positively luxurious. The *General Pike*, launched in 1819, set the fashion. Marble columns, thick carpets, mirrors, and crimson curtains adorned its cabins and public rooms. Soon the finest steamers were floating palaces where passengers could dine, drink, dance, and gamble in luxury as they sped smoothly to their destinations. Yet raft and flatboat traffic *increased*. Farmers, lumbermen, and others with goods from upriver floated down in the slack winter season and returned in comfort by steamer after selling their produce—and their rafts as well, for lumber was in great demand in New Orleans. Every January and February New Orleans teemed with westerners and Yankee sailors, their pockets jingling, bent on a fling before going back to work. The shops displayed everything from the latest Paris fashions to teething rings made of alligator teeth mounted in silver. During the carnival season the city became one great festival, where every human pleasure could be tasted, every vice indulged. "Have you ever been in New Orleans?" one visiting bard sang in the late 1820s.

> . . . If not you'd better go,
> It's a nation of a queer place; day and night a show!
> Frenchmen, Spaniards, West Indians, Creoles, Mustees,
> Yankees, Kentuckians, Tennesseeans, lawyers and trustees.
> Clergymen, priests, friars, nuns, women of all stains;
> Negroes in purple and fine linen, and slaves in rags and chains.
> Ships, arks, steamboats, robbers, pirates, alligators,
> Assassins, gamblers, drunkards, and cotton speculators;
> Sailors, soldiers, pretty girls, and ugly fortunetellers;
> Pimps, imps, shrimps, and all sorts of dirty fellows;
> White men with black wives, *et vice-versa* too,
> A progeny of all colors—an infernal motley crew! . . .
> Snapping turtles, sugar, sugar-houses, water-snakes,
> Molasses, flour, whiskey, tobacco, corn, and johnny-cakes,
> Beef, cattle, hogs, pork, turkey, Kentucky rifles,
> Lumber, boards, apples, cotton, and many other trifles. . . .

The Canal Boom

While the steamboat was conquering western rivers, canals were being constructed that further improved the transportation network. Since the midwestern rivers all emptied into the Gulf of Mexico, they did not provide a direct link with the eastern seaboard. If an artificial waterway could be cut between the great central valley and some navigable stream flowing into the Atlantic, all sections would profit immensely.

Canals were more expensive than roads, but so long as the motive power used in overland transportation was the humble horse, they offered enormous economic advantages to shippers. Because there is less friction to overcome, a team plodding along a towpath can pull a canal barge with a 100-ton load and make better time over long distances than it could pulling a single ton in a wagon on the finest road.

Although canals were as old as Egypt, only about 100 miles of them existed in the United States as late as 1816. Construction costs aside, in a rough and mountainous country canals presented formidable engineering problems. To link the Mississippi Valley and the Atlantic meant somehow circumventing the Appalachian Mountains. Most people thought this impossible.

Mayor De Witt Clinton of New York believed that such a project was feasible in New York State. In 1810, while serving as canal commissioner, he traveled across central New York and convinced himself that it would be practicable to dig a canal from Buffalo, on Lake Erie, to the Hudson River. The Mohawk Valley cuts through the Appalachian chain just north of Albany, and at no point along the route to Buffalo does the land rise more than 570 feet above the level of the Hudson. Marshaling a mass of technical, financial, and commercial information (and using his political influence cannily), Clinton placed his proposal before the New York legislature. In its defense he was eloquent and farsighted:

> As an organ of communication between the Hudson, the Mississippi, the St. Lawrence, the great lakes of the north and west, and their tributary rivers, [the canal] will create the greatest inland trade ever witnessed. The most fertile and extensive regions of America will avail themselves of its facilities for a market. All their surplus . . . will concentrate in the city of New York. . . . That city will, in the course of time, become the granary of the world, the emporium of commerce, the seat of manufactures, the focus of great moneyed operations. . . . And before the revolution of a century, the whole island of Manhattan, covered with habitations and replenished with a dense population, will constitute one vast city.

The legislators were convinced, and in 1817 the state began construction along a route 363 miles long, most of it across densely forested wilderness. At the time the longest canal in the United States ran less than 28 miles!

The construction of the Erie Canal, as it was called, was a remarkable accomplishment. The chief engineer, Benjamin Wright, a surveyor-politician from Rome, New York, had had almost no experience with canal building. One of his chief associates, James Geddes, possessed only an elementary school education and knew virtually nothing about surveying. Both learned rapidly by trial and error. Fortunately, Wright proved to be a

■ The junction of the Erie and Champlain canals, north of Albany, in 1830. The canalboat at the right has been locked down and is being hauled behind two mules, who walk the towpath. Even today a small locomotive used to tow ships through a lock is called a mule.

good organizer and a fine judge of engineering talent. He quickly spotted young men of ability among the workers and pushed them forward. One of his finds, Canvass White, was sent to study British canals. White became an expert on the design of locks; he also discovered an American limestone that could be made into waterproof cement, a vital product in canal construction that had previously been imported at a substantial price from England. Another of Wright's protégés, John B. Jervis, began as an axman, rose in two years to resident engineer in charge of a section of the project, and went on to become perhaps the outstanding American civil engineer of his time. Workers who learned the business digging the "Big Ditch" supervised the construction of dozens of canals throughout the country in later years.

The Erie, completed in 1825, was immediately a financial success. Together with the companion Champlain Canal, which linked Lake Champlain and the Hudson, it brought in over half a million dollars in tolls in its first year. Soon its entire $7 million cost had been recovered, and it was earning profits of about $3 million a year. The effect of this prosperity on New York State was enormous. Buffalo, Rochester, Syracuse, and half a dozen lesser towns along the canal flourished.

New York City had already become the largest city in the nation, thanks chiefly to its merchants, who had established a reputation for their rapid and orderly way of doing business. In 1818 the Black Ball Line opened the first regularly scheduled freight and passenger service between New York and England. Previously, shipments might languish in port for weeks while a skipper waited for additional cargo. Now merchants on both sides of the Atlantic could count on the Black Ball packets to move their goods between Liverpool and New York on schedule whether or not the transporting vessel had a full cargo. This improvement brought much new business to the port. In the same year New York enacted an auction law requiring that imported goods having been placed on the block could not be withdrawn if a bid satisfactory to the seller was not forthcoming. This, too, was a boon to businessmen, who could be assured that if they outbid the competition, the goods would be theirs.

Now the canal cemented New York's position as the national metropolis. Most European manufactured goods destined for the Mississippi Valley entered the country at New York and passed on to the west over the canal. The success of the Erie also sparked a nationwide canal-building boom. Most canals were constructed either by the states, as in the case of the Erie, or as "mixed enterprises" that combined public and private energies.

No state profited as much from this construction as New York, for none possessed New York's geographical advantages. In New England the terrain was so rugged as to discourage all but fanatics. Canals were built connecting Worcester and Northampton, Massachusetts, with the coast, but they were failures financially. The Delaware and Hudson Canal, running from northeastern Pennsylvania across northern New Jersey and lower New York to the Hudson, was completed by private interests in 1828. It managed to earn respectable dividends by barging coal to the eastern seaboard, but it made no attempt to compete with the Erie for the western trade. Pennsylvania, desperate to keep up with New York, engaged in an orgy of construction. In 1834 it completed a complicated system, part canal and part railroad, over the mountains to Pittsburgh. This Mainline Canal cost a staggering sum for that day. With its 177 locks and its cumbersome "inclined-plane railroad" it was slow and expensive to operate and never competed effectively with the Erie. Efforts of Maryland to link Baltimore with the west by water failed utterly.

Beyond the mountains there was even greater zeal for canal construction in the 1820s and still more in the 1830s. Once the Erie opened the way across New York, farmers in the Ohio country de-

manded that links be built between the Ohio River and the Great Lakes so that they could ship their produce by water directly to the east. Local feeder canals seemed equally necessary; with corn worth 20 cents a bushel at Columbus selling for 50 cents at Marietta, on the Ohio, the value of cheap transportation became obvious to Ohio farmers.

Even before the completion of the Erie, Ohio had begun construction of the Ohio and Erie Canal running from the Ohio River to Cleveland. Another, from Toledo to Cincinnati, was begun in 1832. Meanwhile, Indiana had undertaken the 450-mile Wabash and Erie Canal. These canals were well conceived, but the western states overextended themselves building dozens of feeder lines, trying, it sometimes seemed, to supply all farmers west of the Appalachians with water connections from their barns to the New York docks. Politics made such programs almost inevitable, for in order to win support for their pet projects, legislators had to back the schemes of their fellows. The result was frequently financial disaster. There was not enough traffic to pay for all the waterways that were dug. By 1844, $60 million in state "improvement" bonds were in default. Nevertheless, the canals benefited both western farmers and the national economy.

Government Aid to Business

Throughout this period both the United States and the states were active in areas that directly affected the economy. Federal banking, tariff, and land legislation had considerable influence on economic expansion. These political activities, which also contributed to the growth of sectional conflicts in the nation, will be considered in the following chapter; here a number of legal and judicial developments require consideration.

While prejudice against corporations in the manufacturing field continued, the device was such a useful means of bringing together the substantial amounts of capital needed for building roads and canals and for organizing banks and insurance companies that a steadily increasing number of promoters applied for charters. Bills authorizing incorporations became so numerous in some eastern states that legislators found themselves devoting a disconcertingly large portion of their time to them. Therefore they were tempted to issue blanket, though restricted, authorizations. In 1809 Massachusetts passed a law establishing strict rules for all manufacturing corporations in the state. One rule made shareholders individually liable for their company's debts beyond their actual investment. While still requiring separate authorizations for each charter, the Massachusetts legislature could now dispose of applications in a more routine fashion.

Two years later New York enacted the first general incorporation law, permitting the issuance of charters without specific legislative action in each case. Although they held stockholders liable only "to the extent of their respective shares in the . . . company," which was the basic privilege sought by all incorporators, these general charters were not available to companies capitalized at more than $50,000, and they ran for only five years. This was unsatisfactory; after an initial period of enthusiasm (122 charters were issued between 1811 and 1816), the law became nearly a dead letter. Other states did not begin to permit general incorporation until 1837, and businessmen continued to seek, and obtain, special charters for decades thereafter.

Manufacturers in some states received valuable tax benefits. In Vermont no industrial concern paid local taxes. A New York law of 1817 exempted textile mills, and in 1823 Ohio extended similar privileges to textile, iron, and glass companies. Manufacturers benefited from the protection granted inventors by the United States Patent Office, created in 1790, and the attitude of most courts and juries toward labor unions and strikes in this period favored employers. Before the end of the 1820s craft unions had become numerous and active, yet judges tended to consider strikes unlawful conspiracies and to find against unions that tried to establish the closed shop. Though the public's attitude toward organized labor was beginning to change, the legal right of unions to exist was not fully established until the 1840s.

The Marshall Court

The most important legal advantages bestowed upon businessmen in the period were the gift of Chief Justice John Marshall. Historians have tended to forget he had six colleagues on the Supreme Court, and that is easy to understand. Mar-

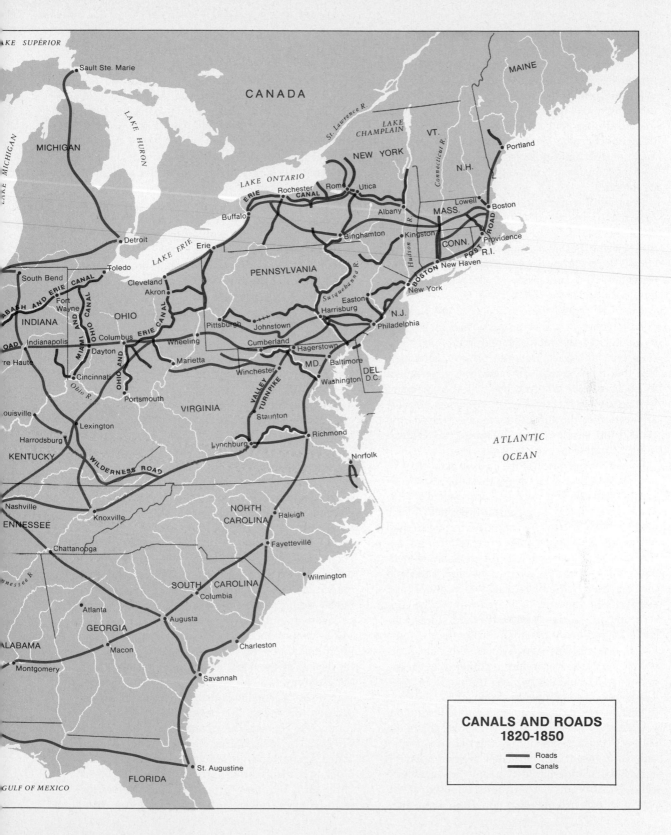

**CANALS AND ROADS
1820-1850**

Roads
Canals

shall's particular combination of charm, logic, and forcefulness made the Court during his long reign, if not a rubber stamp, remarkably submissive to his view of the Constitution. Marshall's belief in a powerful central government explains his tendency to hand down decisions favorable to the manufacturing and business interests. He also thought that "the business community was the agent of order and progress" and tended to interpret the Constitution in a way that would advance its interests.

A series of extremely important cases came before the Court between 1819 and 1824, and in each one Marshall's decision was applauded by most of the business community. The cases involved two major principles: the "sanctity" of contracts and the supremacy of federal legislation over the laws of the states.

Marshall shared the conviction of the Revolutionary generation that property had to be protected against arbitrary seizure if liberty was to be preserved. Contracts between private individuals and between individuals and the government must be strictly enforced, he believed, or chaos will result. He therefore gave the widest possible application to the constitutional provision that no state could pass any law "impairing the Obligation of Contracts."

Two controversies settled in February 1819 illustrate Marshall's views on the subject of contracts. In *Sturges* v. *Crowninshield* he found a New York bankruptcy law unconstitutional. States could pass such laws, he conceded, but they could not make them applicable to debts incurred before the laws were passed, for debts were contracts. In *Dartmouth College* v. *Woodward* he held that a charter granted by a state was a contract and might not be canceled or altered without the consent of both parties. Contracts could scarcely be more sacred than Marshall made them in the Dartmouth College case, which involved an attempt by New Hampshire to alter the charter granted to Dartmouth by King George III in 1769. The state had sought not to destroy the college but to change it from a private to a public institution, yet Marshall held that to do so would violate the contract clause. In the light of this decision, corporations licensed by the states seemed immune against later attempts to regulate their activities, although, of course, restrictions imposed at the time of the chartering were not affected. As a re-

sult, states began to spell out the limitations of corporate charters in greater detail.

Marshall's decisions concerning the division of power between the federal government and the states were even more important. The question of the constitutionality of a national bank, first debated by Hamilton and Jefferson, had not been submitted to the courts during the life of the first Bank of the United States. By the time of the second Bank there were many state banks, and some of them felt that their interests were threatened by the national institution. Responding to pressure from local banks, the Maryland legislature placed an annual tax of $15,000 on "foreign" banks. The Maryland branch of the Bank of the United States refused to pay, whereupon the state brought suit against its cashier, John W. McCulloch. *McCulloch* v. *Maryland* was crucial to the Bank, for five other states had levied taxes on its branches, and others would surely follow suit if the Maryland law were upheld.

Marshall extinguished the threat. The Bank was constitutional, he announced in phrases taken almost verbatim from Hamilton's 1791 memorandum to Washington on the subject; its legality was implied in many of the powers specifically granted to Congress. Full "discretion" must be allowed Congress in deciding exactly how its powers "are to be carried into execution." Since the Bank was legal, the Maryland tax was unconstitutional. Marshall found a "plain repugnance" in the thought of "conferring on one government a power to control the constitutional measures of another." He put this idea in the simplest possible language: "The power to tax involves the power to destroy . . . the power to destroy may defeat and render useless the power to create." The long-range significance of the decision lay in its strengthening of the implied powers of Congress and its confirmation of the Hamiltonian or "loose" interpretation of the Constitution. By establishing the legality of the Bank, it also aided the growth of the economy.

In 1824 Marshall handed down an important decision involving the regulation of interstate commerce. This was the "steamboat case," *Gibbons* v. *Ogden*. In 1815 Aaron Ogden, former United States senator and governor of New Jersey, had purchased the right to operate a ferry between Elizabeth Point, New Jersey, and New York City from Fulton's backer, Robert R. Livingston, who held a New York monopoly of steamboat navigation on the Hudson. When Thomas Gibbons, who held a federal coasting license, set up a competing line, Ogden sued him. Ogden argued in effect that Gibbons could operate his boat (whose captain was Cornelius Vanderbilt, later a famous railroad magnate) on the New Jersey side of the Hudson but had no right to cross into New York waters. After complicated litigation in the lower courts, the case reached the Supreme Court on appeal. Marshall decided in favor of Gibbons, effectively destroying the New York monopoly. A state can regulate commerce which begins and ends in its own territory but not when the transaction involves crossing a state line; then the national authority takes precedence. "The act of Congress," he said, "is supreme; and the law of the state . . . must yield to it."

This decision threw open the interstate steamboat business to all comers, and since an adequate 100-ton vessel could be built for as little as $7,000, dozens of small operators were soon engaged in it.

Their competition tended to keep rates low and service efficient, to the great advantage of the country. More important in the long run was the fact that in order to include the ferry business within the federal government's power to regulate interstate commerce, Marshall had given the word the widest possible meaning. "Commerce, undoubtedly, is traffic, but it is something more,—it is intercourse." By construing the "commerce" clause so broadly, he made it easy for future generations of judges to extend its coverage to include the control of interstate electric power lines and even radio and television transmission.

Many of Marshall's decisions aided the economic development of the country in specific ways, but his chief contribution lay in his broadly national view of economic affairs. When he tried consciously to favor business by making contracts inviolable, his influence was important but limited—and, as it worked out, impermanent. In the steamboat case and in *McCulloch* v. *Maryland*, where he was really deciding between rival property interests, his work was more truly judicial in spirit and far more lasting. In such matters his nationalism enabled him to add form and substance to Hamilton's vision of the economic future of the United States.

Marshall and his colleagues firmly established the principle of judicial limitation on the power of legislatures and made the Supreme Court a vital part of the American system of government. In an age plagued by narrow sectional jealousies, Marshall's contribution was of immense influence and significance, and upon it rests his claim to greatness.

SUPPLEMENTARY READING

Titles marked with an asterisk have been published in paperback

Two splendid works by George Dangerfield provide the best introduction to the Era of Good Feelings: **The Era of Good Feelings*** (1952) and **The Awakening of American Nationalism*** (1965). The best biography of Monroe is Harry Ammon, **James Monroe: The Quest for National Identity** (1971). Shaw Livermore, Jr., **The Twilight of Federalism** (1962), is also useful.

On the forces changing the American economy and stimulating the development of industry, see Stuart Bruchey, **The Roots of American Economic Growth*** (1965), and D. C. North, **The Economic Growth of the United States*** (1961). G. R. Taylor, **The Transportation Revolution*** (1951), a book far broader in scope than its title indicates, also discusses this subject intelligently. On government aid to business, see Oscar and M. F. Handlin, **Commonwealth: A Study of the Role of Government in the American Economy** (1947), Louis Hartz, **Economic Policy and Democratic Thought: Pennsylvania*** (1948), and E. M. Dodd, **American Business Corporations Until 1860** (1954). F. J. Turner, **Rise of the New West*** (1906), is still the best volume on the expansion of the west during the Era of Good Feelings, but see also the appropriate chapters of R. A. Billington, **Westward Expansion** (1967).

On the industrial revolution in America, see A. D. Chandler, Jr., **The Visible Hand: The Managerial Revolution in American Business** (1977), V. S. Clark, **History of Manufactures in the United States** (1929), T. C. Cochran and William Miller, **The Age of Enterprise*** (1942), Roger Burlingame, **March of the Iron Men***

(1938), C. F. Ware, **The Early New England Cotton Manufacture** (1931), and M. T. Parker, **Lowell: A Study in Industrial Development** (1940). R. M. Tryon, **Household Manufactures in the United States** (1917), documents the persistence of one type of production into the 19th century. On the early history of labor, J. R. Commons et al., **History of Labour in the United States** (1918–1935), is the standard work. On the "Lowell girls," see Thomas Dublin, **Women at Work** (1977). B. M. Wertheimer, **We Were There: The Story of Working Women in America** (1977), is a more general history. See also R. A. Mohl, **Poverty in New York** (1971), and A. F. C. Wallace, **Rockdale: The Growth of an American Village** (1978).

On the spread of cotton cultivation in the south, see L. C. Gray, **History of Agriculture in the Southern United States** (1933). There are two excellent biographies of Eli Whitney: Allan Nevins and Jeannette Mirsky, **The World of Eli Whitney*** (1952), and C. McL. Green, **Eli Whitney and the Birth of American Technology*** (1956). W. D. Jordan, **White over Black*** (1968), and L. F. Litwack, **North of Slavery: The Negro in the Free States*** (1961), discuss the fate of blacks. On the colonization movement, see P. J. Staudenraus, **The African Colonization Movement** (1961).

Taylor's **Transportation Revolution** is the best introduction to the changes in transportation that took place. P. D. Jordan, **The National Road** (1948), is useful, as are L. D. Baldwin, **The Keelboat Age on Western Waters** (1941), and Walter Havighurst, **Voices on the River:**

The Story of the Mississippi Waterways (1964). George Dangerfield, **Chancellor Robert R. Livingston of New York** (1960), contains an excellent account of the planning and operation of the *Clermont*, while L. C. Hunter, **Steamboats on the Western Rivers** (1949), is good on later developments. No student should miss Mark Twain, **Life on the Mississippi*** (1883).

On the Erie Canal, see R. E. Shaw, **Erie Water West: A History of the Erie Canal** (1966), Nathan Miller, **The Enterprise of a Free People** (1962), and R. G. Albion, **The Rise of New York Port** (1939). Albion's **Square-Riggers on Schedule** (1938) is also good on the growth of New York City, while Blake McKelvey, **Rochester: The Water-Power City** (1945), discusses the impact of the Erie on that community. Carter Goodrich (ed.), **Canals and American Economic Development** (1961), describes the role of government aid in canal construction authoritatively.

The most important decisions of the Marshall court in this period are discussed in J. A. Garraty (ed.), **Quarrels That Have Shaped the Constitution*** (1964). The fullest account of the Court is Charles Warren, **The Supreme Court in United States History** (1937). See also E. S. Corwin, **John Marshall and the Constitution** (1919), and R. K. Newmyer, **The Supreme Court under Marshall and Taney*** (1968).

9/THE EMERGENCE OF SECTIONALISM

The nationalism and buoyant optimism of the Era of Good Feelings obscured but could not repress the many abrasive conflicts that economic growth and political expansion were creating. Three sectional coalitions, each held together by certain common interests, were giving American political life a new pattern in the 1820s. The richest and most populous group consisted of the states north and east of Maryland. On certain issues Ohio and even Kentucky tended to ally themselves with this region, and in some respects New England was a subgroup with its own special interests. The key to the political unity of the region was manufacturing, although the people and their representatives were deeply concerned with agriculture, commerce, and other matters as well.

The southern states made up a second political unit, this one held together by an amalgam of slavery (as a social institution) and the southern staple crops, especially cotton. The entire Southwest, including Kentucky and Tennessee, tended to become part of the South when the "peculiar institution" or issues affecting cotton were under consideration.

The third political section was the West. Only just beginning to be important enough in Monroe's time to influence national affairs decisively, the region between the Appalachians and the Mississippi was a sprawling, rapidly changing, immensely varied zone. It had less political cohesiveness than either North or South, tending to be pulled abruptly one way and then the other by questions that found the other sections solid and unyielding.

Westerners were acutely aware of their region's special character. When such "western issues" as internal improvements, Indian affairs, and land policy came up for discussion, its representatives quickly united. As the West grew, it became powerful in national affairs out of proportion to its population, for it could usually swing the balance in disputes between the North and the South. And people realized increasingly that the future belonged to the West. More and more this region influenced the tone and spirit of American politics.

Sectional Political Issues

The War of 1812 and the depression that struck the country in 1819 shaped many of the controversies that agitated political life during the Era of Good Feelings. The tariff question was affected by both. Before the War of 1812 the level of duties averaged about 12.5 percent of the value of dutiable products, but to meet the added expenses occasioned by that conflict, Congress doubled all tariffs. In 1816, when the revenue was no longer needed, a new act kept duties close to wartime levels. Infant industries that had grown up during the years of embargo, nonintercourse, and war were able to exert considerable pressure, for they could show that imports had rocketed from $12 million in 1814 to $113 million in 1815 and were still rising. The act especially favored textiles be-

cause the British were dumping cloth in America at bargain prices in their attempt to regain lost markets. The depression added to the strength of the protectionists. Unemployed workers and many farmers became convinced that prosperity would return only if American industry were shielded against foreign competition.

Except for New England, where the shipping interests favored free trade and where the booming mills of the Boston Associates were not seriously injured by foreign competition, the North favored protection. Yet in 1816 there was some backing for high duties in every section. A few southerners hoped that textile mills would spring up in their region; more supported protection on the ground that national self-sufficiency was necessary in case of war. In the West small manufacturers in the towns added their support, and so did farmers, who were counting on workers in the new eastern factories to consume much of their wheat and corn and hogs. But with the passage of time the South rejected protection almost completely. Industry failed to develop, and since they exported most of their cotton and tobacco, southerners soon concluded that besides increasing the cost of nearly everything they bought, high duties on imports would limit the foreign market for southern staples by inhibiting international exchange. As this fact became clear, the West tended to divide on the tariff question: the Northwest and much of Kentucky, which had a special interest in protecting its considerable hemp production, favored high duties; the Southwest, where cotton was the major crop, favored low duties.

National banking policy was another important political issue affected by the war and the depression. Presidents Jefferson and Madison had managed to live with the Bank of the United States despite its supposed unconstitutionality, but its charter was not renewed when it expired in 1811. Aside from the constitutional question, the major opposition to recharter came from state banks eager to take over the business of the Bank for themselves. The fact that English investors owned most of the Bank's stock (the government had sold 2,200 shares to the British banking house of Baring Brothers in 1802) was also used as an argument against recharter.

The war played havoc with American banking. Many more state banks were created after 1811,

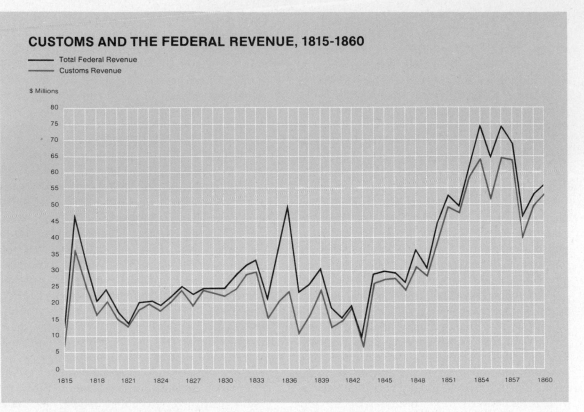

CUSTOMS AND THE FEDERAL REVENUE, 1815-1860

——— Total Federal Revenue
——— Customs Revenue

■ In some years the amounts received from customs duties supplied nearly all the federal revenues—1841, for example—so it is no surprise that the tariff was a major political and sectional issue between the War of 1812 and the Civil War. The jump in federal revenues in the mid 1830s, over and above the usual customs duties, was caused largely by increased public land sales (see chart on page 249).

and most extended credit recklessly. When the British raid on Washington and Baltimore in 1814 sent panicky depositors scurrying to convert their deposits into gold or silver, the overextended financiers could not oblige them. All banks outside New England suspended specie payments; that is, they stopped exchanging their bank notes for hard money on demand. Paper money immediately fell in value; a paper dollar was soon worth only 85 cents in coin in Philadelphia, less in Baltimore. Government business also suffered from the absence of a national bank. In October 1814 Secretary of the Treasury Alexander J. Dallas submitted a plan for a second Bank of the United States, and after considerable wrangling over its precise form, the institution was authorized in April 1816.

The new Bank was much larger than its predecessor, being capitalized at $35 million. However, unlike Hamilton's creation, it was badly managed

at the start. Its first president, William Jones, a former secretary of the treasury, was inept and easygoing. He displayed, according to the historian George Dangerfield, "a kindheartedness which, in his new position, was tantamount to corruption." All kinds of chicanery went on under Jones' nose. According to the charter, no shareholder could have more than 30 votes, regardless of the size of his holdings, yet one director who owned 1,172 shares registered each in a different name, with himself as "attorney" for all, and successfully cast 1,172 votes at meetings. More important, Jones allowed his institution to join in the irresponsible creation of credit. By the summer of 1818 the Bank's 18 branches had issued notes in excess of ten times their specie reserves, far more than was prudent, considering the Bank's responsibilities. When depression struck the country in 1819, the Bank of the United States was as hard pressed as many of the state banks. Jones resigned.

The new president, Langdon Cheves of South Carolina, was as conservative as Jones had been liberal. During the bad times, when easy credit was needed, he pursued a policy of stern curtailment. The Bank thus regained a sound position at the expense of hardship to borrowers. "The Bank was saved," the contemporary economist William Gouge wrote somewhat hyperbolically, "and the people were ruined." Just at the time when John Marshall was establishing its constitutionality, it reached a lowpoint in public favor. Irresponsible state banks resented it, as did the advocates of hard money.

Regional lines were less sharply drawn on the Bank issue than on the tariff. Northern Congressmen voted against the Bank 53 to 44 in 1816—many of them because they objected to the particular proposal, not because they were against *any* national bank. Those from other sections favored it, 58 to 30. The collapse occasioned by the Panic of 1819 produced further opposition to the institution in the West.

Land policy also caused sectional controversy. No one wished to eliminate the system of survey and sale, but there was continuous pressure to reduce the price of public land and the minimum unit offered for sale. The Land Act of 1800 set $2 per acre as the minimum price and 320 acres (a half section) as the smallest unit. Buyers could pay for the land in four annual installments, which meant that one needed only $160 to take possession of a good-sized farm. In 1804 the minimum unit was cut to 160 acres, which could be had for about $80 down.

Since banks were pursuing an easy-credit policy, land sales boomed. The outbreak of the War of 1812 caused a temporary slump, but by 1814 sales had reached an all-time high and were increasing rapidly. Postwar prices of agricultural products were excellent, for the seas were now free and European agriculture had not yet recovered from the ravages of the Napoleonic wars. In 1818 the government sold nearly 3.5 million acres. Thereafter, continuing expansion and the rapid shrinkage of the foreign market as European farmers resumed production led to disaster. Prices fell, the panic struck, and western debtors were forced to the wall by the hundreds.

Sectional attitudes toward the public lands were fairly straightforward. The West wanted cheap land; the North and South tended to look upon the national domain as an asset that should be converted into as much cash as possible. Northern manufacturers feared that cheap land in the West would drain off surplus labor and force wages up, while southern planters were concerned about the competition that would develop when the virgin lands of the Southwest were put to the plough to make cotton. The West, however, was ready to fight to the last line of defense over land policy, while the other regions would usually compromise on the issue to gain support for their own vital interests. Sectional alignments on the question of internal improvements were almost identical, but this issue, soon to become very important, had not greatly agitated national affairs before 1820. As we have seen, the only significant federal internal improvement project undertaken before that date was the National Road.

The most divisive issue was slavery. After the compromises affecting the "peculiar institution" made at the Constitutional Convention, it caused remarkably little conflict in national politics before 1819. Although the importation of blacks rose in the 1790s, Congress abolished the African slave trade in 1808 without major incident. As the nation expanded, free and slave states were added to the Union in equal numbers, Ohio, Indiana, and Illinois being balanced by Louisiana, Mississippi, and Alabama. In 1819 there were 22 states, 11 slave and 11 free. The expansion of slavery occasioned by the cotton boom led southerners to support it more aggressively, which tended to irritate many northerners, but most persons considered slavery mainly a local issue. To the extent that it was a national question, the North opposed it and the South defended it ardently. The West leaned toward the southern point of view, for in addition to the southwestern slave states, the Northwest was sympathetic, partly because much of its produce was sold on southern plantations and partly because at least half of the early settlers of that area came from Virginia, Kentucky, and other slave states.

By 1824 the giants of the Revolutionary generation had completed their work. Washington, Hamilton, Franklin, Samuel Adams, Patrick Henry, and most of their peers were dead. John Adams (88), Thomas Jefferson (81), and James Madison (73) were passing their declining years

■ Asher B. Durand's portrait of an uncompromising John Quincy Adams dates from 1834, when the former president was a congressman from Massachusetts.

quietly on their ancestral acres, full of memories and sage advice, but no longer active in national affairs. In every section new leaders had come forward, men shaped by the past but chiefly concerned with the present. Quite suddenly, between the war and the panic, they had inherited power. They would shape the future of the United States.

Northern Leaders

John Quincy Adams was the best-known political leader of the North in the early 1820s. Just completing his brilliant work as secretary of state under Monroe, he had behind him a record of public service dating to the Confederation period. At 11 he was giving English lessons to the French minister to the Continental Congress and his secretary. ("He shows us no mercy and makes us no compliments," the minister remarked.) While in his teens he served as secretary of legation in Russia and Great Britain. After graduating from Harvard in 1787, he became American minister to the

Netherlands and to Prussia. Chosen United States senator from Massachusetts in 1803 as a Federalist, he gradually switched to the Republican point of view, supporting even the Embargo Act. Madison sent him back to Europe as minister to Russia in 1809. His work at Ghent on the Peace Commission has already been mentioned.

Adams was farsighted, imaginative, hardworking, and extremely intelligent, but inept in personal relations. He had all the virtues and most of the defects of the Puritan, being suspicious both of others and of himself. He suffered in two ways from being his father's child: as the son of a president he was under severe pressure to live up to the Adams name, and his father expected a great deal of him. When the boy was only 7, John Adams wrote his wife: "Train [the children] to virtue. Habituate them to industry, activity, and spirit. Make them consider vice as shameful and unmanly. Fire them with ambition to be useful. . . . Fix their ambition upon great and solid objects, and their contempt upon little, frivolous and useless ones."

Such training made John Quincy an indefatigable worker. Even in winter he normally rose at 5 A.M., and he could never convince himself that most of his associates were not lazy dolts. He was tense, compulsive, conscience-ridden. He set a standard no one could meet and consequently was continually dissatisfied with himself. As one of his grandsons remarked, "he was disappointed because he was not supernatural." Adams had what one Englishman called "a vinegar aspect," passing through life "like a bull-dog among spaniels." Toward enemies he was merciless and overwhelming, toward friends inspiring but demanding.

Like his father and the other great men of the preceding generation, John Quincy Adams was a strong nationalist. While New England was still antiprotectionist, he was at least open-minded on the subject of high tariffs. He supported the second Bank of the United States and, unlike most easterners, he believed that the federal government should spend freely on roads and canals in the West. To slavery he was, like most New Englanders, personally opposed. As Monroe's second term drew toward its close, Adams seemed one of the most likely candidates to succeed him, and at this period his ambition to be president was his great failing. It led him to make certain compromises with his principles, which in turn plagued his oversensitive conscience and had a corrosive effect upon his peace of mind.

Daniel Webster was less prominent in the 1820s than Adams, but he was recognized as one of the coming leaders of New England. Born in New Hampshire in 1782, he graduated from Dartmouth College in 1801, and by the time of the War of 1812 he had made a local reputation as a lawyer and orator. After serving two terms in Congress during the conflict, he moved to Boston to concentrate on his legal practice. He soon became one of the leading constitutional lawyers of the country, prominent in the Dartmouth College controversy, *McCulloch* v. *Maryland*, and other important cases. In 1823 he was again elected to Congress.

Webster owed much of his reputation to his formidable presence and his oratorical skill. Dark, large-headed, craggy of brow, with deep-set, brooding eyes and a firm mouth, he projected a remarkable appearance of heroic power and moral strength. His thunderous voice, his resourceful vocabulary, his manner—all backed by the mastery of every oratorical trick—made him unique. "He . . . is never averse, whilst traversing the thorny paths of political disputation, to scatter the flowers of rhetorical elegance around him," one contemporary admirer recorded.

Webster had a first-rate mind, powerful and logical. His faults were largely those of temperament. He was too fond of good food and fine broadcloth, of alcohol and adulation. Hard work over an extended period of time was beyond him; generally he bestirred himself only with great effort and too often simply to advance his own cause. Webster could have been a lighthouse in the night, guiding his fellow citizens to safe harbor. More often he was a weather vane, shifting to accommodate the strongest breeze. The good opinion of "the best people" meant so much to him that he rarely used his gifts to shape and guide that opinion in the national interest.

Unlike the independent-minded Adams, Webster nearly always reflected the beliefs of the dominant business interests of New England. His opposition to the embargo and the War of 1812 got him into Congress, where he faithfully supported the views of New England merchants. He opposed the high tariff of 1816 because the merchants favored free trade, and he voted against

■ Eyes like "anthracite furnaces," the English historian Thomas Carlyle remarked of Daniel Webster; this is the "Black Dan" portrait by Francis Alexander.

establishing the Bank chiefly on partisan grounds. (His view changed when the Bank hired him as its lawyer.) He was against cheap land and federal construction of internal improvements. His opposition to slavery accorded with the opinion of most of his constituents, but on this question he stood more solidly for principle. Basically he was a nationalist (as was seen in his arguments before the Supreme Court), yet he sometimes allowed political expediency and the prejudices of New England to obscure his feelings. Ahead of him lay fame, considerable constructive service, but also bitter frustration. And one hour of greatness.

Elsewhere in the North there were few outstanding figures among the younger politicians. De Witt Clinton of New York had served briefly in the United States Senate and had run unsuccessfully for the presidency against Madison in 1812, but he was primarily concerned with state and local affairs, especially during the 1820s when the Erie Canal was being constructed. New York's man of the future was a little sandy-haired politico named Martin Van Buren. The Red Fox, as people sometimes called him, was one of the most talented politicians ever to play a part in American affairs. He was born in 1782 and in his teens campaigned for Thomas Jefferson. He studied law and prospered, for he was clever and hardworking, but his ambitions were always political. From 1812 to 1820 he served in the state legislature; in 1820 he was elected United States senator.

Van Buren had great charm and immense tact. By nature affable, he never allowed partisanship to mar his personal relationships with other leaders. The members of his political machine, known as the Albany Regency, were almost fanatically loyal to him, and even his enemies could seldom dislike him as a man. Somehow Van Buren could reconcile deviousness with honesty. He "rowed to his objective with muffled oars," as Randolph of Roanoke said, yet he was neither crooked nor venal. Politics for him was like a game or a complex puzzle: the object was victory, but one must play by the rules or lose all sense of achievement. Only a fool will cheat at solitaire, and despite his gregariousness Van Buren was at heart a solitary operator.

His positions on the issues of the 1820s are hard to determine because he never took a position if he could avoid doing so. In part this was his politician's desire to straddle every fence; it also reflected his quixotic belief that issues were means rather than ends in the world of politics. He opposed rechartering the first Bank yet was not conspicuous among those who fought the second. He did not oppose internal improvements, but De Witt Clinton was his political enemy. No one could say with assurance what he thought about the tariff, and since slavery did not arouse much interest in New York, it is safe to suppose that at this time he had no opinion at all about the institution. Any intelligent observer in the 1820s would have predicted that "the Little Magician" would go far, for he was obviously a master of his craft. How far, and in what direction, no one could have guessed.

Southern Leaders

The most prominent southern leader was William H. Crawford, Monroe's secretary of the treasury. Born in 1772 in the shadow of Virginia's Blue Ridge, he was taken to the Deep South while still a lad, settling finally in Georgia. For a brief time he taught school, then studied law. A giant of a man, ruddy-faced and handsome, he prospered in the law and became a leader in the conservative faction in the state, speaking for the large planters against the interests of the yeomen farmers. Following service in the legislature, he was elected to the Senate in 1807. Later he put in a tour of duty as minister to France, and in 1816 he was appointed secretary of the treasury.

Crawford was direct and friendly, a marvelous storyteller, and a superb manipulator of people. He was one of the few persons in Washington who could teach the fledgling senator Martin Van Buren anything about politics, and Van Buren supported him enthusiastically in the contest for the 1824 presidential nomination. (So, although not publicly, did Jefferson and Madison.) Crawford was one of the first politicians to try to build a national machine. "Crawford's Act" of 1820, limiting the term of minor federal appointees to four years, was passed largely through his efforts, for he realized before nearly anyone else that a handful of petty offices, properly distributed, could win the allegiance of thousands of voters.

Crawford had something interesting to say on most of the important issues of the times. Although predisposed toward the states' rights position, he favored recharter of the Bank and was willing to go along with a moderately protective tariff. During the depression that began in 1819 he devised an excellent relief plan for farmers who were unable to meet installment payments due on land purchased from the government. He suggested a highly original scheme for a flexible paper currency not convertible into hard money. Crawford was controversial. Many of his contemporaries considered him no more than a cynical spoilsman, though his administration of the Treasury was first-rate. Yet he had many friends. His ambition was vast, his power great. Fate, however, was about to strike Crawford a crippling blow.

John C. Calhoun, the other outstanding southern leader, was born in South Carolina in 1782 and graduated from Yale in 1804. He studied law at Tapping Reeve's remarkable law school in Litchfield, Connecticut, which in half a century turned out 15 future United States senators, 10 governors, 2 Supreme Court justices, and a number of other men prominent in public affairs. Returning to South Carolina, Calhoun served in the

■ This striking portrait of John C. Calhoun was painted sometime in the years between 1818 and 1825 by Charles Bird King. The handsome Calhoun was in his thirties.

state legislature; in 1811 he went to Washington as a congressman. A prominent War Hawk, he took a strong nationalist position on all the issues of the day. In 1817 Monroe made him secretary of war.

Although devoted to the South and its institutions, Calhoun took the broadest possible view of political affairs. John Quincy Adams, seldom charitable in his private opinions of colleagues (he called Crawford "a worm"), praised Calhoun's "quick understanding" and "enlarged philosophic views." "He is above all sectional and factional prejudices," Adams wrote. Charles M. Wiltse has summarized Calhoun's views in the early 1820s:

> Ever since its weakness had been exposed by the War of 1812, Calhoun had consciously striven to guide the Government of the United States into the path of power.... To this end he had supported a moderate tariff, a national bank, a large Navy, a well-equipped and well-officered Army, and a unified system of transportation by road and canal; and he had consistently argued that the Constitution granted all the powers necessary to bring these things to fruition.

"Our true system is to look to the country," Calhoun said in 1820, "and to support such measures and such men, without regard to sections, as are best calculated to advance the general interest."

Calhoun was intelligent, bookish, and given to the study of abstractions. Basically a gentle person, he was cold and restrained in most of his relationships. He had no hobbies and was utterly humorless. Legend has it that he once tried to write a poem but after putting down the word "Whereas" gave it up as beyond his powers. Some obscure failing made it impossible for him to grasp the essence of the human condition. An English observer once said that Calhoun had "an imperfect acquaintance with human nature." Yet he burned to lead his fellows. Few contemporaries could maintain themselves in debate against his powerful intelligence, yet that mind—so sharp, so penetrating—was the blind bondsman of his ambition.

Western Leaders

The outstanding western leader of the 1820s was Henry Clay of Kentucky, one of the most charming and colorful of American statesmen. Tall, lean, gray-eyed, Clay was the kind of person who made men cheer and women swoon. On the platform he ranked with Webster; behind the political scenes he was the peer of Van Buren. In every environment he was warm and open—what a modern political scientist might call a charismatic personality. Clay loved to drink, swear, tell tales, and play poker. It was characteristic that at one sitting he won $40,000 from a friend and then cheerfully told him that a note for $500 would wipe out the obligation. He was a reasonable man, skilled at arranging political compromises, but he possessed a reckless streak: like so many westerners, his sense of honor was exaggerated. Twice in his career he called men out for having insulted him. Fortunately, all concerned were poor shots.

Virginia-born, Clay moved to Lexington, Kentucky, in 1797 at the age of 20 and developed a thriving law practice. After some years in the state legislature, he won a seat in Congress in 1810. He led the War Hawks in 1811–1812 and was Speaker of the House from 1811 to 1820 and from 1823 to 1825.

■ Henry Clay was Speaker of the House when he posed for Matthew Jouett in 1824. Jouett worked in Lexington, Kentucky, the self-styled "Athens of the West."

Intellectually second-rate when compared to Adams or Calhoun, or even to Webster, Clay had few original ideas. But he had a perfect temperament for politics. He loved power and understood that in the United States it had to be shared to be exercised. His great gift was in seeing national needs from a broad perspective and fashioning a program that could inspire ordinary citizens with something of his vision. In the early 1820s he was just developing his "American System." In return for eastern support of a policy of federal aid in the construction of roads and canals, the West would back the protective tariff. He justified this deal on the widest national grounds. By stimulating manufacturing, it would increase the demand for western raw materials, while western prosperity would lead to greater consumption of eastern manufactured goods. Washington did not describe the interdependence of the sections better in his Farewell Address than did Clay, repeatedly, in Congress and upon the stump. And, like Washington, Clay was conservative. He opposed the na-

tional bank in 1811 on constitutional grounds but supported the new one in 1816 and thereafter, saying, with typical candor and shrewdness, that "the force of circumstance and the lights of experience" had convinced him that he had previously misread the Constitution. His view of slavery, as his biographer Glyndon Van Deusen has said, was "a combination of theoretical dislike and practical tolerance." He would have preferred to ignore the subject. Nevertheless, slavery repeatedly played a crucial role in Clay's career.

The West had other spokesmen in the 1820s. Thomas Hart Benton, elected to the Senate by the new state of Missouri, was an expansionist and a hard-money man of the uncompromising sort, suspicious of paper currency and therefore of all banks. He championed the small western farmer, favoring free homesteads for pioneers and an extensive federal internal improvements program. Opposed in principle to high tariffs, he tended to vote for them "with repugnance and misgiving" to obtain protection for Missouri's lead and furs. Poor workers should cast aside their tools and head west, he believed.

For 30 years Benton advocated his ideas in the Senate in bluff, colorful language. "Nobody opposes Benton but a few black-jack prairie lawyers," he would roar. "Benton and democracy are one and the same, sir; synonymous terms, sir; synonymous terms, sir." A largehearted man, though vain and pompous, he remained essentially a sectional rather than a national figure.

Another western leader was General William Henry Harrison. Although he sat in the Ohio legislature and in both houses of Congress between 1816 and 1828, Harrison was primarily a soldier. During the Panic of 1819 he took an anti-Bank and pro-high-tariff stand, but he did not identify himself closely with any policy other than the extermination of the Indians. He had little to do with the newly developing political alignments of the 1820s.

Much like Harrison was Andrew Jackson, the "Hero of New Orleans," whose popularity greatly exceeded Harrison's. He had many friends, shrewd in the ways of politics, who were working devotedly, if not entirely unselfishly, to make him president. No one knew his views on most questions, but few cared. His military reputation and his forceful personality were his chief assets.

■ New York's 2,500-seat Park Theatre was depicted in watercolor by John Searle in 1822, the year after it opened. Searle included many prominent New Yorkers of the time in the audience, who are watching a performance of a popular farce called *Monsieur Tonson.*

Northern Social and Cultural Life

New issues and new leaders reflected, in addition to economic change, important alterations in the structure of society and the thinking of the people. Despite the expansion of its industry, New England's population increased scarcely at all when compared to the rest of the country. The best land was already under cultivation, and the price of a farm by American standards was high. The region attracted few immigrants, and much of the natural growth of the population was siphoned off by the West. The other northern states, especially New York, where development had been relatively slow in the colonial period because of restrictive land policies and the domination of the western districts by the Iroquois, expanded rapidly. In 1790 New York ranked fifth among the states with a population of 340,000. By 1820 it had more than quadrupled and was the most populous state in the Union.

Throughout the North the urban population was increasing at a faster pace than in other sections. Boston had only 18,000 inhabitants in 1790; as a result of its rich foreign commerce, its population doubled by 1815 despite the stagnation resulting from the embargo and the war. New England towns such as Salem, Providence, and New Haven expanded at a similar rate, New York and Philadelphia more rapidly.

The manners and attitudes of the people of the northern states were changing too. Society remained anchored to British roots, and socially ambitious people tended, quite consciously, to ape what they took to be the modes and manners of London. But by 1820 "republican" manners, which meant generally a stress on equality, informality, directness (some foreigners called it rudeness), and a disregard for the privacy of others, were everywhere coming into fashion.

Each city had its distinctive qualities. Boston was like a provincial English town both in appearance and population; most citizens had been Boston-bred for generations, and nearly all had British ancestors. New York still displayed a strong Dutch influence, but it had become, with the possible exception of New Orleans, the most cosmopolitan city in the land, as well as its greatest mercantile center. Every European tongue could be heard on its busy streets. Philadelphia retained its Quaker character, with a strong admixture of German. No city was so public-spirited, none better supplied with clubs, charitable organizations, and cultural opportunities.

These northern cities were not yet great centers of industry. Although relatively free of slums, they were dirty, crowded, and crude. Police and fire protection scarcely existed; sewage disposal was generally an individual problem. In Boston streetcleaning was left until the 1820s to farmers who collected the sweepings for fertilizer. Philadelphia, by far the cleanest and most orderly, lacked a decent water system until 1822.

■ An influential and conspicuous example of Charles Bulfinch's "Federal" style is the State House in Boston. This mid 19th-century engraving gives a good idea of how the building looked in its earlier years; it has red brick walls and a shiny gold dome.

The North was the center of American art and culture. All the major towns supported theaters, where the works of Shakespeare and other important dramatists were performed along with a remarkable number of amateurish American plays. Since transportation was slow and expensive, decentralization was essential even in intellectual matters. Towns as small as Worcester and Albany had active publishing businesses, though New York, Boston, and Philadelphia outdistanced all other cities in this field. By 1825 the House of Harper in New York, organized in 1817, was the largest book publisher in the nation. Every town of any size had at least a weekly newspaper, and magazines of various kinds proliferated. Most were short-lived, but Boston's *North American Review,* founded in 1815, was destined to survive for more than a century and to have an influence far out of proportion to its small circulation.

Architecture flourished in the northern cities chiefly as a result of the work of Charles Bulfinch and some of his disciples. Bulfinch, who had studied in England, was influenced by British architects but developed a manner all his own. Thanks to his "Federal" style, parts of Boston achieved a dignity and charm equal to the finest sections of London. The State House, many other public buildings, and, best of all, many of Bulfinch's private houses—austere yet elegant, solid yet airy and graceful—gave the town a distinction it had lacked before the Revolution. Bulfinch and a few of his followers, notably Samuel McIntire and Asher Benjamin, equaled the achievements of the best European architects of their day.

Literature and Painting

Most of the nation's writers in this era lived in the northern states. The *North American Review* set out to "foster American genius," and literary clubs such as Boston's Anthology Club and the Friendly Club in New York sprang up to encourage the production of a distinctively American literature. According to the historian Russel B. Nye, in the period between the Revolution and 1830 "every author of note made at least one attempt to use American history in a major literary work."

Yet as Nye admits, in nearly every case "nothing of consequence appeared." Of the novelists before 1830, only James Fenimore Cooper made

■ James Fenimore Cooper's engraved portrait appeared in London's *New Monthly* magazine under the description "The author of 'The Spy.'" His novels featuring Indians and frontiersmen had wide popularity in Great Britain for decades.

successful use of the national heritage. Beginning with *The Spy* (1821), *The Pioneers* (1823), and *The Last of the Mohicans* (1826), he wrote a long series of tales of Indians and settlers that presented a vivid, if romanticized, picture of frontier life. (Cooper's Indians, Mark Twain quipped, belonged to "an extinct tribe that never existed.") Cooper's work marked a shift from the classicism of the 18th century, which emphasized reason and orderliness in writing, to the romanticism of the early 19th century, with its stress on highly subjective emotional values and its concern for the beauties of nature and the freedom of the individual.

Most novelists of the period slavishly imitated British writers. Some looked to the sentimental novels of Samuel Richardson for a model, others aped satirical writers like Daniel Defoe and Tobias Smollett. Most popular were historical romances done in the manner of the Waverley novels of Sir Walter Scott. None approached the level of the best British writers, and as a result American novelists were badly outdistanced in their own country by the British, both in prestige and popularity. Since foreign copyrights were not recognized in the United States, British books were shamelessly pirated and sold cheaply. Half a million volumes of Scott were sold in America before 1823. American readers benefited but not American writers. Cooper even encouraged a rumor that his first novel, *Precaution* (1820), had been written by an Englishman because he thought this a good way to get it a fair hearing.

New York City was the literary capital of the country during the first three decades of the century. Its leading light was Washington Irving, whose comical *Diedrich Knickerbocker's History of New York* (1809) made its young author famous on both sides of the Atlantic. Yet Irving soon abandoned the United States for Europe. *The Sketch Book* (1819), which included "Rip Van Winkle" and other well-known tales and legends of the Dutch in the Hudson Valley, was written while the author was residing in Birmingham and London. Outside New York there was much less literary activity. New England was only on the verge of its great literary flowering. The Massachusetts-born poet William Cullen Bryant made a stir with "Thanatopsis," published in the *North American Review* in 1817, but he soon moved to New York, where he became editor of the *Evening Post.* In Philadelphia Philip Freneau continued to write excellent verse, and, before his premature death in 1810, Charles Brockden Brown produced some mildly interesting novels, but that was all that was worthy of even passing mention.

American painting in this period reached a level comparable to that of contemporary European work. Like the writers, nearly all American artists came from the North. All received most of their training in Europe. Benjamin West of Philadelphia, the first and in his day the most highly regarded, went to Europe before the Revolution and never returned; he can scarcely be considered an American. John Singleton Copley, whose stern, straightforward portraits display a more distinctly American character than the work of any of his contemporaries, was a Bostonian. No one so well captured the vigor and integrity of the Revolutionary generation. Charles Willson Peale was born in Maryland, but after studying under West in Lon-

don, he settled in Philadelphia, where he established a museum containing fossils, stuffed animals, and various natural curiosities as well as paintings. Peale helped found the Pennsylvania Academy of the Fine Arts, and he did much to encourage American painting. Not the least of his achievements was the production of a large brood of artistic children to whom he gave such names as Rembrandt, Titian, and Rubens. The most talented of Peale's children was (appropriately) Rembrandt, whose portrait of Jefferson, executed in 1800, is one of the finest likenesses of the Sage of Monticello that we have.

Another outstanding artist of this generation was Gilbert Stuart of Rhode Island, best known for his many studies of George Washington. Stuart studied in England with Benjamin West, and his brush was much in demand in London. In America he worked in New York, Philadelphia, and Boston. Stuart was probably the most technically accomplished of the early American portrait painters. He was fond of painting his subjects with ruddy complexions (produced by means of a judicious mixture of vermilion, purple, and white pigment), which made many of his elderly sitters appear positively cherubic. Stuart once remarked that the pallid flesh tones used by a rival looked "like putrid veal a little blown with green flies."

John Vanderlyn of New York was one of the first Americans to study in Paris, where the icy neoclassicism of Jacques Louis David influenced him greatly. Originally a portraitist, in later life he painted a number of curious panoramas covering thousands of square feet of canvas. Henry Inman, who learned his trade as an apprentice to the prolific miniaturist-engraver John Wesley Jarvis, lived most of his life in New York and Philadelphia. Among the many prominent men who sat for Inman were Chief Justice Marshall, President Van Buren, the artist-naturalist John Audubon (whose *Birds of America* [1827–1838] is a landmark in the history of American art), the writer Nathaniel Hawthorne, and Nicholas Biddle, president of the second Bank of the United States (see page 246).

In general the painting of the period was less obviously imitative of European models than the national literature—and of far higher quality. Wealthy merchants, manufacturers, and planters wished their likenesses preserved, and the demand for portraits of the nation's Revolutionary heroes seemed insatiable. Since paintings could

■ In 1801 Charles Willson Peale masterminded the first American scientific expedition, to "exhume" the bones of a prehistoric mastodon found on a New York farm. Peale set up a lift to remove muck from the diggings and painted the entire operation, including himself gesturing in the group at far right.

not be reproduced as books could be, American artists did a flourishing business. And they remained unmistakably in the European tradition.

Exceptions to this generalization can be found in the work of a number of self-trained artists like Jonathan Fisher, Charles Octavius Cole, and J. William Jennys. These primitive painters supplied rural and middle-class patrons in the same way that Copley and Stuart catered to the tastes of the rich and prominent. Jennys, for example, received $24 in 1801 for portraits of Dr. William Stoddard Williams of Deerfield, Massachusetts, and his wife. Cole specialized in New England sea captains, whom he often painted holding brassbound spyglasses. One historian has discovered traces of

more than 20 artisan-painters within the single state of Maine in the 1830s and 1840s. Some of these primitive canvases have great charm and distinction. All show little sign of European influence, yet they are not especially American either. They reflect rather the characteristics of all primitive art: simplicity and distinctness.

Religion and Education

The religious views of the people of the North in the first decade of the 19th century presented no drastic break with past trends. The region remained overwhelmingly Protestant, but most sects took a somewhat more tolerant attitude toward those who disagreed with them than they had in colonial times.

Early in the new century a "Second Great Awakening" broke out sporadically in various sections. The new revivals were as emotionally charged as those of the earlier awakening. Preachers described the tortures awaiting unrepentant sinners just as graphically. But the new evangelists took a more optimistic view of the possibility of salvation. Charles Grandison Finney, probably the most influential preacher of the movement, described a benevolent Deity presiding over a democratic Heaven not unlike the United States of America. If people would only see the light and behave honestly toward one another, the millennium would (literally) arrive. "God always allows his children as much liberty as they are prepared to enjoy," Finney declared.

Pessimistic Calvinistic denominations declined nearly everywhere. After deism began to lose its

force, the liberal Unitarian wing of the Congregational churches of New England absorbed many of its major ideas. William Ellery Channing, pastor of the Federal Street Church in Boston, rejected a God of Vengeance. Channing taught that Christ was merely an exceptionally fine human being, and he decried the emotional aspects of the Puritan approach to God. The Unitarians called upon rational arguments to justify faith; however, they retained the Bible as a prime source of religious truth and did not deny the reality of the biblical miracles. They preserved a Puritan concern for moral earnestness and social improvement.

Calvinists did not abandon the field to the Unitarians in New England, but after 1805, when they "captured" Harvard, where most ministers were educated, the liberals were dominant. Like deism, Unitarianism remained pretty difficult going for an untrained mind, but a simpler form, called Universalism, which stressed the comforting be-

■ A New Bedford, Massachusetts, church congregation had such a bitter quarrel in 1816 that it literally came to a parting of the ways, down to the church building itself. The sketch was made by Charles Lesueur, a French naturalist touring the United States, who came by just as the draft oxen were towing away half the building.

lief that a kind, forgiving God would allow everyone into Heaven, became quite popular.

No spectacular progress was made in education in the northern states until the 1830s and 1840s. Boston established the nation's first public high school in 1821, and in 1824 Massachusetts required all towns of more than 500 families to support similar institutions, but only an insignificant fraction of the youth of the country enrolled in such schools. Massachusetts also led in opening the public schools to blacks; in 1855 the legislature outlawed religious and racial discrimination in schools throughout the state. Elsewhere there were few schools for blacks, nearly all of them segregated.

Secondary and higher education remained primarily for the rich and those of middling wealth. Rousseau's idea that education must be adapted to the age level of the child and the Swiss Johann Pestalozzi's belief in professional training for teachers caused much discussion in the United States but produced little immediate change. The curricula of the schools remained about what they had been in colonial America. Much of the teaching was simply out of date; as late as 1810 some widely used arithmetic texts still employed problems based on shillings and pence and systems of weights and measures that had no practical application for Americans. Salaries were low and many teachers were ill prepared for their jobs. Yet the country as a whole was beginning to accept Jefferson's thesis that in a democracy a decent system of public education was a necessity.

At the college level attendance increased, but not as fast as the population. The largest growth took place in the South and West, but the older northern colleges supplied most of the administrators and teachers for the new institutions and thus made their mark upon them. College teaching was undistinguished, emphasis being placed on rote learning. Classical studies were always emphasized, along with rhetoric, mathematics, and philosophy. After 1800 science and "political economy" appeared, but first-class work in these fields was rare.

Academic standards declined on the whole, for enrollments were rising without a corresponding increase in the number of teachers or in the financial resources of the colleges. Few professors took serious interest in research. However, a few scholars were beginning to go to Germany for advanced work. At least 25 Americans studied at Göttingen, Leipzig, and other German universities before 1830; in time their influence on higher education would be strong.

Society and Culture in the South

Social change in the South resulted chiefly from the reinvigoration of slavery and the spread of cotton. The Upper South grew rather slowly, but the cotton regions expanded almost as rapidly as New York and Pennsylvania. Between 1790 and 1820, South Carolina doubled and Georgia quadrupled in population. Yet the South remained predominantly rural; the only city in the region that grew much was Baltimore, and its economy was tied more to the North than to the South. As late as 1810 Charleston, the one truly southern city, had but 24,000 inhabitants.

Superficially Charleston seemed prosperous and cultivated, with its attractive Georgian houses done in stucco and tile and its procession of concerts and balls. But when the great planters returned to their estates after the social season, Charleston became an empty shell. The small southern towns were shabby—with rutted streets, open sewers, and unpainted houses—and culturally barren.

The great planters dominated southern society though they were only a tiny fraction of the population. Slavery bred a paternalistic point of view, which helps explain why the small farmers usually accepted planter leadership even when they had the political power to overthrow it. The alternative seemed to be identification with the blacks, and even the lowliest white southerner found that unthinkable. The opportunity to rise in the South was almost as great as in the North, and most people preferred making their way by joining rather than by fighting the establishment.

In a slaveholding society a kind of artificial chivalry flourished. Dueling was common; the military arts were highly valued; white women were idealized. This explains the immense popularity of the novels of Sir Walter Scott in the South. Thirty-five towns in the region were named Waverley, and hundreds of girl babies were christened Rowena in honor of the heroine of *Ivanhoe.* While many small colleges were founded, chiefly by religious sects, primary and secondary education lagged and illiteracy was high. The most interesting architecture in the area were the graceful homes of the planters, mostly done in classic style, with tall white columns and broad porches.

Like the North, the South was overwhelmingly Protestant, but the religious trend there ran in a different direction. In colonial and Revolutionary times southern planters were notoriously easygoing about religion. That Jefferson was a deist might be expected in the light of his commitment to the rational point of view, yet even a man of few intellectual interests like Washington, though he attended Episcopal services, looked on the Deity as a sort of impersonal first cause and did not make religion an important part of his life. Around 1800, however, while Unitarianism was undermining orthodoxy in New England, southern churches were becoming more authoritarian and emotional. The expansion of slavery explains this change, for freedom of religious thought—of all thought, for that matter—might lead to conclusions dangerous to existing institutions. A stern, paternalistic God made sense to a society determined to convince a large proportion of the population that obedience to authority was a fact of existence and that this life was but a time of trial in preparation for the next. It may also be that the white southerners' unconscious guilt at their oppression of the slaves predisposed them to the belief that most people are sinners, but such a conclusion must perforce be speculative.

The culture of the southern slaves has been the subject of much recent study. White historians long argued that slaves swiftly lost all but the vaguest awareness of their African origins, that the typical American black, slave or free, was "a man without a past." Ulrich B. Phillips put it this way in *Life and Labor in the Old South* (1929): "Foulahs and Fantyns, Eboes and Angolas begat American plantation Negroes to whom a spear would be strange but a 'languid hoe' familiar, the tomtom forgotten but the banjo inviting." It is now clear that more of African culture was retained than historians realized, that slaves, culturally speaking, were Afro-Americans. Aside from such obvious elements as music, dances, names,

and folklore, subtle motor habits, speech patterns, concepts of time and family organization, methods of treating illnesses—to say nothing of religious attitudes and values—persisted among Afro-Americans generation after generation.

Beyond the question of African survivals among blacks is the question of cultural assimilation generally. Every culture is an amalgam, the American more than most. It would be anthropologically naive to assume that the culture of white Americans, especially in the South, was not in part African, just as it was part Indian. To what extent African and evangelical Christian elements "explain" the religious practices of slaves is a question that can be asked with equal cogency of the practices of many of their masters.

None of this is to deny the enormous impact of white culture on the slaves, especially after the cutting off of importations early in the 19th century. One need only recall how white immigrants lost or "forgot" large elements of their European heritage and then consider how much more difficult it would be for most Africans, forcefully deracinated, scattered, deprived of the common means of preserving and transmitting their culture, to retain their old ways.

Western Life

The civilization of the new West was a mixture of North and South and at the same time something distinct. The "great migration" from Connecticut and Massachusetts into Ohio gave that state a New England cast, both in the appearance of its towns and farms and in the community spirit and general point of view of the people. Settlers in the Southwest and in the southerly parts of the old Northwest, mostly southerners, had brought their ways along with their baggage. Yet many historians have noticed how life in Indiana and Illinois made one Kentucky boy an Abraham Lincoln and how moving to Mississippi made another Kentucky lad a Jefferson Davis.

Few western communities were mere extensions of North or South; the frontier left its mark upon them all. The untapped riches and the huge expanse of the West made the people restless, prodigal, optimistic, boastful, and also industrious and resourceful. Its rawness and remoteness made

■ Mrs. Frances Trollope came to the United States in 1827 and opened a fancy-goods shop in Cincinnati. In her book *Domestic Manners of the Americans* (1832) she was sour and caustic toward everything American. This sketch from her book shows a bedraggled family scratching out a living selling firewood to passing steamboats.

them tough and crude yet openhearted and hospitable, too. Even more than other Americans, westerners believed in equality and democracy, though by some alchemy they convinced themselves that blacks and Indians had no right to these blessings.

The West grew at a furious pace. The population of Ohio increased more than tenfold between 1800 and 1820; by the latter date Ohio was the fifth largest state in the Union, with nearly 600,000 residents. Although far more sparsely populated, Mississippi grew almost as swiftly, and the "older" regions of Kentucky and Tennessee were surging ahead.

While the West remained primarily agricultural, its towns grew as fast as its farms. The expansion of New Orleans following the invention of the steamboat has been mentioned. Cincinnati had nearly 10,000 inhabitants in 1820, Pittsburgh 8,000, Lexington more than 5,000. Western cities served as the harbors and depots of the inner continent, and local manufacturing quickly appeared.

In 1810 a resident described Pittsburgh as "a large workshop"; in 1815 the value of its manufactures exceeded $2.6 million. Western cultural life centered in the cities. Lexington's claim to be the "Athens of the West" was preposterous, but the town offered a remarkably varied intellectual fare for such a small community. Cincinnati possessed an important book publishing industry, and most towns of any size had subscription libraries before 1815. Both amateur and professional theaters existed in Lexington, Louisville, Cincinnati, St. Louis, and New Orleans. By 1820 Cincinnati could boast of its Western Museum, founded by the "Franklin of the West," Dr. Daniel Drake, that indefatigable civic booster and herald of culture who also helped to establish a library, various clubs and educational institutions, and a medical journal.

Most westerners were undoubtedly uncouth and intellectually naive. Much of their "culture" was inferior even to the low level existing in the East. Yet the towns had what Louis B. Wright called in *Culture on the Moving Frontier* "a saving remnant" eager to raise standards. "Often their efforts were pathetic," Wright admits, "but the dream was there and the dream was important."

The western combination of low standards and high zeal can be seen in the educational and religious life of the region. Everyone admitted the need for schools, but despite the provision in the early land ordinances that a section of each township be devoted to educational purposes, schools were poor and not very numerous. Most of the Protestant sects established colleges in the West, but aside from a few institutions like the Presbyterian's Transylvania College in Lexington, most western colleges were pitifully inadequate by any standard. Their religious connections hindered the colleges by committing them to the production of devout members of a particular church rather than young men devoted to the pursuit of knowledge. The reaction of the evangelical religions against the 18th-century rationalism of the deists crippled their intellectual life further. It is significant that Transylvania achieved its greatest distinction under the presidency of a Unitarian, Horace Holley of Boston.

Since westerners preferred plenty of emotion and hellfire in their religion, the Methodists and Baptists attracted the widest support. The Second Great Awakening swept through the region with special force. The George Whitefield of this movement was James McGready, a preacher who "could so array hell before the wicked that they would tremble and quake, imagining a lake of fire and brimstone yawning to overwhelm them."

McGready, and others inspired by his example, preached a simple message: sin (which included drinking, gambling, and disbelief in Christianity as well as the standard vices) was wrong; salvation (through repentance and church membership) could be had by all. An energetic and essentially simple people, surrounded by the dangers and uncertainties of the frontier, took eagerly to McGready's type of exhortation. Their religious camp meetings lasted for days and attracted thousands. Mass hysteria often engulfed the earnest throngs. Men and women sobbed, shrieked, barked like animals, and were seized by the "jerks," transported with what they conceived to be the divine spirit. Disciples of McGready such as Finis Ewing (so named because he was the last of 12 children) tramped tirelessly through the West, taking their message to isolated farms and crowded camp meetings, converting sinners by the thousands. Others were like Peter Cartwright, a reformed gambler, totally uneducated, who took his Methodist "exhorter's license" and traveled a broad circuit through the West. "His self-reliance, his readiness with tongue and fist, his quick sense of humor, all made him dear to the hearts of the frontier," a biographer explained. "If, as not infrequently happened, intruders attempted to break up his meetings, he was quick to meet force with force and seems to have been uniformly victorious in these physical encounters."

The importance of sociocultural differences among the sections can be exaggerated. The Second Awakening began in New England, and a number of Unitarians lived in the West. The average easterners were only a little less crude and brash than most frontier people; their view of blacks differed from those of their slaveholding cousins only slightly. Patriotism of the spread-eagle variety flourished everywhere; loyalty to section did not seem to diminish it. Americans north, south, and west paid little heed to social differences. They believed in the future progress and prosperity of the country. They worked hard, pampered their children, opened wide their doors to strangers. They loved the dollar mightily, exercising remarkable ingenuity in acquiring it, but donated generously to public causes. They were at once vain and pitifully eager to please, tough fighters but sentimental, proud of America yet sedulous apers of European "culture." Nevertheless, they *were* northerners and southerners and westerners. In the decades following the Era of Good Feelings, this fact became increasingly significant.

The Missouri Compromise

The sectional conflicts of the 1820s repeatedly influenced politics. The depression of 1819–1822 increased tensions by making people feel more strongly about the issues of the day. For example, manufacturers who wanted high tariffs in 1816 were more vehemently in favor of protection in 1820 when their business fell off. Even when economic conditions improved, geographical alignments on key issues tended to solidify.

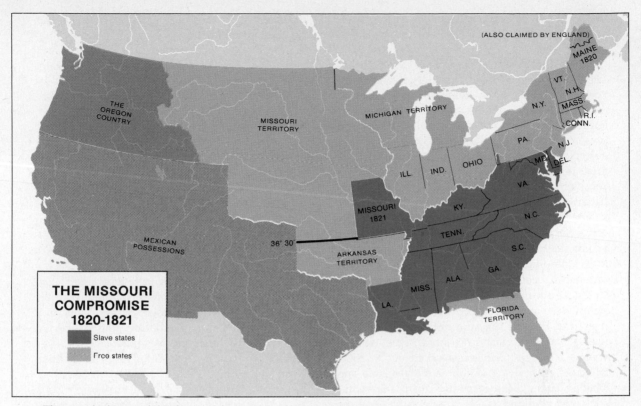

THE MISSOURI
COMPROMISE
1820-1821

Slave states

Free states

(ALSO CLAIMED BY ENGLAND)

THE OREGON COUNTRY

MISSOURI TERRITORY

MICHIGAN TERRITORY

MEXICAN POSSESSIONS

36° 30'

ARKANSAS TERRITORY

MISSOURI 1821

ILL. IND. OHIO

KY.

TENN.

MISS. ALA. GA.

LA.

FLORIDA TERRITORY

S.C.

N.C.

VA.

MD. DEL.

PA. N.J.

N.Y.

VT. N.H. MASS. R.I. CONN.

MAINE 1820

■ This was the lineup of the slave and free states resulting from the Missouri Compromise. The Compromise was repealed by the Kansas-Nebraska Act (1854) and declared unconstitutional in the Dred Scott case (1857).

One of the first and most critical of the sectional contests concerned the admission of Missouri as a slave state. When Louisiana entered the Union in 1812, the rest of the Louisiana Purchase was organized as Missouri Territory. Building upon a nucleus of Spanish and French inhabitants, the region west and north of St. Louis grew rapidly, and in 1817 the Missourians petitioned for statehood. A large percentage of the settlers—the population exceeded 60,000 by 1818—were southerners who had moved into the valleys of the Arkansas and Missouri rivers. Since many of them owned slaves, Missouri would become a slave state.

The admission of new states had always been a routine matter, in keeping with the admirable pattern established by the Northwest Ordinance. But during the debate on the Missouri Enabling Act in February 1819, Congressman James Tallmadge of New York introduced an amendment prohibiting "the further introduction of slavery" and providing that all slaves born in Missouri after the terri-

tory became a state should be freed at age 25.

While Tallmadge was merely seeking to apply in the territory the pattern of race relations that had developed in the states immediately east of Missouri, his amendment represented, at least in spirit, something of a revolution. The Northwest Ordinance had prohibited slavery in the land between the Mississippi and the Ohio, but that area had only a handful of slaveowners in 1787 and little prospect of attracting more. Elsewhere no effort to restrict the movement of slaves into new territory had been attempted. If one assumed (as whites always had) that the slaves themselves should have no say in the matter, it appeared democratic to let the settlers of Missouri decide the slavery question for themselves. Nevertheless, the Tallmadge amendment passed the House, the vote following sectional lines closely. The Senate, however, resoundingly rejected it. The less populous southern part of Missouri was then organized separately as Arkansas Territory, and an attempt to bar slavery there was stifled. The Missouri Enabling Act failed to pass before Congress adjourned.

When the next Congress met in December 1819, the Missouri issue came up at once. The vote on Tallmadge's amendment had shown that the rapidly growing North controlled the House of Representatives. It was vital, southerners felt, to preserve a balance in the Senate. Yet northerners objected to the fact that Missouri extended hundreds of miles north of the Ohio River, which they considered slavery's natural boundary. Angry debate raged in Congress for months.

The debate did not turn on the morality of slavery or the rights of blacks. Northerners objected to adding new slave states because under the Three-fifths Compromise these states would be overrepresented in Congress (60 percent of their slaves would be counted in determining the size of the states' delegations in the House of Representatives) and because they did not relish competing with slave labor. Since no moral issue was involved, a compromise was worked out in 1820. Missouri entered the Union as a slave state and Maine, having been separated from Massachusetts, was admitted as a free state to preserve the balance in the Senate.

To prevent further conflict, Congress adopted a proposal of Senator Jesse B. Thomas of Illinois, which "forever prohibited" slavery in all other parts of the Louisiana Purchase north of 36° 30′ north latitude, the westward extension of Missouri's southern boundary. Although this division would keep slavery out of most of the territory, southerners accepted it cheerfully. The land south of the line, the present states of Arkansas and Oklahoma, seemed ideally suited for the expanded plantation economy, and most persons considered the treeless northern regions little better than a desert. One northern senator, decrying the division, contemptuously described the land north and west of Missouri, today one of the world's richest agricultural regions, as "a prairie without food or water."

The Missouri Compromise did not end the crisis. When Missouri submitted its constitution for approval by Congress (the final step in the admission process), the document, besides authorizing slavery and prohibiting the emancipation of any slave without the consent of the owner, *required*

the state legislature to pass a law barring free blacks and mulattos from entering the state "under any pretext whatever." This provision plainly violated Article IV, Section 2 of the United States Constitution: "The Citizens of each State shall be entitled to all Privileges and Immunities of Citizens in the several States." It did not, however, represent any more of a break with established racial patterns, north or south, than the Tallmadge amendment; many states east of Missouri barred free blacks without regard for the Constitution.

Nevertheless, northern congressmen hypocritically refused to accept the Missouri constitution. Once more the debate raged. Again, since few northerners cared to defend the rights of blacks seriously, the issue was compromised. In March 1821 Henry Clay found a face-saving formula: out of respect for the "supreme law of the land," Congress accepted the Missouri constitution with the demurrer that no law passed in conformity to it should be construed as contravening Article IV, Section 2. Of course this was pure cant.

Every thinking person recognized the political dynamite inherent in the Missouri controversy. The sectional lineup had been terrifyingly compact. What meant the Union if so trivial a matter as one new state could so divide the people? Moreover, despite the timidity and hypocrisy of the North, everyone realized that the immorality of slavery lay at the heart of the conflict. "We have the wolf by the ears, and we can neither safely hold him, nor safely let him go," Jefferson wrote a month after Missouri became a state. The dispute, he said, "like a fire bell in the night, awakened and filled me with terror." Jefferson knew that the compromise had not quenched the flames ignited by the Missouri debates. "This is a reprieve only," he said. John Quincy Adams called it the "title page to a great tragic volume."

Yet the issue had been settled peaceably if ignobly. Tempers subsided. Other controversies that aroused strong feelings did not seem to divide the country so deeply. The question of federal internal improvements caused endless debate that split the country on geographical lines. In 1816 the nationalist-minded Calhoun had pressed a plan to set up a $1.5 million fund for roads and canals. Congress approved this despite strong opposition in New England and a divided South. In 1822 a bill providing money for the upkeep of the National Road caused another sectional split. Both measures were vetoed, but in 1824 Monroe approved a differently worded internal improvement act. Such proposals excited intense reactions. John Randolph, opposing the 1824 bill with his usual ferocity, threatened to employ "every . . . means short of actual insurrection" to defeat it. Yet other prominent southerners favored internal improvements, and no one—not even Randolph, it will be noted—threatened the Union on this issue.

The tariff continued to divide the country. When a new, still higher tariff was enacted in 1824, the slave states voted almost unanimously against it, the North and Northwest in favor, and New England remained of two minds. Clay, who expounded the case for his American System brilliantly in the debates, provided arguments for the tariff that his foes found hard to counter. Webster, continuing to speak for the merchants of New England (he conducted a poll of business leaders before deciding how to vote), made a powerful speech against the act, but the measure passed without creating a major storm.

The Adams Administration

The divisions on these questions were not severely disruptive, in part because the major politicians, competing for the presidency, did not dare risk alienating any section by taking too extreme a position. Calhoun, for example, had changed his mind about protective tariffs by 1824, but he avoided declaring himself because of his presidential ambitions. Another reason was that the old party system had broken down; the Federalists had disappeared as a national party and the Jeffersonians, lacking an organized opposition, had become less aggressive and more troubled by factional disputes.

The presidential fight was therefore waged on personal grounds, though the heat generated by the contest began the process of reenergizing party politics. Besides Calhoun the candidates were Jackson, Crawford, Adams, and Clay. The maneuvering among them was complex, the infighting savage. In March 1824 Calhoun, who was young enough to wait for the White House, withdrew and declared for the vice-presidency, which he won easily. Crawford, who had the support of many congressional leaders, seemed the likely winner, but he suffered a series of paralytic strokes that gravely injured his chances.

Despite the bitterness of the contest, it attracted relatively little public interest; barely a quarter of those eligible took the trouble to vote. In the electoral college Jackson led with 99, Adams had 84, Crawford 41, and Clay 37. Since no one had a majority, the contest was thrown into the House of Representatives, which, under the Constitution, had to choose from among the three leaders, each state delegation having one vote. By employing his great influence in the House, Clay swung the balance. Not wishing to advance the fortunes of a rival westerner like Jackson and feeling, with reason, that Crawford's health made him unavailable, Clay gave his support to Adams, who was thereupon elected.

Although deeply marked by his New England heritage, Adams was a man of the broadest experience and interests. He took a Hamiltonian view of the future of the country and hoped to use the national authority to foster all sorts of useful projects. He asked Congress for a federal program of internal improvements so vast that even Clay boggled when he realized its scope. He came out for aid to manufacturing and agriculture, a variety of scientific and educational projects (including expeditions to explore the West, a national university, and an astronomical observatory), and many administrative reforms. For a nationalist of unchallengeable Jeffersonian origins like Clay or Calhoun to have pressed for so extensive a program would have been politically risky. For the son of John Adams to do so was disastrous; every doubter remembered his Federalist background and decided that he was trying to overturn the glorious "Revolution of 1800."

Adams proved to be his own worst enemy, for he was as inept a politician as ever lived. Knowing that many citizens considered things like observatories impractical extravagances, he urged Congress not to be "palsied by the will of our constituents." To persuade Americans, who were almost pathological on the subject of monarchy, to support his road-building program, he cited with approval the work being done abroad by "the nations of Europe and . . . their rulers," which revived fears that all Adamses were royalists at heart. He was insensitive to the ebb and flow of

■ A comment by David Claypoole Johnston on the 1824 presidential "foot race" has Adams leading by a lead, trailed by Crawford and Jackson. Clay (far right, hand on head), well behind, pulls up in dismay. The many figures and the dreadful puns ("How is Clay now?" "Oh dirt cheap" or "Hurra for our son Jack" "Hurra for our Jack-son") are typical of the cartoons of the era.

public feeling; even when he wanted to move with the tide, he seldom managed to dramatize and publicize his stand effectively. There was wide support in the country for a federal bankruptcy law, but instead of describing himself in plain language as a friend of poor debtors, Adams called for the "amelioration" of the "often oppressive codes relating to insolvency" and buried the recommendation at the tail end of a dull state paper. He refused to use his power of appointment to win support. "I will not dismiss . . . able and faithful political opponents to provide for my own partisans," he said. The attitude was traditional at the time, but Adams carried it to extremes—in four years he removed only 12 men from office. Nevertheless, by appointing Henry Clay secretary of state, he laid himself open to the charge that he had won the presidency by a "corrupt bargain." Thus, despite his politically suicidal attitude toward federal jobs, he was subject to the annoyance of a congressional investigation of his appointments, out of which came no less than six bills designed "to reduce the patronage of the executive."

To be sure, Adams inherited a chaotic political situation. Contending sectional interests clashed angrily, uncurbed by loyalty to a national party. Yet he would neither bend to the prevailing winds nor, by using his power as president, attempt to build an effective party based on the American System and backed by broad public support. He was soon miserable, under attack from every side. As his grandson Brooks Adams later wrote, his service as president made him doubt the existence of God and the purposefulness of life.

The battle to succeed Adams began almost on the day of his election. Jackson quickly established himself as the candidate of what can best be characterized as the "opposition." He felt that he, the man with the largest vote, had been cheated of the presidency in 1824 by Adams and Clay, and he burned for revenge. Relying heavily on his military reputation and on Adams' talent for making enemies, Jackson avoided taking a stand on issues as much as possible. Senator Benton of Missouri urged Jackson to shrink from any "particular confession" on internal improvements and on other questions where his views might displease certain voters. The political situation thus became monumentally confused, one side unable to marshal support for its policies, the other unwilling to adopt policies for fear of losing support.

Tariff of Abominations

The tariff question added to the confusion. High duties, so repulsive to the export-conscious South, attracted more and more favor in the North and West. Besides manufacturers, lead miners in Missouri, hemp raisers in Kentucky, woolgrowers in New York, and many other interests demanded protection against foreign competition. The lack of party discipline provided an ideal climate for "logrolling" in Congress. Legislators who like Senator Benton opposed high tariffs in principle found themselves under constant pressure from their constituents to raise the duties on products of local importance; to satisfy these demands, they traded votes with other congressmen similarly situated. In this way massive "support" for protection was generated.

In 1828 a new tariff was hammered into shape by the House Committee on Manufactures. Northern and western agricultural interests were in command; they wrote into the bill extremely high duties on raw wool, hemp, flax, fur, and liquor. New England manufacturers protested vociferously, for although their products were protected, the proposed law would increase the cost of their raw materials. This gave southerners, now hopelessly in the minority on the tariff question, a chance to block the bill. When the New Englanders proposed amendments lowering the duties on raw materials, the southerners voted nay, hoping to force them to reject the measure on the final vote. This desperate strategy failed. New England had by this time committed its future to manufacturing, a change signalized by the somersault of Webster, who, ever responsive to local pressures, now voted for protection. After winning some minor concessions in the Senate, largely through the intervention of Van Buren, enough New Englanders accepted the so-called Tariff of Abominations to assure its passage.

Vice-President Calhoun, who had watched the debate from the vantage point of his post as president of the Senate, now came to a great turning

point in his career. He had thrown in his lot with Jackson, whose running mate he was to be in the coming election, and had been assured that the Jacksonians would oppose the bill. Yet northern Jacksonians had been responsible for drafting and passing it. The new tariff would impoverish the South, he believed. He warned Jackson that relief must soon be provided or the Union would be shaken to its foundations. Then he returned to his South Carolina plantation and wrote an essay, the *South Carolina Exposition and Protest,* repudiating the nationalist philosophy he had previously championed.

The South Carolina legislature released this document to the country in December 1828, along with eight resolutions denouncing the protective tariff as unfair and unconstitutional. The theorist Calhoun, however, was not content with outlining the case against the tariff. His *Exposition* provided an ingenious defense of the right of the people of a state to reject a law of Congress. Starting with John Locke's revered concept of government as a contractual relationship, he argued that since the states had created the Union, logic dictated that they be the final arbiters of the meaning of the Constitution which was its framework. If a special state convention, representing the sovereignty of the people, decided that an act of Congress violated the Constitution, it could interpose its authority and "nullify" the law within its boundaries. Calhoun did not seek to implement this theory in 1828, for he hoped that the next administration would lower the tariff and make nullification unnecessary.

Election of 1828

The new president was to be Jackson, who defeated Adams handily, though by no means overwhelmingly, in a contest disgraced by character assassination and lies of the worst sort on both sides. Administration supporters denounced Jackson as a bloodthirsty military tyrant, a drunkard, and a gambler. His wife Rachel, ailing and shy, was dragged into the campaign, her good name heartlessly besmirched. Previously married to a cruel, unbalanced man named Lewis Robards, she had begun living with Jackson (whether a marriage ceremony had been performed is to this day uncertain) before her divorce from Robards had been legally completed. When this fact came to light, she and Jackson had to remarry. Seizing upon this incident, an Adams pamphleteer wrote: "Ought a convicted adulteress and her paramour husband be placed in the highest offices of this free and christian land?"

Furious, the Jacksonians (now calling themselves Democrats) replied in kind. They charged that Adams had lived with his wife before marriage and that, while American minister to Russia, he had supplied a beautiful American virgin for the delectation of the czar. Discovering that the president had purchased a chess set and a billiard table for the White House, they accused him of squandering public money on gambling devices. They translated his long and distinguished public

service into the statistic that he had received over the years a sum equal to $16 for every day of his life in government pay. The great questions of the day were largely ignored.

All this was inexcusable, and both sides must share the blame. When inauguration day arrived, Adams refused to attend the ceremonies because Jackson had failed to pay the traditional preinaugural courtesy call on him at the White House, but the Old Puritan may have been equally if unconsciously motivated by shame at tactics he had countenanced during the campaign. In any case, deep personal feelings were uppermost in everyone's mind at the formal changing of the guard. The real issues, however, remained. Andrew Jackson would now have to deal with them.

SUPPLEMENTARY READING

Titles marked with an asterisk have been published in paperback

George Dangerfield, **The Era of Good Feelings*** (1952) and **The Awakening of American Nationalism*** (1965), and F. J. Turner, **The Rise of the New West*** (1906), continue to be useful for this period. On the tariff, see F. W. Taussig, **The Tariff History of the United States*** (1923); on banking, Bray Hammond, **Banks and Politics in America from the Revolution to the Civil War*** (1957); on land policy, R. M. Robbins, **Our Landed Heritage*** (1942).

The outstanding study of the career of Adams is S. F. Bemis, **John Quincy Adams** (1949–1956). R. N. Current, **Daniel Webster and the Rise of National Conservatism*** (1955), is an excellent brief biography. On Clinton, see W. W. Campbell, **The Life and Writings of De Witt Clinton** (1933). Van Buren's early career is treated in R. V. Remini, **Martin Van Buren and the Making of the Democratic Party*** (1959), Jackson's in Remini's **Andrew Jackson and the Course of American Empire, 1767–1821** (1977). Van Buren's **Autobiography** (1920), edited by J. C. Fitzpatrick, is candid and amusing.

For Crawford, see C. C. Mooney, **William H. Crawford** (1974). On Calhoun, the standard study of his early career is C. M. Wiltse, **John C. Calhoun: Nationalist** (1949), an excellent work. Richard Hofstadter, **The American Political Tradition*** (1948), contains a thought-provoking essay on Calhoun; see also R. N. Current, **John C. Calhoun*** (1963), and G. M. Capers, **John C. Calhoun, Opportunist*** (1960). The best biography of Clay is G. G. Van Deusen, **The Life of Henry Clay*** (1937), while Clement Eaton, **Henry Clay and the**

Art of American Politics* (1957), is a stimulating and judicious brief account. W. N. Chambers, **Old Bullion Benton: Senator from the New West** (1956), is first-rate, but see also Benton's **Thirty Years' View** (1854–1856). Freeman Cleaves, **Old Tippecanoe** (1939), covers the life of William Henry Harrison adequately.

Social and cultural trends are discussed in R. B. Nye, **The Cultural Life of the New Nation*** (1960), J. A. Krout and D. R. Fox, **The Completion of Independence*** (1944), M. E. Curti, **The Growth of American Thought** (1951), and Harvey Wish, **Society and Thought in Early America** (1950). Van Wyck Brooks, **The World of Washington Irving** (1944), discusses the principal literary figures, while O. W. Larkin, **Art and Life in America** (1949), is excellent on painting and architecture. On religion, see Perry Miller, **The Life of the Mind in America from the Revolution to the Civil War*** (1965), W. G. McLaughlin, **Modern Revivalism** (1959), Conrad Wright, **The Beginnings of Unitarianism in America*** (1955), W. R. Cross, **The Burned-Over District*** (1950), and B. A. Weisberger, **They Gathered at the River*** (1958). Rush Welter, **Popular Education and Democratic Thought in America*** (1962), is a good introduction to the subject.

Southern life is discussed in Clement Eaton, **The Mind of the Old South*** (1964) and **The Growth of Southern Civilization*** (1961), and also in U. B. Phillips, **Life and Labor in the Old South*** (1929), and T. P. Abernethy, **The South in the New Nation** (1961). Melville Herskovits, **The Myth of the Negro Past*** (1941), is the standard study of African survivals in the culture of American blacks. On the West, L. B. Wright, **Culture on the Moving Frontier*** (1955), and R. C. Wade, **The Urban Frontier*** (1959), are very useful.

On the Missouri Compromise, see Glover Moore, **The Missouri Controversy*** (1953). The election of 1824 can be studied in the biographies of Adams, Clay, and Calhoun mentioned above and in Dangerfield's volumes. See also Marquis James, **The Life of Andrew Jackson*** (1938), and Shaw Livermore, **The Twilight of Federalism** (1962). On the presidency of John Quincy Adams, in addition to the Bemis biography, both Henry Adams, **The Degradation of the Democratic Dogma** (1919), and J. H. Powell, **Richard Rush: Republican Diplomat** (1942), are enlightening. R. V. Remini, **The Election of Andrew Jackson*** (1964), provides an excellent survey of the election of 1828; Remini's **Andrew Jackson and the Course of American Empire** presents new evidence on Jackson's marriage.

10/THE AGE OF JACKSON

 At 11 A.M. on March 4, 1829, a bright sunny day, Andrew Jackson, hatless and dressed severely in black, left his quarters at Gadsby's Hotel. Accompanied by a few close associates, he walked up Pennsylvania Avenue to the Capitol. At a few minutes after noon he emerged on the East Portico with the justices of the Supreme Court and other dignitaries. Before a throng of more than 15,000 people he delivered an almost inaudible and thoroughly commonplace inaugural address and then took the presidential oath. The first man to congratulate him was Chief Justice Marshall, who had administered the oath. The second was "Honest George" Kremer, a Pennsylvania congressman best known for the leopardskin coat that he affected, who led the cheering crowd that brushed past the barricade and scrambled up the Capitol steps to wring the new president's hand.

Jackson shouldered his way through the crush, mounted a splendid white horse, and rode off to the White House. A reception had been announced, to which "the officially and socially eligible as defined by precedent" had been invited. The day was unseasonably warm after a hard winter, and the streets of Washington were muddy. As Jackson rode down Pennsylvania Avenue, the crowds that had turned out to see the Hero of New Orleans followed—on horseback, in rickety wagons, and on foot. Nothing could keep them out of the executive mansion, and the result was chaos. Long tables laden with cakes, ice cream, and orange punch had been set up in the East Room, but these scarcely deflected the well-wishers. Jackson was pressed back helplessly as men tracked mud across valuable rugs and clambered up on delicate chairs to catch a glimpse of him. The White House shook with their shouts. Glassware splintered, furniture was overturned, women fainted.

Jackson was a thin old man despite his toughness, and soon he was in danger. Fortunately, friends formed a cordon and managed to extricate him through a rear door. The new president spent his first night in office at Gadsby's.

Only a generation earlier Jefferson had felt obliged to introduce pell-mell to encourage informality in the White House. Now a man whom John Quincy Adams called "a barbarian" held Jefferson's office, and, as one Supreme Court justice complained, "The reign of King 'Mob' seemed triumphant."

Jacksonian Democracy

Some historians claim that Andrew Jackson was not a democrat at all and anything but a consistent friend of the weak and underprivileged. They point out that he was a wealthy land speculator, owner of a fine Tennessee plantation, the Hermitage, and of many slaves. Before becoming president he had opposed cheap-money schemes, favored the big speculators, pressed lawsuits against more than a hundred individuals who owed him money. Although his supporters liked to cast him as the political heir of Jefferson, he was in many ways like the conservative Washington: a soldier first, an inveterate speculator in western lands, a

man with few intellectual interests and only sketchily educated.

Nor was Jackson quite the roughhewn frontier character he sometimes seemed. He could not spell (again, like Washington), he possessed the unsavory habits of the tobacco chewer, and he had a violent temper. But his manners and life-style were those of a southern planter. As president he spent money lavishly, entertaining guests at great feasts in halls bedecked with flowers and glowing in the light of hundreds of candles. His judgment was intuitive yet usually sound; his reputation for unbridled irascibility was not really deserved. His frequent rages were often feigned—designed to accomplish some carefully thought out purpose. "He would sometimes extemporize a fit of passion in order to overwhelm an adversary," one contemporary noted, "but his self-command was always perfect." Once, after scattering a delegation of protesters with an exhibition of Jovian wrath, he turned to an observer and said impishly, "They thought I was mad."

It is of small importance to anyone interested in Jacksonian Democracy to know exactly how "democratic" Jackson was or how sincere his interest in the welfare of the "common man." Whatever his personal convictions, he stood as the symbol for a movement supported by a new, democratically-oriented generation that had grown up under the spell of the American and French revolutions. That he was both a great hero and in many ways a very ordinary man helps explain his mass appeal. He had defeated a mighty British army and killed hosts of Indians, but he acted on hunches and not always consistently, shouted and pounded his fist when angry, put loyalty to old comrades above efficiency in making appointments, distrusted "aristocrats" and all special privilege. Perhaps he was rich, perhaps conservative, but he was a man of the people, born in a frontier cabin, familiar with the problems of the average citizen.

Jackson epitomized many American ideals. He was intensely patriotic, generous to a fault, natural and democratic in manner (at home alike in the forest and in the ballroom of a fine mansion). He admired good horseflesh and beautiful women, yet no sterner moralist ever lived; he was a fighter, a relentless foe, but a gentleman in the best American sense. That some special providence

■ A figurehead of Andrew Jackson carved by Laban S. Beecher for the frigate *Constitution*. Soon after it was mounted on the ship an anti-Jackson agitator sawed off the head just below the nose! It was later neatly mended by a shipcarving firm. The piece is almost 12 feet tall.

watched over him (as over the United States) appeared beyond argument to those who had followed his career. He seemed, in short, both an average and an ideal American, one the people could identify with and still revere.

For these reasons Jackson drew support from every section and every social class: western farmers and southern planters, urban workers and bankers and merchants. In this sense he was profoundly democratic—and in the sense, too, that whatever his position on public issues, he believed in equality of opportunity, distrusted entrenched status of every sort, and rejected no free American because of humble origins or inadequate education.

Rise of the Common Man

Having been taught by Jefferson that all men are created equal, the Americans of Jackson's day found it easy to believe that every man was as good as his neighbor. The difference between Jeffersonian Democracy and the Jackson variety was one of attitude rather than practice. Jefferson had believed that ordinary citizens could be educated to determine right. Jackson insisted that they knew what was right by instinct. Jefferson's pellmell encouraged the average citizen to hold up his head; by the time of Jackson, the "common man" gloried in ordinariness and made mediocrity a virtue. The slightest hint of distinctiveness or servility became suspect. That President Washington required his footmen to wear uniforms was taken as a matter of course in the 1790s, but the British minister in Jackson's day found it next to impossible to find American servants willing to don his splendid livery. The word "servant" itself fell out of fashion, replaced by the egalitarian "help."

The Founding Fathers had not foreseen all the implications of political democracy for a society like that which existed in the United States. They believed that the ordinary man should have political power in order to protect himself against the superior man, but they assumed that the latter would always lead. The people would naturally choose the best men to manage public affairs. In Washington's day and even in Jefferson's this was generally the case, but the inexorable logic of democracy gradually produced a change. The new western states, unfettered by systems created in a less democratic age, drew up constitutions that eliminated property qualifications for voting and holding office; the eastern states revised their own frames of government to accomplish the same purpose. More public offices were made elective rather than appointive.

Even the presidency, designed to be removed from direct public control by the electoral college, felt the impact of the new thinking. By Jackson's day only two states, Delaware and South Carolina, still provided for the choice of presidential electors by the legislature; in all others they were selected by popular vote. The system of permitting the congressional caucus to name the candidates for the presidency came to an end before 1828. Jackson and Adams were put forward by state legislatures, and soon the still more democratic system of nomination by national party conventions was adopted.

Certain social changes reflected a new way of looking at political affairs. The final disestablishment of churches reveals a dislike of special privilege. The beginnings of the free-school movement, the earliest glimmerings of interest in adult education, and the slow spread of secondary education all bespeak a concern for improving the knowledge and judgment of the ordinary citizen. The rapid increase in the number of newspapers, their declining prices (the first successful penny papers appeared in the 1830s), and their ever greater concentration on political affairs indicate that an effort was being made to bring political news to the common man's attention.

All these changes emphasized the idea that every citizen was equally important and the conviction that all should participate actively in government. Officeholders began to stress the fact that they were *representatives* as well as leaders and to appeal more frankly and much more intensively for votes. The public responded with a surge of interest. At each succeeding presidential election, a larger percentage of the population went to the polls.

As voting became more important, so did party politics, for it took organized effort to run the campaigns and get out the vote. Parties became powerful institutions; as a result, they attracted voters' loyalties powerfully. This development took place first at the state level and at different times in different states. According to Richard P. McCormick, whose book *The Second American Party System* describes the process, the 1828 election stimulated party formation because it pitted two well-known men against each other, forcing local leaders to make a choice and then convince local voters to accept their judgment. This was especially true in states where neither Adams nor Jackson had a preponderance. Thus the new system established itself much faster in New York and Pennsylvania than in New England, where Adams was strong, or Tennessee, where the "native son" Jackson had overwhelming support.

Like most institutions, the parties created bureaucracies to keep them running smoothly. Devoted party workers were rewarded with political office when their efforts were successful. "To the victors belong the spoils," said the New York politician William L. Marcy, and the image, drawn from war and piracy, was appropriate. Although the vigorous wooing of voters constituted a recognition of their importance and a commitment to keeping them informed, campaigning—another military term—frequently degenerated into demagoguery. The most effective way to attract the average voter, politicians soon decided, was by flattery.

Andrew Jackson was the first product of this system to become president. He was chosen because he was popular, not because he was experienced in government. No one knew for sure where he stood on such subjects as the tariff and internal improvements because he did not really know himself, having never been much concerned with them. But he was valiant, honest, patriotic, and eager to do his duty—qualities the position has always required.

The Spoils System

Jackson took office with the firm intention of punishing the "vile wretches" who had attacked him so viciously during the campaign. (Rachel Jackson died shortly after the election, and her devoted husband was convinced that the indignities heaped upon her by Adams partisans had speeded her decline.) The concept of political office as a reward for victory seemed to justify a housecleaning in Washington. Henry Clay captured the fears of anti-Jackson government workers. "Among the official corps here there is the greatest solicitude and apprehension," he said. "The members of it

■ Jackson's spoils-system policies were repeatedly attacked by opposition cartoonists. "Office Hunters for the Year 1834," for example, portrays the president as a demon dangling the spoils of his office, including banquets, money, weapons, appointments, and for some obscure reason, millinery, above his greedy supporters.

feel something like the inhabitants of Cairo when the plague breaks out; no one knows who is next to encounter the stroke of death."

Eager for "the spoils," an army of politicians invaded Washington. "I am ashamed of myself," one such character confessed when he met a friend on the street. "I feel as if every man I meet knew what I came for." "Don't distress yourself," his friend replied, "for every man you meet is on the same business." There was nothing especially innovative about this invasion, for the principle of filling offices with one's partisans was almost as old as the republic. However, the long lapse of time since the last real political shift, and the recent untypical example of John Quincy Adams, who rarely removed or appointed anyone for political reasons, made Jackson's policy appear revolutionary. His removals were not entirely unjustified, for many government workers had grown senile and others corrupt. A number of officials

were found to be short in their accounts, a few were hopeless drunks. Jackson was determined to root out the thieves. Even Adams admitted that some of those Jackson dismissed deserved their fate.

Aside from going along with the spoils system and eliminating crooks and incompetents, Jackson advanced another reason for turning experienced government employees out of their jobs—the principle of rotation. "No man has any more intrinsic right to official station than another," he said. Those who hold government jobs for a long time "are apt to acquire a habit of looking with indifference upon the public interests and of tolerating conduct from which an unpracticed man would revolt." By "rotating" jobholders periodically, more citizens could participate in the tasks of government, an obvious advantage in a democracy. The danger of creating an entrenched bureaucracy would also be eliminated. The problem

238

was that the constant replacing of trained workers by novices was not likely to increase the efficiency of the government. Jackson's response to this argument was typical: "The duties of all public officers are . . . so plain and simple that men of intelligence may readily qualify themselves for their performance."

Contempt for expert knowledge and the belief that ordinary Americans can do anything they set their minds to became fundamental tenets of Jacksonian Democracy. To apply them to present-day government would be to court disaster, but in the early 19th century it was not so preposterous, for the role that government played in American life was simple and nontechnical.

Furthermore, Jackson did not practice what he preached. By and large his appointees were anything but "common men." A majority came from the same social and intellectual elite as those they replaced. As the historian Sidney H. Aronson pointed out, "circumstances made it difficult for him to locate such common men in the crowd." He did not try to rotate civil servants in the War and Navy departments, where to do so might have been harmful. In general he left pretty much alone what a modern administrator would call "middle management," the backbone of every organization. During his two terms he dismissed less than 20 percent of the 10,000-odd government workers.

Nevertheless, the spoilsmen roamed the capital in force during the spring of 1829, seeking, as the forthright Jackson said, "a tit to suck the treasury pap." Their philosophy was well summarized by a New Yorker: "No d - - - - d rascal who made use of his office . . . for the purpose of keeping Mr. Adams in, and Genl. Jackson out of power is entitled to the least lenity or mercy. . . . Whether or not I shall get anything in the general scramble for plunder, remains to be proven, but I rather *guess* I shall."

President of All the People

President Jackson was not cynical about the spoils system. As a strong man who intuitively sought to increase his authority, the idea of making government workers dependent on him made excellent sense. His opponents had pictured him as a simple soldier fronting for a rapacious band of politicians, but he soon proved he would exercise his

authority directly. Except for Martin Van Buren, the secretary of state, his Cabinet was not distinguished, and he did not rely on it for advice. He turned instead to an informal "Kitchen Cabinet," which consisted of the influential Van Buren and a few close friends. But these men were advisers, not directors; Jackson was clearly master of his own administration.

More than any earlier president, he conceived of himself as the direct representative of all the people and therefore the embodiment of national power. From Washington to John Quincy Adams, his predecessors together had vetoed only 9 bills, always on the ground that the measures were unconstitutional. Jackson vetoed 12, some simply because he thought the legislation inexpedient. He was the first president to employ the "pocket veto," the device of killing a bill at the tag end of a session of Congress by refusing either to sign or veto it. Yet he had no ambition to expand the scope of federal authority at the expense of the states. Furthermore, he was a poor administrator, given to penny-pinching and lacking in imagination. His strong prejudices and his contempt for expert advice, even in fields such as banking where his ignorance was almost total, did him no credit and the country considerable harm.

Jackson's great success (not merely his popularity) was primarily the result of his personality. A shrewd French observer, Michel Chevalier, after commenting on "his chivalric character, his lofty integrity, and his ardent patriotism," pointed out what was probably the central element in Jackson's appeal. "His tactics in politics, as well as in war," Chevalier wrote in 1824, "is to throw himself forward with the cry of *Comrades, follow me!*" Sometimes he might be wrong, but always he was a leader.

Sectional Tensions Continue

In office Jackson had to say something about western lands, the tariff, and other issues. He tried to steer a moderate course, urging a slight reduction of the tariff and "constitutional" internal improvements. He suggested that once the rapidly disappearing federal debt had been paid off, the surplus revenues of the government might be "distributed" among the states.

Even these cautious proposals caused conflict,

so complex were the interrelations of sectional disputes. If the federal government turned its expected surplus over to the states, it could not afford to reduce the price of public land without going into the red. This disturbed some westerners, notably Senator Thomas Hart Benton of Missouri. Western anxiety in turn suggested to southern opponents of the protective tariff an alliance of South and West. The southerners argued that a tariff levied only to raise revenue would increase foreign imports, bring more money into the Treasury, and thus make it possible to reduce the price of public land.

The question came up in the Senate in December 1829, when an obscure Connecticut senator, Samuel A. Foot, suggested restricting the sale of government land. Benton promptly denounced the proposal as a plot concocted by eastern manufacturers to check the westward migration of their workers. On January 19, 1830, Senator Robert Y. Hayne of South Carolina, a spokesman for Vice-President Calhoun, supported Benton vigorously, suggesting an alliance of South and West based on cheap land and low tariffs. Daniel Webster then rose to the defense of northeastern interests, cleverly goading Hayne by accusing South Carolina of advocating disunionist policies. Responding to this attack, the South Carolinian, a glib speaker but a rather imprecise thinker, launched into an impassioned exposition of the states' rights doctrine.

Webster then took the floor again and for two days, before galleries packed with the elite of Washington society, cut Hayne's argument to shreds. The Constitution was a compact of the American people, not merely of the states, he insisted, the Union perpetual and indissoluble. Webster made the states' rights position appear close to treason; his "second reply to Hayne" effectively prevented the formation of a West-South alliance.

Jackson and Calhoun

The Webster-Hayne debate revived discussion of the idea of nullification. Although southern-born, Jackson had devoted too much of his life to fighting for the entire United States to countenance disunion. Therefore, when the states' rights faction invited him to a dinner to celebrate the anniversary of Jefferson's birth, he came prepared. The

evening reverberated with speeches and toasts of a states' rights tenor, but when the president was called upon to volunteer a toast, he raised his glass, fixed his eyes grimly on John C. Calhoun, and said: "Our *Federal* Union: It must be preserved!" Calhoun took up the challenge at once. "The Union," he retorted, "next to our liberty, most dear!"

It is difficult to measure the importance of the animosity between Jackson and Calhoun in the crisis to which this clash was a prelude. Calhoun wanted very much to be president. He had failed to inherit the office from John Quincy Adams and had accepted the vice-presidency again under Jackson in hopes of succeeding him at the end of one term, if not sooner, for Jackson's health was known to be frail. Yet Old Hickory showed no sign of passing on or retiring. Jackson also seemed to place special confidence in the shrewd Van Buren, who, as secretary of state, also had claim to the succession.

A silly social fracas in which Calhoun's wife appeared to take the lead in the systematic snubbing of Peggy Eaton, wife of the secretary of war, had estranged the two. (Peggy was supposed to have had an affair with Eaton while she was still married to another man, and Jackson, undoubtedly sympathetic because of the attacks he and Rachel had endured, stoutly defended her good name.) Then, shortly after the Jefferson Day dinner, Jackson discovered that in 1818, when he invaded Florida (see pages 177–178), Calhoun, then secretary of war, had recommended to President Monroe that Jackson be summoned before a court of inquiry and charged with disobeying orders. Since Calhoun had repeatedly led Jackson to believe that he had supported him at the time, the revelation convinced the president that Calhoun was not a man of honor.

The personal difficulties are worth stressing because Jackson and Calhoun were not far apart ideologically except on the ultimate issue of the right of a state to overrule federal authority. Jackson was a strong president, but he did not believe that the area of national power was large or that it should be expanded. His interests in government economy, in the distribution of federal surpluses to the states, and in interpreting the powers of Congress narrowly were all similar to Calhoun's. Like most westerners, he favored internal improvements, but he preferred that local projects be left to the states. In 1830 he vetoed a bill providing aid for the construction of the Maysville Road because the route was wholly within Kentucky. There were political reasons for this veto, which was a slap at Kentucky's hero, Henry Clay, but it could not fail to please Calhoun.

Indian Problems

The president also took a states' rights position in the controversy that arose between the Cherokee Indians and Georgia. While he shared many of the typical westerner's feelings about Indians, Jackson insisted that he did not hate them. He subscribed to the theory, advanced by Jefferson, that Indians were "savage" because they roamed wild in a trackless wilderness. The "original inhabitants of our forests" were "incapable of self-government," Jackson claimed, ignoring the fact that they had governed themselves without trouble before the whites arrived. If they settled on small farms they would become "civilized," and all would be well between them and the whites.

Most Indians preferred to maintain their tribal ways, so Jackson pursued a policy of "removing" them from the path of western settlement. This policy seems heartless to modern critics, but since few Indians were willing to adopt the white way of life, most contemporary whites considered removal the only humane solution if the nation was to continue to expand. Jackson was well aware that removal would impose hardships on what he called "this unhappy race—the original dwellers in our land." He insisted that the Indians receive fair prices for their lands and that the government bear the expense of resettling them. He believed that moving them beyond the Mississippi would

■ In 1832, fighting to retain tribal lands in Illinois, Black Hawk and his followers were attacked by militia. This lithograph, by Henry Lewis, depicts the Indians' slaughter as they fled across the Mississippi.

protect them from the "degradation and destruction to which they were rapidly hastening . . . in the States."

Many tribes resigned themselves to removal without argument. Between 1831 and 1833, 15,000 Choctaws migrated from their lands in Mississippi to the region west of Arkansas Territory. A few tribes, such as Black Hawk's Sac and Fox in Illinois and Osceola's Seminoles in Florida, resisted and had to be subdued by troops. One Indian nation, the Cherokees, sought to hold on to their lands by adjusting to white ways. They took up farming and cattle raising, developed a written language, drafted a constitution, and tried to establish a state within a state in northwestern Georgia. Several treaties with the United States seemed to establish the legality of their government. But Georgia would not recognize the Cherokee Nation. It passed a law in 1828 declaring all Cherokee laws void and the region part of Georgia.

The Indians challenged this law in the Supreme Court. In *Cherokee Nation* v. *Georgia* (1831) Chief Justice John Marshall refused to hear the case. However, in *Worcester* v. *Georgia* (1832), a case involving two missionaries to the Cherokees who had not procured licenses required by Georgia law, he ruled that the state could not control the Cherokees or their territory. Later, when a Cherokee named Corn Tassel, convicted in a Georgia court of the murder of another Indian, appealed on the ground that the crime had taken place in Cherokee territory, Marshall declared the Georgia action unconstitutional on the same ground.

Jackson backed Georgia's position. No independent nation could exist within the United States, he insisted. As for *Worcester* v. *Georgia,* he said: "John Marshall has made his decision. Now let him enforce it." Georgia thereupon hanged poor Corn Tassel. In 1838, after Jackson had left the White House, the United States forced 15,000 Cherokees to leave Georgia for Oklahoma. About 4,000 of them died on the way; the route has been named The Trail of Tears.

Jackson's willingness to allow Georgia to ignore decisions of the Supreme Court persuaded extreme southern states' righters that he would not oppose the doctrine of nullification should it be formally applied to a law of Congress. They deceived themselves egregiously. Jackson did not challenge Georgia because he approved of the state's position. He spoke of "the poor deluded . . .

■ This is Charles Lesueur's 1830 study of a Choctaw, one of the southeastern peoples removed to Indian Territory in what is now Oklahoma.

Cherokees" and called William Wirt, the distinguished lawyer who defended their cause, a "truly wicked" man. Jackson was not one to worry about being inconsistent. When South Carolina revived the talk of nullification in 1832, he acted in quite a different manner.

The Nullification Crisis

The proposed alliance of South and West to reduce the tariff and the price of land had not materialized, partly because Webster had discredited the South in the eyes of western patriots and partly because the planters of South Carolina and Georgia, fearing the competition of fertile new cotton lands in Alabama and Mississippi, opposed the rapid exploitation of the West almost as vociferously as northern manufacturers did. When a new tariff law was passed in 1832, it lowered duties much less than the southerners desired. At once talk of nullifying it began to be heard in South Carolina.

In addition to the economic woes of the up-country cotton planters, the great planter-aristocrats of the rice-growing Tidewater, though relatively prosperous, were troubled by northern criticisms of slavery. In the rice region blacks outnumbered whites by two to one, the densest concentration of blacks in the United States. Thousands of these slaves were African-born, brought in during the burst of importations before Congress outlawed the trade in 1808. Controlled usually by overseers of the worst sort, the slaves seemed to the master race like savage beasts straining to rise up against their oppressors. In 1822 the exposure in Charleston of a planned revolt organized by Denmark Vesey, who had bought his freedom with money won in a lottery, had alarmed many whites. News of a far more serious uprising in Virginia led by the slave Nat Turner in 1831, just as the tariff controversy was coming to a head, added to popular concern. Radical South Carolinians saw protective tariffs and agitation against slavery as the two sides of one coin; against both aspects of what appeared to them the tyranny of the majority, nullification seemed the logical defense. Yield on the tariff, editor Henry L. Pinckney of the influential Charleston *Mercury* warned, and "abolition will become the order of the day."

Endless discussions of Calhoun's doctrine after the publication of his *Exposition and Protest* in 1828 had produced much interesting theorizing without clarifying the issue. William H. Freehling, a modern student of the controversy, sums it up aptly: "The theory of nullification was a veritable snarl of contradictions." Admirers of Calhoun praised his "power of analysis & profound philosophical reasonings," but his idea was ingenious rather than profound. Plausible at first glance, it was based on false assumptions: that the Constitution was subject to definitive interpretation; that one party could interpret a compact unilaterally without destroying it; that a minority of the nation could reassume its sovereign independence but that a minority of a state could not.

President Jackson was in this respect Calhoun's exact opposite. The South Carolinian's mental gymnastics he brushed aside; intuitively he realized the central reality: if a state could nullify a law of Congress, the Union could not exist. "Tell . . . the Nullifiers from me that they can talk and write resolutions and print threats to their hearts' content," he warned a South Carolina representative when Congress adjourned in July 1832. "But if one drop of blood be shed there in defiance of the laws of the United States, I will hang the first man of them I can get my hands on to the first tree I can find."

The warning was not taken seriously in South Carolina. In October the state legislature provided for the election of a special convention, which, when it met, contained a solid majority of nullifiers. On November 24, 1832, the convention passed an Ordinance of Nullification, prohibiting the collection of tariff duties in the state after February 1, 1833. The legislature then authorized the raising of an army and appropriated money to supply it with weapons.

Jackson quickly began military preparations of his own, telling friends that he would have 50,000 men ready to move in a little over a month. He also made a statesmanlike effort to end the crisis peaceably. First he suggested to Congress that it lower the tariff further. On December 10 he addressed a "Proclamation to the People of South Carolina." Nullification could only lead to the destruction of the Union, he said. "The laws of the United States must be executed. I have no discretionary power on the subject. . . . Those who told you that you might peaceably prevent their execution deceived you." Old Hickory added sternly: "Disunion by armed force is *treason*. Are you really ready to incur its guilt?"

Attention now shifted to Congress, where administration leaders introduced both a new tariff bill and a Force Bill granting the president additional authority to execute the revenue laws. Calhoun, having resigned as vice-president to accept appointment as senator from South Carolina, led the fight against the Force Bill. Jackson was eager to see the tariff reduced but determined to enforce the law. As the February 1 deadline approached, he claimed that he could raise 200,000 men if needed to suppress resistance. "Union men, fear not," he said. *"The Union will be preserved."*

Jackson's determination sobered the South Carolina radicals. Their appeal for the support of other southern states fell on deaf ears: all rejected the idea of nullification. The unionist minority in South Carolina added to the radicals' difficulties by threatening civil war if federal authority were defied. Calhoun, though a brave man, was alarmed for his own safety, for Jackson had threatened to "hang him as high as Haman" if nullification were attempted. He was suddenly eager to avoid a showdown. Ten days before the deadline, South Carolina postponed nullification pending the outcome of the tariff debate. Then Calhoun joined forces with Henry Clay to push a compromise tariff through Congress. Its passage early in March 1833 reflected the willingness of the North and West to make concessions in the interest of national harmony. Senator Silas Wright of New York, closely affiliated with Van Buren, explained the situation: "People will neither cut throats nor dismember the Union for protection. There is more patriotism and love of country than that left yet. The People will never balance this happy government against ten cents a pound upon a pound of wool."

And so the Union weathered the storm. Having approached the brink of civil war, the nation had drawn hastily back. The South Carolina legislature professed to be satisfied with the new tariff (in fact it made few immediate reductions, providing for a gradual lowering of rates over a ten-year period) and repealed the Nullification Ordinance, saving face by nullifying the Force Bill, which was now a dead letter. But the radical South Carolina planters—not Calhoun, who continued to count himself a nationalist—were becoming convinced that only secession would protect slavery. The nullification fiasco had proved that they could not succeed without the support of other slave states. Thereafter they devoted themselves ceaselessly to obtaining it.

The Bank War

Jackson's strong stand against South Carolina was the more effective because in the fall of 1832 he had been reelected president. The main issue in this election, aside from Jackson's personal popularity, was the president's determination to destroy the second Bank of the United States. In the "Bank War" Jackson won as complete a victory as in his battle with the nullifiers, yet the effects of his triumph were anything but beneficial to the country.

After *McCulloch* v. *Maryland* had presumably established its legality and the conservative Langdon Cheves had gotten it on a sound footing, the Bank of the United States had flourished. In 1823 Cheves was replaced as president by Nicholas Biddle, who managed it brilliantly. A charming and talented Philadelphian, only 37 when he took over the Bank, Biddle was experienced in literature, the law, and diplomacy as well as in finance. At the suggestion of his friend William Clark, he prepared the first scholarly account of the Lewis and Clark expedition, based on the explorers' voluminous journals.

Almost alone in the United States, Biddle realized that his institution could act as a rudimentary central bank, regulating the availability of credit throughout the nation by controlling the lending policies of the state banks. Small banks, possessing limited amounts of gold and silver, sometimes overextended themselves in making large amounts of bank notes available to borrowers in order to earn interest. All this paper money was legally convertible into hard cash on demand, but in the ordinary run of business people seldom bothered to convert their notes so long as they thought the issuing bank was sound. Bank notes passed freely from hand to hand and from bank to bank in every section of the country.

Eventually much of the paper money of the local banks came across the counter of one or another of the 22 branches of the Bank of the United States. By collecting these notes and presenting them for conversion into specie, Biddle could compel the local banks to maintain adequate reserves of gold and silver—in other words, make them hold their lending policies within bounds. "The Bank of the United States," he explained, "has succeeded in keeping in check many institutions which might otherwise have been tempted into extravagant and ruinous excesses." By exerting what he described as "a mild and gentle but efficient control," he compelled local banks to operate upon "a scale . . . commensurate with their real means."

Biddle's policies in the 1820s were good for his own institution, which earned substantial profits, for the state banks, and probably for the country. Pressures on local bankers to make loans were enormous. The nation had an insatiable need for

■ This miniature of Nicholas Biddle, president of the Bank of the United States, is by Henry Inman who was considered the nation's finest portraitist in his day.

capital, and the general mood of the people was optimistic. Everyone wanted to borrow, and everyone expected values to rise, as *in general* they did. But by making liberal loans to produce merchants, for example, rural bankers indirectly stimulated farmers to expand their output beyond current demand, which eventually led to a decline in prices and an agricultural depression. In every field of economic activity, reckless lending caused inflation and greatly exaggerated the ups and downs of the business cycle. It can be argued, however, that by restricting the lending of state banks, Biddle was slowing the rate of economic growth and that in a predominantly agricultural society an occasional slump was not a large price to pay for rapid economic development.

Thus Biddle's policies acted to stabilize the economy, and many interests, including a substantial percentage of state bankers, supported them. They also roused a great deal of opposition. In part the opposition originated in pure ignorance: distrust of paper money did not disappear,

and those who disliked *all* paper saw the Bank as merely the largest (and thus the worst) of many bad institutions. At the other extreme, some bankers chafed under Biddle's restraints because by discouraging them from lending freely, he was limiting their profits. Few financiers realized what Biddle was trying to accomplish. Bray Hammond, whose researches have thrown much light on the history of American banking, estimated that in this period no more than one banker in four understood what was happening when he made a loan. What *was* "sound" banking practice? Honest people disagreed, and many turned against the ideas of Nicholas Biddle.

Many bankers who understood what Biddle was doing also resisted him. New York bankers resented the fact that a Philadelphia institution could wield so much power over their affairs. New York was the nation's largest importing center; huge amounts of tariff revenue were collected there. Yet, since this money was all deposited to the credit of the Bank of the United States, Biddle controlled it from Philadelphia. Finally, some objected to the Bank because it was a monopoly. Distrust of chartered corporations as agents of special privilege tended to focus on the Bank, which had a monopoly of public funds but was managed by a private citizen and controlled by a handful of rich men. Biddle's wealth and social position aggravated this feeling. Like many brilliant people, he sometimes appeared arrogant. He was unused to criticism and disdainful of ignorant and stupid attacks, failing to see that they were sometimes the most dangerous.

Jackson's Bank Veto

This formidable opposition to the Bank was diffuse and unorganized until Andrew Jackson brought it together. When he did, the Bank was quickly destroyed. Jackson belonged among the ignorant enemies of the institution, a hard-money man suspicious of all commercial banking. "I think it right to be perfectly frank with you," he told Biddle in 1829. "I do not dislike your Bank any more than all banks. But ever since I read the history of the South Sea Bubble I have been afraid of banks."

Jackson's attitude dismayed Biddle. It also mystified him, since the Bank was the country's best defense against a speculative mania like the 18th-century "South Sea Bubble" in which hundreds of naive British investors had been fleeced. Almost against his will, he found himself gravitating toward Clay and the National Republicans, offering advantageous loans and retainers to politicians and newspaper editors in order to build up a following. Thereafter events moved inevitably toward a showdown, for the president's combative instincts were easily aroused. "The Bank," he told Van Buren, "is trying to kill me, *but I will kill it!*"

Henry Clay, Daniel Webster, and other prominent National Republicans hoped to use the Bank controversy against Jackson. They reasoned that the institution was so important to the country that Jackson's opposition to it would undermine his popularity. They therefore urged Biddle to ask Congress to renew the Bank's charter. The charter would not expire until 1836, but by pressing the issue before the 1832 presidential election they could force Jackson either to approve the recharter bill or to veto it (which would give candidate Clay a lively issue in the campaign). The banker yielded to this strategy reluctantly, for he would have preferred to postpone the showdown, and a recharter bill passed Congress early in July 1832. Jackson promptly vetoed it.

Jackson's message explaining why he had rejected the bill was immensely popular. It adds nothing to his reputation as a statesman. Being a good Jeffersonian—and no friend of John Marshall—he insisted that the Bank was unconstitutional. (*McCulloch* v. *Maryland* he brushed aside, saying that as president he had sworn to uphold the Constitution as *he* understood it.) The Bank was inexpedient, he argued. Being a dangerous private monopoly that allowed a handful of rich men to accumulate "many millions" of dollars, the bank was making "the rich richer and the potent more powerful." Furthermore, many of its stockholders were foreigners: "If we must have a bank . . . it should be *purely American.*" Little that he said made any more sense than this absurdity.*

The most unfortunate aspect of Jackson's veto was that he could have reformed the Bank instead of destroying it. The central banking function was too important to be left in private hands. Biddle once boasted that he could put nearly any bank in the United States out of business simply by forcing it to exchange specie for its bank notes; he thought he was demonstrating his forbearance, but in fact he was revealing a dangerous flaw in the system. When the Jacksonians called him Czar Nicholas, they were not far from the mark. Moreover, private bankers *were* making profits that in justice belonged to the people, for the government received no interest from the large sums it kept on deposit in the Bank. Jackson would not consider reforms. He set out to smash the Bank of the United States without any real idea of what might be put in its place—a most foolhardy act.

Biddle considered Jackson's veto "a manifesto of anarchy," its tone like "the fury of a chained panther biting the bars of his cage." A large majority of the voters, however, approved of Jackson's hard-hitting attack. He was easily reelected president, defeating Clay, 219 to 49 in the electoral college.

Buttressed by his election triumph, Jackson acted swiftly. "Until I can strangle this hydra of corruption, the Bank, I will not shrink from my duty," he said. Shortly after the start of his second term, he decided to withdraw the government funds deposited in its vaults. Under the law only the secretary of the treasury could remove the deposits. When Secretary Louis McLane refused to do so, believing that the alternative depositories, the state banks, were less safe, Jackson promptly "promoted" him to secretary of state and appointed William J. Duane, a Pennsylvania lawyer, to the Treasury post. Foolishly, he failed to ask Duane his views on the issue before appointing him. Too late he discovered that the new secretary agreed with McLane! It would not be "prudent" to entrust the government's money to "local and irresponsible" banks, Duane said.

Believing that Cabinet officers should obey the president as automatically as a colonel obeys a general, Jackson dismissed Duane, replacing him with Attorney General Roger B. Taney, who had been advising him closely on Bank affairs. Taney carried out the order by depositing new federal receipts in seven state banks in eastern cities while continuing to meet government expenses with drafts on the Bank of the United States.

---

*The country needed all the foreign capital it could attract. Foreigners owned only $8 million of the $35 million stock, and in any case they could not vote their shares.

The situation was confused and slightly unethical. Set on winning the "Bank War," Jackson lost sight of his fear of unsound paper money. Taney, however, knew exactly what he was doing. One of the state banks receiving federal funds was the Union Bank of Baltimore. Taney owned stock in this institution, and its president was his close friend. Little wonder that Jackson's enemies were soon calling the favored state banks "pet" banks. This charge was not entirely fair because Taney took pains to see that the deposits were placed in financially sound institutions. Furthermore, by 1836 the government's funds had been spread out reasonably equitably in about 90 banks. But neither was the charge entirely unfair; the administration certainly favored institutions that were politically sympathetic to it.

When Taney began to remove the deposits, the government had $9,868,000 to its credit in the Bank of the United States; within three months the figure fell to about $4 million. Faced with the withdrawal of so much cash, Biddle had to contract his operations. He decided to exaggerate the contraction, pressing the state banks hard by presenting all their notes and checks that came across his counter for conversion into specie and drastically limiting his own bank's business loans. He hoped that the resulting shortage of credit would be blamed on Jackson and that it would force the president to return the deposits. "Nothing but the evidence of suffering . . . will produce any effect," he reasoned.

For a time the strategy appeared to be working. Paper money became scarce, specie almost unobtainable. A serious panic threatened. New York banks were soon refusing to make any loans at all. "Nobody buys; nobody can sell," a French visitor to the city observed. Memorials and petitions poured in on Congress. Worried and indignant delegations of businessmen began trooping to Washington seeking "relief." Clay, Webster, and Calhoun thundered against Jackson in the Senate.

The president would not budge. "I am fixed in my course as firm as the Rockey Mountain," he wrote Vice-President Van Buren. No "frail mortals" who worshiped "the golden calf" could change his mind. To others he swore he would sooner cut off his right arm and "undergo the torture of ten Spanish inquisitions" than restore the deposits. When delegations came to him, he

roared at them harshly: "Go to Nicholas Biddle. . . . Biddle has all the money!" And in the end—because he was right—business leaders began to take the old general's advice. Pressure on Biddle mounted swiftly, and in July 1834 he suddenly reversed his policy and began to lend money freely. The artificial crisis ended.

Boom and Bust

While the government insisted that its "pet" banks maintain large reserves, other state banks began to offer credit on easy terms, aided by a large increase in their reserves of gold and silver resulting from causes unconnected with the policies of either the government or Biddle's Bank.* Bank notes in circulation jumped from $82 million in January 1835 to $120 million in December 1836. Bank deposits rose even more rapidly.

Much of the new money flowed into speculation in land; a mania to invest in property swept the country. The increased volume of currency caused prices to soar 15 percent in six months, buoying investors' spirits and making them ever more optimistic about the future. By the summer of 1835 one observer estimated that in New York City, which had about 250,000 residents, enough house lots had been laid out and sold to support a population of 2 million. Chicago at this time had only 2,000 to 3,000 inhabitants, yet most of the land for 25 miles around the village had been sold and resold in small lots by speculators anticipating the growth of the area. Throughout the West farmers borrowed money from local banks by mortgaging their land, used the new bank notes to buy more land from the government, and then borrowed still more money from the banks on the strength of their new deeds.

So long as prices rose, the process could be repeated endlessly. In 1832, while the Bank of the United States still regulated the money supply, federal income from the sale of land was $2.6 million. In 1834 it was $4.9 million, in 1835, $14.8

---

*A decline in the Chinese demand for Mexican silver led to increased exports of the metal to the United States, and the rise of American interest rates attracted English capital into the country. Heavy English purchases of American cotton at high prices also increased the flow of specie into American banks.

PUBLIC LAND SALES, 1814-1860

Millions of Acres

■ During most of this period, the minimum price of public land was $1.25 an acre. In 1854 however, the price was reduced to as low as 12.5 cents for land 30 years or more on the market.

million. In 1836 it rose to $24.9 million, and the government found itself totally free of debt and with a surplus of $20 million!

Finally Jackson became alarmed by the speculative mania. In the summer of 1836 he issued the Specie Circular, which provided that purchasers must henceforth pay for public land in gold or silver. At once the rush to buy land ground to a halt. When demand slackened, prices sagged. Speculators, unable to dispose of lands mortgaged to the banks, had to abandon them to the banks, but the banks could not realize enough on the foreclosed property to recover their loans. Suddenly the public mood changed. Commodity prices tumbled 30 percent between February and May. Hordes of depositors sought to withdraw their money in the form of specie, and soon the banks exhausted their supplies. Panic swept the country in the spring of 1837 as every bank in the nation was forced to suspend specie payments. The boom was over.

Major swings in the business cycle can never be attributed to the actions of a single person, however powerful, but there is no doubt that Jackson's war against the Bank exaggerated the swings of the economic pendulum, not so much by its direct effects as by the impact of its ill-considered policies on popular thinking. His Specie Circular did not *prevent* speculators from buying land—at most it caused purchasers to pay a premium for gold or silver. But it convinced potential buyers that the boom was going to end and led them to make decisions that in fact ended it. Old Hickory's combination of impetuousness, combativeness, arrogance, and ignorance rendered the nation he loved so dearly a serious disservice. He lacked, as Glyndon Van Deusen wrote in *The Jacksonian Era*, "the capacity for that slow and often painful balancing of opposite viewpoints, the fruit of philosophic reflection, which is the characteristic of the man of culture." This was his greatest failing, as a president and as a man.

Jacksonian Foreign Policy

Jackson's emotional and dogmatic side also influenced his handling of foreign affairs. His patriotism was often so extravagant as to be ludicrous; in less peaceful times he might well have embroiled the country in far bloodier battles than his war with Nicholas Biddle produced. By pushing relentlessly for the solution of minor problems, he won a number of diplomatic successes. Several advantageous reciprocal trade agreements were negotiated, including one with Great Britain that finally opened British West Indian ports to American ships. American claims dating from the Napoleonic wars were pressed vigorously. The most important result of this policy came in 1831, when France agreed to pay about $5 million to compensate for damages done to American property during that long conflict.

This settlement, however, led to trouble because the French Chamber of Deputies refused to appropriate the necessary funds. When the United States submitted a bill for the first installment in 1833, it was unable to collect. Jackson at once adopted a belligerent stance, his ire further aroused by a bill for $170,041.18 submitted by Nicholas Biddle for the services of the Bank of the United States in attempting to collect the money. When France ignored the second installment, Jackson sent a blistering message to Congress, full of such phrases as "not to be tolerated" and "take redress into our own hands." He asked for a law "authorizing reprisals upon French property" if the money was not paid.

Jackson's case was ironclad, yet the matter did not merit such vigorous prosecution. Congress wisely took no action. Jackson suspended diplomatic relations with France and ordered the navy readied. The French—in part, no doubt, because they were clearly in the wrong—were insulted by Jackson's manner. Irresponsible talk of war was heard in both countries. Fortunately the French Chamber finally appropriated the money, Jackson moderated his public pronouncements, and the issue subsided.

Similarly, when a snag delayed the negotiation of the West Indian treaty, Jackson had suggested forcing Great Britain to make concessions by imposing a boycott on trade with Canada. In both cases he showed poor judgment, being ready to take monumental risks to win petty victories. His behavior reinforced the impression held by foreigners that the United States was a rash young country with a chip on its shoulder, pathologically mistrustful of the good faith of European powers.

The Jacksonians

Jackson's personality had a large impact on the shape and tone of American politics. When he came to office, nearly everyone professed to be a follower of Jefferson. By 1836 being a Jeffersonian no longer meant much; what mattered was how one felt about Andrew Jackson. He had ridden to power at the head of a diverse political army, but he left behind him an organization with a fairly cohesive, if not necessarily consistent, body of ideas. This Democratic party contained rich citizens and poor, easterners and westerners, abolitionists as well as slaveholders. It was not yet a close-knit national organization, but—always allowing for individual exceptions—the Jacksonians agreed on certain underlying principles. These included suspicion of special privilege and large business corporations, both typified by the Bank of the United States; freedom of economic opportunity, unfettered by private or governmental restrictions; absolute political freedom, for white men at least, and the conviction that any ordinary man is capable of performing the duties of most public offices. Jackson's ability to reconcile his belief in the *supremacy* of the Union with his conviction that the *area* of national authority should be held within narrow limits tended to make the Democrats the party of those who believed that the powers of the states should not be diminished.

Although the Locofoco,* or radical, wing of the party championed the idea, nearly all Jacksonians, like their leader, favored giving the small man his chance—by supporting public education, for example, and by refusing to place much weight on a person's origin, dress, or manners. "One individual is as good as another" (again we must insert the adjective "white") was axiomatic with them.

---

*A locofoco was a type of friction match. The name was first applied in politics when a group of New York Jacksonians used these matches to light candles when a conservative faction tried to break up their meeting by turning off the gaslights.

This attitude helps explain why immigrants, Catholics, and other minority groups usually voted Democratic. However, the Jacksonians showed no tendency either to penalize the wealthy or to intervene actively in economic affairs to aid the underprivileged. The motto "That government is best which governs least" graced the masthead of the chief Jacksonian newspaper, the Washington *Globe*, throughout the era.

Rise of the Whigs

The opposition to Jackson was far less cohesive. Henry Clay's National Republican party provided a nucleus, but Clay never dominated that party as Jackson dominated the Democrats. Its orientation was basically anti-Jackson. It was as though the American people were a great block of granite from which some sculptor had just fashioned a statue of Jackson, the chips scattered about the floor of the studio representing the opposition.

While Jackson was president the impact of his personality delayed the formation of a true two-party system, but as soon as he surrendered power the opposition, taking heart, began to coalesce. Many Democrats could not accept the odd logic of Jacksonian finance. As early as 1834 these men, together with the Clay element, the extreme states' righters who followed Calhoun, and other dissident groups, were calling themselves Whigs, the name (harking back to the Revolution) implying patriotic resistance to the tyranny of "King Andrew." This coalition possessed great resources of wealth and talent. Anyone who understood banking was almost obliged to become a Whig unless he was connected with one of Jackson's "pets." Those spiritual descendants of Hamilton who rejected the administration's refusal to approach economic problems from a broadly national perspective also joined in large numbers. Those who found the coarseness and "pushiness" of the Jacksonians offensive were another element in the new party. The anti-intellectual and antiscientific bias of the administration (Jackson rejected proposals for a national university, an observatory, and a scientific and literary institute) drove many well-educated people into the Whig fold. Whig arguments also appealed to ordinary voters who were predisposed to favor strong governments that would check the "excesses" of unrestricted individualism.

The Whigs were slow to develop an effective party organization. They had too many generals and not enough troops. It was hard for them to agree on any issue more complicated than opposition to Jackson. Furthermore, they stood in conflict with the major trend of their age: the glorification of the common man.

Lacking a dominant leader in 1836, the Whigs relied on "favorite sons," hoping to throw the presidential election into the House of Representatives. Daniel Webster ran in New England. For the West and South, Hugh Lawson White of Tennessee, a former friend who had broken with Jackson, was counted on to carry the fight. General William Henry Harrison was supposed to win in the Northwest and to draw support everywhere from those who liked to vote for military heroes. This sorry strategy failed; Jackson's handpicked candidate, Martin Van Buren, won a majority of both the popular and the electoral votes.

Van Buren's Administration

The Red Fox, the Little Magician—Van Buren's brilliance as a political manipulator has tended to obscure his statesmanlike qualities and his engaging personality. High office sobered Van Buren and improved his judgment. He fought the Bank of the United States as a monopoly, but he also opposed irresponsible state banks. New York's "Safety Fund System," requiring all banks to contribute to a fund, supervised by the state, to be used to redeem the notes of any member bank that failed, was established largely through his efforts. Van Buren believed in public construction of internal improvements, but he favored state rather than national programs, and he urged a rational approach: each project must stand on its own as a useful and profitable public utility.

He continued to equivocate spectacularly on the tariff—in his *Autobiography* he described two of his supporters walking home after listening to him talk on the tariff, each convinced that it had been a brilliant speech, but neither having obtained the slightest idea as to where Van Buren stood on the subject—but he was never in the pocket of any special interest group or tariff lobbyist. He accounted himself a good Jeffersonian, tending to prefer state action to federal, but he was by no means doctrinaire. Basically he approached most questions rationally and pragmatically.

Van Buren had outmaneuvered Calhoun easily in the struggle to succeed Jackson, winning the old hero's confidence and serving him well. In 1832 he was elected vice-president and thereafter was conceded to be the "heir apparent." In 1835 the Democratic National Convention nominated him for president unanimously.

Van Buren took office just as the Panic of 1837 struck the country. Its effects were frightening but short-lived. When the banks stopped converting paper money into gold and silver, they outraged conservatives but in effect eased the pressure on the money market: interest rates declined and business loans again became relatively easy to obtain. In 1836, at the height of the boom in land sales, Congress had voted to "distribute" the new Treasury surplus to the states, and this flow of money, which the states promptly spent, also stimulated the revival. Late in 1838 the banks resumed specie payments.

In 1839 a bumper crop caused a sharp decline in the price of cotton. Then a number of state governments that had overextended themselves in road- and canal-building projects were forced to default on their debts. This discouraged investors, particularly foreigners. A general economic depression ensued that lasted until 1843.

Van Buren was not responsible for the panic or the depression, but his manner of dealing with economic issues was scarcely helpful. He saw his role as being concerned only with problems plaguing the *government*, ignoring the economy as a whole. "The less government interferes with private pursuits the better for the general prosperity," he pontificated. As Daniel Webster scornfully pointed out, Van Buren was following a policy of "leaving the people to shift for themselves," one which many Whigs rejected.

Such a hands-off approach to the depression seems foolish by modern standards. Van Buren's refusal to assume any responsibility for the general welfare appears to explode the theory that the Jacksonians were deeply concerned with the fate of ordinary citizens. In *The Concept of Jacksonian Democracy*, Lee Benson argues that the Whigs, rather than the Democrats, were the "positive liberals" of the era. Benson cites many statements by

Whigs about giving "free scope to the employment of capital and credit" and applying "the means of the state boldly and liberally to aid . . . public works."

This approach helps correct past oversimplifications, but it judges the period by the standards of a later age. The country in the 1830s was still mainly agricultural, and for most farmers the depression, while serious, did not spell disaster. The means, even the statistical information, necessary for regulating the economy effectively did not exist. Moreover, many Jacksonians were perfectly willing to see the *states* act to stimulate economic growth in bad times—as indeed most of them did.

Van Buren's chief goal as president was to find an acceptable substitute for the state banks as a place to keep federal funds. The depression and the suspension of specie payments embarrassed the government along with private depositors. He soon settled on the idea of "divorcing" the government from all banking activities. His Independent Treasury Bill called for the construction of government-owned vaults where federal revenues could be stored until needed. To insure absolute safety, all payments to the government were to be made in hard cash. After a battle that lasted until the summer of 1840, the Independent Treasury Act passed both the House and the Senate.

Opposition to the Independent Treasury had been bitter, and not all of it was partisan. Bankers and businessmen objected to the government's withholding so much specie from the banks, which needed all the hard money they could get to support loans that were the lifeblood of economic growth. It seemed irresponsible for the federal government to turn its back on the banks, which so obviously performed a semipublic function. These criticisms made good sense, but through a lucky combination of circumstances, the system worked reasonably well for many years. By creating suspicion in the public mind, officially stated distrust of banks acted as a useful damper on their tendency to overexpand. No acute shortage of specie developed because heavy agricultural exports and the investment of much European capital in American railroads beginning in the mid 1840s brought in large amounts of new gold and silver. After 1849 the discovery of gold in California added another important source of specie. The supply of money and bank credit kept pace roughly with the growth of the economy, but

■ By the 1840s the daguerreotype—"the mirror with a memory," as Oliver Wendell Holmes described it—was all the rage. This is Martin Van Buren around 1848 when he was the Free Soil nominee for president.

through no fault of the government. "Wildcat" banks proliferated. Fraud and counterfeiting were common, and the operation of everyday business affairs was inconvenienced in countless ways. The disordered state of the currency remained a grave problem until corrected by Civil War banking legislation.

Election of 1840

It was not his financial policy that led to Van Buren's defeat in 1840. The depression naturally hurt the Democrats, and the Whigs were far better organized than in 1836. The Whigs also adopted a different strategy, cynical but effective. The Jacksonians had come to power on the coattails of a popular general whose views on public questions they concealed or ignored. They had maintained themselves by shouting the praises of the common man. Now the Whigs seized upon these techniques and carried them to their logical—or illogical—conclusion. Not even bothering to draft a program, and passing over Clay and Webster, whose views were known and therefore controversial, they nominated General Harrison for president. The Hero of Tippecanoe was counted on to conquer the party created in the image of the Hero of New Orleans. To "balance" the ticket, the Whigs chose a former Democrat, John Tyler of Virginia, an ardent supporter of states' rights, as their vice-presidential candidate.

The Whig argument was specious but effective: General Harrison is a plain man of the people who

■ A cornerstone of Whig strategy in the 1840 campaign was the mass political rally, such as this one held in Cincinnati a month before election day. A "triumphal" arch was erected across Main Street for the occasion, with Harrison banners, flags, and slogans, both patriotic and political, much in evidence. A contemporary etching.

lives in a log cabin (where the latchstring is always out). Contrast him with the suave Van Buren, luxuriating amid "the Regal Splendor of the President's Palace." Harrison drinks ordinary hard cider and eats hog meat and grits, while Van Buren swills expensive foreign wines and fattens on fancy concoctions prepared by a French chef. The general's furniture is plain and sturdy; the president dines off gold plates and treads on Royal Wilton carpets that cost the people $5 a yard. In a country where all are equal, the people will reject an aristocrat like "Martin Van Ruin" and put their trust in General Harrison, a simple, brave, honest, public-spirited common man.

Such nonsense created an irrelevant and mis-

leading impression. Harrison came from a distinguished family, being the son of Benjamin Harrison, a signer of the Declaration of Independence and a former governor of Virginia. He was well educated and in at least comfortable financial circumstances, and he certainly did not live in a log cabin. The Whigs ignored these facts. The log cabin and the cider barrel became their symbols, which every political meeting saw reproduced in a dozen forms. The leading Whig campaign newspaper, edited by a vigorous young New Englander named Horace Greeley, was called the *Log Cabin*. Cartoons, doggerel, slogans, and souvenirs were everywhere substituted for argument.

The Democrats used the same methods as the

Whigs and were equally well organized, but they had little heart for the fight. The president tried to run on his record and to focus public attention on issues. His voice could not be heard above the huzzas of the Whigs, who chanted "Tippecanoe and Tyler too!" and "Van, Van, is a used-up man" and rolled out another barrel of hard cider. A huge turnout (four-fifths of the eligible voters, more than 2.4 million as against 1.5 million four years earlier) carried Harrison to victory by a margin of almost 150,000. The electoral vote was 234 to 60.

The Democrats had been blown up by their own bomb. In 1828 they had portrayed John Quincy Adams as a bloated aristocrat and Jackson as a simple western farmer. The lurid talk of Van Buren dining off golden plates was no different from the stories that made Adams out to be a passionate gambler. If Van Buren was a lesser man than Adams, Harrison was a pale imitation indeed of Andrew Jackson.

The Whigs continued to repeat history by rushing to gather the spoils of victory. Washington was again flooded by office seekers, the political confusion monumental. Harrison had no ambition to be an aggressive leader. He believed that Jackson had misused the veto and professed to put as much emphasis as had Washington on the principle of the separation of legislative and executive powers. This delighted the Whig leaders in Congress, who had had their fill of the "executive usurpation" of Jackson. Either Clay or Webster seemed destined to be the real ruler of the new administration, and soon the two were squabbling over their old general like sparrows over a crust.

At the height of their squabble, less than a month after his inauguration, Harrison fell gravely ill. Pneumonia developed, and on April 4 he died. John Tyler of Virginia, honest, conscientious, but doctrinaire, became president of the United States. The political climate of the country changed drastically. Events began to march in a new direction, one that led ultimately to Bull Run, to Gettysburg, and to Appomattox.

SUPPLEMENTARY READING

Titles marked with an asterisk have been published in paperback

On Jackson's presidency, see. G. G. Van Deusen, **The Jacksonian Era*** (1959). R. V. Remini, **Andrew Jackson and the Course of American Freedom, 1822–1832** (1981), the second volume of Remini's Jackson biography, covers only the first term but is based on solid research. The nature of Jacksonian Democracy was analyzed brilliantly by Alexis de Tocqueville, **Democracy in America*** (1835–1840). A. M. Schlesinger, Jr, **The Age of Jackson*** (1945), stresses the democratic character of Jacksonianism. J. W. Ward, **Andrew Jackson: Symbol for an Age*** (1955), pictures Jackson as typifying certain basic aspects of the American character. D. T. Miller, **Jacksonian Aristocracy** (1967) and two works by Edward Pessen, **Riches, Class and Power Before the Civil War** (1973) and **Jacksonian America*** (1969), describe the growth and extent of economic and class distinctions. Marvin Meyers' **The Jacksonian Persuasion*** (1957) is another interesting attempt to explain the nature of the times. T. P. Abernethy, **From Frontier to Plantation in Tennessee** (1932), portrays Jackson as a conservative, chiefly by stressing his early career. Richard Hofstadter's analysis of Jackson in **The American Political Tradition*** (1948) is also important.

A number of contemporary commentaries by foreigners throw much light on Jacksonian Democracy. See especially, in addition to Tocqueville, Frances Trollope, **Domestic Manners of the Americans*** (1832), Michel Chevalier (J. W. Ward, ed.), **Society, Manners and Politics in the United States*** (1961), Harriet Martineau, **Retrospect of Western Travel** (1838) and **Society in America*** (1837), and F. J. Grund, **Aristocracy in America*** (1959).

On Jackson's administration of the government and the development of the spoils system, see L. D. White, **The Jacksonians*** (1954), and S. H. Aronson, **Status and Kinship in the Higher Civil Service** (1964); on the development of parties, R. P. McCormick, **The Second American Party System*** (1966). For his Indian policy, consult F. P. Prucha, **American Indian Policies in the Formative Years*** (1962), B. W. Sheehan, **Seeds of Extinction*** (1973), R. N. Satz, **American Indian Policy in the Jacksonian Era** (1975), and Grant Foreman, **Indian Removal: The Emigration of the Five Civilized Tribes*** (1953).

By far the best treatment of the nullification controversy is W. W. Freehling, **Prelude to Civil War: The Nullification Controversy in South Carolina*** (1966), which shows the close relationship between the nullifiers and the slavery issue. Also helpful is C. M. Wiltse, **John C. Calhoun: Nullifier** (1949). C. S. Sydnor, **The**

Development of Southern Sectionalism* (1948), locates the crisis in a broader context. Calhoun's character and personality are well described in M. L. Coit, **John C. Calhoun: American Portrait*** (1950).

The struggle with the Bank is discussed in Bray Hammond, **Banks and Politics in America from the Revolution to the Civil War*** (1957), J. M. McFaul, **The Politics of Jacksonian Finance** (1972), and Walter Smith, **Economic Aspects of the Second Bank of the United States** (1953). Peter Temin, **The Jacksonian Economy*** (1969), minimizes the effects of Jackson's policies on economic conditions. Temin also provides an interesting analysis of economic trends throughout the period. T. P. Govan's **Nicholas Biddle: Nationalist and Public Banker*** (1959) is excellent on Biddle's view of banking but too apologetic. C. B. Swisher's **Roger B. Taney** (1935) is a good biography.

The political and economic ideas of Whigs and Democrats are discussed in Lee Benson, **The Concept of Jacksonian Democracy*** (1961), and R. P. Formisano, **The Birth of Mass Politics: Michigan, 1827–1861** (1971). For Jackson's foreign policy, see R. A. McLemore, **Franco-American Diplomatic Relations** (1941). Walter Hugins' **Jacksonian Democracy and the Working Class*** (1960) is a fine scholarly study. On the development of the Whig party, in addition to the biographies of leading Whigs, see E. M. Carroll, **Origins of the Whig Party** (1925), G. R. Poage, **Henry Clay and the Whig Party** (1936), and McCormick's **Second American Party System.**

The election of 1840 is treated in R. G. Gunderson, **The Log-Cabin Campaign** (1957), Freeman Cleaves, **Old Tippecanoe** (1939), O. P. Chitwood, **John Tyler: Champion of the Old South** (1939), J. A. Garraty, **Silas Wright** (1949), and the biographies of Clay and Webster.

Portfolio Three

TOCQUEVILLE'S AMERICA

In 1831 two well-born young Frenchmen, Alexis de Tocqueville and Gustave de Beaumont, set sail from Le Havre for America. Ostensibly they were to study the American prison system, but their real aim was far more ambitious. "We are leaving," Tocqueville wrote, "with the intention of examining, in detail and as scientifically as possible, all the mechanism of that vast American society which everyone talks of and no one knows. . . . We are counting on bringing back the elements of a fine work." In time that "fine work" would become Tocqueville's classic analysis of American society, *Democracy in America;* but first, as Beaumont wrote, they must "see America; . . . its inhabitants, its cities, its institutions, its customs." In the following nine months they did precisely that, traveling virtually the length and breadth of the nation.

The America Tocqueville and Beaumont saw—and they saw a great deal—can be recaptured not only in their notes and letters but in the drawings, prints, and paintings of the period, such as Carl Bodmer's 1832 watercolor above of a steamboat landing in New Jersey. The America that the artists pictured has long since disappeared, yet many of the fundamental traits of the society Tocqueville analyzed may be observed in the America of today.

Portfolio Three /1

City of Commerce

On May 11, 1831, after an Atlantic passage of some 40 days, Tocqueville and Beaumont landed in New York City for a six-week stay. As he looked at the hustle and bustle of New York, Tocqueville saw a city and a society that differed radically from Paris and the still aristocratic society of early 19th-century France. His first impressions were hardly complimentary. "To a Frenchman the aspect of the city is bizarre and not very agreeable," he wrote his mother. "One sees neither dome, nor bell tower, nor great edifice, with the result that one has the constant impression of being in a suburb. In its centre the city is built of brick, which gives it a most monotonous appearance. . . . The streets are very badly paved, but sidewalks for pedestrians are to be found in all of them."

Everywhere he looked Tocqueville saw one kind of business or another, and he noted that "the whole society seems to have melted into a middle class." Soon he was turning this observation into his first major generalization about American society: "We are most certainly in another world here. Political passions here are only on the surface. The profound passion, the only one which profoundly stirs the human heart, the passion of all the days, is the acquisition of riches." Pressing his analysis a step further, he noted that this "thirst for riches . . . brings in its train many hardly honourable passions, such as cupidity, fraud, and bad faith. . . . In addition, [Americans] consider the bankruptcies which are very frequent in all cities as of no importance or of very little account."

While Tocqueville found this business society at first "both vulgar and disagreeably uncultivated" and more the product of "accidental circumstances" than "the will of man," he quickly noted that "before my eyes is none the less an immense spectacle. Never before has a people found for itself such a happy and fruitful basis of life. Here freedom is unrestrained, and subsists by being useful to every one without injuring anybody. There is undeniably something *feverish* in the activity it imparts to industry and to the human spirit. But up to now that fever seems only to increase man's power without affecting his reason. In spite of this activity, nature's resources are inexhaustible. What remains to be done seems to increase in proportion to what has already been done. New York, which had 20,000 souls at the moment of the American Revolution, has 200,000 now, and each year adds immense developments to its greatness."

■ Above is an 1834 aquatint of New York's Broadway, looking north from Canal Street. It is easy to see why Tocqueville concluded that he was in the midst of a highly commercial society: Practically every building houses two or more businesses, and street peddlers are busy hawking ice, firewood, and boots. While the two visitors were in the city they put up at a fashionable boarding house on lower Broadway. As the contemporary views at left and right suggest, they found boarding-house life "very agreeable" if informal. "It upsets all our settled habits," Tocqueville admitted. "We were utterly astounded the first day to see the women come to breakfast at 8 o'clock in the morning carefully dressed for the whole day."

■ *The Dinner Party* was painted about 1825 by the Boston artist Henry Sargent. Tocqueville tolerated but rarely praised American *haute cuisine*. After one banquet, he recorded that the dinner represented the infancy of art: "the vegetables and fish before the meat, the oysters for dessert. In a word, complete barbarism."

High Society

Tocqueville and Beaumont had an unusual opportunity to observe the upper crust of American society, for wherever they went they found that the company of two young French aristocrats was considered a badge of social distinction. Even in the Jacksonian era, democracy was not without its social affectations. In New York Beaumont wrote that "the aristocracy of fortune aims at distinction here as elsewhere. Much is made of the oldness of families. I was astonished to hear these proud champions of equality call themselves *honourable esquires.* They put heraldic arms on their carriages and on their seals. The taste for superiority crops up everywhere. They are besides excessively vain." Tocqueville carried the analysis a step further. "In this republican country they are a thousand times more fond of nobility, of titles, of crosses, and of all the inconsequential distinctions of Europe than we are in France. The greatest equality reigns here in the laws. It is even in appearance in the customs. But I tell you the devil loses nothing by it. And the pride which cannot come out in public finds at the very bottom of the soul a fine corner in which to install itself." The frantic search for emblems of status was fueled, he noted, by the fact that "money is the only social distinction."

Fresh from the excitement of revolution-torn Paris, Tocqueville found social life in mercantile-minded America exceedingly dull. "In the United States," he wrote, "they have neither war, nor pestilence, nor literature, nor eloquence, nor fine arts, nor revolutions; no great excesses. . . . They enjoy there the most insipid happiness which can be imagined." He feared that democracy was leading to mediocrity: "The people grow more enlightened, knowledge is spreading, a middling capacity is becoming common. The outstanding talents, the great characters, are more rare. Society is less brilliant and more prosperous."

■ A Baltimore horse race like the one at top "wasn't quite the style of Europe." Tocqueville thought "the horses were fine but the jockeys ridiculously clothed." The public's fashions for such occasions, however, as illustrated in the 1836 advertisement above, won Tocqueville's commendation: "The French mode dominates."

The Rigors of Travel

The America that Tocqueville and Beaumont set out to explore was, as Tocqueville put it, "one vast forest, in the middle of which they have carved out some clearings." In 1831 American railroads were still in their infancy, and canals provided only slow and cramped transportation which a gentleman avoided whenever possible. This was instead the heyday of the stagecoach and the steamboat, and it was largely with the aid of these two conveyances that the two Frenchmen made their extensive tour of the United States. In nine months they traveled more than 4,000 miles, a remarkable achievement. They saw something of all 24 states, explored the edge of the western frontier, traveled down the Ohio and the Mississippi from Pittsburgh to New Orleans, and visited almost all of the nation's major cities.

Neither stagecoach nor steamboat seems to have treated the somewhat frail Tocqueville kindly, but he never lost his sense of humor, his determination to carry on, or his capacity for objective reporting. The stage road might be "infernal" and the carriage "without springs," yet he could still note the "tranquillity of the Americans over all these inconveniences. They seem to bear them as necessary evils." When he nearly lost his life aboard an Ohio steamboat trapped in ice, he remarked mildly, "water journeys do not go well with us." But above and beyond the hazards and inconveniences, Tocqueville had only praise for the nation's rough yet remarkably extensive network of communications. "The roads, the canals, and the mails," he noted, "play a prodigious part in the prosperity of the Union. . . . In the Michigan forests there is not a cabin so isolated, not a valley so wild, that it does not receive letters and newspapers at least once a week. . . . America has undertaken and is finishing some immense canals. It already has more railroads than France. . . . Of all the countries of the world," he concluded, "America is the one where the movement of thought and human industry is the most continuous and the most swift."

■ As if he were describing John Lewis Krimmel's painting (above) of a country inn, Tocqueville wrote, "We were introduced into the 'barroom' . . . where the simplest as well as the richest . . . smoke, drink, and talk politics together, on the footing of the most perfect exterior equality."

■ The engraving at right, from a mail stage broadside, was labeled, "Thirty-nine hours from Boston to New York." Tocqueville noted ruefully that stages were "drawn at full trot on roads as detestable as those of lower Brittany."

■ The 1832 French lithograph (left) of a *bateau à vapeur américain* shows the type of river craft used by Tocqueville and Beaumont in their travels.

■ Karl Bodmer, a 23-year-old Swiss, painted the above watercolor of an Indiana farmstead in 1832. Although the pioneer's log cabin was often a crude and unfinished dwelling, Tocqueville viewed it as an "ark of civilization." When his steamboat approached Detroit, shown opposite in an 1834 lithograph, he marveled, "Without transition you pass from wilderness into the streets of a city."

■ Beaumont drew this sketch during an excursion to the frontier outpost of Saginaw. Tocqueville relaxes at right while Beaumont gives their Indian guide a water bottle to prevent his desertion.

Edge of the Frontier

Probably no part of his trip provided Tocqueville with as many insights as the two weeks he spent on the edge of the frontier in the forests of Michigan Territory. The deeper he penetrated into the wilderness, the more amazed he was to find that the American was much the same sort of fellow on the frontier as he was in the city. "The man you left in New York," he wrote, "you find again in almost impenetrable solitudes: same clothes, same attitudes, same language, same habits, same pleasures." He attributed this similarity to the fact that "those who inhabit these isolated places have arrived there since yesterday; they have come with the customs, the ideas, the needs of civilization."

If the settler seemed to be trying to shape the frontier in the image of the civilization that had been left behind, the frontier was putting its own stamp on the American character. The pioneer, Tocqueville wrote, "has braved exile, the loneliness and numberless miseries of the savage life, he has slept on the bare ground, he has exposed himself to the forest fevers and the tomahawk of the Indian." Tocqueville was convinced these efforts in pursuit of "the acquisition of riches" would continue "with a perseverance and a scorn for life that one might call heroic, if that name fitted other than virtuous things."

A further effect of pioneering was a remarkable attitude toward change. "The American has no time to tie himself to anything. He grows accustomed only to change, and ends by regarding it as the natural state of man. He feels the need of it, more, he loves it; for the instability, instead of meaning disaster to him, seems to give birth only to miracles all about him." In this world of change, Tocqueville asked, how could the American be anything but an optimist? "The same man has given his name to a wilderness which none before him had traversed, has seen the first forest tree fall and the first planter's house rise in the solitude, where a community came to group itself, a village grew, and today a vast city stretches."

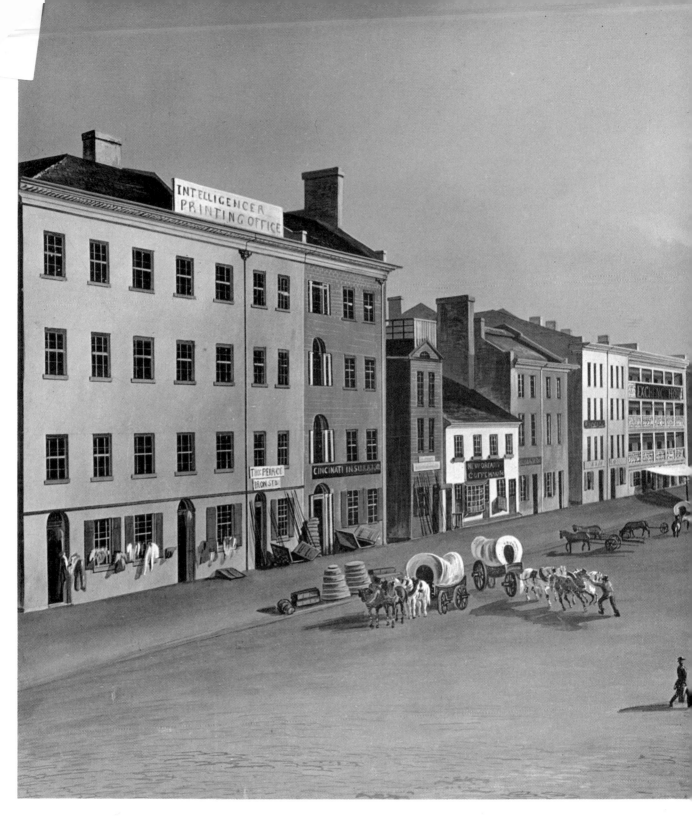

Queen City of the West

On their return from Michigan the two Frenchmen resumed touring the older states, then boarded an Ohio River steamboat for Cincinnati, the "Queen City of the West." What they saw, shown in this 1835 painting by an amateur artist named John Caspar Wild, sent them both scurrying to their notebooks. "I don't believe there exists anywhere on earth a town which has

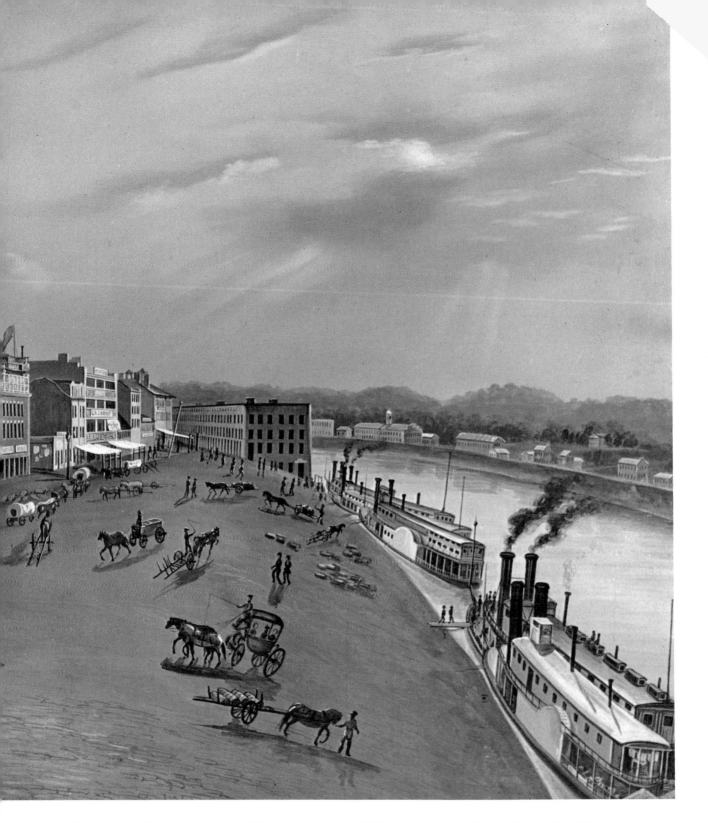

had a growth so prodigious," Beaumont wrote. "Thirty years ago the banks of the Ohio were a wilderness. Now there are 30,000 inhabitants." Tocqueville confessed himself astonished by the spectacle of "a city which seems to want to rise too quickly for people to have any system or plan about it. Great buildings . . . houses under construction, no names on the streets, no numbers on the houses, no outward luxury, but the image of industry and labor obvious at every step."

The South and Slavery

Cincinnati demonstrated the vigor of the western frontier, Tocqueville wrote. "Society is growing more rapidly than man." But when their steamboat headed down the Ohio, he was interested to notice how different were Ohio and Indiana, the free states on their right, from the slave state of Kentucky on their left. "For the first time," he wrote his father, "we have had the chance to examine . . . the effect that slavery produces on society. On the right bank of the Ohio everything is activity, industry; labor is honoured; there are no slaves. Pass to the left bank and the scene changes so suddenly that you think yourself on the other side of the world; the enterprising spirit is gone. There, work is not only painful; it's shameful, and you degrade yourself in submitting yourself to it. To ride, to hunt, to smoke like a Turk in the sunshine: there is the destiny of the white. To do any other kind of manual labor is to act like a slave."

Critical as he was of slavery, Tocqueville's aristocratic heart was warmed by southern charm. "The whites, to the South of the Ohio, form a veritable aristocracy which . . . combines many prejudices with high sentiments and instincts. They say, and I am much inclined to believe, that in the matter of honour these men practice delicacies and refinements unknown in the North. They are frank, hospitable, and put many things before money."

But charm alone did not make a strong society. "You see few churches, no schools," he observed. "Society, like the individual, seems to provide for nothing." The South would end "by being dominated by the North. Every day the latter grows more wealthy and densely populated while the South is stationary or growing poor."

Later, after he had returned from New Orleans, he summed up his thoughts in one of those brilliant flashes of insight that would make him famous. Under the heading "Future of the Union," he wrote, "The first result of this disproportionate growth is a violent change in the equilibrium of power and political influence. Powerful states become weak, territories without a name become states. . . . Wealth, like population, is displaced. These changes cannot take place without injuring interests, without exciting violent passions."

■ The drawing at left by August Köllner and Benjamin Latrobe's watercolor above portray two aspects of slavery: the leisurely life of the plantation owner and the hard lot of the slave. Beaumont caustically noted that "in the house of the whites [slaves are] an obligatory furnishing, as is a chair or a table. . . . The convenience of being served . . . makes the white indolent. . . . His customs are feudal; he spends his time hunting, riding, or doing nothing. . . ."

■ Slavery, Tocqueville observed after witnessing a slave auction like the one below, "brutalizes the black population and debilitates the white." In one blunt sentence he summed up his two-month tour of the South: "Man is not made for servitude."

A Nation of Equals

Despite his disapproval of slavery, Tocqueville believed that equality, both social and political, was the guiding principle of American life. "The great advantage of the Americans," he asserted, "is . . . that they are born equal instead of becoming so." No institution provided proof of this assertion so convincingly as the family. In America, he observed, "the paternal authority is almost reduced to nothing." As soon as the first years of childhood were past, equality, and with it freedom and independence, were given the young—male and female, first-born and last-born alike. Such treatment not only produced the rapid maturing of self-confident men and women ready to extend the frontier but led to the growth of strong ties between father and son, mother and daughter, brother and brother. Tocqueville felt certain that "in proportion as manners and laws become more democratic . . . rules and authority are less talked of, confidence and tenderness are often increased." In a democracy, he believed, this state of affairs boded well for the family, but it raised serious problems for society as a whole. "Democracy loosens social ties, but tightens natural ones; it brings kindred more closely together, while it throws citizens more apart," he concluded.

Thus it appeared to Tocqueville that outside of the family circle equality tended to isolate people and make them selfish. This dangerous situation might lead either to complete conformity or, at the other extreme, to unrestrained individualism. But happily, Tocqueville noticed, the young democracy had created a veritable abundance of social institutions which managed to generate diversity while providing a framework for communal enterprises. "Americans of all ages, all conditions, and all dispositions constantly form associations," he observed. "They have not only commercial and manufacturing companies, in which all take part, but associations of a thousand other kinds, religious, moral, serious, futile, general or restricted, enormous or diminutive. The Americans make associations to give entertainments, to found seminaries, to build inns, to construct churches, to diffuse books, to send missionaries to the antipodes; in this manner they found hospitals, prisons, and schools. If it is proposed to inculcate some truth or to foster some feeling by the encouragement of a great example, they form a society."

To Tocqueville the centrifugal forces in American life, rather than the centripetal ones, were the most dangerous. It seemed to him that "in proportion as the circle of public society is extended, it may be anticipated that the sphere of private intercourse will be contracted; far from supposing that the members of modern society will ultimately live in common, I am afraid that they will end by forming only small coteries."

■ The print above, entitled *The Grand Fantastical Parade,* satirized an 1833 demonstration in New York against the militia system, one of the nation's oldest volunteer organizations. But most Americans were too fond of this highly social institution to be swayed. The sober portrait at the right, ca. 1840, of a typically large family is the work of an unknown primitive artist who found painting the human hand beyond his skill.

A Restless People

As he penned one of his most telling comments on life in America, Tocqueville observed, "In the United States a man builds a house in which to spend his old age, and he sells it before the roof is on; he plants a garden and lets it just as the trees are coming into bearing; he brings a field into tillage and leaves other men to gather the crops; he embraces a profession and gives it up; he settles in a place, which he soon afterwards leaves to carry his changeable longings elsewhere. If his private affairs leave him any leisure, he instantly plunges into the vortex of politics; and if at the end of a year of unremitting labor he finds he has a few days' vacation, his eager curiosity whirls him over the vast extent of the United States, and he will travel fifteen hundred miles in a few days to shake off his happiness. Death at length overtakes him, but it is before he is weary of his bootless chase of that complete felicity which forever escapes him."

Other eyes, such as those of the unknown artist who painted this view of the clamorous commotion of moving day in New York about 1840 (and included himself at the far left), observed the same phenomenon of restlessness. Yet Tocqueville went a step further and pinpointed the potential tragedy of such physical and social mobility.

"Equality," he wrote in *Democracy in America*, "leads by a still shorter path to the various effects [of restlessness] I have just described. When . . . the distinctions of ranks are obliterated and privileges are destroyed, when hereditary property is subdivided and education and freedom are widely diffused, the desire of acquiring the comforts of the world haunts the imagination of the poor, and the dread of losing them that of the rich. Many scanty fortunes spring up; those who possess them have a sufficient share of physical gratifications to conceive a taste for these pleasures, not enough to satisfy it. They never procure them without exertion, and they never indulge in them without apprehension. They are therefore always straining to pursue or to retain gratifications so delightful, so imperfect, so fugitive."

The Religious Impulse

Tocqueville had not been in America more than a month when he observed, "Never have I been so conscious of the influence of religion on the morals and the social and political state of a people." A few weeks later he wrote his first long commentary on "American Government and Religion." "Sunday is rigorously observed," he noted. "As for what we generally understand as faiths, such as customs, ancient traditions, the strength of memories . . . I don't see a trace of them." He observed instead that "the immense majority have *faith* in the wisdom and good sense of human kind." America, in other words, had placed its faith in democracy. "In France, I had almost always seen the spirit of religion and the spirit of freedom marching in opposite directions. But in America I found that they were intimately united." United in spirit but separated in fact, of course; separation spared the church the worldly misfortunes of the state and left it free to be democracy's conscience. Tocqueville concluded that "while the law permits Americans to do what they please, religion prevents them from conceiving, and forbids them to commit what is rash or unjust."

■ Tocqueville greatly admired the moral influence of the socially active sects like the Quakers (above). Americans, he thought, had little taste for symbols, ritual, and complicated theology, preferring to have their religion "bared to the light of day."

■ In the 1830s pioneers worshiped with unrestrained enthusiasm at camp meetings like the one depicted above by Parisian Jacques Gerard Milbert. Below is Englishman George Harvey's 1837 watercolor, *Night Fall, St. Thomas Church, Broadway*. Tocqueville counted on religion to "purify" and "restrain" American materialism.

■ Above is an unknown artist's painting of a women's school about 1840. Although he was not enthusiastic about equal education for women, Tocqueville concluded that there was "no choice." A good education, he philosophized, was "indispensable to protect women from the dangers with which democratic manners surround them."

■ This satirical drawing, also by an unknown artist, shows meteorologist James Pollard Espy delivering a lyceum lecture in New York about 1841. Begun in 1826 and dedicated to the "general diffusion of knowledge," the lyceum movement was a box-office success for years.

Education for Democracy

During most of his tour Tocqueville wrestled with the question, Could a democratic society achieve stable government? Finally, halfway down the Ohio River, he decided that indeed it could. He recorded that "enlightenment," more than anything else, including "virtue," was the prime reason for America's success at self-government: "The Americans are hardly more virtuous than others, but they are infinitely better educated." American education, he continued, was stamped with a democratic character: Primary instruction was "within the reach of everybody"; anyone was "free to found a public school and direct it as he pleases"; and education was "an industry like other industries, the *consumers* being the judges and the state taking no hand whatever." In fact state governments did take a hand, but in 1832 education was still largely a local and a private matter. Almost every town outside the South maintained a primary school, and the churches ran a variety of educational institutions.

Schooling was just one part of an American's education. "The citizen of the United States," Tocqueville observed, "does not acquire his practical science and his positive notions from books; the instruction he has acquired may have prepared him for receiving those ideas, but it did not furnish them. The American learns to know the laws by participating in the act of legislation; and he takes a lesson in the forms of government from governing. The great work of society is ever going on before his eyes, and as it were, under his hands." In addition, as Tocqueville observed, the daily newspaper, which alone "can drop the same thought into a thousand minds at the same moment," helped to keep Americans informed.

All in all, Tocqueville was immensely impressed and concluded that "the mass of those possessing an understanding of public affairs, a knowledge of law and precedents, a feeling for the best interests of the nation, and the faculty of understanding them, is greater in America than in any place else in the world."

■ The informality of the American rural courtroom, as in the painting above, never worried Tocqueville. He was certain the jury system was democracy's best method of adult education—"a gratuitous public school, ever open [that] invests each citizen with a kind of magistracy."

A Sovereign People

John Lewis Krimmel's painting of voting day in Philadelphia pictures the rowdy and colorful confusion which, Tocqueville said, accompanied all American political activity. "No sooner do you set foot upon American ground than you are stunned by a kind of tumult; a confused clamour is heard on every side, and a thousand simultaneous voices demand the satisfaction of their social wants. Everything is in motion around you." By 1832 universal white suffrage was the rule in all but a few states; while only about 60 percent of those eligible had voted in the presidential election of that year, this was double the figure for 1824. "King Caucus" had given way to the national nominating convention, and most state offices were now elective. "The people," Tocqueville said, "reign in the American political world as the Deity does in the universe."

Democracy in America

A few weeks before Tocqueville returned to France he made his only visit to Washington. The capital city, which was then barely 30 years old, did not strengthen his confidence in the vigor of the central government: "Washington offers the sight of an arid plain, burned by the sun, on which are scattered two or three sumptuous edifices and the five or six villages composing the town." He toured Capitol Hill systematically and observed all the institutions of government, including the House of Representatives, shown opposite in a detail from Samuel F. B. Morse's painting of about 1822. He met as many politicians, notably President Andrew Jackson, as time allowed. He found them, as the two drawings on this page by George Caleb Bingham suggest, clever and ambitious but lacking in statesmanship. They offered a clear demonstration of the leveling influence of democracy, he decided. The city, the politicians, even the president, lacked the grandeur and the sense of high purpose that Tocqueville had hoped to find. For the time being it did not matter, he wrote, for in the "New World . . . man has no other enemy than himself. . . . In order to be happy and to be free, he has only to determine that he will be so." The challenge would come when America would have to resort "to *conscription* and to *heavy taxation*." "Democracy," he wrote, "does not always perish from weakness and inability to act. It is not in the nature of a democratic power to lack material means, but rather moral force, stability, and skill."

If dark clouds loomed on the horizon, for the present the United States was a "remarkable spectacle." In *Democracy in America* Tocqueville wrote, "Tangible objects and ideas circulate throughout the Union. . . . Nothing checks the spirit of enterprise. The government invites the aid of all who have talents or knowledge to serve it. Inside of the frontiers of the Union profound peace prevails, as within the heart of some great empire; abroad it ranks with the most powerful nations of the earth; two thousand miles of coast are open to the commerce of the world; and as it holds the keys of a new world its flag is respected in the most remote seas. The union is happy and free as a small people, and glorious and strong as a great nation."

11/THE ROMANTIC AGE

As the United States grew larger, richer, and more centralized, it began to evolve a more distinctive culture. Still the child of Europe, by mid century it was clearly the offspring rather than an imitation of the parent society. Jefferson had drawn most of his ideas from classical authors and 17th-century English thinkers. He gave to these doctrines an American cast, as when he stressed the separation of church and state or the pursuit of happiness instead of property in describing the "unalienable rights" of men. But Ralph Waldo Emerson, whose views were roughly similar to Jefferson's and served later generations of liberals in much the way that Jefferson's did, was an *American* philosopher despite the fact that he was influenced by European thinkers.

The Romantic View of Life

In the western world the romantic movement was a revolt against the bloodless logic of the Age of Reason. It was a noticeable if unnamed point of view in Germany, France, and England as early as the 1780s and in America a generation later; by the second quarter of the 19th century few intellectuals were unmarked by it. "Romantics" believed that change and growth were the essence of life, for individuals and for institutions. They valued feeling and intuition over pure thought, stressed the differences between individuals and societies rather than the similarities. Ardent love of country characterized the movement; individualism, optimism, ingenuousness, emotion were its bywords. Whereas the Puritans, believing that nearly everyone was destined to endure the tortures of Hell for all eternity, contemplated death with dread, romantics, assuming that good people would go to Heaven, professed to look forward to death.

Romanticism perfectly fitted the mood of 19th-century America. Interest in raw nature and in primitive peoples, worship of the individual, praise of folk culture, the subordination of intellect to feeling—were these primarily romantic ideas or American ideas? Jacksonian Democracy with its self-confidence, careless prodigality, contempt for learning, glorification of the ordinary—was it a product of the American experience or a reflection of a wider world view?

The romantic way of thinking found its fullest American expression in the transcendentalist movement. Transcendentalism, a New England creation, is difficult to describe because it emphasized the indefinable and the unknowable. It was a mystical, intuitive way of looking at life that subordinated facts to feelings. Human beings were truly divine because they were part of nature, itself the essence of divinity. Their intellectual capacities did not define their capabilities, for they could "transcend" reason by having faith in themselves and in the fundamental benevolence of the universe. Transcendentalists were complete individualists, seeing the social whole as no more than the sum of its parts. Organized religion, indeed all institutions were unimportant if not counterproductive; what mattered was the single person and that people aspire, stretch *beyond* their known capabilities. Failure resulted only from lack of effort. The expression "hitch your wagon to a star" is of transcendentalist origin.

Emerson and Thoreau

The leading transcendentalist thinker was Ralph Waldo Emerson. Born in 1803 and educated at Harvard, Emerson became a minister, but in 1832 he gave up his pulpit, deciding that "the profession is antiquated." After traveling in Europe, where he met many romantic writers, including Samuel Taylor Coleridge, William Wordsworth, and (especially important) Thomas Carlyle, he settled in Concord, Massachusetts, to a long career as essayist, lecturer, and sage.

Emerson managed to restore to what he called "corpse-cold" Unitarianism the fervor and purposefulness characteristic of 17th-century Puritanism. His philosophy was at once buoyantly optimistic and rigorously intellectual, self-confident and conscientious. In a notable address at Harvard in 1837 on "The American Scholar," he urged Americans to put aside their devotion to things European and seek inspiration in their immediate surroundings. He saw himself as pitting "spiritual powers" against "the mechanical powers and the mechanical philosophy of this time." The new industrial society of New England disturbed him profoundly.

Emerson favored change and believed in progress. It was America's destiny to fulfill "the postponed expectations of the world." Temperamentally, however, he was too serene and too much his own man to fight for the causes other reformers espoused, and he was too idealistic to accept the compromises that most reformers make to achieve their ends.

Because he put so much emphasis on self-reliance, Emerson disliked powerful governments. "The less government we have the better," he said. In a sense he was the prototype of some modern alienated intellectuals, so repelled by the world as it was that he would not actively try to change it. Nevertheless he thought strong leadership essential, perhaps being influenced in this direction by his friend Carlyle's glorification of the role of great men in history. "The wise man is the

State," Emerson argued. He also had a strong practical streak. He made his living by lecturing, tracking tirelessly across the country, talking before every type of audience for fees ranging from fifty to several hundred dollars.

Closely identified with Emerson was his Concord neighbor Henry David Thoreau. After graduating from Harvard in 1837, Thoreau taught school for a time and helped out in a small pencil-making business run by his family. He was a strange man, gentle, a dreamer, content to absorb the beauties of nature almost intuitively, yet stubborn and individualistic to the point of selfishness. "He is the most unmalleable fellow alive," one acquaintance wrote. The hectic scramble for wealth that he saw all about him he found disgusting—and alarming, for he believed it was destroying both the natural and the human resources of the country.

Like Emerson, Thoreau objected to many of society's restrictions on the individual. "That government is best which governs not at all," he said, going both Emerson and the Jeffersonians one better. He was perfectly prepared to see himself as a majority of one. "When were the good and the brave ever in a majority?" he asked. "If a man does not keep pace with his companions," he wrote on another occasion, "perhaps it is because he hears a different drummer."

In 1845 Thoreau decided to put to the test his theory that a person need not depend on society for a satisfying existence. He built a cabin at Walden Pond on some property owned by Emerson and lived there alone for two years. He did not try to be entirely self-sufficient: he was not above returning to his family or to Emerson's for a square meal on occasion, and he generally purchased the building materials and other manufactured articles that he needed. Instead he set out, by experimenting, to prove that *if necessary* an individual could get along without the products of civilization. He used manufactured plaster in building his Walden cabin, but he also gathered a bushel of clamshells and made a small quantity of lime himself, to prove that it could be done.

At Walden Thoreau wrote *A Week on the Concord and Merrimack Rivers* (1849), which utilized an account of a trip he had taken with his brother as a vehicle for a discussion of his ideas about life and literature. He spent much time observing the quiet world around the pond, thinking, and writing in his journal. The best fruit of this period was that extraordinary book, *Walden* (1854). Superficially *Walden* is the story of Thoreau's experiment, moving and beautifully written. It is also an acid indictment of the social behavior of the average American, an attack on unthinking conformity, on subordinating one's own judgment to that of the herd.

The most graphic illustration of Thoreau's confidence in his own values occurred while he was living at Walden. At that time the Mexican War was raging (see pages 295–301). Thoreau considered the war immoral because it advanced the cause of slavery. To protest he refused to pay his Massachusetts poll tax. For this he was arrested and lodged in jail, although only for one night because an aunt promptly paid the tax for him. His essay "Civil Disobedience," explaining his view of the proper relation between the individual and the state, resulted from this experience. Like Emerson, however, Thoreau refused to participate in practical reform movements.

Edgar Allan Poe

The work of all the imaginative writers of the period reveals romantic influences, and it is possibly an indication of the affinity of the romantic approach to American conditions that a number of excellent writers of poetry and fiction first appeared in the 1830s and 1840s. Edgar Allan Poe, one of the most remarkable, seems almost a caricature of the romantic image of the tortured genius. Poe was born in Boston in 1809, the son of poor actors who died before he was 3. He was raised by a wealthy Virginian, John Allan.

Few persons as neurotic as Poe have been able to produce first-rate work. In college he ran up debts of $2,500 in less than a year and had to withdraw. He won an appointment to West Point but was discharged after a few months for disobedience and "gross neglect of duty." He was a lifelong alcoholic and an occasional taker of dope. He married a child of 13. Once he attempted to poison himself; repeatedly he was down and out even to the verge of starvation. He was haunted by melancholia and hallucinations. Yet he was an excellent magazine editor, a penetrating critic, a poet of unique if somewhat narrow talents, and a fine short story writer. Although he died at 40, he turned out a large volume of serious, highly original work.

Poe responded strongly to the lure of romanticism. In his youth he aped Lord Byron, and Coleridge profoundly influenced his approach to writing. His works abound with examples of wild imagination and fascination with mystery, fright, and the occult. He was not, however, an imitator. If he did not invent the detective story, he perfected it; his tales "The Murders in the Rue Morgue" and "The Purloined Letter" stressed the thought processes of a clever detective in solving a mystery by reasoning from evidence. Poe was one

of the earliest writers to deal with what are today called science fiction themes, and "The Pit and the Pendulum" and "The Cask of Amontillado" show that he was a master of the horror tale.

Although dissolute in his personal life, when Poe touched pen to paper, he became a disciplined craftsman. The most fantastic passages in his works are the result of careful, reasoned selection; not a word, he believed, could be removed without damage to the whole. And despite his rejection of most of the values prized by middle-class America, Poe was widely read in his own day. His poem "The Raven" won instantaneous popularity when it was published in 1845. Had he been a little more stable, he might have made a good living with his pen—but in that case he might not have written as he did.

Nathaniel Hawthorne

Another product of the prevailing romanticism was Nathaniel Hawthorne of Salem, Massachusetts. Hawthorne was born in 1804. When he was a small child, his father died and his grief-stricken mother became a recluse. Left largely to his own devices, he grew to be a lonely, introspective person, bookish and imaginative. Wandering about New England by himself in summertime, he soaked up local lore, which he drew upon in writing short stories. For a time he lived in Concord, where he came to know most of the leading transcendentalists. However, he disliked the egoism of the transcendental point of view and rejected its bland optimism outright. "Emerson," he said, was an "everlasting rejector of all that is, and seeker for he knows not what." Emerson, for his part, could not enjoy Hawthorne's writings because of their pervasive air of gloom.

Hawthorne was fascinated by the past, particularly by the Puritan heritage of New England and its continuing influence on his own generation. He scorned "minute fidelity" to the real world in his fiction, seeking "a severer truth . . . the truth of the human heart." But he was active in politics, and an admirer of Andrew Jackson. Three Democratic presidents—Van Buren, Polk, and Franklin Pierce, the last a classmate of his at Bowdoin College— appointed him to minor political offices.

Hawthorne's early stories, originally published in magazines, were brought together in *Twice-Told*

■ Both Poe (above, in a portrait by Samuel Osgood) and Hawthorne (below) won popular recognition in their day. Poe's *The Raven and Other Poems* (1845) sold widely, while Hawthorne's *The Scarlet Letter* (1850) became a best seller the year it was published.

Tales (1837). They made excellent use of New England culture and history for background but were concerned chiefly with the struggles of individuals with sin, guilt, and especially the pride and isolation that often afflict those who place too great reliance on their own judgment. His greatest works were two novels written after the Whigs turned him out of his government job in 1849. *The Scarlet Letter* (1850), a grim yet sympathetic analysis of adultery, condemned not the woman, Hester Prynne, but the people who presumed to judge her. *The House of the Seven Gables* (1851) was a gripping account of the decay of an old New England family.

Like Poe, Hawthorne was appreciated in his own day and widely read; unlike Poe, he made a modest amount of money from his work. Yet he was never very comfortable in the society he inhabited. Thoreau considered him "simple and childlike," and another writer spoke of his "tenderness" and "boundless sympathy with all forms of being." Nevertheless, there was a certain gruffness in him too. He had no patience with the second-rate. And despite his success in creating word pictures of a somber, mysterious world, he considered America too prosaic a country to inspire good literature. "There is no shadow, no antiquity, no mystery, no picturesque and gloomy wrong, nor anything but a commonplace prosperity," he complained.

Herman Melville

In 1850, while writing *The House of the Seven Gables*, Hawthorne was introduced by his publisher to another writer in the midst of a novel. This was Herman Melville, the book *Moby Dick.* The two became good friends at once, for despite their dissimilar backgrounds, they had a great deal in common. Melville was a New Yorker, born in 1819, one of eight children of a merchant of distinguished lineage. His father, however, lost all his money and died when the boy was 12. Herman left school at 15, worked briefly as a bank clerk, and in 1837 went to sea. For 18 months, in 1841–1842, he was crewman on the whaler *Acushnet.* Then he jumped ship in the South Seas. For a time he lived among a tribe of cannibals in the Marquesas; later he made his way to Tahiti, where he idled away nearly a year. In August 1843 he secured a berth on a passing American warship, the frigate *United States*. After another year at sea he returned to America in the fall of 1844.

Although he had never before attempted serious writing, in 1846 he published *Typee*, an account of his life in the Marquesas. The book was a great success, for Melville had visited a part of the world almost unknown to Americans, and his descriptions of his bizarre experiences suited the taste of a romantic age. "The man who had lived among the cannibals" became suddenly a well-known figure. Success inspired him to write a sequel, *Omoo* (1847); other books followed quickly.

As he wrote Melville became conscious of deeper powers. He read widely, thought profoundly. In 1849 he began a systematic study of Shakespeare, pondering the bard's intuitive grasp of human nature. *Antony and Cleopatra* and *King Lear* particularly intrigued him. Like Hawthorne, Melville could not accept the prevailing optimism of his generation. Unlike his friend, he admired Emerson, seconding the Emersonian demand that Americans reject European ties and develop their own literature. "Believe me," he wrote, "men not very much inferior to Shakespeare are this day being born on the banks of the Ohio." Yet he considered Emerson's vague talk about striving and the inherent goodness of mankind complacent nonsense, his individualism "a self-conceit so intensely intellectual and calm that at first one hesitates to call it by its right name."

Experience made Melville too aware of the evil in the world to be a transcendentalist. His novel *Redburn* (1849), based on his adventures on a Liverpool packet, was, as the critic F. O. Matthiessen put it, "a study in disillusion, of innocence confronted with the world, of ideals shattered by facts." Yet Melville was no cynic; he expressed deep sympathy for the Indians and for immigrants, crowded like animals into the holds of transatlantic vessels. He denounced the brutality of discipline in the United States Navy in *White-Jacket* (1850). His essay "The Tartarus of Maids," a moving if somewhat overdrawn description of young women working in a paper factory, protested the subordination of human beings to machines.

Hawthorne, whose dark view of human nature coincided with his own, encouraged Melville to press ahead with *Moby Dick* (1851). This book, Melville said, was "broiled in hellfire." Against

■ During the creative surge that produced *Moby Dick*, Melville overflowed with new ideas, asking a friend for "fifty fast-writing youths with an easy style."

the background of a whaling voyage (no better account of whaling has ever been written), he dealt subtly and symbolically with the problems of good and evil, of courage and cowardice, of faith, stubbornness, pride. In Captain Ahab, driven relentlessly to hunt down the huge white whale Moby Dick, which had destroyed his leg, Melville created one of the great figures of literature; in the book as a whole, he produced one of the finest novels written by an American, comparable to the best in any language.

As Melville's work became more profound, it lost its appeal to the average reader, and its originality and symbolic meaning escaped most of the critics. *Moby Dick*, his masterpiece, received little attention and most of that unfavorable. Melville had not expected the book to be popular. "Dollars damn me," he told Hawthorne, to whom *Moby Dick* was dedicated. "What I feel most moved to write, that is banned,—it will not pay." He kept on writing until his death in 1891 but was virtually ignored. Only in the 1920s did the critics rediscover him and give him his merited place in the history of American literature.

■ A daguerreotype of Whitman, taken during the late 1840s when he was a journalist in New York and, briefly, the editor of the Brooklyn *Eagle*.

Walt Whitman

Walt Whitman, whose *Leaves of Grass* (1855) was the last of the great literary works of this brief outpouring of genius, was the most romantic and by far the most distinctly American writer of his age. He was born on Long Island, outside New York City, in 1819. At 13 he left school and became a printer's devil; thereafter he held a succession of newspaper jobs in the metropolitan area. He was an ardent Jacksonian and later a Free Soiler, which got him into hot water with a number of the publishers for whom he worked.

Although genuinely a "common man," thoroughly at home among tradesmen and laborers, he was surely not an ordinary man. Deeply introspective, he read omnivorously, if in a rather disorganized fashion. He soaked up Homer, Dante, Shakespeare, Goethe, Carlyle, Scott, and many others, meanwhile working out a new, intensely personal mode of expression. During the early 1850s, while employed as a carpenter and composing the poems that made up *Leaves of Grass*, he regularly carried a book of Emerson in his lunch box. "I was simmering, simmering, simmering,"

he later recalled. "Emerson brought me to a boil." The transcendental idea that inspiration and aspiration are at the heart of all achievement captivated him. A poet could best express himself, he believed, by relying uncritically on his natural inclinations without regard for rigid metrical forms. In this sense Whitman was the opposite of Poe, the careful literary craftsman (whose work he characterized as "brilliant and dazzling, but with no heat").

Leaves of Grass consisted of a preface, in which Whitman made the extraordinary statement that Americans had "probably the fullest poetical nature" of any people in history, and 12 strange poems in free verse: rambling, uneven, appearing to most readers shocking both in the commonplace nature of the subject matter and the coarseness of the language. Emerson, Thoreau, and a few others saw a fresh talent in these poems, but most readers and reviewers found them offensive. Indeed, the work was so undisciplined and so much of it had no obvious meaning that it was easy to miss the many passages of great beauty and originality that were scattered throughout.

Part of Whitman's difficulty arose because there was much of the charlatan in his makeup; often his writing did not ring true. He loved to use foreign words and phrases, and since he had no more than a smattering of any foreign language, he frequently sounded pretentious and sometimes downright foolish when he did so. In reality a sensitive, effeminate person, he tried to pose as a great, rough character. (Later in his career he bragged of fathering no less than six illegitimate children, which was assuredly untrue.) He never married, and his work suggests that his strongest emotional ties were with men. He displayed a great deal of the American love of show and bombast. Thomas Carlyle once remarked shrewdly that Whitman thought he was a big man because he lived in a big country.

Whitman's work was more authentically American than that of any contemporary. His egoism—he titled one of his finest poems "Song of Myself"—was tempered by his belief that he was typical of all humanity.

> I celebrate myself, and sing myself,
> And what I assume you shall assume,
> For every atom belonging to me as good
>   belongs to you.

He had a remarkable ear for rendering common speech poetically, for employing slang, for catching the breezy informality of Americans and their faith in themselves.

> Earth! you seem to look for something at my hands,
> Say, old top-knot, what do you want?
>
> I bequeath myself to the dirt to grow from the
> grass I love,
> If you want me again look for me under your
> boot-soles.

Because of these qualities and because in his later work, especially during the Civil War, he occasionally struck a popular chord, Whitman was never as neglected as Melville. When he died in 1892, he was, if not entirely understood, at least widely appreciated.

"The Flowering of New England"

Emerson, Thoreau, Poe, Hawthorne, Melville, and Whitman were the great figures of American literature before the Civil War. A number of others, if they lacked genius, are worth reading. One was Henry Wadsworth Longfellow. In 1835, while still in his twenties, Longfellow became professor of modern languages at Harvard. Although he published a fine translation of Dante's *The Divine Comedy* and was expert in many languages, his fame came from his poems, "The Village Blacksmith," "Paul Revere's Ride," *The Courtship of Miles Standish*, a sentimental tale of Pilgrim days, and *The Song of Hiawatha*, the romantic retelling of an Indian legend. These brought him excellent critical notices and considerable fortune; his work was widely translated and reprinted.

Though musical, polished, full of vivid images, Longfellow's poetry lacked profundity, originality, and force, as he did himself. But it was neither cheap nor trivial. When Longfellow wrote

> Life is real! life is earnest!
> And the grave is not its goal . . .

he expressed the heartfelt belief of most of his generation. In this sense he captured the spirit of his times better than any of his great contemporaries, better even than Whitman.

Longfellow was the most talented of a group of minor New England writers who collectively gave that section great intellectual vitality in the decades before the Civil War. Prominent in this "flowering of New England" was John Greenleaf Whittier, a poet nearly as popular as Longfellow in his day. Whittier believed ardently in the abolition of slavery and worked actively in politics and journalism. A few of his poems can still be read with pleasure, among them "The Barefoot Boy," dealing with his rural childhood. Somewhat more weighty was the achievement of James Russell Lowell, the first editor of the *Atlantic Monthly*, founded in Boston in 1857. Lowell's first series of *Biglow Papers* (1848), humorous stories written in the New England dialect, made an original and influential contribution to the national literature. Dr. Oliver Wendell Holmes, professor of medicine at Harvard, was widely known as a poet and essayist. A few of his poems, such as "The Chambered Nautilus" and "Old Ironsides," are interesting examples of American romantic verse, and his "Autocrat of the Breakfast-Table" series in the *Atlantic Monthly* became a regional if not a national institution.

Collectively these minor writers had a salutary effect on American culture, for if rather smug and narrow, they were serious and industrious. If they did not often soar, at least they fixed their gaze upward and encouraged their readers to do likewise.

So did the important historians of the period, all of them New Englanders. George Bancroft, one of the first Americans to study in Germany, began in 1834 to publish a 10-volume *History of the United States* based on thorough research. William Hickling Prescott, though nearly blind, wrote extensively on the history of Spain and Spain's American empire, his *Conquest of Mexico* (1843) and *Conquest of Peru* (1847) being his most important works. John Lothrop Motley, another German-trained historian, published his *Rise of the Dutch Republic* in 1856, and Francis Parkman began his great account of the struggle between France and Great Britain for the control of North America with *Conspiracy of Pontiac* in 1851.

The public read these histories avidly. They suited the taste of the times, they were written with a mass audience in mind, and they were thoroughly in the romantic tradition. As David Levin said in his important study *History as Romantic*

Art, "they all shared an 'enthusiastic' attitude toward the Past, an affection for grand heroes, an affection for Nature and the 'natural.'"

Southern Writers

Southern literature was even more markedly romantic than that of New England. John Pendleton Kennedy of Baltimore wrote several novels with regional historical themes, much in the manner of Sir Walter Scott. Kennedy was also a Whig politician of some importance who served several terms in Congress; in 1852 he became secretary of the navy in the Fillmore Cabinet. The more versatile and influential William Gilmore Simms of South Carolina wrote nearly two dozen novels, several volumes of poetry, and a number of biographies. At his peak in the 1830s he earned as much as $6,000 a year with his pen. His favorite theme was the South Carolina frontier, which he portrayed in *The Partisan* (1835), one of a series of novels dealing with the Revolution, and *The Yemassee* (1835), the story of an early 18th-century Indian war. His novels seem too melodramatic for modern tastes; the plots lack variety, the style lacks discipline. His portraits of the planter class are too bloodless and reverential to be convincing, and his female characters are nearly all pallid and fragile. Only when he wrote of the frontier life and its people did his work possess much power, yet along with Kennedy he contributed largely to the glamorous legend of the Old South.

The Spread of Culture

As the population grew and became more concentrated, and as society, especially in the North, was permeated by a middle-class point of view, popular concern for "culture" in the formal sense increased. A literate and prosperous people, committed to the idea of education but not generally well educated, became devoted to "self-improvement," to being "refined" and "civilized." Industrialization made it easier to satisfy the demand for culture, though at the same time the new machines tended to make the artifacts of culture more stereotyped. Efficient printing techniques reduced the cost of books, magazines, and newspa-

pers. By the late 1850s one publisher was able to offer a 50-volume set of the ever popular Sir Walter Scott for $37.50.

The first penny newspaper was the New York *Sun* (1833), but James Gordon Bennett's New York *Herald,* founded in 1835, brought the new cheap journalism to perfection. The penny papers depended on sensation, crime stories, and society gossip to attract readers, and they covered the important news too.

In the 1850s the moralistic and sentimental "domestic" novel was in its prime. The most successful writers in this genre were women, which led Hawthorne to complain bitterly that "a d - - - - d mob of scribbling women" was taking over American writing. Typical were Susan Warner's *The Wide, Wide World* (1850), a sad tale about a pious, submissive girl who cried "more readily and more steadily than any other tormented child in a novel of the time," and Maria Cummins' *The Lamplighter* (1854), the story of little Gerty, an orphan rescued by a kindly lamplighter named Trueman Flint. *The Lamplighter* sold 70,000 copies within a year of publication. As Carl Bode wrote in *The Anatomy of American Popular Culture,* these works were "the great-grandmother" of the 20th-century soap opera.

Besides reading countless volumes of sentimental nonsense (the books of another novelist, Mary Jane Holmes, sold over a million copies in these years), Americans consumed many volumes of religious literature. In 1840 the American Tract Society disposed of 3 million copies of its publications; in 1855 the total exceeded 12 million. The society had hundreds of missionary-salesmen, called colporteurs, who roamed the country preaching the gospel and selling or giving away tracts and religious books. These publications avoided denominational controversies and advocated an evangelical brand of Christianity. They bore titles such as "Quench Not the Spirit" (over 900,000 copies distributed by 1850) and "The Way to Heaven." The American Bible Society flourished, issuing hundreds of thousands of copies of the Old and New Testaments each year. Americans also devoured many books on self-improvement, some aimed at uplifting the reader's character, others, which would today be called "how-to-do-it" books, at teaching everything from raising chickens to carving tombstones.

Education and Art

The popular thirst for knowledge and culture led to improvements in education. All the states had some public schools by the 1850s, and the idea that free schools were only for paupers was gradually dying. Even in the South, where wealthy planters employed tutors for their children and had little interest in public education, the trend was toward schooling at state expense. During the 1850s school attendance in the section increased by 40 percent, the number of schools by 50 percent, public money spent for education by almost 100 percent.

Some historians believe that the advocates of public support for high schools were not really interested in improving the education of the masses. They point out that most of the students in these schools came from middle-class families. Less well-to-do children usually had to work; their parents tended to oppose or to be indifferent to secondary school training. *Compulsory* education

was still almost nonexistent. This view is controversial, but whatever the motives of the friends of public education, the result of their efforts was a gradual improvement in the general level of education in the nation. And leaders of the public education movement, such as Horace Mann, first secretary of the Massachusetts Board of Education, and Henry Barnard of Connecticut, editor of the *American Journal of Education* and in later years the first United States commissioner of education, were also laying the foundations for the development of teaching as a true profession.

Much remained to be accomplished. Many conservatives objected to public education on the ground that it undermined individual self-reliance. Some of them, however, gave generous support to private schemes designed to help the masses gain knowledge. Rich men such as John Jacob Astor of New York and George Peabody of Massachusetts endowed libraries and colleges. The Lowell Institute, established in Boston in 1836 to sponsor free public lectures, and the Cooper

■ From one extreme to another: a Shaker chair (left) notable for its perfectly plain and uncluttered lines contrasted with a fantasia of an armchair (right) which is described as a "rich and fanciful" piece whose decorations are emblems of "repose profound."

Union, set up by the industrialist Peter Cooper in the late 1850s to offer courses in practical subjects for workers, were but the most important of many such institutions. Mechanics' libraries sprang up in every industrial center and attracted so many readers that pressure was soon applied to grant them state funds. In 1848 Massachusetts led the way by authorizing the use of public money to back the Boston Public Library, and soon several states had authorized local communities to found tax-supported libraries.

The surge of desire for knowledge and culture in America is well illustrated by the success of the mutual improvement societies known as lyceums. The movement began in Great Britain; in the United States its father was Josiah Holbrook, an itinerant lecturer and sometime schoolmaster from Connecticut. Holbrook founded the first lyceum in 1826 at Millbury, Massachusetts; within five years there were over a thousand scattered across the country. The lyceums conducted discussions, established libraries, and lobbied for

better schools. Soon they began to sponsor lecture series on topics of every sort. Many of the nation's political and intellectual leaders, such as Emerson, Melville, Webster, Holmes, and Lowell, regularly graced their platforms along with other, less demanding speakers.

In the 1830s and 1840s new techniques made it possible to weave colored patterns into cloth by machine, to manufacture wallpaper printed with complicated designs, and to produce rugs and hangings that looked like tapestries. Combined with the use of machine methods in the furniture business, these inventions had a powerful impact on public taste. That impact, at least in the short run, was aesthetically unfortunate; manufacturers were carried away by the possibilities opened up by their new machinery. As Russell Lynes writes in his entertaining study *The Tastemakers*, "Styles ran riot. The new mechanical methods of making furniture gave designers a free hand to indulge their delight in ornamentation. . . . The new chairs and sofas, bedecked with fruit, flowers, and beast-

■ This front elevation of a Gothic "ornamented cottage" is taken from *The Model Architect: A Series of Original Designs For Cottages, Villas, Suburban Residences, Etc.*, published in Philadelphia by Samuel Sloan in 1868.

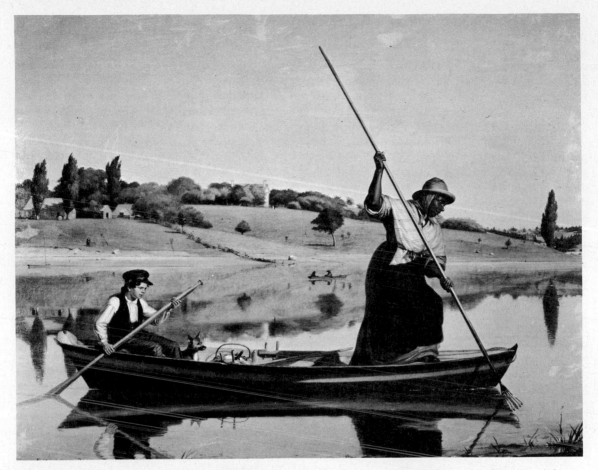

■ A lifelong resident of rural Long Island, William Sidney Mount took everyday life of that corner of America as his inspiration. *Eel Spearing at Setauket* (1845) is one of his most characteristic canvases. Mount's subject matter had universal appeal; his art sold widely in engraved form in Europe.

ies and standing on twisted spindles, crowded into living rooms and parlors."

The new wood-turning machinery added to the popularity of the elaborately decorated "Gothic" style of architecture. The irregularity and uniqueness of Gothic buildings suited the prevailing romanticism; their aspiring towers, steeples, and arches and their flexibility (a new wing or extension could always be added without spoiling the effect) made them especially attractive to a people enamored of progress. The huge pile of pink masonry of the Smithsonian Institution in Washington, with its nine distinct types of towers, represents American Gothic at its most giddy and lugubrious stage. Designed in 1846 by James Renwick, the building confounded generations of architects, but with the passage of time it came to

seem the perfect setting for the vast collection of mementoes that fill "the nation's attic." The best of the Gothic designers was probably Andrew Jackson Downing, author of *The Architecture of Country Houses* (1850). "Greek" and "Italian" styles also flourished in this period, the former particularly in the South; elsewhere the Gothic was by all odds the most popular.

Increasingly, Americans of the period were purchasing native art. George Catlin, who painted hundreds of pictures of Indians and their surroundings, all rich in authentic detail, displayed his work before admiring crowds in many cities. Outstanding genre painters (artists whose canvases told stories, usually drawn from everyday life), most notably William Sidney Mount of New York and George Caleb Bingham of Missouri, were successful with both genre paintings and portraits. Rumor had it that Mount received $1,000 for his first important canvas; Bingham's paintings commanded excellent prices; and the public bought engravings of the work of both men in enormous numbers.

The more academic artists of the period were popular as well. The "luminists" and members of the romantic Hudson River school specialized in grandiose pictures of wild landscapes. Their best work was distinctively American, and some of them disposed of their canvases at good prices. In the 1840s Thomas Doughty regularly collected $500 each for his paintings. The works of Asher B.

■ Miniature copies of Hiram Powers' *The Greek Slave*, Henry James said, stood "exposed under little glass covers" in parlors from Boston to San Francisco.

Durand, John Kensett, and Thomas Cole were in demand. The collector Luman Reed commissioned five large Cole canvases for an allegorical series, *The Course of Empire*, and crowds flocked to see another of Cole's series, *The Voyage of Life*, when it was exhibited in New York.

In 1839 the American Art-Union was formed in New York to encourage native art. The Art-Union hit on the ingenious device of selling what were in effect lottery tickets and using the proceeds to purchase paintings, which became the prizes in the lottery. Annual "memberships" sold for $5; 814 subscribed in 1839, nearly 19,000 10 years later. Soon the Art-Union was giving every member an engraving of one of its principal prizes. The organization had to disband after a New York court outlawed the lottery in 1851, but in 1854 a new Cosmopolitan Art-Union was established in Ohio. In the years before the Civil War it boomed, reaching a peak of 38,000 members and paying as much as $6,000 for an individual work—the sculptor Hiram Powers' boneless female nude, *The Greek Slave*. It also distributed an art magazine and each year gave a young artist a gold medal and $2,000 for foreign study.

The art-unions made little effort to encourage innovators, but they were a boon to many artists. The American Art-Union paid out as much as $40,000 for its prizes in a single year. By distributing thousands upon thousands of engravings and colored prints, they introduced competent American works of art into middle-class homes.

Beginning in the late 1850s the prints of the firm of Currier and Ives brought a crude but charming kind of art to a still wider audience. Currier and Ives lithographs portrayed horse racing, trains, rural landscapes, and "every tender domestic moment, every sign of national progress, every regional oddity, every private or public disaster from a cut finger to a forest fire." They were issued in very large editions and sold for as little as 15 cents.

An Age of Reform

Why reform movements proliferated at this time can be explained in a number of ways, none entirely satisfactory but all enlightening. The new optimism of revivalistic religion, with its rejection of the Calvinist view of original sin and predestination and its emphasis on the idea that eternal salvation was available to all good Christians, made people confident that life on earth was potentially rewarding for all. But if sin were, so to speak, voluntary, every decent person must try to eliminate it. Although transcendentalists like Emerson and Thoreau were seldom active in reform movements, the transcendental stress on striving played a role, and so did the Jeffersonian faith in the power of reason and the belief in progress shared by frontier farmers and middle-class eastern businessmen.

On the other hand, many Americans were disturbed by the persistence of social problems in the Republic. Crime and vice, they discovered, did not disappear simply because the people now governed themselves. The question is complicated by the varying motives of the reformers, some of whom interpreted change as meaning a return to an older, golden age rather than a march toward a new utopia. Not all reforms were democratic in spirit, not all reformers optimists about human nature.

Belief in progress, however, was almost axiomatic among Americans; people who had accomplished so much found it easy to believe that nothing was impossible. "Everything may be made better," a Massachusetts clergyman said in 1844, a remark that would have appeared almost blasphemous to his Puritan predecessors. At the same time, progress led to social dislocations that stimulated interest in reform. Industrialization posed problems affecting labor, city life, and economic organization. The more society improved, the more it required tinkering—or so it seemed.

The same sense of destiny that had influenced the decisions of the Founding Fathers when they shaped the country's political institutions now possessed the minds of persons interested in social institutions. The key word here is *institutions.* Most reformers were environmentalists; they believed that human beings were shaped by their surroundings—by the way they were brought up and by the society in which they lived. "Criminals," Professor Francis Lieber wrote in 1835, are "led to crime by the bad example of their parents." "To the defects of our social organization," another reformer claimed, "we chiefly owe the increase of evil doers." The fact of rapid growth lent an air of urgency to the reform spirit; it made reformers more radical and more intolerant. For the

moment all was in flux, society was indeed malleable. But how long would this last? In discussing educational reform in 1848, Horace Mann spoke of "a futurity, now fluid" but soon "to be struck into adamant."

The idea that Americans should create new institutions and the transcendental, individualistic distrust of all institutions (combined with the easy availability of land) led many reformers to test their theories by establishing experimental communities. The "communitarian" point of view aimed at "commencing a wholesale social reorganization by first establishing and demonstrating its principles completely on a small scale." The first communitarians were religious reformers. In a sense the Pilgrims fall into this category, along with a number of other groups in colonial times, but only in the 19th century did the idea flourish.

One of the earliest significant groups was founded by George Rapp, who brought some 600 Germans to western Pennsylvania in 1804. Rappites renounced marriage and sex and took every word in the Bible literally. They believed that the millennium was at hand; people must have their affairs constantly in order so as to be ready to meet their Maker on short notice. Industrious, pious, and isolated from other Americans by their language and beliefs, the Rappites prospered but had little influence on their neighbors.

More influential were the Shaker communities founded by an English woman, Ann Lee, who came to America in 1774. Mother Ann, as she was called, saw visions which convinced her that Christ would come to earth again as a woman and that she was that woman. With a handful of followers she founded a community near Albany, New York. The group grew rapidly, and after her death in 1784 her movement continued to expand. By the 1830s her followers had established about 20 successful communities.

Like the Rappites, the Shakers practiced celibacy; believing that the millennium was imminent, they saw no reason for perpetuating the human race. Each group lived in a large Family House, the sexes strictly segregated. Property was held in common but controlled by a ruling hierarchy. So much stress was placed on equality of labor and reward and on voluntary acceptance of the rules, however, that the system does not seem to have been oppressive.

The Shaker religion, joyful and fervent, was

marked by much group singing and dancing, which provided the members with emotional release from their tightly controlled regimen. An industrious, skillful people, they made a special virtue of simplicity; some of their designs for buildings and, especially, furniture achieved a classic beauty seldom equaled among untutored artisans. Despite their odd customs, the Shakers were universally tolerated and even admired.

There were many other religious colonies, such as the Amana Community, which flourished in New York and Iowa in the 1840s and 1850s, and John Humphrey Noyes' Oneida Community, where the members practiced "complex" marriage—a form of promiscuity based on the principle that every man in the group was married to every woman—and prospered by developing a number of manufacturing skills. Brook Farm, the famous transcendental retreat founded "to combine the thinker and the worker" and "do away with the necessity of menial services," was essentially a religious experiment at the start. Brook Farm experimenters tried to accomplish through cooperation what Thoreau sought to do at Walden by himself, "to impart," as their constitution stated, "a greater freedom, simplicity, truthfulness, refinement, and moral dignity, to our mode of life."

The most important of the religious communitarians were the Mormons. A remarkable Vermont farm boy, Joseph Smith, founded the religion in western New York in the 1820s. Smith saw visions; he claimed to have discovered and translated an ancient text, the *Book of Mormon*, written in hieroglyphics on plates of gold, which described the adventures of a tribe of Israelites that had populated America from biblical times until their destruction in a great war in 400 A.D. With a small band of followers, Smith established a community in Ohio in 1831. The Mormons' dedication and economic efficiency attracted large numbers of converts, but their unorthodox religious views and their exclusivism, product of their sense of being a chosen people, roused resentment among unbelievers. They were forced to move first to Missouri and then back to Illinois, where in 1839 they founded the town of Nauvoo.

Nauvoo flourished—by 1844 it was the largest city in the state, with a population of 15,000—but once again the Mormons ran into local trouble.

They quarreled among themselves, especially after Smith secretly authorized polygamy (he called it "celestial marriage") and a number of other unusual rites for members of the "Holy Order," the top leaders of the church.* They created a paramilitary organization, the Nauvoo Legion, headed by Smith, envisaging themselves as a kind of semi-independent state within the federal Union. Smith announced that he was a candidate for president of the United States. Rumors circulated that the Mormons intended to take over the entire Northwest for their "empire." Once again local "gentiles" rose against them; Smith was arrested, then murdered by a mob.

Under a new leader, Brigham Young, the Mormons sought a haven beyond the frontier. In 1847 they marched westward, pressing through the mountains until they reached the desolate wilderness on the shores of Great Salt Lake. There, at last, they established their Zion and began to make their truly significant impact on American history. Irrigation made the desert flourish, precious water wisely being treated as a community asset. Hard, cooperative, intelligently directed effort spelled growth and prosperity; more than 11,000 people were living in the area when it became part of Utah Territory as a result of the Compromise of 1850. In time the communal Mormon settlement broke down, but the religion has remained, along with a distinctive Mormon culture that has been a major force in the shaping of the West. The Mormon church is still by far the most powerful single influence in Utah and a thriving organization in many other parts of the United States and in Europe.

Despite their many common characteristics, the religious communities varied enormously; subordination of the individual to the group did not destroy group individualism. Their sexual practices, for example, ranged from the "complex marriage" of the Oneidans through Mormon polygamy and the ordinary monogamy of the Brook Farmers to the reluctant acceptance of sexual intercourse by the Amana Community and the absolute celibacy of the Rappites and Shakers. The

---

*The justification of polygamy, paradoxically, was that marriage was a sacred, eternal state. If a man remarried after his wife's death, eventually he would have two wives in Heaven. Therefore why not on earth?

■ These scenes are from a canvas scroll painted by C.C.A. Christensen which illuminated early Mormon history. Above, a mob attacks a Mormon settlement in Missouri in the 1830s. Moving to Illinois, Joseph Smith organized the Nauvoo Legion (below) to defend his people.

communities are more significant as reflections of the urgent reform spirit of the age than they are for their accomplishments.

The communities had some influence on reformers who wished to experiment with social organization. When Robert Owen, a British utopian socialist who believed in economic as well as political equality and who considered competition debasing, decided to create an ideal community in America, he purchased the Rappite settlement at New Harmony, Indiana. Owen's advocacy of free love and "enlightened atheism" did not add to the stability of his group or to its popularity among outsiders. The colony was a costly failure.

The American followers of Charles Fourier, a French utopian socialist who proposed that society should be organized in cooperative units called phalanxes, fared better. Fourierism did not seek to tamper with sexual and religious mores. Its advocates included important journalists such as Horace Greeley of the New York *Tribune* and Parke Godwin of the New York *Evening Post* and many of the leading Massachusetts transcendentalists. In the 1840s several dozen Fourierist colonies were established in the northern and western states; Brook Farm, in its last years, became one of them. Members worked at whatever tasks they wished and only as much as they wished. Wages were paid according to the "repulsiveness" of the tasks performed; the person who "chose" to clean out a cesspool would receive more than someone hoeing corn or mending a fence or engaging in some task requiring complex skills. As might be expected, none of the communities lasted very long.

Practical Reformers

The communitarians were the most colorful of the reformers, their proposals the most spectacular. More effective, however, were the many individuals, some sensible, some fanatical, who worked for limited practical goals. The educational administrator Horace Mann insisted that by educating the masses class conflicts could be eradicated and the "obdurate and dark mass of avarice and ignorance and prejudice" swept out of existence. At a humbler level, many teachers tried to improve the schools by introducing new ideas drawn principally from the work of European educators.

The writings of the Swiss Johann Pestalozzi were especially influential. Pestalozzi stressed adapting the curriculum to the changing needs of the growing child. Knowledge should be acquired in a logical and orderly pattern, rote learning deemphasized. The child should be prepared to take its place in society, Pestalozzi taught, not stuffed drum-tight with useless facts. Improved education for women also got a start in this period. Emma Hunt Willard's Female Seminary at Troy, New York, was established in 1821. Mary Lyon opened Mount Holyoke College in 1837; four years earlier Oberlin had admitted women students and become the first coeducational college.

The work of Thomas Hopkins Gallaudet in developing methods for educating the deaf, culminating by 1851 in the establishment of special schools in 14 states, reflects the spirit of the times. Dr. Samuel Gridley Howe did similar work for the blind, devising means for making books with raised letters* that the blind could "read" with their fingers, and heading a school for the blind in Boston, the pioneering Perkins Institution. Howe was also interested in trying to educate the mentally defective and in other causes. "Every creature in human shape should command our respect," he insisted. "The strong should help the weak, so that the whole should advance as a band of brethren."

One of the most striking aspects of the reform movement was the emphasis on establishing special facilities for dealing with social problems. In the colonial period, orphans, indigent persons, the insane, and the feebleminded were usually cared for in private homes. Even criminals were seldom sentenced to jail terms; punishment commonly consisted of whipping, being placed in stocks in the town square, or (for serious crimes) execution. The new conviction that people were shaped by their surroundings led reformers to demand that the weak and the deviant be placed in special environments where they could be properly trained, or re-formed. The result, in the words of the historian David J. Rothman, was "the discovery of the asylum" as a place for orphans, criminals, the poor, and the insane. In the 1830s institutions of this kind were springing up in the United States like mushrooms in a forest after a summer rain.

---

*The Braille system of raised dots, invented in France, was not introduced in the United States until later in the century.

The rationale for this trend was scientific. Its spirit, however, was humane, though many of the institutions would seem anything but humane to the modern eye. The highly regarded Philadelphia prison system was based on strict solitary confinement, which was supposed to lead culprits to reflect upon their sins and then reform their ways. The prison was literally a penitentiary, a place to repent. In fact the system often drove inmates mad, and soon a rival "Auburn System" was developed in New York State, which allowed for some social contact and for work in shops and stone quarries. This system was incredibly harsh by modern standards. Absolute silence was required at all times. The prisoners were herded about in lock step and punished by brutal flogging for the slightest infraction of the rules. Nonetheless, considerable "moral and religious instruction" was provided, and the authorities sincerely intended the system to reform the inmates. When Alexis de Tocqueville and his companion Gustave de Beaumont visited the United States in the 1830s, they made a thorough study of American prisons for the French government. The Philadelphia System, they concluded, produced "the deepest impression on the soul of the convict." The Auburn System made the convict "more conformable to the habits of man in society."

The hospitals for mental patients were intended to cure inmates, not merely to confine them. The emphasis was on isolating them from the pressures of society; on order, quiet, routine; on control but not on punishment. The unfortunates were seen as *de*ranged; the task was to *ar*range their lives in a rational manner. In practice, shortages of trained personnel, niggardly legislative appropriations, and the inherent difficulty of managing violent and irrational patients often produced deplorable conditions in the asylums. This situation led Dorothea Dix, a woman of almost saintlike selflessness, to devote 30 years of her life to a campaign to improve the care of the insane. She traveled to every state in the Union and as far afield as Turkey and Japan, inspecting asylums and poorhouses. Some she praised, others she denounced. Insane persons in Massachusetts, she wrote in a memorial to the state legislature, were being kept in cages and closets, *"chained, naked, beaten with rods, and lashed into obedience!"* Her reports led to some improvement in conditions in Massachusetts and other states, but in the long

■ Dorothea Lynde Dix, the pioneer reformer who tried to improve the plight of the insane in the United States, also traveled to Europe, where she urged Queen Victoria and Pope Pius IX to support her efforts.

run the bright hopes of the reformers were never realized.

Reformers must of necessity interfere in the affairs of others; thus there is often something of the busybody and arrogant meddler in them. How they are regarded usually depends on the observer's own attitude toward their objectives. Consider the temperance movement. Most foes of alcohol opposed drinking on moral and religious rather than medical grounds, and the campaign for temperance was conducted in a spirit of religious revivalism—which might suggest to a psychologist that the reformers found in this activity the same emotional release that the drunkard finds in alcohol.

The foundation of the American Temperance Union in 1826 signaled the start of a great crusade. Employing lectures, pamphlets, rallies, essay contests, and many other techniques, the union set out to persuade people to "sign the pledge" not to drink liquor. Primitive sociological studies of the effects of drunkenness (as early as 1833 statisticians discovered a high correlation between alcoholic consumption and crime) added to the effectiveness of the campaign. Soon the union claimed a million members. In 1840 an organization of reformed drunkards, the Washingtonians, began a campaign of its own to reclaim alcoholics. One of the most effective of its workers was John B. Gough, rescued by the organization in 1842 after seven years in the gutter. "Crawl from the slimy ooze, ye drowned drunkards," Gough would shout, "and with suffocation's blue and livid lips speak out against the drink!"

The methods and the objectives of the temperance people, some of whom were demanding the prohibition of alcohol rather than mere restraint, roused bitter opposition. But they were very well organized. In a number of states they obtained strict licensing systems, heavy liquor taxes, and local option laws, then outright prohibition. In 1851 Maine passed the first effective law prohibiting the manufacture and sale of alcoholic beverages. The leader of the campaign was Mayor Neal Dow of Portland, a businessman who became a prohibitionist after seeing the damage done by drunkenness among workers in his tannery. By 1855 a dozen other states had passed laws based on the Maine statute.

The Protestant "crusade" against the Catholic church in America was also seen by its supporters as a reform. In the name of freedom, democracy, and "true" Christianity, certain Protestant groups deluged the country with tracts and sermons and at times resorted to violence against worshipers of "the whore of Babylon." Hatred of Roman Catholics, of course, antedated the first English settlements in America and had much to do with the long colonial conflict with the French in Canada. It flared up in this period chiefly because of the influx of Catholic immigrants from Ireland and Germany. Between 1830 and 1860 the Catholic population of the United States multiplied almost tenfold, rising from 318,000 to 3.1 million. Distaste for Catholics was related to dislike of cities because so many of the new immigrants, especially the Irish, were urban dwellers. (Heavy drinking by his Irish workers led Neal Dow to become anti-Catholic and to oppose unlimited immigration.)

The Abolitionist Crusade

No reform movement of this era was more significant, more ambiguous in character, or more provocative of later historical investigation than the drive to abolish slavery. That slavery should have been a cause of indignation to reformers was inevitable. Humanitarians were outraged by the master's whip and by the practice of disrupting families. Democrats protested the denial of political and civil rights to slaves. Perfectionists of all kinds deplored the fact that slaves had no chance to improve themselves.

For many years the abolition movement attracted few followers, for there seemed no way to get rid of slavery in the United States short of revolution. While a few theorists argued that the Fifth Amendment, which provides that no one may be "deprived of life, liberty, or property, without due process of law" could be interpreted to mean that the Constitution outlawed slavery, the great majority believed that the institution was not subject to federal control.

Antislavery northerners neatly compartmentalized their thinking. Slavery was wrong; they would not tolerate it in their own communities. But since the Constitution obliged them to tolerate it in the states where it existed, they felt no responsibility to fight it. Moreover, the issue was explosive enough even when limited to the question of the expansion of the institution into the territories. Those who advocated any kind of *forced* abolition seemed completely irresponsible. Most early critics of slavery therefore confined themselves to urging "colonization" or persuading slaveowners to treat their property humanely.

To blacks, the typical white northerner promised that somehow, someday, wrongs would be righted. Meanwhile, slaves should "cultivate feelings of piety and gratitude" for the "blessings" they enjoyed. What these blessings were they seldom specified. As the historian Benjamin Quarles remarked acidly, their advice was "bear and forbear."

In the highly charged atmosphere of the 1830s and 1840s a few zealots would not listen to reason. These abolitionists sought to win converts and to disrupt the slave system. They wrote pamphlets describing the horrors of slavery, edited newspapers, drafted petitions to Congress, organized

■ For 35 years *The Liberator*, edited by William Lloyd Garrison, was one of the nation's leading antislavery organs.

FAIR....FAIR!!!

The Ladies' Anti-Slavery Committee are most happy to announce to the citizens of Syracuse and vicinity, that they have received very elegant additions to what has been prepared in this place, from the ladies of Rochester, Waterloo, Cazenovia, Utica, Albany, and many other places, making up in all a most desirable and splendid assortment of

USEFUL AND FANCY ARTICLES,

which will be sold at reasonable market prices. The Committee most confidently invite the patronage of the humane and philanthropic to come and buy; remembering that it is for the poorest of the poor—even the poor slave.

☞The doors will be open at 10 o'clock on Tuesday morning, August 1st, and the sales will continue two days. Admittance 12 1-2 cents.

A Soiree will be given at the Fair on the evening of August 1st, in commemmoration of the WEST INDIA EMANCIPATION.

₊ Doors open at 7 o'clock—Collation at 8.—Speeches from the most accomplished orators of Boston and other places.

ELIZABETH RUSSELL, Syracuse;
P. S. WRIGHT, Utica;
MARY SPRINGSTEAD, Cazenovia;
SARAH VAN EPS, Vernon;
ABBY MOTT, Albany.

■ This 1834 abolitionist fund-raiser involved women from a 200-mile geographical area of upstate New York. In that same year Great Britain freed the slaves in its overseas dependencies, which explains the "Soiree" in honor of "West India Emancipation."

meetings, and lectured on the subject wherever they could attract an audience. They encouraged slaves to run away and protected and supported those who managed to escape. Concepts like equality and progress had become so great a part of their mental baggage that the logic of circumstances had little influence on them. "If we express frankly and freely our opinions," one of them pontificated, "they will give up their slaves."

Among the stern believers in principle was the Quaker Benjamin Lundy, editor of a paper called *The Genius of Universal Emancipation.* Lundy was no fanatic; he urged the use of persuasion in the South rather than interference by the federal government. But he refused to mince words and consequently he was subject to frequent harassment.

Even more provocative was Lundy's youthful assistant, William Lloyd Garrison of Massachusetts. Garrison believed in "immediate" abolition. A mild-mannered man, humanitarian in outlook, backer of many reforms, a pacifist, he was abso-

lutely unyielding in his opposition to slavery. The slaves must be freed and treated as equals, he preached. Compensated emancipation would be criminal, colonization unthinkable. Because the United States countenanced slavery, Garrison refused to engage in political activity to achieve his ends. He openly burned a copy of the Constitution—he called it an "agreement with hell"—to show his contempt for a system that tolerated human bondage. His method was to denounce and demand; he would neither compromise nor negotiate nor wait.

In 1831 Garrison established his own paper, *The Liberator.* "I am in earnest," he announced in the first issue. "I will not equivocate—I will not excuse—I will not retreat a single inch—and *I will be heard.*" Working incessantly for the cause, he organized the New England Anti-Slavery Society (1831) and the American Anti-Slavery Society (1833).

Few white Americans found Garrison's line of

argument convincing. More influential in attracting recruits was Theodore Dwight Weld, a young minister who had been converted to evangelical Christianity by Charles Grandison Finney (see page 222). Unlike Garrison, Weld was willing to advance step by step (he spoke of "immediate" emancipation "gradually" achieved) and to engage in political activity to achieve his ends. He used the methods of the evangelist to win converts; his antislavery meetings sometimes ran for days.

Of course many blacks had been abolitionists long before the white movement began to attract attention; some 50 black antislavery societies existed in 1830, and thereafter these groups grew in size and importance, being generally associated with the Garrisonian wing. White abolitionists eagerly used black speakers, especially runaway slaves, whose heartrending accounts of their experiences roused sympathies and who, merely by speaking clearly and with conviction, stood as living proof that blacks were neither animals nor fools.

Frederick Douglass, the most influential black abolitionist, was one of the most remarkable Americans of that generation. Douglass was a slave who had escaped from Maryland in 1838. Although slavery had brought him a full portion of beatings and other indignities, he had been taught to read and write and had learned a trade, opportunities denied the vast majority of bondsmen. Settling in Massachusetts, he became an agent of the Massachusetts Anti-Slavery Society and a frequent speaker at abolitionist meetings.

Douglass was a tall, majestically handsome man who radiated determination and indignation. Slavery, he told white audiences, "brands your republicanism as a sham, your humanity as a base pretense, your Christianity as a lie." In 1845 he published his autobiography, one of the most gripping accounts of a slave's life in the literature. The book attracted wide attention in America and in Europe. Douglass insisted that freedom for blacks required not merely emancipation but full equality, social and economic as well as political. Not many white northerners accepted his reasoning, but few who heard him or read his works could maintain the illusion that all blacks were dull-witted or resigned to inferior status.

At first Douglass was, in his own words, "a faithful disciple" of Garrison, prepared to tear up the Constitution and destroy the Union to gain his

■ Frederick Douglass posed for this daguerreotype in the 1840s, when he was one of the most effective spokesmen of the Massachusetts Anti-Slavery Society.

ends. In the late 1840s, however, he changed his mind, deciding that the Constitution, created to "establish Justice, insure domestic Tranquility . . . and secure the Blessings of Liberty," as its preamble states, "could not well have been designed at the same time to maintain and perpetuate a system of rapine and murder like slavery." Thereafter he fought slavery and race prejudice from within the system. This Garrison was never willing to do.

Garrison's importance and his understanding of the problem of slavery cannot be measured by the number of his followers, which was never large. He recognized that abolitionism was a revolutionary movement, not a mere reform; that achieving racial equality, not simply "freeing" the slaves, was the only way to reach the professed objective: justice for blacks. And he saw clearly how few American whites, even among the abolitionists, believed that blacks were their equals. This understanding led him to the conclusion, totally out of keeping with the view of most reformers of that day, that American society was rotten to the core; hence his refusal to make any concession to the existing establishment. He was hated in the North precisely because he rejected the idea that a Constitution that supported slavery still merited reverence, because he demanded that people choose between love of country and love of liberty.

This is not to deny that Garrison was an opinionated fanatic. He was a perfectionist, a trafficker in moral absolutes of the most rigid sort. Nevertheless, the totality of his commitment impressed many persons in spite of themselves. And events played into his hands.

Thousands of northerners, while not necessarily proslavery, were deathly afraid of what would happen if the slaves were freed. Either race war or racial intermixture (what they called "amalgamation") was sure to follow, they believed. Many antiabolitionists resorted to mob action in the effort to suppress the abolitionist movement. Throughout the North abolitionists were repeatedly insulted, jailed, manhandled, and prevented from expressing their views. One, Elijah Lovejoy, editor of an abolitionist paper in Alton, Illinois, was killed trying to defend his press against a mob. In Connecticut a young abolitionist, Prudence Crandall, opened a boarding school for black girls. She was harassed unmercifully. The legislature passed a law making her school illegal, and when she refused to close down she was thrown in jail.

In the long run such violence was counterproductive. It led more and more people with moderate views to rethink their positions, and many ended in the Garrisonian camp.

The actions of extremist southerners also aided the abolitionists. The bloody Nat Turner slave rebellion, occurring shortly after *The Liberator* began to appear, fired southern tempers against Garrison. While he had only a handful of readers in the

■ An "advertisement" for the underground railroad (which, of course, wasn't a railroad at all but individuals who smuggled escaped slaves to safety via predetermined routes), from an abolitionist journal. Escapes on the so-called Liberty Line reached a peak during the 1850s. The most successful of the 3,200 known "conductors" was Harriet Tubman, herself an escaped slave, who guided some 300 to freedom in the North.

North, southern editors, by denouncing him at length, gave his views wide publicity in their own region.

This was bad tactics but understandable, for "immediate" abolitionists like Garrison were utterly indifferent to what effect the sudden freeing of the slaves would have on the South. They adopted an oversimplified and distorted view of the problem—all southern whites were villains, all blacks saints. Garrison said he would rather be governed by "the inmates of our penitentiaries" than by southern congressmen, whom he characterized as "desperadoes." The life of a slaveowner, he wrote, "is but one of unbridled lust, of filthy amalgamation, of swaggering braggadocio, of haughty domination, of cowardly ruffianism, of boundless dissipation, of matchless insolence, of infinite self-conceit, of unequalled oppression, of more than savage cruelty." Rather than accept slavery, another abolitionist raved, "let races be swept from the face of the earth—let nations be dismembered—let dynasties be dethroned—let laws and governments, religions and reputations be cast out." "Slavery and cruelty cannot be disjoined," still another wrote, "consequently every slaveholder must be inhuman." Such specious reasoning was typical and, in the charged atmosphere of the times, destructive.

Defense of Slavery

Nearly every southerner found the abolitionists' arguments egregiously provocative. Slavery might be a less than perfect institution—what human institution was not?—yet for generations it had been accepted as part of southern life. Had not Washington, Jefferson, Jackson, indeed all the early presidents except the Adamses been slaveholders? Goaded by abolitionist assaults and by political controversy over slavery in the territories, southerners began to crack down unmercifully on every kind of dissent. They tried unsuccessfully to force the post office to bar antislavery literature from the mails and then accomplished their purpose by passing state laws making it illegal for postmasters to accept such material. Southern congressmen objected even to the routine reception of petitions urging the abolition of the slave trade in the District of Columbia. In 1836 they managed to pass a "gag rule" in the House of Representatives under which such petitions were automatically laid on the table without "further action whatever."

This denial of the right of petition outraged John Quincy Adams, now a congressman from Massachusetts. Although not an abolitionist, "Old Man Eloquent" battled furiously against the gag rule. Timorous opponents quailed before his indignation and his remorseless logic, and he succeeded in rousing the North. Petitions poured into Washington, 225,000 of them in a single session. In 1844 the gag rule was finally rescinded, but the long struggle pointed up the southerners' willingness to suppress the liberties of whites as well as blacks. Perhaps it also reflected their guilt feelings, for their policy was self-destructive—bound to attract sympathy to the very ideas they opposed. The gag rule accomplished what can only be called a political miracle: it made a popular hero of John Quincy Adams.

Within the South, freedom of expression practically disappeared. Schoolbooks were censored, dissident teachers fired. After about 1830 southerners who spoke out against slavery were whipped, beaten, driven away. Northern abolitionists who appeared openly in the region would have been taking their lives in their hands. While humanitarian southerners participated in movements to improve prisons, aid the blind and the insane, and similar causes, in an age when the rest of the nation teemed with social experiments, the South remained a bastion of conservatism. Free labor was almost as tightly controlled as slave. "The courts were openly antagonistic to striking workers," Richard B. Morris has written. Southerners considered "that strike action, like antislavery agitation, was an attack on their 'peculiar' institution."

Southerners worked out an interesting and varied justification of slavery. The most sophisticated presentation of the southern position was *The Pro-Slavery Argument* (1853), the work of several authors, which rejected the Jeffersonian theory that all men were created equal as a pernicious abstraction. People *differed* in natural endowments of all kinds—strength, intelligence, race. A high civilization depended on social order, "which implies distinctions and differences of conditions." Equality was in this sense unnatural. Others argued that since blacks were racially inferior to whites, slavery was better for them than freedom. "Providence has placed [the slave] in our hands for his own good," a southern governor claimed.

Writers such as George Fitzhugh, a Virginia lawyer and philosopher, and William J. Grayson, a South Carolina planter, argued that slavery was *better* than freedom for all workers. "Wage slaves" in northern factories, they said, suffered far more than southern slaves, both materially and psychologically. "Liberty and equality throw the whole weight of society on its weakest members," Fitzhugh wrote in *Sociology for the South* (1854). "A Southern farm is the beau ideal of Communism; it is a joint concern, in which the slave consumes more than the master, of the coarse products, and is far happier, because . . . he is always sure of a support." Describing the lot of slaves in "The Hireling and the Slave" (1856), Grayson wrote:

Secure they toil, uncursed their peaceful life,
With labor's hungry broils and wasteful strife.
No want to goad, no faction to deplore,
The slave escapes the perils of the poor.

Other propagandists, tossing about pseudoscientific language with confident abandon, stressed the theory that Negroes were racially inferior. Blacks belonged to the "prognathous" species of mankind, one "authority" proclaimed. They had a nervous system "somewhat like the ourang outang." Even men of the cloth contributed their mite to the cause, quoting the Bible ("Both thy bondmen and thy bondmaids, which thou shalt have, shall be of the heathen that are round about you . . . and they shall be your possession."—Leviticus) and adding such comments as this, from the pen of the Reverend Thornton Stringfellow of Virginia: "Job himself was a great slaveholder, and, like Abraham, Isaac, and Jacob, won no small portion of his claims to character . . . from the manner in which he discharged his duty to his slaves." By 1860 it was possible for a Louisiana minister to deliver a sermon entitled "Slavery, a Divine Trust."

The self-serving character of such arguments is clear enough, yet those who made them, and indeed many ordinary southerners, were not necessarily hypocrites or cynics. Many planters really were concerned for the welfare of their slaves, and if their assumptions about racial inferiority had been correct, their philosophy would not have been entirely indefensible. And their criticism of the crass, grasping competitiveness of northern capitalism had much to recommend it. Their difficulty (aside from their fundamental errors about the capacities of blacks) came in living up to their ideals. Many paid lip service to the gracious, aristocratic, nonmaterialistic values of a neofeudal society; few practiced what they preached.

While a large majority of the people, North and South, rejected the positions of both the abolitionists and the fanatical defenders of slavery, events in both sections played into the hands of extremists. Abolitionist exaggerations angered moderate southerners and made them more receptive to the talk of their own hotheads. The plight of fugitive slaves, hounded relentlessly across the land, often by professional slave catchers, aroused many northerners who might otherwise have avoided commitment. The famous "underground railroad," a loose-knit organization of individuals who helped to spirit fugitives to safety in the North or in Canada, was neither as important nor as successful as it has sometimes been portrayed; but only the most heartless northerner could turn a hunted runaway from his door, and once involved, a "conductor" on the railroad became an accomplice, committed to the movement against slavery. After the Supreme Court decided, in the case of *Prigg* v. *Pennsylvania* (1842), that the states did not have to enforce the federal Fugitive Slave Act, the northern states passed "personal liberty" laws barring state officials from aiding in the capture and return of fugitives. Southern resentment of these acts led to the much more stringent federal act of 1850, part of the Great Compromise, which in turn drove more northern moderates to abolitionism.

Women's Rights

The question of slavery was related to another major reform movement of the era, the crusade for women's rights. The relationship was personal and ideological, direct and indirect, simple and profound. Superficially, the connection can be explained in this way: Women were as likely as men to find slavery offensive and to protest against it. When they did so, they ran into even more adamant resistance, the prejudices of those who objected to abolitionists being reinforced by their feelings that women should not speak in public or participate in political affairs. Thus female abolitionists, driven by the urgencies of conscience,

■ This sweetly sentimental young woman decorated the cover of the sheet music for a polka. Her costume of short skirt and pantalettes was designed by Mrs. Amelia Bloomer. "Bloomers" were an easy target for much of the ridicule aimed at the early women's rights movement.

were almost forced to become advocates of women's rights. "We have good cause to be grateful to the slave," the feminist Abby Kelley wrote. "In striving to strike his irons off, we found most surely, that we were manacled *ourselves.*"

At a more profound level, the reference that abolitionists made to the Declaration of Independence to justify their attack on slavery radicalized women with regard to their own place in society. Were only all *men* created equal and endowed by God with unalienable rights? For many women the question was a consciousness-raising experience; they began to believe that, like blacks, they were imprisoned from birth in a caste system, le-

gally subordinated and assigned menial social and economic roles that prevented them from developing their full potentialities. Such women considered themselves in a sense worse off than blacks, who had at least the psychological advantage of confronting an openly hostile and repressive society rather than one concealed behind the cloying rhetoric of romantic love.

With the major exception of Margaret Fuller, whose book *Women in the Nineteenth Century* (1844) made a frontal attack on all forms of sexual discrimination, the leading advocates of equal rights for women were active in the abolitionist movement. Among the first were Sarah and Angelina

Grimké, South Carolinians who abandoned their native state because of their detestation of slavery and devoted themselves to stirring up the North against it. Male objections to their activities soon made them advocates of women's rights. Similarly, the refusal of delegates to the World Anti-Slavery Convention held in London in 1840 to let women participate in their debates precipitated the decision of two American abolitionists, Lucretia Mott and Elizabeth Cady Stanton, to turn their energies to the woman question.

Slavery aside, there were other aspects of this feminist consciousness raising. With the development of industrialization, the economy became more diversified and occupations more specialized. One result of this was that women were expected to confine themselves to the "women's sphere," principally child rearing and housekeeping. But as the historian Nancy F. Cott has shown, the very effort to enforce specialization made women aware of their second-class citizenship and thus more likely to be dissatisfied. They lacked not merely the right to vote, of which they did not make a major issue, but if married, the right to own property or to make a will. Lydia Maria Child, a popular novelist, found this last restriction particularly offensive. It excited her "towering indignation" that her husband had to sign her will. David Child was not what today would be called a male chauvinist, but, as she explained, "I was indignant for womankind made chattels personal from the beginning of time."

As Lydia Child noted, the subordination of women was as old as civilization. The attack on it came not because of any new discrimination but for the same reasons that roused reformers against other forms of injustice: belief in progress, a sense of personal responsibility, the conviction that institutions *could* be changed and that the time for changing them was limited.

When women sought to involve themselves in reform, they became aware of perhaps the most serious handicap that society imposed upon them—the conflict between their roles as wives and mothers and their urge to participate in the affairs of the larger world. Elizabeth Cady Stanton has left a striking description of this dilemma. She lived in the 1840s in Seneca Falls, a small town in central New York. Her husband was frequently away on business; she had a brood of growing children and little domestic help. When, stimu-

■ A rare, early portrait of Elizabeth Cady Stanton. In 1848 she helped draft the Declaration of Principles, spelling out the injustices of men to women. The conclusion: "He has endeavored, in every way he could, to destroy her confidence in her own powers, to lessen her self-respect, and to make her willing to lead a dependent and abject life."

lated by her interest in abolition and women's rights, she sought to become active in the movements, even to read about them, her family responsibilities made the task almost impossible.

"I now fully understood the practical difficulties most women had to contend with," she recalled in her autobiography, *Eighty Years and More* (1898). "The general discontent I felt with woman's portion as wife, mother, housekeeper, physician, and spiritual guide, the chaotic condition into which everything fell without her constant supervision, and the wearied, anxious look of the majority of women, impressed me with the strong feeling that some active measures should be taken." Active measures she took. Together with Lucretia Mott and a few others of like mind, she organized a meeting, the Seneca Falls Convention (July 1848), and drafted a Declaration of Principles patterned on the Declaration of Independence. "We hold these truths to be self-evident: that all men and women are created equal," it stated, and it went on to list the "injuries and usurpations" of men, just as Jefferson had outlined those of George III.

From this seed the movement grew. During the 1850s a series of national conventions was held; more and more reformers, including some prominent male activists such as William Lloyd Garrison, joined the cause. Of the recruits Susan B. Anthony was the most influential, for she was the first to see the need for thorough organization if effective pressure was to be brought to bear on male-dominated society. Her first campaign, mounted in 1854–1855 in behalf of a petition to the New York legislature calling for reform of the property and divorce laws, accumulated 6,000 signatures. But the petition did not persuade the legislature to act. Indeed, the feminists achieved very few practical results during the age of reform. Their leaders, however, were persevering types, most of them extraordinarily long-lived. Their major efforts lay in the future.

Despite the aggressiveness of many reformers and the extremity of some of their proposals, little social conflict blighted these years. Most citizens readily accepted the need for improving society and at the same time were prepared to shrug off impractical schemes as the work of harmless visionaries. When Sylvester Graham, inventor of the graham cracker, traveled up and down the land praising the virtues of hard mattresses, cold showers, and homemade bread, he was mobbed by the professional bakers, but in general, as his biographer says, "he was the subject of jokes, lampoons, and caustic editorials" rather than violence. Americans argued about everything from women's rights to phrenology, from prison reform to mesmerism, and they seldom came to blows. Even the abolitionist movement might not have caused serious social strife if the conflict over the western territories had not repeatedly dragged the slavery issue into politics. When that happened, the romantic age of reform came to an end.

SUPPLEMENTARY READING

Titles marked with an asterisk have been published in paperback

Useful surveys of cultural and intellectual currents in this period are Merle Curti, **The Growth of American Thought** (1951), R. B. Nye, **Society and Culture in America*** (1974), and Harvey Wish, **Society and Thought in Early America** (1950). C. R. Fish, **The Rise of the Common Man*** (1927), and A. C. Cole, **The Irrepressible Conflict*** (1934), deal more specifically with these years, while Clement Eaton, **The Mind of the Old South*** (1964), contains interesting essays on representative southern intellectual leaders. R. B. Davis, **Intellectual Life in Jefferson's Virginia** (1964), is also helpful. F. O. Matthiessen, **American Renaissance: Art and Expression in the Age of Emerson and Whitman*** (1941), is especially valuable.

The standard treatment of transcendentalism is still O. B. Frothingham, **Transcendentalism in New England*** (1876). R. L. Rusk, **The Life of Ralph Waldo Emerson** (1949), and J. W. Krutch, **Henry David Thoreau*** (1948), are first-rate biographies. On American literature, Van Wyck Brooks, **The Flowering of New England*** (1936), and Lewis Mumford, **The Golden Day*** (1926), are useful surveys. Biographies of the writers of the age include Edward Wagenknecht, **Edgar Allan Poe** (1963), J. R. Mellow, **Nathaniel Hawthorne and His Times** (1980), Leon Howard, **Herman Melville*** (1951), Justin Kaplan, **Walt Whitman** (1980), and Newton Arvin, **Longfellow: His Life and Work*** (1963). The student should also sample the works of these writers and those of the great romantic historians, which are available in many editions. David Levin, **History as Romantic Art*** (1959), is an excellent analysis of the assumptions and attitudes of the historians, but see also Harvey Wish, **The American Historian*** (1960).

Popular culture is discussed in Carl Bode, **The Anatomy of American Popular Culture** (1959), and Russell Lynes, **The Tastemakers*** (1954). Bode's **The American Lyceum*** (1956) is also useful. On education, see L. A. Cremin, **American Education: The National Experience** (1980), Merle Curti, **The Social Ideas of American Educators*** (1935), Jonathan Messerli, **Horace Mann** (1972), and T. R. Sizer (ed.), **The Age of the Academies*** (1964). M. B. Katz, **The Irony of Early School Reform*** (1968), questions the motives of the reformers. O. W. Larkin, **Art and Life in America** (1949), surveys American painting and architecture and Neil Harris, **The Artist in American Society*** (1966), puts art in its social setting. See also Barbara Novak, **Nature and Culture: American Landscape Painting** (1980).

Books treating the reform movements of these years include A. F. Tyler, **Freedom's Ferment*** (1944), and A. M. Schlesinger, **The American as Reformer*** (1950). H. S. Commager (ed.), **The Era of Reform*** (1960), provides a convenient sampling of the writing of reformers. A. E. Bestor, **Backwoods Utopias*** (1950), is excellent, but see also R. L. Muncy, **Sex and Marriage in Utopian Communities** (1973). F. M. Brodie's biography of

Joseph Smith, **No Man Knows My History** (1945), is critical of Mormonism; see also R. B. Flanders, **Nauvoo: Kingdom on the Mississippi*** (1965). Volumes helpful for the understanding of specific reform movements include H. E. Marshall, **Dorothea Dix** (1937), D. J. Rothman, **The Discovery of the Asylum*** (1971), F. L. Byrne, **Prophet of Prohibition: Neal Dow and His Crusade** (1961), N. H. Clark, **Deliver Us from Evil: an Interpretation of Prohibition*** (1976), and R. A. Billington, **Protestant Crusade*** (1938).

The abolition movement is considered in Louis Filler, **The Crusade Against Slavery*** (1960), D. L. Dumond, **Antislavery*** (1961), Benjamin Quarles, **Black Abolitionists*** (1969), and G. H. Barnes, **The Anti-Slavery Impulse*** (1933). L. L. Richards, **"Gentlemen of Property and Standing"** (1970), treats northern opposition to abolitionism. R. B. Nye, **Fettered Freedom*** (1949), discusses the impact of slavery on civil liberties. Nye's **William Lloyd Garrison and the Humanitarian Reformers*** (1955) is an excellent brief biography. For a more detailed account of Garrison's career, consult J. L. Thomas, **The Liberator: William Lloyd Garrison** (1963);

for a stimulating interpretation, stressing his conscious radicalism, see A. S. Kraditor, **Means and Ends in American Abolitionism: Garrison and His Critics on Strategy and Tactics** (1969). R. H. Abzug, **Passionate Liberator** (1980), is a good biography of Theodore Dwight Weld. See also N. I. Huggins, **Slave and Citizen: The Life of Frederick Douglass*** (1980), and Douglass' autobiography, **Life and Times of Frederick Douglass*** (1962). E. L. McKitrick (ed.), **Slavery Defended*** (1963), covers the arguments of the southern slaveholders.

Eleanor Flexner, **Century of Struggle: The Woman's Rights Movement in the United States*** (1959), provides an excellent account of the origins of feminism and its relation to abolitionism. See also Gerda Lerner, **The Grimké Sisters from South Carolina*** (1967), Katherine Anthony, **Susan B. Anthony** (1954), and L. W. Banner, **Elizabeth Cady Stanton** (1980). Ann Douglas, **The Feminization of American Culture** (1977), and N. F. Cott, **The Bonds of Womanhood** (1977), are helpful. Gerda Lerner (ed.), **The Female Experience*** (1977), is a valuable collection of source materials.

12/EXPANSION AND SLAVERY

 President John Tyler was a thin, rather delicate appearing man with pale blue eyes and a long nose. Courteous, tactful, soft-spoken, he gave the impression of being weak, an impression reinforced by his professed belief that the president should defer to Congress in the formulation of policy. This was a false impression; John Tyler was stubborn and proud, and these characteristics combined with an almost total lack of imagination to make him worship consistency, as so many second-raters do. He had turned away from Jackson because of the aggressive way the president had used his powers of appointment and the veto, but he also disagreed with Henry Clay and the northern Whigs about the Bank, protection, and federal internal improvements. Being a states' rights southerner, he considered such measures unconstitutional. Nevertheless, he was prepared to cooperate with Clay as the leader of what he called the "more immediate representatives" of the people, the members of Congress. He asked all of Harrison's Cabinet to remain in office.

The Tyler Administration

Tyler and Clay did not get along, and for this Clay was chiefly to blame. He behaved in an overbearing manner that was out of keeping with his nature, the best explanation for it being his resentment at having been passed over by the Whigs in 1840. (When news of Harrison's nomination reached him in Washington he was half drunk. His face darkened. "I am the most unfortunate man in the history of parties," he said, "always run . . . when sure to be defeated, and now betrayed for a nomination when I, or anyone, would be sure of an election.") He considered himself the real head of the Whig party and intended to exercise his leadership.

In Congress Clay announced a comprehensive "program" that ignored Tyler's states' rights view of the Constitution. Most important was his plan to set up a new Bank of the United States. A bill to repeal the Independent Treasury Act caused no difficulty, but when Congress passed a new Bank bill, Tyler vetoed it. The entire Cabinet except Secretary of State Webster thereupon resigned in protest.

Cast out by the Whigs, Tyler attempted to build a party of his own, and for the remainder of his term the political squabbling in Washington was continuous. Clay wanted to distribute the proceeds from land sales to the states, presumably to bolster their sagging finances but actually to reduce federal revenues in order to justify raising the tariff. To win western votes for distribution, he agreed to support a preemption bill legalizing the right of squatters to occupy unsurveyed land and to buy it later at $1.25 an acre without bidding for it at auction. The Preemption Act of 1841 put this compromise into effect. However, the southerners insisted on an amendment pledging that distribution would be stopped if the tariff were raised above the 20 percent level, and when the Whigs blithely tried to ignore this proviso by pushing a high tariff through Congress without repealing the Distribution Act, Tyler vetoed the bill. Finally, the

■ John Tyler posed for a daguerreotypist about 1850, after he had retired from public life. Tyler voted in favor of Virginia's secession ordinance in 1861.

Distribution Act was repealed and Tyler signed the new Tariff Act of 1842, raising duties to about the levels of 1832.

Webster's decision to remain in the Cabinet was motivated in part by his desire to complete several important negotiations with Great Britain. The unsettled boundary between Maine and New Brunswick was the most important issue. The intent of the peace treaty of 1783 had been to award the United States all land in the area drained by rivers flowing into the Atlantic rather than the St. Lawrence, but the wording was obscure and the old maps conflicting. The issue became critical in 1838 when Canadians began cutting timber in the Aroostook Valley, which was claimed by the United States. When Maine sent an agent to remonstrate with the lumberjacks, he was arrested. Maine and New Brunswick each called up militia and the Aroostook "War" followed. No one was killed, yet the danger of a real war was great. Acting with admirable restraint, Van Buren sent General Winfield Scott to the area, and Scott managed to arrange a truce. At the time that Webster took over the State Department, nothing further had been accomplished.

Slavery also caused Anglo-American friction. The British outlawed the slave trade in 1807 and in 1834 abolished slavery throughout the empire. While the United States also forbade the trade, it was still touchy because of British aggressiveness before 1812, and it refused to permit visit and search of American vessels by British warships under any circumstances. This cause of ill feeling was aggravated late in 1841 when the American brig *Creole*, out of Hampton Roads, Virginia, put in at Nassau in the British West Indies. *Creole* had been en route to New Orleans with a cargo of slaves (a perfectly legal voyage) when the slaves had broken loose. They seized the ship and put into Nassau to claim asylum. The British promptly arrested the ringleaders, charging them with mutiny and murder, but the bulk of the slaves were freed despite protests from the State Department.

Webster-Ashburton Treaty

In 1842 the British sent a new minister, Lord Ashburton, to the United States to try to settle all outstanding disputes. Ashburton, head of a London banking house that had large investments in the United States, made an ideal ambassador. He and Webster easily worked out a compromise boundary. The British cared relatively little about the Aroostook Valley timber but needed part of the territory to the north to build a military road connecting Halifax and Quebec. Webster, who thought any settlement desirable simply to eliminate a possible cause of war, willingly agreed.

The problem of placating Maine and Massachusetts, which wanted every acre of the land in dispute, Webster solved in an extraordinary manner. It was known that during the peace negotiations ending the Revolution, Franklin had marked the boundary between Maine and Canada on a map with a heavy red line, but no one could locate the Franklin map. Webster obtained an old map of the area and had someone mark off in red a line that followed the British version of the boundary. He showed this document to representatives of Maine and Massachusetts, convincing them that

they had better agree to his compromise before the British got wind of it and demanded the whole region! It later came out that the British had a true copy of the Franklin map, which showed that the entire area rightfully belonged to the United States.

Webster's generosity made excellent sense. Lord Ashburton, gratified by having obtained the strategic territory, made concessions elsewhere along the Canadian and American border (see map, page 307). Through a foolish error, the United States had built a million-dollar fort at the northern end of Lake Champlain on what turned out to be Canadian soil. Ashburton agreed to cede this strip of land along the New York and Vermont border to the United States. He also yielded 6,500 square miles of wild land between Lake Superior and Lake of the Woods, which later proved to contain one of the richest deposits of iron ore in the world. Webster and Ashburton agreed to maintain separate but cooperating naval squadrons off the African coast to aid in the suppression of the slave trade.

The Senate ratified the Webster–Ashburton Treaty in August 1842. Its importance, more symbolic than practical, was nonetheless great. British dependence on foreign foodstuffs was increasing; America's need for British capital was rising. War, or even unsettled affairs, would have injured vital business relations and produced no compensating gains. Although no Era of Good Feelings between the two nations had arrived, the spirit of mutual concession that characterized the Webster–Ashburton negotiations was encouraging.

The Texas Question

The settlement with Great Britain won support in every section of the United States, but the same could not be said for Tyler's attempt to annex the Republic of Texas, for this involved the question of slavery. In the Transcontinental Treaty of 1819 with Spain, the boundary of the United States had been drawn in such a way as to exclude Texas. This seemed unimportant at the time, yet within months of the ratification of the treaty in February 1821, Americans led by Stephen F. Austin had begun to settle in the area, then part of an independent Mexico. Cotton flourished on the fertile Texas plains, and the Mexican authorities offered

■ A painting done in 1885, after a study of available sources, is probably the most accurate view of the final storming of the Alamo. Mexican troops poured through two openings made in the walls by their artillery fire; others scaled ladders to gain the interior of the fort. The Texans made their last stand in the mission at right.

free land to groups of settlers. By 1830 there were some 20,000 white Americans in Texas, together with about 2,000 slaves, while only a few thousand Mexicans lived there.

John Quincy Adams had offered Mexico $1 million for Texas, and Jackson was willing to pay $5 million, but Mexico would not sell. Nevertheless the flood of American settlers alarmed the Mexican authorities. The immigrants apparently felt no loyalty to Mexico. Most were Protestants, though Mexican law required that all immigrants be Catholics; few attempted to learn more than a few words of Spanish. When Mexico outlawed slavery, they evaded the law by "freeing" their slaves and then signing them to lifetime contracts as indentured servants. For these reasons Mexico prohibited further immigration of Americans into Texas in 1830, though again the law proved impossible to enforce.

As soon as the Mexican government began to restrict them, the Texans began to seek independence. In 1835 a series of skirmishes escalated into a full-scale rebellion, the Texans receiving much military and financial aid from American "volunteers." The Mexican president, Antonio López de Santa Anna, marched north with 6,000 soldiers to subdue the rebels. Late in February 1836 he reached San Antonio, where a force of 187 men under Colonel William B. Travis held the city. The Texans took refuge behind the stout walls of

a former mission called the Alamo. For 10 days they beat off Santa Anna's assaults, inflicting terrible casualties on the attackers. Finally, on March 6, the Mexicans carried the walls. Inside they killed everyone, even the wounded, then soaked the corpses in oil and burned them. Among the dead were the legendary Davy Crockett and Jim Bowie, inventor of the Bowie knife.

After the Alamo and the slaughter of another garrison at Goliad, southeast of San Antonio, peaceful settlement of the dispute between Texas and Mexico was impossible. On March 2, 1836, the Texans declared their independence. Sam Houston, a former congressman and governor of Tennessee and an experienced Indian fighter, was placed in charge of the rebel army. For a time Houston retreated before Santa Anna's troops, who greatly outnumbered his own. At the San Jacinto River he took a stand. On April 21, 1836, shouting "Forward! Charge! Remember the Alamo! Remember Goliad!" he ordered the attack. The Texans routed the Mexican army, which soon retreated across the Rio Grande. In October Houston was elected president of the Republic of Texas, and a month later a plebiscite revealed that an overwhelming majority favored annexation by the United States.

President Jackson hesitated. To take Texas might mean war with Mexico. Assuredly it would stir up the slavery controversy. On his last day in

■ In an 1844 cartoon a slave awaits the outcome of the "Great Prize-Fight" matching the American eagle against Spanish and British contenders, with Texas and California the prize. The ghost of Washington encourages the Republic with "Go it, my Boy, you will beat them all." Britain's John Bull bets Canada while Spain's Don Quixote bets Cuba.

office he recognized the republic, but he made no move to accept it into the Union, nor did Van Buren. Texas thereupon went its own way, developing friendly ties with Great Britain. An independent Texas suited British tastes perfectly, for it could provide an alternative supply of raw cotton and a market for manufactures unfettered by tariffs.

These events caused alarm in the United States, especially among southerners, who dreaded the possibility that a Texas dominated by Great Britain might abolish slavery. As a southerner, Tyler shared these feelings; as a beleaguered politician, spurned by the Whigs and held in contempt by most Democrats, he saw in annexation a chance to revive his fortunes. When Webster resigned as secretary of state in 1843, Tyler replaced him with a fellow Virginian, Abel P. Upshur, whom he or-

dered to seek a treaty of annexation. The South was strong for taking Texas, and in the West and even the Northeast the patriotic urge to add such a magnificent new territory to the national domain was great. Counting noses, Upshur convinced himself that the Senate would approve annexation by the necessary two-thirds majority. He negotiated a treaty in February 1844, but before he could sign it he was killed by the explosion of a cannon on U.S.S. *Princeton* during a weapons demonstration.

To insure the winning of Texas, Tyler appointed John C. Calhoun secretary of state. This was a blunder; Calhoun was so closely associated with the South and with slavery that his appointment alienated thousands of northerners who might otherwise have welcomed annexation. Suddenly Texas was a hot political issue. Clay and

Van Buren, who seemed assured of the 1844 Whig and Democratic presidential nominations, promptly announced that they opposed annexation, chiefly on the ground that it would probably lead to war with Mexico. With a national election in the offing, northern and western senators refused to vote for annexation, and in June the Senate rejected the treaty, 35 to 16. The Texans were angry and embarrassed, the British eager again to take advantage of the situation.

Manifest Destiny

The Senate, Clay, and Van Buren had all misinterpreted public opinion. John C. Calhoun, whose world was so far removed from that of the average citizen, in this case came much closer to comprehending the mood of the country than any of its other leaders.

For two centuries Americans had been gradually conquering a continent. While the first colonists had envisaged a domain extending from the Atlantic to the Pacific, they had not realized the immensities of the New World. By the time their descendants came to appreciate its size, they had been chastened by the experience of battling the Indians for possession of the land and then laboriously developing it. The Revolution and its aftermath of nationalism greatly stimulated expansion, and then, before the riches of trans-Appalachia had even been inventoried, Jefferson had stunned the country with Louisiana, an area so big that the mere thought of it left Americans giddy.

The westward march from the 17th century to the 1840s had seemed fraught with peril, the prize

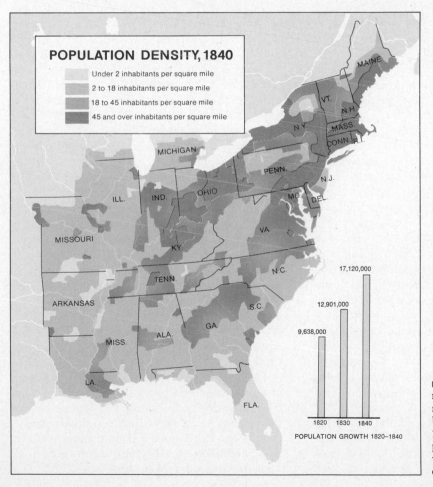

POPULATION DENSITY, 1840

- Under 2 inhabitants per square mile
- 2 to 18 inhabitants per square mile
- 18 to 45 inhabitants per square mile
- 45 and over inhabitants per square mile

POPULATION GROWTH 1820–1840

■ The accelerating westward movement is evident in this map. Arkansas entered the Union in 1836, Michigan in 1837. During the 1830s the population of the nation as a whole increased by nearly one-third.

golden but attainable only through patient labor and fearful hardships. Wild animals and wild men, mighty forests and mighty foreign powers beset the path. John Adams wrote of "conquering" the West "from the trees and rocks and wild beasts." He was "enflamed" by the possibilities of "that vast scene which is opening in the West," but to win it the United States would have to "march *intrepidly* on."

Quite rapidly (as historians measure time) the atmosphere changed. Each year of national growth increased the power and confidence of the people, and every forward step revealed a wider horizon. Now the West seemed a ripe apple, to be plucked almost casually. Where pioneers had once stood in awe before the majesty of the Blue Ridge, then hesitated to venture from the protective shadows of the forest into the open prairies of Illinois, they now shrugged their shoulders at great deserts and began to talk of the Rocky Mountains as "mere molehills" along the road to the Pacific. After 200 years of westward expansion had brought them as far as Missouri and Iowa, Americans suddenly perceived their destined goal. *The whole continent was to be theirs!* Theirs to exploit, and theirs to make into one mighty nation, a land of opportunity, a showcase to display the virtues of democratic institutions, living proof that Americans were indeed God's chosen people. A journalist named John L. O'Sullivan captured the new mood in a sentence. Nothing must interfere, he wrote in 1845, with "the fulfilment of our *manifest destiny* to overspread the continent allotted by Providence for the free development of our yearly multiplying millions."

The politicians did not sense the new mood in 1844; even Calhoun, who saw the acquisition of Texas as part of a broader program, was thinking of balancing sectional interests rather than of national expansion. In fact the expansion, stimulated by the natural growth of the population and by a revived flood of immigration, was going on in every section and with little regard for political boundaries. New settlers rolled westward in hordes. Between 1830 and 1835, 10,000 entered "foreign" Texas, and this was a trickle compared to what the early 1840s were to bring. By 1840 many Americans had also settled far to the west in California, which was unmistakably Mexican territory, and in the Oregon country, jointly claimed by the United States and Great Britain.

California and Oregon

California was a huge and sparsely settled land dominated by Mexican cattlemen and a network of 21 Catholic missions running north from San Diego to beyond San Francisco. The mission friars controlled more than 30,000 Indian converts who lived and worked on their properties. By the 1830s a handful of Americans had established themselves in California. Richard Henry Dana's *Two Years Before the Mast* (1840) describes what life was like for these people: "There is no working class (the Indians being practically serfs and doing all the hard work) and every rich man looks like a grandee, and every poor scamp like a broken-down gentleman."

Oregon, a vaguely defined area between California and Russian Alaska, proved still more alluring to Americans. Captain Robert Gray had sailed up the Columbia River in 1792, and Lewis and Clark had visited the region on their great expedition. In 1811 John Jacob Astor's Pacific Fur Company had established trading posts on the Columbia. Some two decades later Methodist, Presbyterian, and Catholic missionaries began to find their way into the Willamette Valley, immediately to the south. Gradually a small number of settlers followed, until by 1840 there were about 500 Americans in the Willamette area, a beautiful green land of rich soil, mild climate, and tall forests teeming with game.

In the early 1840s, fired by the spirit of manifest destiny, the country suddenly burned with "Oregon fever." In dozens upon dozens of towns, societies were founded to collect information and organize groups to make the march to the Pacific. Land hunger (stimulated by the glowing reports of those on the scene) drew the new migrants most powerfully, but the patriotic concept of manifest destiny gave the trek across the 2,000 miles of wilderness separating Oregon from the western edge of American settlement in Missouri the character of a crusade. In 1843 nearly a thousand pioneers made the long trip.

The Oregon Trail began at the western border of Missouri and followed the Kansas River and the perverse, muddy Platte ("a mile wide and six inches deep") past Fort Laramie to the Rockies. It crossed the Continental Divide by the relatively easy South Pass, veered south to Fort Bridger, on Mexican soil, and then ran north and west

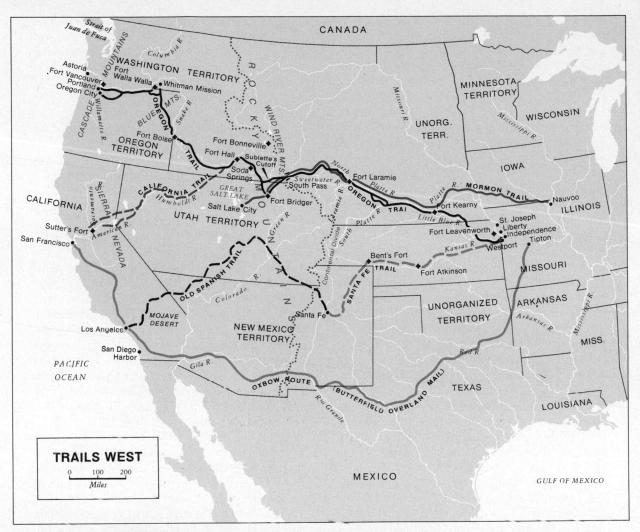

TRAILS WEST

0 100 200
Miles

■ The Old Spanish Trail was the earliest. Part of it was mapped in 1776 by a Franciscan missionary. The Santa Fe Trail came into wide use after 1823. The Oregon Trail was pioneered by trappers and missionaries. The first party traversed the Mormon Trail in 1847, while the Oxbow Route, developed under a federal mail contract, was used from 1858 to 1861.

through the valley of the Snake River and eventually, by way of the Columbia, to Fort Vancouver, a British post guarding the entrance to the Willamette Valley.

Over this tortuous path wound the canvas-covered caravans with their scouts and their accompanying herds. Each group became a self-governing community on the march, with regulations democratically agreed upon "for the purpose of keeping good order and promoting civil and military discipline." For a party of a thousand-odd like the group of 1843, the Indians posed no great threat (though constant vigilance was necessary),

but the five-month trip was full of labor, discomfort, and uncertainty, in the words of the historian David Lavender, a "remorseless, unending, weather-scoured, nerve-rasping plod on and on and on and on, foot by aching foot." And at the end lay the regular tasks of pioneering. The spirit of the trailblazers is caught in an entry from the diary of James Nesmith:

Friday, October 27.—Arrived at Oregon City at the falls of the Willamette.
Saturday, October 28.—Went to work.

Behind the dreams of the Far West as an

American Eden lay the commercial importance of the three major West Coast harbors: San Diego, San Francisco, and the Strait of Juan de Fuca leading into Puget Sound. Eastern merchants considered these harbors the keys to the trade of the Orient. That San Diego and San Francisco were Mexican and the Puget Sound district was claimed by Great Britain did not lessen their desire to possess them. As early as 1835, Jackson tried to buy the San Francisco region. Even Calhoun called San Francisco the future New York of the Pacific and proposed buying all California from Mexico.

Election of 1844

In the spring of 1844 expansion did not seem likely to affect the presidential election. The Whigs nominated Clay unanimously and made no statement about Texas in their party platform. When the Democrats gathered in convention at Baltimore in May, Van Buren appeared to have the nomination in his pocket, and he too wanted to keep Texas out of the campaign. That a politician of Van Buren's caliber, controlling the party machinery, could be upset in a national convention seemed unthinkable. But upset he was, for the southern delegates rallied round the Calhoun policy of taking Texas to save it for slavery. "I can beat Clay and Van Buren put together on this issue," Calhoun boasted. "They are behind the age." With the aid of a few northern expansionists the southerners forced through a rule requiring that the choice be by a two-thirds majority. This Van Buren could not muster. After a brief deadlock, a "dark horse," James K. Polk of Tennessee, swept the convention.

Polk was a good Jacksonian. He opposed high tariffs and was dead set against establishing another national bank. But he believed in taking Texas, and he favored expansion generally. To mollify the Van Burenites, the convention nominated Senator Silas Wright of New York for vice-president, but Wright was Van Buren's loyal friend and equally opposed to annexation. When the word was flashed to him in Washington over the new "magnetic telegraph" which Samuel F. B. Morse had just installed between the convention hall in Baltimore and the Capitol, he refused to run. The delegates then picked George M. Dallas of Pennsylvania. The Democratic platform de-

manded that Texas be "reannexed" (implying that it had been part of the Louisiana Purchase) and that all of Oregon be "reoccupied" (suggesting that the joint occupation of the region with Great Britain, which had been agreed to in the Convention of 1818, be abrogated).

Texas was now in the campaign. The friends of Tyler, convening in Baltimore, had nominated the president on a "Tyler and Texas" ticket, which threatened to split the expansionist vote; old Andrew Jackson, who had nothing but contempt for "Tiler," was persuaded to write a letter professing "real regard" for him and praising his "good sense and patriotism." This, together with more flattery from Polk, convinced Tyler that he should withdraw.

When Clay sensed the new expansionist sentiment of the voters, he tried to hedge on his opposition to annexation, but he probably lost as many votes as he gained by his surrender of principle to expediency, especially among the antislavery element in the northern states. The election was extremely close. The campaign followed the pattern established in 1840, with stress on parades, mass meetings, and slogans. Polk carried the country by only 38,000 of 2.7 million votes. In the electoral college the vote was 170 to 105.

The decisive factor in the contest was the Liberty party, an antislavery splinter group organized in 1840. Only 62,000 voters supported candidate James G. Birney, a "reformed" Kentucky slaveholder, but nearly 16,000 of them lived in New York, most in the western part of the state, a Whig stronghold. Since Polk carried New York by barely 5,000, the votes for Birney probably cost Clay the state. Had he won New York's 36 electoral votes, he would have been elected, 141 to 134.

Polk's victory was nevertheless taken as a mandate for expansion. Tyler promptly called on Congress to take Texas by joint resolution, which would avoid the necessity of obtaining a two-thirds majority in the Senate. This was done a few days before Tyler left the White House. Under the resolution Texas retained title to all public lands within its boundaries but accepted full responsibility for debts incurred while an independent republic. As many as four new states might be carved from its territory, but only with its approval. Polk accepted this arrangement, and in December 1845 Texas became a state.

Polk as President

President Polk, a slightly built, erect, handsome man with large, grave, steel gray eyes, was approaching 50. His mind was not of the first order, for he lacked imagination and was too tense and calculating to allow his intellect free rein. He was an efficient, hard worker with a strong will and a tough skin, qualities that stood him in good stead in the White House, and he made politics his whole life. It was typical of the man that he developed a special technique of handshaking in order better to cope with the interminable reception lines that every leader has to endure. "When I observed a strong man approaching," he once explained, "I generally took advantage of him by being a little quicker than he was and seizing him by the tip of his fingers, giving him a hearty shake, and thus preventing him from getting a full grip upon me." In four years in office he was away from his desk in Washington for a total of only six weeks.

Polk was uncommonly successful as president. He was determined to lower the tariff of 1842 and to restore the Independent Treasury, and both goals he achieved. He opposed federal internal improvements and managed to have his way. He made himself the spokesman of American expansion by committing himself to obtaining, in addition to Texas, both Oregon and the great Southwest. Here again, he succeeded.

Oregon was the first order of business. In his inaugural address Polk stated the American claim to the entire region in the plainest terms, but from the American point of view the remote northern half of the Oregon country had little value, and after allowing the British time to digest his demand for everything, he informed the British minister in Washington, Richard Pakenham, that he would accept a boundary following the 49th parallel to the Pacific.

Pakenham rejected this proposal without submitting it to London, and Polk thereupon decided to insist again on the whole area. When Congress met in December 1845, he asked for authority to give the necessary one year's notice for abrogating the 1818 treaty of joint occupation. "The only way to treat John Bull," he told one congressman, "was to look him straight in the eye." Following considerable discussion, Congress complied. It was, Representative Robert Winthrop of Massachusetts

proclaimed in the debate, "our manifest destiny to spread over this whole continent." In May 1846 Polk notified Great Britain that he intended to terminate the joint occupation.

The British were now eager to compromise. Officials of the Hudson's Bay Company had become alarmed by the rapid growth of the American settlement in the Willamette Valley. By 1845 there were some 5,000 people there, whereas the country north of the Columbia contained no more than 750 British subjects. A clash between the groups could have but one result; the company decided to shift its base from the Columbia to Vancouver Island. And British experts outside the company reported that the Oregon country could not possibly be defended in case of war. Thus, when Polk accompanied the one-year notice with a hint that he would again consider a compromise, the British foreign secretary, Lord Aberdeen, hastened to suggest dividing the Oregon territory along the 49th parallel. Polk, abandoning his belligerent attitude, agreed. The treaty followed that line from the Rockies to Puget Sound, but Vancouver Island, which extends below the line, was left entirely to the British, so both nations retained free use of the Strait of Juan de Fuca (see map, page 293). Although some northern Democrats accused Polk of treachery because he had failed to fight for all of Oregon, the treaty so obviously accorded with the national interest that the Senate approved it by a large majority in June 1846.

War with Mexico

One reason for the popularity of the Oregon compromise was that the country was already at war with Mexico and wanted no trouble with Great Britain. While the expansionist spirit and the confidence born of its overwhelming advantages of size and wealth certainly encouraged the United States to bully Mexico, the war had broken out in large measure because of the Mexicans' stubborn pride. Texas had been independent for the better part of a decade and Mexico had made no serious effort to reconquer it; nevertheless the government promptly broke off diplomatic relations when the United States annexed the republic.

Polk, who did not want to fight if he could obtain what he wanted by negotiation, ordered General Zachary Taylor into Texas only to protect the border. However, the location of that border was in dispute. Texas claimed the Rio Grande; Mexico insisted that the boundary was the Nueces River, which emptied into the Gulf about 150 miles to the north. Taylor reached the Nueces in July 1845 with about 1,500 troops and crossed into the disputed territory. He stopped on the southern bank at Corpus Christi, not wishing to provoke the Mexicans by marching to the Rio Grande.

In November Polk sent an envoy, John Slidell, on a secret mission to Mexico to try to obtain the disputed territory by negotiation. Mexico was in default on some $2 million owed American citizens for losses suffered during political upheavals in the country. Polk authorized Slidell to cancel this debt in return for recognition of the annexation of Texas and acceptance of the Rio Grande boundary. The president also empowered him to offer as much as $30 million if Mexico would sell the United States all or part of New Mexico and California.

It would have been to Mexico's long-range advantage to have made a deal with Slidell. The country could well have used the money, and the area Polk wanted, lying in the path of American expansion, was likely to be engulfed as Texas had

been, without regard for the actions of the American or Mexican governments.

Not illogically, Polk believed his tough stance would persuade the Mexicans to give in. But the Mexican government did not dare even to receive Slidell. The Mexican people had little love for the undemocratic regime of President José Herrera. They loved their country, however, and their despair over local conditions exaggerated their patriotism. The mere news that Slidell was in Mexico City hastened the overthrow of Herrera, and the new president, General Mariano Paredes, promptly reaffirmed his country's claim to *all* Texas. In March 1846 Slidell returned to Washington convinced that the Mexicans could not negotiate until they had been "chastised."

Polk had already decided to fight and had ordered Taylor to advance to the Rio Grande. By March 28 his army, swelled to about 4,000, was drawn up on the north bank of the river, across from the Mexican town of Matamoros. When a Mexican force crossed the river on April 25 and attacked an American mounted patrol, the president had an ideal pretext. His message to Congress treated the matter as a *fait accompli:* "War exists," he stated flatly. He asked for authority not

■ This 1846 daguerreotype is the earliest known American war photograph. U.S. General John E. Wool poses with his staff in Saltillo, Mexico.

merely to drive the Mexicans back but to prosecute the war to "a speedy and successful termination." Congress accepted this reasoning and without actually declaring war voted to raise and supply an additional 50,000 troops. For the first time (but not the last) a president had led the nation into war without the formal declaration required by the Constitution.

The outcome of the Mexican War was never in doubt from the moment of the first battles. At Palo Alto, north of the Rio Grande, 2,300 Americans scattered a Mexican force more than twice their number. Then, hotly pursuing, 1,700 Americans routed 7,500 Mexicans at Resaca de la Palma. Fewer than 50 United States soldiers lost their lives in these engagements, while Mexican losses in killed, wounded, and captured exceeded 1,000. Within a week of the declaration of war the Mexicans had been driven across the Rio Grande and General Taylor had his troops firmly established on the southern bank.

The Mexican army was poorly equipped and, despite a surfeit of high-ranking officers, poorly led. The well-supplied American forces had a hard core of youthful West Pointers eager to make their reputations and regulars trained in Indian warfare to provide the leadership needed to turn volunteer soldiers into first-rate fighting men. Yet Mexico was a large, rugged country with few decent roads; conquering it was a formidable task.

Northern Mexico and California

President Polk insisted not only on directing grand strategy (he displayed real ability as a military planner) but on supervising hundreds of petty details, down to the purchase of mules and the promotion of enlisted men. His partisanship caused unnecessary turmoil in army ranks. He wanted, as Thomas Hart Benton said, "a small war, just large enough to require a treaty of peace, and not large enough to make military reputations dangerous for the presidency." Both Taylor and Winfield Scott, the commanding general in Washington, were Whigs. Polk, who tended to suspect the motives of anyone who disagreed with him, feared that one or the other would make political capital of his popularity as a military leader. The examples of his hero, Jackson, and of General Harrison loomed large in Polk's thinking.

Polk's attitude was narrow, almost unpatriotic, but not unrealistic. Zachary Taylor was not a brilliant soldier. Polk believed that he lacked the "grasp of mind" necessary for high command, and General Scott complained of his "comfortable, laborsaving contempt for learning of every kind." But Taylor commanded the love and respect of his men (they called him Old Rough and Ready and even Zack), and he knew how to deploy them in the field. He had joined the army in 1808 and made it his whole life; he cared so little for politics that he had never bothered to cast a ballot in an election. Yet the dust had barely settled on the field of Resaca de la Palma when Whig politicians began to pay him court. "Great expectations and great consequences rest upon you," a Kentucky politician explained to him. "People everywhere begin to talk of converting you into a political leader, when the War is done."

Polk's concern was heightened because domestic opposition to the war was growing. Many northerners, Whigs and Democrats alike, feared that the war would lead to the expansion of slavery. Other citizens felt that Polk had misled Congress about the original outbreak of fighting and that the United States was the aggressor. The farther from the Rio Grande one went in the United States, the less popular "Mr. Polk's War" became; in New England opposition was almost as widespread as it had been to "Mr. Madison's War" in 1812.

Polk's design for prosecuting the war consisted of three parts. First, he would clear the Mexicans from Texas and occupy the northern provinces of Mexico. Second, he would take possession of California and New Mexico. Finally, he would march on Mexico City. Proceeding west from the Rio Grande, Taylor captured the Mexican fortified town of Monterrey after a hard, five-day battle in September 1846. The following February he defeated a Mexican army of 15,000 at Buena Vista, effectively ending the war in the northern provinces.

Meanwhile, the entire Southwest was falling into American hands. In June 1846 American settlers in the Sacramento Valley seized Sonoma and raised the "Bear Flag" of the Republic of California. Another group, headed by Captain John C. Frémont, leader of an American exploring party which happened to be in the area, clashed with the Mexican authorities around Monterey, California,

■ This satiric 1846 cartoon reflects an anti-Mexican War bias, with its deadpan title "Volunteers for Texas," and its caricatured line-up of unsavory-looking enlistees—a black man carrying an umbrella rather than a gun, an Irishman, a drunk (possibly German)—being eyed disdainfully through a monocle by an effete officer.

and then joined with the Sonoma rebels. Most important was a United States naval squadron under Commodore John D. Sloat, which captured Monterey and San Francisco in July 1846 and then moved against the remaining Mexican troops in the southern part of California. A force of 1,700 horsemen commanded by General Stephen Watts Kearny hurried across the Rockies from Fort Leavenworth to capture Santa Fe. Kearny then sped on with a small contingent of dragoons to California, where he joined the other American units in mopping-up operations around San Diego and Los Angeles. By February 1847 the United States had won control of nearly all of Mexico north of the capital city.

On to Mexico City

The campaign against Mexico City was the most difficult of the war and the best managed. Fearful of Taylor's growing popularity and entertaining certain honest misgivings about his ability to oversee a complicated campaign, Polk put Winfield Scott in charge of the offensive. He tried to per-

suade Congress to make Thomas Hart Benton a lieutenant general so as to have a Democrat in nominal control, but the Senate displayed enough sense to vote down this absurd proposal.

About Scott's competence no one entertained a doubt, yet he seemed even more of a threat to the Democrats than Taylor, for he had political ambitions as well as military ability. In 1840 the Whigs had considered running him for president. Scion of an old Virginia family, Scott was nearly six and a half feet tall; in uniform his presence was commanding. He was intelligent, even-tempered, and cultivated, if somewhat punctilious and pompous, as his nickname, Old Fuss and Feathers, indicated. After a sound but not spectacular record in the War of 1812, he had added to his reputation by helping to modernize military administration and strengthen the professional training of officers. The vast difference between the army of 1812 and that of 1846 was chiefly his doing. On the record, and despite the politics of the situation, Polk had no choice but to give him this command.

Scott landed his army south of Veracruz, Mexico, on March 9, 1847, laid siege to the city, and obtained its surrender in less than three weeks with the loss of only a handful of his 10,000 men.

Marching westward through hostile country, he maintained effective discipline, avoiding atrocities that might have inflamed the countryside against him. Finding his way blocked by well-placed artillery and a large army at Cerro Gordo, where the national road rose steeply toward the central highlands, Scott outflanked the Mexican position and then carried it by storm, capturing more than 3,000 prisoners and much equipment. By mid May he had advanced to Puebla, only 80 miles southeast of Mexico City.

After delaying until August for the arrival of reinforcements, he pressed on, won two hard-fought victories at the outskirts of the capital, and on September 14 hammered his way into the city. In every engagement the American troops had been outnumbered, yet they were not once defeated and always exacted a far heavier toll from the defenders than they themselves were forced to pay. In the fighting on the edge of Mexico City, for example, Scott's army sustained about 1,000 casualties, for the Mexicans defended their capital bravely. But 4,000 Mexicans were killed or wounded in the engagements, and 3,000 (including eight generals, two of them former presidents of the republic) were taken prisoner.

The Treaty of Guadalupe Hidalgo

The Mexicans were thoroughly beaten, but they refused to accept the situation. As soon as the news of the capture of Veracruz reached Washington, Polk sent Nicholas P. Trist, chief clerk of the State Department, to accompany Scott's army and to act as peace commissioner after the fall of Mexico City. Trist, a competent though somewhat pompous man, possessed impeccable credentials as a Democrat, for he had married a granddaughter of Thomas Jefferson and had served for a time as secretary to Andrew Jackson. Long residence as United States consul at Havana had given him an excellent command of Spanish.

Trist joined Scott at Veracruz in May. The two men, both rather vain, took an instant dislike to each other. Scott considered it a "personal dishonor" to be asked to defer to what he considered a State Department flunky, and his feelings were not salved when Trist sent him an officious, 30-page letter discoursing upon the nature of his as-

signment. However, Scott was eager to end the war and realized that a petty quarrel with the president's emissary would not advance that objective. Trist fell ill, and Scott sent him a jar of guava marmalade; after that they became good friends.

Because of the confused state of affairs following the fall of Mexico City, Trist could not commence negotiations with Mexican peace commissioners until January 1848. Polk, unable to understand the delay, became impatient. Originally he had authorized Trist to pay $30 million for New Mexico, Upper and Lower California, and the right of transit across Mexico's narrow Isthmus of Tehuantepec. Now, observing the disorganized state of Mexican affairs, he began to consider demanding more territory and paying less for it. He summoned Trist home.

Trist, with Scott's backing, ignored the order. He realized that unless a treaty was arranged soon the Mexican government might disintegrate, leaving no one in authority to sign a treaty. He dashed off a 65-page letter to the president, in effect refusing to be recalled, and proceeded to negotiate. Early in February the Treaty of Guadalupe Hidalgo was completed. By its terms Mexico accepted the Rio Grande as the boundary of Texas and ceded New Mexico and Upper California to the United States. In return the United States agreed to pay Mexico $15 million and to take on the claims of American citizens against Mexico, which by that time amounted to another $3.25 million.

Trist sent the treaty to Polk in the care of a New Orleans newspaperman. When he learned that Trist had ignored his orders, the president seethed. Trist was "contemptibly base," he thought, an "impudent and unqualified scoundrel." He ordered him placed under arrest and fired him from his State Department job.* Yet he had no choice but to submit the treaty to the Senate, for to have insisted on more territory would have meant more fighting, and the war was becoming increasingly unpopular. The relatively easy military victory made some people ashamed that their country was crushing a small neighbor. Pacifists denounced the war as immoral. Aboli-

---

*Trist was retired to private life without being paid for his time in Mexico. In 1870, when he was on his deathbed, Congress finally awarded him $14,299.20.

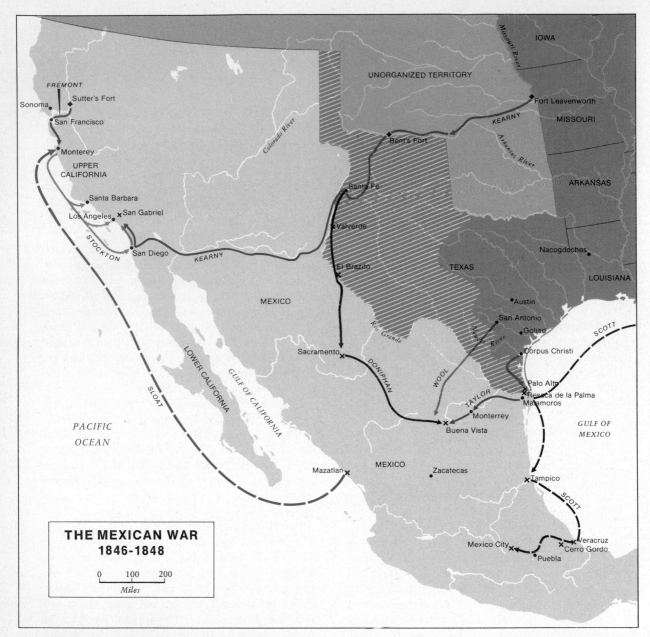

THE MEXICAN WAR
1846-1848

0   100   200
Miles

■ American naval power proved a decisive factor in the Mexican War. The Pacific Squadron, under John D. Sloat and Robert F. Stockton, secured California, and a 200-vessel fleet conveyed Winfield Scott's army to Veracruz. The striped area was later ceded to the United States by Texas.

tionists, led by William Lloyd Garrison, called it an "invasion . . . waged solely for the detestable and horrible purpose of extending and perpetuating American slavery." The Senate, subject to the same pressures as the president, ratified the agreement by a vote of 38 to 14.

The Aftermath

The Mexican War, won quickly and at relatively small cost in lives and money, brought huge territorial gains. The Pacific Coast from south of San Diego to the 49th parallel and all the land between the coast and the Continental Divide had become the property of the American people. Immense amounts of labor and capital would have to be invested before this new territory could be made to yield its bounty, but the country clearly had the capacity to accomplish the job.

In this atmosphere came what seemed a sign from the heavens. In January 1848, while Scott's veterans rested upon their victorious arms in Mexico City, a mechanic named James W. Marshall was building a sawmill on the American River in the Sacramento Valley east of San Francisco. One day, while supervising the deepening of the millrace, he noticed a few flecks of yellow in the bed of the stream. These he gathered up and tested. They were pure gold.

Other strikes had been made in California and been treated skeptically or as matters of local curiosity; since the days of Jamestown, too many pioneers had run fruitlessly in search of El Dorado, too much fool's gold had been passed off as the real thing. Yet this discovery produced an international sensation. The gold was real and plentiful— $200 million of it was extracted in the first four years—but equally important was the fact that everyone was ready to believe the news. The gold rush reflected the heady confidence inspired by Guadalupe Hidalgo; it seemed the ultimate justification of manifest destiny. Surely an era of continental prosperity and harmony had dawned.

Slavery in the Territories

Prosperity came in full measure but not harmony, for once again expansion brought the nation face to face with the divisive question of slavery. This giant chunk of North America, most of it vacant, its future soon to be determined—should it be slave or free? The question, in one sense, seems hardly worth the national crisis it provoked. Slavery had little future in New Mexico, less in California, none in Oregon. Why did the South fight so hard for the *right* to bring slaves into a region so unsuited to their exploitation? Why did southern congressmen vote against barring slavery in Oregon Territory, and why, for that matter, did their northern colleagues insist that it be legally barred there, when everyone, North and South, knew that forbidden, encouraged, or ignored, the institution would never gain a foothold in the area?

The answers to these questions are complicated and tragic. Narrow partisanship is part of the explanation. In districts where slavery was entrenched, a congressman who watched over the institution with the eyes of Argus, ever ready to defend it against the most trivial slight, usually found himself a popular hero. In the northern states the representatives who were vigilant in what they might describe as "freedom's cause" seldom regretted it on election day. But slavery raised a moral question. Most Americans tried to avoid confronting this truth; as patriots they assumed that any sectional issue could be solved by compromise. However, while the majority of whites had little respect for blacks, slave or free, few persons, northern or southern, could look upon the ownership of one human being by another as simply an alternative form of economic organization and argue its merits as they would those of the protective tariff or a national bank. Twist the facts as they might, slavery was either right or it was wrong; being on the whole honest and moral, they could not, having faced that truth, stand by unconcerned while the question was debated.

The question could come up in Congress only indirectly, for the Constitution did not give the federal government any control over slavery in the states. But Congress had complete control in the territories. Therefore the fact that slavery had no future in the Mexican cession was unimportant— in fact, for the foes of slavery it was an advantage. By attacking slavery where it did not and probably never could exist, they could conceal from the slaveholders—and perhaps even from themselves—their hope ultimately to extinguish the institution.

Slavery had complicated the Texas problem from the start, and it beclouded the future of the Southwest even before the Mexican flag had been stripped from the staffs at Santa Fe and Los Angeles. The northern, Van Burenite wing of the Democratic party had become increasingly uneasy about the proslavery cast of Polk's policies, which were unpopular in their part of the country. Once it became likely that the war would bring new territory into the Union, these northerners felt compelled to try to check the president and to assure their constituents that they would resist the admission of further slave territory. On August 8, 1846, during the debate on a bill appropriating

■ Two leading lights of the day, Webster at the left and Clay at the right, as they looked about the time they played major roles in the Compromise of 1850. The daguerreotype of Clay dates from the late 1840s, that of Webster (by the noted Boston firm of Southworth and Hawes) from 1851, a year before he died.

money for the conduct of the war, Congressman David Wilmot of Pennsylvania, normally a staunch supporter of the Polk administration, introduced an amendment that provided "as an express and fundamental condition to the acquisition of any territory from the Republic of Mexico" that "neither slavery nor involuntary servitude shall ever exist in any part of said territory, except for crime, whereof the party shall first be duly convicted."

The Wilmot Proviso passed the House but met defeat in the Senate. To counter it, Calhoun, again senator from South Carolina, introduced a series of resolutions the following February that argued that Congress had no right to bar slavery from any territory; since territories belonged to all the states, slave and free, all should have equal rights in them. From this position it was only a step (soon taken) to demanding that Congress guarantee the right of slaveowners to bring slaves into the territories and establish federal slave codes in the territories. Most northerners considered this

proposal as repulsive as southerners found the Wilmot Proviso.

Calhoun's resolutions could never pass the northern-dominated House of Representatives, and Wilmot's Proviso had no chance in the Senate. Yet their very existence threatened the Union; as Senator Benton remarked, they were like the blades of a pair of scissors, ineffective separately, an efficient cutting tool taken together.

To resolve the territorial problem, two compromises were offered. One, eventually backed by President Polk, would extend the Missouri Compromise line to the Pacific. The majority of southerners were willing to go along with this scheme, but most northerners would no longer agree to the reservation of *any* new territory for slavery. The other possibility, advocated by Senator Lewis Cass of Michigan, called for organizing new territories without mention of slavery, thus leaving it to local settlers, through their territorial legislatures, to determine their own institutions. Cass' "popular sovereignty," known more vulgarly as "squatter sovereignty," had the superficial merits of appearing to be democratic and of enabling the members of Congress to escape the responsibility of deciding the question themselves.

Election of 1848

One test of strength occurred in August, before the 1848 presidential election. After six months of acrimonious debate, Congress passed a bill barring slavery from Oregon. The test, however, proved little. If it required half a year to settle the question for Oregon, how could an answer ever be found for California and New Mexico? Plainly the time had come, in a democracy, to go to the people. The coming presidential election seemed to provide an ideal opportunity.

In this crisis politicians of both parties hedged, fearful of losing votes in one section or another. With the issues blurred, the electorate had no real choice. That the Whigs should behave in such a manner was perhaps to be expected of the party of "Tippecanoe and Tyler too," but in 1848 they outdid even their 1840 performance, nominating Zachary Taylor for president. They chose the general despite his total lack of political sophistication and after he had flatly refused to state his opinion on any current subject. The party offered no platform. Taylor was a brave man and a fine general; the Democrats had mistreated him; he was a common, ordinary fellow, unpretentious and warmhearted. Such was the Whig "argument." Taylor's contribution to the campaign was so naive as to be pathetic. "I am a Whig, *but not an ultra Whig*. . . . If elected . . . I should feel bound to administer the government untrammeled by party schemes."

The Democratic party had little better to offer. All the drive and zeal characteristic of it in the Jackson period had gradually seeped away. Polk's espousal of Texas annexation had driven many northerners from its ranks. Individuals like James Buchanan of Pennsylvania, Polk's secretary of state, and William L. Marcy of New York, his secretary of war—cautious, cynical politicians interested chiefly in getting and holding office—now came to the fore in northern Democratic politics.

The Democratic nominee was Lewis Cass, the father of popular sovereignty, but the party did not endorse that or any other solution to the territorial question. Cass was at least an experienced politician, having been governor of Michigan Territory, secretary of war, minister to France, and senator. Nevertheless, he was vain, aloof, and conservative. His approach to life was exemplified by an annoying habit he displayed at Washington social functions: a teetotaler, he would circulate among the guests with a glass in hand, raising it to his lips repeatedly but never swallowing a drop.

The Van Buren wing of the Democratic party, now known as Barnburners,* could not stomach Cass, in part because he was willing to countenance the extension of slavery into new territories, in part because he had led the swing to Polk in the 1844 Democratic convention. Combining with the Liberty party, they formed the Free Soil party and nominated Van Buren.

Van Buren knew he could not be elected, but he believed the time had come to take a stand. "The minds of nearly all mankind have been penetrated by a conviction of the evils of slavery," the onetime "Fox" and "Magician" declared. The Free Soil party polled nearly 300,000 votes, about 10 percent of the total, in a very dull campaign. Offered a choice between honest ignorance and cynical opportunism, the voters—by a narrow margin—chose the former, Taylor receiving 1.36 million votes to Cass' 1.22 million. Taylor carried 8 of the 15 slave states and 7 of the 15 free states, proof that the sectional issue had been avoided.

The Compromise of 1850

The issue was not avoided for long. The discovery of gold had brought an army of prospectors into California. By the summer of 1848 San Francisco had become almost a ghost town, and an estimated two-thirds of the adult males of Oregon had hastened south to the gold fields. After President Polk confirmed the "extraordinary character" of the strike in his annual message of December 1848, there was no containing the gold seekers. During 1849, 25,000 Americans made their way to California from the East by ship; more than 55,000 others crossed the continent by overland routes. About 8,000 Mexicans, 5,000

---

*To call attention to their radicalism—supposedly they would burn down the barn to get rid of the rats.

■ The hard road to El Dorado as sketched by J. Goldsborough Bruff, a Washington, D.C., draftsman who led a company "to see the elephant" (in the phrase of the day) in 1849. At right, the gold seekers "circle up" for the night. The two self-portraits below from Bruff's diary neatly sum up the journey. His pencil notes are: Below left, "Seeing the Elephant. Leaving Home (No. 1)." Under his sketch, "D--n your $3 when one can make $100 a day easy." Below right, "Seeing the Elephant. No. 5. Arrival in California." Above the sketch, "The mule understands breaking better than being broke." Below the sketch, "40 miles more without fodder! rather tight, but then the jig's up and I'll soon have my pile! So I'll drive on." On the tree, "Only 40 mi. to the Settlements. Flour $2.25 lb."

South Americans, and numbers of Europeans joined the rush.

The rough limits of the gold country had been quickly marked out. For 150 miles and more along the western slope of the Sierras stretched the great mother lode. Along the expanse any stream or canyon, any ancient gravel bed might conceal a treasure in nuggets, flakes, or dust. Armed with pickaxes and shovels, with washing pans, even with knives and spoons, the eager prospectors hacked and dug and sifted, each accumulating a horde, some great, some small, of gleaming yellow metal.

The impact on the region was enormous. Almost overnight the Spanish-American population was reduced to the status of a minority. Disregarding justice and reason alike, the newcomers from the east, as one observer noted, "regarded every man but a native [North] American as an interloper." They referred to everyone of Latin American origin as a "greaser" and sought by law and by violence to keep them from mining for gold. Even the local Californians (now American citizens) were discriminated against.

The ethnic conflict was only part of the problem. Rough, hard men, separated from women, lusting for gold in a strange wild country where fortunes could be made in a day, gambled away in an hour, or stolen in an instant—the situation demanded the establishment of a territorial government. President Taylor appreciated this, and in his gruff, simplehearted way he suggested an uncomplicated answer: admit California directly as a state, letting the Californians decide for themselves about slavery. The rest of the Mexican Cession could be formed into another state. No need for Congress, with its angry rivalries, to meddle at all, he believed. In this way the nation could avoid the divisive effects of sectional debate.

The Californians reacted favorably to Taylor's proposal. They were overwhelmingly opposed to slavery, though not for humanitarian reasons. On the contrary, they tended to look upon blacks as they did Mexicans and feared that if slavery were permitted, white gold seekers would be disadvantaged. "They would be unable," one delegate to the California constitutional convention predicted, "to compete with the bands of negroes who would be set to work under the direction of capitalists. It would become a monopoly." By October 1849 they had drawn up a constitution that outlawed

slavery, and by December the new state government was functioning.

At this the South stood aghast. Taylor was the owner of a large plantation and many slaves; southerners had assumed (without bothering to ask) that he would fight to keep the territories open to slavery. To admit California would destroy the balance between free and slave states in the Senate; to allow all the new land to become free would doom the South to wither in a corner of the country, surrounded by hostile free states. Should that happen, how long could slavery sustain itself even in South Carolina? Radicals were already saying that the South would have to choose between secession and surrender. Taylor's plan played into the hands of extremists.

This was no longer a squabble over territorial governments. With the Union itself at stake, Henry Clay rose to save the day. He had been as angry and frustrated when the Whigs nominated Taylor as he was when they passed him over for Harrison. Now, well beyond 70 and in ill health, he put away his ambition and his resentment and for the last time concentrated his remarkable vision on a great, multifaceted national problem. California must be free and soon admitted to the Union, but the South must have some compensation. For that matter, why not seize the opportunity to settle every outstanding sectional conflict related to slavery? Clay pondered long and hard, drew up a plan, then consulted his old Whig rival Webster and obtained his general approval. On January 29, 1850, he laid his proposal, "founded upon mutual forbearance," before the Senate. A few days later he defended it on the floor of the Senate in the last great speech of his life.

California should be brought directly into the Union as a free state, he argued. The rest of the Southwest should be organized as a territory without mention of slavery: the southerners would retain the right to bring slaves there, while in fact none would do so. "You have got what is worth more than a thousand Wilmot Provisos," Clay pointed out to his northern colleagues. "You have nature on your side." The empty lands in dispute along the Texas border should be assigned to New Mexico Territory, Clay continued, but in exchange the United States should take over Texas' preannexation debts. The slave trade should be abolished in the District of Columbia (but not slavery itself), and a more effective federal fugitive slave

'CONQUERING PREJUDICE,'
or
"Fulfilling a Constitutional duty with alacrity."

■ New Englanders severely criticized Webster for his support of the fugitive slave bill that became part of the Compromise of 1850. In this lithograph he is the central figure. "He exceeds my most sanguine expectation," cries a slave catcher (right).

law should be enacted and strictly enforced in the North.

Clay's proposals occasioned one of the most magnificent debates in the history of the Senate. Every important member had his say. Calhoun, perhaps even more than Clay, realized that the future of the nation was at stake and that his own days were numbered.* Too feeble to deliver his speech himself, he sat impassive, wrapped in a great cloak, while Senator James M. Mason of Virginia read it to the crowded Senate. Calhoun thought his plan would save the Union, but his speech was an argument for secession; he demanded that the North yield completely on every point, ceasing even to discuss the question of slavery. Clay's compromise was unsatisfactory; he himself had no other to offer. If you will not yield, he said to the northern senators, "let the States . . . agree to separate and part in peace. If you are unwilling we should part in peace, tell us so, and we shall know what to do. . . ."

Three days later, on March 7, Daniel Webster

*He died on March 31.

took the floor. He too had begun to fail; the brilliant volubility and the thunder were gone, and when he spoke his face was bathed in sweat and there were strange pauses in his delivery. But his argument was lucid. Clay's proposals should be adopted. Since the future of all the territories had already been fixed by geographical and economic factors, the Wilmot Proviso was unnecessary. The North's constitutional obligation to yield fugitive slaves, he said, braving the wrath of New England abolitionists, was "binding in honor and conscience." (A cynic might say that once again Webster was placing property rights above human rights, yet his sincerity was beyond question.) The Union, he continued, could not be sundered without bloodshed. At the thought of the dread possibility, the old fire flared: "Peaceable secession!" Webster exclaimed, "Heaven forbid! Where is the flag of the republic to remain? Where is the eagle still to tower?"

The debate did not end with the aging giants. Every possible viewpoint was presented, argued, rebutted, rehashed. Senator William H. Seward of New York, a new Whig leader, close to Taylor's

The Compromise of 1850 / 307

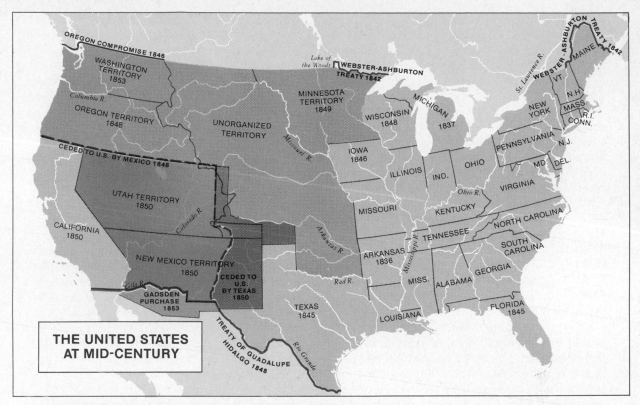

THE UNITED STATES
AT MID-CENTURY

■ This map indicates the provisions of the Compromise of 1850 that applied to the Mexican cession. Beginning with the annexation of Texas in 1845 and ending with the Gadsden Purchase in 1853 (to furnish a route for a southern transcontinental railroad), the United States added more than 869 million acres of territory.

ear, caused a stir while arguing against concessions to the slave interests by saying that despite the constitutional obligation to return fugitive slaves, a "higher law" than the Constitution, the law of God, forbade anything that countenanced the evil of slavery.

The majority clearly favored some compromise, but nothing could have been accomplished without the death of President Taylor on July 9. Obstinate, probably resentful because few people paid him half the heed they paid Clay and other prominent members of Congress, he had insisted on his own plan to bring both California and New Mexico directly into the Union. When Vice-President Millard Fillmore succeeded him, the deadlock between the White House and Capitol Hill was broken. Even so, each part of the compromise had to be voted upon separately, for too many stubborn congressmen were willing to overturn the whole plan because they objected to specific parts of it.

Senator Benton, for example, announced against Clay's Omnibus Bill because he objected to the fugitive slave provision and the Texas boundary settlement.

The final congressional maneuvering was managed by another relative newcomer, Senator Stephen A. Douglas of Illinois, who took over when Washington's summer heat prostrated the exhausted Clay. Partisanship and economic interests complicated Douglas' problem. According to rumor, Clay had persuaded an important Virginia newspaper editor to back the compromise by promising him a $100,000 government printing contract. This inflamed many southerners. New York merchants, fearful of the disruption of their southern business, submitted a petition bearing 25,000 names in favor of compromise, a document that had a favorable effect in the South. The prospect of the federal government's paying the debt of Texas made ardent compromisers of a horde of speculators. Between February and September, Texas bonds rose erratically from 29 to over 60, while men like W. W. Corcoran, whose Washington bank held more than $400,000 of these securities, entertained legislators and supplied lobbyists with large amounts of cash.

In the Senate and then in the House tangled combinations pushed through the separate measures, one by one. California became the thirty-first state. The rest of the Mexican cession was divided into two territories, New Mexico and Utah, each to be admitted to the Union when qualified, "with or without slavery as [its] constitution may prescribe." Texas received $10 million to pay off its debt in return for accepting a narrower western boundary. The slave trade in the District of Columbia was abolished as of January 1, 1851. The Fugitive Slave Act of 1793 was amended to provide for the appointment of federal commissioners with authority to issue warrants, summon posses, and compel citizens under pain of fine or imprisonment to assist in the capture of fugitives. The fugitives were to be returned to the South without jury trial merely upon the submission of an affidavit by their "owner," and they could not testify in their own defense.

Only 4 senators and 28 representatives voted for all these bills. In general, the Democrats gave more support to the compromise than the Whigs, but party lines never held firmly. For example, 17 Democrats and 15 Whigs voted to admit California as a free state. A large number of congressmen absented themselves when parts of the settlement unpopular in their home districts came to a vote; 21 senators and 36 representatives failed to commit themselves on the new fugitive slave bill. Senator Jefferson Davis of Mississippi voted for the fugitive slave measure and the bill creating Utah Territory, remained silent on the New Mexico bill, and opposed the other measures. Senator Salmon P. Chase of Ohio, an abolitionist, supported only the admission of California and the abolition of the slave trade.

In this piecemeal fashion the Union was preserved. The credit belongs mostly to Clay, whose original conceptualization of the compromise enabled lesser minds to understand what they must do.

Everywhere sober and conservative citizens sighed with relief. Mass meetings throughout the country "ratified" the result. Hundreds of newspapers gave the compromise editorial approval. In Washington patriotic harmony reigned. "You would suppose that nobody had ever thought of disunion," Webster wrote. "All say they always meant to stand by the Union to the last." When Congress met again in December, it seemed that party asperities had been buried forever. "I have determined never to make another speech on the slavery question," Senator Douglas told his colleagues. "Let us cease agitating, stop the debate, and drop the subject." If this were done, he predicted, the compromise would be accepted as a "final settlement." So, indeed, it seemed, as the year 1850 passed into history.

SUPPLEMENTARY READING

Titles marked with an asterisk have been published in paperback

G. G. Van Deusen, **The Jacksonian Era*** (1959), provides a convenient summary of the period. For the Tyler administration, see O. D. Lambert, **Presidential Politics in the United States: 1841–1844** (1936), R. J. Morgan, **A Whig Embattled: The Presidency under John Tyler** (1954), G. R. Poage, **Henry Clay and the Whig Party** (1936), and Robert Seager, **And Tyler Too!** (1963), which is useful chiefly for its portrayal of Tyler's personal life.

On diplomatic affairs, see P. A. Varg, **United States Foreign Relations: 1820–1860** (1979), and D. M. Pletcher, **The Diplomacy of Annexation: Texas, Oregon, and the Mexican War** (1973). E. C. Barker, **Mexico and Texas** (1928) and **Life of Stephen F. Austin*** (1925), dis-

cuss the migration of Americans into the Texas region, while W. C. Binkley, **The Texas Revolution** (1952), and Marquis James, **The Raven*** (1929), the latter a biography of Sam Houston, are good accounts of the Texans' struggle for independence.

The new expansionism is discussed in A. K. Weinberg, **Manifest Destiny*** (1935), and in Frederick Merk, **Manifest Destiny and Mission in American History*** (1963) and **The Monroe Doctrine and American Expansionism** (1966). H. N. Smith, **Virgin Land*** (1950), is also important for an understanding of this subject. The course of western development is treated in R. A. Billington, **The Far Western Frontier*** (1956). On Oregon see O. O. Winther, **The Great Northwest** (1947), David

Lavender, **Westward Vision: The Story of the Oregon Trail*** (1963), and Francis Parkman's classic account, **The Oregon Trail*** (1849). The history of the American penetration of California is covered in R. G. Cleland, **From Wilderness to Empire** (1944).

For the election of 1844, see J. C. N. Paul, **Rift in the Democracy*** (1961). The best biography of Polk is C. G. Sellers' **James K. Polk** (1957–1966), but see also C. A. McCoy, **Polk and the Presidency** (1960), and Allan Nevins (ed.), **Polk: The Diary of a President** (1929). N. A. Graebner, **Empire on the Pacific** (1955), is the fullest analysis of the factors influencing the Oregon boundary compromise.

There are a number of good brief accounts of the Mexican War, including A. H. Bill, **Rehearsal for Conflict** (1947), and O. A. Singletary, **The Mexican War*** (1960). See also Holman Hamilton, **Zachary Taylor: Soldier of the Republic** (1946), and C. W. Elliott, **Winfield Scott** (1937). J. H. Schroeder, **Mr. Polk's War** (1973), discusses American opposition to the conflict. Allan Nevins' masterpiece, **The Ordeal of the Union** (1947–1960), commences with 1847 and so covers part of the Mexican conflict. For the discovery of gold in California, in addition to the work of Billington mentioned above, see R. W. Paul, **California Gold: The Beginning of Mining in the Far West*** (1947), and J. W. Caughey, **Gold Is the Cornerstone** (1948). On the treatment of Mexicans and blacks, see R. F. Heizer and A. J. Almquist, **The Other Californians*** (1971), and R. M. Lapp, **Blacks in Gold Rush California** (1977).

The fullest study of the Compromise of 1850 is Holman Hamilton, **Prologue to Conflict*** (1964). See also Allan Nevins' **Ordeal of the Union,** the biographies of Clay, Calhoun, and Webster cited in earlier chapters, C. B. Going, **David Wilmot: Free-Soiler** (1924), R. W. Johannsen, **Stephen A. Douglas** (1973), Holman Hamilton, **Zachary Taylor: Soldier in the White House** (1951), and A. O. Craven, **The Growth of Southern Nationalism** (1953).

13/AN ERA OF ECONOMIC CHANGE

 A nation growing as rapidly as the United States in the middle decades of the 19th century changed continually in hundreds of ways. The country was developing a *national* economy marked by the dependence of each area upon all the others, the production of goods in one region for sale in all, the increased specialization of agricultural and industrial producers, and the growth in size of the average unit of production. Basic adjustments were taking place, sometimes unnoticed. Cotton remained the most important southern crop and the major American export; however, after the mid 1840s the mainsprings of national economic growth were the manufacturing of the Northeast and the railroads, which revolutionized transportation and communication.

The continuing westward movement of agriculture had significant new effects. American foreign commerce changed radically, and the flood of European immigration had an impact on manufacturing, town life, and farming.

Agriculture in the Old South

The South was changing less than any other section. Cotton remained "king" of the region, slavery its most distinctive institution. Nevertheless, a number of significant agricultural developments occurred. Cotton continued to march westward until by 1859, 1.3 million of the 4.3 million bales grown in the United States came from beyond the Mississippi. In the Upper South, Virginia held its place as the leading tobacco producer, but states beyond the Appalachians were raising more than half the crop by the 1850s. Early in that decade the introduction of Bright Yellow, a mild variety of tobacco that (miraculously) grew best in poor soil, gave a great stimulus to production. The older sections of Maryland, Virginia, and North Carolina shifted to the kind of diversified farming usually associated with the Northeast. By 1849 the wheat crop of Virginia was worth twice as much as the tobacco crop.

In the time of Washington and Jefferson, progressive Virginia planters had experimented with crop rotation and fertilizers. In the mid 19th century, pressed by the exhaustion of their soils after decades of tobacco cultivation, many Virginia farmers adopted advanced methods. Edmund Ruffin introduced the use of marl, an earth rich in calcium, to counteract the acidity of worn-out tobacco fields. Ruffin discovered that dressings of marl, combined with the use of fertilizers and with proper drainage and plowing methods, doubled and even tripled the yield of corn and wheat. In his *Essay on Calcareous Manures* (1832), which went through five editions, and in his magazine *The Farmers' Register*, Ruffin described the advantages of scientific farming. In the 1840s some southerners began to import Peruvian guano, a high-nitrogen fertilizer of bird droppings, which increased yields. Others experimented with contour plowing to control erosion, with improved breeds of livestock, new types of plows, and agricultural machinery.

Slavery as an Economic Institution

The increased importance of cotton in the South strengthened the hold of slavery on the region. The price of slaves rose until by the 1850s a prime field hand was worth as much as $1,800, roughly three times the cost in the 1820s. While the prestige value of owning this kind of property affected its price, the rise chiefly reflected the increasing value of the South's agricultural output. "Crop value per slave" jumped from less than $15 early in the century to more than $125 in 1859.

In the cotton fields of the Deep South slaves brought several hundred dollars per head more than in the older regions; thus the tendency to sell them "down the river" continued. Mississippi took in some 10,000 slaves a year throughout the period; as a result, in 1830 the black population of the state exceeded the white. Slave trading became a big business. There were about 50 dealers in Charleston in the 1850s and 200 in New Orleans. The largest traders were Isaac Franklin and John Armfield, who collected slaves from Virginia and Maryland at their "model jail" in Alexandria and shipped them by land and sea to a huge depot near Natchez. Each of the partners cleared half a million dollars before retiring, and other, smaller operators did proportionately well.

The impact of the trade on the slaves was frequently disastrous. Husbands were often separated from wives, parents from children. But because the business was so profitable, the prejudice against slave traders tended to disappear. Men of high social status became traders, and persons of humble origin who had prospered in the trade had little difficulty in buying land and setting up as respectable planters.

As blacks became more expensive, the ownership of slaves became more concentrated. On the eve of the Civil War only one white southern family in four owned any at all. In 1850 only 254 persons owned 200 or more slaves. In 1860 only about 46,000 of the 8 million white residents of the slave states had as many as 20. When one calculates the cost of 20 slaves and the land to keep them profitably occupied, it is easy to understand why this figure is so small. The most efficient size of a plantation worked by gangs of slaves ranged between 1,000 and 2,000 acres. In

■ "Anderson . . . , 24, a No. 1 bricklayer and mason," brought the top price of $2,700 in a New Orleans slave auction in 1856.

every part of the South the majority of farmers cultivated no more than 200 acres, in many sections less than 100 acres. A few large plantations and many small farms—this was the pattern. However, the *trend* in the South was toward larger agricultural units.

There were few genuine economies of scale in southern agriculture. Small farmers grew the staple crops, and many of them owned a few slaves, often working beside them in the fields. These yeomen farmers were the backbone of the South—hardworking, self-reliant, and moderately prosperous, quite unlike the "poor white trash" of the pine barrens and the remote valleys of the Appalachians who scratched a meager subsistence from substandard soils and lived in ignorance and squalor.

Well-managed plantations yielded annual profits of 10 percent and more, and in general, money invested in southern agriculture earned at least a modest return. Considering the way the work force was exploited, this is hardly surprising. Recent estimates indicate that after allowing for the cost of land and capital, the average plantation slave "earned" cotton worth $78.78 in 1859. It cost masters about $32 a year to feed, clothe, and house a slave. In other words, almost 60 percent of the product of slave labor was expropriated by the masters.

However, the South failed to develop locally owned marketing and transportation facilities, and for this slavery was at least partly responsible. In 1840 *Hunt's Merchant Magazine* estimated that it cost $2.85 to move a bale of cotton from the farm to a seaport and that additional charges for storage, insurance, port fees, and freight to a European port exceeded $15. Middlemen from outside the South commonly earned most of this money. New York capitalists gradually came to control much of the South's cotton from the moment it was picked, and a large percentage of the crop found its way into New York warehouses before being sold to manufacturers. The same middlemen supplied most of the foreign goods that the planters purchased with their cotton earnings.

Southerners complained about this state of affairs but did little to correct it. Capital tied up in the ownership of labor could not be invested in anything else, and social pressures in the South militated against investment in trade and commerce. Ownership of land and slaves yielded a kind of psychic income not available to any middleman. Moreover, the system made underconsumers of 4 million southerners. As one British visitor pointed out, slaves were "a nonconsuming class." Finally, the enormous reservoir of intelligence and skill that the blacks represented was almost entirely wasted, as, unfortunately, so much of it is still wasted in America. Many slave craftsmen worked on the plantations, and a few free blacks made their way in the South remarkably well, but the amount of talent unused, energy misdirected, and imagination smothered can only be guessed.

Foreign observers in New England frequently noted the alertness and industriousness of ordinary laborers and attributed this, justifiably, to the high level of literacy. Less than 1 percent of the

■ **This Richmond slave-market scene was painted about 1853 by an English artist, Eyre Crowe. The quiet dignity of the slave family and the businesslike demeanor of the prospective buyers reminded a commentator on the painting of Hannah Arendt's indictment of Nazi death-camp bureaucracy: "the banality of evil."**

population in New England could not read and write. Correspondingly, the stagnation and inefficiency of southern labor could be attributed in part to the high degree of illiteracy, for over 20 percent of *white* southerners could not read or write, a tragic squandering of human resources.

Slavery as a Social Institution

It is difficult to generalize about the "peculiar institution" because so much depended on the individual master's behavior. Owners exercised power over their human possessions "as absolute . . . as the Khan of Tartary." Yet the system was fundamentally paternalistic. Most owners felt responsibilities toward their slaves, and slaves were dependent on and imitative of white values. However, powerful fears and resentments, not always recognized, existed on both sides. The plantation environment forced the two races to live in close proximity. From this circumstance could rise

every sort of human relationship. One planter, using the appropriate pseudonym Clod Thumper, could write: "Africans are nothing but brutes, and they will love you better for whipping, whether they deserve it or not." Another, describing a slave named Bug, could say: "No one knows but myself what feeling I have for him. Black as he is we were raised together."

The United States was the only place in the Western Hemisphere where the slave population grew by natural increase. After the ending of the slave trade the black population increased at about the same proportion as the white, rising from 1 million to 4 million by 1860. Put differently, during the entire period from the founding of Jamestown to the Civil War only a little more than half a million slaves were imported into the country, about 5 percent of the number of Africans carried by slavers to the New World. Surely this proves that American slaves were not driven to extinction.

Most owners provided adequate clothing, hous-

■ These reportorial views of slavery were sketched by a young Austrian, Franz Hölzlhuber, who toured the South between 1856 and 1860. Above is a rice plantation on the Arkansas River. The slaves below, harvesting sugar cane in Louisiana, are dressed in striped garb to discourage attempts at escape.

ing, and food for their slaves, for only a fool or a sadist would fail to take care of such valuable property. But the slave diet (chiefly corn and hog fat) was deficient in protein, and this could make slaves disease-prone. Vital statistics indicate that infant mortality among slaves was twice the white rate, life expectancy at least five years less. The most careful student of this subject, Richard Sutch, concludes: "the returns from slavery were maximized by using force to extract the maximum amount of work from the slaves while providing them only with sufficient food, shelter, clothing, and health care to keep them healthy and hard working."

Slaves were without rights; they developed a distinctive way of life by attempting to resist oppression and injustice while accommodating themselves to the system. Their marriages had no legal status, but their partnerships seem to have been as loving and stable as those of their masters. Certainly they were acutely conscious of family relationships and responsibilities. Slave religion, on the surface an untutored form of Christianity tinctured with some African survivals, seemed to most slaveowners a useful instrument for teaching meekness and resignation and for providing harmless emotional release, as indeed it was and did. It also, however, sustained the slaves' sense of their own worth as creatures made in the image of God, and it taught them, therefore, that while human beings can be enslaved in body, their spirits cannot be enslaved without their consent.

Nearly every white observer claimed that slaves were congenitally lazy; George Washington, for example, wrote that "when an overlooker's back is turned, the most of them will slight their work, or be idle altogether." In part this tendency can be explained as a rational response to forced, uncompensated labor. As one planter confessed, they "are not stimulated to care and industry as white people are, who labor for themselves." "Laziness" was also a reflection of a peasantlike view of the world, one that was a product of their surroundings, not of their servile status. The historian Eugene D. Genovese says that owners would have liked their slaves to behave like clock-punching factory workers, but plantations were not factories, and no one, least of all the masters, punched a clock. "Do as I say, not as I do," is not an effective way of teaching anything. Moreover, it must be remembered that under slavery the "overlook-er's back" was rarely turned. Slaves worked long and hard, whatever their innate tendencies might have been.

Observing that slaves were often happy and only rarely overtly rebellious, whites persuaded themselves that most blacks accepted the system without resentment and indeed preferred slavery to the uncertainties of freedom. There was much talk about "loyal and faithful servants." The Civil War, when slaves flocked to the Union lines once assured of freedom and fair treatment, disabused them of this illusion. "This war has taught us the perfect impossibility of placing the least confidence in the negro," one planter explained in 1862. After the war this planter wrote: "I believed that these people were content, happy, and attached to their masters . . . [but] we were all laboring under a delusion."

As slaves became more valuable and as northern opposition to the institution grew more vocal, the system hardened perceptibly. Southerners made much of the danger of insurrection. When a plot was uncovered or a revolt took place, instant and savage reprisals resulted. In 1822, after the conspiracy of Denmark Vesey was exposed by informers, 37 slaves were executed and another 30-odd deported, although no overt act of rebellion had occurred. After a rising in Louisiana, 16 blacks were decapitated, their heads left to rot on poles along the Mississippi as a grim warning. The Nat Turner revolt in Virginia in 1831 was the most sensational of the slave uprisings; 57 whites lost their lives before it was suppressed. Southerners treated runaways almost as brutally as rebels, though they posed no real threat to whites. The authorities tracked down fugitives with bloodhounds and subjected captives to merciless lashings.

As the years passed, interest in doing away with slavery simply vanished in the South. The southern states made it increasingly difficult, if not impossible, for masters to free their slaves. During 1859 in all the South only about 3,000 in a slave population of nearly 4 million were given their freedom, and many of them were elderly and thus of little or no economic value.

Some unscrupulous southerners engaged in smuggling fresh supplies from Africa. About 54,000 slaves entered America illegally after the trade was outlawed in 1808, not a very large number relative to the slave population. In *American*

SLAVERY RECORD.

INSURRECTION IN VIRGINIA!

Extract of a letter from a gentleman to his friend in Baltimore, dated

'RICHMOND, August 23d.

An express reached the governor this morning, informing him that an insurrection had broken out in Southampton, and that, by the last accounts, there were seventy whites massacred, and the militia retreating. Another express to Petersburg says that the blacks were continuing their destruction ; that three hundred militia were retreating in a body, before six or eight hundred blacks. A shower of rain coming up as the militia were making an attack, wet the powder so much that they were compelled to retreat, being armed only with shot-guns. The negroes are armed with muskets, scythes, axes, &c. &c. Our volunteers are marching to the scene of action. A troop of cavalry left at four o'clock, P. M. The artillery, with four field pieces, start in the steam boat Norfolk, at 6 o'clock, to land at Smithfield. Southampton county lies 80 miles south of us, below Petersburg.'

From the Richmond Whig, of Tuesday.

Disagreeable rumors have reached this city of an insurrection of the slaves in Southampton County, with loss of life. In order to correct exaggeration, and at the same time to induce all salutary caution, we state the following particulars :

An express from the Hon. James Trezvant states that an insurrection had broken out, that several families had been murdered, and that the negroes were embodied, requiring a considerable military force to reduce them.

The names and precise numbers of the families are not mentioned. A letter to the Post Master corroborates the intelligence. Prompt and efficient measures are being taken by the Governor, to call out a sufficient force to put down the insurrection, and place lower Virginia on its guard.

Serious danger of course there is none. The deluded wretches have rushed on assured destruction.

The Fayette Artillery and the Light Dragoons will leave here this evening for Southampton ; the artillery go in a steamboat, and the troop by land.

We are indebted to the kindness of our friend Lyford for the following extract of a letter from the Editors of the Norfolk Herald, containing the particulars of a most murderous insurrection among the blacks of Southampton County,* Virginia.—*Gaz.*

NORFOLK, 24th Aug. 1831.

I have a horrible, a heart rending tale to relate, and lest even its worst feature might be distorted by rumor and exaggeration, I have thought it proper to give you all and the worst information, that has as yet reached us through the best sources of intelligence which the nature of the case will admit.

A gentleman arrived here yesterday express from Suffolk, with intelligence from the upper part of Southampton county, stating that a band of insurgent slaves (some of them believed to be runaways from the neighboring Swamps,) had turned out on Sunday night last, and murdered several whole families, amounting to 40 or 50 individuals. Some of the families were named, and among them was that of Mrs. Catharine Whitehead, sister of our worthy townsman, Dr. N. C. Whitehead,—who, with her son and five daughters, fell a sacrifice to the savage ferocity of these demons in human shape.

■ The abolitionist *Liberator* reprinted southern accounts of the Nat Turner Revolt.

Slavers and Federal Law, a fascinating volume, Warren S. Howard estimates that over 30,000 were spirited into the United States and Cuba in the brief period 1857–1860, but he suspects that most of this number went to Cuba. British, French, Portuguese, and American naval vessels patrolled the African coast continuously. The American navy alone seized more than 50 suspected slavers in the two decades before 1860. However, the fast, sharklike pirate cruisers were hard to catch, the anti-slave-trade laws imperfectly worded and unevenly enforced. Many accounts tell of slaves in America long after 1808 with filed teeth, tattoos, and other signs of African origin, yet no one owning such a person was ever charged with the possession of contraband goods.

Psychological Effects of Slavery

The injustice of slavery needs no proof; less obvious is the fact that it had a corrosive effect on the personalities of southerners, slave and free alike. By "the making of a human being an animal without hope," the system bore heavily on all slaves' sense of their own worth. Some found the condition absolutely unbearable. They became the habitual runaways who collected whip scars like medals; the "loyal" servants who struck out in rage against a master knowing that the result would be certain death; the leaders of slave revolts.

Denmark Vesey of South Carolina, even after buying his freedom, could not stomach the subservience demanded of slaves by the system. When he saw Charleston slaves step into the gutter to make way for whites, he taunted them: "You deserve to remain slaves!" For years he preached resistance to his fellows, drawing his texts from the Declaration of Independence and the Bible and promising help from black Haiti. So vehemently did he argue that some of his followers claimed they feared Vesey more than their masters, even more than God. He planned his uprising for five years, patiently working out the details, only to see it aborted at the last moment when a few of his recruits lost their nerve and betrayed him. For Denmark Vesey, death was probably preferable to living with such rage as his soul contained.

Yet Veseys were rare. Most slaves appeared, if not contented, at least resigned to their fate. Some seemed even to accept the whites' evaluation of their inherent abilities and place in society. The historian Stanley Elkins has drawn an interesting parallel between the behavior of slaves and that of the inmates of Adolf Hitler's concentration camps, arguing that in both cases such factors as the fear of arbitrary punishment and the absence of any hope of escape led to the disintegration of the victim's personality—to childishness, petty thievery, chronic irresponsibility, and even to a degrading identification with the master race itself.

The comparison is overdrawn, for plantations were not concentration camps. Slaves had strong family and group attachments and a complex culture of their own, maintained, so to speak, under the noses of their masters. By a mixture of subterfuge, accommodation, and passive resistance, they erected subtle defenses against exploitation, achieving a sense of community that helped sustain the psychic integrity of individuals. And if some slaves indeed became fawning "Sambos" and "Uncle Toms," it must be remembered that the slave system was designed to make blacks submissive. It discouraged, if it did not extinguish, independence of judgment and self-reliance. These qualities are difficult enough to develop in human beings under the best circumstances; when every element in society encouraged slaves to let others do their thinking for them, to avoid questioning the status quo, to lead a simple, animal existence, many, probably most, did so willingly enough. Was this not slavery's greatest shame?

Slavery warped whites perhaps even more severely than it did blacks. This subject too has attracted the attention of psychoanalytically inclined historians, who have suggested, among other things, that the system encouraged whites to conceal their animal natures from themselves by projecting on the helpless slaves their own base passions. Many planters, these historians note, took advantage of their position to avail themselves of slave women. (Estimates of the proportion of the slave population fathered by whites range from 4 to 8 percent.) To avoid facing the fact that they were rapists, the whites pictured *blacks* as lustful, superpotent, and incapable of self-restraint. In a related manner idle slaveowners exacted labor from their slaves by brute force and justified their cruel whips by claiming that blacks were inher-

ently lazy. The harm done to the slaves by such mental distortions is obvious. More obscure is the effect on the masters: self-indulgence is perhaps only contemptible; self-delusion is pitiable.

Such a description of master-slave relations is one-sided. Probably the large majority of owners respected the most fundamental personal rights of their slaves. Indeed, so far as sexual behavior is concerned, there are countless known cases of lasting relationships based on love and mutual respect between owners and what law and the community defined as their "property."

And the psychological injury inflicted on whites by slavery can be demonstrated without resort to Freudian insights. By associating working for others with servility, it discouraged many poor southerners from hiring out to earn a stake. It provided the weak, the shiftless, and the unsuccessful with a scapegoat that made their own miserable state easier to bear but harder to escape. A few slaveowning sadists could not resist the temptations that the possession of human beings put before them. Such types could speak of "amusing" themselves with "the old strap." Growing up in Hannibal, Missouri, Sam Clemens, the future Mark Twain, once saw an angry overseer brain a clumsy slave for some minor ineptitude. "He was dead in an hour," Clemens later recalled. "Nobody in the village approved of that murder, but of course no one said much about it. . . . Considerable sympathy was felt for the slave's owner, who had been bereft of valuable property by a worthless person who was not able to pay for it."

More significant were the countless petty cruelties that the system allowed. "I feel badly, got very angry, and whipped Lavinia," one Louisiana woman wrote in her diary. "O! for government over my temper." But for slavery, she would surely have had better self-control. Similar though more subtle was the interaction of the institution with the American tendency to brag and bluster. "You can manage ordinary niggers by lickin' 'em and by givin' 'em a taste of hot iron once in a while when they're extra ugly," one uncouth Georgian was heard to say at a slave auction shortly before the Civil War. "But if a nigger ever sets himself up against me, I can't never have any patience with him. I just get my pistol and shoot him right down; and that's the best way." With the price of slaves as high as it was, this was probably just talk, but bad talk, harmful to speaker and listener alike. Northern braggarts, perforce, were less objectionable.

Still, braggarts are inconsequential in most social situations; historians need seldom pay them much heed. However, the finest white southerners were often warped by the institution. Even those who abhorred slavery sometimes let it corrupt their thinking: "I consider the labor of a breeding woman as no object, and that a child raised every 2 years is of more profit than the crop of the best laboring man." This cold appraisal was written by the author of the Declaration of Independence.

Manufacturing in the South

Although the temper of southern society discouraged business and commercial activity, considerable manufacturing developed. Small flour and lumber mills flourished. Iron and coal were mined in Virginia, Kentucky, and Tennessee. The Tredegar Iron Works in Richmond did an annual business of about $1 million.

Cotton textiles could be manufactured in the South because of the availability of the raw material and the abundance of waterpower along the Appalachian slopes. By 1825 a thriving factory was functioning at Fayetteville, North Carolina, and soon others sprang up in North Carolina and in adjoining states. William Gregg's factory at Graniteville, South Carolina, established in 1846, was a constant money-maker. An able propagandist as well as a good businessman, Gregg saw the textile business not only as a source of profit but as a device for improving the lot of the South's poor whites. He worked hard to weaken the southern prejudice against manufacturing and made his plant a model of benevolent paternalism similar to that of the early mills of Lowell. As with every other industry, however, southern textile manufacturing amounted to very little when compared with that of the North. Gregg employed only about 300 textile workers in 1850, the whole state of South Carolina fewer than 900. Lowell, Massachusetts, had more spindles turning in 1860 than did the entire South.

Less than 15 percent of all the goods manufactured in the United States in 1860 came from the South; the region did not really develop an industrial society. Its textile manufacturers depended on the North for machinery and for skilled workers and technicians. When the English geologist Charles Lyell visited New Orleans in 1846, he was astounded to discover that the thriving city supported not a single book publisher. Even a local guidebook that he purchased bore a New York imprint. As Clement Eaton has written in *The Growth of Southern Civilization,* "the agrarian ideal undoubtedly hampered the growth of the business class."

Industrial Expansion

The most obvious change in the North in the decades before the Civil War was the rapid expansion of industry. The best estimates suggest that immediately after the War of 1812 the United States was manufacturing annually less than $200 million worth of goods. In 1859 the northeastern states alone produced $1.27 billion of the national total of almost $2 billion. The rate of growth was accelerating; in 1837 Massachusetts, a typical industrial state, turned out manufactured products worth over $86 million; in 1845, about $125 million; in 1855, nearly $300 million.

Manufacturing expanded in so many directions that it is difficult to portray or to summarize its evolution. The factory system made great strides. The development of rich anthracite coalfields in Pennsylvania was particularly important in this connection. The coal could be floated cheaply on canals to convenient sites and used to produce both heat for smelting and metalworking and steam power to drive machinery. Steam permitted greater flexibility in locating factories and in organizing work within them, and since waterpower was already being used to capacity, steam was essential for the expansion of output.

American industry displayed a remarkable receptivity to technological change. In his *March of the Iron Men,* Roger Burlingame lists half a page of new inventions and processes developed between 1825 and 1850, including—besides such obviously important items as the sewing machine, the vulcanization of rubber, and the cylinder press—the screwmaking machine, the friction match, the lead pencil, and an apparatus for making soda water. A society in flux put a premium on resourcefulness; an environment that offered so much freedom to the individual encouraged experimentation. The

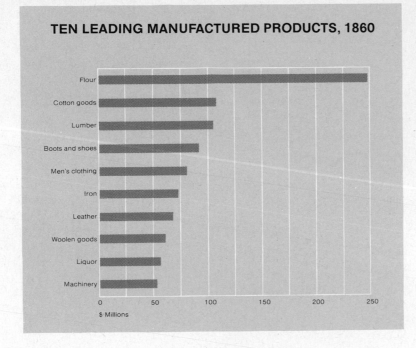

TEN LEADING MANUFACTURED PRODUCTS, 1860

Flour
Cotton goods
Lumber
Boots and shoes
Men's clothing
Iron
Leather
Woolen goods
Liquor
Machinery

0   50   100   150   200   250
$ Millions

■ The leading American industries as listed in the 1860 census of manufacturers are ranked here by value of product. The boots and shoes industry employed the most workers, 123,000. Next were cotton goods and men's clothing, each with just under 115,000 workers.

expanding market inspired businessmen to use new techniques. With skilled labor always in short supply, the pressure to substitute machines for trained hands was great.

In the 1820s a foreign visitor noted: "Everything new is quickly introduced here, and all the latest inventions. There is no clinging to old ways; the moment an American hears the word 'invention' he pricks up his ears." Twenty years later a Frenchman wrote: "If they continue to work with the same ardor, they will soon have nothing more to desire or to do. All the mountains will be flattened, the valleys filled, all matter rendered productive." By 1850 the United States led the world in the manufacture of goods that required the use of precision instruments, and in certain industries the country was well on the way toward modern mass-production methods. American clocks, pistols, rifles, and locks were outstanding.

The American exhibits at the London Crystal Palace Exhibition of 1851 so impressed the British that they sent two special commissions to the United States to study manufacturing practices. After visiting the Springfield Arsenal, the British investigators placed a large order for gunmaking machinery and hired a number of American technicians to help organize what became the Enfield rifle factory. They were amazed by the lock and clock factories of New England and by the plants where screws, files, and similar metal objects were turned out in volume by automatic machinery. Instead of resisting new laborsaving machines, they noted, "the workingmen hail with satisfaction all mechanical improvements."

Invention alone does not account for the industrial advance. Every year new natural resources were discovered and made available by the westward march of settlement, and the expansion of agriculture produced an ever larger supply of raw materials for the mills and factories. Of the ten leading industries in 1860, *eight* (flour milling, cotton textiles, lumber, shoes, men's clothing, leather, woolen goods, and liquor) relied on farm products for their raw materials.

In the 1850s the prejudice against the corporation began to break down; by the end of the decade the northern and northwestern states had all passed general incorporation laws. Of course the corporate device made possible larger accumulations of capital. While the federal government did not charter business corporations, two actions of Congress illustrate the shift in public attitudes. In 1840 a group of scientists sought a federal charter for a National Institution for the Promotion of Sci-

■ An elaborate 1851 chromolithograph applauds Yankee triumphs at the Crystal Palace Exhibition, ranging from artificial limbs to Hiram Powers' sculpture, *The Greek Slave* (page 270). At center is the yacht, *America*, winner of the first America's Cup in that year.

ence. They were turned down on constitutional grounds; if Congress "went on erecting corporations in this way," one legislator said, "they would come, at last, to have corporations for everything." In 1863, however, the bill creating the National Academy of Science went through both houses without debate.

Industrial growth led to a great increase in the demand for labor. The effects, however, were mixed. Skilled artisans, technicians, and toolmakers earned good wages and found it relatively easy to set themselves up as small manufacturers. The expanding frontier drained off much agricultural labor that might otherwise have been attracted to industry, and the thriving new towns of the West absorbed large numbers of eastern artisans of every kind. At the same time, the pay of an unskilled worker was never enough to support a family decently, and the new machines tended to weaken the bargaining power of the ordinary artisan by making skill superfluous.

Many other forces acted to stimulate manufacturing. Immigration increased rapidly during the period; an avalanche of strong backs and willing hands and thousands of keen, well-trained minds descended upon the country from Europe. Europeans invested large sums in the booming American economy, and the savings of millions of

Americans and the great hoard of new California gold added to the supply of capital. Improvements in transportation, the growth of the population, the absence of internal tariff barriers, and the relatively high per capita wealth of the people all meant an ever expanding market for manufactured goods.

Self-generated Expansion

The *pace* of the advance is best explained by many interactions, the "backward and forward linkages" produced by industrial activity. The cotton textile business was clearly the most important example. Samuel Slater built his first machines in his own little plant, but soon the industry spawned dozens of companies devoted to the manufacture of looms, spinning frames, and other machines. They in turn stimulated the growth of machine-tool production, metalworking companies, and eventually the mining and refining of iron. "For a considerable . . . period," George S. Gibb writes in his study of *Textile Machinery Building in New England, 1813–1849,* "the manufacture of textile machinery appears to have been America's greatest heavy goods industry. . . . From the textile mills and the textile machine shops came the men who supplied most of the tools for the American Industrial Revolution. From these mills and shops sprang directly the machine-tool and locomotive industries together with a host of less basic metal fabricating trades."

The booming mills stimulated what another historian calls "a vast array of final consumer goods industries to meet the needs of the northeastern urban dweller, the southern slave and planter, and the western farmer." Examples abound. The invention of the sewing machine in 1846 by Elias Howe (who got his early training in a Lowell cotton-machine factory) resulted in the creation of the ready-made clothing industry. The sewing machine soon revolutionized the shoe industry, speeding the trend toward factory production and triggering the same kind of forward and backward linkages that characterized the textile business. The new agricultural machinery business, besides stimulating other industries, made possible a huge expansion of farm production, which stimulated economic growth.

The New Industrial Society

Rapid industrialization influenced American life in countless ways, none more significant than its effect on the character of the work force and consequently on the structure of society. The jobs created by industrial expansion attracted European immigrants by the tens of thousands. It is a truism that America is a nation of immigrants—even the ancestors of the Indians came to the New World from Asia. But only with the development of nationalism, that is, with the establishment of the independent United States, did the word *immigrant,* meaning a foreign-born resident, come into existence.

The flow of newcomers was for several decades slow, first because of European wars and then because of bad times following the defeat of Napoleon. Fewer than 300,000 people entered the United States between 1775 and 1820. As late as 1840 less than 8 percent of the population was foreign-born or the children of immigrants. Then 1.5 million people came to the United States in the 1840s, and 2.6 million in the 1850s. In proportion to the population, this was the heaviest immigration in American history.

Most of this human tide came from two countries, Ireland and Germany. This was especially true between 1847 and 1854, when the Irish potato blight and a series of crop failures in Germany drove thousands to try their luck in America. Many thousands of substantial Germans and Scandinavians pushed on directly into the western regions. But the poorer immigrants could not afford to do this; farming required capital that the majority did not have. The Irish, "the poorest and most wretched population that can be found in the world," one of their priests called them, tended to settle in the large eastern seaports, which grew even more rapidly than the country as a whole. In 1830 New York had about 200,000 inhabitants; 20 years later it had 515,000; in 1860 there were over a million, more than half of whom were immigrants and their American-born children.

Viewed in historical perspective, immigration has stimulated the American economy and increased social mobility. Each increase in the labor force has made possible expanded production, and each new wave of migrants has pushed earlier arrivals up the social scale and on to better jobs. In

■ "Damned plague ships and swimming coffins," was the New York *Journal of Commerce's* blunt assessment of the transatlantic immigrant vessels crowding American ports in the 1840s and 1850s. This woodcut of immigrant families jammed into the steerage of one of these ships appeared in a French newspaper in 1849.

the short run, however, the influx of the 1840s and 1850s depressed living standards, weakened the social fabric, and sharpened class divisions. For the first time the nation had a culturally distinctive working class with its own habits and values. Irish immigrants in particular were so desperately poor that they would accept whatever wage employers offered them. They thus roused resentment among native workers, resentment exacerbated by the unfamiliarity of the Irish with city ways and by their Roman Catholic faith, which the Protestant majority associated with Old World authoritarianism and corruption.

The Irish developed their own prejudices, particularly against blacks, with whom they often competed for work. One of their leaders in the old country, Daniel O'Connell, admitted that the American Irish were "among the worst enemies of the colored race." And of course blacks responded with equal bitterness. "Every hour sees us elbowed out of some employment to make room for some newly-arrived emigrant from the Emerald Isle, whose hunger and color entitle him to special favor," one of them complained. Antiblack prejudice was less noticeable among other immigrant

groups but by no means absent; most immigrants adopted the views of the local native majority.

Social and racial rivalries aside, unskilled immigrants caused serious disruptions of economic patterns wherever they appeared. Their absorption into the factories of New England speeded the disintegration of the system of hiring young farm women. Already competition and technical advances in the textile industry were increasing the pace of the machines and reducing the number of skilled workers needed to run them. Fewer young farm women were willing to work under these conditions. Recent immigrants, who demanded less coddling and who seemed to provide the mills with a "permanent" working force, replaced the women in large numbers. By 1860 Irish immigrants alone made up more than 50 percent of the labor force in the New England mills.

The influx of immigrants does not entirely explain the wretched state of industrial workers during this period. Low wages and the crowding that resulted from the swift expansion of city populations produced slums that would make the most noisome modern ghetto seem a paradise. A Boston investigation in the late 1840s described one district as "a perfect hive of human beings . . . huddled together like brutes." In New York tens of thousands of the poor lived in dark, rank cellars, those in the waterfront districts often invaded by high tides. Tenement houses like great gloomy prisons rose back to back, each with many windowless rooms and often without heat or running water.

Outside the "home," city life for the poor was almost equally squalid. Slum streets were littered with garbage and trash. Recreational facilities were almost nonexistent, police and fire protection pitifully inadequate. "Urban problems" were less critical than a century later only because they affected a smaller part of the population; for those who experienced them they were, all too often, crushing. In the mid 1850s large numbers of children in New York scrounged a bare existence by begging and scavenging. They took shelter at night in coal bins and empty barrels.

■ New York's notorious Five Points District, about 1829. "Reeking everywhere with dirt and filth," Charles Dickens wrote of Five Points in 1842. "Where dogs would howl to lie, men and women and boys slink off to sleep, forcing the dislodged rats to move."

Most town workers maintained small vegetable gardens and a few chickens; low wage rates did not necessarily reflect a low standard of living. In the new industrial slums even a blade of grass was unusual. In 1851 the editor Horace Greeley's New York *Tribune* published a minimum weekly budget for a family of five. The budget, which allowed nothing for savings, medical bills, recreation, or other amenities (Greeley did include 12 cents a week for newspapers) came to $10.37. Since the weekly pay of a factory hand seldom reached $5, the wives and children of most workers labored in the factories merely to survive. And child labor in the 1850s differed fundamentally from child labor in the 1820s. The pace of the machines was faster, the surrounding environment more depressing.

Relatively few workers belonged to unions. Local federations of craft unions sprang up in the major cities, and during the boom that preceded the Panic of 1837, a National Trades' Union representing a few northeastern cities managed to hold conventions. Early in the Jackson era, "workingmen's" political parties enjoyed a brief popularity, occasionally electing a few local officials. These organizations were made up mostly of skilled craftsmen, professional reformers, and even businessmen. They soon expired, destroyed by internal bickering over questions that had little or nothing to do with working conditions.

The depression of the late thirties led to the demise of most trade unions. Nevertheless, *skilled* workers improved their lot somewhat in the 1840s and 1850s. The working day declined gradually from about 12.5 hours to 10 or 11 hours. Many states passed 10-hour laws and laws regulating child labor, but they were poorly enforced. Most states, however, enacted effective mechanic's lien laws, giving workers first call on the assets of bankrupt and defaulting employers, and the Massachusetts court's decision in the case of *Commonwealth* v. *Hunt* (1842), establishing the legality of labor unions, became a judicial landmark when other state courts followed the precedent.

The flush times of the early 1850s caused the union movement to revive. Many strikes occurred and a few new national organizations appeared. Most unions were local institutions, weak and with little control over their membership. The Panic of 1857 dealt the labor movement another body blow. Thus there was no trend toward the general unionization of labor between 1820 and the Civil War. For this the workers themselves were partly to blame: craftsmen took little interest in unskilled workers except to keep them down. Few common laborers considered themselves part of a permanent working class with different objectives from those of their employers. The traditional individualism of Americans, the fluidity of society, the constant influx of job-hungry immigrants, and the widespread use of women and children in unskilled jobs made labor organization difficult, for the assumption was that nearly anyone who was willing to work could eventually escape from the wage-earning class. "If any continue through life in the condition of the hired laborer," Abraham Lincoln declared in 1859, "it is . . . because of either a dependent nature which prefers it, or improvidence, folly, or singular misfortune."

Any investigation of American society before the Civil War reveals a paradox that is obvious but difficult to resolve. The United States was a land of opportunity, a democratic society with a prosperous, expanding economy and few class distinctions. Its people had a high standard of living in comparison with the citizens of European countries. Yet within this rich, confident nation there existed a class of miserably underpaid and depressed unskilled workers, mostly immigrants, who were worse off materially than nearly any southern slave. The literature is full of descriptions of needleworkers earning 12 cents a day, of women driven to prostitution because they could not earn a living decently, of hunger marches and soup kitchens, of disease and crime and people sunk into apathy by hopeless poverty. In 1848 more than 56,000 New Yorkers, about a quarter of the population, were receiving some form of public relief. A police drive in that city in 1860 brought in nearly 500 beggars.

The middle-class majority seemed indifferent to or at best unaware of these conditions. Reformers conducted investigations, published exposés, and labored to help the victims of urbanization and industrialization. They achieved little. Great fires burned in these decades to release the incredible energies of America. The poor were the ashes, sifting down silent and unnoticed beneath the dazzle and the smoke. While the industrial revolution was making the United States the richest nation in the world, it was also creating, as the historian Robert H. Bremner has said, "a poverty problem, novel in kind and alarming in size." Industrialization produced poverty (in Marxian terminology, a proletarian class) and a capitalistic aristocracy. Tenements sprang up cheek by jowl with the urban palaces of the new rich and the tree-lined streets of the prosperous middle class.

In colonial times Americans (as we have seen) believed in a stratified, deferential society, but in practice their civilization became increasingly democratic. After the Revolution, ideology rapidly caught up with practice, and for a brief moment reality and theory were in close accord. But as the researches of Edward Pessen have shown, by the time of Andrew Jackson large economic and social distinctions were rapidly developing. In the early 1840s about 300 residents of New York City owned property assessed at $100,000 or more, a sum equivalent to $4 million or more today, and the situation was similar in Boston, Philadelphia, and other cities. Most of these wealthy individuals were not self-made; they were scions of well-to-do and socially prominent families—in New York this was true of about 95 percent of them.

Economic opportunities were great, taxation minimal. Little wonder that as the generations passed, the rich got richer. Industrialization accelerated the process and, by stimulating the immigration of masses of poor workers, skewed the social balance still further. Society became more stratified, differences in wealth and status among citizens greater. But the ideology of egalitarian democracy reigned supreme. By the mid 19th century Americans were convinced that all men were equal, and indeed all *white* men had equal political rights. Socially and economically, however, the distances between top and bottom were widening. This situation endured for the rest of the century, and in some respects it still endures.

Foreign Commerce

Changes in the pattern of foreign commerce were less noticeable than those in manufacturing but were nevertheless significant. After increasing erratically during the 1820s and 1830s, both imports and exports leaped forward in the next 20 years. The nation remained primarily an exporter of raw materials and an importer of manufactured goods, and in most years it imported more than it exported. Cotton continued to be the most valuable

export, in 1860 accounting for a record $191 million of total exports of $333 million. Despite America's own thriving industry, textiles still held the lead among imports, with iron products second. As in earlier days, Great Britain was both the best customer of the United States and its leading supplier.

The success of sailing packets, those "square-riggers on schedule," greatly facilitated the movement of passengers and freight. Fifty-two packets were operating between New York and Europe by 1845, and many more plied between New York and other American ports. The packets accelerated the tendency for trade to concentrate in New York and to a lesser extent in Boston, Philadelphia, Baltimore, and New Orleans. The commerce of smaller towns like Providence and New Haven, which had flourished in earlier days, now languished.

New Bedford and a few other southern New England towns shrewdly saved their prosperity by concentrating on whaling, which boomed between 1830 and 1860. The supply of whales seemed unlimited—as indeed it was, given the primitive hunting techniques of the age of sail. By the mid 1850s, with sperm oil selling at over $1.75 a gallon and the country exporting an average of $2.7 million worth of whale oil and whalebone a year, New Bedford boasted a whaling fleet of well over 300 vessels and a population approaching 25,000. The whalers ranged the oceans of the world; they lived a hard, lonely life punctuated by moments of exhilaration when they sighted the great mammoths of the deep and drove the harpoon home. They also made magnificent profits: to clear 100 percent in a single voyage was merely routine.

The increase in the volume and value of trade and its concentration at larger ports had a marked effect on the construction of ships. By the 1850s the average vessel was three times the size of those built 30 years earlier. Startling improvements in design, culminating in the long, sleek, white-winged clipper ships, made possible speeds previously undreamed of. Appearing just in time to supply the need for fast transportation to the California gold fields, the clippers cut sailing time around the Horn to San Francisco from five or six months to three, the record of 89 days being held jointly by *Andrew Jackson* and by Donald McKay's famous *Flying Cloud*. Another McKay-designed clipper, *Champion of the Seas*, once logged 465 nau-

■ This minutely detailed engraving of New York in the late 1830s, looking across the East River from Brooklyn, is the work of Thomas Horner. Manhattan's wharves are packed solid with merchant ships, and the river teems with vessels of every description.

tical miles in 24 hours, far in excess of the best efforts of any modern yacht. To achieve such speeds, cargo capacity had to be sacrificed, making clippers uneconomical for carrying the bulky produce that was the mainstay of commerce. But for specialty goods, in their brief heyday the clippers were unsurpassed. Hong Kong merchants, never known for extravagance, willingly paid 75 cents a cubic foot to ship teas by clipper to London even though slower vessels charged only 28 cents. In the early 1850s clippers sold for as much as $150,000; with decent luck they might earn their full cost in a voyage or two.

Steam Conquers the Atlantic

The reign of the clipper ship was short. Like so many other things, ocean commerce was being mechanized. Steamships conquered the high seas more slowly than the rivers because early models were unsafe in rough waters and uneconomical. A river boat could take on fuel along its route, while an Atlantic steamer had to carry tons of coal across the ocean, thereby reducing its capacity for cargo. However, by the late 1840s steamers were capturing most of the passenger traffic, mail contracts, and first-class freight. Although unable to keep up with the clippers in a heavy breeze, their average speed was far greater, especially on the westward voyage against the prevailing winds. By 1860 the Atlantic had been crossed in less than ten days. Nevertheless, for very long voyages, such as the 15,000-mile haul around South America to California, fast sailing ships held their own for many years.

The steamship, and especially the iron ship, which had greater cargo-carrying capacity and was stronger and less costly to maintain, took away the advantages that American shipbuilders had held since colonial times. American lumber was cheap, but the British excelled in iron technology. Although the United States invested about $14.5 million in subsidies for the shipping industry, the funds were not employed intelligently and did little good. In 1858 all government effort to aid shipping was abandoned.

The combination of competition, government

subsidy, and technological advance drove shipping rates down drastically. Between the mid twenties and the mid fifties the cost of moving a pound of cotton from New York to Liverpool fell from 1 cent to about a third of a cent. Transatlantic passengers could obtain the best accommodations on the fastest ships for under $200 and good accommodations on slower packets for as little as $75.

Rates were especially low for European emigrants willing to travel to America on cargo vessels. By the 1840s at least 4,000 ships were engaged in carrying bulky American cotton and Canadian lumber to Europe. On their return trips with manufactured goods they had much unoccupied space, which they converted into rough quarters for passengers. Conditions on these ships were crowded, stuffy, and foul. Frequently epidemics took a fearful toll among steerage passengers. On one crossing of the ship *Lark,* 158 of 440 passengers died of typhus. Yet without this cheap means of transportation, thousands of poor immigrants would simply have remained at home. Bargain freight rates also help explain the clamor of American manufacturers for high tariffs, for transportation costs added relatively little to the price of European goods.

Railroads and Canals

Another dramatic change in the United States in the pre-Civil War years was the shift in the direction of the nation's internal commerce and its immense increase. From the time of the first settlers in the Mississippi Valley, the Great River had controlled the flow of goods from farm to market. The completion of the Erie Canal in 1825 heralded a shift, speeded by the feverish canal construction of the following decade.* However, even in the late 1830s the bulk of the trade of the valley still flowed down to New Orleans.

Each year saw more western produce moving to market through the canals. In 1845 the Erie was still drawing over two-thirds of its west-east traffic from within New York, but by 1847, despite the fact that this local business held steady, more than

half of its traffic came from west of Buffalo, and by 1851 more than two-thirds. The volume of western commerce over the Erie in 1851 amounted to more than twenty times what it had been in 1836, while the value of western goods reaching New Orleans in this period increased only two and a half times.

The expanding traffic and New York's enormous share of it caused businessmen in other eastern cities whose canal projects had been unsuccessful to respond promptly when a new means of transport, the railroad, became available. The first railroads were built in England in the 1820s. In 1830 the first American line, the ambitiously named Baltimore and Ohio Railroad, carried in its first year 80,000 passengers over a 13-mile stretch of track. By 1833 Charleston, South Carolina, had a line reaching 136 miles to Hamburg, on the Savannah River. Two years later the first cars rolled over the Boston and Worcester Railroad. The Panic of 1837 slowed construction, but by 1840 the United States had 3,328 miles of track, equal to the canal mileage and nearly double the railroad mileage of all Europe.

The first railroads did not compete with the canals for intersectional traffic. The through connections needed to move goods economically over great distances materialized slowly. Of the 6,000 miles of track operating in 1848, nearly all lay east of the Appalachians, and little of it had been coordinated into railroad *systems.* The intention of most early builders had been to monopolize the trade of surrounding districts, not to establish connections with competing centers. Frequently railroads used different gauges deliberately to prevent other lines from tying into their tracks.

Engineering problems held back growth. Steep grades and sharp curves—unavoidable in many parts of the country if the cost of the roads was not to be prohibitive—required more powerful and flexible engines than yet existed. Sparks from wood-burning locomotives caused fires. Wooden rails topped with strap iron wore out quickly and broke loose under the weight and vibration of heavy cars. In time, hard work and ingenuity solved these difficulties. The iron T-rail and the use of crossties set in loose gravel to reduce vibration increased the durability of the tracks and made possible heavier, more efficient equipment. Modifications in the design of locomotives en-

---

*In 1830 there were 1,277 miles of canal in the United States; by 1840 there were 3,326 miles.

■ An early Baltimore and Ohio locomotive (the date given is 1848), painted by an unknown artist.

abled the trains to negotiate sharp curves. Engines that could burn hard coal appeared, thereby eliminating the danger of starting fires along the right of way and reducing fuel costs.

Between 1848 and 1852 railroad mileage nearly doubled. Three years later it had doubled again, and by 1860 the nation had 30,636 miles of track. During this extraordinary burst of activity, four companies drove lines of gleaming iron from the Atlantic seaboard to the great interior valley. In 1851 the Erie, longest road in the world with 537 miles of track, linked the Hudson River north of New York City with Dunkirk on Lake Erie. Late the next year the Baltimore and Ohio reached the Ohio River at Wheeling, and in 1853 a banker named Erastus Corning consolidated eight short lines connecting Albany and Buffalo to form the New York Central. Finally, in 1858 the Pennsylvania Railroad completed a line across the mountains from Philadelphia to Pittsburgh.

In the states beyond the Appalachians building went on at an even more feverish pace. In the 1850s Ohio laid more than 2,300 miles of track, Illinois more than 2,600, Wisconsin nearly 900. In the South, where construction was slower, Mississippi laid about 800 miles, Alabama over 600. By 1855 passengers could travel from Chicago or St. Louis to the East Coast entirely by railroad at a cost ranging from about $20 to $30, the trip taking, with luck, less than 48 hours. A generation earlier such a trip required two to three weeks.

Financing the Railroads

This building program consumed immense amounts of labor and capital at a time when many demands for these resources existed. Immigrants or (in the South) slaves did most of the heavy work. Raising the necessary money proved a more complex task.

Private investors supplied about three-quarters of the money invested in railroads before 1860, over $800 million in the 1850s alone. Much of this capital, especially in the early days, came from local merchants and businessmen and from farmers along the proposed rights of way. Funds were easy to raise because subscribers seldom had to lay out the full price of their stock at one time; instead they were subject to periodic "calls" for a percentage of their commitment as construction progressed. If the road made money, much of the additional mileage could be paid for out of earnings from the first sections built. The Utica and Schenectady Railroad, one of the lines that became part of the New York Central, was capitalized in 1833 at $2 million (20,000 shares at $100). Only $75 per share was ever called; in 1844 the road had been completed, shares were selling at $129, and shareholders were receiving handsome cash dividends.

The Utica and Schenectady was a short road in a rich territory; for less favorably situated lines, stocks were hard to sell and bonds, backed by the property of the line, were more commonly used to raise money. In the West, where the population was thin, the distances great, and property values relatively low, outside capital had to be found. Much of it came from New England, where investors like the China merchant John Murray Forbes were increasingly active in railroad finance. They dealt mainly in bonds, using stock chiefly to maintain control of the companies whose bonds they held. Most foreign investors preferred bonds over stocks; by 1853 Europeans owned about a quarter of all American railroad bonds.

Of the lines connecting the seaboard with the Middle West, the New York Central alone needed no public aid, chiefly because it ran through prosperous, well-populated country and across level terrain. The others were all "mixed enterprises," drawing about half their capital from state and local governments.

Public aid took many forms. Towns, counties, and the states themselves lent money to railroads and invested in their stock. Special privileges, such as exemption from taxation and the right to condemn property, were often granted, and in a few cases states built and operated roads as public corporations. In all, the proportionate contribution of state and local governments to the cost of railroad building—between 25 and 30 percent—was much less than their contribution to canals, and it declined steadily as the rail network expanded and matured.

As with earlier internal improvement proposals, federal financial aid to railroads was usually blocked in Congress by a combination of eastern and southern votes. But in 1850 a scheme for granting federal lands to the states to build a line from Lake Michigan to the Gulf of Mexico won considerable southern and eastern support and passed both houses. The main beneficiary was the Illinois Central Railroad, which received a 200-foot right of way and alternate strips of land along the track 1 mile wide and 6 miles deep, a total of almost 2.6 million acres. By mortgaging this land and by selling portions of it to farmers, the Illinois Central raised nearly all the $23.4 million it spent on construction. The success of this operation led to additional grants of almost 20 million acres in the 1850s, benefiting more than 40 railroads. Far larger federal grants were made after the Civil War, when the transcontinental lines were built.

Frequently the capitalists who promoted railroads were more concerned with making money out of the *construction* of the lines than with operating them. Erastus Corning was a good railroad man; his lines were well maintained and efficiently run. Yet he was also a banker and a manufacturer of iron. He accepted no salary as president of the Utica and Schenectady, "asking only that he have the privilege of supplying all the rails, running gear, tools and other iron and steel articles used." When he could not himself produce rails of the proper quality, he purchased them in England, charging the railroad a commission for his services. Corning's actions led to stockholder complaints, and a committee was appointed to investigate. He managed to control this group easily enough, but it did report that "the practice of buying articles for the use of the Railroad Company from its own officers might in time come to lead to abuses of great magnitude." The prediction proved all too accurate in the generation following the Civil War.

Corning, it must be emphasized, was honest enough; his mistake, if mistake it was, lay in overestimating his own impartiality a little. Others in the business were unashamedly crooked and avidly took advantage of the public passion for railroads. Some officials issued stock to themselves without paying for it and then sold the shares to gullible investors for hard cash. Others manipulated the books of their corporations, used inside information to make killings in the stock market, and set up special construction companies and paid them exorbitant returns out of railroad assets. These practices did not become widespread until after the Civil War, but all of them first sprang up in the period now under discussion.

Railroads and the National Economy

The effects of so much railroad construction were profound. While the main reason that farmers put more land under the plow was an increase in the price of agricultural products, the railroad helped determine just what land was utilized and how profitably it could be farmed. Much of the fertile prairie through which the Illinois Central ran had been available for settlement for many years before 1850, but development had been slow because it was remote from navigable waters and had no timber. In 1840 the three counties immediately northeast of Springfield had a population of about 8,500. They produced about 59,000 bushels of wheat and 690,000 bushels of corn. In the next decade the region grew slowly by the standards of that day: the three counties had about 14,000 people in 1850 and produced 71,000 bushels of wheat and 2.2 million bushels of corn. Then came the railroad and with it an agricultural revolution. By 1860 the population of the three counties had soared to over 38,000, wheat production had topped 550,000 bushels, and corn 5.7 million bushels. "Land-grant" railroads such as the Illinois Central stimulated agricultural expansion by advertising their lands widely and selling farm sites at low rates on liberal terms.

Access to world markets gave the farmers of the upper Mississippi Valley an incentive to increase output. Land was plentiful and cheap, but farm labor was scarce; consequently agricultural wages rose sharply, especially after 1850. New tools and machines appeared in time to ease the labor shortage. First came the steel plowshare, invented by John Deere, necessary because the prairie sod was tough and sticky. In 1839 Deere turned out ten such plows in his little shop; by 1857 he was selling 10,000 a year. More important was the perfection of the mechanical reaper, for the real limit on wheat production was set by the amount that farmers could handle during the brief harvest season. Although many inventors made significant contributions and no single company monopolized production, the major figure in the development of the reaper was Cyrus Hall McCormick. McCormick's horse-drawn reaper bent the grain against the cutting knife and then deposited it neatly on a platform, whence it could easily be raked into windrows. With this machine, two workers could cut 14 times as much wheat as with scythes.

■ The great decade of railroad building is shown here in impressive detail. Certain towns and cities owed most of their spectacularly rapid growth to the railroad, Chicago being the outstanding example. The map also suggests the strong influence of the railroads on the expansion and economic prosperity of smaller cities such as Fort Wayne, Milwaukee, and Nashville. At the outbreak of the Civil War in 1861, the relative lack of railroads in the South was a bad omen for the Confederacy.

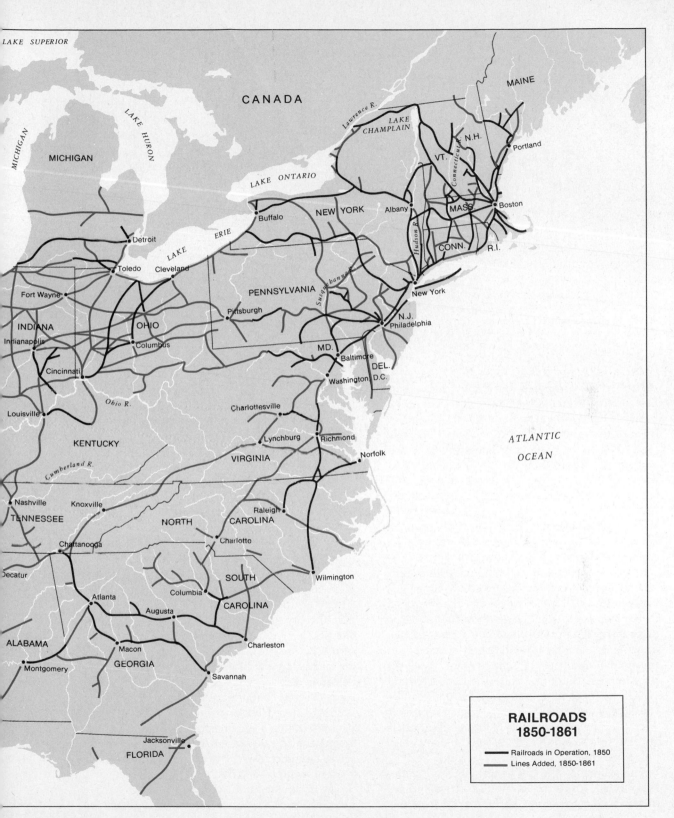

LAKE SUPERIOR

CANADA

Lawrence R.

MAINE

LAKE CHAMPLAIN

MICHIGAN

LAKE HURON

N.H.

VT.

Portland

LAKE ONTARIO

Albany

MASS.

Boston

Buffalo

NEW YORK

Connecticut R.

Hudson R.

CONN.

R.I.

Detroit

LAKE ERIE

New York

Toledo

Cleveland

N.J.

Philadelphia

Fort Wayne

PENNSYLVANIA

Susquehanna R.

INDIANA

OHIO

Pittsburgh

MD.

Baltimore

Indianapolis

Columbus

Washington, D.C.

DEL.

Cincinnati

Charlottesville

Louisville

Ohio R.

Lynchburg

Richmond

KENTUCKY

VIRGINIA

Norfolk

ATLANTIC OCEAN

Cumberland R.

Nashville

Knoxville

Raleigh

TENNESSEE

NORTH CAROLINA

Chattanooga

Charlotte

Decatur

SOUTH

Wilmington

Atlanta

Columbia

CAROLINA

Augusta

ALABAMA

Macon

Charleston

Montgomery

GEORGIA

Savannah

Jacksonville

FLORIDA

**RAILROADS
1850-1861**

━━━ Railroads in Operation, 1850
─── Lines Added, 1850-1861

■ John Roebling's railroad bridge at Niagara Falls, the first to be suspended from wire cables, was memorialized by a Currier lithograph upon its completion in 1855. "No one is afraid to cross," Roebling reported happily.

McCormick prospered, but despite his patents he could not keep other manufacturers out of the business. Competition led to continual improvement of the machines and kept prices within the reach of most farmers. Installment selling added to demand. By 1860 nearly 80,000 reapers had been sold; their efficiency helps explain why wheat output rose by nearly 75 percent in the 1850s.

The railroad had an equally powerful impact on American cities. The seaports that formed the eastern terminuses of the network benefited, and so did countless intermediate centers such as Buffalo and Cincinnati. Most especially Chicago advanced. In 1850 not a single line had reached there; five years later it was terminal for 2,200 miles of track and controlled the commerce of an imperial domain. By extending half a dozen lines west to the Mississippi, it drained off nearly all the river traffic north of St. Louis. The Illinois Central sucked the expanding output of the prairies into Chicago as well. Most of this freight went eastward over the new railroads or on the Great Lakes and the Erie Canal. Nearly 350,000 tons of shipping plied the lakes by 1855.

The railroads, like the textile industry, stimulated other kinds of economic activity. They transformed agriculture, as we have seen; both real estate values and buying and selling of land increased whenever the iron horse puffed into a new district. The railroads spurred regional concentration of industry and an increase in the size of business units. Their insatiable need for capital stimulated the growth of investment banking. The complexity of their operations made them, as the historian Alfred D. Chandler, Jr., writes, "the first modern business enterprises," the first to employ large numbers of salaried managers and to develop "a large internal organizational structure with carefully defined lines of responsibility."

Although they apparently did not have a very great effect on general manufacturing before the Civil War, the roads consumed large amounts of iron, thereby helping the mining and smelting industries. New foundries sprang up to turn out locomotives. In 1860 railroads purchased nearly half the nation's output of bar and sheet iron. Railroad demands also led to technological advances that were of great importance in the iron industry. Probably more labor and more capital were occupied in economic activities resulting from the development of railroads than in the roads themselves—another way of saying that the railroads were immensely valuable internal improvements.

The proliferation of trunk lines and the competition of the canal system (for many products the slowness of canal transportation was not a serious handicap) led to a sharp decline in freight and passenger rates. Periodically, railroads engaged in "wars" to capture business. At times a person could travel from New York to Buffalo for as little as $4; anthracite was being shipped from the Pennsylvania mines to the coast for $1.50 a ton. The Erie Canal reduced its toll charges by more than two-thirds in the face of railroad competition, and the roads in turn cut rates drastically until, on the eve of the Civil War, it cost less than 1 cent per ton-mile to send produce through the canal and only slightly more than 2 cents a mile on the railroads. By that time one could ship a bushel of wheat from Chicago to New York by railroad for less than 35 cents.

Cheap transportation had a revolutionary effect on western agriculture. Farmers in Iowa could now raise grain to feed the factory workers of Lowell and even of Manchester, England. Two-thirds of the meat consumed in New York City was soon arriving by rail from beyond the Appalachians. The center of American wheat production shifted westward to Illinois, Wisconsin, and Indiana. When the Crimean War (1853–1856) and European crop failures increased foreign demand, these regions boomed. Success bred success for farmers and for the railroads. Profits earned carrying wheat enabled the roads to build feeder lines that opened up still wider areas to commercial agriculture and made it easy to bring in lumber, farm machinery, household furnishings, and the settlers themselves at very low cost. "Immigration, settlement, farm development, and railroad construction were all dependent upon each other," Paul W. Gates writes in *The Farmer's Age*.

Railroads and the Sectional Conflict

Increased production and cheap transportation boosted the western farmer's income and thus his standard of living. The days of isolation and self-sufficiency, even for the family on the edge of the frontier, rapidly disappeared. Frontiersmen became businessmen and, to a far greater extent than their forebears, consumers, buying all sorts of manufactured articles that their ancestors had made for themselves or done without. This was not entirely beneficial. Like southern planters,

they now became dependent on middlemen and lost some of their feeling of self-reliance. Overproduction became a problem. It began to take more capital to buy a farm, for as profits increased, so did the price of land. Machinery was an additional expense. The percentage of farm laborers and tenants tended to rise.

The linking of East and West had fateful effects on politics. The increased ease of movement from section to section and the ever more complex social and economic integration of East and West stimulated nationalism and thus became a force for the preservation of the Union. Without the railroads and canals, Illinois and Iowa would scarcely have dared to side against the South in 1861. When the Mississippi ceased to be essential to them, citizens of the upper valley could afford to be more hostile to slavery and especially to its westward extension. Economic ties with the Northeast reinforced cultural connections.

The South might have preserved its influence in the Northwest if it had pressed forward its own railroad-building program. It failed to do so. There were many southern lines but nothing like a southern *system*. As late as 1856 one could get from Memphis to Richmond or Charleston only by very indirect routes. As late as 1859 the land-grant road extending the Illinois Central to Mobile, Alabama, was not complete, nor did any economical connection exist between Chicago and New Orleans. This state of affairs could be accounted for in part by the scattered population of the South, the paucity of passenger traffic, the seasonal nature of much of the freight business, and the absence of large cities. Southerners placed too much reliance on the Mississippi: the fact that traffic on the river continued heavy throughout the 1850s blinded them to the precipitous rate at which their *relative* share of the nation's trade was declining. But the fundamental cause of the South's backwardness in railroad construction was the attitude of its leaders. Southerners of means were no more interested in commerce than in industry; their capital found other outlets.

The Economy on the Eve of Civil War

Between the mid forties and the mid fifties the United States experienced one of the most remarkable periods of growth in its history. Manufacturing output increased an astounding 69 percent in 10 years. Every economic indicator surged forward: grain and cotton production, population, gold production, sales of public land. The building of the railroads stimulated business, and by making transportation cheaper the completed lines energized the nation's economy. The "American System" that Henry Clay had dreamed of arrived with a rush just as Clay was passing from the scene.

Inevitably this growth caused dislocations, these aggravated by the boom psychology that once again infected the popular mind. In 1857 there was a serious collapse. The return of Russian wheat to the world market after the Crimean War caused grain prices to fall. This checked agricultural expansion, which hurt the railroads and cut down on the demand for manufactures.

People called this abrupt downturn the Panic of 1857 and worried about a depression. Yet the vigor of the economy was such that the bad times did not last long. The upper Mississippi Valley suffered most, for so much new land had been opened up that supplies of farm produce greatly exceeded demand, and the world situation remained unhelpful. Elsewhere conditions improved rapidly. Gold-mad California had escaped the depression entirely. The South, somewhat out of the hectic rush to begin with, was affected very little by the collapse of 1857, for cotton prices continued high. Manufacturers experienced a moderate revival in 1859.

Before a new upward swing could become well established, however, the sectional crisis between North and South shook people's confidence in the future. Then the war came, and a new set of forces began to shape economic development.

SUPPLEMENTARY READING

Titles marked with an asterisk have been published in paperback

Most of the volumes dealing with economic developments mentioned in Chapter 8 continue to be useful for this period. See especially G. R. Taylor, **The Transportation Revolution*** (1951), P. W. Gates, **The Farmer's Age*** (1960), D. C. North, **The Economic Growth of the United States*** (1961), and Stuart Bruchey, **The Roots of American Economic Growth*** (1965). Allan Nevins has interesting chapters on economic developments in **The Ordeal of the Union** (1947).

An excellent survey of the antebellum South is Clement Eaton, **The Growth of Southern Civilization*** (1961). For more detailed coverage, see C. S. Sydnor, **The Development of Southern Sectionalism*** (1948), and A. O. Craven, **The Growth of Southern Nationalism** (1953).

The literature on slavery is extensive and of high quality. See especially K. M. Stampp, **The Peculiar Institution*** (1956), S. M. Elkins, **Slavery*** (1959), E. D. Genovese, **Roll, Jordan, Roll*** (1975), L. H. Owens, **This Species of Property*** (1976), J. W. Blassingame, **The Slave Community*** (1972), L. W. Levine, **Black Culture and Black Consciousness** (1977), N. I. Huggins, **Black Odyssey** (1977), H. G. Gutman, **Black Family in Slavery and Freedom** (1976), and P. D. Escott, **Slavery Remembered*** (1979). Among specialized volumes, P. D. Curtin, **The Atlantic Slave Trade*** (1970), and W. S. Howard's **American Slavers and the Federal Law** (1963), which discusses the illegal slave trade. On the internal trade, see Frederic Bancroft, **Slave-Trading in the Old South*** (1931), on slave insurrections, E. D. Genovese, **From Rebellion to Revolution: Afro-American Slave Revolts** (1979), and S. B. Oates, **The Fires of Jubilee: Nat Turner's Fierce Rebellion** (1975), are excellent, and William Styron's novel, **The Confessions of Nat Turner*** (1967), is a fine example of how historical research can be put to effective use by a writer of fiction. R. C. Wade, **Slavery in the Cities*** (1964), contains much interesting material, as does W. K. Scarborough, **The Overseer: Plantation Management in the Old South** (1966). On southern manufacturing, see Broadus Mitchell, **William Gregg: Factory Master of the Old South** (1941).

On industrial developments, in addition to the books mentioned in Chapter 8, see A. C. Cole, **The Irrepressible Conflict*** (1934), H. J. Habbakuk, **American and British Technology in the Nineteenth Century*** (1962), and G. S. Gibb, **The Saco-Lowell Shops: Textile Machinery Building in New England** (1950). On labor history, F. R. Dulles, **Labor in America*** (1960), is a good introduction. N. J. Ware, **The Industrial Worker, 1840–1860*** (1924), and W. A. Sullivan, **The Industrial Worker in Pennsylvania** (1955), are more specialized. See also Thomas Dublin, **Women at Work** (1977), R. A. Mohl, **Poverty in New York** (1971), and B. M. Wertheimer, **We Were There** (1977). For workingmen's political activities, see Edward Pessen, **Most Uncommon Jacksonians: The Radical Leaders of the Early Labor Movement*** (1967).

Immigration is dealt with in M. A. Jones, **American Immigration*** (1960), and M. L. Hansen, **The Immigrant in American History*** (1940). More specialized works include Hansen's **The Atlantic Migration*** (1940), Oscar Handlin, **Boston's Immigrants*** (1941), and Robert Ernst, **Immigrant Life in New York City** (1949). Poverty in America is examined by R. H. Bremner, **From the Depths*** (1956), and in Mohl's **Poverty in New York.**

Taylor's **Transportation Revolution** is outstanding on developments in commerce and communication. On the age of sail, see S. E. Morison, **The Maritime History of Massachusetts*** (1921), C. C. Cutler, **Greyhounds of the Sea** (1960), and Robert Carse, **The Moonrakers** (1961). J. F. Stover, **Iron Road to the West** (1978), is a good survey of railroad building in the 1850s. Among the specialized studies of railroad development are T. C. Cochran, **Railroad Leaders** (1953), P. W. Gates, **The Illinois Central Railroad and Its Colonization Work** (1934), E. C. Kirkland, **Men, Cities, and Transportation** (1948), A. D. Chandler, Jr., **Henry Varnum Poor** (1956), R. W. Fogel, **Railroads and American Economic Growth*** (1964), and Albert Fishlow, **American Railroads and the Transformation of the Ante-Bellum Economy** (1965).

14/THE COMING OF THE CIVIL WAR

The political settlement between North and South designed by Henry Clay in 1850 lasted only four years. One specific event wrecked it, but it was probably doomed in any case. Americans continued to migrate westward by the thousands, and as long as slaveholders could carry their human property into federally controlled territories, northern resentment would smolder. Slaves continued to seek freedom in the North, and the stronger federal Fugitive Slave Act did not guarantee their capture and return. Abolitionists intensified their propaganda. With wisdom and forbearance, perhaps a real reconciliation of the sections could have been negotiated, but the historian who searches for examples of intelligent and tolerant statesmanship in the period 1850–1854 seeks almost in vain.

Enforcing the Fugitive Slave Act

The new fugitive slave law caused a sharp increase in the efforts of southerners to recover escaped slaves. Something approaching panic reigned in the black communities of northern cities after its passage. Hundreds of former slaves fled to Canada, but many more remained. A few were arrested, generally without incident. However, not all the captives were in fact runaways, and northerners frequently refused to stand aside while these people were dragged off in chains.

Shortly after the passage of the act, a New Yorker, James Hamlet, was seized, convicted, and rushed off to slavery in Maryland without even being allowed to communicate with his wife and children. The New York black community was outraged, and with help from white neighbors it swiftly raised $800 to buy his freedom. In 1851 Euphemia Williams, who had lived for years as a free woman in Pennsylvania, was seized, her presumed owner claiming also her six children, all Pennsylvania-born. A federal judge released Mrs. Williams, but the case created alarm in the North.

Abolitionists often interfered with the enforcement of the law in cases where the black was unquestionably a runaway. When two Georgians came to Boston to reclaim William and Ellen Craft, admitted fugitives, an abolitionist "Vigilance Committee" forced them to return home empty-handed. The Crafts prudently—or perhaps in disgust—decided to leave the United States for England. Early in 1851 a Virginia agent captured Frederick "Shadrach" Wilkins, a waiter in a Boston coffee house. While Wilkins was being held for deportation, a mob of blacks broke into the courthouse and freed him. That October a slave named Jerry, who had escaped from Missouri, was arrested in Syracuse, New York. Within minutes the whole town had the news. Crowds surged through the streets, and when night fell, a mob smashed into the building where Jerry was being held and spirited him away to safety.

Incidents of these types exacerbated feelings. Southerners accused the North of reneging on one of the main promises made in the Compromise, while the sight of harmless human beings being hustled off to a life of slavery disturbed many northerners who were not abolitionists. Although most white northerners were probably not pre-

■ A broadside written in 1851 by Boston abolitionist Theodore Parker alerted the city's black community to the dangers posed by the new Fugitive Slave Act.

pared to break it, in some states the Fugitive Slave Act became virtually unenforceable. Massachusetts passed a strong personal liberty law. When a newspaperman in Wisconsin was convicted of rousing a mob to free a captured runaway, the state supreme court declared the Fugitive Slave Act unconstitutional and released him. After long delays the United States Supreme Court overruled this decision (*Ableman* v. *Booth*, 1859), but in the meantime the act was a dead letter in Wisconsin and in other states as well. In all, in the decade of the act's existence, about 300 fugitives were returned to their owners.

Uncle Tom's Cabin

Tremendously important in increasing sectional tensions was Harriet Beecher Stowe's novel *Uncle Tom's Cabin* (1852). Mrs. Stowe was neither a professional writer nor an abolitionist and had almost no firsthand knowledge of slavery. Her conscience was roused by the Fugitive Slave Act, which she called a "nightmare abomination." She dashed off her book quickly; as she later recalled, it seemed to write itself. Its success was immediate: 10,000 copies were sold in a week, 300,000 in a year, and soon it was being translated into dozens of languages. Dramatized versions were staged in countries throughout the world.

Uncle Tom's Cabin had little literary merit, for Mrs. Stowe was a second-rate writer. Her approach to the subject explains the book's success.

This tale of the pious, patient slave Uncle Tom, the saintly white child Eva, and the callous slave driver Simon Legree appealed to an audience far wider than that reached by the abolitionists. It avoided the self-righteous, accusatory tone of most abolitionist tracts. Many of the southern characters were fine, sensitive people, while the cruel Simon Legree was a transplanted Yankee. There were many heartrending scenes of pain, self-sacrifice, and heroism. The story proved especially effective on the stage: the slave Eliza crossing the frozen Ohio River to freedom, the death of

■ The frontispiece of a children's edition of *Uncle Tom's Cabin* shows highpoints from the book; in the center circle, Eliza crosses the ice to freedom on the Ohio shore.

Little Eva, Eva and Tom ascending to heaven—these scenes left audiences in tears.

Southern critics pointed out, correctly enough, that Mrs. Stowe's picture of plantation life was distorted, her slaves atypical. They called her a "coarse, ugly, long-tongued woman" and accused her of trying to "awaken rancorous hatred and malignant jealousies" that would undermine national unity. Most northerners, having little basis on which to judge the accuracy of the book, tended to discount southern criticism as biased. In any case, *Uncle Tom's Cabin* raised questions in many minds that transcended the issue of accuracy. Did it matter if all slaves were not as kindly as Uncle Tom, as determined as George Harris? What if only *one* white master was as evil as Simon Legree? No earlier white American writer had looked at slaves as *people*.

Uncle Tom's Cabin touched the hearts of millions. Some became abolitionists, others, still hesitating to step forward, asked themselves as they put the book down: Is slavery just?

"Young America"

A distraction was needed to help keep the lid on sectional troubles. Some hoped to find one in foreign affairs, for American diplomacy in the fifties was active and aggressive. The spirit of manifest destiny explains this in large part; once the United States had reached the Pacific, expansionists began to seek new worlds to conquer. In the late 1840s they talked about transmitting the dynamic, democratic spirit of the United States to other countries, aiding local revolutionaries, opening up new markets, perhaps annexing foreign lands.

To an extent this "Young America" spirit was purely emotional, a mindless confidence that democracy would triumph everywhere, that public opinion was "stronger than the Bayonet." At the time of the European revolutions of 1848, Americans talked freely about helping the liberals in their struggles against autocratic governments. Horace Greeley's New York *Tribune* predicted that all Europe would soon become "one great and splendid Republic . . . and we shall all be citizens of the world." When the Austrians crushed a rebellion in Hungary, Secretary of State Daniel Webster addressed an insulting note full of vague threats to the Austrian chargé in Washington. Hungarian revolutionary hero Louis Kossuth visited the United States in search of aid in 1851–1852; President Fillmore put the U.S.S. *Mississippi* at his disposal, and great crowds turned out to cheer him.

The United States had no intention of going to war to win independence for the Hungarians, as Kossuth soon learned to his sorrow. However, the same democratic-expansionist sentiment led to dreams of conquests in the Caribbean area. In 1855 a freebooter named William Walker, backed by an American company engaged in transporting migrants to California across Central America, seized control of Nicaragua and elected himself president. He was ousted two years later but made repeated attempts to regain control until, in 1860, he died before a Honduran firing squad. Another would-be dictator, "General" George W. L. Bickley, claiming that he was disturbed by that "crookedest of all boundary lines, the Rio Grande," tried to organize an expedition to conquer Mexico.

While many northerners suspected them of engaging in dastardly plots to obtain more territory for slavery, Walker and Bickley were primarily adventurers trying to use the prevailing mood of buoyant expansionism for selfish ends. They attracted southern recruits by suggesting that slavery might follow in their wake—Bickley proposed that Mexico be divided into 25 slave states—but at the same time some northerners proposed colonizing ex-slaves in the Caribbean in order to "build up a free black power" in the area to prevent the extension of slavery there.

The rapid development of California created a need for improved communication with the West Coast. A canal across Central America would cut weeks from the sailing time between New York and San Francisco. In 1850 Secretary of State John M. Clayton and the British minister to the United States, Henry Lytton Bulwer, negotiated a treaty providing for the demilitarization and joint Anglo-American control of any canal across the isthmus. Although no canal was built at the time, the United States had officially staked out its interest in the region.

As this area began to assume strategic importance to the United States, the desire to obtain Cuba grew stronger. In 1854 President Franklin Pierce instructed his minister to Spain, Pierre

■ Commodore Perry confronts Japanese leaders in 1853. The "black ships" of Perry's squadron are in the background. A watercolor by a Japanese artist.

Soulé of Louisiana, to offer $130 million for the island. Since Soulé was a hotheaded bungler, the administration arranged for him first to confer in Belgium with the American ministers to Great Britain and France, James Buchanan and John Y. Mason, to work out a plan for persuading Spain to sell. Out of this meeting came the Ostend Manifesto, a confidential dispatch to the State Department proposing that the United States try to buy Cuba and suggesting that if Spain refused to sell, "the great law of self-preservation" might justify "wresting" it from Spain by force.

News of the manifesto leaked out, and it had to be published. Northern opinion was outraged by this "slaveholders' plot." Europeans claimed to be shocked by such "dishonorable" and "clandestine" diplomacy. The government had to disavow the manifesto, and any hope of obtaining Cuba or any other territory in the Caribbean vanished.

The goals of Young America explain President Fillmore's dispatching an expedition under Commodore Matthew C. Perry to try for commercial concessions in the isolated kingdom of Japan in 1852. Perry's expedition was a great success. The Japanese, impressed by American naval power, agreed to establish diplomatic relations. In 1858 an American envoy, Townsend Harris, negotiated a commercial treaty that opened six Japanese ports to American ships. President Pierce's negotiation of a Canadian reciprocity treaty with Great Britain in 1854 and an unsuccessful attempt, also made under Pierce, to annex the Hawaiian Islands are further illustrations of the vigorous foreign policy of the period.

Stephen A. Douglas

The most prominent spokesman of the Young America movement was Stephen A. Douglas. The senator from Illinois was the Henry Clay of his generation, capable of seeing the United States and its national needs in the broadest perspective. He was born in Vermont in 1813 and moved to Illinois when barely 20. There he studied law and was soon deep in Democratic politics. From 1835 to 1843 he held a succession of state offices; then he was elected to Congress. In 1847, after two terms in the House, he was chosen United States senator.

Douglas succeeded at almost everything he attempted; rarely has a man seemed so closely attuned to his time and place in history. His law practice was large and prosperous. He dabbled in Chicago real estate and made a large fortune. Politics suited him to perfection. Although very short, he had powerful shoulders, a large head, strong features, and deep-set, piercing eyes. His high forehead was made to appear even bolder by the way he wore his hair, swept back in a pompadour and hanging over his collar. His appearance was so imposing that friends called him the Little Giant. "I live with my constituents," he once boasted, "drink with them, lodge with them, pray with them, laugh, hunt, dance, and work with them. I eat their corn dodgers and fried bacon and sleep two in a bed with them." Yet he was more than a backslapper. He read widely, wrote poetry, financed a number of young American artists, served as a regent of the Smithsonian Institution, and was interested in scientific farming.

The foundations of Douglas' politics were expansion and popular sovereignty. He had been willing to fight for all of Oregon in 1846, and he supported the Mexican War to the hilt in Congress. That local settlers should determine their own institutions was, to his way of thinking, axiomatic. Arguments over the future of slavery in the territories he believed a foolish waste of energy and time since natural conditions would keep the institution out of the West. The main thing, he insisted, was to get on with the development of the United States. Let the nation build railroads, acquire new territory, expand its trade. He believed slavery "a curse beyond computation" for both blacks and whites, but he refused to admit that any moral issue was involved. He cared not, he boasted, whether slavery was voted up or voted down. This was not really true, but the question was interfering with the rapid exploitation of the continent; Douglas wanted it settled so that the

■ **"By God, sir, I made James Buchanan, and by God, sir, I will unmake him!" Douglas remarked characteristically during the debate over Kansas.**

country could concentrate on more important matters.

Douglas' success in steering the Compromise of 1850 through Congress added to his already considerable reputation, and in 1851, although only 38, he set out to win the Democratic presidential nomination. He reasoned that since he was the brightest, most imaginative, and hardest-working Democrat around, he had a right to press his claim. His brash aggressiveness proved his undoing. He expressed open contempt for James Buchanan and said of his other chief rival, Lewis Cass, who had served in the diplomatic corps, that his "reputation was beyond the C."

At the 1852 Democratic convention Douglas had no chance. Cass and Buchanan killed each other off and the delegates finally chose a dark horse, Franklin Pierce of New Hampshire. The Whigs, rejecting the colorless Fillmore, nominated General Winfield Scott. In the campaign both sides supported the Compromise of 1850. The Democrats won an easy victory, 254 electoral votes to 42.

So handsome a triumph seemed to insure stability, but in fact it was a prelude to political chaos. The Whig party was crumbling fast. The "Cotton Whigs" of the South, alienated by the antislavery attitude of their northern brethren, were flocking into the Democratic fold; the radical "Conscience" and the conservative "Silver Gray" Whig factions in the North found themselves more and more at odds with each other. Congress fell overwhelmingly into the hands of proslavery southern Democrats, a development profoundly disturbing to most of their northern colleagues.

Kansas-Nebraska Act

Franklin Pierce was a youthful-appearing 48 when he took office. He was generally well liked by politicians. His career had included service in the New Hampshire legislature and in both houses of Congress. Alcohol had become a problem for him in Washington, however, and in 1842 he had resigned from the Senate. The setback proved temporary; his New Hampshire law practice boomed, and he added to his reputation by serving as a brigadier general during the Mexican War. While his nomination for president had been a surprise, once made, it had appeared perfectly reasonable. Great things were expected of his administration, especially after he surrounded himself with men of all factions: to balance his appointment of a radical states' rights Mississippian, Jefferson Davis, as secretary of war, for example, he named a conservative Unionist, William L. Marcy of New York, as secretary of state.

Only a strong man, however, can manage a ministry of all talents, and Pierce was weak. He followed, as Allan Nevins has written, a "policy of smiling on everybody but specially favoring both ends against the middle." The ship of state was soon drifting; Pierce seemed incapable of holding firm the helm.

This was the situation in January 1854 when Senator Douglas, chairman of the Committee on Territories, introduced what looked like a routine bill organizing the land west of Missouri and Iowa as Nebraska Territory. Since settlers were beginning to trickle into the area, the time had arrived to set up a civil administration, but Douglas also acted because a territorial government was essential to railroad development. As a director of the Illinois Central line and as a land speculator, he hoped to make Chicago the terminus of a transcontinental railroad, but construction could scarcely begin before the entire route was cleared of Indians and brought under some kind of civil control.

Southerners, wishing to bring the transcontinental line to Memphis or New Orleans, pointed out that a right of way through organized territory already existed across Texas and New Mexico Territory. In 1853 the United States minister to Mexico, James Gadsden, a prominent southern railroad executive, had engineered the purchase of more than 29,000 square miles of Mexican territory south of the Gila River, which provided an easy route over the mountains for such a railroad (see map, page 307). Douglas, whose vision of the economic potentialities of the nation was Hamiltonian, would have been willing to support the construction of two or even three transcontinental railroads, but he knew that Congress would not go that far. In any case, he believed that the Nebraska region must be organized promptly.

The powerful southern faction in Congress would not go along with Douglas' proposal as it stood. The railroad question aside, Nebraska would presumably become a free state, for it lay north of latitude 36°30′ in a district from which slavery had been excluded since 1820 by the Missouri Compromise. To win over the southerners, Douglas agreed first to divide the region into two territories, Kansas and Nebraska, and then—a fateful concession—to repeal the part of the Missouri Compromise that excluded slavery from land north of 36°30′. Whether the new territories should become slave or free, he argued, should be left to the decision of the settlers in accordance with the democratic principle of popular sovereignty. No one, he thought, could legitimately object; the region, unsuited to plantation agriculture, would surely become free. The fact that he might advance his presidential ambitions by making concessions to the South must have influenced Douglas too, as must the local political situation in Missouri, where the fear of being "surrounded" on three sides by free states was great.

Douglas' miscalculation of northern sentiment was monumental. It was one thing to apply popular sovereignty to the new territories in the Southwest as a way of avoiding a confrontation with the slave states, quite another to apply it to a region that had been part of the United States for half a century and free soil for 34 years. Word that the area was to be reopened to slavery caused an indignant outcry; many moderate opponents of slavery were radicalized. A group of abolitionist congressmen issued an "Appeal of the Independent Democrats" (actually, all were Free Soilers and Whigs) denouncing the Kansas-Nebraska bill as "a gross violation of a sacred pledge" and calling for a campaign of letter writing, petitions, and public meetings to prevent its passage. The unanimity and force of the northern public's reaction was like nothing in America since the days of the Stamp Act and the Intolerable Acts.

Protests could not defeat the bill. Southerners in both houses backed it regardless of party. Douglas, at his best when under attack, pushed it with all his power. The authors of the "Appeal," he charged, were "the pure unadulterated representatives of Abolitionism, Free Soilism, [and] Niggerism." President Pierce added whatever force the administration could muster. As a result, the northern Democrats split and the bill became law late in May 1854. Thus the nation took the greatest single step in its blind march toward the abyss of secession and civil war.

Bleeding Kansas

The repeal of the Missouri Compromise struck the North like a slap in the face—at once shameful and challenging. Presumably the question of slavery in the territories had been settled forever; now, without justification, it had been reopened. Two days after the Kansas–Nebraska bill passed the House of Representatives, Anthony Burns, a slave who had escaped from Virginia by stowing away on a ship, was arrested in Boston. A mob tried to free him but was thrown back. Troops were rushed to the scene to restrain the swelling crowds. Burns was a runaway, and the federal commissioner ruled that he should be returned to his master. This was done, but, as one eyewitness scornfully pointed out, it required two companies of artillery and a thousand police and marines to take "one trembling colored man to the vessel which was to carry him to slavery." As the grim parade marched past buildings festooned with black crepe, the crowd shouted "Kidnapers! Kidnapers!" at the soldiers. Estimates of the cost of returning this single slave to his owner ran as high as $100,000. In previous cases the conservative majority had tended to hold back; after the Kansas–Nebraska Act, nearly everyone opposed the return of fugitive slaves.

■ A cartoon of the "Know-Nothing" era, with savage caricatures of the drunken Irishman and the beer-sodden German stealing the big-city ballot box.

344 / THE COMING OF THE CIVIL WAR

The Democratic party lost heavily in the North as a result of the Kansas-Nebraska Act—there were 91 free-state Democrats in the House of Representatives when the act was passed, only 25 after the next election. With the Whig party already moribund, dissidents flocked to two new parties. The American, or "Know-Nothing," party (its members used the password "I don't know") sought to take advantage of the anxieties and frustrations generated by the slavery controversy, by the rapid social and economic changes of the times, and by the growing popular dissatisfaction with political leaders who were not solving these problems. The party denounced both abolitionists and southern fire-eaters; it appealed at once to the patriotism of the voters and to their meanest emotions. Its program was nativist—a kind of defensive nationalism that idealized the virtues of "native" Protestant Americans and denounced Catholics and recent immigrants. These "new" elements, it claimed, were undermining American values.

The argument was simplistic and wrongheaded, but for a time this "politics of impatience" achieved considerable success. Operating often in tacit alliance with the antislavery forces (dislike of slavery did not prevent many abolitionists from being prejudiced against Catholics and immigrants), the Know-Nothings won a string of local victories in 1854 and elected more than 40 congressmen.

Far more important was the new Republican party, made up of former Free Soilers, Conscience Whigs, and "Anti-Nebraska" Democrats. The Know-Nothing party made a pretense of being a national organization, but the Republican party was purely sectional. It sprang up spontaneously throughout the old Northwest and caught on with a rush in New England. Republicans presented themselves as the party of freedom. They were not abolitionists (though most abolitionists were soon voting Republican), but they insisted that slavery be kept out of the territories. The heart of their reasoning was that if America was to remain a land of opportunity, free white labor must have exclusive access to the West. In 1854 the Republicans won over a hundred seats in the House of Representatives and control of many state governments.

Still the furor might have died down if settlement of the new territories had proceeded in an orderly manner. Almost none of the settlers who flocked to Kansas owned slaves, relatively few of them were primarily interested in the slavery question, and most had a low opinion of blacks. ("I kem to Kansas to live in a free state," one northerner explained. "I don't want niggers a-trampin' over my grave.") Like nearly all frontiersmen, they wanted land and local political office, lucrative government contracts, and other business opportunities.

When Congress opened the gates to settlement in May 1854, *none* of the land in the territory was available for sale. Treaties extinguishing Indian titles had yet to be ratified, and public lands had not been surveyed. In July Congress authorized squatters to occupy unsurveyed federal lands, but much of this property was far to the west of the frontier and practically inaccessible. The situation led to confusion over property boundaries, to graft and speculation, and to general uncertainty among settlers, thereby exacerbating the difficulty of establishing an orderly government.

The legal status of slavery in Kansas became the focus of all these conflicts. Both North and South were determined to have Kansas. They made of the territory first a testing ground and then a battlefield, thus exposing the fatal flaw in the Kansas–Nebraska Act and the idea of popular sovereignty. The law said that the people of Kansas were "perfectly free" to decide the slavery question. But the citizens of territories were *not* entirely free; by definition, territories were not sovereign political units. The act had created a political vacuum, which its vague statement that the settlers must establish their domestic institutions "subject . . . to the Constitution" did not adequately fill. When should the institutions be established? Was it democratic to let a handful of early arrivals make decisions that would affect the lives of the thousands soon to follow? The virtues of the time-tested system of congressional control established by the Northwest Ordinance became fully apparent only when the system was discarded.

More serious was the fact that outsiders, North and South, refused to permit Kansans to work out their own destiny. The contest for control began at once. A New England Emigrant Aid Society was formed, with grandiose plans for transporting antislavery settlers to the area. The society was mostly bluff; it transported only a handful of New

Englanders to Kansas. Yet the New Englanders were very conspicuous and undoubtedly encouraged other antislavery settlers to make the move.

They also stirred southerners to fight back, and in the early days the proslavery forces had many advantages. The first inhabitants in frontier regions nearly always came from lands immediately to the east. In this case they were proslavery Missourians. When word spread that "foreigners" from New England were seeking to "steal" Kansas, these men rushed to protect their "rights."

In November 1854 an election was held in Kansas to pick a territorial delegate to Congress. A large band of Missourians crossed over specifically to elect a proslavery man and carried it easily. In March 1855 some 5,000 "Border Ruffians" again descended upon Kansas and elected a territorial legislature. A census had recorded 2,905 eligible voters, but 6,307 votes were cast. The legislature promptly enacted a slave code and laws prohibiting abolitionist agitation. Antislavery settlers refused to recognize this regime and held elections of their own. By January 1856 two governments existed in Kansas, one based on fraud, the other extralegal.

By denouncing the free-state government located at Topeka, President Pierce encouraged the proslavery settlers to assume the offensive. In May they sacked the antislavery town of Lawrence. A psychopathic Free Soiler named John Brown then took the law into his own hands in retaliation. Together with six companions (four of them his sons) Brown stole into a proslavery settlement on Pottawatomie Creek in the dead of night. They dragged five unsuspecting settlers from their rude cabins and murdered them. This senseless slaughter brought men on both sides to arms by the hundreds. Irregular fighting broke out, and by the end of 1856 some 200 persons had lost their lives. Exaggerated accounts of "Bleeding Kansas" filled the pages of northern newspapers.

A certain amount of violence was normal in any frontier community, but it suited the political interests of the Republicans to make the situation in Kansas seem worse than it was. The Democrats were also partly to blame, for although residents of nearby states often tried to influence elections in new territories, the actions of the Missouri Border Ruffians made a mockery of the democratic process. However, the main responsibility for the Kansas tragedy must be borne by the Pierce administration in Washington. Under popular sovereignty the national government was supposed to see that elections were orderly and honest. Instead, the president acted as a partisan. When the first governor of the territory objected to the manner in which the proslavery legislature had been elected, Pierce replaced him with a man who backed the southern group without question.

Charles Sumner

As counterpoint to the fighting in Kansas there rose an almost continuous cacophony in the halls of Congress. Every event in Kansas brought forth tirades in the Capitol. Red-faced legislators traded insults and threats. Epithets like "liar" were freely tossed about. Prominent in these angry outbursts was a new senator, Charles Sumner of Massachusetts. Brilliant, learned, and articulate, Sumner had made a name for himself in New England as a reformer interested in the peace movement, prison reform, and the abolition of slavery. He possessed great magnetism and was, according to the tastes of the day, an accomplished orator, but he suffered inner torments of a complex nature that warped his personality. He was egotistical and humorless. His unyielding devotion to his principles was less praiseworthy than it seemed on casual examination, for it resulted from his complete lack of respect for the principles of others. Reform movements evidently provided him a kind of emotional release; he became combative and totally lacking in objectivity when espousing a cause.

In the Kansas debates Sumner displayed vindictiveness and an icy disdain for his foes. Colleagues threatened him with assassination, called him a "filthy reptile" and a "leper." He was impervious to such hostility. In the spring of 1856 he loosed a dreadful blast at "the crime against Kansas." Characterizing administration policy as tyrannical, imbecilic, absurd, and infamous, he demanded that Kansas be admitted to the Union at once as a free state. Then he began a long and intemperate personal attack on both Douglas and the elderly Senator Andrew P. Butler of South Carolina, who was not present to defend himself.

Sumner described Butler as a "Don Quixote" who had taken "the harlot, slavery" as his mistress. While he was still talking, Douglas, who

■ A well-known contemporary drawing gives a dramatic view of Brooks caning Sumner. Beneath Sumner's left hand is a scroll inscribed Kansas. The cartoon was originally titled "Southern Chivalry—Arguments vs. Clubs."

shrugged off such language as part of the game, was heard to mutter, "That damn fool will get himself killed by some other damn fool."

Such a "fool" quickly materialized in the person of Congressman Preston S. Brooks of South Carolina, a nephew of Senator Butler. Since Butler was absent from Washington, Brooks, who was probably as mentally unbalanced as Sumner, assumed the responsibility of defending his kinsman's honor. A southern romantic par excellence, he decided that caning Sumner would reflect his contempt more effectively than challenging him to a duel. Two days after the speech, Brooks entered the Senate as it adjourned. Sumner remained at his desk writing. After waiting with exquisite punctilio until a talkative woman in the lobby had left so that she would be spared the sight of violence, Brooks walked up to Sumner and rained blows upon his head with a guttapercha cane until he fell, unconscious and bloody, upon the floor. "I . . . gave him about 30 first-rate stripes," Brooks later boasted. "Towards the last he bellowed like a calf. I wore my cane out completely but saved the head which is gold." The physical damage suffered by Sumner was relatively superficial, but the incident so affected him psychologically that he was unable to return to his seat in Congress until 1859.

Both sides made much of this disgraceful incident. When the House censured him, Brooks resigned, returned to his home district, and was triumphantly reelected. A number of well-wishers even sent him souvenir canes. Northerners viewed the affair as illustrating the brutalizing effect of slavery on southern whites and made a hero of Sumner.

Buchanan Tries His Hand

Such was the atmosphere surrounding the 1856 presidential election. The Republican party now dominated much of the North, and it must be emphasized that it stood not for abolition but for restricting slavery to areas where it already existed. It nominated John C. Frémont, "the Pathfinder," one of the heroes of the conquest of California. Frémont fitted the Whig tradition of presidential candidates: a popular military man with almost no political experience. However, he was sound and articulate on the issue of slavery in the territories.

■ Buchanan "never made a witty remark, never wrote a memorable sentence, and never showed a touch of distinction," according to historian Allan Nevins.

Although men of diverse interests had joined the party, Republicans expressed their objectives in one simple slogan: "Free soil, free speech, and Frémont."

The Democrats cast aside the ineffectual Pierce, but they did not dare nominate Douglas because he had raised such a storm in the North. They settled on James Buchanan, chiefly because he had been out of the country serving as minister to Great Britain during the long debate over Kansas! The Know-Nothing party nominated ex-president Fillmore, a choice the remnants of the Whigs ratified.

The Democrats concentrated on denouncing the Republicans as a sectional party that threatened to destroy the Union. On this issue they carried the day. Buchanan won only a minority of the popular vote, but he had strength in every section. He got 174 electoral votes to Frémont's 114 and Fillmore's 8. The significant contest took place in the populous states just north of slave territory, Pennsylvania, Ohio, Indiana, and Illinois. Buchanan carried all but Ohio, though by narrow margins.

No one could say that James Buchanan lacked political experience. He had been elected to the Pennsylvania legislature in 1815 when only 24. He served for well over 20 years in Congress and had been minister to Russia, then Polk's secretary of state, then minister to Great Britain under Pierce. Personally, Buchanan was a bundle of contradictions. Dignified in bearing and by nature cautious, he could consume enormous amounts of liquor without showing the slightest sign of inebriation. A big, heavy man, he was nonetheless remarkably graceful and light on his tiny feet, of which he was inordinately proud. He wore a very high collar to conceal a scarred neck, and because of an eye defect he habitually carried his head to one side and slightly forward, which gave him, as his most recent biographer says, "a perpetual attitude of courteous deference and attentive interest" that sometimes led individuals to believe they had won a greater share of his attention and support than was actually the case. In fact he was extremely stubborn and sometimes vindictive.

Buchanan was popular with women and attracted to them as well, but although he contemplated marriage on more than one occasion, he never took the final step. Over the years many strong men in politics had held him in contempt. Yet he was patriotic, conscientious, moderate. While Republican extremists called him a "Doughface"—they believed he lacked the force of character to stand up against southern extremists—many voters in 1856 thought they saw in him the qualities necessary to steer the nation to calmer waters.

The Dred Scott Decision

Before Buchanan could fairly take the Kansas problem in hand, an event occurred that drove another deep wedge between North and South. Back in 1834 Dr. John Emerson of St. Louis joined the army as a surgeon and was assigned to duty at Rock Island, Illinois. Later he was transferred to Fort Snelling, in Wisconsin Territory. In 1838 he returned to Missouri. Accompanying him on these travels was his body servant, Dred Scott, a slave. In 1846, after Emerson's death, Scott, with the help of a friendly lawyer, brought suit in the Missouri courts for his liberty, arguing that residence in Illinois, where slavery was barred under the Northwest Ordinance, and in Wisconsin Territory, where the Missouri Compromise outlawed it, had made him a free man.

The future of Dred Scott mattered not at all to the country or the courts; at issue was the question of whether Congress or the local legislatures had the power to outlaw slavery in the territories. After many years of litigation, the case reached the Supreme Court. On March 6, 1857, two days after Buchanan's inauguration, the high tribunal acted. Blacks, the Court declared, were not citizens; therefore Scott could not sue in a federal court. This dubious legal logic settled Scott's fate. However, the Court went further. Since the plaintiff had returned to Missouri, the laws of Illinois no longer applied to him. His residence in Wisconsin Territory—this was the most controversial part of the decision—did not make him free because the Missouri Compromise was unconstitutional. According to the Bill of Rights (the Fifth Amendment), the federal government cannot deprive any person of life, liberty, or property without due process of law.* Therefore, Chief Justice Roger B. Taney reasoned, "an Act of Congress which deprives a person . . . of his liberty or property merely because he came himself or brought his property into a particular Territory . . . could hardly be dignified with the name of due process of law."

The Dred Scott decision has been widely criticized on legal grounds. Each justice filed his own opinion, and in several important particulars there was no line of argument that any five of the nine agreed upon. Some critics have argued that the justices should not have gone beyond the minimum of argument necessary to settle the case, and many have made much of the fact that a majority of the justices were southerners. It would be going too far, however, to accuse the Court of plotting to extend slavery. The judges were trying to settle the vexing question of slavery in the territories once and for all. If this admirable objective could only be accomplished by fuzzy reasoning—well, it

---

*Some state constitutions had similar provisions, but the slave states obviously did not. The Fourteenth Amendment to the Constitution extended the ban to the states (see pages 398–399).

would not be the first time in the history of jurisprudence that an important result rested on shaky logic.

In addition to invalidating the Missouri Compromise, which had already been repealed, the decision threatened Douglas' principle of popular sovereignty, for if Congress could not exclude slaves from a territory, how could a mere territorial legislature do so? Until statehood was granted, slavery seemed as inviolate as freedom of religion or speech or any other civil liberty guaranteed by the Constitution. Where formerly freedom (as guaranteed in the Bill of Rights) was a national institution and slavery a local one, now, according to the Court, slavery was nationwide, excluded only where states had specifically abolished it.

The irony of employing the Bill of Rights to keep blacks in chains did not escape northern critics. Now slaves could be brought into Minnesota Territory, even into Oregon. In his inaugural address Buchanan had sanctimoniously urged the people to accept the forthcoming ruling—"whatever this may be"—as a final settlement. Many assumed (indeed, it was true) that certain judges had "leaked" word of the decision to him in advance of his speech. If this "greatest crime in the judicial annals of the Republic" was allowed to stand, northerners argued, the Republican party would have no reason to exist: its program had been declared unconstitutional! The Dred Scott decision convinced thousands that the South was engaged in an aggressive attempt to extend the peculiar institution so far that it could no longer be considered peculiar.

The Lecompton Constitution

Kansas soon provided a test for northern suspicions. Initially Buchanan handled the problem of Kansas well by appointing Robert J. Walker of Mississippi as governor. Although a southerner, Walker had no desire to foist slavery on the territory against the will of its inhabitants. He was a small man but a courageous one, patriotic, vigorous, tough-minded, much like Douglas in temper and belief. A former senator and Cabinet member, he had more political stature by far than any previous governor. The proslavery leaders in Kansas had managed to convene a constitutional convention at Lecompton, but the Free Soil forces had refused to participate in the election of delegates. When this rump body drafted a proslavery constitution and then refused to submit it to a fair vote of all the settlers, Walker denounced its work and hurried back to Washington to explain the situation to Buchanan.

The president refused to face reality. His prosouthern advisers were clamoring for him to "save" Kansas. Instead of rejecting the Lecompton constitution, he asked Congress to admit Kansas to the Union with this document as its frame of government.

Buchanan's decision brought him head-on against Stephen A. Douglas, and the repercussions of their clash shattered the Democratic party. Principle and self-interest (an irresistible combination) forced Douglas to oppose the leader of his party. If he stood aside while Congress admitted Kansas, he would not only be abandoning popular sovereignty, he would be committing political suicide. He was up for reelection to the Senate in 1858. Fifty-five of the 56 newspapers in Illinois had declared editorially against the Lecompton constitution; if he supported it, defeat was certain. In a dramatic confrontation at the White House he and Buchanan argued the question at length, tempers rising. Finally, the president tried to force him into line. "Mr. Douglas," he said, "I desire you to remember that no Democrat ever yet differed from an Administration of his own choice without being crushed." "Mr. President," Douglas replied contemptuously, "I wish *you* to remember that General Jackson is dead!" And he stalked out of the room.

Buchanan compounded his error by putting tremendous political pressure on Douglas, cutting off his Illinois patronage on the eve of his reelection campaign. Of course Douglas persisted, openly joining the Republicans in the fight. Congress rejected the bill.

Meanwhile, the extent of the fraud perpetrated at Lecompton became clear. In October 1857 a new legislature had been chosen in Kansas, the antislavery voters participating in the balloting. It ordered a referendum on the Lecompton constitution in January 1858. The constitution was overwhelmingly rejected, this time the proslavery settlers boycotting the test. When Buchanan persisted in pressing Congress to admit Kansas under the Lecompton constitution, Congress ordered another referendum. To slant the case in favor of approval, the legislators stipulated that if the constitution was voted down, Kansas could not be admitted into the Union until it had a population of 90,000. Nevertheless, the Kansans rejected it by a ratio of six to one.

More than opposition to slavery influenced this vote, for by 1858 most Kansans were totally alienated from the Democratic administration in Washington because of its bungling and corrupt management of the public lands. After delaying sales unconscionably, Buchanan suddenly put 8 million acres up for auction in 1858. Squatters on this land were faced, in the midst of a depression, with finding $200 in cash to cover the minimum price of their quarter sections or losing their improvements. Local protests forced a delay of the sales, but Kansans by the thousands were convinced that Buchanan had thrown the land on the market out of pique at their original rejection of the Lecompton constitution.

The Emergence of Lincoln

These were dark days. During the summer of 1857 a panic struck the New York stock market, heralding a sharp downturn of the economy. This depression was probably unavoidable after the feverish expansion and speculation of the previous ten years, but northerners blamed the southern-dominated Congress, which had just reduced tariff duties to the lowest levels in nearly half a century. As prices plummeted and unemployment rose, they attributed the collapse to foreign competition and accused the South of having sacrificed the prosperity of the rest of the nation for its selfish advantage. The South in turn read in the panic proof of the superiority of the slave system, for the depression had little effect on the southern economy, chiefly because the world price of cotton remained high.

Dissolution threatened the Union. To many Americans Stephen A. Douglas seemed to offer the best hope of preserving it. For this reason unusual attention was focused on his campaign for reelection to the Senate in 1858. The importance of the contest and Douglas' national prestige put great pressure on the Republicans of Illinois to nominate someone who would make a good showing against him. The man they chose was Abraham Lincoln.

After a towering figure has passed from the stage, it is always difficult to discover what he was like before his rise to prominence. This is especially true of Lincoln, who changed greatly when power and responsibility and fame came to him. Lincoln was not unknown in 1858, but his career had not been distinguished. He was born in Kentucky in 1809, and the story of his early life can be condensed, as he once said himself, into a single line from Gray's *Elegy:* "The short and simple annals of the poor." His illiterate, ne'er-do-well father, Thomas Lincoln, was a typical frontier wanderer. When Abraham was 7 the family moved to Indiana. In 1830 they pushed west again into southern Illinois. The boy received almost no formal schooling, but he had a good mind and was extremely ambitious. He cut loose from his family, made a trip to New Orleans, and for a time managed a general store in New Salem, Illinois. When barely 25 he won a seat in the Illinois legislature as a Whig. He studied law and was admitted to the bar in 1836.

Lincoln remained in the legislature until 1842, displaying a perfect willingness to adopt the Whig position on all issues. In 1846 he was elected to Congress. While not engaged in politics he worked at the law, maintaining an office in Springfield and following the circuit, taking a variety of cases, few of much importance. He earned a decent but by no means sumptuous living. After one term in Congress his political career petered out. He seemed fated to pass his remaining years as a typical small-town lawyer.

Even during this period Lincoln's personality was enormously complex. His bawdy sense of humor and his endless fund of stories and tall tales made him a legend first in Illinois and then in Washington. He was admired in Illinois as a powerful and expert axman and a champion wrestler. He was thoroughly at home with toughs like the "Clary's Grove Boys" of New Salem and in the convivial atmosphere of a party caucus. But in a society where most men drank heavily, he never touched liquor. And he was subject to periods of melancholy so profound as to appear almost psychopathic. Friends spoke of him as having "cat fits," and he wrote of himself in the early 1840s: "I

■ Alexander Hesler's portrait, taken in Springfield on June 3, 1860, shortly after the Republican national convention, is generally considered to be the finest of the pre-Civil War photographs of Lincoln.

am now the most miserable man living. If what I felt were equally distributed to the whole human family, there would not be one cheerful face on earth."

In a region swept by repeated waves of religious revivalism, Lincoln managed to be at once a man of calm spirituality and a skeptic without appearing offensive to conventional believers. He was a party wheelhorse, a corporation lawyer, even a railroad lobbyist, yet his reputation for integrity was stainless.

The revival of the slavery controversy in 1854 stirred Lincoln deeply. No abolitionist, he had always tried to take a "realistic" view of the problem. The Kansas–Nebraska bill led him to see the moral issue more clearly. "If slavery is not wrong, nothing is wrong," he stated with the clarity and

simplicity of expression for which he later became famous. Compromises made for the sake of sectional harmony had always sought to preserve as much territory as possible for freedom. Yet unlike most northern Free Soilers, he did not blame the southerners for slavery. "They are just what we would be in their situation," he confessed.

The fairness and moderation of his position combined with its moral force won Lincoln many admirers in the great body of citizens who were trying to reconcile their generally low opinion of blacks and their patriotic desire to avoid an issue that threatened the Union with their growing conviction that slavery was sinful. *Anything* that aided slavery was wrong, Lincoln argued. But before casting the first stone, every northerner should look into his own heart: "If there be a man amongst us who is so impatient of [slavery] as a wrong as to disregard its actual presence among us and the difficulty of getting rid of it suddenly in a satisfactory way . . . that man is misplaced if he is on our platform." And Lincoln confessed:

> If all earthly power were given to me, I should not know what to do as to the existing institution. But . . . [this] furnishes no more excuse for permitting slavery to go into our free territory than it would for reviving the African slave trade.

Thus Lincoln was at once compassionate toward the slaveowner and stern toward the institution. "'A house divided against itself cannot stand,'" he warned. "I believe this government cannot endure permanently half slave and half free." Without minimizing the difficulties or urging a hasty and ill-considered solution, Lincoln demanded that the people look toward a day, however remote, when not only Kansas but the entire country would be free.

The Lincoln-Douglas Debates

As Lincoln developed these ideas his reputation grew. In 1855 he almost won the Whig nomination for senator. In 1856, at the first Republican National Convention, he received 110 votes for the vice-presidential nomination. He seemed the logical man to pit against Douglas in 1858.

In July Lincoln challenged Douglas to a series of seven debates. The senator accepted. The debates were well attended and widely reported, for the idea of a direct confrontation between candidates for an important office captured the popular imagination. The candidates presented a sharp physical contrast that must have helped ordinary voters in sorting out their differing points of view.* Douglas was short and stocky, Lincoln long and lean. Douglas gave the impression of irrepressible energy. While speaking, he roamed the platform; he used broad gestures and bold, exaggerated arguments. He did not hesitate to call "Honest Abe" a liar. Lincoln on his part was slow and deliberate of speech, his voice curiously high-pitched. He seldom used gestures or oratorical tricks, trying rather to create an impression of utter sincerity to add force to his remarks.

The two employed different political styles, each calculated to project a particular image. Douglas epitomized efficiency and success. He dressed in the latest fashion, favoring flashy vests and the finest broadcloth. Ordinarily he arrived in town in a private railroad car, to be met by a brass band, then to ride at the head of a parade to the appointed place. Lincoln appeared before the voters as a man of the people. He wore ill-fitting black suits and a stovepipe hat—repository for letters, bills, scribbled notes, and other scraps—that exaggerated his great height. He presented a worn and rumpled appearance, partly because he traveled from place to place on day coaches, accompanied by only a few advisers. When local supporters came to meet him at the station, he preferred to walk with them through the streets to the scene of the debate.

Lincoln and Douglas maintained a high intellectual level in their speeches, but these were *political* debates. They were seeking not to influence future historians (who have nonetheless pondered their words endlessly) but to win votes. They tended to exaggerate their differences, which were not in fact enormous. Neither wanted to see slavery in the territories or thought it economically efficient, and neither sought to abolish it by political action or force. Both believed blacks congenitally inferior to whites.

Douglas' strategy was to make Lincoln look like an abolitionist. He accused the Republicans of favoring racial equality and refusing to abide by the decision of the Supreme Court in the Dred Scott case. Himself he pictured as a heroic champion of democracy, attacked on one side by the "black" Republicans and on the other by the Buchananites, yet ready to fight to his last breath for popular sovereignty.

Lincoln tried to picture Douglas as proslavery and a *defender* of the Dred Scott decision. "Slavery is an unqualified evil to the negro, to the white man, to the soil, and to the State," he said. "Judge Douglas," he also said, "is blowing out the moral lights around us, when he contends that whoever wants slaves has a right to hold them." However, he often weakened the impact of his arguments, being perhaps too eager to demonstrate his conservatism. The historian David M. Potter drew a

---

*The choice of the next senator lay, of course, in the hands of the state legislature. Technically, Douglas and Lincoln were campaigning for candidates for the legislature who were pledged to support them for the Senate seat.

nice distinction in Lincoln's position between "what he would do for the slave" and "what he would do for the Negro." "All men are created equal," he would say, on the authority of the Declaration of Independence, only to add: "I am not, nor ever have been, in favor of bringing about in any way the social and political equality of the white and black races." He opposed allowing blacks to vote, to sit on juries, to marry whites, even to be citizens. He predicted the "ultimate extinction" of slavery, but when pressed he predicted that it would not occur "in less than a hundred years at the least." He took a fence-sitting position on the question of abolition in the District of Columbia and stated flatly that he did not favor repeal of the Fugitive Slave Act.

In the debate at Freeport, a town northwest of Chicago near the Wisconsin line, Lincoln cleverly asked Douglas if, considering the Dred Scott decision, the people of a territory could exclude slavery *before* the territory became a state. Unhesitatingly Douglas replied that they could, simply by not passing the local laws essential for holding blacks in bondage. "It matters not what way the Supreme Court may hereafter decide as to the abstract question," he said. "The people have the lawful means to introduce or exclude it as they please, for the reason that slavery cannot exist . . . unless it is supported by local police regulations."

This argument saved Douglas in Illinois. The Democrats carried both houses of the legislature by a narrow margin, whereas it is almost certain that if Douglas had accepted the Dred Scott decision outright, the balance would have swung to the Republicans. But the "Freeport Doctrine" cost him heavily two years later when he made his bid for the Democratic presidential nomination. "It matters not what way the Supreme Court may hereafter decide"—southern extremists would not accept a man who suggested that the Dred Scott decision could be circumvented, though in fact Douglas had only stated the obvious.

Probably Lincoln had not thought beyond the senatorial election when he asked the question; he was merely hoping to keep Douglas on the defensive and perhaps injure him in southern Illinois, where considerable proslavery sentiment existed. In any case, defeat did Lincoln no harm politically. He had more than held his own against one of the most formidable debaters in politics, and his distinctive personality and point of view had im-

pressed themselves upon thousands of minds. Indeed, his political career was revitalized.

The campaign of 1858 marked Douglas' last triumph, Lincoln's last defeat. Elsewhere the elections in the North went heavily to the Republicans. When the old Congress reconvened in December, northern-sponsored economic measures (a higher tariff, the transcontinental railroad, river and harbor improvements, a free homestead bill) were all blocked by southern votes.

Whether the South could continue to prevent the passage of this legislation in the new Congress was problematical. In early 1859 even many moderate southerners were uneasy about the future. The radicals, made panicky by Republican victories and their own failure to win in Kansas, spoke openly of secession if a Republican was elected president in 1860. Lincoln's "house divided" speech was quoted out of context, while Douglas' Freeport Doctrine added to southern woes. When Senator William H. Seward of New York spoke of an "irrepressible conflict" between freedom and slavery, southerners became still more alarmed.

Naturally they struck back. Led by William L. Yancey of Alabama and Senators Jefferson Davis of Mississippi, John Slidell of Louisiana, and James H. Hammond of South Carolina, they demanded a federal slave code for the territories and talked of annexing Cuba and reviving the African slave trade. "Issues were becoming emotionalized," the historian David Herbert Donald wrote of these unhappy times. "Slogans were reducing public sentiment to stereotyped patterns; social psychology was approaching a hair-trigger instability."

John Brown's Raid

In October 1859 John Brown, the scourge of Kansas, made his second tragic contribution to the unfolding sectional drama. Gathering a group of 18 followers, white and black, he staged an attack on Harpers Ferry, Virginia, a town on the Potomac upstream from Washington. He planned to seize the federal arsenal there, arm the slaves who he thought would flock to his side, establish a black republic in the mountains of Virginia, and then press ahead with a sort of private war against the South.

Simply by overpowering a few night watchmen,

■ The image of John Brown as martyr was memorialized in art as well as in song and story. Here is a sentimental interpretation, *The Last Moments of John Brown,* painted in 1884 by American genre artist Thomas Hovenden.

Brown and his men occupied the arsenal and a nearby rifle factory. They captured several hostages, one of them Colonel Lewis Washington, a great-grandnephew of George Washington. But no slaves came forward to join them. Federal troops commanded by Robert E. Lee soon trapped Brown's men in an engine house of the Baltimore and Ohio Railroad. After a two-day siege in which the attackers picked off ten of his men, Brown was captured.

No incident so well illustrates the role of emotion and irrationality in the sectional crisis as John Brown's raid. Over the years before his Kansas escapade, Brown had been a drifter, horse thief, and swindler, several times a bankrupt, a failure in everything he attempted. His maternal grand-

mother, his mother, and five aunts and uncles were certifiably insane, as were two of his own children and many collateral relatives. After his ghastly Pottawatomie murders it should have been obvious to anyone that he was mad: some of the victims were hacked to bits. Yet numbers of supposedly high-minded northerners, including Emerson and Thoreau, had supported him and his antislavery "work" after 1856, and some contributed directly and knowingly to his Harpers Ferry enterprise. After Brown's capture, Emerson, in an essay on "Courage," called him a martyr who would "make the gallows as glorious as the cross."

Many southerners reacted to Harpers Ferry with an equal irrationality, some with a rage similar to Brown's. Dozens of hapless northerners in the southern states were arrested, beaten, or driven off. One, falsely suspected of being an accomplice of Brown, was lynched.

Brown's fate lay in the hands of the Virginia authorities. Ignoring his obvious derangement, they charged him with treason, conspiracy, and murder. He was speedily convicted and hanged. (It would have been wiser and more just to have committed him to an asylum; then his dreadful act could have been seen in proper perspective.)

"Old Brown" had still one more contribution to make to the developing sectional tragedy. Despite the furor he had created, cool heads everywhere called for calm and denounced his attack. Most leading Republican politicians repudiated him and tried to reassure the South that they would never condone the use of violence against slavery. Even execution would probably not have made a martyr of Brown had he behaved like a madman after his capture. Instead, an enormous dignity descended upon him as he lay in his Virginia jail awaiting death. "If it is deemed necessary that I should forfeit my life for the furtherance of the ends of justice, and mingle my blood further with the blood of . . . millions in this slave country whose rights are disregarded by wicked, cruel, and unjust enactments," he said before the judge pronounced sentence, "I say, let it be done."

This John Brown, with his patriarchal beard and sad eyes, so apparently incompatible with the bloody terrorist of Pottawatomie and Harpers Ferry, led thousands in the North to ignore his past and their own better judgment and treat him as a martyr—thus a saint. Thoreau compared his execution to Christ's crucifixion.

And so a megalomaniac became to the North a hero and to the South a symbol of northern ruthlessness. The historian C. Vann Woodward put it this way: "Paranoia continued to induce counterparanoia, each antagonist infecting the other reciprocally, until the vicious spiral ended in war." Soon, as the popular song had it, Brown's body lay "a-mouldering in the grave," and the memory of his bloody act did indeed go "marching on."

Election of 1860

By 1860 the nation was teetering on the brink of disunion. Radicals North and South were heedlessly provoking one another. When a disgruntled

North Carolinian, Hinton Rowan Helper, published *The Impending Crisis of the South,* an attempt to demonstráte statistically that slavery was ruining the South's economy and corrupting its social structure, the Republicans flooded the country with an abridged edition, though they knew that southerners considered the book an appeal for social revolution. "I have always been a fervid Union man," one southerner wrote in 1859, "but I confess the [northern] endorsement of the Harpers Ferry outrage and Helper's infernal doctrine has shaken my fidelity." In February 1860 the legislature of Alabama formally resolved that the state ought to secede if a Republican was elected president.

Extremism was more evident in the South, and to any casual observer that section must have seemed the aggressor in the crisis. Yet even in demanding the reopening of the African slave trade, southern radicals believed they were defending themselves against attack. They felt surrounded by hostility. The North was growing at a much faster rate; if nothing were done, they feared, a flood of new free states would soon be able to amend the Constitution and emancipate the slaves. The decline of slavery in border states from Maryland to Missouri seemed to be bringing that day closer, and the increasing worldwide condemnation of the institution added a further psychological burden. John Brown's raid, with its threat of black insurrection, reduced them to a state of panic.

When legislatures in state after state in the South cracked down on freedom of expression, made the manumission of slaves illegal, banished free blacks, and took other steps that northerners considered blatantly provocative, the advocates of these policies believed that they were only defending the status quo. Perhaps, by seceding from the Union, the South could raise a dike against the tide of abolitionism and preserve its way of life. Secession also provided an emotional release—a way of dissipating tension by striking back at criticism.

Stephen A. Douglas was probably the last hope of avoiding a rupture between North and South, but when the Democrats met at Charleston, South Carolina, in April 1860 to choose their presidential candidate, the southern delegates would not accept him unless he promised not to disturb slavery in the territories. Indeed, they went further in

■ In this 1860 election cartoon, candidates Lincoln (at left), Douglas, and Breckinridge are tearing the nation apart, while candidate Bell futilely tries to apply glue from a tiny pot using an even tinier brush.

their demands. The North, William L. Yancey of Alabama insisted, must accept the proposition that slavery was not merely tolerable but *right*. Of course the northerners would not go so far. "Gentlemen of the South," said Senator George E. Pugh of Ohio in replying to Yancey, "you mistake us— you mistake us! We will not do it!" When southern proposals were voted down, most of the delegates from the Deep South walked out. Without them Douglas could not obtain the required two-thirds majority, and the convention adjourned without naming a candidate.

In June the Democrats reconvened at Baltimore. Again they failed to reach agreement. The two wings then met separately, the northerners nominating Douglas, the southerners John C. Breckinridge of Kentucky, Buchanan's vice-president. On the question of slavery in the territories, the

northerners promised to "abide by the decision of the Supreme Court," which meant, in effect, that they stood for Douglas' Freeport Doctrine. The southerners announced their belief that neither Congress nor any territorial government could prevent citizens from settling *"with their property"* in any territory.

Meanwhile the Republicans, meeting in Chicago in mid May, had drafted a platform attractive to all classes and all sections of the northern and western states. For manufacturers they proposed a high tariff, for farmers a homestead law providing free land for settlers. Internal improvements "of a National character," notably a railroad to the Pacific, should receive federal aid. No restrictions should be placed on immigration. As to slavery in the territories, the Republicans did not equivocate: "The normal condition of all the territory of the United States is that of freedom." Neither Congress nor a local legislature could "give legal existence to Slavery in any Territory."

In choosing a presidential candidate the convention displayed equally shrewd political judgment. Seward was the front-runner, but he had taken too extreme a stand and appeared unlikely to carry the crucial states Pennsylvania, Ohio, and Illinois. He led on the first ballot but could not get a majority. Then the delegates began to look closely at Abraham Lincoln. His thoughtful and moderate views on the main issue of the times attracted many, and so did his political personality. "Honest Abe," the "Railsplitter," a man of humble origins (born in a log cabin), self-educated, self-made, a common man but by no means an ordinary man—the combination seemed unbeatable.

Lincoln had an excellent team of convention managers. Taking advantage of the fact that the

convention was meeting in Lincoln's home state, they packed the gallery with leather-lunged ward heelers assigned the task of shouting for their man. They also made a series of deals with the leaders of other state delegations to win additional votes. "I authorize no bargains and will be bound by none," Lincoln telegraphed the convention. "Lincoln ain't here and don't know what we have to meet," one of his managers remarked—and proceeded to trade off two Cabinet posts for the votes of key states. On the second ballot Lincoln drew shoulder to shoulder with Seward, on the third he was within two votes of victory. Before the roll could be called again, delegates began to switch their votes, and in a landslide, soon made unanimous, Lincoln was nominated.

A few days earlier the remnants of the Know-Nothing and Whig parties had formed the Constitutional Union party and nominated John Bell of Tennessee for president. "It is both the part of

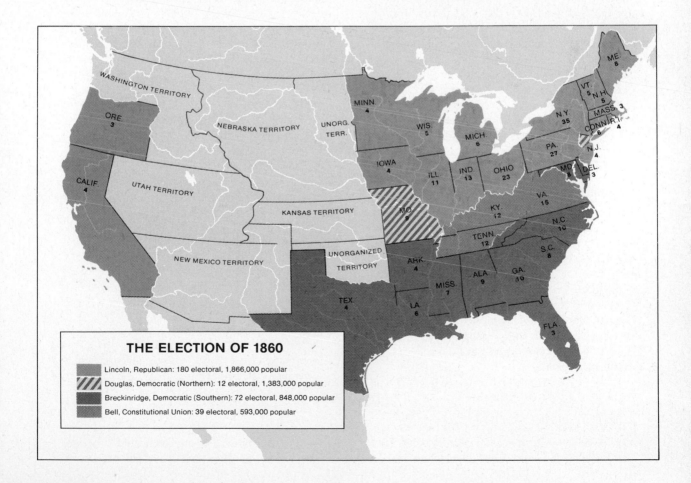

THE ELECTION OF 1860

Lincoln, Republican: 180 electoral, 1,866,000 popular
Douglas, Democratic (Northern): 12 electoral, 1,383,000 popular
Breckinridge, Democratic (Southern): 72 electoral, 848,000 popular
Bell, Constitutional Union: 39 electoral, 593,000 popular

patriotism and of duty," they resolved, "to recognize no political principle other than the Constitution of the country, the union of the states, and the enforcement of the laws." Ostrichlike, the Constitutional Unionists ignored the conflicts rending the nation. Only in the border states, where the consequences of disunion were sure to be most tragic, did they make much headway.

With four candidates in the field, no one could win a popular majority, but it soon became clear that Lincoln was going to be elected. Breckinridge had most of the slave states in his pocket and Bell would run strong in the border regions, but the populous northern and western states had a large majority of the electoral vote, and there the choice lay between the Republicans and the Douglas Democrats. In such a contest the Republicans, with their attractive economic program and their strong stand against slavery in the territories, were sure to come out on top.

Lincoln avoided campaigning and made no public statements. Douglas, recognizing the certainty of Lincoln's victory, accepted his fate and for the first time in his career rose above ambition. "We must try to save the Union," he said. "I will go South." Everywhere, even in the heart of the Cotton Kingdom, he appealed to the voters to stand by the Union whoever was elected. He was the only candidate to do so; the others refused to remind the voters that their election might result in secession and civil war.

When the votes were counted, Lincoln had 1,866,000, almost a million fewer than the combined total of his three opponents, but he swept the North and West, which gave him 180 electoral votes and the presidency. Douglas received 1,383,000 votes, so distributed that he carried only Missouri and part of New Jersey. Breckinridge, with 848,000 popular votes, won most of the South; Bell, with 593,000, carried Virginia, Tennessee, and Kentucky. Lincoln was thus a minority president, but his title to the office was unquestionable. Even if his opponents could have combined their *popular* votes in each state, Lincoln would have won.

The Secession Crisis

A few days after Lincoln's victory, the South Carolina legislature ordered an election of dele-gates to a convention to decide the state's future course. On December 20 the convention voted unanimously to secede, basing its action on the logic of Calhoun. "The State of South Carolina has *resumed* her position among the nations of the world," the delegates announced.

By February 1, 1861, all the other states of the Lower South had followed suit. A week later, at Montgomery, Alabama, a provisional government of the Confederate States of America was established. Virginia, Tennessee, North Carolina, and Arkansas did not leave the Union but announced that if the federal government attempted to use force against the new Confederacy, they too would secede.

Why were southerners willing to wreck the Union their grandfathers had put together with so much love and labor? No simple explanation is possible. The danger that the expanding North would overwhelm them was for neither today nor tomorrow. Lincoln had assured them that he would respect slavery where it existed. The Democrats had retained control of Congress in the election; the Supreme Court was firmly in their hands as well. If the North *did* try to destroy slavery, *then* secession was perhaps a logical tactic, but why not wait until the threat materialized? To leave the Union meant abandoning the very objectives for which the South had been contending for over a decade: a share of the federal territories and an enforceable fugitive slave act.

One reason why the South rejected this line of thinking was the tremendous economic energy generated in the North, which seemed to threaten the South's independence:

> From the rattle with which the nurse tickles the ear of the child born in the South to the shroud which covers the cold form of the dead, everything comes from the North [one southerner complained at a commercial convention in 1855]. We rise from between sheets made in Northern looms, and pillows of Northern feathers, to wash in basins made in the North. . . . We eat from Northern plates and dishes; our rooms are swept with Northern brooms, our gardens dug with Northern spades . . . and the very wood which feeds our fires is cut with Northern axes, helved with hickory brought from Connecticut and New York.

Secession, southerners argued, would "liberate" the South and produce the kind of balanced economy that was proving so successful in the North.

The other reasons were emotional. The years of sectional conflict, the growing northern criticism of slavery, perhaps even an unconscious awareness that this criticism was well founded, had undermined and in many cases destroyed the patriotic feelings of southerners. Because of the constant clamor set up by the New England antislavery groups, the South tended to identify all northerners as "Yankee abolitionists" and to resent them with increasing passion. "I look upon the whole New England race as a troublesome unquiet set of meddlers," one Georgian wrote. Moreover, a Republican president did not need the consent of Congress to flood the South with unfriendly federal officials: abolitionists and perhaps even blacks. Such a possibility most southerners found unsupportable. Fear approaching panic swept the region.

Although states' rights provided the legal justification for leaving the Union, and southerners expounded the strict-constructionist interpretation of the Constitution with great ingenuity, the economic and emotional factors were far more basic. Thus the Lower South decided to go ahead with secession regardless of the cost. "Let the consequences be what they may," an Atlanta newspaper proclaimed. "Whether the Potomac is crimsoned in human gore, and Pennsylvania Avenue is paved ten fathoms in depth with mangled bodies . . . the South will never submit. . . ."

Not every slaveowner, it must be repeated, could contemplate secession with such bloodthirsty equanimity. Some believed that the risks of war and slave insurrection were too great. Others retained a profound loyalty to the United States. Many accepted secession only after the deepest examination of conscience. But almost without exception, in the end they did accept it. Lieutenant Colonel Robert E. Lee of Virginia was typical of thousands. "I see only that a fearful calamity is upon us," he wrote during the secession crisis. "There is no sacrifice I am not ready to make for the preservation of the Union save that of honour. If a disruption takes place, I shall go back in sorrow to my people & share the misery of my native state."

In the North there was a foolish but understandable reluctance to believe that the South really intended to break away permanently; in the South, an equally unrealistic expectation that the North would not resist secession forcibly. President-elect Lincoln was inclined to write off secession as a bluff designed to win concessions he was determined not to make. Lincoln also showed a lamentable political caution in refusing to announce his plans or to cooperate with the outgoing Democratic administration before taking over on March 4.

As for President Buchanan, he recognized the seriousness of the situation but professed himself powerless. Secession, he said, was illegal, but the federal government had no legal way to prevent it. He urged making concessions to the South yet lacked the forcefulness to take the situation in hand. Of course he faced unprecedented difficulties. His term was about to run out, and since he could not commit his successor, his influence was minuscule. Yet a bolder man might still have rallied the Unionists of the South by some dramatic stroke. And Buchanan ought to have denounced secession in uncompromising terms. Instead he vacillated between compromise and aimless drift. His friendly biographer, Philip Klein, has written: "Importuned, threatened, warned, begged, pushed, pulled, and shoved in every direction . . . the president at length became distraught and despaired of achieving a solution."

Appeasers, well-meaning believers in compromise, and those prepared to fight to preserve the Union were alike incapable of effective action. A group of moderates headed by Henry Clay's disciple, Senator John J. Crittenden of Kentucky, proposed a constitutional amendment in which slavery would be "recognized as existing" in all territories south of latitude 36°30'. The amendment also promised that no future amendment would tamper with the institution in the slave states and offered other guarantees to the South. But Lincoln refused to consider any arrangement that would open new territory to slavery. "On the territorial question," he wrote, "I am inflexible." The Crittenden Compromise got nowhere.

The new southern Confederacy set vigorously to work drafting a constitution, choosing Jefferson Davis as provisional president, seizing arsenals and other federal property within its boundaries, and preparing to dispatch diplomatic representatives to enlist the support of foreign powers. Buchanan bumbled helplessly in Washington. And out in Illinois, Abraham Lincoln juggled Cabinet posts and grew a beard.

SUPPLEMENTARY READING

Titles marked with an asterisk have been published in paperback

The events leading to the Civil War have been analyzed by dozens of historians. Of modern authorities, Allan Nevins provides the fullest and most magisterial treatment in his **The Ordeal of the Union** (1947) and **The Emergence of Lincoln*** (1950). An excellent briefer summary is D. M. Potter, **The Impending Crisis*** (1976). See also the interpretation of A. O. Craven, more sympathetic to the South, in **The Coming of the Civil War*** (1942) and **Civil War in the Making*** (1959). R. F. Nichols, **The Disruption of American Democracy*** (1948), discusses the political developments of 1856–1861 exhaustively and perceptively. Eric Foner, **Free Soil, Free Labor, Free Men*** (1970), is a good analysis of Republican ideas and policies.

The works on the abolitionists mentioned in Chapter 11 cover the enforcement of the Fugitive Slave Act and **Uncle Tom's Cabin.*** R. F. Wilson, **Crusader in Crinoline** (1941), is a satisfactory biography of Harriet Beecher Stowe. E. L. McKitrick (ed.), **Slavery Defended*** (1963), contains a typical southern review of **Uncle Tom's Cabin.** Two recent studies stress the anti-black feelings of whites in the western states and their relation to the sectional crisis: E. H. Berwanger, **The Frontier Against Slavery: Western Anti-Negro Prejudice and the Slavery Extension Controversy*** (1967), and V. J. Voegeli, **Free but Not Equal: The Midwest and the Negro During the Civil War*** (1967).

For the foreign policy of the 1850s, see Dexter Perkins, **The Monroe Doctrine: 1826–1867** (1933), D. S. Spencer, **Louis Kossuth and Young America** (1977), Basil Rauch, **American Interests in Cuba** (1948), R. F. Nichols, **Advance Agents of American Destiny** (1956), Arthur Walworth, **Black Ships Off Japan** (1946), I. D. Spencer, **The Victor and the Spoils: A Life of William L. Marcy** (1959), and P. S. Klein, **President James Buchanan** (1962).

On Stephen A. Douglas, see R. W. Johannsen, **Stephen A. Douglas** (1973), and G. M. Capers' **Stephen A. Douglas*** (1959). Nevins is particularly good on the whole Kansas controversy, but see also R. F. Nichols' biography of Franklin Pierce, **Young Hickory of the Granite Hills** (1931), P. W. Gates, **Fifty Million Acres: Conflicts Over Kansas Land Policy*** (1954), H. H. Simms, **A Decade of Sectional Controversy** (1942), and J. C. Malin's **The Nebraska Question** (1953) and **John Brown and the Legend of Fifty-Six** (1942).

Sumner's role in the deepening crisis is brilliantly discussed in David Donald, **Charles Sumner and the Coming of the Civil War** (1960). Klein's life of Buchanan is careful and judicious. On the Dred Scott case, see D. E. Fehrenbacher, **The Dred Scott Case** (1978), and Vincent Hopkins, **Dred Scott's Case*** (1951).

The best modern biographies of Lincoln are B. P. Thomas, **Abraham Lincoln** (1952), and Stephen Oates, **With Malice Toward None*** (1977). On his early career, see A. J. Beveridge, **Abraham Lincoln** (1928), and D. E. Fehrenbacher, **Prelude to Greatness*** (1962). The text of the Lincoln-Douglas debates is conveniently reprinted in R. W. Johannsen (ed.), **The Lincoln–Douglas Debates of 1858*** (1965). The best analysis of the debates is H. V. Jaffa, **Crisis of the House Divided*** (1959).

S. B. Oates, **To Purge This Land with Blood** (1970), is a good modern biography of John Brown, but Nevins' **Ordeal of the Union** provides the finest account of the raid on Harpers Ferry. C. V. Woodward's essay, "John Brown's Private War," in his **The Burden of Southern History*** (1960), is excellent on the effects of the Harpers Ferry raid. Nichols' **The Disruption of American Democracy*** describes the breakup of the Democratic party and the election of 1860. For the secession crisis and the outbreak of the Civil War, consult K. M. Stampp, **And the War Came*** (1950), D. M. Potter, **Lincoln and His Party in the Secession Crisis*** (1950), S. A. Channing, **Crisis of Fear*** (1970), and J. L. Roark, **Masters Without Slaves*** (1977).

15/THE WAR TO SAVE THE UNION

 The nomination of Lincoln had succeeded brilliantly for the Republicans, but had his election been a good thing for the country? As the inauguration approached, many Americans had their doubts. Honest Abe was a clever politician who had spoken well about the central issue of the times, but would he act decisively in this crisis? His behavior as president-elect was not reassuring. He spent much time closeted with politicians. Was he too obtuse to understand the grave threat to the Union posed by secession? People remembered uneasily that he had never held executive office, that his congressional career had been short and undistinguished. When finally he uprooted himself from Springfield in February 1861, his occasional speeches en route to the capital were vague, almost flippant in tone. He kissed babies, shook hands, mouthed platitudes. Some thought it downright cowardly that he would let himself be spirited in the dead of night through Baltimore, where feeling against him ran high.

The Lincoln Administration

Everyone waited tensely to see whether he would oppose secession with force or, as many persons such as the influential Horace Greeley of the New York *Tribune* were suggesting, allow the "wayward sisters" to "depart in peace." Lincoln seemed concerned only with organizing his Cabinet. The final slate was not ready until the morning of inauguration day, and shrewd observers found it alarming, for the new president had chosen to construct a "balanced" Cabinet representing a wide range of opinion instead of putting together a group of harmonious advisers who could help him face the crisis.

William H. Seward, the secretary of state, was the ablest and best known of the appointees. Despite his reputation for radicalism, the hawk-nosed, chinless, tousle-haired Seward hoped to conciliate the South and was thus in bad odor with the Radical wing of the Republican party. In time Seward proved himself Lincoln's strong right arm, but at the start he badly underestimated the president and expected to dominate him. Senator Salmon P. Chase, a bald, square-jawed, antislavery leader from Ohio, whom Lincoln named secretary of the treasury, represented the Radicals. Chase was humorless and vain but able; he detested Seward, agreeing with him only in thinking Lincoln a weakling. Simon Cameron of Pennsylvania, the secretary of war, was a politician of dubious integrity; Lincoln picked him to honor a deal made at the convention by his managers. Many of the president's selections worried thoughtful people.

Lincoln's inaugural address was conciliatory but firm. Southern institutions were in no danger from his administration. Secession, however, was illegal, the Union "perpetual." Federal property in the South would be held and protected. "A husband and wife may be divorced," Lincoln said, employing one of his homely and, by the Victorian standards of the day, slightly risqué metaphors, "but the different parts of our country cannot . . . . Intercourse, either amicable or hostile, must continue between them." The tone throughout was calm and warm. His concluding words catch the spirit of the inaugural perfectly:

> I am loath to close. We are not enemies, but friends. We must not be enemies. Though passion may have strained, it must not break, our bonds of affection. The mystic chords of memory, stretching from every battlefield and patriot grave to every living heart . . . will yet swell the chorus of the Union when again touched, as surely they will be, by the better angels of our nature.

Border-state moderates found the speech encouraging; so did the fiery Charles Sumner, who shared the opinion of many intellectuals that Lincoln was a dolt. The Confederates, however, read Lincoln's denial of the right of secession as justifying their decision to secede.

Fort Sumter

While stoutly denying the legality of secession, Lincoln had in fact taken a temporizing position. The Confederates had seized most federal property in the Deep South. Lincoln admitted frankly that he would not attempt to reclaim this property. However, two strongpoints, Fort Sumter, on an island in Charleston harbor, and Fort Pickens, at Pensacola, Florida, were still in loyal hands. Most Republicans, Lincoln included, did not want to surrender them without a show of resistance. To do so, one wrote, would be to convert the American eagle into a "debilitated chicken."

Yet to reinforce the forts might mean bloodshed that would make reconciliation impossible. After weeks of indecision, Lincoln took the moderate step of sending a naval expedition to supply the beleaguered Sumter garrison with food. Unwilling to permit this, the Confederates opened fire on the fort on April 12 before the supply ships arrived. After holding out against the bombardment of shore batteries for 34 hours, Major Robert Anderson and his men surrendered.

The attack precipitated an outburst of patriotic indignation in the North. Lincoln promptly issued a call for 75,000 volunteers, and this caused Virginia, North Carolina, Arkansas, and Tennessee to secede. After years of conflict and compromise, the nation chose to settle the great quarrel between the sections by force of arms.

Southerners considered Lincoln's call for troops an act of naked aggression. They were seeking to exercise what a later generation would call the right of self-determination. How, they asked, could the North square its professed belief in democratic free choice with its refusal to permit the southern states to leave the Union peaceably when a majority of their citizens wished to do so?

Lincoln took the position that secession was a *rejection* of democracy. If the South could refuse to abide by the result of an election in which it had freely participated, then everything that monarchists and other conservatives had said about the instability of republican governments would be proved true. "The central idea of secession is the essence of anarchy," he said. The United States must "demonstrate to the world" that "when ballots have been fairly and constitutionally decided, there can be no successful appeal except to ballots themselves, at succeeding elections."

This was the proper ground for Lincoln to take, both morally and politically. A war against slavery would not have been in keeping with his many pronouncements, and it would not have been supported by a majority of the people. Slavery was the root cause of secession but not of the North's determination to resist secession, which resulted from the people's love of the Union. Although abolition was to be one of the major results of the Civil War, the war was fought for nationalistic reasons, not to destroy slavery. Lincoln made this plain beyond argument when he wrote, more than a year after the outbreak of hostilities: "I would save the Union. . . . If I could save the Union without freeing *any* slave, I would do it; and if I could save it by freeing *all* the slaves, I would do it; and if I could do it by freeing some and leaving others alone, I would also do that." He added, however, "I intend no modification of my oft-expressed *personal* wish that all men, everywhere, could be free."

The Blue and the Gray

In any test between the United States and the 11 states of the Confederacy, the former possessed tremendous advantages. There were 20.7 million people in the northern states (excluding Kentucky and Missouri, where opinion was divided), only 9 million in the South, of which about 3.5 million

---

THE WAR.

Highly Important News from Washington.

Offensive War Measures of the Administration.

The President's Exposition of His Policy Towards the Confederate States.

A WAR PROCLAMATION.

Seventy-five Thousand Men Ordered Out.

Thirteen Thousand Required from New York.

Call for an Extra Session of Congress.

Preparations for the Defence of the National Capital.

The Great Free States Arming for the Conflict.

Thirty Thousand Troops to be Tendered from New York.

Strong Union Demonstrations in Baltimore.

THE BATTLE AT CHARLESTON.

EVACUATION OF FORT SUMTER.

Major Anderson to Sail for New York.

IMPORTANT NEWS FROM MONTGOMERY.

■ In April 1861 the New York *Herald* summarized the events triggered by the bombardment of Fort Sumter. Lincoln based his proclamation on an old law giving the president power to federalize state militias.

were slaves, whom the whites hesitated to trust with arms. The North's economic capacity to wage war was even more preponderant, for it had seven times as much manufacturing and a far larger and more efficient railroad system than the South. Northern control of the merchant marine and the navy made possible a blockade of the Confederacy, a particularly potent threat to a region so dependent on foreign markets.

The Confederates discounted these advantages. Many doubted that public opinion in the North would sustain Lincoln if he attempted to meet secession with force. Northern manufacturers needed southern markets, and merchants depended heavily on southern business. Many western farmers were still sending their produce down the Mississippi. War would threaten the prosperity of all these groups, southerners maintained. Should the North try to cut Europe off from southern cotton, the powers, particularly Great Britain, would descend upon the land in their might, force open southern ports, and provide the Confederacy with the means of defending itself forever. "You do not dare to make war on cotton," Senator Hammond of South Carolina had taunted his northern colleagues in 1858. "No power on earth dares to make war upon it. Cotton is king."

The Confederacy also counted on certain military advantages. The new nation need only hold what it had; it could fight a defensive war, less costly in men and material and of great importance in maintaining morale and winning outside sympathy. Southerners would be defending not only their social institutions but their homes and families.

To some extent the South benefited from superior military leadership. Both armies relied on West Pointers for their top commanders. Since most professionals followed the decisions of their home states when the war broke out, about 300 West Pointers became northern generals, about 180 southern. Among officers of lesser rank, the southerners probably excelled in the first years of the struggle, for the military tradition was strong in the South, and many young men had attended military academies. Luck played a part too; the Confederacy quickly found a great commander, while the highest-ranking northern generals in the early stages of the war proved either bungling or indecisive. In battle after battle Union armies were defeated by forces equal or inferior in size. Since there was little to choose between northern and southern common soldiers, superior generalship clearly made some difference.

Both sides faced massive difficulties in organizing for a war long feared but never properly anticipated. After southern defections, the regular army consisted of only 13,000 officers and men, far too few to absorb the 186,000 who had joined the colors by early summer. Recruiting was left to the states, each being assigned a quota; there was little central organization. Natty companies of "Fire Zouaves" and "Garibaldi Guards" in gorgeous uniforms rubbed shoulders with slovenly units composed of toughs and criminals and with regiments of farm boys from Iowa, Illinois, and Michigan. Few knew even the rudiments of soldiering. The hastily composed high command, headed by the elderly Winfield Scott, debated grand strategy endlessly while regimental commanders lacked decent maps of Virginia.

The Union mustered its military, economic, and administrative resources slowly because it had had little experience with war, none with civil war. The Whig prejudice against powerful presidents was part of Lincoln's political heritage; consequently he controlled neither Congress nor his own administration with the firmness of a Jackson or a Polk. He replaced nearly all the Democratic civil servants he could, but he failed to develop an efficient team of advisers. Fortunately, in the early stages of the war Congress was cooperative. Douglas, while critical of Lincoln before the attack on Sumter, devoted all his energies to rallying the Democrats as soon as war broke out. His death in June 1861 was a great loss to the country.

Lincoln proved capable of handling heavy responsibilities. His strength lay in his ability to think problems through, to accept their implications, and then to act unflinchingly. Anything but a tyrant by nature, he boldly exceeded the conventional limits of presidential power in the emergency, expanding the army without congressional authorization, suspending the writ of habeas corpus, even emancipating the slaves when he thought military necessity demanded that action. He displayed a remarkable patience and depth of character: he would willingly accept snubs and insults from lesser men in order to advance the cause. He kept a close check on every aspect of the war effort, yet he found time for thought too. His young secretary John Nicolay reported seeing him sit sometimes for a whole hour like "a petrified image," lost in contemplation. Gradually his stock rose—first with men like Seward who saw him close up and experienced both his steel and his gentleness, then with the people at large, who sensed his compassion, his humility, his wisdom. He was only 52 when he became president, and already people were calling him Old Abe. Before long they would call him Father Abraham.

The Confederacy faced far greater problems than the North, for it had to create an entire administration under pressure of war, with the additional handicap of the states' rights philosophy to which it was committed. The Confederate Constitution explicitly recognized the sovereignty of the states and contained no broad authorization for laws designed to advance the general welfare. State governments repeatedly defied the central administration, located at Richmond after Virginia seceded, even with regard to military affairs.

Of course the Confederacy made heavy use of the precedents and administrative machinery taken over from the United States. The government quickly decided that all federal laws would remain in force until specifically repealed, and many former federal officials continued to perform their duties under the new auspices.

The call to arms produced a turnout in the Confederacy perhaps even more impressive than that in the North; by July 1861 about 112,000 men were under arms. As in the North, men of every type enlisted and morale was high. Ordinary militia companies sporting names like "Tallapoosa Thrashers," "Cherokee Lincoln Killers," and "Chickasaw Desperadoes" marched in step with troops of "character, blood, and social position" bearing names like "Richmond Howitzers" and "Louisiana Zouaves." (A "Zouave" mania swept both North and South, prospective soldiers evidently considering the broad sashes and baggy red breeches the embodiment of military splendor.)

President Jefferson Davis represented the best type of southern slaveowner. A graduate of West Point, he was a fine soldier and a successful planter, noted for his humane treatment of his slaves. In politics he had pursued a somewhat unusual course. While senator from Mississippi, he opposed the Compromise of 1850 and became a leader of the southern radicals. After Pierce made him secretary of war, however, he took a more nationalistic position, one close to that of Douglas.

■ This daguerreotype portrait of Jefferson Davis was probably taken in Washington about 1860, when Davis was senator from Mississippi.

He supported the transcontinental railroad idea and spoke in favor of the annexation of Cuba and other Caribbean areas. He rejected Douglas' position during the Kansas controversy but tried to close the breach that Kansas had opened in Democratic ranks. In the crisis after the 1860 election he supported secession only reluctantly, preferring to give Lincoln a chance to prove that he meant the South no harm.

Davis was courageous, industrious, and intelligent, but he was rather too reserved and opinionated to make either a good politician or a popular leader. As president he devoted too much time to details and failed to delegate authority. He fancied himself a military expert because of his West Point training and his Mexican War service, often neglecting pressing administrative problems to concentrate on devising strategy. Unfortunately for the South, he was a mediocre military thinker. Unlike Lincoln, he quarreled frequently with his subordinates, held grudges, and allowed personal feelings to distort his judgment. "He was abnormally sensitive to disapprobation," his wife admitted. "He felt how much he was misunderstood, and the sense of mortification and injustice gave him a repellent manner." Ordinary southerners respected him for his devotion to the Confederacy, but few could feel for him the affection that Lincoln inspired.

The Test of Battle

As summer approached, the two nations prepared for battle, full of pride, enthusiasm, and ignorance. The tragic confrontation was beginning. "Forward to Richmond!" "On to Washington!" Such shouts propelled the troops into battle long before they were properly trained. On July 21, at Manassas Junction, Virginia, some 20 miles below Washington, on a branch of the Potomac called Bull Run, 30,000 men under General Irwin McDowell attacked a roughly equal force of Confederates commanded by the "Napoleon of the South," Pierre G. T. Beauregard. McDowell swept back the Confederate left flank. Victory seemed sure. Then a Virginia brigade under Thomas J. Jackson, rushed to the field by rail from the Shenandoah Valley in the nick of time, held doggedly to a key hill, and the advance was checked. (A South Carolina general, seeking to rally his own men, pointed to the hill and shouted: "Look, there is Jackson with his Virginians, standing like a stone wall against the enemy." Thus "Stonewall" Jackson received his nickname.)

The southerners then counterattacked, driving the Union soldiers back. As often happens with green troops, retreat quickly turned to rout. McDowell's men fled toward the defenses of Washington, abandoning their weapons, stumbling through lines of supply wagons, trampling foolish sightseers who had come out to watch the battle. Panic engulfed Washington and Richmond exulted, both sides expecting the northern capital to fall within hours.

The inexperienced southern troops were too disorganized to follow up their victory. Casualties on both sides were light, and the battle had little direct effect on anything but morale. Southern confidence increased, while the North began to realize how immense the task of subduing the Confederacy would be.

After Bull Run, Lincoln devised a broader, more systematic strategy for winning the war. The navy

■ A hasty pencil sketch by an unknown artist captures the panic that swept the Union ranks after the Bull Run defeat. The scene is the main road leading through Centreville to Washington.

would clamp a tight blockade on all southern ports. In the West operations designed to gain control of the Mississippi would be undertaken. Most important, a new army would be mustered at Washington to invade Virginia. Congress promptly authorized the enlistment of 500,000 three-year volunteers. To lead this army and—after General Scott's retirement in November—to command the Union forces, Lincoln appointed a 34-year-old major general, George B. McClellan.

McClellan was the North's first military hero. Units under his command had driven the Confederates from the pro-Union western counties of Virginia, clearing the way for the admission of West Virginia as a separate state. The fighting had been on a small scale, but McClellan, an incurable romanticizer and something of an egomaniac, managed to inflate its importance. "You have annihilated two armies," he proclaimed in a widely publicized message to his troops. Few Americans noticed that there were only about 250 victims of this "annihilation."

Despite his penchant for self-glorification, McClellan had solid qualifications for command. One was experience. After graduation from West Point in 1846, he had served in the Mexican War. During the Crimean War he spent a year in the field, talking with British officers and studying fortifications. McClellan had a fine military bearing, a flair for the dramatic, the ability to inspire troops. He was a talented administrator and organizer. He had a sublime faith in his own destiny. He liked to concoct bold plans, dreamed of striking swiftly at the heart of the Confederacy to capture Richmond, Nashville, even New Orleans. Yet he was sensible enough to insist on massive logistical support, thorough training for the troops, iron discipline, and meticulous staff work before making a move.

Behind the Union Lines

After Bull Run, this policy was exactly right. By the fall of the year a real army was taking shape along the Potomac: disciplined, confident, adequately supplied. Northern shops and factories were producing guns, ammunition, wagons, uniforms, shoes, and the countless other supplies needed to fight a great war. Most manufacturers operated on a small scale, but with the armed forces soon wearing out 3 million pairs of shoes and 1.5 million uniforms a year, and with men leaving their jobs by the hundreds of thousands to fight, the tendency of industry to mechanize and to increase the size of the average manufacturing unit became ever more pronounced.

At the beginning of the war Secretary of the Treasury Salmon P. Chase, inexperienced in monetary matters, greatly underestimated the financial needs of the government and the probable duration of the conflict. He failed to ask Congress for enough money to fight the war properly. In August 1861 Congress passed an income tax law (3 percent on incomes over $800, later raised to a top of 10 percent on incomes over $10,000) and assessed a direct tax on the states. Loans amounting to $140 million were authorized. As the war dragged on and expenses mounted, new excise taxes on every imaginable product and service were passed, and still further borrowing was necessary. In 1863 the banking system was overhauled.

During the war the federal government borrowed a total of $2.2 billion and collected $667 million in taxes. These unprecedentedly large sums proved inadequate. Some obligations were met by printing paper money unredeemable in coin. About $431 million in "greenbacks"—the term distinguished this fiat money from the redeemable yellowback bills—were issued during the course of the war.

Printing-press money roused heated emotions; some considered it plain fraud, others a necessary way of mobilizing the national wealth in an emergency. From the modern point of view the latter position seems correct. Public confidence in all paper money vacillated with each change in the fortunes of the Union armies. Whenever the war seemed to be going badly, citizens rushed to convert their paper money into gold. Long before the first greenbacks were issued, the banks had been forced to suspend specie payments on their notes—a fortunate thing because it enabled them to ease their lending policies and thus to finance necessary industrial expansion.

On balance, the heavy emphasis on borrowing and currency inflation was expensive but not irresponsible. In a country still chiefly agricultural, people had relatively low cash incomes and therefore could not easily bear a heavy tax load. Many Americans considered it reasonable to expect fu-

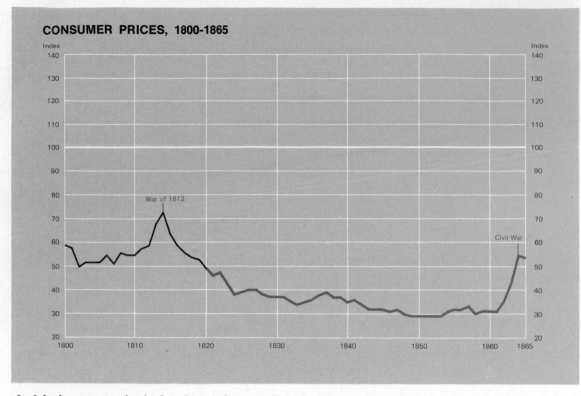

CONSUMER PRICES, 1800-1865

■ Look back at page 190 for the first chart in the series. Note that the information that is new on this chart (the period from 1820 to 1865), is drawn in color while older data appear in black.

ture generations to pay part of the dollar cost of saving the Union when theirs was contributing so heavily in labor and blood.

Partisan politics was altered by the war but not suspended. The secession of the southern states left the Republicans with large majorities in both houses of Congress. Most Democrats supported measures necessary for the conduct of the war but objected to the way the Lincoln administration was conducting it. The sharpest conflicts came when slavery and race relations were under discussion, the Democrats adopting a conservative stance and the Republicans dividing into Moderate and Radical wings. Political divisions on economic issues such as tariffs and land policy tended to cut across party lines and—so far as the Republicans were concerned—to bear little relation to slavery and race.

As the war progressed, the Radical faction became increasingly influential. In 1861 the most prominent Radical senator was Charles Sumner, finally recovered from his caning by Preston Brooks and brimful of hatred for slaveholders. In the House, Thaddeus Stevens of Pennsylvania was the rising power. Sumner and Stevens represented the extreme left wing on all questions relating to slaves; they insisted not merely on abolition but on granting full political and civil rights to blacks. Moderate Republicans objected vehemently to treating blacks as equals and opposed making abolition a war aim, and even many of the so-called Radicals disagreed with Sumner and Stevens on race relations. Senator Benjamin Wade of Ohio, for example, was a lifelong opponent of slavery, yet he had convinced himself that blacks (he habitually called them "niggers") had a distinctive and unpleasant smell. He considered the common white prejudice against blacks perfectly understandable. But prejudice, he maintained, gave no one the right "to do injustice to anybody"; he insisted that blacks were at least as intelligent as whites and were entitled not merely to freedom but to full political equality.

At the other end of the political spectrum stood

the so-called Peace Democrats. These "Copperheads" (apparently the reference was not to the poisonous snake but to an earlier time when some hard-money Democrats wore copper pennies around their necks) opposed all measures in support of the war and organized secret societies, such as the Knights of the Golden Circle, in an effort to win control of Congress and force a negotiated peace. Few were actually disloyal, but their activities at a time when thousands of men were risking their lives in battle infuriated many northerners.

Lincoln treated dissenters with a curious mixture of repression and tolerance. He suspended the writ of habeas corpus in critical areas and applied martial law freely. Over 13,000 persons were arrested and held without trial, many, as it later turned out, unjustly. The president argued that the government dared not stand on ceremony in a national emergency. His object, he insisted, was not to punish but to *prevent*. Arbitrary arrests were not made for purely political purposes, and elections were held in complete freedom throughout the war.

The federal courts compiled an admirable record in defending civil liberties, though when in conflict with the military, they could not enforce their decrees. In *Ex parte Merryman* (1861) Chief Justice Taney held General George Cadwalader in contempt for failing to produce a prisoner for trial when ordered to do so, but Cadwalader went unpunished and the prisoner continued to languish behind bars. After the war, in *Ex parte Milligan* (1866), the Supreme Court declared illegal the military trials of civilians in areas where the regular courts were functioning, but by that time the question was of only academic interest.

The most notorious domestic foe of the administration was the Peace Democrat Congressman Clement L. Vallandigham of Ohio. There were two rebellions in progress, Vallandigham claimed, "the Secessionist Rebellion" and "the Abolitionist Rebellion." "I am against both," he added. In 1863, after he had made a speech urging that the war be ended by negotiation, Vallandigham was seized by the military and thrown into jail. Of course his followers protested indignantly. Lincoln ordered him released and banished to the Confederacy. Once at liberty Vallandigham moved to Canada, from which refuge he ran unsuccessfully for governor of Ohio.

Vallandigham was a zealot who "chose to ignore expediency," as his biographer put it. "Perish offices," he once said, "perish life itself, but do the thing that is right." In 1864 he returned to Ohio. Although he campaigned against Lincoln in the presidential election, he was not molested.

David Herbert Donald's judgment of Lincoln's policy toward dissenters is worth quoting:

> The arbitrary arrests cannot be passed over lightly: to do so would allow too small a value to civil guarantees. On the other hand a search of the full record will show that anything like a drastic military régime was far from Lincoln's thoughts. The harshness of war regulations was often tempered by leniency. . . . The word "dictator" in its twentieth-century connotation would be utterly inappropriate if applied to the Civil War President.

The Confederate War Effort

The South also revised its strategy after Bull Run. While it might have been wiser to risk everything on a bold invasion of the North, President Davis relied primarily on a strong defense to wear down the Union's will to fight. When volunteering slackened in 1862, the Confederate Congress passed a conscription act that contained many glaring inequities. It permitted the hiring of substitutes and exempted many classes of people (including college professors and mail carriers) whose work could hardly have been deemed essential. A provision deferring the owners of 20 or more slaves led many to grumble about "a rich man's war and a poor man's fight." In Alabama alone, nearly 1,500 planters were exempted from military service.

Although the Confederacy did not develop a two-party system, there was plenty of internal political strife. Davis made enemies easily, and his tenure was marked by bickering and needless argument. The widespread southern devotion to states' rights and individual liberty (for white men) caused endless trouble, especially when Davis found it necessary to suspend the writ of habeas corpus under certain circumstances. Throughout the war conflicts were continually erupting between Davis and southern governors jealous of their prerogatives as heads of "sovereign" states.

Finance was the Confederacy's most vexing problem. The blockade made it impossible to raise money through tariffs. The Confederate Congress passed an income tax together with many excise taxes, but the most effective levy was a tax-in-kind, amounting to one-tenth of each farmer's production. The South borrowed as much as it could ($712 million), even mortgaging cotton undeliverable because of the blockade in order to gain European credits. But it relied mainly on printing paper currency; over $1.5 billion poured from the presses during the war. Considering the amount issued, this currency held its value well until late in the war, when the military fortunes of the Confederacy began to decline. Then the bottom fell out, and by early 1865 the Confederate dollar was worth less than two cents in gold.

Because of the shortage of manufacturing facilities, the task of outfitting the army strained southern resources to the limit. Large supplies of small arms (some 600,000 weapons during the entire war) came from Europe through the blockade, along with other valuable materiel. As the block-

ade became more efficient, however, it became increasingly difficult to obtain European goods. The Confederates did manage to build a number of munitions plants, and they captured huge amounts of northern arms. No battle was lost because of a lack of guns or other military equipment, though shortages of shoes and uniforms handicapped the Confederate forces on some occasions.

Foreign policy loomed large in Confederate thinking, for the "cotton is king" theory presupposed that the great powers would break any northern blockade to get cotton for their textile mills. Southern expectations were not realized, however. The European nations would have been delighted to see the United States broken up, but none was prepared to support the Confederacy directly. The attitude of Great Britain was decisive. The cutting off of cotton did not hit the British as hard as the South had hoped. They had a large supply on hand when the war broke out, and when that was exhausted, alternative sources in India and Egypt took up part of the slack. Furthermore, British crop failures necessitated the impor-

■ The Confederate commerce raider *Nashville* (left), assisted by two small steamers, runs the blockade in 1862. The northern navy began the war with far too few warships to effectively blockade the 3,500-mile southern coastline.

■ The Tredegar Iron Works in Richmond, Virginia, was one of the major manufacturing facilities already in existence in the South before the Civil War. As the blockade intensified, its importance to the Confederate war effort increased.

tation of large amounts of northern wheat, providing a powerful reason for not antagonizing the United States. The fact that the mass of ordinary people in Great Britain favored the North was also of great importance in determining British policy.

Nevertheless the Civil War hurt the British economy, and the government gave serious thought to recognizing the Confederacy. Had it done so, the result would almost certainly have been war with the United States, and in that event the South might well have won its independence.

Several times the two nations came to the brink of war. In November 1861 the American warship *San Jacinto* stopped a British vessel, the *Trent*, on the high seas and forcibly arrested two Confederate envoys, James M. Mason and John Slidell, who were en route to London. This violation of international law would probably have led to war had not Lincoln decided to turn the southerners loose. In 1862 two powerful cruisers, the *Florida* and the *Alabama*, were built for the Confederates in English shipyards under the most transparent of subterfuges. Despite American protests, they were permitted to put to sea and were soon wreaking havoc among northern merchantmen. When two ironclad "rams" were also built in Britain for the

Confederates, the United States made it clear that it would declare war if they were delivered. The British government then confiscated the vessels, avoiding a showdown.

The northern cause was aided by the brilliant diplomacy of Charles Francis Adams, the son of John Quincy, who served as American minister in London throughout the conflict. In the last analysis, however, the military situation determined British policy; once the North obtained a clear superiority on the battlefield, the possibility of intervention vanished.

War in the West: Shiloh

Northern superiority was achieved slowly and at enormous cost. After Bull Run no heavy fighting took place until early 1862. Then, while McClellan continued his deliberate preparations to attack Richmond, Union forces in the West, led by a shabby, cigar-smoking West Pointer named Ulysses S. Grant, invaded Tennessee from a base at Cairo, Illinois. Making effective use of armored gunboats, Grant captured forts Henry and Donelson, strongpoints on the Tennessee and Cumber-

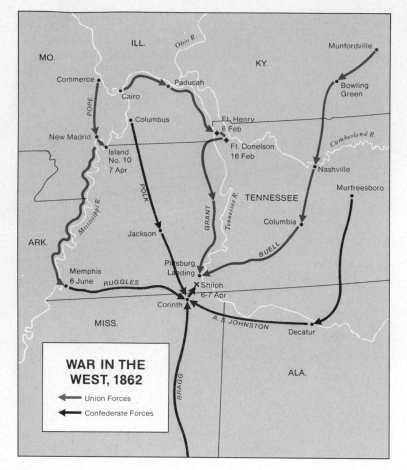

■ The Confederacy massed its western forces at Corinth for an unavailing counterstroke at Shiloh. The South's Mississippi River defenses also crumbled; by June of 1862 the river was open to Yankee gunboats as far south as Memphis.

land rivers in northern Tennessee, taking 14,000 prisoners. Next he marched toward Corinth, Mississippi, an important railroad junction.

To check Grant's invasion the Confederates massed 40,000 men under Albert Sidney Johnston. On April 6, while Grant slowly concentrated his forces, Johnston struck suddenly at Shiloh, 20 miles north of Corinth. Some Union soldiers were caught half-dressed, others in the midst of brewing their morning coffee. A few died in their blankets. "We were more than surprised," one Illinois officer later admitted. "We were astonished." However, Grant's men stood their ground. At the end of a day of ghastly carnage the Confederates held the advantage, but fresh Union troops under General Don Carlos Buell poured in during the night, and in the course of the second day of battle the tide turned. The Confederates fell back toward Corinth, exhausted and demoralized.

Grant was too shaken by the unexpected attack and too appalled by his huge losses to apply the *coup de grâce;* he allowed the enemy to escape. This cost him the fine reputation he had won in capturing Fort Henry and Fort Donelson. He was relieved of his command and his battle-tested army was broken up, its strength dissipated in a series of uncoordinated campaigns. Although Corinth eventually fell and New Orleans was captured by a naval force under the command of Captain David Farragut, Vicksburg, key to control of the Mississippi, remained firmly in Confederate hands. A great opportunity had been lost.

Shiloh had other results. The staggering casualties shook the confidence of both belligerents. More Americans fell there in two days than in all the battles of the Revolution, the War of 1812, and the Mexican War combined. Union losses exceeded 13,000 out of 63,000 engaged; the Confederates lost 10,699, including General Johnston. The generals began to reconsider their tactics and to experiment with field fortifications and other defensive measures. And the people, North and South, stopped thinking of the war as a romantic test of courage and military guile.

McClellan versus Lee

In Virginia, General McClellan, after unaccountable delays, was finally moving against Richmond. Instead of trying to advance across the difficult terrain of northern Virginia, he transported his army by water to the tip of the peninsula formed by the York and James rivers in order to attack Richmond from the southeast. After the famous battle (March 9, 1862) between U.S.S. *Monitor* and the Confederate *Merrimack*, the first fight in history between armored warships, control of these waters was securely in northern hands.

While McClellan's plan alarmed many congressmen because it seemed to leave Washington relatively unprotected, it simplified the problem of keeping the army supplied in hostile country. But McClellan now displayed the weaknesses that eventually ruined his career. To him the Civil War was not a mighty struggle over fundamental beliefs but a sort of complex game that generals played at a leisurely pace and for limited stakes. He believed it more important to capture Richmond than to destroy the army protecting it. With their capital in northern hands, surely the southerners (outwitted and outmaneuvered by a brilliant general) would abandon the contest in gentlemanly fashion and agree to return to the Union. The idea of crushing the South seemed to him wrongheaded and uncivilized.

Beyond this, McClellan was temperamentally unsuited for a position of so much responsibility. Beneath the swagger and the charm he was a profoundly insecure man. He talked like Napoleon, but he did not like to fight. Repeatedly he called for more men; when he got them, he demanded still more. He knew how to get ready, but he was never ready in his own mind.

McClellan began the Peninsula campaign in mid March. Proceeding deliberately, he floated an army of 112,000 men down the Potomac and by May 14 had established a base at White House

■ Lee in 1863, by Julian Vannerson. "So great is my confidence in General Lee," Stonewall Jackson remarked, "that I am willing to follow him blind-folded."

Landing, less than 25 miles from Richmond. A swift thrust might have ended the war quickly, but McClellan delayed, despite the fact that he had 80,000 men in striking position and large reserves. As he pushed forward slowly, the Confederates caught part of his force separated from the main body by the rain-swollen Chickahominy River and attacked. The Battle of Seven Pines was indecisive yet resulted in more than 10,000 casualties.

At Seven Pines the Confederate commander, General Joseph E. Johnston, was severely wounded; leadership of the Army of Northern Virginia then fell to Robert E. Lee. Although no enthusiast about secession, Lee was a superb soldier. During the Mexican War his gallantry under fire inspired the most lavish praise from hardened professionals. General Scott called him the bravest man in the army; another officer rhapsodized over his "daring reconnaissances pushed up to the can-

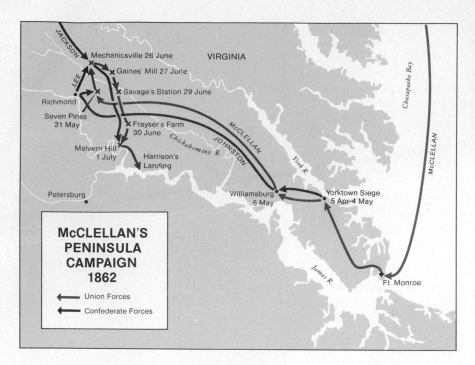

McCLELLAN'S PENINSULA CAMPAIGN 1862

← Union Forces
← Confederate Forces

■ On June 1 Lee succeeded Joseph E. Johnston as head of the Army of Northern Virginia. On June 26 he attacked McClellan and by July 2 had pushed him back to the James River.

non's mouth." He displayed an almost instinctive mastery of tactics. Admiral Raphael Semmes, who accompanied Scott's army on the march to Mexico City, recalled in 1851 that Lee "seemed to receive impressions intuitively, which it cost other men much labor to acquire."

Lee was the antithesis of McClellan, being gentle, courtly, tactful, and entirely without McClellan's swagger and vainglorious belief that he was a man of destiny. McClellan seemed almost deliberately to avoid understanding his foes, acting as though every southern general was an Alexander. Lee, a master psychologist on the battlefield, cleverly took the measure of each Union general and devised his tactics accordingly. Where McClellan was complex, egotistical, perhaps even unbalanced, Lee was a man of almost perfect character. Yet on the battlefield Lee's boldness skirted the edge of foolhardiness.

As a staff officer he had planned a brilliant maneuver to relieve the pressure on Richmond, sending General "Stonewall" Jackson, soon to be his most trusted lieutenant, on a diversionary raid in the Shenandoah Valley, west of Richmond and Washington. Jackson struck hard and swiftly at scattered Union forces in the region, winning a

series of battles and capturing vast stores of equipment. Lincoln dispatched 20,000 reserves to the Shenandoah to check him—to the dismay of McClellan, who wanted the troops to move against Richmond from the north. But after Seven Pines, Lee ordered Jackson back to Richmond. While Union armies streamed toward the valley, Jackson slipped stealthily between them. On June 25 he reached Ashland, directly north of the Confederate capital.

Before that date McClellan had possessed a clear numerical superiority yet had only inched ahead; now the advantage lay with Lee. The very next day he launched a massive surprise attack. For seven days the battle raged. Lee's plan was brilliant but too complicated for an army yet untested: the full weight of his force never hit the northern army at any one time. Nevertheless the shock was formidable. McClellan, who excelled in defense, fell back, his lines intact, exacting a fearful toll. Under difficult conditions he managed to transfer his troops to a new base on the James River at Harrison's Landing, where the guns of the navy could shield his position. Again the loss of life was terrible: northern casualties totaled 15,800, those of the South nearly 20,000.

Lee Counterattacks

McClellan was still within striking distance of Richmond, in an impregnable position with secure supply lines and 86,000 soldiers ready to resume the battle. Lee had absorbed heavy losses without winning any significant advantage. Yet Lincoln was exasperated with McClellan for having surrendered the initiative and, after much deliberation, reduced his authority by placing him under General Henry W. Halleck. Halleck called off the Peninsula campaign and ordered McClellan to move his army from the James to the Potomac, near Washington. He was to join General John Pope, who was gathering a new army between Washington and Richmond.

For the president to have lost confidence in McClellan was understandable. Nevertheless, to allow Halleck to pull back the troops was a bad mistake. Had the federal army poised at Harrison's Landing made any aggressive thrust, Lee would not have dared to move from the defenses of Richmond. When it withdrew, Lee seized the initiative. With typical decisiveness and daring, he marched rapidly north against Pope. Late in August, after some complex maneuvering, the Confederates drove Pope's confused troops from the field. It was the same ground, Bull Run, where the first major engagement of the war had been fought.

Thirteen months had passed since the first failure at Bull Run, and despite the expenditure of thousands of lives and millions of dollars the Union army stood as far from Richmond as ever. Dismayed by Pope's incompetence, Lincoln turned in desperation back to McClellan. When his secretary protested that McClellan had expressed contempt for the president, Lincoln replied gently: "We must use what tools we have."

While McClellan was regrouping the shaken Union Army, Lee once again took the offensive. He realized that no number of individual southern triumphs could destroy the enormous material advantages of the North. Unless some dramatic blow, delivered on northern soil, persuaded the people of the United States that military victory was impossible, the South would surely be crushed in the long run by the weight of superior resources. Lee therefore marched rapidly northwest around the defenses of Washington.

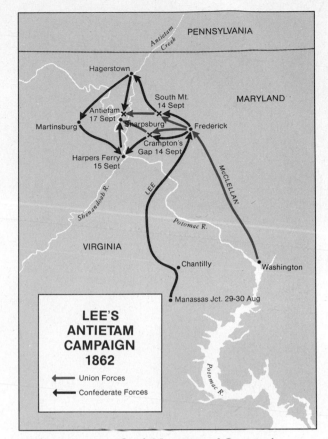

■ Delaying actions at South Mountain and Crampton's Gap, east of Sharpsburg, bought Lee enough time to pull together his forces to meet McClellan's troops.

Acting with even more than his usual boldness, Lee divided his army of 60,000 into a number of units. One, under Stonewall Jackson, descended upon weakly defended Harpers Ferry, capturing more than 11,000 prisoners. Another pressed as far north as Hagerstown, Maryland, nearly to the Pennsylvania line. McClellan pursued with his usual deliberation until a captured dispatch revealed to him Lee's dispositions. Then he acted more swiftly, forcing Lee to stand and fight on September 17 at Sharpsburg, Maryland, between the Potomac and Antietam Creek.* On a field that offered Lee no room to maneuver, 70,000 Union

---

*Southerners tended to identify battles by nearby towns, northerners by bodies of water. Thus Manassas and Bull Run, Sharpsburg and Antietam, Murfreesboro and Stone's River, etc.

■ Part of the human wreckage left by the armies at Antietam. Alexander Gardner took this photograph of Confederate dead by the Cornfield, a nondescript piece of ground that earned a grim fame on September 17, 1862.

soldiers clashed with 40,000 Confederates. When darkness fell, more than 22,000 lay dead or wounded on the bloody field.

Although casualties were evenly divided and the Confederate lines intact, Lee's position was perilous. His men were exhausted. McClellan had not yet thrown in his reserves, and new federal units were arriving hourly. A bold northern general would have continued the fight without respite through the night. One of ordinary aggressiveness would have waited for first light and then struck with every soldier who could hold a rifle, for with the Potomac at his back, Lee could not retreat under fire without inviting disaster. McClellan, however, did nothing. For an entire day, while Lee scanned the field in futile search of some weakness in the Union lines, he held his fire.

That night the Confederates slipped back across the Potomac into Virginia.

Lee's invasion had failed, his army had been badly mauled, the gravest threat to the Union in the war had been checked. But McClellan had let victory slip through his fingers. Soon Lee was back behind the defenses of Richmond, rebuilding his army.

Once again, this time finally, Lincoln dismissed McClellan from his command.

The Emancipation Proclamation

Antietam provided Lincoln with an excuse to take a step that changed the character of the war. As we have seen, when the fighting started, only a few extremists wanted to free the slaves by force. The fear of alienating the border states was reason enough for not making emancipation a war aim. However, pressures to act against the peculiar institution mounted steadily. Slavery had divided the nation; now it was driving Americans to war within themselves. Love of country led them to fight to save the Union, but fighting roused hatreds and caused many to desire to smash the enemy. Sacrifice, pain, and grief made abolitionists of many who had no love for blacks—they sought to free the slave only to injure the master. To make abolition an object of the war might encourage the slaves to revolt.

Lincoln disclaimed this objective; nevertheless the possibility existed. Already the slaves seemed to be looking to the North for freedom: whenever Union troops invaded Confederate territory, they flocked into their lines. For a time Lincoln tried to check the enthusiasm of certain generals who issued proclamations freeing these slaves, but little could be done to prevent the disintegration of slavery in captured territories.

As the war progressed, the Radicals in Congress gradually chipped away at slavery. In April 1862 they pushed through a bill abolishing it in the District of Columbia; two months later another measure outlawed it in the territories; in July a Confiscation Act "freed" all slaves owned by persons in rebellion against the United States. In fighting for these measures and in urging general emancipation, some Radicals made statements harshly critical of Lincoln; but while he carefully avoided being identified with them or with any other faction, the president was never very far from their position. He resisted emancipation because he feared it would divide the country and injure the war effort, not because he personally disapproved. Indeed, he frequently offered Radical pressure as an excuse for doing what he wished to do on his own, this being an excellent device for keeping reluctant Moderates and war Democrats in line.

Lincoln would have preferred to see slavery done away with by state law, with compensation for slaveowners and federal aid for all freedmen willing to leave the United States. He tried repeatedly to persuade the loyal slave states to adopt this policy, but without success. He moved cautiously. By the summer of 1862 he was convinced that for military reasons and to win the support of liberal opinion in Europe, the government should adopt an antislavery policy. He delayed temporarily, fearing that a statement in the face of military reverses would be taken as a sign of weakness. The victory at Antietam gave him his opportunity, and on September 22 he made public the Emancipation Proclamation. After January 1, 1863, it said, all slaves in areas in rebellion against the United States "shall be then, thenceforward, and forever free."

No single slave was freed directly by Lincoln's announcement, which did not apply to the border states or to those sections of the Confederacy, like New Orleans and Norfolk, Virginia, already controlled by federal troops. It differed in philosophy, however, from the Confiscation Act in striking at the institution, not at the property of rebels. Henceforth every Union victory would speed the destruction of slavery without regard for the attitudes of individual masters.

Some of the president's advisers thought the Proclamation inexpedient and others considered it illegal. Lincoln justified it as a way to weaken the enemy. He drew on his power as commander in chief of the armed forces for the necessary authority. The Proclamation is full of phrases like "as a fit and necessary war measure" and "warranted by the Constitution upon military necessity."

Southerners considered the Proclamation an incitement to slave rebellion—as one of them put it, an "infamous attempt to incite flight, murder, and rapine . . . and convert the quiet, ignorant, dependent black son of toil into a savage incendiary and brutal murderer." Most antislavery groups approved but thought it did not go far enough. Foreign opinion was mixed: liberals tended to applaud, conservatives to react with alarm or contempt. "The principle is not that a human being cannot justly own another," the London *Spectator* sneered, "but that he cannot own him unless he is loyal to the United States."

As Lincoln anticipated, the Proclamation had a subtle but continuing impact in America. Its immediate effect was to aggravate racial prejudices. Millions of white Americans disapproved of slavery yet abhorred the idea of equality for blacks. David Wilmot, for example, insisted that his famous Proviso was designed to preserve the territories for whites rather than to weaken slavery, and as late as 1857 the people of Iowa rejected Negro

■ The genesis of the Emancipation Proclamation seen from diametrically opposed viewpoints. The drawing above is by Adalbert Johann Volck, a Baltimore dentist and vitriolic propagandist for the Confederate cause. A satanical Lincoln, one foot on the Constitution, is inspired by a portrait of John Brown with a halo and a depiction of the alleged excesses of the Saint Domingue slave revolt of the 1790s. David Gilmore Blythe, a staunch administration supporter, left no doubt in his painting below that the sources of Lincoln's inspiration were of a much higher order.

■ A woodcut from *Leslie's Illustrated* shows an orphanage for blacks destroyed by a mob during the New York draft riots. The rioters were dispersed by combat troops fresh from the Battle of Gettysburg.

suffrage by a vote of 49,000 to 8,000. To some emancipation seemed to herald an invasion of the North by blacks who would compete with them for jobs, drive down wages, commit crimes and spread diseases, and—eventually—destroy the "purity" of the white race.*

The Democrats spared no effort to make political capital of these fears and prejudices during the congressional election campaign of 1862, and they made large gains, especially in the Northwest. So strong was antiblack feeling that most of the Republican politicians who defended emancipation did so with racist arguments. Far from encouraging southern blacks to move north, they claimed, the ending of slavery would lead to a mass migration of northern blacks to the South.

When the Emancipation Proclamation began actually to free slaves, the government pursued a policy of "containment," that is, of keeping the freedmen in the South. Panicky fears of an inundation of blacks subsided in the North. Nevertheless, emancipation remained a cause of social dis-

content. In March 1863, volunteering having fallen off, Congress passed a conscription act. The law applied to all men between 20 and 45, but it allowed draftees to hire substitutes and even to buy exemption for $300, provisions that were patently unfair to the poor. Moreover, it represented an enormous expansion of national authority, since in effect it gave the government the power of life and death over individual citizens. Draft riots erupted in parts of the nation.

By far the most serious disturbance occurred in New York City in July 1863. Many workers resented conscription in principle and were embittered by the $300 exemption fee (which represented a year's wages). The idea of being forced to risk their lives to free slaves who would then, they believed, compete with them for jobs infuriated them. On July 13 a mob attacked the office where the names of conscripts were being drawn. Most of the rioters were poor Irish laborers who resented what seemed to them the special attention blacks were suddenly receiving. For four days the city was an inferno. Public buildings, shops, and private residences were put to the torch. What began as a protest against the draft became a campaign to exterminate blacks. Over a hundred were run down "as hounds would chase a fox" and beaten to death, some of them burned alive. It took federal troops and the temporary suspension

---

*The word *miscegenation* was coined in 1863 by David G. Croly, an editor of the New York *World*, directly as a result of the Emancipation Proclamation. Its original meaning was: "The mingling of the white and black races on the continent *as a consequence of the freedom of the latter.*" Of course miscegenation in its current, more general meaning long antedated the freeing of any slave.

of the draft in the city to put an end to the rioting.

The Emancipation Proclamation does not entirely account for the draft riots. The new policy neither reflected nor triggered a revolution in white thinking about the race question. Its significance was subtle but real; both the naive view that Lincoln freed the slaves on January 1, 1863, and the cynical one that his action was a meaningless propaganda trick are incorrect. Northern hostility to emancipation rose from fear of change more than from hatred of blacks, while liberal disavowals of any intention to treat blacks as equals were in large measure designed to quiet this fear. To a degree the racial backlash that the Proclamation inspired reflected the public's awareness that a change, frightening but irreversible, *had occurred*.

Most white northerners did not surrender their comforting belief in black inferiority, and Lincoln was no exception. Yet Lincoln was evolving. He talked about deporting ex-slaves to the tropics, but he did not send any there. And he began to receive black leaders in the White House and to allow black groups to hold meetings on the grounds.

Many other Americans were changing too. The brutality of the New York riots horrified many white citizens. Over $40,000 was swiftly raised to aid the victims, and some conservatives were so appalled by the Irish rioters that they began to talk of giving blacks the vote. The influential *Atlantic Monthly* commented: "It is impossible to name any standard . . . that will give a vote to the Celt and exclude the negro."

A revolutionary shift occurred in white thinking about using black men as soldiers. Although they had fought in the Revolution and in the Battle of New Orleans during the War of 1812, a law of 1792 barred blacks from the army. During the

■ Company E, 4th U.S. Colored Infantry at Fort Lincoln, Virginia, was part of one of the black regiments that came into existence after 1863.

early stages of the rebellion, despite the eagerness of thousands of free blacks to enlist, the prohibition remained in force. By 1862, however, the need for manpower was creating pressure for change. In August Secretary of War Edwin M. Stanton, who had replaced the incompetent Simon Cameron, authorized the military government of the captured South Carolina sea islands to enlist slaves in the area. In January 1863 Stanton allowed the governor of Massachusetts to organize a black regiment, the famous Massachusetts 54th. Swiftly thereafter other states began to recruit black soldiers, and in May 1863 the federal government established a Bureau of Colored Troops to supervise their enlistment. By the end of the war one soldier in eight in the Union army was black.

Black soldiers were segregated and commanded by white officers. At first they received only $7 a month, about half what white soldiers were paid. But they soon proved themselves in battle; 38,000 were killed, a rate of loss about 40 percent higher than that among white troops. Their bravery under fire convinced thousands of white soldiers that blacks were not by nature childish or cowardly. Even southerners were impressed. The Confederates threatened to kill or enslave black soldier-prisoners, but they almost never did. Fear of reprisals undoubtedly restrained them. So did the grudging respect that southern soldiers had to yield to men taken while charging fixed positions under fire and otherwise demonstrating their courage.

To blacks, both slave and free, the Emancipation Proclamation served as a beacon. Even if it failed immediately to liberate one slave or to lift the burdens of prejudice from one black back, it stood as a promise of future improvement. "I took the proclamation for a little more than it purported," Frederick Douglass recalled in his autobiography, "and saw in its spirit a life and power far beyond its letter." Lincoln was by modern standards a racist, but his most militant black contemporaries respected him deeply. The *Anglo-African,* an uncompromising black newspaper (the position of which is revealed in an 1862 editorial that asked: "Poor, chicken-hearted, semi-barbarous Caucasians, when will you learn that 'the earth was made for MAN?'"), referred in 1864 to Lincoln's "many noble acts" and urged his reelection. Douglass said of him: "Lincoln was not . . . either

our man or our model. In his interests, in his associations, in his habits of thought and in his prejudices, he was a white man." On the other hand, he spoke of Abraham Lincoln as "one whom I could love, honor, and trust without reserve or doubt."

As for the slaves of the South, after January 1, 1863, whenever the "Army of Freedom" approached, they laid down their plows and hoes and stole away in droves. "We-all knows about it," one black confided to a northern clergyman early in 1863. "Only we darsen't let on. We *pretends* not to know." Such behavior came as a shock to the owners. "[Those] who loved us best—as we thought—were the first to leave us," one planter mourned. Talk of slave "ingratitude" increased. Instead of referring to their workers as "servants" or "my black family," many owners began to describe them as "slaves" or "niggers."

Antietam to Gettysburg

It was well that Lincoln seized upon Antietam to release the Proclamation; had he waited for a more impressive victory, he would have waited nearly a year. To replace McClellan, he chose General Ambrose E. Burnside, best known to history for his magnificent side-whiskers, ever after called sideburns. Burnside, a West Pointer, had compiled a good record as a corps commander, but he lacked the self-confidence essential to anyone who takes responsibility for major decisions. He knew his limitations and tried to avoid high command, but patriotism and his sense of duty compelled him, when pressed, to accept leadership of the Army of the Potomac. He prepared to march on Richmond.

Unlike McClellan, Burnside was aggressive—too aggressive. He planned to ford the Rappahannock at Fredericksburg. Supply problems and bad weather delayed him until mid December, giving Lee time to concentrate his army in impregnable positions behind the town. Although he had more than 120,000 men against Lee's 75,000, Burnside should have called off the attack when he saw Lee's advantage; instead he ordered the troops forward. Crossing the river over pontoon bridges, his divisions occupied Fredericksburg. Then, in wave after wave, they charged the Confederate defense line while Lee's artillery riddled them from nearby Marye's Heights. Watching the battle from his command post on the heights, General Lee was deeply moved. Turning to General James Longstreet, he said: "It is well that war is so terrible—we should grow too fond of it!"

On December 14, the day following this futile assault, General Burnside, tears streaming down his cheeks, ordered the evacuation of Fredericksburg. Shortly thereafter General Joseph Hooker replaced him.

Unlike Burnside, "Fighting Joe" Hooker was ill-tempered, vindictive, and devious. In naming him to command the Army of the Potomac, Lincoln sent him a letter, now famous for what it reveals of the president's character:

> I think that during Gen. Burnside's command of the Army, you have taken counsel of your ambition, and thwarted him as much as you could, in which you did a great wrong to the country. . . . I have heard, in such a way as to believe it, of your recently saying that both the Army and the Government need a Dictator. Of course it is not *for* this, but in spite of it, that I have given you the command. Only those generals who gain successes, can set up dictators. What I now ask of you is military success, and I will risk the dictatorship. . . . Beware of rashness, but with energy and sleepless vigilance, go forward, and give us victories.

Hooker proved no better than his predecessor. By the spring of 1863 he had 125,000 men ready for action. Late in April he forded the Rappahannock and quickly concentrated at Chancellorsville, about 10 miles west of Fredericksburg. His army outnumbered the Confederates by more than two to one; he should have forced a battle at once. Instead he delayed, and while he did, Lee sent Stonewall Jackson's corps (28,000 men) across tangled countryside to a position directly athwart Hooker's unsuspecting flank. At 6 P.M. on May 2, Jackson attacked.

Completely surprised, the Union right crumbled, brigade after brigade overrun before it could wheel to meet Jackson's charge. At the first sound of firing, Lee had struck along the entire front to impede Union troop movements. If the battle had begun earlier in the day, the Confederates might have won a decisive victory; as it happened, nightfall brought a lull, and the next day the Union troops rallied and held their ground. Heavy fighting continued until May 5, when Hooker aban-

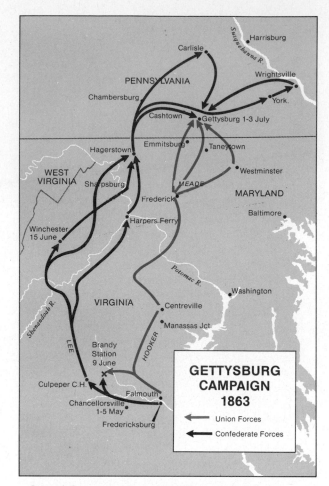

■ General George G. Meade, the fifth man to head the Army of the Potomac in less than a year, had to challenge Lee at Gettysburg just two days after assuming command.

doned the field and retreated in good order behind the Rappahannock.

Chancellorsville cost the Confederates dearly, for their losses, in excess of 12,000, were almost as heavy as the North's and harder to replace. They also lost Stonewall Jackson, struck down by the bullets of his own men while returning from a reconnaissance. Nevertheless, the Union army had suffered another fearful blow to its morale.

Lee now took the offensive. He knew that time was still on the side of the North; to defend Richmond was not enough. Already federal troops in the West were closing in on Vicksburg, threatening to cut Confederate communications with Arkansas and Texas. Now was the time to strike, while the morale of the northern people was at low ebb. With 75,000 soldiers he crossed the Potomac again, a larger Union force dogging his right flank. By late June his army had fanned out across southern Pennsylvania in a 50-mile arc from Chambersburg to the Susquehanna. Gray-clad soldiers ranged 50 miles *northwest* of Baltimore, within 10 miles of Harrisburg.

On July 1 Confederate troops looking for shoes in the town of Gettysburg clashed with a Union cavalry unit stationed there. Both sides sent out calls for reinforcements. Like iron filings drawn to a magnet, the two armies converged. The Confederates won control of the town, but the Union army, now commanded by General George G. Meade, took a strong position on Cemetery Ridge, a hook-shaped stretch of high ground just to the south. Lee's men occupied Seminary Ridge, a parallel position. On this field the fate of the Union was probably decided. For two days the Confederates attacked Cemetery Ridge, pounding it with the heaviest artillery barrage ever seen in America and sweeping bravely up its flanks in repeated assaults. General George E. Pickett's famous charge of 15,000 men actually carried the Union lines on the afternoon of July 3, but reserves drove them back before they could consolidate their position. By nightfall the Confederate army was spent and bleeding, the Union lines unbroken.

The following day was the Fourth of July. The two weary forces rested on their arms. Had the Union army attacked in force, the Confederates might have been crushed, but just as McClellan had hesitated after Antietam, Meade let opportunity pass. On July 5 Lee retreated to safety. For the first time he had been clearly bested on the field of battle.

Vicksburg: Lincoln Finds a General

On that same Independence Day, far to the west, federal troops won another great victory. When General Halleck was called east in July 1862, Ulysses S. Grant reassumed command of the Union troops. Grant was one of the most controversial officers in the army. At West Point he had compiled an indifferent record, ranking twenty-first in a class of 39. During the Mexican War he served well, but when he was later assigned to a lonely post in Oregon, he took to drink and was forced to resign his commission. Thereafter he failed at a number of civilian occupations. In 1861, approaching 40, he seemed headed for a life of frustration and mediocrity.

The war gave him a second chance. Back in service, however, his reputation as a ne'er-do-well and his unmilitary bearing worked against him, as did the heavy casualties suffered by his troops at

■ The Union navy played a key role in Grant's Vicksburg plan, slugging its way past the city's guns to transport the Federals across the Mississippi. Grant reestablished his supply line via the Yazoo River when he laid siege to Vicksburg.

■ U.S. Grant, photographed by Matthew Brady in 1863. As a strategist, Grant was a total realist. His conquest of Vicksburg was as bold and imaginative a campaign as the war produced, yet in Virginia in 1864–1865 he adjusted to different circumstances and fought a slow and grinding war of attrition.

Shiloh. Yet the fact that he knew how to manage a large army and win battles did not escape Lincoln. When a gossip tried to poison the president against him by referring to his drinking, Lincoln remarked that if he knew what brand Grant favored, he would send a barrel of it to some of his other generals. Grant never used alcohol as a substitute for courage.

Grant's major aim was to capture Vicksburg, a city of tremendous strategic importance. Together with Port Hudson, a bastion north of Baton Rouge, Louisiana, it guarded a 150-mile stretch of the Mississippi. The river between these points was inaccessible to federal gunboats. So long as Vicksburg remained in southern hands, the trans-Mississippi region could send men and supplies to the rest of the Confederacy.

Vicksburg sits on a high bluff overlooking a sharp bend in the river. When it proved unapproachable from either west or north, Grant devised an audacious scheme for getting at it from

the *east.* He descended the Mississippi from Memphis to a point a few miles north of the city. Then, leaving part of his force behind to create the impression that he planned to attack from the north, he crossed to the west bank and slipped quickly southward. Recrossing the river below Vicksburg, he abandoned his communications and supply lines and struck at Jackson, the capital of Mississippi. In a series of swift engagements he captured Jackson, cutting off the army of General John C. Pemberton, defending Vicksburg, from other Confederate units. Turning next on Pemberton, he defeated him in two battles and drove him inside the Vicksburg fortifications. By mid May the city was under siege. Grant applied relentless pressure, and on July 4 Pemberton surrendered. With Vicksburg in Union hands, federal gunboats could range the entire length of the Mississippi.* Texas

---

*Port Hudson, isolated by Vicksburg's fall, surrendered on July 9.

and Arkansas were isolated, for all practical purposes lost to the Confederacy.

Lincoln had disliked Grant's plan for capturing Vicksburg. Now he generously confessed his error and placed Grant in command of all federal troops west of the Appalachians. Grant promptly took charge of the fighting around Chattanooga, where Confederate advances, beginning with the Battle of Chickamauga (September 19–20), were threatening to develop into a major disaster for the North. Shifting corps commanders and bringing up fresh units, he won another decisive victory at Chattanooga in a series of battles ending on November 25, 1863. This cleared the way for an invasion of Georgia. Suddenly this unkempt, stubby little man, who looked more like a tramp than a general, emerged as the military leader the North had been so desperately seeking. In March 1864 Lincoln summoned him to Washington, named him lieutenant general, and gave him supreme command of the armies of the United States.

Economic Effects, North and South

Though much blood would yet be spilled, by the end of 1863 the Confederacy was on the road to defeat. Northern military pressure, gradually increasing, was eroding the South's most precious resource, manpower. An ever tightening naval blockade was reducing its economic strength. Shortages developed that, combined with the flood of currency pouring from the presses, led to a drastic inflation. By 1864 an officer's coat cost $2,000 in Confederate money, cigars sold for $10 each, butter was $25 a pound and flour $275 a barrel. The southern railroad network gradually wore out, the major lines maintaining operations only by cannibalizing less vital roads. Imported products such as coffee disappeared; salt became scarce. Efforts to increase manufacturing were only moderately successful because of the shortage of labor, capital, and technical knowledge. In general, southern prejudice against centralized authority prevented the Confederacy from making effective use of its scarce resources. Even blockade running was left in private hands until 1864. Precious cargo space that should have been reserved for medical supplies and arms was often devoted to high-priced luxuries.

In the North, after a brief depression in 1861 caused by the uncertainties of the situation and the loss of southern business, the economy boomed. Government purchases greatly stimulated certain lines of manufacturing; the railroads operated at close to capacity and with increasing efficiency; a series of bad harvests in Europe boosted agricultural prices. Congress passed a number of economic measures long desired but held up in the past by southern opposition: (1) the Homestead Act (1862) gave 160 acres to any settler who would farm the land for five years; (2) the Morrill Land Grant Act of the same year provided the states with land at the rate of 30,000 acres for each member of Congress to support state agricultural colleges; (3) various tariff acts raised the duties on manufactured goods to an average rate of 47 percent in order to protect domestic manufacturers from foreign competition; (4) the Pacific Railway Act (1862) authorized subsidies in land and money for the construction of a transcontinental railroad; (5) the National Banking Act of 1863 gave the country, at last, a uniform currency. Under this last act, banks could obtain federal charters by investing at least one-third of their capital in United States bonds. They might then issue currency up to 90 percent of the value of those bonds. A 10 percent tax on the issues of state banks drove state bank notes out of circulation.

All these laws stimulated the economy and added to public confidence. Whether the overall economic effect of the Civil War was beneficial is less clear. It was fought mostly with rifles, light cannon, horses, and wagons rather than with masses of heavy artillery, tanks, and trucks. Consequently it had much less effect than later wars on heavy industry. Although production expanded, it did so more slowly during the 1860s than in the decades preceding and following. Prices soared beginning in 1862, averaging about 80 percent over the 1860 level by the end of the war. Wages, however, did not keep pace. This condition did not make for a healthy economy—nor did the fact that there were chronic shortages of labor in many fields, shortages aggravated by a sharp drop in the number of immigrants entering the country.

The war had a demoralizing effect on many businessmen. Inflation and shortages encouraged speculation and fostered a selfish, materialistic attitude toward life. "The intense desire to buy almost any kind of securities amounted almost to insanity," one observer commented in 1862. By 1864 cotton was worth $1.90 a pound in New England. It could be had for 20 cents a pound in the South. While it was illegal to traffic in the staple across the lines, unscrupulous operators did so and made huge profits. Many contractors took advantage of wartime confusion to sell the government "shoddy" goods and to swindle the public in other ways.

Yet the war undoubtedly helped prepare the way for modern industrial society in the United States. It posed problems of organization and planning, both military and civilian, that challenged the talents of creative persons and thus led to a more complex and efficient economy. The mechanization of industry, the growth of large corporations, the creation of a better banking system, and the emergence of business leaders attuned to these conditions would surely have occurred in any case, for industrialization was under way long before the South seceded. Nevertheless the war greatly speeded economic change.

Grant, Sherman, and Victory

Grant's strategy as supreme commander was simple, logical, and ruthless. He would attack Lee and try to capture Richmond. General William Tecumseh Sherman would drive from Chattanooga toward Atlanta, Georgia. Like a lobster's claw, the two armies could then close to crush all resistance. Early in May 1864 Grant and Sherman commenced operations, each with more than 100,000 men.

Grant marched the Army of the Potomac directly into the tangled wilderness area south of the Rappahannock, where Hooker had been routed a year earlier. Lee, having only 60,000 men, forced the battle in the roughest possible country, where Grant found it difficult to make efficient use of his larger force. For two days (May 5–6) the Battle of the Wilderness raged. When it was over, the North had sustained another 18,000 casualties, far more than the Confederates. But unlike his predecessor, Grant did not fall back after being checked, nor did he expose his army to the kind of devastating counterattack at which Lee was so expert. Instead he shifted his troops to the southeast,

attempting to outflank the Confederates. Divining his intent, Lee rushed his divisions southeastward and disposed them behind hastily thrown up earthworks in well-placed positions around Spotsylvania Court House. Grant attacked. After five more days, which cost the Union army another 12,000 men, the Confederate lines were still intact.

Grant remained undaunted. He had grasped the fundamental truth that the war could be won only by grinding the South down beneath the weight of numbers. His own losses of men and equipment could be replaced; those of Lee could not. When critics complained of the cost, he replied doggedly that he intended to fight on in the same manner if it took all summer. Once more he pressed southeastward in an effort to outflank the enemy. At Cold Harbor, 9 miles from Richmond, he found the Confederates once more in strong defenses. At dawn on June 3 he attacked. It was a battle as foolish and nearly as one-sided as General Pakenham's assault on Jackson's line outside New Orleans in 1815. "At Cold Harbor," the forthright Grant confessed in his memoirs, "no advantage whatever was gained to compensate for the heavy losses we sustained."

Sixty thousand casualties in less than a month! The news sent a wave of dismay through the North. There were demands that "Butcher" Grant be removed from command. Lincoln, however, stood firm. Although the price was fearfully high, Grant was gaining his objective. At Cold Harbor, Lee had to fight without a single regiment in general reserve while Grant's army was larger than at the start of the offensive. When Grant next swung round his flank, striking south of the James River toward Petersburg, Lee had to rush his troops to that city to hold him.

As the Confederates dug in, Grant put Petersburg under siege. Soon both armies had constructed complicated lines of breastworks and trenches, running for miles in a great arc south of Petersburg, much like the fortifications that would be used so extensively in World War I in France. Methodically the Union forces extended their lines, seeking to weaken the Confederates and cut the rail connections supplying Lee's troops and the city of Richmond. Grant could not overwhelm him, but by late June, Lee was pinned to earth. Moving again would mean having to abandon Richmond—tantamount, in southern eyes, to surrender.

■ Confederate troops at Petersburg built these incredibly complex fortifications during the long siege. In the background are rows of sharpened sticks (*chevaux-de-frise*) intended to repel cavalry attacks.

The summer of 1864 saw the North submerged in pessimism. The Army of the Potomac held Lee at bay but appeared powerless to defeat him. In Georgia, General Sherman inched forward methodically against the wily Joseph E. Johnston, but when he tried a direct assault at Kennesaw Mountain on June 27, he was thrown back with heavy casualties. In July daring Confederate raiders under General Jubal Early dashed suddenly across the Potomac from the Shenandoah Valley to within 5 miles of Washington before being turned back. A draft call for 500,000 additional men did not improve the public temper. Huge losses and the absence of decisive victory were taxing the northern will to continue the fight.

In June Lincoln had been renominated on a National Union ticket, with the staunch Tennessee Unionist Andrew Johnson, a former Democrat, as his running mate. He was under attack not only from the Democrats, who nominated George B. McClellan and came out for a policy that might almost be characterized as peace at any price, but from the Radical Republicans, many of whom had wished to dump him in favor of Secretary of the Treasury Chase.

Then, almost overnight, the atmosphere changed. On September 2 General Sherman's army fought its way into Atlanta. When the Confederates countered with an offensive northward toward Tennessee,* Sherman did not follow. Instead he abandoned his communications with Chattanooga and marched unopposed through Georgia, "from Atlanta to the sea."

---

*This force was crushed before Nashville in December by a Union army under General George Thomas.

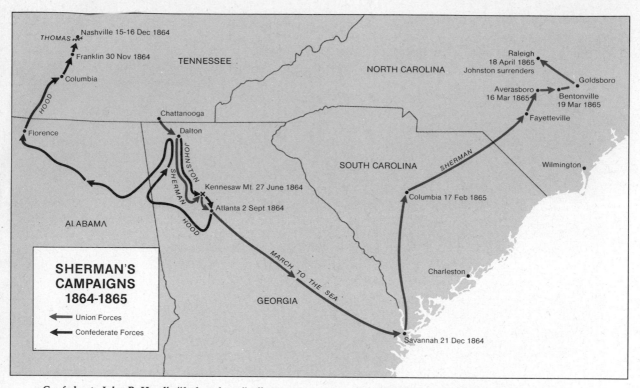

SHERMAN'S
CAMPAIGNS
1864-1865

← Union Forces
← Confederate Forces

■ Confederate John B. Hood's "forlorn hope" offensive toward Nashville failed to deter Sherman from marching through Georgia. Joseph E. Johnston could offer little resistance to Sherman's drive through the Carolinas.

Far more completely than most military men of his generation, Sherman believed in total war—in appropriating or destroying everything that might help the enemy continue the fight. "War is cruelty, and you cannot refine it," he said. Before taking Atlanta he wrote his wife: "We have devoured the land. . . . All the people retire before us and desolation is behind. To realize what war is one should follow our tracks." His army moved through Georgia like a harvester through a field of ripe wheat. "I suppose Jeff Davis will now have to feed the people of Georgia instead of collecting provisions of them to feed his armies," he said coldly.

Sherman's victories staggered the Confederacy and the anti-Lincoln forces in the North. In November the president was easily reelected, 212 electoral votes to 21. The country was determined to carry on the struggle.

At last the South's will to resist began to crack. Sherman entered Savannah on December 22, having denuded a strip of Georgia 60 miles wide.

Early in January 1865 he marched northward, leaving behind "a broad black streak of ruin and desolation—the fences all gone; lonesome smokestacks, surrounded by dark heaps of ashes and cinders, marking the spots where human habitations had stood." In February his troops captured Columbia, South Carolina. Soon they were in North Carolina, advancing relentlessly In Virginia Grant's vise grew daily tighter, the Confederate lines thinner and more ragged.

On March 4 Lincoln took the presidential oath and delivered his second inaugural address. Photographs taken at about this time show how four years of war had marked him. Somehow he had become both gentle and steel-tough, both haggard and inwardly calm. With victory sure, he spoke for tolerance, mercy, and reconstruction. "Let us judge not," he said after stating again his personal dislike of slavery, "that we be not judged." He urged all Americans to turn without malice to the task of mending the damage and to make a just and lasting peace between the sections.

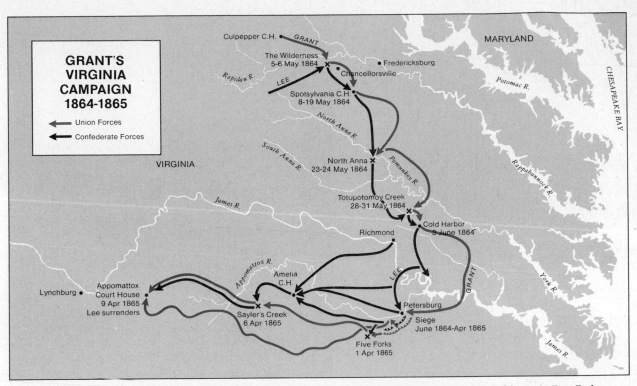

GRANT'S VIRGINIA CAMPAIGN 1864-1865

→ Union Forces
→ Confederate Forces

MARYLAND

Culpepper C.H. • ·GRANT·

The Wilderness
5-6 May 1864

Fredericksburg

Rapidan R.

LEE

Chancellorsville

Spotsylvania C.H.
8-19 May 1864

North Anna R.

South Anna R.

North Anna
23-24 May 1864

Pamunkey R.

VIRGINIA

James R.

Totopotomoy Creek
28-31 May 1864

Cold Harbor
3 June 1864

Richmond

Potomac R.

CHESAPEAKE BAY

Rappahannock R.

Appomattox R.

Amelia
C.H.

LEE

GRANT

York R.

Lynchburg •

Appomattox
Court House
9 Apr 1865
Lee surrenders

Sayler's Creek
6 Apr 1865

Petersburg

Siege
June 1864-Apr 1865

James R.

Five Forks
1 Apr 1865

■ Grant's repeated and costly attempts (60,000 casualties the first month) to outflank Lee are detailed here. At Five Forks the long siege of Petersburg was broken; Richmond was evacuated. A week later Lee surrendered.

Now the Confederate troops around Petersburg could no longer withstand the federal pressure. Desperately Lee tried to pull his forces back to the Richmond and Danville Railroad, but the swift wings of Grant's army enveloped him. Richmond fell on April 3. With fewer than 30,000 effectives to oppose Grant's 115,000, Lee recognized the futility of further resistance. On April 9 he and Grant met by prearrangement at Appomattox Court House.

It was a scene at once pathetic and inspiring. Lee was noble in defeat, Grant, despite his rough-hewn exterior, sensitive and magnanimous in victory. "I met you once before, General Lee, while we were serving in Mexico," Grant said after they had shaken hands. "I have always remembered your appearance, and I think I should have recognized you anywhere." They talked briefly of that earlier war, and then, acting upon Lincoln's instructions, with which he was in full accord, Grant outlined his terms. All that would be required was that the Confederate soldiers lay down

their arms. They could return to their homes in peace. When Lee hinted (he was too proud to ask outright for the concession) that his men would profit greatly if allowed to retain possession of their horses, Grant generously offered to let them do so.

Costs and Prospects

And so the war ended. It cost the nation 600,000 lives. The story of one of the lost thousands must stand for all. Jones Budbury, a tall, 19-year-old redhead, was working in a Pennsylvania textile mill when the war broke out, and he enlisted at once. His regiment first saw action at Bull Run. He took part in McClellan's Peninsula campaign. He fought at Second Bull Run, at Chancellorsville, and at Gettysburg. A few months after Gettysburg he was wounded in the foot and spent some time in an army hospital. By the spring of 1864 he had risen through the ranks to first sergeant and his

■ The men of Lee's Army of Northern Virginia march between Union ranks to lay down their arms at Appomattox, sketched by northern combat artist J.R. Chapin. Describing the scene, a federal officer wrote in his diary: "On our part [there was] not a sound of trumpet . . . nor roll of drum; not a cheer . . . but an awed stillness rather . . . ."

hair had turned gray. In June he was captured and sent to Andersonville military prison, but he fell ill and the Confederates released him. In March 1865 he was back with his regiment in the lines besieging Richmond. On April 6, three days before Lee's surrender, Jones Budbury was killed while pursuing Confederate units near Sailor's Creek, Virginia.

The war also caused enormous property losses, especially in the Confederacy. All the human and material destruction explains the eroding hatred and bitterness that the war implanted in millions of hearts. The corruption, the gross materialism, and the selfishness generated by wartime conditions were other disagreeable by-products of the conflict. Such sores fester in any society, but the Civil War bred conditions that inflamed and multiplied them. The war produced many examples

of charity, self-sacrifice, and devotion to duty as well, yet if the general moral atmosphere of the postwar generation can be said to have resulted from the experiences of 1861–1865, the effect overall was bad.

What had been obtained at this price? Slavery was dead. The concept of an indissoluble Union had won almost universal acceptance: secession was no longer possible after Appomattox. In a strictly political sense, as Lincoln had predicted from the start, the northern victory heartened friends of republican government and democracy throughout the world. A better integrated society and a more technically advanced and productive economic system also resulted from the war.

The Americans of 1865 estimated the balance between cost and profit according to their individual fortunes and prejudices. Only the wisest realized that no final accounting could be made until the people had decided what to do with the fruits of victory. That the physical damage would be repaired no one could reasonably doubt; that even the loss of human resources would be restored in short order was equally apparent. But would the nation make good use of the *opportunities* the war had made available? What would the ex-slaves do with freedom? How would whites, northern and southern, react to emancipation? To what end would the new technology and social efficiency be directed? Would the people be able to forget the recent past and fulfill the hopes for which so many brave soldiers had given their "last full measure of devotion"?

SUPPLEMENTARY READING
Titles marked with an asterisk have been published in paperback

Allan Nevins, **Ordeal of the Union** (1947–1971), continues to be the fullest and most judicious interpretation of the period down to 1863. It excels both as an account of the fighting and as an analysis of political, social, and economic developments. J. G. Randall, **Lincoln, the President*** (1945–1955), is an excellent scholarly study; the last volume of this work was completed after Randall's death by R. N. Current. The best one-volume survey of the period is J. G. Randall and David Donald, **The Civil War and Reconstruction** (1961), while Donald's collection of essays, **Lincoln Reconsidered*** (1956), is original and thought-provoking.

Political and constitutional problems are dealt with in J. G. Randall, **Constitutional Problems Under Lincoln** (1926). Lincoln's dealings with the Radicals have been extensively investigated, most recently in H. L. Trefousse, **The Radical Republicans: Lincoln's Vanguard for Racial Justice*** (1969), which praises Lincoln's management of the Radicals and minimizes his differences with them. See also, however, T. H. Williams, **Lincoln and the Radicals*** (1941). W. B. Hesseltine, **Lincoln and the War Governors** (1948), F. L. Klement, **The Copperheads in the Middle West** (1960), J. H. Silbey, **A Respectable Minority: The Democratic Party in the Civil War Era*** (1977), and Wood Gray, **The Hidden Civil War*** (1942), consider other aspects of the political history of the period.

For the movement to make abolition a war aim and the reaction to it, see J. M. McPherson, **The Struggle for Equality: Abolitionists and the Negro in the Civil War and Reconstruction*** (1964), G. M. Frederickson, **The Inner Civil War: Northern Intellectuals and the Crisis of the Union*** (1965), and V. J. Voegeli, **Free but Not Equal: The Midwest and the Negro During the Civil War*** (1967). The activities and attitudes of blacks during the war are summarized in D. T. Cornish, **The Sable Arm: Negro Troops in the Union Army*** (1956), Benjamin Quarles, **The Negro in the Civil War*** (1969), and B. I. Wiley, **Southern Negroes*** (1938). J. M. McPherson (ed.), **The Negro's Civil War*** (1965), is a convenient collection of source material on this subject.

For aspects of economic and social history, see P. W. Gates, **Agriculture and the Civil War** (1965), and R. P. Sharkey, **Money, Class, and Party: An Economic Study of Civil War and Reconstruction*** (1959). E. D. Fite, **Social and Industrial Conditions in the North During the Civil War** (1910), is still useful, and so is Margaret Leech, **Reveille in Washington*** (1941).

Clement Eaton, **A History of the Southern Confederacy*** (1954), is an excellent brief account of the South during the war, but see also R. S. Henry, **The Story of the Confederacy*** (1957), and E. M. Coulter, **The Confederate States of America** (1950). The fullest biography of Jefferson Davis is Hudson Strode, **Jefferson Davis** (1955–1964). Other useful volumes on the Confederacy include C. W. Ramsdell, **Behind the Lines in the Southern Confederacy** (1944), R. W. Patrick, **Jefferson Davis and His Cabinet** (1944), and B. J. Hendrick, **Statesmen of the Lost Cause** (1939).

The voluminous literature on the military history of the Civil War can only be sampled. K. P. Williams, **Lincoln Finds a General** (1949–1952), is exhaustive and judicious. T. H. Williams, **Lincoln and His Generals*** (1952), is briefer and more lively. Bruce Catton, **The Centennial History of the Civil War** (1961–1965), is vivid and detailed, as are Catton's volumes on the war in the eastern theater, **Mr. Lincoln's Army*** (1951), **Glory Road*** (1952), and **A Stillness at Appomattox*** (1953). The famous **Battles and Leaders of the Civil War,** written during the 1880s by participants, is available in condensed form in Ned Bradford (ed.), **Battles and Leaders of the Civil War** (1956). H. S. Commager (ed.), **The Blue and the Gray*** (1951), is an exciting collection of contemporary accounts of the fighting. R. M. Ketchum (ed.), **The American Heritage Picture History of the Civil War** (1960), is excellent. B. I. Wiley, **The Life of Billy Yank*** (1952), discusses the role of the common soldier. For the naval side of the conflict, see V. C. Jones, **The Civil War at Sea** (1960–1962), and R. S. West, Jr., **Mr. Lincoln's Navy** (1957).

For books dealing with the Confederate military effort, see Frank Vandiver, **Rebel Brass** (1956), A. B.

Moore, **Conscription and Conflict in the Confederacy** (1942), D. S. Freeman, **Lee's Lieutenants** (1942–1944), and B. I. Wiley, **The Life of Johnny Reb*** (1943); see also David Donald (ed.), **Why the North Won the Civil War*** (1960).

Among the biographies of Civil War generals, northern and southern, the following are especially noteworthy: W. S. McFeely, **Grant: A Biography** (1981), W. W. Hassler, Jr., **General George B. McClellan** (1957), Lloyd Lewis, **Sherman, Fighting Prophet** (1932), D. S. Free-man, **R. E. Lee** (1934–1935), and Frank Vandiver, **Mighty Stonewall** (1957). U. S. Grant, **Personal Memoirs*** (1885–1886), should not be missed.

The diplomacy of the Civil War period is covered in H. D. Jordan and E. J. Pratt, **Europe and the American Civil War** (1931), Jay Monaghan, **Diplomat in Carpet Slippers*** (1945), E. D. Adams, **Great Britain and the American Civil War** (1925), M. B. Duberman, **Charles Francis Adams*** (1961), and F. L. Owsley, **King Cotton Diplomacy** (1931).

16/RECONSTRUCTION AND THE SOUTH

 On April 5, 1865, Abraham Lincoln visited Richmond. The fallen capital lay in ruins, sections blackened by fire, but the president was able to walk the streets unmolested and almost unattended. The townspeople seemed to have accepted defeat without resentment. A few days later, in Washington, Lincoln delivered an important speech on Reconstruction, urging compassion and open-mindedness. On April 14 he held a Cabinet meeting at which postwar readjustment was considered at length. That evening, while Lincoln was watching a performance of the play *Our American Cousin* at Ford's Theater, a half-mad actor, John Wilkes Booth, slipped into his box and shot him in the back of the head with a small pistol. Early the next morning, without having regained consciousness, Lincoln died.

The murder was part of a complicated plot organized by die-hard prosoutherners. Seldom have fanatics displayed so little understanding of their own interests, for with Lincoln perished the South's best hope for a mild peace. After his body had been taken home to Illinois, the national mood hardened. It was not a question of avenging the beloved Emancipator; rather a feeling took possession of the public mind that the time of pain and suffering was not yet over, that the awesome drama was still unfolding, that retribution and a final humbling of the South were inevitable.

Presidential Reconstruction

Despite its bloodiness, the Civil War had caused less intersectional hatred than might have been expected. Although civilian property was often seized or destroyed, the invading armies treated the southern population with remarkable forbearance, both during the war and after Appomattox. While he was ensconced in Richmond behind Lee's army, northerners boasted that they would "hang Jeff Davis to a sour apple tree," and when he was captured in Georgia in May 1865, he was at once clapped into irons preparatory to being tried for treason and murder. But feeling against him subsided quickly. In 1867 the military turned him over to the civil courts, which released him on bail. He was never brought to trial. A few other Confederate officials spent short periods behind bars, but the only southerner executed for war crimes was Major Henry Wirz, the commandant of Andersonville military prison.

The legal questions related to bringing the defeated states back into the Union were extremely complex. Since southerners believed that secession was legal, logic should have compelled them to argue that they were out of the Union and would thus have to be formally readmitted. Northerners should have taken the contrary position, for they had fought to prove that secession was illegal. Yet the people of both sections did just the opposite. Senator Charles Sumner and Congressman Thaddeus Stevens, in 1861 uncompromising expounders of the theory that the Union was indissoluble, now insisted that the Confederate states had "committed suicide" and should be treated like "conquered provinces." Erstwhile states' rights southerners claimed that their states were still within the Union. Lincoln believed the issue a "pernicious abstraction" and tried to ignore it.

The process of readmission began in 1862, when Lincoln appointed provisional governors for those parts of the South that had been occupied by federal troops. On December 8, 1863, he issued a proclamation setting forth a general policy. With the exception of high Confederate officials and a few other special groups, all southerners could reinstate themselves as United States citizens by taking a simple loyalty oath. When, in any state, a number equal to ten percent of those voting in the 1860 election had taken this oath, they could set up a state government. Such governments had to be republican in form, must recognize the "permanent freedom" of the slaves, and must provide for black education. The plan, however, did not require that blacks be given the right to vote.

This "ten percent plan" reflected Lincoln's lack of vindictiveness and his political wisdom. He realized that any government based on such a small minority of the population would be, as he put it, merely "a tangible nucleus which the remainder . . . may rally around as fast as it can," a sort of puppet regime, like the paper government established in those sections of Virginia under federal control.* The regimes established under this plan in Tennessee, Louisiana, and Arkansas bore, in the president's mind, the same relation to finally reconstructed states that an egg bears to a chicken. "We shall sooner have the fowl by hatching it than by smashing it," he remarked. He knew that eventually representatives of the southern states would again be sitting in Congress, and he wished to lay the groundwork for a strong Republican party in the section. Yet he realized that Congress had no intention of seating representatives from the "ten percent" states at once.

The Radicals in Congress disliked the ten percent plan, partly because of its moderation and partly because it enabled Lincoln to determine Union policy toward the recaptured regions. In July 1864 they passed the Wade-Davis bill, which provided for constitutional conventions only after a *majority* of the voters in a southern state had

---

*By approving the separation of the western counties that had refused to secede, this government provided a legal pretext for the creation of West Virginia.

■ Andrew Johnson, as recorded by Mathew Brady's camera in 1865. Johnson, Charles Dickens reported, radiated purposefulness but no "genial sunlight."

taken a loyalty oath. Confederate officials and anyone who had "voluntarily borne arms against the United States" were barred from voting in the election or serving at the convention. Besides prohibiting slavery, the new state constitutions would have to repudiate Confederate debts. Lincoln disposed of the Wade-Davis bill with a pocket veto and thus managed to retain the initiative in Reconstruction for the remainder of the war. There matters stood when Andrew Johnson became president following the assassination.

Lincoln had picked Johnson for a running mate in 1864 because he was a border-state Unionist Democrat and something of a hero as a result of his courageous service as military governor of Tennessee. From origins even more lowly than Lincoln's, Johnson had risen to be congressman, governor of Tennessee, and United States senator. He was able and ambitious but fundamentally unsure of himself, as could be seen in his boastful-

ness and stubbornness. His political strength came from the poor whites and yeomen farmers of eastern Tennessee, and he was inordinately fond of extolling the common man and attacking "stuck-up aristocrats." Thaddeus Stevens called him a "rank demagogue" and a "damned scoundrel," and it is true that he was a masterful rabble-rouser. But few men of his generation labored so consistently in behalf of small farmers. Free homesteads, public education, absolute social equality—such were his objectives. The father of communism, Karl Marx, a close observer of American affairs at this time, wrote approvingly of Johnson's "deadly hatred of the oligarchy."

Johnson was a Democrat, but because of his record and his reassuring penchant for excoriating southern aristocrats, the Republicans in Congress were ready to cooperate with him. "Johnson, we have faith in you," said Radical Senator Ben Wade, author of the Wade–Davis bill, the day after Lincoln's death. "By the gods, there will be no trouble now in running the government!"

Johnson's reply, "Treason must be made infamous," delighted the Radicals, but the president proved temperamentally unable to work with them. As Eric L. McKitrick has shown in *Andrew Johnson and Reconstruction*, he was an "outsider," a "lone wolf" in every way. "The only role whose attributes he fully understood was that of the maverick," McKitrick writes. "For the full nourishment and maximum functioning of his mind, matters had to be so arranged that all the organized forces of society could in some sense, real or symbolic, be leagued against him." Like Randolph of Roanoke, his antithesis intellectually and socially, opposition was his specialty; he soon alienated every powerful Republican in Washington.

Radical Republicans listened to Johnson's diatribes against secessionists and the great planters and assumed that he was antisouthern. Nothing could have been further from the truth. He shared most of his poor white Tennessee constituents' prejudices against blacks. "Damn the negroes, I am fighting these traitorous aristocrats, their masters," he told a friend during the war. "I wish to God," he said on another occasion, "every head of a family in the United States had one slave to take the drudgery and menial service off his family."

The new president did not want to injure or humiliate the entire South. On May 29, 1865, he issued an amnesty proclamation only slightly

■ Brady photographed two of the stalwart Radical Republicans, Thaddeus Stevens of Pennsylvania (top) and Benjamin Wade of Ohio (bottom). Stevens served in the House from 1859 until his death in 1868. During the Civil War, Senator "Bluff Ben" Wade chaired the Joint Committee on the Conduct of the War.

more rigorous than Lincoln's. It assumed, correctly enough, that with the war over most southern voters would freely take the loyalty oath; thus it contained no ten percent clause. More classes of Confederates, including those who owned taxable property in excess of $20,000, were excluded from the general pardon. By the time Congress convened in December, all the southern states had organized governments, ratified the Thirteenth Amendment abolishing slavery, and elected senators and representatives. Johnson promptly recommended these new governments to the attention of Congress.

Republican Radicals

Peace found the Republicans in Congress no more united than they had been during the war. A small group of "ultra" Radicals were demanding immediate and absolute racial equality. Senator Sumner led this faction. A second group of Radicals, headed by Thaddeus Stevens in the House and Ben Wade in the Senate, agreed with the ultras' objectives but were prepared to accept half a loaf if necessary to win the support of less radical colleagues.* The moderate Republicans wanted to protect ex-slaves from exploitation and guarantee their basic rights but were unprepared to push for full political and social equality. A handful of Republicans sided with the Democrats in support of Johnson's approach, but all the rest insisted at least on the minimum demands of the moderates. Thus Johnsonian Reconstruction had no chance of winning congressional approval.

Johnson's proposal that Congress accept Reconstruction as completed and admit the new southern representatives was also doomed for reasons having little to do with black rights. The Thirteenth Amendment had the effect of increasing the representation of the southern states in Congress because it made the Three-fifths Compromise (see page 121) meaningless. Henceforth those who had been slaves would be counted as

*When Stevens died, he was buried in a black cemetery. Here is his epitaph, written by himself: "I repose in this quiet and secluded spot, not from any natural preference for solitude, but finding other cemeteries limited as to race, by charter rules, I have chosen this that I might illustrate in my death the principles which I advocated through a long life, equality of man before his Creator."

whole persons in apportioning seats in the House of Representatives. If Congress seated the southerners, the balance of power might swing to the Democrats. To expect the Republicans to surrender power in such a fashion was unrealistic. Former Copperheads gushing with extravagant praise for Johnson put them instantly on guard. And northerners remained suspicious of ex-Confederates. Although most of them were ready to reenter the Union, they were not overflowing with goodwill toward their conquerors.

Some of the new state governments were less than straightforward about accepting the most obvious results of the war. South Carolina, instead of repudiating secession, merely repealed its secession ordinance. A minority of southerners would have nothing to do with amnesties and pardons:

Oh, I'm a good old rebel,
Now that's just what I am;
For the "fair land of freedom,"
I do not care a dam.
I'm glad I fit against it—
I only wish we'd won
And I don't want no pardon
For anything I done.

Southern voters had further provoked northern resentment by their choice of congressmen. Georgia elected Alexander H. Stephens, vice-president of the Confederacy, to the Senate, though he was still in a federal prison awaiting trial for treason! Several dozen men who had served in the Confederate Congress had been elected to either the House or the Senate, together with four generals and many other high officials. The southern people understandably selected locally respected and experienced leaders, but it was equally reasonable that these choices would sit poorly with northerners.

Finally, the so-called Black Codes enacted by southern governments to control former slaves alarmed the North. These varied in severity from state to state. When seen in historical perspective, even the strictest codes represented a considerable improvement over slavery. Most permitted blacks to sue and to testify in court, at least in cases involving members of their own race. Blacks were allowed to own certain kinds of property; marriages were made legal; other rights were guaranteed. However, blacks could not bear arms, be employed in occupations other than farming and

domestic service, or leave their jobs without forfeiting back pay. The Louisiana code required them to sign labor contracts for the year during the first ten days of January. In Mississippi any "vagrant" who could not pay the stiff fine assessed was to be "hired out . . . at public outcry" to the white person who would take him for the shortest period in return for paying his fine. Such laws, apparently designed to get around the Thirteenth Amendment, outraged even moderate northerners.

For all these reasons the Republicans in Congress rejected Johnsonian Reconstruction. Quickly they created a joint committee on Reconstruction, headed by Senator William P. Fessenden of Maine, a moderate, to study the question of readmitting the southern states.

The committee held extensive public hearings that produced much evidence of the mistreatment of blacks. Colonel George A. Custer, stationed in Texas, testified: "It is of weekly, if not of daily occurrence that Freedmen are murdered." The nurse Clara Barton told a gruesome tale about a pregnant woman who had been brutally whipped. Others described the intimidation of blacks by poor whites. The hearings played into the hands of the Radicals, who had been claiming all along that the South was perpetuating slavery under another name.

President Johnson's attitude speeded the swing toward the Radical position. While the hearings were in progress, Congress passed a bill expanding and extending the Freedmen's Bureau, which had been established in March 1865 to care for refugees. The bureau, a branch of the War Department, was already exercising considerable coercive and supervisory power in the South. Now Congress sought to add to its authority in order to protect the black population. The bill had wide support even among moderates. Nevertheless Johnson vetoed it, arguing that it was an unconstitutional extension of military authority in peacetime. Congress then passed a Civil Rights Act that, besides declaring that blacks were citizens of the United States, denied the states the power to restrict their rights to testify in court and to hold property.

Once again the president refused to go along, though his veto was sure to drive more moderates into the arms of the Radicals. On April 9, 1866, Congress repassed the Civil Rights Act by a two-thirds majority, the first time in American history that a major piece of legislation became law over the veto of a president. This event marked a revolution in the history of Reconstruction. Thereafter Congress, not President Johnson, had the upper hand, and it placed progressively stricter controls on the South.

In the clash between the president and Congress, Johnson was his own worst enemy. His language was often intemperate, his handling of men inept, his analysis of southern conditions incorrect. He had assumed that the small southern farmers who made up the majority in the Confederacy shared his prejudices against the planter class. They did not, as their choices in the postwar elections demonstrated. In fact, Johnson's hatred of the southern aristocracy may have been based more on jealousy than on principle. Under the Reconstruction plan, persons excluded from the blanket amnesty could apply individually for the restoration of their rights. When wealthy and socially prominent southerners flocked to Washington, hat in hand, he found their flattery and humility exhilarating. He issued pardons wholesale, saying: "I did not expect to keep out all who were excluded from the amnesty. . . . I intended they should sue for pardon, and so realize the enormity of their crime."

The president misread northern opinion. He believed that Congress had no right to pass laws affecting the South before southern representatives had been readmitted to Congress. However, in the light of the refusal of most southern whites to grant any real power or responsibility to the freedmen (an attitude that Johnson did not condemn) the public would not accept this point of view. Johnson placed his own judgment over that of the overwhelming majority of northern voters, and this was a great error, morally and tactically. By encouraging southerners to resist efforts to improve the lot of blacks, Johnson played into the hands of northern extremists.

The Radicals encountered grave problems in fighting for their program. Northerners might object to the Black Codes and to seating "rebels" in Congress, but few believed in racial equality. Between 1865 and 1868 Wisconsin, Minnesota, Connecticut, Nebraska, New Jersey, Ohio, Michigan, and Pennsylvania all rejected bills granting blacks the vote.

The Radicals were in effect demanding not merely equal rights for freedmen but *extra* rights: not merely the vote but special protection of that right against the pressure that southern whites would surely apply to undermine it. This idea flew in the face of conventional American beliefs in equality before the law and individual self-reliance. Such protection would involve interference by the federal government in local affairs, a concept at variance with American practice. Events were to show that the Radicals were correct—that what amounted to a political revolution in state-federal relations was essential if blacks were to achieve real equality. But in the climate of that day their proposals encountered bitter resistance, and not only from southerners.

Thus, while the Radicals sought partisan advantage in their battle with Johnson and sometimes played on war-bred passions in achieving their ends, they were taking large political risks in defense of genuinely held principles. One historian has aptly called them the "moral trustees" of the Civil War.

The Fourteenth Amendment

In June 1866 Congress submitted to the states a new amendment to the Constitution. The Fourteenth Amendment was a milestone along the road to the centralization of political power, for it significantly reduced the power of *all* the states. In this sense it confirmed the great change wrought by the Civil War: the growth of a more complex, more closely integrated social and economic structure requiring closer national supervision. Few people understood this aspect of the amendment at the time.

First the amendment supplied a broad definition of American citizenship: "All persons born or naturalized in the United States, and subject to the jurisdiction thereof, are citizens of the United States and of the State wherein they reside." Obviously this included blacks. Then it struck at discriminatory legislation like the Black Codes: "No State shall make or enforce any law which shall abridge the privileges or immunities of citizens of the United States; nor shall any State deprive any person of life, liberty, or property, without due process of law." The next section attempted to force the southern states to permit blacks to vote. If a state denied the vote to any class of its adult male citizens, its representation was to be reduced proportionately. Under another clause, former federal officials who had served the Confederacy were barred from holding either state or federal office unless specifically pardoned by a two-thirds vote of Congress. Finally, the Confederate debt was repudiated.

While the amendment did not specifically outlaw segregation or prevent a state from disfranchising blacks if it was willing to see its representation in Congress reduced, the southern states would have none of it. Without them the necessary three-fourths majority of the states could not be obtained. The governor of Mississippi denounced it as "an insulting outrage" to those "who have shed glory and lustre upon our section and our race." Women's rights groups in the North objected to the implication that black men were more fitted to vote than white women. Elizabeth Cady Stanton warned that the amendment would create "an antagonism between black men and all women."

President Johnson vowed to make the choice between the Fourteenth Amendment and his own policy the main issue of the 1866 congressional elections. He embarked on "a swing around the circle" to rally the public to his cause. He failed dismally. Northern opinion had hardened; a large majority was determined that blacks must have at least formal legal equality. The Republicans won better than two-thirds of the seats in both houses, together with control of all the northern state governments. Johnson emerged from the campaign discredited, the Radicals stronger and determined to have their way. The southern states, Congressman James A. Garfield of Ohio said in February 1867, have "flung back into our teeth the magnanimous offer of a generous nation. It is now our turn to act."

The Reconstruction Acts

Had the southern states been willing to accept the Fourteenth Amendment, coercive measures might have been avoided. Their recalcitrance and continuing indications that local authorities were persecuting blacks finally led to the passage, on March 2, 1867, of the First Reconstruction Act. This law divided the former Confederacy—exclusive of Tennessee, which had ratified the Four-

teenth Amendment—into five military districts, each controlled by a major general. It gave these officers almost dictatorial power to protect the civil rights of "all persons," maintain order, and supervise the administration of justice. To rid themselves of military rule, the former states were required to adopt constitutions guaranteeing blacks the right to vote and disfranchising broad classes of ex-Confederates. If the new constitutions proved satisfactory to Congress, and if the new governments ratified the Fourteenth Amendment, their representatives would be admitted to Congress and military rule ended. Johnson's veto of the act was easily overridden.

Although drastic, the Reconstruction Act was so vague that it proved unworkable. Military control was easily established, for federal bayonets were already exerting considerable authority throughout the South. But in deference to moderate Republican views, the law had not spelled out the process by which the new constitutions were to be drawn up. Southern whites preferred the status quo, even under army control, to enfranchising blacks and retiring their own respected leaders. They made no effort to follow the steps laid down in the law. Congress therefore passed a second act, requiring the military authorities to register voters and supervise the election of delegates to constitutional conventions. A third act further clarified procedures.

Still white southerners resisted. The laws required that the constitutions be approved by a majority of the registered voters. Simply by staying away from the polls, whites prevented ratification in state after state. At last, in March 1868, a full year after the First Reconstruction Act, Congress changed the rules again. The constitutions were to be ratified by a majority of the *voters*. In June 1868 Arkansas, having fulfilled the requirements, was readmitted to the Union, and by July a sufficient number of states had ratified the Fourteenth Amendment to make it part of the Constitution. But it was not until July 1870 that the last southern state, Georgia, qualified to the satisfaction of Congress.

Congress versus the President

To carry out this program in the face of determined southern resistance required a degree of single-mindedness over a long period seldom demonstrated by an American legislature. The persistence resulted in part from the suffering and frustrations of the war years. The refusal of the South to accept the spirit of even the mild reconstruction designed by Johnson goaded the North to ever more overbearing efforts to bring the ex-Confederates to heel. President Johnson's stubbornness also influenced the mood of Congress; Republican leaders became obsessed with the need to defeat him. The unsettled times and the large Republican majorities, always threatened by the possibility of a Democratic resurgence if "unreconstructed" southern congressmen were readmitted, sustained their determination.

These considerations led Republicans to attempt a kind of grand revision of the federal government, one that almost destroyed the balance between judicial, executive, and legislative power established in 1789. A series of measures passed between 1866 and 1868 increased the authority of Congress over the army, over the process of amending the Constitution, and over Cabinet members and lesser appointive officers. Even the Supreme Court felt the force of the congressional drive for power; its size was reduced, as was the range of its jurisdiction over civil rights cases. Finally, in a showdown caused by emotion more than by practical considerations, the Republicans attempted to remove President Johnson from office.

Johnson was a poor president and out of touch with public opinion, but he had done nothing to merit ejection from office. While he had a low opinion of blacks, his opinion was so widely shared by whites that it is unhistorical to condemn him as a reactionary on this ground. Johnson believed that he was fighting to preserve constitutional government. He was honest and devoted to duty, and his record easily withstood the most searching examination. When Congress passed laws taking away powers granted him by the Constitution, he refused to submit.

The chief issue was the Tenure of Office Act of 1867, which prohibited the president from removing officials who had been appointed with the consent of the Senate without first obtaining Senate approval. In February 1868 Johnson "violated" this act by dismissing Secretary of War Edwin M. Stanton, who had been openly in sympathy with the Radicals for some time. The House, acting under the procedure set up in the Constitution for removing the president, promptly impeached him before the bar of the Senate, Chief Justice Salmon P. Chase presiding.

This "great act of ill-directed passion," as it has been characterized by one historian, was conducted in a partisan and vindictive manner. Johnson's lawyers easily established that he had removed Stanton only in an effort to prove the Tenure of Office Act unconstitutional. They demonstrated that the act did not protect Stanton to begin with, since it gave Cabinet members tenure "during the term of the President by whom they may have been appointed," and Stanton had been appointed by Lincoln! Nevertheless the Radicals pressed the charges (11 separate articles) relentlessly. To the argument that Johnson had committed no crime, the learned Senator Sumner retorted that the proceedings were "political in character" rather than judicial. Thaddeus Stevens, directing the attack on behalf of the House, warned the senators that although "no corrupt or wicked motive" could be attributed to Johnson, they would "be tortured on the gibbet of everlasting obloquy" if they did not convict him. Tremendous pressure was applied to the handful of Republican senators who were unwilling to disregard the evidence.

Seven of them resisted to the end, and the Senate failed by a single vote to convict Johnson. This was probably fortunate. Had he been forced from office on such flimsy grounds, the independence of the executive might have been permanently weakened. Then the legislative branch would have become supreme.

The Fifteenth Amendment

The failure of the impeachment did not affect the course of Reconstruction. The president was acquitted on May 16, 1868. A few days later the Republican National Convention nominated General Ulysses S. Grant for the presidency. At the Democratic convention Johnson had considerable support, but the delegates nominated Horatio Seymour, a former governor of New York. In November Grant won an easy victory in the electoral college, 214 to 80, but the popular vote was close: 3 million to 2.7 million. Although he would probably have carried the electoral college in any case,

■ In honor of the Fifteenth Amendment, the black community of New York City held a parade in April, 1870. Many of the marchers represented social and political clubs, and carried identifying banners for these groups such as the "Grant and Colfax Club, No. 1" and the "2nd Ward Grant Club."

Grant's margin in the popular vote was supplied by southern blacks enfranchised under the Reconstruction Acts, about 450,000 of whom supported him. A majority of white voters probably preferred Seymour. Since many citizens undoubtedly voted Republican because of personal admiration for General Grant, the election statistics suggest that a substantial white majority opposed the policies of the Radicals.

The ratification of the Fourteenth Amendment and the Reconstruction Acts achieved the purpose of enabling black southerners to vote. The Radicals, however, were not satisfied; despite the unpopularity of the idea in the North, they wished to guarantee the right of blacks to vote in every state. Another amendment seemed the only way to accomplish this objective, but passage of such an amendment appeared impossible. The Republican platform in the 1868 election had smugly distinguished between blacks voting in the South ("de-

manded by every consideration of public safety, of gratitude, and of justice") and in the North (where the question "properly belongs to the people").

However, after the election had demonstrated how crucial the votes of ex-slaves could be, Republican strategy shifted. Grant had carried Indiana by less than 10,000 votes and lost New York by a similar number. If blacks in these and other closely divided states had voted, Republican strength would have been greatly enhanced.

Suddenly Congress blossomed with suffrage amendments. After considerable bickering over details, the Fifteenth Amendment was sent to the states for ratification in February 1869. It forbade *all* the states to deny the vote to anyone "on account of race, color, or previous condition of servitude." Once again nothing was said about denial of the vote on the basis of sex.

Most southern states, still under federal pressure, ratified the amendment swiftly. The same was true in most of New England and in some western states. Bitter battles were waged in Connecticut, New York, Pennsylvania, and the states immediately north of the Ohio River, but by March 1870 most of them had ratified the amendment and it became part of the Constitution. The debates occasioned by these contests show that partisan advantage was not the only reason why voters approved black suffrage at last. The unfairness of a double standard of voting, North and South, the contribution of black soldiers during the war, and the hope that by passing the amendment the strife of Reconstruction could finally be ended all played a part.

When the Fifteenth Amendment went into effect, President Grant called it "the greatest civil change and . . . the most important event that has occurred since the nation came to life." The American Anti-Slavery Society formally dissolved itself, its work apparently completed. One prominent Radical Republican called this triumph over prejudice "hardly explicable on any other theory than that God willed it."

Many of the celebrants lived to see the amendment subverted in the South. That it could be evaded by literacy tests and other restrictions was apparent at the time and may even have influenced some persons who voted for it. But a stronger amendment—one, for instance, that positively granted the right to vote to all men and put the supervision of elections under national control—could not have been ratified.

"Black Republican" Reconstruction

The Radicals had at last succeeded in imposing their will upon the South. Throughout the region former slaves voted, held office, and exercised the "privileges" and enjoyed the "immunities" guaranteed them by the Fourteenth Amendment. Almost to a man they voted Republican.

The spectacle of blacks not five years removed from slavery in positions of power and responsibility attracted much attention at the time and has since been examined exhaustively by historians. The subject is controversial, but certain facts are beyond argument. Black officeholders were nei-

ther numerous nor inordinately influential. None was ever elected governor of a state; fewer than a dozen and a half during the entire period served in Congress; only one (in South Carolina) rose to be a justice of a state supreme court. Blacks held many minor offices and were influential in southern legislatures, though (except in South Carolina) they never made up the majority. Certainly they did not share the spoils of office in proportion to their numbers.

The real rulers of the "black Republican" governments were white: the "carpetbaggers"—northerners who went to the South as idealists eager to help the freedmen, as employees of the federal government, or more commonly as settlers hoping to improve their lot—and the "scalawags"—southerners willing to cooperate with the freedmen out of principle or to advance their own interests. A few scalawags were well-to-do planters and merchants who had been Whigs until the crises of the 1850s destroyed that party in the South, but most were former opponents of secession from sections that had small slave populations before the war.

That blacks should fail to dominate southern governments is certainly understandable. They lacked experience in politics and were mostly poor and uneducated. They were nearly everywhere a minority. Those blacks who held office during Reconstruction tended to be better educated and more prosperous. In his interesting analysis of South Carolina black politicians, Thomas Holt shows that a disproportionate number of them had been free before the war. Of those freed by the Thirteenth Amendment, a large percentage had been house servants or artisans, not field hands. Mulatto politicians were also disproportionately numerous and (as a group) more conservative and economically better off than other black leaders.

In South Carolina and elsewhere, black officeholders proved in the main able and conscientious public servants: able because the best tended to rise to the top in such a fluid situation and conscientious because most of those who achieved importance sought eagerly to demonstrate the capacity of their race for self-government. Extensive studies of states such as Mississippi show that even at the local level, where the quality of officials was usually poor, there was little difference

■ **South Carolina's House of Representatives in session during Reconstruction, from** *Frank Leslie's Illustrated Newspaper.* **Black voters were in the majority in South Carolina.**

in the degree of competence displayed by white and black officeholders. In power, the blacks were not vindictive; by and large they did not seek to restrict the rights of ex-Confederates.

Not all black legislators and administrators were paragons of virtue. In South Carolina, despite their control of the legislature, they broke up into factions repeatedly and failed to press for laws that would improve the lot of poor black farm workers. And waste and corruption were common among them. Legislators paid themselves large salaries and surrounded themselves with armies of useless, incompetent clerks. Half the budget of Louisiana in some years went for salaries and "mileage" for representatives and their staffs. In South Carolina the legislature ordered an expensive census in 1869, only one year before the regular federal census was to be taken. Large sums were appropriated for imposing state capitols and other less than essential buildings. As for corruption, in *The South During Reconstruction* Professor E. Merton Coulter described dozens of de-

falcations that occurred during these years. One Arkansas black took $9,000 from the state for repairing a bridge that had cost only $500 to build. A South Carolina legislator was voted an additional $1,000 in salary after he lost that sum on a horse race.

However, the corruption must be seen in perspective. The big thieves were nearly always white; blacks got mostly crumbs. Furthermore, graft and callous disregard of the public interest characterized government in every section and at every level during the decade after Appomattox. Big-city bosses in the North made off with sums that dwarfed the most brazen southern frauds. The New York City Tweed Ring probably made off with more money than all the southern thieves, black and white, combined. While the evidence does not justify the southern corruption, it suggests that the unique features of Reconstruction politics—black suffrage, military supervision, carpetbagger and scalawag influence—do not explain it.

The "black Republican" governments displayed qualities that grew directly from the ignorance and political immaturity of the former slaves. There was a tragicomic aspect to the South Carolina legislature during these years, its many black members—some dressed in old frock coats, others in rude farm clothes—rising to points of order and personal privilege without reason, discoursing ponderously on subjects they did not understand. "A wonder and a shame to modern civilization," one northern observer called this spectacle.

The country might have been better served if blacks had been enfranchised gradually, as Lincoln suggested. But those who complained about the ignorance and irresponsibility of blacks conveniently forgot that the tendency of 19th-century American democracy was away from educational, financial, or any other restrictions on the fran-

chise. Thousands of white southerners were as illiterate and uncultured as the freedmen, yet no one suggested depriving them of the ballot.

Despite the corruption, confusion, and conflict, the Radical southern governments accomplished a great deal. They spent money freely but not entirely wastefully. Tax rates zoomed, but the money financed the repair and expansion of the South's dilapidated railroad network, rebuilt crumbling levees, and expanded social services. Before the Civil War, public education in the South had lagged far behind the rest of the country, and the education of blacks was illegal. During Reconstruction an enormous gap had to be filled, and it took a great deal of money to fill it. The Freedmen's Bureau made a start, and northern religious and philanthropic organizations did important work. Eventually, however, the state

■ The Freedmen's Bureau established 4,329 schools, attended by some 250,000 ex-slaves, in the South in the postwar period. *Harper's Weekly* artist Alfred Waud did this sketch of a Freedmen's Bureau school in Vicksburg, Mississippi, in 1866. Many of the teachers were northern white women.

Retered, according to act of Congress in the year 1872 by Currier & Ives in the Office of the Librarian of Congress at Washington.

ROBERT C. DE LARGE, M.C. of S. Carolina.   JEFFERSON H. LONG, M.C. of Georgia.

U.S. Senator H.R. REVELS of Mississippi   BENJ. S. TURNER, M.C. of Alabama.   JOSIAH T. WALLS, M.C. of Florida.   JOSEPH H. RAINY, M.C. of S. Carolina.   R. BROWN ELLIOT, M.C. of S. Carolina.

THE FIRST COLORED SENATOR AND REPRESENTATIVES.
In the 41st. and 42nd. Congress of the United States.

■ A Currier & Ives print honoring the first black senator—Hiram R. Revels of Mississippi, seated at the left—and representatives who served in the 41st and 42nd Congresses from 1869 to 1873.

governments established and supported systems of free public education that, while segregated, greatly benefited everyone, whites as well as blacks.

The former slaves grasped eagerly at the opportunity to learn. Nearly all appreciated the immense importance of knowing how to read and write; the sight of elderly men and women poring laboriously over elementary texts beside their grandchildren was common everywhere. Schools and other institutions were supported chiefly by property taxes, and these, of course, hit well-to-do white farmers hard. Hence much of the complaining about the "extravagance" of Reconstruction governments concealed selfish objections to pay-ing for public projects. Eventually the benefits of expanded government services to the entire population became clear, and when white supremacy was reestablished, most of the new services, together with the corruption and inefficiency inherited from the carpetbagger governments, were retained.

Southern Economic Problems

The South's grave economic problems complicated the rebuilding of its political system. The section had never been as prosperous as the North, and wartime destruction left it desperately poor by any standard. In the long run the abolition of slavery released immeasurable quantities of human energy previously stifled, but the immediate effect was to create confusion. Understandably, many former slaves at first equated legal freedom with freedom from having to earn a living, a tendency reinforced for a time by the willingness of the Freedmen's Bureau to provide rations and other forms of relief in war-devastated areas. Freedom to move about without a pass, to "see the world," was one of the most cherished benefits of emancipation. "I's want to be free man, cum when I please, and nobody say nuffin to me, nor order me roun'," one Alabama black told a northern journalist after Appomattox. Thousands flocked to southern towns and cities where there was little they could do to earn a living.

Others expected that freedom would also mean free land, and the slogan "forty acres and a mule" achieved wide popularity in the South in 1865. This idea was forcefully supported by the relentless Congressman Thaddeus Stevens, whose ha-

tred of the planter class was pathological. "The property of the chief rebels should be seized," he stated. If the lands of the richest "70,000 proud, bloated and defiant rebels" were confiscated, the federal government would obtain 394 million acres. Every adult male ex-slave could easily be supplied with 40 acres. The beauty of his scheme, Stevens insisted, was that "nine-tenths of the [southern] people would remain untouched." Dispossessing the great planters would make the South "a safe republic," its lands cultivated by "the free labor of intelligent citizens." If the plan drove the planters into exile, "all the better."

Although Stevens' figures were faulty, many Radicals agreed with him. "We must see that the freedmen are established on the soil," Senator Sumner declared. "The great plantations, which have been so many nurseries of the rebellion, must be broken up, and the freedmen must have the pieces." Stevens, Sumner, and others who wanted to give land to the freedmen weakened their case by associating it with the idea of punish-

■ Among the few blacks to emigrate to the West and obtain land under the provisions of the Homestead Act was the Shores family. S.D. Butcher took this family portrait in Custer County, Nebraska, in the 1880s. Black homesteaders received limited aid from the Freedmen's Relief Association and eastern philanthropists.

ing the former rebels; the average American had too much respect for property rights to support a policy of confiscation.

Aside from its vindictiveness, the extremists' view was simplistic. Land without tools, seed, and other necessities would have done the freedmen little good. Congress did throw open 46 million acres of poor-quality federal land in the South to blacks under the Homestead Act, but few settled upon it. Establishing former slaves on small farms with adequate financial aid would have been of incalculable benefit to them and to the nation. This would have been practicable, but it was not done.

The freedmen therefore had to work out their destiny within the established framework of southern agriculture. White planters predicted that the ex-slaves, being incapable of self-directed effort, would either starve to death or descend into barbarism. Of course the blacks did neither. True, the output of cotton and other southern staples declined precipitously after slavery was abolished. Observers soon came to the conclusion that a free black produced no more than half as much as a slave had produced, and modern econometric studies indicate that this estimate was not far off.

However, the decline in productivity was not caused by the *inability* of free blacks to work independently. What happened was that since they now held, in the pithy phrase of the economist Robert Higgs, "property rights over their own bodies," they chose no longer to work like slaves. They let their children play instead of forcing them into the fields. Mothers devoted more time to child care and housework, less to farm labor. Elderly blacks worked less.

Noting these changes, white critics spoke scornfully of black laziness and shiftlessness. "You cannot make the negro work without physical compulsion," was the common view. As the economic historians Roger Ransom and Richard Sutch have said, the perfectly reasonable desire of ex-slaves to devote more time to leisure was "taken as 'evidence' to support racist characterizations of blacks as lazy, incompetent, and unwilling to work." A leading southern magazine complained in 1866 that black women now expected their husbands "to support them in idleness" (it would never have made such a comment about white housewives). Ransom and Sutch also point out that, while working less, emancipated blacks were far better off materially than under slavery. Their earnings brought them almost 30 percent more than the value of the subsistence provided by their former masters.

In the beginning blacks usually worked for wages, but the wage system did not function well in the postwar South. Money was scarce, and banking capital, never adequate even before the collapse of the Confederacy, accumulated slowly. Interest rates were extremely high. This situation made it difficult for landowners to meet their labor bills. More important, blacks did not like working for wages because it kept them under the direction of whites. Since the voluntary withdrawal of so much black labor from the work force had produced a shortage, they had their way.

A new agricultural system known as sharecropping emerged. Instead of cultivating the land by gang labor as in antebellum times, planters broke up their estates into small units and established on each a black family. The planter provided housing, agricultural implements, draft animals, seed, and other supplies, and the family provided labor. The crop was divided between them, usually on a fifty-fifty basis. If the landlord supplied only land and housing, the laborer got a larger share. This was called share tenancy.

Sharecropping gave blacks at least the hope of earning enough to buy a small farm. But few achieved this ambition because whites resisted their efforts adamantly. As late as 1880 blacks owned less than 10 percent of the agricultural land in the South, though they made up more than half of the region's farm population. Mississippi actually prohibited the purchase of farmland by blacks.

The main cause of southern rural poverty for whites as well as blacks was the lack of enough capital to finance the sharecropping system. Like their colonial ancestors, the landowners had to borrow against October's harvest to pay for April's seed. Thus the crop-lien system developed, and to protect their investments, lenders tended to insist that the grower concentrate on readily marketable cash crops: tobacco, sugar, and especially cotton.

The system injured everyone. Diversified farming would have reduced the farmers' need for cash, preserved the fertility of the soil, and, by placing a premium on imagination and shrewd-

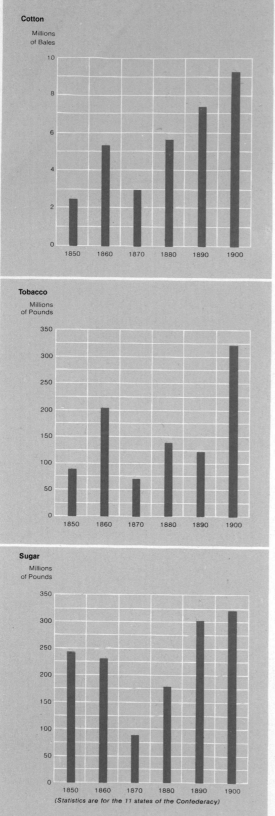

SOUTHERN AGRICULTURE, 1850-1900

Cotton

Millions
of Bales

Tobacco

Millions
of Pounds

Sugar

Millions
of Pounds

(Statistics are for the 11 states of the Confederacy)

ness, aided the best of them to rise in the world. Under the crop-lien system, both landowner and sharecropper depended on credit supplied by local bankers, merchants, and storekeepers for everything from seed, tools, and fertilizer to overalls, coffee, and salt. Crossroads stores proliferated, and a new class of small merchants appeared. The prices of goods sold on credit were high, adding to the burden borne by the rural population. The small southern merchants were almost equally victimized by the system, for they also lacked capital, bought goods on credit, and had to pay high interest rates.

Seen in broad perspective, the situation is not difficult to understand. The South, drained of every resource by the war, was competing for funds with the North and West, both vigorous and expanding and therefore voracious consumers of capital. Reconstruction, in the literal sense of the word, was accomplished chiefly at the expense of the standard of living of the producing classes. The crop-lien system and the small storekeeper were only agents of an economic process dictated by national, perhaps even worldwide, conditions.

This does not mean that the South's economy was paralyzed by the shortage of capital or that recovery and growth did not take place. But compared with the rest of the country, progress was slow. Just before the Civil War cotton harvests averaged about 4 million bales. During the conflict, output fell to about half a million, and the former Confederate states did not enjoy a 4 million bale year again until 1870. Only after 1874 did the crop begin to top that figure consistently. In contrast, national wheat production in 1859 was 175 million bushels and in 1878, 449 million. About 7,000 miles of railroad were built in the South between 1865 and 1879; in the rest of the nation nearly 45,000 miles of track were laid.

In manufacturing the South made important gains after the war. The tobacco industry, stimulated by the sudden popularity of the cigarette, expanded rapidly. The town of Durham, North Carolina, home of the famous Bull Durham pipe

■ Cotton production recovered to its prewar level by 1880, but tobacco and sugar production lagged. Not until 1900 did tobacco growers have a better year than they had in 1860.

and cigarette tobacco, flourished. So did Virginia tobacco towns like Richmond, Lynchburg, and Petersburg. The exploitation of the coal and iron deposits of northeastern Alabama in the early 1870s made a boom town of Birmingham. The manufacture of cotton cloth increased, productive capacity nearly doubling between 1865 and 1880. Yet the mills of Massachusetts alone had eight times the capacity of the entire South in 1880. Despite the increases, the South's share of the national output of manufactured goods declined sharply during the Reconstruction era.

The White Counterrevolution

Radical southern governments could sustain themselves only so long as they had the support of a significant proportion of the white population, for except in South Carolina and Louisiana, the blacks were not numerous enough to win elections alone. The key to Radical survival lay in the hands of the wealthy merchants and planters, mostly former Whigs. People of this sort had nothing to fear from black economic competition. Taking a broad view, they could see that improving the lot of the former slaves would benefit all classes.

These southerners exercised a restraining influence on the rest of the white population. Poor white farmers, the most "unreconstructed" of all southerners, bitterly resented blacks, whose every forward step seemed to weaken their own precarious economic and social position. When the Republicans began to organize and manipulate the new voters in much the way big-city bosses were managing voters in the North, the poor whites seethed with resentment.

Southern Republicans used the Union League of America, a patriotic club founded during the war, to control the black vote. Employing secret rituals, exotic symbols, and other paraphernalia calculated to impress unsophisticated people, they enrolled the freedmen in droves, made them swear to support the League list of candidates at elections, and then marched them to the polls en masse.

Powerless to check the League by open methods, dissident southerners established a number of secret terrorist societies, bearing such names as the Ku Klux Klan, the Knights of the White Camelia, and the Pale Faces. The most notorious of these organizations was the Klan, which originated in Tennessee in 1866. At first it was purely a social club, but by 1868 it had been taken over by vigilante types dedicated to driving blacks out of politics, and it was spreading rapidly across the South. Sheet-clad nightriders roamed the countryside, frightening the impressionable and chastising the defiant. Klansmen, using a weird mumbo

■ A graphic warning by the Alabama Klan to scalawags and carpetbaggers, "those great pests of Southern society"; from the Tuscaloosa *Independent Monitor* for September 1, 1868.

jumbo and claiming to be the ghosts of Confederate soldiers, spread horrendous rumors and published broadsides designed to persuade the freedmen that it was unhealthy for them to participate in politics:

> Niggers and Leaguers, get out of the way,
> We're born of the night and we vanish by day.
> No rations have we, but the flesh of man—
> And love niggers best—the Ku Klux Klan;
> We catch 'em alive and roast 'em whole,
> Then hand 'em around with a sharpened pole.
> Whole Leagues have been eaten, not leaving a man,
> And went away hungry—the Ku Klux Klan. . . .

When intimidation failed, the Klansmen beat their victims and in hundreds of cases murdered them, often in the most gruesome manner. Congress struck at the Klan with three Force Acts (1870–1871), which placed elections under federal jurisdiction and imposed fines and prison sentences on persons convicted of interfering with any citizen's exercise of the franchise. Troops were dispatched to areas where the Klan was strong, and by 1872 the federal authorities had arrested enough Klansmen to break up the organization.

Nevertheless the Klan contributed substantially to the destruction of Radical regimes in the South. Its depredations weakened the will of white Republicans (few of whom really believed in racial equality), and it intimidated many blacks, who gave up trying to exercise their rights.

Gradually it became respectable to intimidate black voters. Beginning in Mississippi in 1874 a number of terrorist movements spread through the South. Instead of hiding behind masks and operating in the dark, these terrorists donned red shirts, organized into military companies, and paraded openly. The Mississippi red-shirts seized militant blacks and whipped them publicly. Killings were frequent. When blacks dared to fight back, the well-organized whites easily put them to rout. In other states similar organizations sprang up, and the same tragic results followed.

Terrorism fed on fear, fear on terrorism. White violence led to fear of black retaliation and thus to even more brutal attacks. The slightest sign of resistance came to be seen as the beginning of race war, and when the blacks suffered indignities and persecutions in silence, the awareness of how much they must resent the mistreatment made them appear more dangerous still. Thus self-hatred was displaced, guilt suppressed, aggression justified as self-defense, individual conscience submerged in the animality of the mob.

Before long the blacks learned to stay home on election day. One by one, "Conservative" parties—Democratic in national affairs—took over southern state governments. Angry northern Radicals attributed the Democratic victories entirely to intimidation, but intimidation was only a partial explanation. The increasing solidarity of whites, northern and southern, was equally significant.

Many northerners had supported the Radical policy only out of irritation with President Johnson. After his retirement their enthusiasm waned. The war was fading into the past and with it the worst of the bad feeling it had generated. Northern voters could still be stirred by references to the sacrifices Republicans had made to save the Union and by reminders that the Democratic party was the organization of rebels, Copperheads, and the Ku Klux Klan. Yet emotional appeals could not push legislation through Congress or convince northerners that it was still necessary to maintain a large army in the South. In 1869 the occupying forces were down to 11,000 men.

Nationalism was reasserting itself. Had not Washington and Jefferson been Virginians? Was not Andrew Jackson Carolina-born? Since most northerners had little real love or respect for blacks, their interest in racial equality flagged once they felt reasonably certain that blacks would not be reenslaved if left to their own devices in the South.

Another, much subtler force was also at work. The prewar Republican party had stressed the common interest of workers, manufacturers, and farmers in a free and mobile society, a land of equal opportunity where all could work in harmony. Southern whites had insisted that laborers must be disciplined if large enterprises were to be run efficiently. By the 1870s, as large industrial enterprises developed in the northern states, the thinking of business leaders changed—the southern argument began to make sense to them, and therefore they became more sympathetic to the southern demand for more control over "their" labor force.

Grant as President

Other matters occupied the attention of northern voters. The expansion of industry and the rapid development of the West, stimulated by a new wave of railroad building, loomed more important to many than the fortunes of ex-slaves. Beginning in 1873, when a stock market panic struck at public confidence, economic difficulties plagued the country for nearly a decade. Heated controversies arose over tariff policy, with western agricultural interests seeking to force reductions from the high levels established during the war, and over the handling of the wartime greenback paper money, with debtor groups and many manufacturers favoring further expansion of the supply of dollars and conservative merchants and bankers arguing for retiring the greenbacks in order to return to a "sound" currency. These controversies tended to divert attention from conditions in the South.

More damaging to the Republicans was the failure of Ulysses S. Grant to live up to expectations as president. Qualities that had made Grant a fine military leader for a democracy—his dislike of political maneuvering and his simple belief that the popular will could best be observed in the actions of Congress—made him a poor chief executive. When Congress failed to act on his suggestion that the quality of the civil service needed improvement, he announced meekly that if Congress did nothing, he would assume the country did not want anything done, and he dropped the subject. Grant was honest, but his honesty was of the naive type that made him the dupe of unscrupulous friends and schemers. In fact he disliked being president and avoided the responsibilities of the office whenever he could.

His most serious weakness as president was his failure to deal effectively with economic and social problems, but the one that injured him and the

■ The cartoonist Thomas Nast was a staunch Grant man; in a *Harper's Weekly* drawing made during the 1872 campaign, Greeley (center) and Charles Sumner urge a black to "clasp hands" with a Klansman and a Tammany Hall instigator of Civil War draft riots.

Republicans most was his inability to cope with government corruption. Grant did not cause the corruption, nor did he participate in the remotest way in the rush to "fatten at the public trough," as the reformers of the day might have put it. But he did nothing to prevent the scandals that disgraced his administration. Out of a misplaced belief in the sanctity of friendship, he protected some of the worst culprits and allowed calculating tricksters to use his good name and the prestige of his office to advance their own interests at the country's expense.

The worst of the scandals—such as the Whiskey Ring affair, which implicated Grant's private secretary, Orville E. Babcock, and cost the government millions in tax revenue, and the defalcations of Secretary of War William W. Belknap in the management of Indian affairs—did not become public knowledge during Grant's first term. However, in 1872 a reform group in the Republican party, alarmed by rumors of corruption and disappointed by Grant's failure to press for civil service reform, organized the Liberal Republican party and nominated Horace Greeley, the able but eccentric editor of the New York *Tribune*, for president. The Democrats also nominated Greeley, though he had devoted his political life to flailing the Democratic party in the *Tribune*. That surrender to expediency, together with Greeley's temperamental unsuitability for the presidency, made the campaign a fiasco for the reformers. Grant triumphed easily, with a popular majority of nearly 800,000.

Nevertheless the defection of the Liberal Republicans hurt the Republican party in Congress. In the 1874 elections, no longer hampered as in the presidential contest by Greeley's notoriety and Grant's fame, the Democrats carried the House of Representatives. It was clear that the days of military rule in the South were ending. By the end of 1875 only three southern states, South Carolina, Florida, and Louisiana, were still under Republican control. The Republican party in the South was "dead as a doornail," a reporter noted. He reflected the opinion of thousands when he added: "We ought to have a sound sensible republican . . . for the next President as a measure of safety; but only on the condition of absolute noninterference in Southern local affairs, for which there is no further need or excuse."

The Disputed Election of 1876

Against this background the presidential election of 1876 took place. Since corruption in government was the most widely discussed issue, the Republicans passed over their most attractive political personality, the dynamic James G. Blaine, Speaker of the House of Representatives, who had been connected with some chicanery involving railroad securities. Instead they nominated Governor Rutherford B. Hayes of Ohio, a former general with an unsmirched reputation. The Democrats picked Governor Samuel J. Tilden of New York, who had attracted national attention for his part in breaking up the Tweed Ring in New York City.

In November Tilden triumphed easily in all the southern states from which the Radical regimes had been ejected. He also carried New York, New Jersey, Connecticut, and Indiana. In the three "unredeemed" southern states, Florida, South Carolina, and Louisiana, he won apparent majorities. This seemed to give him 203 electoral votes to Hayes' 165, with a popular plurality in the neighborhood of 250,000 out of more than 8 million votes cast.

Republican leaders had anticipated the possible loss of Florida, South Carolina, and Louisiana and were prepared to use their control of the election machinery in those states to throw out sufficient Democratic ballots to alter the results if doing so would change the national outcome. Realizing that the 19 electoral votes of those states were exactly enough to elect their man, they telegraphed their henchmen on the scene, ordering them to go into action. The board of canvassers in each of the states invalidated Democratic ballots in wholesale lots and filed returns showing Hayes the winner. Naturally the local Democrats protested vigorously and filed their own returns.

The Constitution provides that presidential electors must meet in their respective states to vote and forward the results to "the Seat of the Government." There, it adds, "the President of the Senate shall, in the Presence of the Senate and House of Representatives, open all the Certificates, *and the Votes shall then be counted*." But who was to do the counting? The House was Democratic, the Senate Republican; neither would agree to allow the other to do the job. On January 29,

1877, scarcely a month before inauguration day, Congress created an electoral commission to decide the disputed cases. The commission consisted of five senators (three Republicans and two Democrats), five representatives (three Democrats and two Republicans), and five justices of the Supreme Court (two Democrats, two Republicans, and one "independent" judge, David Davis). Since it was a foregone conclusion that the others would vote for their party no matter what the evidence, Davis would presumably swing the balance in the interest of fairness.

But before the commission met the Illinois legislature elected Davis senator! He had to resign from the Court and the commission. Since independents were rare even on the Supreme Court, no neutral was available to replace him. The vacancy went to Associate Justice Joseph P. Bradley of New Jersey, a Republican.

Evidence presented before the commission revealed a disgraceful picture of election shenanigans. On the one hand, in all three disputed states Democrats had clearly cast a majority of the votes; on the other, it was unquestionable that many blacks had been forcibly prevented from voting.

The sordid truth was that both sides had been shamefully corrupt. Lew Wallace, a northern politician later famous as the author of the novel *Ben Hur,* visited Louisiana and Florida shortly after the election. "It is terrible to see the extent to which all classes go in their determination to win," he wrote his wife from Florida. "Money and intimidation can obtain the oath of white men as well as black to any required statement. . . . If we win, our methods are subject to impeachment for possible fraud. If the enemy win, it is the same thing." The governor of Louisiana was reported willing to sell his state's electoral votes for $200,000. The Florida election board was supposed to have offered itself to Tilden for the same price. "That seems to be the standard figure," Tilden remarked ruefully.

Most modern authorities take the view that in a fair election the Republicans would have carried South Carolina and Louisiana but that Florida would have gone to Tilden, giving him the election, 188 electoral votes to 181. In the last analysis, this opinion has been arrived at simply by counting white and black noses: blacks were in the majority in South Carolina and Louisiana. Amid the tension and confusion of early 1877, however,

even a Solomon would have been hard pressed to judge rightly amid the rumors, lies, and contradictory statements, and the electoral commission was not composed of Solomons. The Democrats had some hopes that Justice Bradley would be sympathetic to their case, for he was known to be opposed to harsh Reconstruction policies. On the eve of the commission's decision in the Florida controversy, he was apparently ready to vote in favor of Tilden. But the Republicans subjected him to tremendous political pressure. When he read his opinion on February 8, it was for Hayes. Thus, by a vote of 8 to 7, the commission awarded Florida's electoral votes to the Republicans.

The rest of the proceedings were routine. The atmosphere of judicial inquiry and deliberation was a façade. With the spitefulness common to rejected suitors, the Democrats assailed Bradley until, as the New York *Times* put it, he seemed like "a middle-aged St. Sebastian, stuck full of Democratic darts." Unlike Sebastian, however, Bradley was protected from the arrows by the armor of his Republican faith. The commission assigned all the disputed electoral votes (including one in Oregon, where the Democratic governor had seized on a technicality to replace a single Republican elector with a Democrat) to Hayes.

To such a level had the republic of Jefferson and John Adams descended. Democratic institutions, shaken by the South's refusal to go along with the majority in 1860 and by the suppression of civil rights during the rebellion, and further weakened by military intervention and the intimidation of blacks in the South during Reconstruction, seemed now a farce. According to Tilden's campaign manager, angry Democrats in 15 states, chiefly war veterans, were readying themselves to march on Washington to force the inauguration of Tilden. Tempers flared in Congress, where some spoke ominously of a filibuster that would prevent the recording of the electoral vote and leave the country, on March 4, with no president at all.

The Compromise of 1877

Fortunately, forces for compromise had been at work behind the scenes in Washington for some time. Although northern Democrats threatened to fight to the last ditch, many southern Democrats

THE COMPROMISE OF 1877

	Electoral	Popular
Hayes (Rep.) } Disputed*	185	4,037,000
Tilden (Dem.)	184	4,284,000

*Assigned to Hayes by congressional commission.

were willing to accept Hayes if they could gain something in exchange. If Hayes would promise to remove the troops and allow the southern states to manage their internal affairs by themselves, they would be sorely tempted to go along with his election. A more specialized but extremely important group consisted of the ex-Whig planters and merchants who had reluctantly abandoned the carpetbag governments and who were always uncomfortable in alliance with poor whites. If Hayes would agree to let the South alone and perhaps appoint a conservative southerner to his Cabinet, these men would support him willingly, hoping eventually to restore the two-party system that had been destroyed in the South during the 1850s.

Other southerners favored Republican policies because of their economic interests. The Texas and Pacific Railway Company, chartered to build a line from Marshall, Texas, to San Diego, had many southern backers, and supporters of Hayes were quick to point out that a Republican administration would be more likely to help the Texas and Pacific than a retrenchment-minded Democratic one. Ohio Congressman James A. Garfield urged Hayes to find "some discreet way" of show-

ing these southerners that he favored "internal improvements." Hayes replied: "Your views are so nearly the same as mine that I need not say a word."

Tradition has it that a great compromise between the sections was worked out during a dramatic meeting at the Wormley Hotel in Washington on February 26. Actually, as C. Vann Woodward has demonstrated in his important book *Reunion and Reaction,* the negotiations were long-drawn-out and informal, and the Wormley conference was but one of many. With the tacit support of many Democrats, the electoral vote was counted by the president of the Senate on March 2, and Hayes was declared elected, 185 votes to 184.

Like all compromises, this agreement was not entirely satisfactory; like most, it was not honored in every detail. Hayes recalled the last troops from South Carolina and Louisiana in April. He appointed a former Confederate general, David M. Key of Tennessee, postmaster general and delegated to him the congenial task of finding southerners willing to serve their country as officials of a Republican administration. The new alliance of ex-Whigs and northern Republicans did not flourish, however, and the South remained solidly Democratic. The hoped-for federal aid for the Texas and Pacific did not materialize. The major significance of the compromise, one of the great intersectional political accommodations of American history, has been well summarized by Professor Woodward:

> The Compromise of 1877 marked the abandonment of principles and force and a return to the traditional ways of expediency and concession. The compromise laid the political foundation for reunion. It established a new sectional truce that proved more enduring than any previous one and provided a settlement for an issue that had troubled American politics for more than a generation. It wrote an end to Reconstruction and recognized a new regime in the South. More profoundly than Constitutional amendments and wordy statutes it shaped the future of four million freedmen and their progeny for generations to come.

For most of the former slaves, this future was to be bleak. Forgotten in the North, manipulated and then callously rejected by the South, rebuffed by the Supreme Court, voiceless in national affairs, they and their descendants were condemned in the interests of sectional harmony to lives of poverty, indignity, and little hope. Meanwhile, the rest of the United States continued its golden march toward wealth and power.

SUPPLEMENTARY READING

Titles marked with an asterisk have been published in paperback

J. G. Randall and David Donald, **The Civil War and Reconstruction** (1961), is as excellent on postwar readjustments as it is on the war years. K. M. Stampp, **The Era of Reconstruction*** (1964), and J. H. Franklin, **Reconstruction: After the Civil War*** (1961), are outstanding. E. M. Coulter, **The South During Reconstruction** (1947), presents a prosouthern point of view and is strong on economic developments. The older approach to the period, stressing the excesses of black-influenced governments and criticizing the Radicals, derives from the seminal work of W. A. Dunning, **Reconstruction, Political and Economic*** (1907). W. E. B. Du Bois, **Black Reconstruction in America*** (1935), militantly pro-black, was the pioneering counterattack against the Dunning view. See also Eric Foner, **Politics and Ideology in the Age of the Civil War** (1980).

Lincoln's ideas about Reconstruction are analyzed in W. B. Hesseltine, **Lincoln's Plan of Reconstruction*** (1960), and in many of the Lincoln volumes mentioned in earlier chapters. There is no satisfactory biography of Andrew Johnson; both G. F. Milton, **The Age of Hate: Andrew Johnson and the Radicals** (1930), and Milton Lomask, **Andrew Johnson: President on Trial** (1960), are far too sympathetic in approach. Of the special studies of Johnson's battle with the congressional Radicals, H. K. Beale, **The Critical Year** (1930), takes Johnson's side, but recent studies have been critical of the president. See H. L. Trefousse, **The Radical Republicans: Lincoln's Vanguard for Racial Justice*** (1969), E. L. McKitrick, **Andrew Johnson and Reconstruction*** (1960), and W. R. Brock, **An American Crisis: Congress and Reconstruction*** (1963), the last a particularly thoughtful analysis of the era.

A number of biographies provide information helpful in understanding the Radicals. These include B. P. Thomas and H. M. Hyman, **Stanton** (1962), F. M. Brodie, **Thaddeus Stevens*** (1959), R. N. Current, **Old Thad Stevens** (1942), and H. L. Trefousse, **Benjamin Franklin Wade** (1963); J. M. McPherson, **The Struggle for Equality: Abolitionists and the Negro in the Civil War and Reconstruction*** (1964), is also valuable. On the Fourteenth Amendment, see Joseph James, **The Framing of the Fourteenth Amendment*** (1956); on the Fifteenth Amendment, see William Gillette, **The Right to Vote: Politics and the Passage of the Fifteenth Amendment*** (1965).

Conditions in the South during Reconstruction are discussed in all the works cited in the first paragraph. Of state studies, see V. L. Wharton, **The Negro in Mississippi*** (1947), C. E. Wynes, **Race Relations in Virginia** (1961), W. L. Rose, **Rehearsal for Reconstruction: The Port Royal Experiment*** (1964), Thomas Holt, **Black over White: Negro Political Leadership in South Carolina** (1977), and Joel Williamson, **After Slavery: The Negro in South Carolina During Reconstruction*** (1965). G. R. Bentley, **A History of the Freedmen's Bureau** (1955), discusses the work of that important organization, but see also W. S. McFeely, **Yankee Stepfather: General O. O. Howard and the Freedmen*** (1968). On the Ku Klux Klan, see A. W. Trelease, **White Terror: The Ku Klux Klan Conspiracy and Southern Reconstruction** (1971).

On the economic and social effects of Reconstruction, see R. L. Ransom and Richard Sutch, **One Kind of Freedom: The Economic Consequences of Emancipation*** (1977), Robert Higgs, **Competition and Coercion: Blacks in the American Economy, 1865–1914** (1977), and C. F. Oubre, **Forty Acres and a Mule** (1978). F. A. Shannon, **The Farmer's Last Frontier*** (1945), is also useful on southern agriculture. For the growth of industry, see Broadus Mitchell, **The Rise of Cotton Mills in the South** (1921), and J. F. Stover, **The Railroads of the South** (1955).

On Grant's presidency, see W. S. McFeely, **Grant** (1981), but Allan Nevins, **Hamilton Fish: The Inner History of the Grant Administration** (1936), and Matthew Josephson, **The Politicos*** (1938), contain much additional information. On the election of 1868, see C. H. Coleman, **The Election of 1868** (1933), and Stewart Mitchell, **Horatio Seymour** (1938); on the reform movement of the period within the Republican party, see J. G. Sproat, **"The Best Men": Liberal Reformers in the Gilded Age*** (1968), and M. B. Duberman, **Charles Francis Adams*** (1961). For the disputed election of 1876 and the compromise following it, consult C. V. Woodward, **Reunion and Reaction*** (1951), Harry Barnard, **Rutherford B. Hayes and His America** (1954), K. I. Polakoff, **The Politics of Inertia: The Election of 1876 and the End of Reconstruction** (1973), and Allan Nevins, **Abram S. Hewitt** (1935). P. H. Buck, **The Road to Reunion*** (1937), traces the gradual reconciliation of North and South after 1865. William Gillette, **Retreat from Reconstruction** (1980), is an important recent study.

THE DECLARATION OF INDEPENDENCE

When in the Course of human events, it becomes necessary for one people to dissolve the political bands which have connected them with another, and to assume among the Powers of the earth, the separate and equal station to which the Laws of Nature and of Nature's God entitle them, a decent respect to the opinions of mankind requires that they should declare the causes which impel them to the separation.

We hold these truths to be self-evident, that all men are created equal, that they are endowed by their Creator with certain unalienable Rights, that among these are Life, Liberty and the pursuit of Happiness. That to secure these rights, Governments are instituted among Men, deriving their just powers from the consent of the governed, That whenever any Form of Government becomes destructive of these ends, it is the Right of the People to alter or to abolish it, and to institute new Government, laying its foundation on such principles and organizing its powers in such form, as to them shall seem most likely to effect their Safety and Happiness. Prudence, indeed, will dictate that Governments long established should not be changed for light and transient causes; and accordingly all experience hath shown, that mankind are more disposed to suffer, while evils are sufferable, than to right themselves by abolishing the forms to which they are accustomed. But when a long train of abuses and usurpations, pursuing invariably the same Object evinces a design to reduce them under absolute Despotism, it is their right, it is their duty, to throw off such Government, and to provide new Guards for their future security.—Such has been the patient sufferance of these Colonies; and such is now the necessity which constrains them to alter their former Systems of Government. The history of the present King of Great Britain is a history of repeated injuries and usurpations, all having in direct object the establishment of an absolute Tyranny over these States. To prove this, let Facts be submitted to a candid world.

He has refused his Assent to Laws, the most wholesome and necessary for the public good.

He has forbidden his Governors to pass Laws of immediate and pressing importance, unless suspended in their operation till his Assent should be obtained; and when so suspended, he has utterly neglected to attend to them.

He has refused to pass other Laws for the accommodation of large districts of people, unless those people would relinquish the right of Representation in the Legislature, a right inestimable to them and formidable to tyrants only.

He has called together legislative bodies at places unusual, uncomfortable, and distant from the depository of their Public Records, for the sole purpose of fatiguing them into compliance with his measures.

He has dissolved Representative Houses repeatedly, for opposing with manly firmness his invasions on the rights of the people.

He has refused for a long time, after such dissolutions, to cause others to be elected; whereby the Legislative Powers, incapable of Annihilation, have returned to the People at large for their exercise; the State remaining in the mean time exposed to all the dangers of invasion from without, and convulsions within.

He has endeavoured to prevent the population of these States; for that purpose obstructing the Laws of Naturalization of Foreigners; refusing to pass others to encourage their migration hither, and raising the conditions of new Appropriations of Lands.

He has obstructed the Administration of Justice, by refusing his Assent to Laws for establishing Judiciary Powers.

He has made Judges dependent on his Will alone, for the tenure of their offices, and the amount and payment of their salaries.

He has erected a multitude of New Offices, and sent hither swarms of Officers to harass our People, and eat out their substance.

He has kept among us, in times of peace, Standing Armies without the Consent of our legislature.

He has affected to render the Military independent of and superior to the Civil Power.

He has combined with others to subject us to a jurisdiction foreign to our constitution, and unacknowledged by our laws; giving his Assent to their acts of pretended legislation:

For quartering large bodies of armed troops among us:

For protecting them, by a mock Trial, from Punishment for any Murders which they should commit on the Inhabitants of these States:

For cutting off our Trade with all parts of the world:

For imposing taxes on us without our Consent:

For depriving us in many cases, of the benefits of Trial by Jury:

For transporting us beyond Seas to be tried for pretended offences:

For abolishing the free System of English Laws in a neighbouring Province, establishing therein an Arbitrary government, and enlarging its Boundaries so as to render it at once an example and fit instrument for introducing the same absolute rule into these Colonies:

For taking away our Charters, abolishing our most valuable Laws, and altering fundamentally the Forms of our Governments:

For suspending our own Legislature, and declaring themselves invested with Power to legislate for us in all cases whatsoever.

He has abdicated Government here, by declaring us out of his Protection and waging War against us.

He has plundered our seas, ravaged our Coasts, burnt our towns, and destroyed the lives of our people.

He is at this time transporting large armies of foreign mercenaries to compleat the works of death, desolation and tyranny, already begun with circumstances of Cruelty & perfidy scarcely paralleled in the most barbarous ages, and totally unworthy the Head of a civilized nation.

He has constrained our fellow Citizens taken Captive on the high Seas to bear Arms against their Country, to become the executioners of their friends and Brethren, or to fall themselves by their Hands.

He has excited domestic insurrections amongst us, and has endeavoured to bring on the inhabitants of our frontiers, the merciless Indian Savages, whose known rule of warfare, is an undistinguished destruction of all ages, sexes and conditions.

In every stage of these Oppressions We have Petitioned for Redress in the most humble terms: Our repeated Petitions have been answered only by repeated injury. A Prince, whose character is thus marked by every act which may define a Tyrant, is unfit to be the ruler of a free People.

Nor have We been wanting in attention to our British brethren. We have warned them from time to time of attempts by their legislature to extend an unwarrantable jurisdiction over us. We have reminded them of the circumstances of our emigration and settlement here. We have appealed to their native justice and magnanimity, and we have conjured them by the ties of our common kindred to disavow these usurpations, which, would inevitably interrupt our connections and correspondence. They too have been deaf to the voice of justice and of consanguinity. We must, therefore, acquiesce in the necessity, which denounces our Separation, and hold them, as we hold the rest of mankind, Enemies in War, in Peace Friends.

We, therefore, the Representatives of the united States of America, in General Congress, Assembled, appealing to the Supreme Judge of the world for the rectitude of our intentions, do, in the Name, and by Authority of the good People of these Colonies, solemnly publish and declare, That these United Colonies are, and of Right ought to be Free and Independent States; that they are Absolved from all Allegiance to the British Crown, and that all political connection between them and the State of Great Britain, is and ought to be totally dissolved; and that as Free and Independent States, they have full Power to levy War, conclude Peace, contract Alliances, establish Commerce, and to do all other Acts and Things which Independent States may of right do. And for the support of this Declaration, with a firm reliance on the Protection of Divine Providence, we mutually pledge to each other our Lives, our Fortunes and our sacred Honor.

THE CONSTITUTION OF THE UNITED STATES

We the people of the United States, in Order to form a more perfect Union, establish Justice, insure domestic Tranquility, provide for the common defence, promote the general Welfare, and secure the Blessings of Liberty to ourselves and our Posterity, do ordain and establish this CONSTITUTION for the United States of America.

ARTICLE I

Section 1. All legislative Powers herein granted shall be vested in a Congress of the United States, which shall consist of a Senate and House of Representatives.

Section 2. The House of Representatives shall be composed of Members chosen every second Year by the People of the several States, and the Electors in each State shall have the Qualifications requisite for Electors of the most numerous Branch of the State Legislature.

No Person shall be a Representative who shall not have attained to the Age of twenty-five Years, and been seven Years a Citizen of the United States, and who shall not, when elected, be an Inhabitant of that State in which he shall be chosen.

Representatives and direct Taxes shall be apportioned among the several States which may be included within this Union, according to their respective Numbers, which shall be determined by adding to the whole Number of free Persons, including those bound to Service for a Term of Years, and excluding Indians not taxed, three fifths of all other Persons. The actual Enumeration shall be made within three Years after the first Meeting of the Congress of the United States, and within every subsequent Term of ten Years, in such Manner as they shall by Law direct. The Number of Representatives shall not exceed one for every thirty Thousand, but each State shall have at Least one Representative; and until such enumeration shall be made, the State of New Hampshire shall be entitled to chuse three, Massachusetts eight, Rhode-Island and Providence Plantations one, Connecticut five, New-York six, New Jersey four, Pennsylvania eight, Delaware one, Maryland six, Virginia ten, North Carolina five, South Carolina five, and Georgia three.

When vacancies happen in the Representation from any State, the Executive Authority thereof shall issue Writs of Election to fill such Vacancies.

The House of Representatives shall chuse their Speaker and other Officers; and shall have the sole Power of Impeachment.

Section 3. The Senate of the United States shall be composed of two Senators from each State, chosen by the Legislature thereof, for six Years; and each Senator shall have one Vote.

Immediately after they shall be assembled in Consequence of the first Election, they shall be divided as equally as may be into three Classes. The Seats of the Senators of the first Class shall be vacated at the Expiration of the second Year, of the second Class at the Expiration of the fourth Year, and of the third Class at the Expiration of the sixth Year, so that one-third may be chosen every second Year; and if Vacancies happen by Resignation, or otherwise, during the Recess of the Legislature of any State, the Executive thereof may make temporary Appointments until the next Meeting of the Legislature, which shall then fill such Vacancies.

No Person shall be a Senator who shall not have attained to the Age of thirty Years, and been nine Years a Citizen of the United States, and who shall not, when elected, be an Inhabitant of that State in which he shall be chosen.

The Vice President of the United States shall be President of the Senate, but shall have no vote, unless they be equally divided.

The Senate shall chuse their other Officers, and also a President pro tempore, in the absence of the Vice President, or when he shall exercise the Office of the President of the United States.

The Senate shall have the sole Power to try all Impeachments. When sitting for that purpose, they shall be on Oath or Affirmation. When the President of the United States is tried, the Chief Justice shall preside: And no person shall be convicted without the Concurrence of two thirds of the Members present.

Judgment in Cases of Impeachment shall not extend further than to removal from Office, and disqualification to hold and enjoy any Office of honor, Trust, or Profit under the United States: but the Party convicted shall nevertheless be liable and subject to Indictment, Trial, Judgment, and Punishment, according to Law.

Section 4. The Times, Places and Manner of holding Elections for Senators and Representatives, shall be prescribed in each state by the Legislature thereof; but the Congress may at any time by Law make or alter such Regulations, except as to the Places of Chusing Senators.

The Congress shall assemble at least once in every Year, and such Meeting shall be on the first Monday in December, unless they shall by Law appoint a different Day.

Section 5. Each House shall be the Judge of the Elections, Returns and Qualifications of its own Members, and a Majority of each shall constitute a Quorum to do Business; but a smaller number may adjourn from day to day, and may be authorized to compel the Attendance of absent Members, in such Manner, and under such Penalties, as each House may provide.

Each House may determine the Rules of its Proceedings, punish its Members for disorderly Behavior, and, with the Concurrence of two thirds, expel a Member.

Each House shall keep a Journal of its Proceedings, and from time to time publish the same, excepting such Parts as may in their Judgment require Secrecy; and the Yeas and Nays of the Members of either House on any question shall, at the Desire of one fifth of those Present, be entered on the Journal.

Neither House, during the Session of Congress, shall, without the Consent of the other, adjourn for more than three days, nor to any other Place than that in which the two Houses shall be sitting.

Section 6. The Senators and Representatives shall receive a Compensation for their Services, to be ascertained by Law, and paid out of the Treasury of the United States. They shall in all Cases, except Treason, Felony, and Breach of the Peace, be privileged from Arrest during their Attendance at the Session of their respective Houses, and in going to and returning from the same; and for any Speech or Debate in either House, they shall not be questioned in any other Place.

No Senator or Representative shall, during the Time for which he was elected, be appointed to any civil Office under the Authority of the United States, which shall have been created, or the Emoluments whereof shall have been increased, during such time;

and no Person holding any Office under the United States shall be a Member of either House during his continuance in Office.

Section 7. All Bills for raising Revenue shall originate in the House of Representatives; but the Senate may propose or concur with Amendments as on other bills.

Every Bill which shall have passed the House of Representatives and the Senate, shall, before it become a Law, be presented to the President of the United States; If he approve he shall sign it, but if not he shall return it, with his Objections, to that House in which it shall have originated, who shall enter the Objections at large on their Journal, and proceed to reconsider it. If after such Reconsideration two thirds of that House shall agree to pass the bill, it shall be sent, together with the objections, to the other House, by which it shall likewise be reconsidered, and if approved by two thirds of that House, it shall become a Law. But in all such Cases the Votes of both Houses shall be determined by Yeas and Nays, and the Names of the Persons voting for and against the Bill shall be entered on the Journal of each House respectively. If any Bill shall not be returned by the President within ten Days (Sundays excepted) after it shall have been presented to him, the Same shall be a Law, in like Manner as if he had signed it, unless the Congress by their Adjournment prevent its Return, in which Case it shall not be a Law.

Every Order, Resolution, or Vote to which the Concurrence of the Senate and House of Representatives may be necessary (except on a question of Adjournment) shall be presented to the President of the United States; and before the Same shall take Effect, shall be approved by him, or being disapproved by him, shall be repassed by two thirds of the Senate and House of Representatives, according to the Rules and Limitations prescribed in the Case of a Bill.

Section 8. The Congress shall have Power To lay and collect Taxes, Duties, Imposts and Excises, to pay the Debts and provide for the common Defence and general Welfare of the United States; but all Duties, Imposts and Excises shall be uniform throughout the United States;

To borrow money on the credit of the United States;

To regulate Commerce with foreign Nations, and among the several States, and with the Indian Tribes;

To establish an uniform Rule of Naturalization, and uniform Laws on the subject of Bankruptcies throughout the United States;

To coin Money, regulate the Value thereof, and of foreign Coin, and fix the Standard of Weights and Measures;

To provide for the Punishment of counterfeiting the Securities and current Coin of the United States;

To establish Post Offices and post Roads;

To promote the Progress of Science and useful Arts, by securing for limited Times to Authors and Inventors the exclusive Right to their respective Writings and Discoveries;

To constitute Tribunals inferior to the Supreme Court;

To define and punish Piracies and Felonies committed on the high Seas, and Offences against the Law of Nations;

To declare War, grant Letters of Marque and Reprisal, and make Rules concerning Captures on Land and Water;

To raise and support Armies, but no Appropriation of Money to that Use shall be for a longer Term than two Years;

To provide and maintain a Navy;

To make Rules for the Government and Regulation of the land and naval forces;

To provide for calling forth the Militia to execute the Laws of the Union, suppress Insurrections and repel Invasions;

To provide for organizing, arming, and disciplining the Militia, and for governing such Part of them as may be employed in the Service of the United States, reserving to the States respectively, the Appointment of the Officers, and the Authority of training the Militia according to the discipline prescribed by Congress;

To exercise exclusive Legislation in all Cases whatsoever, over such District (not exceeding ten Miles square) as may, by Cession of particular States, and the acceptance of Congress, become the Seat of Government of the United States, and to exercise like Authority over all Places purchased by the Consent of the Legislature of the State in which the Same shall be, for the Erection of Forts, Magazines, Arsenals, dock-Yards, and other needful Buildings;—And

To make all Laws which shall be necessary and proper for carrying into Execution the foregoing Powers, and all other Powers vested by this Constitution in the Government of the United States, or in any Department or Officer thereof.

Section 9. The Migration or Importation of such Persons as any of the States now existing shall think proper to admit, shall not be prohibited by the Congress prior to the Year one thousand eight hundred and eight, but a tax or duty may be imposed on such Importation, not exceeding ten dollars for each Person.

The privilege of the Writ of Habeas Corpus shall not be suspended, unless when in Cases of Rebellion or Invasion the public Safety may require it.

No Bill of Attainder or ex post facto Law shall be passed.

No capitation, or other direct, Tax shall be laid unless in Proportion to the Census or Enumeration herein before directed to be taken.

No Tax or Duty shall be laid on Articles exported from any State.

No Preference shall be given by any Regulation of Revenue to the Ports of one State over those of another: nor shall Vessels bound to, or from, one State, be obliged to enter, clear, or pay Duties in another.

No Money shall be drawn from the Treasury, but in Consequence of Appropriations made by Law; and a regular Statement and Account of the Receipts and Expenditures of all public Money shall be published from time to time.

No Title of Nobility shall be granted by the United States: And no Person holding any Office of Profit or Trust under them, shall, without the Consent of the Congress, accept of any present, Emolument, Office, or Title, of any kind whatever, from any King, Prince, or foreign State.

Section 10. No State shall enter into any Treaty, Alliance, or Confederation; grant Letters of Marque and Reprisal; coin Money; emit Bills of Credit; make any Thing but gold and silver Coin a Tender in Payment of Debts; pass any Bill of Attainder, ex post facto Law, or Law impairing the Obligation of Contracts, or grant any Title of Nobility.

No State shall, without the Consent of the Congress, lay any Imposts or Duties on Imports or Exports, except what may be absolutely necessary for executing its inspection Laws: and the net Produce of all Duties and Imposts, laid by any State on Imports or Exports, shall be for the Use of the Treasury of the United States; and all such Laws shall be subject to the Revision and Control of the Congress.

No State shall, without the Consent of Congress, lay any duty of Tonnage, keep Troops, or Ships of War in time of Peace, enter into any Agreement or Compact with another State, or with a foreign Power, or engage in War, unless actually invaded, or in such imminent Danger as will not admit of delay.

ARTICLE II

Section 1. The executive Power shall be vested in a President of the United States of America. He shall hold his Office during the Term of four years, and, together with the Vice-President, chosen for the same Term, be elected, as follows:

Each State shall appoint, in such Manner as the Legislature thereof may direct, a Number of Electors, equal to the whole Number of Senators and Representatives to which the State may be entitled in the Congress; but no Senator or Representative, or Person holding an Office of Trust or Profit under the United States, shall be appointed an Elector.

The Electors shall meet in their respective States, and vote by Ballot for two persons, of whom one at least shall not be an Inhabitant of the same State with themselves. And they shall make a List of all the Persons voted for, and of the Number of Votes for each; which List they shall sign and certify, and transmit sealed to the Seat of the Government of the United States, directed to the President of the Senate. The President of the Senate shall, in the Presence of the Senate and House of Representatives, open all the Certificates, and the Votes shall then be counted. The Person having the greatest Number of Votes shall be the President, if such Number be a Majority of the whole Number of Electors appointed; and if there be more than one who have such Majority, and have an equal Number of Votes, then the House of Representatives shall immediately chuse by Ballot one of them for President; and if no Person have a Majority, then from the five highest on the List the said House shall in like Manner chuse the President. But in chusing the President, the Votes shall be taken by States, the Representation from each State having one Vote; a quorum for this Purpose shall consist of a Member or Members from two-thirds of the States, and a Majority of all the States shall be necessary to a Choice. In every Case, after the Choice of the President, the Person having the greatest Number of Votes of the Electors shall be the Vice President. But if there should remain two or more who have equal votes, the Senate shall chuse from them by Ballot the Vice-President.

The Congress may determine the Time of chusing the Electors, and the Day on which they shall give their Votes; which Day shall be the same throughout the United States.

No person except a natural-born Citizen, or a Citizen of the United States, at the time of the Adoption of this Constitution, shall be eligible to the Office of President; neither shall any Person be eligible to that Office who shall not have attained to the Age of thirty-five years, and been fourteen Years a Resident within the United States.

In Case of the Removal of the President from Office, or of his Death, Resignation, or Inability to discharge the Powers and Duties of the said Office, the same shall devolve on the Vice President, and the Congress may by Law provide for the Case of Removal, Death, Resignation, or Inability, both of the President and Vice President, declaring what Officer shall then act as President, and such Officer shall act accordingly, until the disability be removed, or a President shall be elected.

The President shall, at stated Times, receive for his Services a Compensation, which shall neither be increased nor diminished during the Period for which he shall have been elected, and he shall not receive within that Period any other Emolument from the United States, or any of them.

Before he enter on the execution of his Office, he shall take the following Oath or Affirmation:—"I do solemnly swear (or affirm) that I will faithfully execute the Office of President of the United States, and will, to the best of my Ability, preserve, protect, and defend the Constitution of the United States."

Section 2. The President shall be Commander in Chief of the Army and Navy of the United States, and of the Militia of the several States, when called into the actual Service of the United States; he may require the Opinion, in writing, of the principal Officer in each of the executive Departments, upon any subject relating to the Duties of their respective Offices, and he shall have Power to Grant Reprieves and Pardons for Offences against the United States, except in Cases of Impeachment.

He shall have Power, by and with the Advice and Consent of the Senate, to make Treaties, provided two thirds of the Senators present concur; and he shall nominate, and by and with the Advice and Consent of the Senate, shall appoint Ambassadors, other public Ministers and Consuls, Judges of the supreme Court, and all other Officers of the United States, whose Appointments are not herein otherwise provided for, and which shall be established by Law: but the Congress may by Law vest the Appointment of such inferior Officers, as they think proper, in the President alone, in the Courts of Law, or in the Heads of Departments.

The President shall have Power to fill up all Vacancies that may happen during the Recess of the Senate, by granting Commissions which shall expire at the End of their next Session.

Section 3. He shall from time to time give to the Congress Information of the State of the Union, and recommend to their Consideration such Measures as he shall judge necessary and expedient; he may, on extraordinary occasions, convene both Houses, or either of them, and in Case of Disagreement between them, with respect to the Time of Adjournment, he may adjourn them to such Time as he shall think proper; he shall receive Ambassadors and other public Ministers; he shall take Care that the Laws be faithfully executed, and shall Commission all the Officers of the United States.

Section 4. The President, Vice President and all civil Officers of the United States, shall be removed from Office on Impeachment for, and Conviction of, Treason, Bribery, or other high Crimes and Misdemeanors.

ARTICLE III

Section 1. The judicial Power of the United States, shall be vested in one supreme Court, and in such inferior Courts as the Congress may from time to time ordain and establish. The Judges, both of the supreme and inferior Courts, shall hold their Offices during good Behaviour, and shall, at stated Times, receive for their Services, a Compensation, which shall not be diminished during their Continuance in Office.

Section 2. The judicial Power shall extend to all Cases, in Law and Equity, arising under this Constitution, the Laws of the United States, and treaties made, or which shall be made, under their Authority;—to all Cases affecting ambassadors, other public ministers and consuls;—to all cases of admiralty and maritime Jurisdiction;—to Controversies to which the United States shall be a Party;—to Controversies between two or more States;—between a State and Citizens of another State;—between Citizens of different States,—between Citizens of the same State claiming Lands under Grants of different States, and between a State, or the Citizens thereof, and foreign States, Citizens or Subjects.

In all Cases affecting Ambassadors, other public Ministers and Consuls, and those in which a State shall be Party, the supreme Court shall have original Jurisdiction. In all the other Cases before mentioned, the supreme Court shall have appellate Jurisdiction, both as to Law and Fact, with such Exceptions, and under such Regulations as the Congress shall make.

The trial of all Crimes, except in Cases of Impeachment, shall be by Jury; and such Trial shall be held in the State where the said Crimes shall have been committed; but when not committed within any State, the Trial shall be at such Place or Places as the Congress may by Law have directed.

Section 3. Treason against the United States, shall consist only in levying War against them, or in adhering to their Enemies, giving them Aid and Comfort. No Person shall be convicted of Treason unless on the Testimony of two Witnesses to the same overt Act, or on Confession in open Court.

The Congress shall have power to declare the Punishment of Treason, but no Attainder of Treason shall work Corruption of Blood, or Forfeiture except during the Life of the Person attainted.

ARTICLE IV

Section 1. Full Faith and Credit shall be given in each State to the public Acts, Records, and judicial Proceedings of every other State. And the Congress may by general Laws prescribe the Manner in which such Acts, Records and Proceedings shall be proved, and the Effect thereof.

Section 2. The Citizens of each State shall be entitled to all Privileges and Immunities of Citizens in the several States.

A Person charged in any State with Treason, Felony, or other Crime, who shall flee from Justice, and be found in another State, shall on demand of the executive Authority of the State from which he fled, be delivered up, to be removed to the State having Jurisdiction of the crime.

No Person held to Service or Labour in one State, under the Laws thereof, escaping into another, shall, in Consequence of any Law or Regulation therein, be discharged from such Service or Labour, but shall be delivered up on Claim of the Party to whom such Service or Labour may be due.

Section 3. New States may be admitted by the Congress into this Union; but no new State shall be formed or erected within the Jurisdiction of any other State; nor any State be formed by the Junction of two or more States, or parts of States, without the Consent of the Legislatures of the States concerned as well as of the Congress.

The Congress shall have Power to dispose of and make all needful Rules and Regulations respecting the Territory or other Property belonging to the United States; and nothing in this Constitution shall be so construed as to Prejudice any Claims of the United States, or of any particular State.

Section 4. The United States shall guarantee to every State in this Union a Republican Form of Government, and shall protect each of them against Invasion; and on Application of the Legislature, or the Executive (when the Legislature cannot be convened) against domestic Violence.

ARTICLE V

The Congress, whenever two-thirds of both Houses shall deem it necessary, shall propose Amendments to this Constitution, or, on the Application of the Legislatures of two-thirds of the several States, shall call a Convention for proposing Amendments, which, in either Case, shall be valid to all Intents and Purposes, as part of this Constitution, when ratified by the Legislatures of three-fourths of the several States, or by Conventions in three-fourths thereof, as the one or the other Mode of Ratification may be proposed by the Congress; Provided that no Amendment which may be made prior to the Year One thousand eight hundred and eight shall in any Manner affect the first and fourth Clauses in the Ninth Section of the first Article; and that no State, without its Consent, shall be deprived of its equal Suffrage in the Senate.

ARTICLE VI

All Debts contracted and Engagements entered into, before the Adoption of this Constitution, shall be as valid against the United States under this Constitution, as under the Confederation.

This Constitution, and the Laws of the United States which shall be made in Pursuance thereof; and all Treaties made, or which shall be made, under the Authority of the United States, shall be the supreme Law of the Land; and the Judges in every State shall be bound thereby, any Thing in the Constitution or Laws of any State to the Contrary notwithstanding.

The Senators and Representatives before mentioned, and the Members of the several State Legislatures, and all executive and judicial Officers, both of the United States and of the several States, shall be bound by Oath or Affirmation to support this Constitution; but no religious Test shall ever be required as a qualification to any Office or public Trust under the United States.

ARTICLE VII

The Ratification of the Conventions of nine States shall be sufficient for the Establishment of this Constitution between the States so ratifying the same.

Done in Convention by the Unanimous Consent of the States present the Seventeenth Day of September in the Year of our Lord one thousand seven hundred and Eighty seven, and of the Independence of the United States of America the Twelfth. In Witness whereof We have hereunto subscribed our Names.

Articles in Addition to, and Amendment of, the Constitution of the United States of America, Proposed by Congress, and Ratified by the Legislatures of the Several States, Pursuant to the Fifth Article of the Original Constitution.

AMENDMENT I [1791]

Congress shall make no law respecting an establishment of religion, or prohibiting the free exercise thereof; or abridging the freedom of speech, or of the press; or the right of the people peaceably to assemble, and to petition the Government for a redress of grievances.

AMENDMENT II [1791]

A well regulated Militia, being necessary to the security of a free State, the right of the people to keep and bear Arms shall not be infringed.

AMENDMENT III [1791]

No Soldier shall, in time of peace, be quartered in any house, without the consent of the Owner, nor in time of war, but in a manner to be prescribed by law.

AMENDMENT IV [1791]

The right of the people to be secure in their persons, houses, papers, and effects, against unreasonable searches and seizures, shall not be violated, and no Warrants shall issue, but upon probable cause, supported by Oath or affirmation, and particularly describing the place to be searched, and the persons or things to be seized.

AMENDMENT V [1791]

No person shall be held to answer for a capital or otherwise infamous crime, unless on a presentment or indictment of a Grand Jury, except in cases arising in the land or naval forces, or in the Militia, when in actual service in time of War or public danger; nor shall any person be subject for the same offence to be twice put in jeopardy of life or limb; nor shall be compelled in any criminal case to be a witness against himself, nor be deprived of life, liberty, or property, without due process of law; nor shall private property be taken for public use, without just compensation.

AMENDMENT VI [1791]

In all criminal prosecutions, the accused shall enjoy the right to a speedy and public trial, by an impartial jury of the State and district wherein the crime shall have been committed, which district shall have been previously ascertained by law, and to be informed of the nature and cause of the accusation; to be confronted with the witnesses against him; to have compulsory process for obtaining witnesses in his favor, and to have the Assistance of Counsel for his defence.

AMENDMENT VII [1791]

In suits at common law, where the value in controversy shall exceed twenty dollars, the right of trial by jury shall be preserved, and no fact tried by a jury, shall be otherwise reexamined in any Court of the United States, than according to the rules of the common law.

AMENDMENT VIII [1791]

Excessive bail shall not be required, nor excessive fines imposed, nor cruel and unusual punishments inflicted.

AMENDMENT IX [1791]

The enumeration in the Constitution, of certain rights, shall not be construed to deny or disparage others retained by the people.

AMENDMENT X [1791]

The powers not delegated to the United States by the Constitution, nor prohibited by it to the States, are reserved to the States respectively, or to the people.

AMENDMENT XI [1798]

The Judicial power of the United States shall not be construed to extend to any suit in law or equity, commenced or prosecuted against one of the United

States by Citizens of another State, or by Citizens or Subjects of any Foreign State.

AMENDMENT XII [1804]

The Electors shall meet in their respective States and vote by ballot for President and Vice-President, one of whom, at least, shall not be an inhabitant of the same State with themselves; they shall name in their ballots the person voted for as President, and in distinct ballots the person voted for as Vice-President, and they shall make distinct lists of all persons voted for as President, and of all persons voted for as Vice-President, and of the number of votes for each, which lists they shall sign and certify, and transmit sealed to the seat of the government of the United States, directed to the President of the Senate;—The President of the Senate shall, in the presence of the Senate and House of Representatives, open all the certificates and the votes shall then be counted;—The person having the greatest number of votes for President, shall be the President, if such number be a majority of the whole number of Electors appointed; and if no person have such majority, then from the persons having the highest numbers not exceeding three on the list of those voted for as President, the House of Representatives shall choose immediately, by ballot, the President. But in choosing the President, the votes shall be taken by states, the representation from each state having one vote; a quorum for this purpose shall consist of a member or members from two-thirds of the states, and a majority of all the states shall be necessary to a choice. And if the House of Representatives shall not choose a President whenever the right of choice shall devolve upon them, before the fourth day of March next following, then the Vice-President shall act as President, as in the case of the death or other constitutional disability of the President.—The person having the greatest number of votes as Vice-President, shall be the Vice-President, if such number be a majority of the whole number of Electors appointed, and if no person have a majority, then from the two highest numbers on the list, the Senate shall choose the Vice-President; a quorum for the purpose shall consist of two-thirds of the whole number of Senators, and a majority of the whole number shall be necessary to a choice. But no person constitutionally ineligible to the office of President shall be eligible to that of Vice-President of the United States.

AMENDMENT XIII [1865]

Section 1. Neither slavery nor involuntary servitude, except as a punishment for crime whereof the party shall have been duly convicted, shall exist within the United States, or any place subject to their jurisdiction.

Section 2. Congress shall have power to enforce this article by appropriate legislation.

AMENDMENT XIV [1868]

Section 1. All persons born or naturalized in the United States, and subject to the jurisdiction thereof, are citizens of the United States and of the State wherein they reside. No State shall make or enforce any law which shall abridge the privileges or immunities of citizens of the United States; nor shall any State deprive any person of life, liberty, or property, without due process of law; nor deny to any person within its jurisdiction the equal protection of the laws.

Section 2. Representatives shall be apportioned among the several States according to their respective numbers, counting the whole number of persons in each State, excluding Indians not taxed. But when the right to vote at any election for the choice of electors for President and Vice-President of the United States, Representatives in Congress, the Executive and Judicial officers of a State, or the members of the Legislature thereof, is denied to any of the male inhabitants of such State, being twenty-one years of age, and citizens of the United States, or in any way abridged, except for participation in rebellion, or other crime, the basis of representation therein shall be reduced in the proportion which the number of such male citizens shall bear to the whole number of male citizens twenty-one years of age in such State.

Section 3. No person shall be a Senator or Representative in Congress, or elector of President and Vice-President, or hold any office, civil or military, under the United States, or under any State, who, having previously taken an oath, as a member of Congress, or as an officer of the United States, or as a member of any State legislature, or as an executive or judicial officer of any State, to support the Constitution of the United States, shall have engaged in insurrection or rebellion against the same, or given aid or comfort to the enemies thereof. But Congress may by a vote of two-thirds of each House, remove such disability.

Section 4. The validity of the public debt of the United States, authorized by law, including debts incurred for payment of pensions and bounties for services in suppressing insurrection or rebellion, shall not be questioned. But neither the United States nor any State shall assume or pay any debt or obligation incurred in aid of insurrection or rebellion against the United States, or any claim for the loss or emancipation of any slave; but all such debts, obligations, and claims shall be held illegal and void.

Section 5. The Congress shall have the power to enforce, by appropriate legislation, the provisions of this article.

AMENDMENT XV [1870]

Section 1. The right of citizens of the United States to vote shall not be denied or abridged by the United States or by any State on account of race, color, or previous condition of servitude—

Section 2. The Congress shall have power to enforce this article by appropriate legislation.

AMENDMENT XVI [1913]

The Congress shall have power to lay and collect taxes on incomes, from whatever source derived, without apportionment among the several States, and without regard to any census or enumeration.

AMENDMENT XVII [1913]

The Senate of the United States shall be composed of two Senators from each State, elected by the people thereof, for six years; and each Senator shall have one vote. The electors in each State shall have the qualifications requisite for electors of the most numerous branch of the State legislatures.

When vacancies happen in the representation of any State in the Senate, the executive authority of such State shall issue writs of election to fill such vacancies: *Provided,* That the legislature of any State may empower the executive thereof to make temporary appointments until the people fill the vacancies by election as the legislature may direct.

This amendment shall not be so construed as to affect the election or term of any Senator chosen before it becomes valid as part of the Constitution.

AMENDMENT XVIII [1919]

Section 1. After one year from the ratification of this article the manufacture, sale, or transportation of intoxicating liquors within, the importation thereof into, or the exportation thereof from the United States and all territory subject to the jurisdiction thereof for beverage purposes is hereby prohibited.

Section 2. The Congress and the several States shall have concurrent power to enforce this article by appropriate legislation.

Section 3. This article shall be inoperative unless it shall have been ratified as an amendment to the Constitution by the legislatures of the several States, as provided in the Constitution, within seven years from the date of the submission hereof to the States by the Congress.

AMENDMENT XIX [1920]

The right of citizens of the United States to vote shall not be denied or abridged by the United States or by any State on account of sex.

Congress shall have power to enforce this article by appropriate legislation.

AMENDMENT XX [1933]

Section 1. The terms of the President and Vice-President shall end at noon on the 20th day of January, and the terms of Senators and Representatives at noon on the 3d day of January, of the years in which such terms would have ended if this article had not been ratified; and the terms of their successors shall then begin.

Section 2. The Congress shall assemble at least once in every year, and such meeting shall begin at noon on the 3d day of January, unless they shall by law appoint a different day.

Section 3. If, at the time fixed for the beginning of the term of the President, the President elect shall have died, the Vice-President elect shall become President. If a President shall not have been chosen before the time fixed for the beginning of his term, or if the President elect shall have failed to qualify, then the Vice-President elect shall act as President until a President shall have qualified; and the Congress may by law provide for the case wherein neither a President elect nor a Vice-President elect shall have qualified, declaring who shall then act as President, or the manner in which one who is to act shall be selected, and such person shall act accordingly until a President or Vice-President shall have qualified.

Section 4. The Congress may by law provide for the case of the death of any of the persons from whom the House of Representatives may choose a President whenever the right of choice shall have devolved upon them, and for the case of the death of any of the persons from whom the Senate may choose a Vice-President whenever the right of choice shall have devolved upon them.

Section 5. Sections 1 and 2 shall take effect on the 15th day of October following the ratification of this article.

Section 6. This article shall be inoperative unless it shall have been ratified as an amendment to the Constitution by the legislatures of three-fourths of the several States within seven years from the date of its submission.

AMENDMENT XXI [1933]

Section 1. The eighteenth article of amendment to the Constitution of the United States is hereby repealed.

Section 2. The transportation or importation into any State, Territory, or possession of the United States for delivery or use therein of intoxicating liquors, in violation of the laws thereof, is hereby prohibited.

Section 3. This article shall be inoperative unless it shall have been ratified as an amendment to the Constitution by conventions in the several States, as provided in the Constitution, within seven years from the date of the submission hereof to the States by the Congress.

AMENDMENT XXII [1951]

No person shall be elected to the office of the President more than twice, and no person who has held the office of President, or acted as President, for more than two years of a term to which some other person was elected President shall be elected to the office of the President more than once.

But this Article shall not apply to any person holding the office of President when this Article was proposed by the Congress, and shall not prevent any person who may be holding the office of President, or acting as President, during the term within which this Article becomes operative from holding the office of President or acting as President during the remainder of such term.

AMENDMENT XXIII [1961]

Section 1. The District constituting the seat of Government of the United States shall appoint in such manner as the Congress may direct:

A number of electors of President and Vice President equal to the whole number of Senators and Representatives in Congress to which the District would be entitled if it were a State, but in no event more than the least populous State; they shall be in addition to those appointed by the States, but they shall be considered, for the purposes of the election of President and Vice President, to be electors appointed by a State; and they shall meet in the District and perform such duties as provided by the twelfth article of amendment.

Section 2. The Congress shall have power to enforce this article by appropriate legislation.

AMENDMENT XXIV [1964]

Section 1. The right of citizens of the United States to vote in any primary or other election for President or Vice President, for electors for President or Vice President, or for Senator or Representative in Congress, shall not be denied or abridged by the United States or any State by reason of failure to pay any poll tax or other tax.

Section 2. The Congress shall have the power to enforce this article by appropriate legislation.

AMENDMENT XXV [1967]

Section 1. In case of the removal of the President from office or his death or resignation, the Vice President shall become President.

Section 2. Whenever there is a vacancy in the office of the Vice President, the President shall nominate a Vice President who shall take the office upon confirmation by a majority vote of both houses of Congress.

Section 3. Whenever the President transmits to the President pro tempore of the Senate and the Speaker of the House of Representatives his written declaration that he is unable to discharge the powers and duties of his office, and until he transmits to them a written declaration to the contrary, such powers and duties shall be discharged by the Vice President as Acting President.

Section 4. Whenever the Vice President and a majority of either the principal officers of the executive departments, or of such other body as Congress may by law provide, transmit to the President pro tempore of the Senate and the Speaker of the House of Representatives their written declaration that the President is unable to discharge the powers and duties of his office, the Vice President shall immediately assume the powers and duties of the office as Acting President.

Thereafter, when the President transmits to the President pro tempore of the Senate and the Speaker of the House of Representatives his written declaration that no inability exists, he shall resume the powers and duties of his office unless the Vice President and a majority of either the principal officers of the executive departments, or of such other body as Congress may by law provide, transmit within four days to the President pro tempore of the Senate and the Speaker of the House of Representatives their written declaration that the President is unable to discharge the powers and duties of his office. Thereupon Congress shall decide the issue, assembling within 48 hours for that purpose if not in session. If the Congress, within 21 days after receipt of the latter written declaration, or, if Congress is not in session, within 21 days after Congress is required to assemble, determines by two-thirds vote of both houses that the President is unable to discharge the powers and duties of his office, the Vice President shall continue to discharge the same as Acting President; otherwise, the President shall resume the powers and duties of his office.

AMENDMENT XXVI [1971]

Section 1. The right of citizens of the United States, who are 18 years of age or older, to vote shall not be denied or abridged by the United States or any state on account of age.

Section 2. The Congress shall have the power to enforce this article by appropriate legislation.

PRESIDENTIAL ELECTIONS, 1789–1980

Year	Candidates	Party	Popular Vote	Electoral Vote
1789	**George Washington**			69
	John Adams			34
	Others			35
1792	**George Washington**			132
	John Adams			77
	George Clinton			50
	Others			5
1796	**John Adams**	Federalist		71
	Thomas Jefferson	Democratic-Republican		68
	Thomas Pinckney	Federalist		59
	Aaron Burr	Democratic-Republican		30
	Others			48
1800	**Thomas Jefferson**	Democratic-Republican		73
	Aaron Burr	Democratic-Republican		73
	John Adams	Federalist		65
	Charles C. Pinckney	Federalist		64
1804	**Thomas Jefferson**	Democratic-Republican		162
	Charles C. Pinckney	Federalist		14
1808	**James Madison**	Democratic-Republican		122
	Charles C. Pinckney	Federalist		47
	George Clinton	Independent-Republican		6
1812	**James Madison**	Democratic-Republican		128
	DeWitt Clinton	Federalist		89
1816	**James Monroe**	Democratic-Republican		183
	Rufus King	Federalist		34
1820	**James Monroe**	Democratic-Republican		231
	John Quincy Adams	Independent-Republican		1
1824	**John Quincy Adams**	Democratic-Republican	108,740 (30.5%)	84
	Andrew Jackson	Democratic-Republican	153,544 (43.1%)	99
	Henry Clay	Democratic-Republican	47,136 (13.2%)	37
	William H. Crawford	Democratic-Republican	46,618 (13.1%)	41

Year	Candidates	Party	Popular Vote	Electoral Vote
1828	**Andrew Jackson**	Democratic	647,231 (56.0%)	178
	John Quincy Adams	National Republican	509,097 (44.0%)	83
1832	**Andrew Jackson**	Democratic	687,502 (55.0%)	219
	Henry Clay	National Republican	530,189 (42.4%)	49
	William Wirt	Anti-Masonic	33,108 (2.6%)	7
	John Floyd	National Republican		11
1836	**Martin Van Buren**	Democratic	761,549 (50.9%)	170
	William H. Harrison	Whig	549,567 (36.7%)	73
	Hugh L. White	Whig	145,396 (9.7%)	26
	Daniel Webster	Whig	41,287 (2.7%)	14
1840	**William H. Harrison** (**John Tyler**, 1841)	Whig	1,275,017 (53.1%)	234
	Martin Van Buren	Democratic	1,128,702 (46.9%)	60
1844	**James K. Polk**	Democratic	1,337,243 (49.6%)	170
	Henry Clay	Whig	1,299,068 (48.1%)	105
	James G. Birney	Liberty	62,300 (2.3%)	
1848	**Zachary Taylor** (**Millard Fillmore**, 1850)	Whig	1,360,101 (47.4%)	163
	Lewis Cass	Democratic	1,220,544 (42.5%)	127
	Martin Van Buren	Free Soil	291,263 (10.1%)	
1852	**Franklin Pierce**	Democratic	1,601,474 (50.9%)	254
	Winfield Scott	Whig	1,386,578 (44.1%)	42
1856	**James Buchanan**	Democratic	1,838,169 (45.4%)	174
	John C. Frémont	Republican	1,335,264 (33.0%)	114
	Millard Fillmore	American	874,534 (21.6%)	8
1860	**Abraham Lincoln**	Republican	1,865,593 (39.8%)	180
	Stephen A. Douglas	Democratic	1,382,713 (29.5%)	12
	John C. Breckinridge	Democratic	848,356 (18.1%)	72
	John Bell	Constitutional Union	592,906 (12.6%)	39
1864	**Abraham Lincoln** (**Andrew Johnson**, 1865)	Republican	2,206,938 (55.0%)	212
	George B. McClellan	Democratic	1,803,787 (45.0%)	21
1868	**Ulysses S. Grant**	Republican	3,013,421 (52.7%)	214
	Horatio Seymour	Democratic	2,706,829 (47.3%)	80
1872	**Ulysses S. Grant**	Republican	3,596,745 (55.6%)	286
	Horace Greeley	Democratic	2,843,446 (43.9%)	66
1876	**Rutherford B. Hayes**	Republican	4,036,572 (48.0%)	185
	Samuel J. Tilden	Democratic	4,284,020 (51.0%)	184

Year	Candidates	Party	Popular Vote	Electoral Vote
1880	**James A. Garfield** (**Chester A. Arthur**, 1881)	Republican	4,449,053 (48.3%)	214
	Winfield S. Hancock	Democratic	4,442,035 (48.2%)	155
	James B. Weaver	Greenback-Labor	308,578 (3.4%)	
1884	**Grover Cleveland**	Democratic	4,874,986 (48.5%)	219
	James G. Blaine	Republican	4,851,981 (48.2%)	182
	Benjamin F. Butler	Greenback-Labor	175,370 (1.8%)	
1888	**Benjamin Harrison**	Republican	5,444,337 (47.8%)	233
	Grover Cleveland	Democratic	5,540,050 (48.6%)	168
1892	**Grover Cleveland**	Democratic	5,554,414 (46.0%)	277
	Benjamin Harrison	Republican	5,190,802 (43.0%)	145
	James B. Weaver	People's	1,027,329 (8.5%)	22
1896	**William McKinley**	Republican	7,035,638 (50.8%)	271
	William J. Bryan	Democratic; Populist	6,467,946 (46.7%)	176
1900	**William McKinley** (**Theodore Roosevelt**, 1901)	Republican	7,219,530 (51.7%)	292
	William J. Bryan	Democratic; Populist	6,356,734 (45.5%)	155
1904	**Theodore Roosevelt**	Republican	7,628,834 (56.4%)	336
	Alton B. Parker	Democratic	5,084,401 (37.6%)	140
	Eugene V. Debs	Socialist	402,460 (3.0%)	
1908	**William H. Taft**	Republican	7,679,006 (51.6%)	321
	William J. Bryan	Democratic	6,409,106 (43.1%)	162
	Eugene V. Debs	Socialist	420,820 (2.8%)	
1912	**Woodrow Wilson**	Democratic	6,286,820 (41.8%)	435
	Theodore Roosevelt	Progressive	4,126,020 (27.4%)	88
	William H. Taft	Republican	3,483,922 (23.2%)	8
	Eugene V. Debs	Socialist	897,011 (6.0%)	
1916	**Woodrow Wilson**	Democratic	9,129,606 (49.3%)	277
	Charles E. Hughes	Republican	8,538,221 (46.1%)	254
1920	**Warren G. Harding** (**Calvin Coolidge**, 1923)	Republican	16,152,200 (61.0%)	404
	James M. Cox	Democratic	9,147,353 (34.6%)	127
	Eugene V. Debs	Socialist	919,799 (3.5%)	
1924	**Calvin Coolidge**	Republican	15,725,016 (54.1%)	382
	John W. Davis	Democratic	8,385,586 (28.8%)	136
	Robert M. La Follette	Progressive	4,822,856 (16.6%)	13
1928	**Herbert C. Hoover**	Republican	21,392,190 (58.2%)	444
	Alfred E. Smith	Democratic	15,016,443 (40.8%)	87

Year	Candidates	Party	Popular Vote	Electoral Vote
1932	**Franklin D. Roosevelt**	Democratic	22,809,638 (57.3%)	472
	Herbert C. Hoover	Republican	15,758,901 (39.6%)	59
	Norman Thomas	Socialist	881,951 (2.2%)	
1936	**Franklin D. Roosevelt**	Democratic	27,751,612 (60.7%)	523
	Alfred M. Landon	Republican	16,681,913 (36.4%)	8
	William Lemke	Union	891,858 (1.9%)	
1940	**Franklin D. Roosevelt**	Democratic	27,243,466 (54.7%)	449
	Wendell L. Wilkie	Republican	22,304,755 (44.8%)	82
1944	**Franklin D. Roosevelt** **(Harry S Truman**, 1945)	Democratic	25,602,505 (52.8%)	432
	Thomas E. Dewey	Republican	22,006,278 (44.5%)	99
1948	**Harry S Truman**	Democratic	24,105,812 (49.5%)	303
	Thomas E. Dewey	Republican	21,970,065 (45.1%)	189
	J. Strom Thurmond	States' Rights	1,169,063 (2.4%)	39
	Henry A. Wallace	Progressive	1,157,172 (2.4%)	
1952	**Dwight D. Eisenhower**	Republican	33,936,234 (55.2%)	442
	Adlai E. Stevenson	Democratic	27,314,992 (44.5%)	89
1956	**Dwight D. Eisenhower**	Republican	35,590,472 (57.4%)	457
	Adlai E. Stevenson	Democratic	26,022,752 (42.0%)	73
1960	**John F. Kennedy** **(Lyndon B. Johnson**, 1963)	Democratic	34,227,096 (49.9%)	303
	Richard M. Nixon	Republican	34,108,546 (49.6%)	219
1964	**Lyndon B. Johnson**	Democratic	43,126,233 (61.1%)	486
	Barry M. Goldwater	Republican	27,174,989 (38.5%)	52
1968	**Richard M. Nixon**	Republican	31,783,783 (43.4%)	301
	Hubert H. Humphrey	Democratic	31,271,839 (42.7%)	191
	George C. Wallace	Amer. Independent	9,899,557 (13.5%)	46
1972	**Richard M. Nixon** **(Gerald R. Ford**, 1974)	Republican	45,767,218 (60.6%)	520
	George S. McGovern	Democratic	28,357,668 (37.5%)	17
1976	**Jimmy Carter**	Democratic	40,828,657 (50.6%)	297
	Gerald R. Ford	Republican	39,145,520 (48.4%)	240
1980	**Ronald Reagan**	Republican	43,899,248 (51%)	489
	Jimmy Carter	Democrat	36,481,435 (41%)	49
	John B. Anderson	Independent	5,719,437 (6%)	

Because only the leading candidates are listed, popular vote percentages do not always total 100. The elections of 1800 and 1824, in which no candidate received an electoral-vote majority, were decided in the House of Representatives.

THE VICE-PRESIDENCY AND THE CABINET, 1789–1982

Vice-President

John Adams	1789–97
Thomas Jefferson	1797–1801
Aaron Burr	1801–05
George Clinton	1805–13
Elbridge Gerry	1813–17
Daniel D. Tompkins	1817–25
John C. Calhoun	1825–33
Martin Van Buren	1833–37
Richard M. Johnson	1837–41
John Tyler	1841
George M. Dallas	1845–49
Millard Fillmore	1849–50
William R. King	1853–57
John C. Breckinridge	1857–61
Hannibal Hamlin	1861–65
Andrew Johnson	1865
Schuyler Colfax	1869–73
Henry Wilson	1873–77
William A. Wheeler	1877–81
Chester A. Arthur	1881
Thomas A. Hendricks	1885–89
Levi P. Morton	1889–93
Adlai E. Stevenson	1893–97
Garret A. Hobart	1897–99
Theodore Roosevelt	1901
Charles W. Fairbanks	1905–09
James S. Sherman	1909–13
Thomas R. Marshall	1913–21
Calvin Coolidge	1921–23
Charles G. Dawes	1925–29
Charles Curtis	1929–33
John Nance Garner	1933–41
Henry A. Wallace	1941–45
Harry S Truman	1945
Alben W. Barkley	1949–53
Richard M. Nixon	1953–61
Lyndon B. Johnson	1961–63
Hubert H. Humphrey	1965–69
Spiro T. Agnew	1969–73
Gerald R. Ford	1973–74
Nelson Rockefeller	1974–77
Walter F. Mondale	1977–81
George Bush	1981–

Secretary of State (1789–)

Thomas Jefferson	1789
Edmund Randolph	1794
Timothy Pickering	1795
John Marshall	1800
James Madison	1801
Robert Smith	1809
James Monroe	1811
John Q. Adams	1817
Henry Clay	1825
Martin Van Buren	1829
Edward Livingston	1831
Louis McLane	1833
John Forsyth	1834
Daniel Webster	1841
Hugh S. Legaré	1843
Abel P. Upshur	1843
John C. Calhoun	1844
James Buchanan	1845
John M. Clayton	1849
Daniel Webster	1850
Edward Everett	1852
William L. Marcy	1853
Lewis Cass	1857
Jeremiah S. Black	1860
William H. Seward	1861
E.B. Washburne	1869
Hamilton Fish	1869
William M. Evarts	1877
James G. Blaine	1881
F.T. Frelinghuysen	1881
Thomas F. Bayard	1885
James G. Blaine	1889
John W. Foster	1892
Walter Q. Gresham	1893
Richard Olney	1895
John Sherman	1897
William R. Day	1897
John Hay	1898
Elihu Root	1905
Robert Bacon	1909
Philander C. Knox	1909
William J. Bryan	1913
Robert Lansing	1915
Bainbridge Colby	1920
Charles E. Hughes	1921
Frank B. Kellogg	1925
Henry L. Stimson	1929
Cordell Hull	1933
E.R. Stettinius, Jr.	1944
James F. Byrnes	1945
George C. Marshall	1947
Dean Acheson	1949
John Foster Dulles	1953
Christian A. Herter	1959
Dean Rusk	1961
William P. Rogers	1969
Henry A. Kissinger	1973
Cyrus R. Vance	1977
Alexander M. Haig, Jr.	1981

Secretary of the Treasury (1789–)

Alexander Hamilton	1789
Oliver Wolcott	1795
Samuel Dexter	1801
Albert Gallatin	1801
G.W. Campbell	1814
A.J. Dallas	1814
William H. Crawford	1816

Richard Rush	1825	Henry Morgenthau,		Jefferson Davis	1853	Smith Thompson	1818
Samuel D.		Jr.	1934	John B. Floyd	1857	S.L. Southard	1823
Ingham	1829	Fred M. Vinson	1945	Joseph Holt	1861	John Branch	1829
Louis McLane	1831	John W. Snyder	1946	Simon Cameron	1861	Levi Woodbury	1831
William J. Duane	1833	George M.		Edwin M. Stanton	1862	Mahlon	
Roger B. Taney	1833	Humphrey	1953	Ulysses S. Grant	1867	Dickerson	1834
Levi Woodbury	1834	Robert B.		Lorenzo Thomas	1868	James K.	
Thomas Ewing	1841	Anderson	1957	John M. Schofield	1868	Paulding	1838
Walter Forward	1841	C. Douglas		John A. Rawlins	1869	George E. Badger	1841
John C. Spencer	1843	Dillon	1961	William T.		Abel P. Upshur	1841
George M. Bibb	1844	Henry H. Fowler	1965	Sherman	1869	David Henshaw	1843
Robert J. Walker	1845	David M.		William W.		Thomas W.	
William M.		Kennedy	1969	Belknap	1869	Gilmer	1844
Meredith	1849	John B. Connally	1970	Alphonso Taft	1876	John Y. Mason	1844
Thomas Corwin	1850	George P. Shultz	1972	James D.		George Bancroft	1845
James Guthrie	1853	William E. Simon	1974	Cameron	1876	John Y. Mason	1846
Howell Cobb	1857	W. Michael		George W.		William B.	
Philip F. Thomas	1860	Blumenthal	1977	McCrary	1877	Preston	1849
John A. Dix	1861	G. William Miller	1979	Alexander		William A.	
Salmon P. Chase	1861	Donald T. Regan	1981	Ramsey	1879	Graham	1850
Wm. P.				Robert T. Lincoln	1881	John P. Kennedy	1852
Fessenden	1864			William C.		James C. Dobbin	1853
Hugh McCulloch	1865	**Secretary of War**		Endicott	1885	Isaac Toucey	1857
George S.		**(1789–1947)**		Redfield Proctor	1889	Gideon Welles	1861
Boutwell	1869			Stephen B. Elkins	1891	Adolph E. Borie	1869
William A.		Henry Knox	1789	Daniel S. Lamont	1893	George M.	
Richardson	1873	Timothy		Russell A. Alger	1897	Robeson	1869
Benjamin H.		Pickering	1795	Elihu Root	1899	R.W. Thompson	1877
Bristow	1874	James McHenry	1796	William H. Taft	1904	Nathan Goff, Jr.	1881
Lot M. Morrill	1876	John Marshall	1800	Luke E. Wright	1908	William H. Hunt	1881
John Sherman	1877	Samuel Dexter	1800	J.M. Dickinson	1909	William E.	
William Windom	1881	Roger Griswold	1801	Henry L. Stimson	1911	Chandler	1881
Charles J. Folger	1881	Henry Dearborn	1801	L.M. Garrison	1913	William C.	
Walter Q.		William Eustis	1809	Newton D. Baker	1916	Whitney	1885
Gresham	1884	John Armstrong	1813	John W. Weeks	1921	Benjamin F.	
Hugh McCulloch	1884	James Monroe	1814	Dwight F. Davis	1925	Tracy	1889
Daniel Manning	1885	William H.		James W. Good	1929	Hilary A. Herbert	1893
Charles S.		Crawford	1815	Patrick J. Hurley	1929	John D. Long	1897
Fairchild	1887	Isaac Shelby	1817	George H. Dern	1933	William H.	
William Windom	1889	George Graham	1817	H.A. Woodring	1936	Moody	1902
Charles Foster	1891	John C. Calhoun	1817	Henry L. Stimson	1940	Paul Morton	1904
John G. Carlisle	1893	James Barbour	1825	Robert P.		Charles J.	
Lyman J. Gage	1897	Peter B. Porter	1828	Patterson	1945	Bonaparte	1905
Leslie M. Shaw	1902	John H. Eaton	1829	Kenneth C.		Victor H. Metcalf	1907
George B.		Lewis Cass	1831	Royall	1947	T.H. Newberry	1908
Cortelyou	1907	Benjamin F.				George von L.	
Franklin		Butler	1837			Meyer	1909
MacVeagh	1909	Joel R. Poinsett	1837			Josephus Daniels	1913
William G.		John Bell	1841	**Secretary of the Navy**		Edwin Denby	1921
McAdoo	1913	John McLean	1841	**(1798–1947)**		Curtis D. Wilbur	1924
Carter Glass	1919	John C. Spencer	1841			Charles F. Adams	1929
David F. Houston	1919	James M. Porter	1843	Benjamin		Claude A.	
Andrew W.		William Wilkins	1844	Stoddert	1798	Swanson	1933
Mellon	1921	William L. Marcy	1845	Robert Smith	1801	Charles Edison	1940
Ogden L. Mills	1932	George W.		Paul Hamilton	1809	Frank Knox	1940
William H.		Crawford	1849	William Jones	1813	James V.	
Woodin	1933	Charles M.		B.W.		Forrestal	1945
		Conrad	1850	Crowninshield	1814		

Secretary of Defense (1947–)

James V. Forrestal	1947
Louis A. Johnson	1949
George C. Marshall	1950
Robert A. Lovett	1951
Charles E. Wilson	1953
Neil H. McElroy	1957
Thomas S. Gates, Jr.	1959
Robert S. McNamara	1961
Clark M. Clifford	1968
Melvin R. Laird	1969
Elliot L. Richardson	1973
James R. Schlesinger	1973
Harold Brown	1977
Caspar W. Weinberger	1981

Postmaster General (1789–1971)

Samuel Osgood	1789
Timothy Pickering	1791
Joseph Habersham	1795
Gideon Granger	1801
Return J. Meigs, Jr.	1814
John McLean	1823
William T. Barry	1829
Amos Kendall	1835
John M. Niles	1840
Francis Granger	1841
Charles A. Wickliffe	1841
Cave Johnson	1845
Jacob Collamer	1849
Nathan K. Hall	1850
Samuel D. Hubbard	1852
James Campbell	1853
Aaron V. Brown	1857
Joseph Holt	1859
Horatio King	1861
Montgomery Blair	1861
William Dennison	1864
Alexander W. Randall	1866
John A.J. Creswell	1869
James W. Marshall	1874
Marshall Jewell	1874
James N. Tyner	1876
David M. Key	1877
Horace Maynard	1880
Thomas L. James	1881
Timothy O. Howe	1881
Walter Q. Gresham	1883
Frank Hatton	1884
William F. Vilas	1885
Don M. Dickinson	1888
John Wanamaker	1889
Wilson S. Bissel	1893
William L. Wilson	1895
James A. Gary	1897
Charles E. Smith	1898
Henry C. Payne	1902
Robert J. Wynne	1904
George B. Cortelyou	1905
George von L. Meyer	1907
F.H. Hitchcock	1909
Albert S. Burleson	1913
Will H. Hays	1921
Hubert Work	1922
Harry S. New	1923
Walter F. Brown	1929
James A. Farley	1933
Frank C. Walker	1940
Robert E. Hannegan	1945
J.M. Donaldson	1947
A.E. Summerfield	1953
J. Edward Day	1961
John A. Gronouski	1963
Lawrence F. O'Brien	1965
W. Marvin Watson	1968
Winton M. Blount	1969

Attorney General (1789–)

Edmund Randolph	1789
William Bradford	1794
Charles Lee	1795
Theophilus Parsons	1801
Levi Lincoln	1801
Robert Smith	1805
John Breckinridge	1805
Caesar A. Rodney	1807
William Pinkney	1811
Richard Rush	1814
William Wirt	1817
John M. Berrien	1829
Roger B. Taney	1831
Benjamin F. Butler	1833
Felix Grundy	1838
Henry D. Gilpin	1840
John J. Crittenden	1841
Hugh S. Legaré	1841
John Nelson	1843
John Y. Mason	1845
Nathan Clifford	1846
Isaac Toucey	1848
Reverdy Johnson	1849
John J. Crittenden	1850
Caleb Cushing	1853
Jeremiah S. Black	1857
Edwin M. Stanton	1860
Edward Bates	1861
Titian J. Coffey	1863
James Speed	1864
Henry Stanbery	1866
William M. Evarts	1868
Ebenezer R. Hoar	1869
Amos T. Ackerman	1870
George H. Williams	1871
Edward Pierrepont	1875
Alphonso Taft	1876
Charles Devens	1877
Wayne MacVeagh	1881
Benjamin H. Brewster	1881
A.H. Garland	1885
William H.H. Miller	1889
Richard Olney	1893
Judson Harmon	1895
Joseph McKenna	1897
John W. Griggs	1897
Philander C. Knox	1901

William H. Moody	1904
Charles J. Bonaparte	1907
G.W. Wickersham	1909
J.C. McReynolds	1913
Thomas W. Gregory	1914
A. Mitchell Palmer	1919
H.M. Daugherty	1921
Harlan F. Stone	1924
John G. Sargent	1925
William D. Mitchell	1929
H.S. Cummings	1933
Frank Murphy	1939
Robert H. Jackson	1940
Francis Biddle	1941
Tom C. Clark	1945
J.H. McGrath	1949
J.P. McGranery	1952
H. Brownell, Jr.	1953
William P. Rogers	1957
Robert F. Kennedy	1961
Nicholas Katzenbach	1964
Ramsey Clark	1967
John N. Mitchell	1969
Richard G. Kleindienst	1972
Elliot L. Richardson	1973
William Saxbe	1974
Edward H. Levi	1975
Griffin B. Bell	1977
Benjamin R. Civiletti	1979
William French Smith	1981

Secretary of the Interior (1849–)

Thomas Ewing	1849
T.M.T. McKennan	1850
Alexander H.H. Stuart	1850
Robert McClelland	1853
Jacob Thompson	1857

Caleb B. Smith	1861	Edward T.	
John P. Usher	1863	Meredith	1920
James Harlan	1865	Henry C. Wallace	1921
O.H. Browning	1866	Howard M. Gore	1924
Jacob D. Cox	1869	William M.	
Columbus Delano	1870	Jardine	1925
Zachariah		Arthur M. Hyde	1929
Chandler	1875	Henry A.	
Carl Schurz	1877	Wallace	1933
Samuel J.		Claude R.	
Kirkwood	1881	Wickard	1940
Henry M. Teller	1881	Clinton P.	
L.Q.C. Lamar	1885	Anderson	1945
William F. Vilas	1888	Charles F.	
John W. Noble	1889	Brannan	1948
Hoke Smith	1893	Ezra Taft Benson	1953
David R. Francis	1896	Orville L.	
Cornelius N. Bliss	1897	Freeman	1961
E.A. Hitchcock	1899	Clifford M.	
James R. Garfield	1907	Hardin	1969
R.A. Ballinger	1909	Earl L. Butz	1971
Walter L. Fisher	1911	Bob S. Bergland	1977
Franklin K. Lane	1913	John R. Block	1981
John B. Payne	1920		
Albert B. Fall	1921		
Hubert Work	1923	**Secretary of**	
Roy O. West	1928	**Commerce and Labor**	
Ray L. Wilbur	1929	**(1903–1913)**	
Harold L. Ickes	1933		
Julius A. Krug	1946	George B.	
Oscar L.		Cortelyou	1903
Chapman	1949	Victor H. Metcalf	1904
Douglas McKay	1953	Oscar S. Straus	1906
Fred A. Seaton	1956	Charles Nagel	1909
Stewart L. Udall	1961		
Walter J. Hickel	1969		
Rogers C.B.		**Secretary of**	
Morton	1971	**Commerce**	
Stanley K.		**(1913–)**	
Hathaway	1975		
Thomas S.		William C.	
Kleppe	1975	Redfield	1913
Cecil D. Andrus	1977	Joshua W.	
James G. Watt	1981	Alexander	1919
		Herbert Hoover	1921
		William F.	
Secretary of		Whiting	1928
Agriculture		Robert P. Lamont	1929
(1889–)		Roy D. Chapin	1932
		Daniel C. Roper	1933
Norman J.		Harry L. Hopkins	1939
Colman	1889	Jesse Jones	1940
Jeremiah M.		Henry A.	
Rusk	1889	Wallace	1945
J. Sterling		W.A. Harriman	1946
Morton	1893	Charles Sawyer	1948
James Wilson	1897	Sinclair Weeks	1953
David F. Houston	1913	Lewis L. Strauss	1958
		F.H. Mueller	1959

Luther Hodges	1961	Anthony J.	
John T. Connor	1965	Celebrezze	1962
A.B. Trowbridge	1967	John W. Gardner	1965
C.R. Smith	1968	Wilbur J. Cohen	1968
Maurice H. Stans	1969	Robert H. Finch	1969
Peter G. Peterson	1972	Elliot L.	
Frederick B. Dent	1973	Richardson	1970
Rogers C.B.		Caspar W.	
Morton	1975	Weinberger	1973
Elliot L.		F. David	
Richardson	1976	Matthews	1975
Juanita M. Kreps	1977	Joseph A.	
Philip M.		Califano, Jr.	1977
Klutznick	1979		
Malcolm Baldrige	1981		

Secretary of Labor (1913–)

William B.	
Wilson	1913
James J. Davis	1921
William N. Doak	1930
Frances Perkins	1933
L.B.	
Schwellenbach	1945
Maurice J. Tobin	1948
Martin P. Durkin	1953
James P. Mitchell	1953
Arthur J.	
Goldberg	1961
W. Willard Wirtz	1962
George P. Shultz	1969
James D.	
Hodgson	1970
Peter J. Brennan	1973
John T. Dunlop	1975
William J. Usery,	
Jr.	1976
F. Ray Marshall	1977
Raymond J.	
Donovan	1981

Secretary of Health, Education, and Welfare (1953–1980)

Oveta Culp	
Hobby	1953
Marion B. Folsom	1955
Arthur S.	
Flemming	1958
Abraham A.	
Ribicoff	1961

Secretary of Housing and Urban Development (1966–)

Robert C. Weaver	1966
George W.	
Romney	1969
James T. Lynn	1973
Carla A. Hills	1975
Patricia Roberts	
Harris	1977
Moon Landrieu	1979
Samuel Pierce, Jr.	1981

Secretary of Transportation (1967–)

Alan S. Boyd	1967
John A. Volpe	1969
Claude S.	
Brinegar	1973
William T.	
Coleman, Jr.	1975
Brock Adams	1977
Neil E.	
Goldschmidt	1979
Andrew L. Lewis,	
Jr.	1981

Secretary of Energy (1977–)

James R.	
Schlesinger	1977
Charles W.	
Duncan, Jr.	1979
James B. Edwards	1981

Secretary of Housing and Human Services (1980–)

Patricia Roberts
  Harris   1979
Richard S.
  Schweiker   1981

Secretary of Education (1980–)

Shirley Mount
  Hufstedler   1979
T.H. Bell   1981

TERRITORIAL EXPANSION

Louisiana Purchase	1803
Florida	1819
Texas	1845
Oregon	1846
Mexican Cession	1848
Gadsden Purchase	1853
Alaska	1867
Hawaii	1898
The Philippines	1898–1946
Puerto Rico	1899
Guam	1899
Amer. Samoa	1900
Canal Zone	1904
U.S. Virgin Islands	1917
Pacific Islands Trust Terr.	1947

POPULATION, 1790–1980

Year	Population
1790	3,929,214
1800	5,308,483
1810	7,239,881
1820	9,638,453
1830	12,866,020
1840	17,069,453
1850	23,191,876
1860	31,443,321
1870	39,818,449
1880	50,155,783
1890	62,947,714
1900	75,994,575
1910	91,972,266
1920	105,710,620
1930	122,775,046
1940	131,669,275
1950	151,325,798
1960	179,323,175
1970	204,765,770
1980	226,504,825

PICTURE CREDITS

Main Text

3 The Granger Collection 6 Palazzo Comunale, Genoa; Brogi 9 William L. Clements Library, University of Michigan 12 National Portrait Gallery, London 13 BOTH: British Museum 15 BOTH: New York Public Library, Picture Collection 17 New York Public Library, Picture Collection 18 New York Public Library, Picture Collection 21 Stokes Collection, New York Public Library 30 The Fine Arts Museum of San Francisco 32 Library of Congress 34-35 Charleston Museum 37 Rare Book Room, New York Public Library 46 The Granger Collection 48 ALL: British Museum 49 Princeton University Observatory 50 Culver Pictures, Inc. 52 Burgerbibliothek, Bern 63 H. Dunscombe Colt Collection 65 Courtesy of the New-York Historical Society, New York City 66 Rare Book Room, New York Public Library 68 Royal Artillery Institute, London 75 Print Department, Metropolitan Museum of Art 77 Rare Book Room, New York Public Library 78 Museum of Fine Arts, Boston 79 Print Department, Metropolitan Museum of Art 80 Print Department, Metropolitan Museum of Art 81 Culver Pictures, Inc. 83 LEFT: Colonial Williamsburg BOTH RIGHT: Chicago Historical Society 88 The Connecticut Historical Society 91 Yale University Art Gallery 98 Historical Society of Pennsylvania 101 Henry Francis du Pont Winterthur Museum 103 Anne S. K. Brown Military Collection, Brown University Library 106 The Granger Collection 116 Mrs. Warren M. Saris Collection 120 Albert E. Leeds Collection 122 Independence National Historical Park, Philadelphia 125 The New-York Historical Society, N.Y. 126 Stokes Collection, New York Public Library 129 National Portrait Gallery, Smithsonian Institution 134 The Granger Collection 138 The New-York Historical Society, N.Y. 141 Historical Society of Pennsylvania 144 The Granger Collection 146 Maryland Historical Society 147 Worcester Art Museum 149 The Granger Collection 154 American Philosophical Society Library 158 Mellon Collection, National Gallery of Art 159 The New-York Historical Society, N.Y. 162 The New-York Historical Society, N.Y. 166 Field Museum of Natural History, Chicago 169 Chicago Historical Society 172 Library of Congress 174 Isaac Delgado Museum, Edgar William and Bernice Garbisch Gift 186 Slater Mill Historical Site 189 The Bettmann Archive, Inc. 194 Oberlin College 195 BOTH: Museum of Science and Industry 196 Museum of Fine Arts, Boston, M. & M. Karolik Collection 198 Randall J. Le Boeuf, Jr., Collection 200 The New-York Historical Society, N.Y. 205 Boston Athenaeum 212 The New-York Historical Society, N.Y. 213 Dartmouth College 215 National Portrait Gallery, Smithsonian Institution 216 Chicago Historical Society 217 The New-York Historical Society, N.Y. 218 The Granger Collection 219 Culver Pictures 221 The Peale Museum, Gift of Mrs. Harry White 222 Museé d'Histoire Naturelle, Le Havre 225 The Granger Collection 230 The Granger Collection 236 Museum of the City of New York 238 Corcoran Gallery 240-241 The Granger Collection 242 H. Lewis, *Das Illustrierte Mississippithal*, 1857 242 Museé d'Histoire Naturelle, Le Havre 246 Brig. Gen. Nicholas Biddle Collection 252 Chicago Historical Society 254 Cincinnati Historical Society 260 The Bettmann Archive 262 TOP: The New-York Historical Society, N.Y. BOTTOM: Culver Pictures 263 Harvard College Library 264 Walt Whitman Foundation 267 UPPER LEFT: New York Public Library UPPER RIGHT: Culver Pictures 268 New York Public Library 269 New York State Historical Association 270 Newark Museum, Gift of Franklin Murphy, Jr., 1926 273 BOTH: Brigham Young University Art Museum Collection 275 Brown Brothers 277 TOP: Metropolitan Museum of Art, Gift of L. N. Phelps Stokes, Edward S. Hawes, Alice Mary Hawes, Marion Augusta Hawes, 1937 BOTTOM: American Antiquarian Society 278 Private Collection 279 Chicago Historical Society 282 Culver Pictures 283 Library of Congress 287 Chicago Historical Society 289 Library of Congress 290 The New-York Historical Society, N.Y. 296 Beinecke Library, Yale University 298 Library of Congress 302 BOTH: Metropolitan Museum of Art, Gift of L. N. Phelps Stokes, Edward S. Hawes, Alice Mary Hawes, Marion Augusta Hawes, 1937 304 TOP: The Huntington Library BOTTOM: BOTH: Yale University Library, Copyright © 1944, by the Columbia University Press 306 Worcester Art Museum, Goodspeed Collection 312 American Antiquarian Society 313 Mr. and Mrs. Samuel J. Henry Collection 314 BOTH: Glenbow Foundation, Calgary, Alberta 316 American Antiquarian Society 320 Lawrence G. Zimmerman Collection 322 L'Illustracion, Paris, 1849 323 Mr. and Mrs. Screven Lorillard Collection 326 Eno Collection, New York Public Library 328 The Granger Collection 332 Library of Congress 337 New York Public Library, Picture Collection 338 The New-York Historical Society, N.Y. 340 United States Naval Academy Museum 341 Library of Congress 343 New York Public Library 345 Kansas State Historical Society, Topeka 346 New York Public Library 347 The New-York Historical Society, N.Y. 351 Chicago Historical Society 354 Metropolitan Museum of Art, Gift of Mr. and Mrs. Carl Stoeckel, 1897 356 New York Public Library, Picture Collection 363 New York *Herald*, April, 1861 365 Chicago Historical Society 366 M. & M. Karolik Collection, Museum of Fine Arts, Boston 370 TOP: Mariner's Museum BOTTOM: The Granger Collection 373 Library of Congress 376 Library of Congress 378 TOP: M. & M. Karolik Collection, Museum of Fine Arts, Boston BOTTOM: Museum of Art, Carnegie Institute, Pittsburgh 379 J. Clarence Davies Collection, Museum of the

City of New York *380* The Granger Collection *384* TOP: GAF Historical Photo Collection *387* The Granger Collection *390* Library of Congress *395* Brady-Handy Collection, Library of Congress *396* BOTH: Brady-Handy Collection, Library of Congress *401* Library of Congress *403* Frank Leslie's Illustrated Newspaper, January 6, 1877 *404* Malcolm F. J. Burns Collection *405* Library of Congress *406* Nebraska State Historical Society *409* Alabama Department of Archives and History *411* Harper's Weekly, August 24, 1872

Portfolios

Portfolio One: *P. One/page 2:* F. Shoberl, *The World in Miniature, 1817–1821 P. One/3:* TOP: Dr. and Mrs. Ernst Anspach Collection; Werner Forman BOTTOM: P. Verite Collection; Andre Held LEFT: National Museet, Copenhagen; Eliot Elisofon *P. One/4:* RIGHT: Museum of Primitive Art; Werner Forman LEFT: Mr. and Mrs. Paul Tishman Collection; Marc and Evelyne Bernheim-Rapho Guillumette CENTER: Museum of Primitive Art *P. One/5:* RIGHT: Museum of Primitive Art; Lisa Little LEFT: Mr. and Mrs. Paul Tishman Collection; Marc and Evelyne Bernheim-Rapho Guillumette *P. One/6:* Wallace Collection *P. One/7:* TOP: T. E. Bowdich, *A Mission from Cape Coast Castle to Ashantee,* 1819 BOTTOM: Nelson Gallery–Atkins Museum *P. One/8:* TOP: ALL: Trustees of the British Museum BOTTOM: LEFT: Margaret W. Plass Collection CENTER AND RIGHT: Trustees of the British Museum *P. One/9* TOP LEFT: Margaret W. Plass Collection TOP CENTER AND RIGHT: Trustees of the British Museum BOTTOM: H. Storrer Collection; Werner Forman *P. One/10:* Mr. and Mrs. Paul Tishman Collection; Marc and Evelyne Bernheim-Rapho Guillumette *P. One/11:* TOP LEFT: Bibliothèque National; Claude Michaelides TOP RIGHT: Musée de L'homme BOTTOM: Palace, Abomey; Marc and Evelyne Bernheim-Rapho Guillumette *P. One/12* Musée de l'homme; Giraudon *P. One/13:* TOP: Dr. and Mrs. Ernst Anspach Collection; Werner Forman BOTTOM: Department of Antiquities, Nigeria; Werner Forman LEFT: Museum of Primitive Art; Lisa Little *P. One/14:* Museum of Primitive Art; Lee Boltin *P. One/15* Department of Antiquities, Nigeria; Werner Forman *P. One/16–17:* Museum fur Volkerkunde, Berlin; Werner Forman BOTTOM: THREE PLAQUES: Trustees of the British Museum; Andre Held RIGHT: Museum of Primitive Art; Lee Boltin *P. One/18:* RIGHT: Department of Antiquities, Nigeria; Werner Forman TOP LEFT: American Museum of Natural History BOTTOM LEFT: Katherine White Reswick Collection; Werner Forman *P. One/19:* RIGHT: Trustees of the British Museum; Hamlyn Publishing Co. LEFT: Mr. and Mrs. Paul Tishman Collection; Marc and Evelyne Bernheim-Rapho Guillumette *P. One/20:* RIGHT: Dr. and Mrs. Ernst Anspach Collection LEFT: Rijksmuseum voor volkenkunde, Leiden; Andre Held *P. One/21:* TOP: Musée Royale d'Afrique Centrale; Andre Held RIGHT: Charles Ratton Collection; Andre Held BOTTOM: Musée de l'homme; Claude Michaelides *P. One/22:* Ishbrandtsen Collection, On loan to the South Street Museum *P. One/23:* TOP: Mr. and Mrs. John Friede Collection; Werner Forman BOTTOM: Buell, *Heroes of the Dark Continent,* 1890 *P. One/24:* Musée des Beaux Arts, Nantes

Portfolio Two: *P. Two/1:* New York State Historical Association, Cooperstown *P. Two/4:* Smithsonian Institution, Photo No. 51,604 *P. Two/5:* TOP: National Gallery of Art, gift of Edgar William and Bernice Chrysler Garbisch BOTTOM: David Hiser, The Image Bank *P. Two/6:* The Historical Society of Pennsylvania *P. Two/7:* TOP LEFT: The Historical Society of Pennsylvania TOP RIGHT: Museum of Fine Arts, Boston, gift of Henry Lee Shattuck CENTER: The Historical Society of Pennsylvania BOTTOM: The New York Public Library, Astor, Lenox and Tilden Foundations, Print Collection *P. Two/8:* TOP: Dementi-Foster Studios, Richmond, courtesy of Gibbs Art Museum, Charleston LEFT: Courtesy of American Heritage Publishing Co., Inc. *P. Two/9:* TOP: Williamsburg Publishing Company BOTTOM: Smithsonian Institution, Photo No. 36–F *P. Two/10–11:* TOP: Courtesy of Dover Publications, Inc. (from republication of Gerard's *Herbal,* 1633 edition) *P. Two/10:* BOTTOM LEFT: Library of Congress BOTTOM RIGHT: Smithsonian Institution, Photo No. 42163D *P. Two/11:* BOTTOM: Library of Congress *P. Two/12:* TOP: American Jewish Historical Society *P. Two/13:* TOP: The Bostonian Society *P. Two/12–13* BOTTOM: Library Company of Philadelphia *P. Two/14:* TOP: Museum of Fine Arts, Boston, gift of Henry Davis Sleeper BOTTOM: Museum of Fine Arts, Boston, gift of Joseph W., William B., and Edward H. R. Revere *P. Two/15:* TOP LEFT: Library of Congress TOP RIGHT: American Antiquarian Society CENTER: American Antiquarian Society *P. Two/16:* LEFT: National Gallery of Art, gift of Edgar William and Bernice Chrysler Garbisch RIGHT: The New-York Historical Society *P. Two/17:* TOP: Abby Aldrich Rockefeller Folk Art Center BOTTOM LEFT: Museum of the City of New York, Toy Collection BOTTOM RIGHT: Essex Institute, Salem, Massachusetts *P. Two/18–19:* Virginia Museum of Fine Arts *P. Two/20:* TOP LEFT: American Antiquarian Society TOP RIGHT: Connecticut Historical Society BOTTOM: National Gallery of Art, gift of Edgar William and Bernice Chrysler Garbisch *P. Two/21:* Abby Aldrich Rockefeller Folk Art Center *P. Two/22:* LEFT: Library of Congress RIGHT: Connecticut Historical Society *P. Two/23:* TOP: New-York Historical Society BOTTOM: Princeton University Library *P. Two/24:* Howard Millard *P. Two/25:* TOP: American Antiquarian Society BOTTOM: Culver Pictures

Portfolio Three: *P. Three/1:* Northern Natural Gas Company Collection, Joslyn Art Museum *P. Three/2:* TOP: Stokes Collection, New York Public Library BOTTOM: American Antiquarian Society *P. Three/3:* Museum of the City of New York *P. Three/4:* Museum of Fine Arts, Boston *P. Three/7:* TOP: Toledo Museum of Art, Gift of Florence Scott Libbey BOTTOM: American Antiquarian Society *P. Three/8* TOP: Northern Natural Gas Company Collection, Joslyn Art Museum BOTTOM: Beinecke Library, Yale University *P. Three/9:* Stokes Collection, New York Public Library *P. Three/10–11:* Cincinnati Historical Society *P. Three/12:* Kennedy Galleries *P. Three/13:* TOP: Maryland Historical Society BOTTOM: Chicago Historical Society *P. Three/15:* TOP: Museum of the City of New York BOTTOM: M. & M. Karolik Collection, Museum of Fine Arts, Boston *P. Three/16:* Mr. and Mrs. Screven Lorillard Collection *P. Three/18:* M. & M. Karolik Collection, Museum of Fine Arts, Boston *P. Three/19* TOP: New York Historical Society BOTTOM: Museum of the City of New York *P. Three/20:* TOP: M. & M. Karolik Collection, Museum of Fine Arts, Boston BOTTOM: Museum of the City of New York *P. Three/21* Museum of Art, Rhode Island School of Design *P. Three/22–23:* Historical Society of Pennsylvania *P. Three/24:* BOTH: Mercantile Library, St. Louis © 1959 University of Oklahoma Press *P. Three/25:* Corcoran Gallery of Art

INDEX

INDEX

MINNESOTA
May 11, 1858

LAKE SUPERIOR

St.
Paul

WISCONSIN
May 29, 1848

Madison

IOWA
Dec. 28, 1846

Des Moines

LAKE MICHIGAN

LAKE HURON

MICHIGAN
Jan. 26, 1837

Lansing

VERMONT
Mar. 4, 1791

MAINE
Mar. 15, 1820

Augusta

Montpelier

NEW HAMPSHIRE
June 21, 1788

Concord

Boston

MASSACHUSETTS
Feb. 6, 1788

LAKE ONTARIO

NEW YORK
July 26, 1788

Albany

Hartford

Providence

RHODE ISLAND
May 29, 1790

LAKE ERIE

PENNSYLVANIA
Dec. 12, 1787

CONNECTICUT
Jan. 9, 1788

ILLINOIS
Dec. 3, 1818

Springfield

INDIANA
Dec. 11,
1816

Indianapolis

OHIO
Mar. 1, 1803

Columbus

Harrisburg

Trenton

NEW JERSEY
Dec. 18, 1787

Dover

DELAWARE
Dec. 7, 1787

MISSOURI
Aug. 10, 1821

Jefferson
City

WEST
VIRGINIA
June 20, 1863

Charleston

Annapolis

MARYLAND
Apr. 28, 1788

VIRGINIA
Richmond
June 25, 1788

Frankfort

KENTUCKY
June 1, 1792

ARKANSAS
June 15, 1836

Little
Rock

Nashville

TENNESSEE
June 1, 1796

NORTH CAROLINA
Nov. 21, 1789

Raleigh

SOUTH
CAROLINA

Columbia

May 23, 1788

MISSISSIPPI
Dec. 10, 1817

ALABAMA
Dec. 4, 1819

Atlanta

GEORGIA
Jan. 2, 1788

LOUISIANA
Apr. 30, 1812

Jackson

Montgomery

Baton Rouge

Tallahassee

FLORIDA
Mar. 3,
1845

GULF OF MEXICO

ATLANTIC OCEAN

POLITICAL MAP
OF
THE UNITED STATES

0   100   200   300   400
MILES

PUERTO RICO
Territory, 1899

VIRGIN ISLANDS
Territory, 1917

San Juan

Charlotte
Amalie

0   40   80
MILES

82 83 84 85 9 8 7 6 5 4 3 2 1